EIGHTH TO TWELFTH CENTURIES AD

The Archaeology of
Medieval Europe

Edited by James Graham-Campbell with Magdalena Valor

Acta Jutlandica LXXXIII:1
Humanities Series 79

Aarhus University Press |

The Archaeology of Medieval Europe, vol. 1

© Aarhus University Press and the Authors

Graphic design and cover design by Jørgen Sparre

Cover illustration: The Bayeux Tapestry (c1070) depicts

the construction of a fortification at Hastings (Sussex),

for Duke William of Normandy, following his invasion

of England in 1066 (Municipale de Bayeux).

Typeset by Anne Marie Kaad

Printed by Narayana Press, Denmark

Printed in Denmark 2007

ISBN 978 87 7934 288 0 (Hb)

ISBN 978 87 7934 290 3 (Pb)

This book has been peer reviewed

Aarhus University Press

Langelandsgade 177

DK-8200 Aarhus N

www.unipress.dk

White Cross Mills

Hightown, Lancaster, LA1 4XS

United Kingdom

www.gazellebookservices.co.uk

PO Box 511

Oakville, CT 06779

www.oxbowbooks.com

This book is published with the financial support of

The Augustinus Foundation

The Charles University, Prague: Faculty of Philosophy and Arts (project 0021620827 MSM)

The University of Galway

The Ghent University: Department of Archaeology (Research Unit Medieval Archaeology)

The University of Lund: Faculty of Humanity and Theology

The University of Seville: HUM-712

The University of Aarhus: Department of Medieval and Renaissance Archaeology

The Aarhus University Research Foundation

CONTENTS

FOREWORD

At the 'Fourth European Symposium for Teachers of Medieval Archaeology' (ESTMA) held in Seville in 1999, I proposed the idea of a collaborative textbook on the medieval archaeology of Europe. This was triggered by recognition of the need to provide students across the Continent with a basis on which to build an appreciation of the European dimension of a discipline that has undergone rapid expansion over the last 50 years, but one that has remained largely based on somewhat nationally-focussed research which, as a result, is mostly published in national books and journals. This book – an eventual product of this proposal – is the first of two volumes that, I hope, will together provide a geographically and methodologically wide-ranging synthesis of this still fast-developing subject. It attempts to outline the coherences, diversities and developments of European culture in a period when Europe began to form itself into the national and cultural provinces that we recognise today.

The idea, so blithely proposed, met with enthusiasm and was gradually developed during the 1999 symposium; but, as with all such bright ideas, it had to be put on a realistic footing. A working-group was set up and a planning meeting took place in 2000, in Brussels, when the basic outline, structure and contents of the publication were discussed, and an Advisory Committee and editors were chosen. There were to be no theoretical or ideological straight-jackets; on the contrary, the project was intended to mirror the very diverse approaches to the discipline of Medieval Archaeology across Europe.

After much discussion, it was decided that there should be two volumes: the first dealing with the eighth to the twelfth centuries; the second with the twelfth to the sixteenth centuries. Both volumes would follow the same thematic pattern, and each chapter would contain some specific studies in the form of 'Box-texts'. In order to secure a broad approach, two authors, normally from different parts of Europe, were proposed for each chapter, with additional authors for some of the Boxes. We endeavoured (not entirely successfully) to cover all those medieval European countries or regions that came to adhere to Roman Christianity – a practical and oft-used, although not entirely satisfactory, demarcation. In all, forty-one authors from fifteen modern countries have contributed to this volume (see p 453). To all of them we are immensely grateful, as also to the two anonymous referees who kindly undertook the essential task of peer-review, to the great advantage of all concerned.

The complexity of the project called for further meetings between 2001 and 2004; these took place in Brussels, Bamberg, Tübingen and Seville, and we are very grateful to Johnny De Meulemeester, Barbara Scholkmann and Magdalena Valor for having organised them. Subsequent editorial meetings were held in Seville, London and Aarhus.

The editors of this first volume, James Graham-Campbell and Magdalena Valor, have, however, done all the really hard work, and to them we are particularly grateful. To James Graham-Campbell, however, must go our greatest gratitude. He it was who accepted the burden of the final organisation of all the texts and illustrations into a full manuscript and who adapted the various versions of English to his own language. We also wish to express our deep gratitude to Martin Comey for his efficient and engaging editorial assistance. Aarhus University Press accepted our, already finalised, publication proposal with enthusiasm, and Sanne Lind Hansen has seen it through the press, with design by Jørgen Sparre and Anne Marie Kaad. We also wish to express our gratitude to them. Finally, we thank those institutions which have contributed towards the cost of this publication (p 4).

Else Roesdahl
University of Aarhus, Denmark
Chairman, ESTMA Advisory Committee

ESTMA Advisory Committee for 'The Archaeology of Medieval Europe' : Vols 1-2

Terry Barry, Trinity College Dublin, Ireland
Reidar Bertelsen, University of Tromsø, Norway
James Graham-Campbell, University College London, England
Anne-Marie Flambard Héricher, University of Rouen, France
Anne Nissen Jaubert, University of Tours, France
Jan Klápště , Charles University, Prague, Czech Republic
Johnny De Meulemeester, Ghent University, Belgium (Vice-Chair)
Tadhg O'Keeffe, University College Dublin, Ireland
Else Roesdahl, University of Aarhus, Denmark (Chair)
Barbara Scholkmann, University of Tübingen, Germany
Przemysław Urbańczyk, Polish Academy of Sciences, Warsaw, Poland
Magdalena Valor, University of Seville, Spain

INTRODUCTION

James Graham-Campbell

What is to be understood by 'Medieval Europe'? Physically, of course, it consisted of the westernmost part of the Eurasian landmass, which is not in itself immediately identifiable, geographically speaking, as a continent. It is true that in the west, Europe faces the Atlantic Ocean, but the Mediterranean Sea to the south is a much more ambiguous space. Today, it divides Europe from Africa; however, during the period of the Roman Empire, the Mediterranean was not a boundary but a central space, being the essential means of communication with those who lived in the 'civilized world', all around its shores. In the north, on the other hand, it was only during the early Middle Ages that the Baltic Sea began to cease being a divide between peoples of different ethnic origins, with differing languages and religious traditions.

In the case of south-east Europe, it has become accepted that Turkey is a country in two continents, separated by the Bosphorus. However, Constantinople (the antecedent of Istanbul) was for long the capital city of a great Christian empire that can certainly be said to have blurred the boundaries of what is currently considered to be Europe (as described below). In the east, the continent of Europe is today considered to extend across the broad expanses of Russia and the Ukraine as far as the Ural Mountains; these have, however, been described as 'comparatively insignificant' and thus as providing 'no real geographical basis' for defining the extent of a continent (Jordan 1973).

The fact is, therefore, that Europe is a cultural construct with uncertain boundaries because of it having no objective geographical basis; likewise, it lacks a common family of languages (hence the importance of the spread of Latin as an essential element in the conversion of Western Christendom). Ultimately, the historical concept of Europe is firmly rooted in the Classical world.

The geographical scope of this over-view of the current state of medieval archaeology thus covers only part of the continent of Europe as it is known today. Its actual extent is considered below, as also the chronological scope of the survey. On the other hand, matters concerning the nature of 'Medieval Archaeology at the Outset of the Third Millennium' are the subject of Chapter 1.

Geographical scope

The geographical scope of this two-volume survey is Latin Europe, meaning that part of medieval Europe, or 'Christendom', in which the majority religion became Roman Catholic (so providing it with a degree of coherence), rather than Greek Orthodox. This results in the omission of the territories of the Byzantine Empire, together with Russia and the Ukraine; however, this division is standard practice in medieval studies when space is at a premium. What is, however, different from standard practice is the full inclusion of the Islamic presence in the Iberian Peninsula, given that the contributions of al-Andalus to medieval Europe were far reaching in many fields – from art and architecture to technology and food.

It is not, however, the case that the Byzantine world is absent from this account, if only because of the extensive diplomatic and trading connections that existed between the two 'Europes' (see Chapter 10). In 726, there was a schism between Western and Eastern Christendom, with the Pope excommunicating both the Byzantine Emperor and the Patriarch in Constantinople. Breaks between the two Churches were, however, periodically patched up, although the mid-eighth century witnessed the creation of the Papal State in central Italy, under Frankish military protection (see Chapter 13). Eventually, there was to be the so-called 'Great Schism', in 1054, on points of theology, ritual and Church discipline.

In the eighth century, the Byzantine Empire embraced not only Asia Minor, Greece and the Aegean, but also Sicily, the heel and toe of Italy and the Dalmatian coast, as well as Cyprus in the Eastern Mediterranean (cf. map: Fig 2.5). This was, however, already a greatly reduced area from that of its sixth- and seventh-century predecessor, the Eastern Roman Empire. By the mid-twelfth century, the Byzantine Empire had further contracted both in the east, with the Moslem Seljuks established in Anatolia, and in the west with the Norman kings of Sicily also having control over southern Italy. The Byzantines had, however, succeeded in taking possession of the West Bulgarian Empire (1018) and had reduced the Serbs to vassalage, although both Bulgaria and the Serbs had previously adopted the Eastern Orthodox rite (cf. map: Fig 2.9). Indeed, even as the Byzantine Empire was shrinking, the authority of the Patriarch of Constantinople was increasing, most notably with the tenth-century conversion of Russia. On the other hand, after the First Crusade and the capture of Jerusalem (in 1099), the territories reconquered from Islam were created independent states, but as an extension of Western Christendom, rather than being returned to the Byzantine Emperor as their rightful sovereign.

Chronological coverage

This book covers the period from the eighth to the late twelfth century, but has no fixed chronological boundaries. The decision to commence this survey with the eighth century, rather than in the fifth (thus marking the end of the Roman Empire), was taken for several reasons, the principle ones of which are outlined below. On the other hand, the decision that the period from the eighth to sixteenth centuries would be divided during the twelfth century was largely one of convenience, although this period does witness some change in the available sources, e.g. the increased preservation of buildings (in stone, but also brick), as also the multiplication of written records. However, given that there is no artificially selected date to form a *terminus ante/post quem* for this first volume, it is to be anticipated that there will be some overlap with the second.

In many European regions, the eighth century was a period of increasing agricultural production that facilitated urban growth and the development of an associated life-style, supported by advances in manufacturing, technology and trade (including transport and communication). It was a period when Christianity had become well established in the territories that had once formed the western part of the Roman Empire, with the addition of Ireland, even if the Iberian Peninsula was then undergoing Islamisation. There followed the spread of Christianity, accompanied by development in Church organisation and institutional consolidation. These aspects of economic, social and religious life provide the major themes of the five centuries under review, which are said to have witnessed 'the Birth of Europe'.

Following Conversion, the previously widespread custom of burying the dead fully clothed, and even with additional grave-goods, went out of fashion across the greater part of Western Europe, generally speaking in the late seventh century. This factor makes for a significant change in the nature of the archaeological data-base after the early Middle Ages. For instance, certain types of luxury artefact manufactured on the Continent during the ninth-tenth centuries are best known from their deposition in the pagan graves of Scandinavia or elsewhere in the Viking world.

Ultimately, however, the eighth century was an important turning-point in the history of Europe because of the formation of the Carolingian Empire – the work of Charlemagne, or Charles the Great (cf. Story (ed) 2005), who reigned as King of the Franks, and subsequently also of the Lombards (in Italy), from 768-814. Even if the Empire that he created, after fifty-three military campaigns, began to fall apart after his death, medieval Europe had embarked on a new course, with Charlemagne having consummated a new relationship with the papacy. On Christmas Day in 800, the Pope in Rome crowned him the first Catholic Emperor in Western Christendom. Afterwards, he knelt in homage before Charlemagne – but only the Pope could create an Emperor. There was thus, from the start, a built-in tension to this new relationship.

Charlemagne ruled over what is properly described as the 'first Europe' (for which see also the 'Afterword'), although his Empire did not even comprise the full extent of Western Christendom during this period. This concept did not, however, last for long after his death, but nevertheless there can be no more appropriate period than the eighth century with which to commence *The Archaeology of Medieval Europe*.

Background

There is consensus that, by the ninth century at the latest, those parts of Europe that had formed part of the Roman Empire had been 'transformed' during the period since 'Late Antiquity'. Indeed, the centuries following its collapse in the fifth century have formed the subject of a major European Science Foundation Research Project (1993-98), which resulted in several publications and exhibitions, including *The Transformation of the Roman World, AD 400-900*, edited by L Webster and M Brown (1997). Other volumes in the series are cited elsewhere in this book, particularly those relating to 'Urbanism' (Chapter 4).

Following this initiative, there have been several important publications that have likewise concentrated on these formative centuries, e.g. M McCormick, *Origins of the European Economy. Communications and Commerce, AD 300-900* (2001); C Wickham, *Framing the Middle Ages: Europe and the Mediterranean, 400-800* (2005); and J Knight, *The End of Antiquity: Archaeology, Society and Religion AD 235-700* (2007).

Reference works

Students of the Middle Ages will need to familiarise themselves with an historical survey of Europe during the eighth-twelfth centuries to take full advantage of this book. One such is 'The Short Oxford History of Europe', with the relevant volumes being: *The Early Middle Ages: Europe 400-1000*, edited by R Mckitterick (2001); *From the Vikings to the Normans*, edited by W Davies (2003); and *The Central Middle Ages, 950-1320*, edited by D Power (2006).

There are various reference works, such as historical atlases and medieval encyclopedias, as well as exhibition catalogues, which students will likewise need to make use of, as essential companions to this book. Amongst the former may be noted: *The New Penguin Atlas of Medieval History*, by C McEvedy (1992); *The Penguin Historical Atlas of the Medieval World*, by A Jotischky & C Hull (2005); and the second edition of *The Atlas of Medieval Europe*, edited by D Ditchburn, S MacLean & A Mackay (2007). Obviously, such works cover the whole medieval period, as do many other historical surveys and compilations, such as *The Medieval World*, edited by P Linehan and J Nelson (2001).

Mention needs also to be made to both the *Dictionary of the Middle Ages*, in 13 volumes (1982-89), edited by J-R Strayer, and the continuing series of *Routledge Encyclopedias of the Middle Ages*, which commenced (in 1993) with *Medieval Scandinavia*, edited by P Pulsiano & K Wolf. Exhibition catalogues (such as those listed on p 260) are also a most valuable resource for medieval archaeologists because they provide numerous illustrations of artefacts and generally also contain a series of up-to-date essays. Indeed, some catalogues, such as that published for the Council of Europe's (1992) Exhibition, 'From Viking to Crusader: Scandinavia and Europe 800-1200', are available in more than one language (in this instance: English, French, German and Scandinavian; edited by E Roesdahl & DM Wilson).

Readers of German will benefit from the comprehensive contents of the recently completed 35 volumes of the *Reallexikon der Germanische Altertumskunde* (1973-2007), established by Johannes Hoops (although this does contain some contributions in English), and the *Lexikon des Mittelalters* (1977-99). Readers of Scandinavian languages have at their disposal the 22 volumes of the *Kulturhistorisk Leksikon for Nordisk Middelalder* (1956-78).

Contributors and contents

In a book of this kind, there are inevitably going to be biases in geographical coverage – not even when two (or more) authors are combined from different parts of Europe will they have equal knowledge of every region. Some authors have chosen to merge their contributions into a single text, whereas in other chapters they have remained separate. In the merged chapters, where one of the authors has been responsible for the greater part of its contents, as with 'Death, Life and Memory' (Chapter 15), the authorship is listed as being by 'Thomas Meier, with James Graham-Campbell'.

Amongst the many topics covered here, there are some that are only touched upon because of their having much increased importance from the twelfth century onwards, meaning that they will be treated more fully in Volume 2. Some topics have been deliberately omitted, such as art-history, other than in the form of a brief survey for architectural purposes, given the ever-increasing importance of buildings archaeology. There are several medieval technologies, crafts and industries, such as mining or leatherworking, which might readily have been included alongside those considered in Chapter 7. This is, however, where the chapter bibliographies (and such reference works as those noted above) need to be followed up. It is for this very reason that several authors have extended the scope of their bibliographies beyond the works actually cited by them in their chapters.

Medieval chronologies

There is no agreement amongst European medievalists, not even between historians and archaeologists, as to a standard chronology and terminology for the periodisation of the Middle Ages as a whole, quite apart from there being many long-established regional chronologies.

The following terms have been used here: 'early medieval period' or 'early Middle Ages', and 'late medieval' or 'late Middle Ages', with the 'High Middle Ages' inbetween, but without a too exact definition. The systems presented below are those that are currently in use in Germany (courtesy of Thomas Meier) and by the Society of Medieval Archaeology (in Britain).

Germany (archaeology)
Early Middle Ages: 450 to 8thC
Carolingian/Ottonian: 9th-10thC
High Middle Ages: 1000-1250
Late Middle Ages: 1250-1500

Germany (history)
Early Middle Ages: 476-1024
High Middle Ages: 1024-1250
Late Middle Ages: 1250-1492

Society of Medieval Archaeology
Early Middle Ages: 5th to mid-11thC (to the Norman Conquest, i.e. 1066)
High Middle Ages: mid-11th to mid-14thC (to the Black Death)
Late Middle Ages: mid-14th to mid-16thC

There would have been much to say for having followed here the German archaeological system, confining the 'early medieval period' to that ending in the eighth century (which is what, in practice, happens in England, where the ninth to mid-eleventh centuries are generally known as either the 'late Saxon' or the 'Viking' period). Scandinavian usage, on the other hand, does not allow for this because there the 'Viking period' marks the transition from prehistory (late Iron Age) to the early Middle Ages, which are not therefore considered to commence before the eleventh century (these are matters further considered in Chapter 1).

The fact remains that the chronological scope of this book cuts across the most widely used and long-established chronologies, such as those listed above, and it clearly encompasses parts of both the 'early Middle Ages/early medieval period' and the 'High Middle Ages'. For present purposes therefore, but only as a rule of thumb (given the imprecision of much archaeological dating), these terms may be taken as representing: (i) the eighth-tenth centuries (although inevitably sometimes embracing earlier centuries); and (ii) the eleventh and twelfth centuries (although allowing for some continuity into the thirteenth).

Sources: TG Jordan, *The European Culture Area: a Systematic Geography* (New York, 1973); D Austin & L Alcock (eds), *From the Baltic to the Black Sea: Studies in Medieval Archaeology* (London, 1990); N Davies, *Europe: a History* (Oxford, 1996); J Story (ed), *Charlemagne: Empire and Society* (Manchester, 2005).

CHAPTER 1

MEDIEVAL ARCHAEOLOGY at the Outset of the Third Millennium: Research and Teaching

Hans Andersson, Barbara Scholkmann and Mette Svart Kristiansen

Different Countries: Different Medieval Archaeologies

Medieval archaeology developed late as a university discipline. Nevertheless, medieval archaeology has been in existence at least since the nineteenth century in many countries and, as we shall see later, this means that the discipline has been defined in differing ways in different countries. Chronologically, it depends on the various definitions of the Middle Ages that are to be found in different parts of Europe: from southern Europe, where the fall of the Roman Empire in the fifth century AD marks the beginning of the Middle Ages, to Scandinavia where the transition to the Middle Ages is dated to c1050. It means that what is still prehistory in the north is already the medieval period in the south. Another important factor, which has influenced medieval archaeology, is from (or within) which discipline it developed: prehistory, art-history or history. This has inevitably influenced the particular character of the discipline in different countries.

Although that situation still exists, medieval archaeologists from different traditions agree on the main tasks of 'medieval archaeology': the study of a period in the past with a variety of sources, making use not only of material remains, but also of documentary and pictorial evidence. The archaeologist must of course lay stress on the physical material, but needs also to work to integrate this evidence with the other source material. This has consequences for the theory, methods and teaching of medieval archaeology. This situation is common ground for all historical archaeologies, which work together with text and objects (Andrén 1998). Many departments today are extending their study of medieval archaeology into later periods – and so the name may be changed, for example, into 'historical archaeology'. This means that the traditional termination of the Middle Ages, at the end of the fifteenth or the beginning of the sixteenth century, signifies less for archaeologists than it did before. This has to do with the new themes that are engaging researchers. Many of them, including urbanisation, landscape archaeology, industrial archaeology and the archaeology of religion, cannot be restricted to certain periods. Also of importance are discussions of general human problems, in which medieval archaeologists can participate with essential data and can then, on their part, gain inspiration from others. Even if the discipline of medieval archaeology is not an extensive one, there exists a broad context within which to work.

The Development of Medieval Archaeology

The history of medieval archaeology is difficult to encapsulate. Whereas prehistoric archaeology was well defined and established as an independent discipline by the turn of the twentieth century, no such development took place for medieval archaeology much before the 1960s or 1970s. This is not to say, however, that there had been no substantial professional archaeological studies of medieval material before this period; indeed, lively activity may be identified as early as the 1800s, but this was broadly dependent on a general rise in interest in the Middle Ages. There are also significant differences in the discipline's emergence and growth in various parts of Europe. In the Mediterranean countries, classical archaeology long dominated, and it was only after the Second World War (1939-45) that medieval archaeology came into its own, in many cases with academic influence from Britain. In Eastern Europe the situation was divided. Given the role that the Slavs played in shaping early medieval society, research emphasis was placed on a 'Slavic archaeology'. In part for political reasons, therefore, the later Middle Ages did not receive the same attention. During the last few decades, however, the later medieval period has been incorporated into archaeological research programmes and, in general, more pan-European historical developments have attracted greater interest in Eastern Europe. In contrast, in Spain and Portugal, archaeology has been strongly influenced by the fact that these countries were, in large part, incorporated into the Muslim world for much of the Middle Ages.

It is in Western and Northern Europe that the different approaches to medieval archaeology have had the longest development (cf. van Regteren Altena 1990). One may recognise nuanced variations between those areas that had formed part of the Roman Empire and those that were beyond its borders. Nevertheless, there was a common ground to the emergence of medieval archaeology with the rise of Romanticism in the early 1800s, when there occurred a strong growth in interest in the Middle Ages. From a purely archaeological point of view, the nineteenth-century excavations of Merovingian graves in southern Germany represent a key development. Another manifestation of the growing interest in the Middle Ages involved the restoration and reconstruction of buildings, including both churches and castles. These helped to give rise to 'buildings archaeology' as a well-defined sub-discipline. Examples of this may be found in France, England and Scandinavia, as well as other areas. It is important to note that these initial developments were also influenced by a romantic interest in monuments, a focus that was to affect medieval archaeology for a long time. It is also worth observing that, before medieval archaeology achieved academic status as a discipline in its own right, other areas of study – including art-history, architecture and history – had been setting the agenda and organising archaeological investigations.

The development that took off after the Second World War was initiated by settlement studies, both archaeological and historical. These concerned the countryside as well as towns, with somewhat different emphases being evident once again in the research traditions of different countries. Urban archaeology certainly existed from the beginning of the twentieth century, and even somewhat earlier. In Lund, southern Sweden, there was actually a late nineteenth-century excavation programme that focused on the medieval town. During 1915-18, parts of Nya Lödöse were discovered and excavated within the borders of modern-day Gothenburg in western Sweden. This excavation is significant because it was a professional academic study of an historic late medieval town, carried out with what were then advanced methods. While a few other isolated medieval archaeological studies were carried out before World War II, it remains true that the major development of the discipline occurred post-war. Among the pioneering work, which immediately followed the war, was W Neugebauer's excavation of the partially destroyed Lübeck and, for example, similar studies were carried out in Hamburg, as also by WF Grimes in London (Neugebauer 1980; Schindler 1957; Grimes 1968). The excavation of medieval Novgorod by AV Artsikhovsky began in the 1930s; after the war, work was re-started by BA Kolchin, with open-area excavation being carried out on a large-scale from 1951-62, with the discovery of well-preserved wooden streets, log-constructed buildings and a vast quantity of artefacts, including letters written on birch bark (see Thompson 1967, for an English summary); work continues (cf. Yanin et al 1992), but this material lies outside the scope of this book.

It was only towards the end of the 1950s that there took place a truly rapid expansion in the archaeology of towns in the West. The leading innovator in Western Europe was Asbjörn Herteig, in Bergen, western Norway. In 1955, parts of the so-called 'German Wharf' were destroyed by fire in Bergen's harbour. This was indeed the area of medieval town where Hanseatic trade activity had been focused. Herteig's large-scale excavations (Clarke 1989) allowed him to trace how settlement and building activity had developed, as well as the manner in which the harbour area had expanded. By considering related sources, Herteig was able to establish a better understanding of the town's evolution. This manner of thinking and of planning this archaeological research had a substantial influence, especially in Sweden. From the beginning of the 1960s, archaeologists working in Lund carried out several new, extensive excavations. British participants in both the Bergen and Lund studies carried their experiences with them back to England, and it can be said, for example, that the excavations of King's Lynn reflected this methodological influence (Clarke & Carter 1977). Many other European countries followed with the adoption of large-scale urban archaeological investigations. The timing and focus of the work depended in part on how cultural heritage legislation was shaped in the different countries. An effect of these early, large-scale studies was that comprehensive artefact and site-inventory work was also carried out in many European countries. Indeed, these efforts were often aimed at protecting historical-cultural deposits against destruction and buildings that were threatened by rapid post-war reconstruction and city-centre development, especially in Northern and Western Europe. Here, inspiration came mainly from England: Martin Biddle's analysis of London (Biddle & Hudson 1972), and CW Heighway's overview of the risks to cultural deposits in English cities (Heighway 1972), were established as model approaches. Perhaps the largest project of this sort to have then been carried out was 'Medieval Towns in Sweden and Finland' (Andersson 1992).

In Eastern Europe, the development of medieval archaeology followed a somewhat different course. Nevertheless, the archaeology of towns emerged as a driving force in the growing discipline. For example, Poland has a tradition of medieval archaeological research that can be traced back to the inter-war period, and there, after the Second World War, the study of medieval towns was integrated into a broader project concerning the rise of the Polish state. The same pattern characterised the then Czechoslovakia, where archaeological investigations concerned Great Moravia, as well as East Germany, where the Slavs became the focus of research (Leciejewicz 1993).

As for research interest into the medieval countryside, there is a virtually parallel trend in which post-World War II developments played a major role. In 1950, excavations began at Wharram Percy, in northern England, which in many ways were to set the standard for village studies in Northern Europe. From 1960 to 1962, Walter Janssen investigated the complex of ruins at Königshagen vid Harz. In 1961, Gabrielle Damians d'Archimbaud started her excavations in Rougiers, Provence. In Denmark, the ethnologist Axel Steensberg had already completed his first rural excavation by the end of the 1930s and he continued with the large-scale excavations of Store Valby (Steensberg et al 1974) and Borup Ris (Steensberg 1983). These projects were one of the inspirations for the work undertaken at Wharram Percy (Beresford & Hurst 1990). Nevertheless, these three early post-war excavations together formed the threshold for modern research into medieval rural archaeology. In England, interest in deserted medieval villages became a key focus for historical archaeology, and Italy was inspired by the research being undertaken in England, with many landscape studies carried out – often as collaborations between Italian and English research institutions.

Other significant research foci have also contributed to the modern development of medieval archaeology. For example, research on castles and fortifications took a major step-forward with the establishment of the important Chateau Gaillard conferences, which started in 1962 on the initiative of Michel de Bouard (Caen).

Major field-projects were clearly important contributors in defining the discipline in the 1950s, 60s and 70s, but there are other indications that medieval archaeology was seeking self-consciously to establish its identity as an independent discipline during these decades. This is to be seen most clearly in the creation of new university positions and institutions. In 1951, Michel de Bouard established the *Centre de Recherches Archéologiques Médiévales* at the University of Caen. In Lund, Erik Cinthio became Docent in Art-History and Medieval Archaeology (and subsequently the first Professor of Medieval Archaeology in Sweden), when the topic was formally offered for study at the university in 1962. In 1971, David Wilson became the first Professor of Medieval Archaeology in Britain, at University College London (where he had been Reader in the Archaeology of the Anglo-Saxon Period since 1964); in addition, Olaf Olsen became Professor of Medieval Archaeology at the University of Aarhus, Denmark, in the same year. In Italy, Ricardo Francovich has shown how academic work in medieval archaeology can be traced back to the 1960s. At the same time, there was the establishment of new specialised academic journals: the first was *Medieval Archaeology* (1957), followed among others by *Archéologie médiévale* (1971), *Zeitschrift für Archäologie des Mittelalters* (1973) and *Archeologia medievale* (1974).

By the beginning of the 1970s, the discipline of medieval archaeology had generally taken shape and had become thoroughly professionalized throughout Europe. A consensus concerning the contents of the study of medieval archaeology had more or less been achieved by this time, and the following years reflect a period of consolidation. Urban archaeology experienced further growth. New research topics were integrated, such as metalworking, with a substantial emphasis on iron production. In general, both Italy and Scandinavia played an important role in the development of the discipline at this stage and, as happened in Eastern Europe a few decades earlier, medieval archaeology was incorporated into larger interdisciplinary projects. At the same time, the discussion of theory took on a more central importance, influenced not least by prehistoric archaeology, but also by history (e.g. the study of mentality).

As mentioned above, the discipline of medieval archaeology was for long closely tied to antiquarian activity and this is reflected today in an interest in historical preservation. Rescue archaeology has had a particularly tangible influence, not least concerning urban archaeology, although the scale and rate of development in cities has declined somewhat since the early post-war period, if not everywhere across Europe. The agenda of historical preservation has become so strong that fewer structures are now torn down in medieval urban centres. Instead, large-scale infrastructural projects – including motorways, railways and industrial parks – have impacted on the countryside to an unprecedented degree. It is therefore hardly surprising that the archaeology of villages has become an important topic in recent years, in some ways overshadowing urban archaeology.

Objectives and Research Topics

Modern medieval archaeology considers all material remains, in the broadest sense, to be the objects of its research, integrating the investigation of archaeological evidence with that of monuments and standing buildings. However, the importance and consideration given to these different sources varies from country to country. This is the result of independent national development and, consequently, the varying emphasis accorded to them within research agendas (Andersson & Wienberg 1993; Decaëns & Flambard Héricher 1999; Valor & Carmona 2001).

The general topics of medieval archaeology may be divided into three main fields:

- the formation of the medieval world, i.e. the transition from Late Antique or prehistoric structures and societies to those of the European Middle Ages;

- the developments and changes to the conditions that existed during the Middle Ages, related to structures, societies and material culture; and
- the transformation from the late medieval to the post-medieval world.

These aspects are investigated by analysing their reflection in the material record.

The differing histories of the various regions of Europe are reflected by the different periods during which the Middle Ages are considered to have begun (with the associated creation of medieval archaeology). In those regions that were at least partly integrated into the Roman Empire, until its collapse, Late Antiquity and the Palaeo-Christian period represent the onset of the Middle Ages. For the rest of Europe, conversion to Christianity accompanied by the introduction of writing is the turning-point, since it marks the beginning of the co-existence of written and material evidence. As Christianity was introduced into the northernmost and easternmost parts of Europe as late as the twelfth/thirteenth century, the initial limit of the period investigated by medieval archaeology varies significantly. In a number of countries, such societies as the Anglo-Saxons, Franks, Alamans and Vikings form part of the research topics of early medieval archaeology.

As for the end of the Middle Ages (and thus the termination of medieval archaeology), some countries have made rather a sharp division between medieval and post-medieval archaeology, similar to the distinction between medieval and modern history. Nowadays, efforts are frequently made to overcome this conception so as to try and comprehend structures and processes crossing this limit, following Jacques Le Goff's (1985) notion of the 'Long Middle Ages'. Medieval archaeology can therefore also be concerned with the study of the post-medieval period without needing to be labelled as 'post-medieval archaeology'.

There exists a corresponding concept throughout medieval archaeology in Europe with regards to fields of research. Nevertheless, there is significant variation within national schools concerning the importance of, and thus focus on, different topics, as also variation in the extent to which the perspective focuses on historical regions, thereby overcoming present-day frontiers. On the one hand, the traditional areas of research that have formed the basic canon since the infancy of medieval archaeology (i.e. towns, rural settlements, churches and monasteries, castles and fortifications) have become more and more diversified. On the other, new questions and topics have been developed, such as:

- the investigation of historical regions and past environments (landscape archaeology; environmental archaeology), with its particular interdisciplinary approach;
- exchange and trade in an overall perspective, including means of transport and historic routes;
- the archaeology of ships, which has shown significant potential for the coastal areas surrounding the Mediterranean, as well as the North and Baltic Seas, and, in some cases also, for inland navigation;
- the archaeology of death and burial in a Christian context;

- the archaeology of Jewish settlements and religious buildings, especially in Central Europe;
- the archaeology of production, focusing on technological processes and innovations, whereby the primary industries, such as mining, smelting and glass-working, are given particular attention; and, finally,
- the entire area of material culture, constituting a central field of research in which artefacts are integrated into research topics going beyond typological or chronological problems, such as everyday life, lifestyles and social differentiation within medieval society.

At the moment, some international trends are evident within medieval archaeology. For example, the importance of archaeometry is increasing within all fields of research. The archaeology of buildings is coming into greater focus, especially in those countries where medieval archaeology emerged from prehistory. Landscape archaeology has also an increasing role; whereas the landscape was traditionally viewed as the framework for sites and monuments, it has now become an independent subject for investigation, as a stage (Gerrard 2003, 141f, 149f, with refs; Muir 2000). There is also a tendency to develop comprehensive research topics extending beyond the analysis of single sites, although the intensity of such approaches varies between countries and universities.

The Position of the Discipline, among other Academic Disciplines

Reviewing the current situation of medieval archaeology, it is evident that the subject has become established as an independent scientific discipline in most European countries (Andersson & Wienberg 1993; Decaëns & Flambard Héricher 1999). It has also been firmly integrated into the canon of those sciences dealing with the emergence and development of the Middle Ages, and the history of the peoples who lived during this period. The specific position among these sciences varies in individual countries and is conditioned by the national development of the discipline and its different scientific traditions.

The particular nature of medieval archaeology is both interdisciplinary and transdisciplinary. It is closely tied to prehistory, from which the discipline has adopted important methods and techniques for the exploitation and analysis of the material record. In addition, the periods investigated by later prehistory and medieval archaeology partially overlap. As far as the objectives of research are concerned, the linkage to medieval history is of vital significance. The investigations of medieval archaeologists are based on the analysis of the material record and are confronted with the results of the latter working on the documentary evidence. The problem of the inter-relationship between the two disciplines is therefore of fundamental importance for the development of theoretical concepts of interpretation within medieval archaeology. Other disciplines related to medieval archaeology include some auxiliary historical sciences, such as numismatics and epigraphy, which several countries have in fact incorporated into medieval archaeology.

In some countries, history of art and architecture played a crucial role in the emergence of medieval archaeology, e.g. in France (Hubert 1961). In these countries, the inter-relationship between the two disciplines has thus been strong – and in some cases still is. In general, its role within modern medieval archaeology is less important, and the inter-relationship is subject to discussion (Wicker 1999). On the other hand, the importance of historical geography – especially in its genetically oriented approach to settlement research – has been increasing in the context of comprehensive questions about the development of historical regions. Finally, medieval archaeology – in the manner of most other archaeological disciplines – has opened up a broad co-operation with the natural sciences. Most important are geophysics and geochemistry, with their non-invasive methods of exploration, the wide range of scientific dating methods, and all those disciplines that apply archaeometric methods in the analysis of the medieval material record, such as palaeobiology, physical anthropology and archaeochemistry.

The Teaching of Medieval Archaeology

The position of medieval archaeology within universities and teaching is again formatively influenced by the differing national tendencies and histories of research. This can be seen by its integration into different faculties or departments. In France, for example, medieval archaeology is closely linked to medieval history and history of art, whereas in Scandinavia or Germany, it is assigned to prehistory. In consequence, this has had an affect on the various curricula.

Today, many European countries offer courses in medieval archaeology, with the possibilities being most extensive in the United Kingdom. The range of different courses and degrees at European universities has been presented during the conferences of the 'European Symposium for Teachers of Medieval Archaeology' (ESTMA Lund 1990, see Andersson & Wienberg 1993; ESTMA II Budapest 1993; ESTMA III Caen 1996, see Decaëns & Flambard Héricher 1999; ESTMA IV Seville/Cordoba 1999; see Valor & Carmona 2001; ESTMA V Bamberg 2002). This has revealed significant variation in structures and subjects. On the other hand, due to the ongoing establishment of the standardised European Higher Education Area within the European Union, all universities will adopt the Anglo-American system and thus a threefold system of degrees. This system has already been implemented in some countries and is due to come into place throughout the EU by 2010. All taught students will then be awarded a bachelor's or master's degree; however, the contents of these degrees are not to be standardised.

Differences in the contents of teaching are especially distinct regarding the extent to which courses in medieval art-history or prehistory are integrated. This is equally valid for the emphasis put on methods, and on whether the perspective focuses on present-day or historical regions. Similarly, the consideration of theoretical aspects and the integration of natural sciences differ in the individual countries. The focus on specific topics is determined by the varying research priorities. Nevertheless, some common standards can be observed, especially concerning the basic education. At most universities, the acquisition of basic competence in the exploitation of the material record (methods of excavation) plays an important part during the first years, as well as courses on the classic fields of research, such as rural settlements, towns, religious architecture, castles and fortifications. The study of material culture is variously incorporated within different curricula. In summary, one may state that there is no uniform study of medieval archaeology, rather that it takes on different forms, specific to different countries and universities. However, the acquired knowledge and skills are broadly comparable.

The Theoretical Framework

In most European countries, the approaches of archaeology remain positivistic, i.e. the exploration and extensive exploitation of archaeological data is given special emphasis, whereas a critical reflection on theoretical aspects is rarely undertaken. Some time ago – mainly in Scandinavia and the Anglophone world – archaeology opened up a discussion of the theoretical framework for the interpretation of the material record (Hodder 1991). This 'new archaeology' followed an approach which was ahistorical in the final analysis so that it had hardly any impact on medieval archaeology (Moreland 1991), whereas the concepts of 'post-processual archaeology' were to be far more intensively discussed and integrated into research agenda. This is especially true for 'symbolic and structural archaeology' and its 'contextual' approach (Gerrard 2003, 217f), which seems particularly appropriate for developing models for an interpretation of medieval material culture, based on theoretical reflections. Simultaneously, new perspectives evolved, such as 'identity and society', 'artefacts and meaning' or 'medieval archaeology in modern society'. The elaboration of a gender perspective on archaeological sources from the Middle Ages is one aspect of these developments (Gilchrist 1997).

Medieval archaeology is an historical archaeology. From a theoretical point of view, all historical archaeologies share the vital fact that their genuine archaeological sources are tied up within a framework of parallel records, including writings and pictures (Andrén 1998). This is equally valid for all European regions, even though the beginning and the density of such parallel records vary significantly. The possibilities of connecting written and pictorial evidence with archaeological remains offers a special potential for their interpretation and, from its beginnings, medieval archaeology has taken up this opportunity.

The linking of these parallel records in the course of interpretation is therefore a vital problem on the theoretical level. Problems concerning pictorial sources and their relation to the material record have attracted little attention so far (but see, e.g. Carver 1986, on late Anglo-Saxon artefacts, and various studies of the Bayeux Tapestry: e.g. Flambard Héricher 2004; Renaudeau 2004; Lewis 2005). In contrast, the inter-relationships between documentary and material sources, and thus also between the disciplines of medieval history and archaeology, have been discussed in several countries since the latter came into being (Scholkmann 2003; Carver 2002). Although there have always been some scholars who have understood the discipline more as a cultural history (Cinthio 1963), the problem maintains a prominent position in current theoretical discussions.

These issues have been discussed both at a national level and independently. However, there is some conformity concerning the problems and the results. Especially during its infancy, but sometimes still today, medieval archaeology has been considered as complementary to the discipline of medieval history, thus to be regarded as an auxiliary science, providing evidence mainly for those periods and topics for which written records are scarce or non-existent. This is indicated by the focus that some countries put on the early medieval period. Such an approach narrows the potential of the material record to a mere supplement, verifying documentary sources, or simply to the illustration of historical processes. For a long time also, medieval archaeology accepted exclusively historical questions, raised by historians, as a starting-point for archaeological research (de Bouard 1975). Contrarily, current theoretical discussion calls for a detachment from historical questions and for the elaboration of genuine questions with an archaeological agenda (Austin 1990; Champion 1990; Moreland 2001).

At the same time, models for a new understanding of the relations between material and written sources, of connecting artefacts and texts, have been developed (Andrén 1998; Moreland 2001). These models regard the material record and written sources as 'discursive contexts' and define and interpret material sources as texts. This approach could offer a potential for the further development of the discipline. The contribution of medieval archaeology in assembling an overall understanding of the medieval world, and the visibility of its share in so doing, will determine the future relevance of the discipline within modern society.

The European Perspective

In all European countries, medieval archaeology emerged from an interest in monuments and archaeological relics of the national past. Thus, in the initial phase, and sometimes until recently, it focused entirely on the material culture of a particular country; it was therefore often regarded as a study of the national heritage from the Middle Ages. Transnational approaches usually considered historical regions, while any approach to a comprehensive view, encompassing problems and research topics throughout Europe, took a back-seat. For example, the establishment of the conference series *Château Gaillard* in 1962, offering a European platform for the presentation of research on medieval castles and fortifications, only gained a companion as late as 1995, when an equivalent series *Ruralia* was established, dealing with rural settlements.

The recent development of vital importance is thus the transition from a national perspective to a wider view over the entirety of medieval Europe (hence the need for this text-book). The conference 'Medieval Europe: York 1992' (*Medieval Europe 1992*) was the first attempt to offer such a platform, where the results of research from all European countries could be presented, and thus to create an opportunity to view research topics in a specifically European perspective. It has been further developed at the following international conferences: 'Medieval Europe: Bruges 1997' (de Boe & Verhaeghe 1997); 'Medieval Europe: Basel 2002' (Helmig et al 2002); and 'Medieval Europe: Paris' (2007). By now, the 'European perspective' can be perceived of as an integral part of medieval archaeology in Europe.

Archaelogical Investigation

The basis for medieval archaeology is the study of the many physical remains of the period, consisting of objects, cultural layers, standing buildings and other *in situ* structures. Pictorial and written sources provide a unique approach to this study, which is one of the most important characteristics of the discipline. The great variety of the source material adds up to an extremely complex area of endeavour, associated with enormously different methodological problems and challenges: diving to shipwrecks at the bottom of the sea; the use of heavy machinery to uncover the subsurface of many square kilometres of open countryside, with thousands of postholes from ploughed-over villages; the excavation of individual skeletons with a trowel; the survey of fossil roads, systems of cultivation and building foundations hidden in brushwood and thorn thickets, or visible as 'mosaics' on grassy meadows and moors; the interpretation of complex cultural layers of garbage, metres thick, and the remains of structures in the core of a medieval city; the laboratory analysis of macro-fossils; the processing of items found in the soil, or items that were never in the soil, such as works of art used in churches or forgotten in attics; and the recording of roofing, masonry and the layout of buildings, such as churches, monasteries, fortresses and castles still in use. The many areas of research have much in common, rooted as they are in archaeology – but are still so varied that, from a methodological and technical point of view, they can be regarded as specialised branches with their own distinguishing characteristics. The following is a brief introduction to both the core and some more specialised areas of the field.

Archaeological investigations cover all forms of recording, processing and interpretation of the physical remains of the period. Some types of investigation are destructive, such as archaeological excavation or certain methods for determining the composition of objects; others are non-destructive, such as reconnaissance in the field, the archaeological study of standing buildings, and the study of items from excavations and museum collections. Thus excavation is only one part of archaeological investigation – although it is an important part, being very characteristic of the discipline. These days, when archaeological remains are more clearly than ever seen to constitute a finite and vulnerable archive, the development of non-destructive methods of investigation is a growing field of activity.

Data and interpretation

Archaeological remains are the result of a long chain of naturally and culturally determined processes of transformation that, during the course of time, have altered their extent, appearance, and context. Archaeological investigation, which ranges from various types of preliminary investigation through to excavation, or to other types of investigation, leading to the recording and storage of data, is the last link in this series of processes. The methods and tools of the profession have developed concurrently with its themes and theoretical directions. From the simple exposure of monuments in the early days of medieval archaeology, combined with its focus on individual objects, a demand for professionalism and methods of handling large quantities of data has developed, especially as a result of the rise in the great urban excavations during the phase when the profession reached maturity. At the same time, there has been increasing understanding of the relationship between data and interpretation. Where the emphasis in processual archaeology is on distinguishing between the two of them, e.g. between the description of layers and their interpretation during excavation, we have become more aware that 'interpretation occurs at the trowel's edge': that the methods used in excavation and collection of data depend themselves on interpretation (Hodder 1999, 83).

It is impossible to reconstruct fully the Middle Ages. The Middle Ages are long over and exist only as relics – or as shadows in our imaginations. But the study of these physical remains allows us to produce qualified stories of the medieval period; it is the task of the archaeologist to build bridges to connect the paths of the present with those of the past. Clarifying this position is an important basis for understanding source-production, i.e. the observations, selections and rejections that are made in the course of the work process, from start to finish. The choice and interpretation of data, and the general establishment of a fund of knowledge, are dependent on the individual researcher. Results are never better than the starting-point: that is the nature of the investigation and the abilities of the archaeologists involved in it.

Archaeological excavation

It has been said many times over, and it must be repeated again: excavation is an unrepeatable experiment. Whereas written sources, pictures and maps, objects and buildings can be studied over and over again by various researchers, bringing new approaches to the evidence, every archaeological excavation is unique, and a sod can only be turned once. This means that carrying out an excavation makes special demands on meticulousness, as does the choice of method for excavation and recording. Every excavation requires that a problem be formulated, and then an exploratory design drawn up to address it, but the design also needs to be sufficiently flexible to be able to register the unexpected and to pose new questions.

It is impossible to investigate and record everything, but it is possible to document for better or for worse what has been investigated. There is available a considerable body of literature treating the entire process, from the preparatory stages through the investigation itself and the subsequent processing of data, along with the various techniques required for carrying out excavation and its documentation (e.g. Drewett 1999; Roskams 2001, both with comprehensive refs).

There are many possible choices of method for investigation and recording and they will be closely linked to the purpose of the individual project. The background for the investigation, whether rescue or research excavation, also offers a number of choices. Excavation is often initiated as a result of construction work and, in this case, it is not the excavating body that defines the extent of the task, but the developer. Heritage legislation in Europe varies greatly with regard to the protection of physical remains, possible archaeological investigation, its economic framework and the responsibilities of those concerned. As the 1992 Malta Convention (*The European Convention on the Protection of the Archaeological Heritage*) is ratified and implemented, minimum European standards will be established in a number of these areas; among other things, the focus on preservation of remains *in situ* will become more common.

Prior to an archaeological survey, defined in this case as an excavation, preliminary investigation should take place, if at all possible, in order to determine the type and extent of the task ahead, both in relation to such administrative aspects as the budget and timetable, and in relation to the investigation's historical and archaeological perspectives: What is presently known about the area, site or monument to be explored? How will the investigation contribute to answering a series of research questions, either locally or in a wider perspective? The availability of archives, collections and other sources will vary locally and nationally, as will the possibility of carrying out in-depth investigation, so that this introduction can only mention some of the most common sources and methods that need to be taken into consideration.

In order to acquire a preliminary impression of a locality, antiquarian archives (such as Sites and Monuments Records) should be consulted for an overview of known physical remains and earlier investigations. In addition, written sources and maps of the area can provide important information on earlier topographical conditions, such as the original locations of institutions that no longer exist, as well as for the infrastructure and patterns of land-ownership. Place-names on historical maps provide an important source for the identification of older settlement patterns in the countryside.

There are varying possibilities for supplementary investigation on the site itself. These can be invasive or non-invasive, including a whole range of techniques for remote-sensing (Clark 1996). Aerial photographs and field-walking can be used to identify new sites in open landscapes. Geophysical methods, based on resistivity or magnetic anomalies from sub-surface structures and cultural layers, can be used for the further mapping of sites, for such purposes as estimating their horizontal extent, the depth and character of their cultural layers, and any special areas of activity (Fig 1.1). Geochemical mapping methods can also be employed, especially phosphate analysis, which is now widely used. A more direct examination of a site can be made by using coring or mechanically dug test-pits (*sondages*). Preliminary excavations should be used with care in city centres, as they can destroy important stratigraphic relationships; if possible 'free' sections from modern excavations should be examined in order to answer preliminary questions as to the complexity and extent of the cultural layers to be encountered.

Preliminary work also includes consulting with the various partners who may be going to assist with specific tasks during the excavation and with the processing of any artefacts found, such as zoologists, anthropologists, macrofossil botanists and museum conservators. Finally, the work must be co-ordinated with the site-developer and construction-workers, if any. This is especially important in complicated urban excavations, where archaeologists and builders must often work closely together because of safety considerations, but also for technical reasons.

Settlements excavated in cultivated landscapes are often characterised by the absence of their cultural layers as a result of ploughing. In these investigations, the plough-layer is usually stripped mechanically, exposing the subsoil, after which recording and excava-

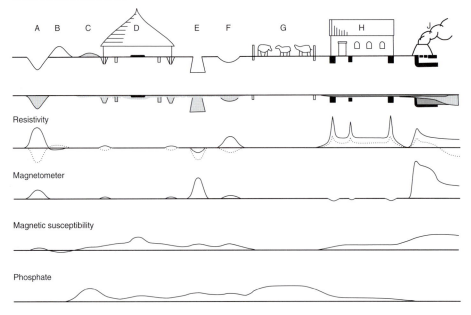

Choice of method: choice of site

Resistivity

Magnetometer

Magnetic susceptibility

Phosphate

Fig 1.1　*Using remote-sensing, it is possible to clarify the extent of a site, the positions of burials, and certain types of features and activities. Here a selection of methods can be seen used on a settlement that has been ploughed over. Top: the settlement with ditch (A) and earthworks (B), midden (C), a building with post-holes and a hearth on its central axis (D), with two pits (E and F), a fold for animals (G) and a massive building (H) with foundations for solid walls. There is also a kiln (J). Next the settlement is shown as it would appear under the plough-layer, and how it can be revealed using the different detection methods available (after Clark 1996).*

tion of the surviving sunken features can begin. Occasionally, the area investigated may be very large, such as with the excavation of the precursors of the village of Vorbasse, in Denmark, where over 200,000 m² were uncovered. This makes it possible to achieve a comprehensive image of the structural development of the settlement, as well as its social and economic conditions, through time (cf. Hamerow 2002). In this type of excavation, the main challenge is to connect the many, stratigraphically more-or-less unrelated, features into a meaningful whole (cf. the method presented in Holst 1999). When a settlement comprises a number of phases, this can be an extremely complex task (Fig 1.2).

Using machines to remove the surface soil in order to expose the undisturbed subsoil is, of course, effective, but this can in some cases have a price to pay because it has been shown that important information can be lost in this way. As Peter Drewett has observed: 'People in the past, as today, lived and undertook their daily tasks on surfaces, not down pits and postholes' (1999, 98). On some sites it can be advantageous to carry out three-dimensional recording of artefacts, using detectors and intra-site reconnaissance, both before and during the removal of the overburden in spits. Some items will

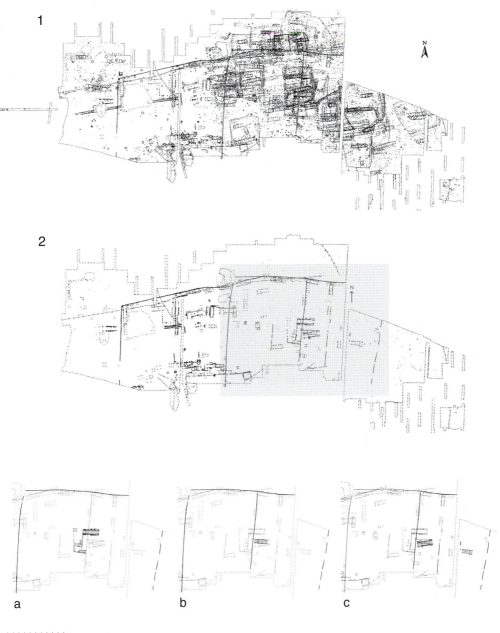

Østergård, Hyrup, Denmark: (1) the settlement can be separated into several phases from 1500 BC
to AD 1200; with (2) a plan of the medieval features. The structural development in the eastern
section of the area (grey) is suggested. The foundation farm from the Viking period was succeeded in
the mid-11th century by another large single farm (a). This farm was divided up through inheritance
during the 11th and 12th centuries (b & c: showing only the splitting of the eastern farm), before it
evolved into a small village (Hans Peter Jørgensen, after Sørensen 2003).

Fig 1.2

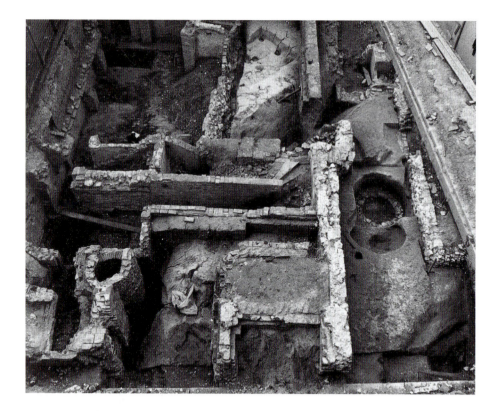

Fig 1.3   *Complex stratigraphic situation at the urban excavation 'Vor dem Neuen Bau' in Ulm, south-western Germany, in 1988. Apart from some post-holes, the oldest structure is the Grubenhaus (H), an SFB with post-holes, dating to the late 11th/early 12th century. It was partly disturbed when a 4m wide ditch was dug, in the early 12th century, from east to west (3); part of a similar ditch was found in the southernmost corner (4), both belonging to the fortification of the royal palace. The large moat at left (1) cuts the ditch (3) and dates to the 12th century; it was thus part of the early town fortification. When the town was extended in the late Middle Ages, the moat was filled in, after which several late medieval and post-medieval walls and foundations were constructed over it, as well as a cess-pit (LA), two wells (BR) and a cellar (Keller) (after Bräuning 1998).*

have been introduced to the area through later manuring, but others will derive from the settlement in question and, despite the fact that many years of cultivation will have torn them from their original contexts, their overall distribution can still reflect the situations under which they were originally deposited. Likewise, on less complex sites with few phases, phosphate analysis and measuring magnetic susceptibility can be helpful in revealing areas of activity, if this has not already been carried out as part of the preliminary investigation.

In urban excavations and on other sites with preserved cultural layers, the archaeologist is faced with further challenges (Fig 1.3). While excavation in an open landscape can be extensive, covering up to a half, and even occasionally whole villages, urban excava-

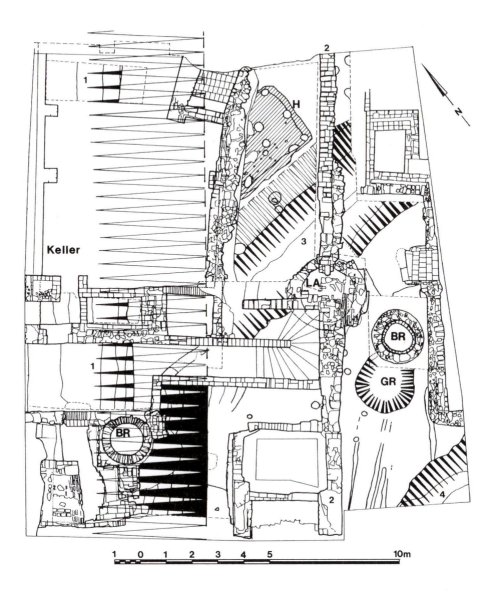

Keller

tions rarely extend beyond a few plots or tenements. In return, cultural layers in urban locations are often preserved to a considerable depth, so that whereas excavation in open fields is calculated in square metres, urban excavations are calculated in cubic metres of metre-thick cultural layers. In this type of excavation, description of the often complex stratigraphy, with its thousands of individual contexts, is of central importance. The challenges of urban archaeology have increased the understanding of the potential for knowledge contained within cultural layers. Where interest was earlier concentrated primarily on exposing structures (according to the principle of 'find a wall and then follow it'), the next step was arbitrary excavation of the cultural layers in horizontal spits, with no consideration of the actual extent of the deposits, perhaps working in square

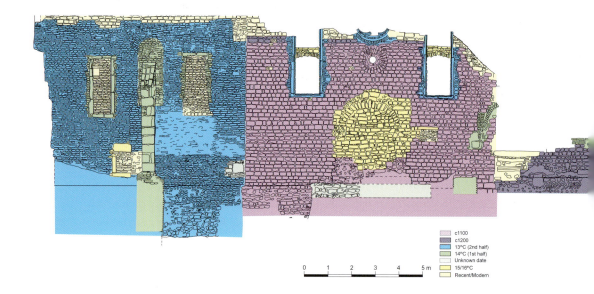

	c1100
	c1200
	13ᵗʰC (2nd half)
	14ᵗʰC (1st half)
	Unknown date
	15/16ᵗʰC
	Recent/Modern

0   1   2   3   4   5 m

Fig 1.4   *The medieval synagogue at Speyer, Germany: building and analysis (reproduced by permission of Sigmar Fitting (photo) & Pia Heberer (drawing), Landesamt für Denkmalpflege Rheinland Pfalz).*

sections, but nevertheless concentrating on *cultural layers* in contrast to *structures*. A further development of this was the stratigraphic excavation, where the emphasis is on *contexts/entities*. These designations are a signal that cultural layers and constructions are now considered equally worthwhile in the archaeological data-set. From this point of view, *surfaces/interfaces* also form an important part of the stratigraphic sequence and are vital to its interpretation. Surfaces are the stages on which the people of the Middle Ages acted, while postholes and middens are merely the results of these actions. The stratigraphic method of excavation is therefore the essential starting point for many of the questions posed within the framework of post-processual archaeology.

Methods for recording and systematizing data have developed concurrently, especially in connection with English excavations during the 1970s. The development of the Harris Matrix (Box 1.1), systematizing data on pre-printed sheets, as well as emphasising individual contexts, can be seen as a coherent concept (Pearson & Williams 1993). Such sheets for recording data are constantly being developed and refined. For instance, the recording of cultural layers now includes a description of the composition of the deposit and its stratigraphic relationships, of the artefacts that it contains, with lists of samples taken, photos, etc; the extent of the deposit is registered three-dimensionally with the aid of a plan, section and measurements, including heights. As a final consequence of the stratigraphic method of excavation, a single-context plan can be drawn up for each layer. Composite plans are problematic as primary documentation, as only the youngest deposits are completely visible, whereas other (just as important) deposits can only be hinted at. Consequently, this method does not allow for a full re-evaluation of correlations, or for new questions, given that the decision as to which deposits and relationships would be documented was made at the documentation phase. Finally, the context is interpreted before it is removed.

Following the gradual introduction of electronic data processing (EDP) to archaeology during the early 1980s, the digital medium has had an explosive affect on the recording, processing and representation of data, and the possibilities for further development seem unending.

After excavation come data processing and report writing, as well as the organisation of relevant scientific research projects, together with the preparation of finds for conservation and storage (see Box 1.2). One could say that the many square/cubic metres are converted into running metres of shelving in archaeological archives, and the results of this phase of the project are just as dependent on the financial situation as the previous phases.

Buildings archaeology

Medieval buildings, whether ruins or still in use, comprise a special object of study (Morris 2000); in contrast to 'traditional archaeology', they are visible in the landscape and are thus, in principle, available for repeated study with new questions aimed at a building's manifest as well as latent features (Fig 1.4). Such research includes not only the archaeological investigation of the construction and development of buildings as the

BOX 1.1 STRATIGRAPHIC RELATIONSHIPS

In 1973, Edward Harris developed the so-called Harris Matrix, resulting from the complex urban excavations that took place in Winchester, England, during 1969-71. It provides a 2-dimensional graphic presentation of the relative stratigraphic correlations of different contexts (Harris 1979; 1989). A Harris Matrix visualises the chronology of activities, but neither their duration nor whether they occurred simultaneously. It is most often used in excavations with deep cultural layers, where it is an important tool during the excavation and recording process and forms the basis for interpretation during the final processing. Use of the Harris Matrix has also begun to gain a footing in buildings archaeology.

A Harris Matrix recognizes three types of stratigraphic relationship (Fig 1). While the first two relationships are unambiguous, the third is more problematic because it deals with contexts found on either side of an intersection, which is believed to have been cut through them (Fig 2). In contrast to the first two relationships, there is an interpretive element involved here – an element that Harris otherwise disclaims (Harris 1979, 82; cf. the discussion in Roskams 2001, 155f).

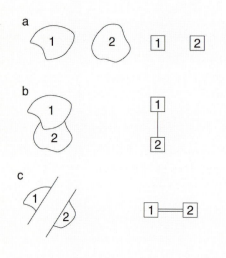

Fig 1

Stratigraphic entities can: (a) 'have no direct stratigraphic relationship'; (b) be 'in superimposition'; or (c) be 'correlated as parts of the same original deposit'.

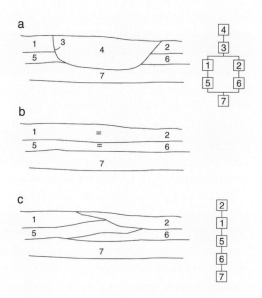

Fig 2

(a) Contexts (1 & 2, 5 & 6) on either side of an intersection (3: note that the burial's interface is recorded separately) may have been identical (b), but other correlations (c) are also possible. Interpretation will here scramble the stratigraphy and should be avoided.

It can also be important to record and visualise the physical relationships of contexts (Fig 4). This is usually done for individual contexts on separate layer-sheets, from which a Harris Matrix is prepared. By preparing a matrix of physical relationships, knowledge can be gained of simultaneity, and surfaces connected across the entire excavation area, together with an explanation of the horizontal and vertical distribution of artefacts. This can, however, be a time-consuming business and so when undertaken needs to be of considerable importance to the questions raised by the investigation.

By Mette Svart Kristiansen

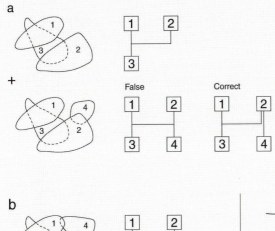

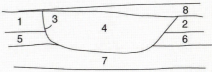

Fig 3

False H-structures (a) are a common error appearing during the construction of a Harris matrix. H-structures can, however, be correct (b). Note that two contexts opposite each other (1 & 2), with both on their own strings, do not indicate simultaneity.

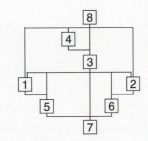

Fig 4

The physical relationships of contexts (in section).

BOX 1.2   FROM EXCAVATION TO PUBLICATION

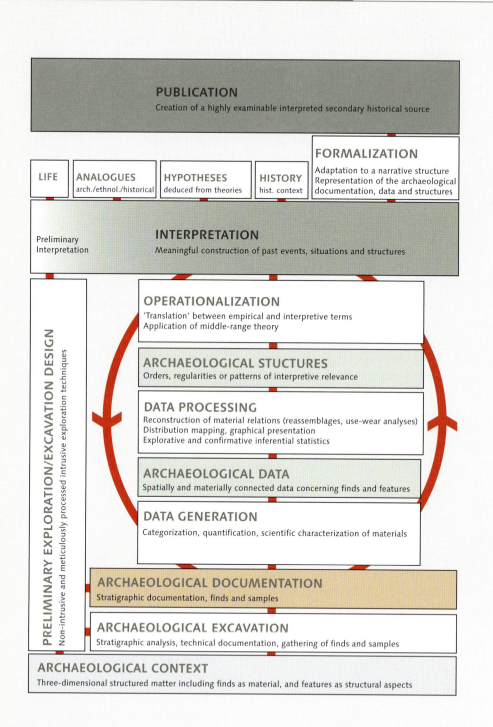

PUBLICATION
Creation of a highly examinable interpreted secondary historical source

FORMALIZATION
Adaptation to a narrative structure
Representation of the archaeological documentation, data and structures

| LIFE | ANALOGUES arch./ethnol./historical | HYPOTHESES deduced from theories | HISTORY hist. context |

Preliminary Interpretation

INTERPRETATION
Meaningful construction of past events, situations and structures

PRELIMINARY EXPLORATION/EXCAVATION DESIGN
Non-intrusive and meticulously processed intrusive exploration techniques

OPERATIONALIZATION
'Translation' between empirical and interpretive terms
Application of middle-range theory

ARCHAEOLOGICAL STUCTURES
Orders, regularities or patterns of interpretive relevance

DATA PROCESSING
Reconstruction of material relations (reassemblages, use-wear analyses)
Distribution mapping, graphical presentation
Explorative and confirmative inferential statistics

ARCHAEOLOGICAL DATA
Spatially and materially connected data concerning finds and features

DATA GENERATION
Categorization, quantification, scientific characterization of materials

ARCHAEOLOGICAL DOCUMENTATION
Stratigraphic documentation, finds and samples

ARCHAEOLOGICAL EXCAVATION
Stratigraphic analysis, technical documentation, gathering of finds and samples

ARCHAEOLOGICAL CONTEXT
Three-dimensional structured matter including finds as material, and features as structural aspects

This chart pivots around the interpretations of the active archaeologist (Frommer 2007), given that this individual is exclusively involved in the entire 'archaeological process'. During the first stage, interpretation governs the process of planning and excavation (light green), taking the form of preliminary interpretation, which at this stage is unable to take fully into account the archaeological record. The archaeologist's interpretation further controls the evaluation of the documentation resulting from the excavation (green) and, ultimately, influences the structure and content of the final publication (dark green).

Since the intrusive access to the archaeological context is unique (represented by the narrow bars in the graph in contrast to the repeatable processes represented by the thick bars), the initial phase of planning and excavation plays a fundamental role. The common separation between the planning and excavation phases, on the one hand, and the subsequent evaluation of the results on the other, with regard to the staff as well as to its design, directly affects the quality and adequacy of this stage of the interpretative process.

The web of interactions during the interpretive evaluation takes up a large part of the archaeologist's work. Just like the overall chart, this web represents a non-linear hermeneutic process of perception. It is, however, strongly oriented by the data. Quantitative-deductivist procedures that determine the individual steps are thereby integrated into an overall hermeneutic framework. Within such an integrating approach, hermeneutics and deductivism are not dichotomous, but fruitfully compatible (Kosso 1991; Patrick 1985; Hodder & Hudson 2003, 239-42). The sequence of the representations (coloured boxes) of the archaeological record used here follows in part the 'Archaeological Method' of Evžen Neustupný (1993); the term 'archaeological structures' has likewise been adapted from this work. Within archaeological practice, the documentation resulting from excavation is meaningfully transcended by phenomenological access, as well as by conversion into data for processing. The potential of 'Life', 'Analogues', 'Hypotheses' and 'History' (small boxes), as sources of comparative knowledge, has been widely used ever since. These factors – understood as unrecognised influences – cannot anyway be avoided, a fact that has been stressed by both processual and post-processual archaeologists, from their distinct perspectives.

By Sören Frommer

Fig 1

The 'archaelogical process'.

basis for such studies as their place in an architectural cultural context, but also, under the influence of recently developed archaeological theory, as an expression of social conditions and everyday practices (Grenville 1997, 17-22).

The archaeological investigation of standing buildings involves moving from two to three dimensions, where the laws of stratigraphy relating to superimposition are partly annulled, and where the object is altered from soil to bricks and mortar, as well as having load-bearing walls and floors. Naturally, it is also possible to find remains of buildings underground. Here, the three-dimensional aspect often no longer exists, but the ability to read the different materials and structures is still important. In the archaeological investigation of a building, it is an advantage to carry out documentation and analysis during the surveying process. Another possibility is to do a photogrammetric survey, where the analysis is undertaken afterwards.

Throughout Europe different traditions exist for the inclusion of buildings archaeology as a specialised area of interest in the profession, and in many places it occupies only a small niche. This is remarkable in the light of the origins of medieval archaeology, with its basis in existing buildings. In addition, the numerous medieval buildings spread across Europe comprise a central part of the material culture of the period and open the way to a cross-disciplinary field of activity in cooperation with architects and restorers. Here the special expertise of the medieval archaeologist contributes the analysis of buildings as historical source material, according to archaeological principles of investigation and documentation, preferably including excavation – forming a combination of archaeological research above and below ground.

Artefacts

The study of artefacts is a core topic of medieval archaeology – and thus they form the backbone of this book. Artefacts can be studied individually, as types, and as part of an archaeological context. An explosive growth in the number of artefacts found in excavations has meant a similar growth in specialised studies of finds. An important task for many years has been to draw up typologies for groups of artefacts and their dating, especially those based on the dendrochronological (tree-ring) dating of well-documented urban stratigraphical excavations. Even though there is now a solid base, the task is not yet complete and there is still room for pioneers in this field. Based on existing knowledge and published material, it has become possible to pose new types of question, such as those based on finds-contexts that can illuminate trade, crafts or regionalism. In recent years, inspired by post-processual theories, there has been an increased focus on social conditions, such as strategies for everyday life, including the relationships between the sexes, and the use of artefacts to emphasise or blur social status. In this connection, the focus on the three-dimensional recording of artefacts during excavation has increased, and also considerations of their relation to primary, re-deposited or postdepositional layers. All types of layer, and their content of artefacts, can provide important if differing information.

Scientific methods of investigation and dating

The natural sciences hold a central position in medieval archaeology. Since the discipline has become a profession, and with increasing understanding of the inter-disciplinary opportunities available, cooperation between archaeologists, geologists, nuclear physicists, biologists, anthropologists and others has grown. Depending on the financial framework and questions posed by the excavation, it is now possible to include a wide range of scientific analyses. The areas of endeavour are many and are constantly being renewed, but are in general to be divided into four main areas: methods of dating; determination of materials; anthropology; and nutrition and environment (Brothwell & Pollard 2001).

The Middle Ages must be characterised as but a brief period in the calendar of the natural sciences, but of the various scientific dating methods, interest can be concentrated on a few. Dendrochronology, with its possibility of dating the felling of a tree to a half-year, when the bark is preserved, is an extremely precise method of dating, vital to the study of the medieval period. Radiocarbon (C14) dating is considerably less precise, but in some cases can provide a useful alternative (although more refined methods are in development), as also can thermoluminescence dating, e.g. for dating hearths, kilns, and the phases of brick buildings.

Archaeobotanical and zoological investigations are widespread given that since macrofossils and animal bones are found in great numbers in excavations (Box 6.1). Macrofossils are found in almost all archaeological layers, but in varying amounts and conditions depending on the state of preservation. They can be used specifically to evaluate the functions of individual structures or the formation of series of layers, and more generally to illuminate questions concerning economy and everyday life, the development of vegetation and the cultivated landscape, and thus the interaction between humans and nature. Zoological material is often the most comprehensive of the groups of material found in an excavation. It provides a unique opportunity to illustrate the composition of the animal population, the agricultural economy and patterns of consumption.

BIBLIOGRAPHY

Andersson, H (1992) 'The era of town inventories: a kind of evaluation', in Addyman, P and Roskams, S (eds), *Urbanism. Medieval Europe 1992: Preprinted Papers*, Vol 1, York, 15-20

Andersson, H and Wienberg, J (eds) (1993) *The Study of Medieval Archaeology*, European Symposium for Teachers of Medieval Archaeology, Lund, 11-15 June 1990, Stockholm

Andrén, A (1998) *Between Artifacts and Texts: Historical Archaeology in Global Perspective. Contributions to Global Historical Archaeology*, New York

Austin, D (1990) 'The "proper study" of medieval archaeology', in Austin, D and Alcock, L (eds), *From the Baltic to the Black Sea: Studies in Medieval Archaeology*, Boston, 43-78

Beresford, M and Hurst, J (1990) *Wharram Percy. Deserted Medieval Village*, London

Biddle, M and Hudson, D (1972) *The Future of London's Past*, London

Bräuning, A (1998) *Um Ulm herum. Untersuchungen zu mittelalterlichen Befestigungsanlagen in Ulm*, Forschungen und Berichte der Archäologie des Mittelalters in Baden-Württemberg 23, Stuttgart

Brothwell, DR and Pollard, AM (eds) (2001) *Handbook of Archaeological Sciences*, Chichester

Carver, MOH (1986) 'Contemporary artifacts illustrated in late Saxon manuscripts', *Archaeologia* 108, 117-45

Carver, M (2002) 'Marriages of true minds: archaeology with texts', in Cunliffe, B, Davies, W and Renfrew, C (eds), *Archaeology: the Widening Debate*, British Academy, London, 465-96

Champion, TC (1990) 'Medieval archaeology and the tyranny of the historical record', in Austin, D and Alcock, L (eds), *From the Baltic to the Black Sea: Studies in Medieval Archaeology*, Boston, 79-95

Chateau Gaillard (1964): *Etudes de Castellologie européenne*, 1

Cinthio, E (1963) 'Medieval archaeology as a research subject', *Meddelanden från Lunds Universitets Historiska Museum 1962-1963*, 186-202

Clark, A (1996) *Seeing Beneath the Soil. Prospecting Methods in Archaeology*, London

Clarke, H (1989) 'Asbjørn Herteig: archaeologist and pioneer', in Myrvoll, S and Herteig, AE (eds), *Archaeology and the Urban Economy: Festschrift to Asbjørn E. Herteig*, Bergen, 23-7

Clarke, H and Carter, A (1977) *Excavations in King's Lynn 1963-1970*, Society for Medieval Archaeology Monograph Series 7, London

de Boe, G and Verhaeghe, F (1997) *Papers of the 'Medieval Europe Brugge 1997' Conference*, Zellik

de Bouard, M (1975) *Manuel d'archéologie médiévale: De la fouille à l'histoire*, Paris

Decaëns, J and Flambard Héricher, A-M (1999) *Estma III: Actes du IIIe Colloque Européen des Professeurs d'Archéologie Médiévale*, Caen

Drewett, PL (1999) *Field Archaeology: an Introduction*, London

The European Convention on the Protection of the Archaeological Heritage, Valetta, January 1992 www.coe.int/T/E/Cultural_Co-operation/Heritage/Archaeology/2Convention.asp

Flambard Héricher, A-M (2004) 'Archaeology and the Bayeux Tapestry', in Bouet, P, Levy, B and Neveux, F (eds), *The Bayeux Tapestry: Embroidering the Facts of History*, Caen, 261-87

Frommer, S (2007) *Historische Archäologie. Versuch einer geschichtswissenschaftlichen Grundlegung der Archäologie des Mittelalters und der Neuzeit*, Tübinger Forschungen zur historischen Archäologie 2, Büchenbach

Gerrard, C (2003) *Medieval Archaeology. Understanding Traditions and Contemporary Approaches*, London

Gilchrist, R (1997) 'Ambivalent bodies: gender and medieval archaeology', in Moore, J and Scott, E (eds), *Invisible People and Processes. Writing Gender and Childhood into European Archaeology*, Leicester/London, 42-58

Grenville, J (1997) *Medieval Housing*, London

Grimes, WF (1968) *The Excavation of Roman and Mediaeval London*, London

Hamerow, H (2002) *Early Medieval Settlements. The Archaeology of Rural Communities in Northwest Europe 400-900*, Oxford

Harris, EC (1979; 1989, 2nd ed) *Principles of Archaeological Stratigraphy*, London/New York

Heberer, P (2004) 'Die mittelalterliche Synagoge in Speyer. Bauforschung und Rekonstruktion', in Haverkamp, A (ed), *Historisches Museum Der Pfalz Speyer, Europas Juden im Mittelalter*, Ostfildern

Heighway, CM (ed) (1972) *The Erosion of History. Archaeology and Planning in Towns: a Study of Historic Towns affected by Modern Development in England, Wales and Scotland*, London

Helmig, G, Scholkmann, B and Untermann, M (2002) *Centre – Region – Periphery: Medieval Europe Basel 2002*, Hertingen

Hodder, I (1991) *Archaeological Theory in Europe*, London

Hodder, I (1999) *The Archaeological Process. An Introduction*, Oxford

Hodder, I and Hudson, S (2003, 3rd ed) *Reading the Past. Current Approaches to Interpretation in Archaeology*, Cambridge

Holst, MK (1999) 'The dynamic of the Iron-age village. A technique for the relative-chronological analysis of area-excavated Iron-age settlements', *Journal of Danish Archaeology* 13, 95-119

Hubert, J (1961) 'Archéologie médiévale', in Samaran, C (ed), *L'Histoire et ses méthodes*, Paris, 322-3

Kosso, P (1991) 'Method in archaeology: middle range theories as hermeneutics', *American Antiquity* 56, 621-7

Leciejewicz, L (1993) 'Medieval Archaeology in Eastern Europe', in Andersson, H and Wienberg, J (eds), *The Study of Medieval Archaeology. European Symposium for Teachers of Medieval Archaeology, Lund, 11-15 June 1990*, Lund Studies in Medieval Archaeology 13, Lund, 75-84

Le Goff, J (1985) *L'imaginaire médiéval: essais. Bibliothèque des histoires*, Paris

Lewis, MJ (2005) *The Archaeological Authority of the Bayeux Tapestry*, British Archaeological Reports 404, Oxford

Medieval Europe 1992; Conference on Medieval Archaeology in Europe: Preprinted Papers, Vols 1-8, York

Moreland, J (1991) 'Method and theory in medieval archaeology in the 1990s', *Archeologia medievale* 18, 7-42

Moreland, J (2001) *Archaeology and Text*, London

Morris, RK (2000) 'What is buildings archaeology?', in Morris, RK, *The Archaeology of Buildings*, Gloucestershire, 10-19

Muir, R (2000) *The New Reading the Landscape*, Fieldwork in Landscape History I, Exeter

Neugebauer, W (1980) 'Vorgeschichtsforschung und Bodendenkmalpflege in der Hansestadt Lübeck bis zum Jahre 1973', *Archäologie in Lübeck. Erkenntnisse von Archäologie und Bauforschung zur Geschichte und Vorgeschichte der Hansestadt*, 4-7, Lübeck

Neustupný, E (1993) *Archaeological Method*, Cambridge

Patrick, LE (1985) 'Is there an archaeological record?', *Advances in Archaeological Method and Theory* 8, 27-62

Pearson, N and Williams, T (1993) 'Single-context planning: its role in on-site recording procedures and in post-excavation analysis at York', in Harris, EC, Brown MR and Brown GJ (eds), *Practices of Archaeological Stratigraphy*, London, 89-103

Regteren Altena, HH van (1990) 'On the growth of young medieval archaeology: a recollection', in Besteman, JC, Bos, JM and Heidinga, HA (eds), *Medieval Archaeology in the Netherlands: Studies presented to H.H. van Regteren Altena*, Assen, 1-7

Renaudeau, O (2004) 'The Bayeux Tapestry and its depiction of costume: the problems of interpretation', in Bouet, P, Levy, B and Neveux, F (eds), *The Bayeux Tapestry: Embroidering the Facts of History*, Caen, 237-59

Roskams, S (2001) *Excavation*, Cambridge Manuals in Archaeology, Cambridge

Ruralia 1- (1996-)

Schindler, R (1958) *Ausgrabungen in Alt Hamburg. Neue Ergebnisse zur Frühgeschichte der Hansestadt. Hamburger Heimatbücher*, Hamburg

Scholkmann, B (2003) 'Die Tyrannei der Schriftquellen? Überlegungen zum Verhältnis materieller und schriftlicher Überlieferung in der Mittelalterarchäologie', in Heinz, M, Eggert, KHM and Veit, U (eds), *Zwischen Erklären und Verstehen?*, Tübingen, 239-57

Steensberg, A (1983) *Borup AD 700-1400. A Deserted Settlement and its Fields in South Zealand, Denmark*, 2 vols, Copenhagen

Steensberg, A, Østergaard Christensen, JL, Hatting, T and Liversage, D (1974) *Store Valby. Historisk-arkæologisk undersøgelse af en nedlagt landsby på Sjælland*, Det Kongelige Danske Videnskabernes Selskab, Historisk-filosofiske Skrifter 8:1, Copenhagen

Sørensen, AB (2000) 'Østergård: a medieval rural settlement in southern Jutland through time, emphasizing the period 1000-ca.1200', in Klápstě, J (ed), *Ruralia 3, Conference III, 3–9 September 1999*, Památky Archeologické – Supplementum 14, Prague, 156-67

Sørensen, AB (2003) 'Middelalderens fødsel – tiden 1000-1340 – huse gårde og bebyggelser', in *Det Sønderjyske Landbrugs Historie. Jernalder, Vikingetid og Middelalder. Skrifter udgivet af Historisk Samfund for Sønderjylland* 82, Haderslev, 434-57

Thompson, MW (1967) *Novgorod the Great: Excavations at the Medieval City 1951-62 directed by A.V. Artsikhovsky and B.A. Kolchin*, London

Valor, M and Carmona, MA (2001) *IV European Symposium for Teachers of Medieval Archaeology*, Seville

Wicker, NL (1999) 'Archaeology and art history: common ground for the new millennium', *Medieval Archaeology* 43, 161-71

Yanin, VL, Nosov, EN, Khoroshev, AS, Sorokin, AN, Rybina, EA, Pvetkin, VI and Gaidukov, PG (1992) *The Archaeology of Novgorod, Russia*, Society of Medieval Archaeology Monograph Series 13, Leeds

CHAPTER 2

PEOPLES AND ENVIRONMENTS

Lech Leciejewicz and Magdalena Valor

The Natural Landscape

The natural landscape has always played an important role in the development of human culture. It creates specific opportunities that help humans, depending on the level of their ability, to adjust as best as possible to the conditions of their surroundings. Such was certainly the case with medieval Europe when, as never before, the process of environmental change became accelerated.

Geomorphology and natural resources

The shape of the European continent had changed little over several millennia, since the retreat of the continental ice-sheet with the onset of the geological age known as the Holocene. Shifts in coastline and land-levels, caused in the south primarily by seismic movement of the Earth's crust, and in the north, by eustatic movement of the sea, were of limited and local character. In some areas, however, they did result in the transgression of the sea. During the Middle Ages, the division of Europe into a southern mountainous zone, its boundaries marked by relatively young mountain ranges (the Alps, Pyrenees, Carpathians and their older foothills), and the northern lowland zone (with only the British Isles and Fennoscandia being dissected by old mountain ranges), was the most noticeable (Leciejewicz 2004). A special position was occupied by Iceland, situated near the Arctic Circle, owing to the presence of active volcanoes. Most of the rivers in the south belong to the drainage basin of the Mediterranean and Black Seas, on the western peripheries of the Continent to the Atlantic Ocean, and in the north to the North Sea and the Baltic.

This topography was far-reaching in its consequences (Fig 2.1). The mountains abounded in many useful natural resources, particularly minerals. The Iberian Peninsula, Gaul, the British Isles and the Scandinavian Peninsula, with Transylvania in the east, held rich deposits of valuable metal ores which had begun to be exploited during prehistory, namely iron, bronze, copper, lead, silver and gold. New reserves were to be found, such as the silver deposits discovered during the tenth century in the Harz mountains

The natural landscape of Europe: geomorphology and vegetation zones (after Leciejewicz 2004).   **Fig 2.1**
Key: (a) land above 500m; (b) bog; (c) tundra/taiga boundary; (d) taiga/mixed forest & grasslands
boundary; (e) mixed forest & grasslands/forest-steppe boundary; (f) forest-steppe/steppe boundary;
and (g) temperate zone/subtropical plants boundary.

of central Germany and, only slightly later, in the Vosges mountains of France and the Black Forest. Bog-iron ores, in their meadow, lake and marsh varieties, occurred in many places in the European lowlands.

Stone resources were also highly useful. Apart from the traditional use of marble (much of which was obtained during the medieval period from the ruins of Classical cities), other deposits of special importance included basalt lava in the Eiffel mountains on the Rhine, used for making quernstones (p 310 & Fig. 10.7), porphyry and granite, quarried in the northern foothills of the Ore mountains (on the modern border between Germany and the Czech republic) and the Sudety mountains (the modern boundary between the Czech Republic and Poland), and Norwegian soapstone, used in Scandinavia for making vessels (pp 310-11). Amber continued to be popular, obtained on the North Sea coast of Denmark and the southern shores of the Baltic. There was also an intensification of salt production (pp 188-9 & 232-3). It was mined, in crystalline form, in the Alps and Transylvania, and from brine rising here and there on the European Lowland and in the northern foothills of the Carpathians. On the coasts of the Atlantic Ocean and the Mediterranean Sea, salt was obtained from sea-water – an activity that gained special importance on the Venetian Lagoon.

A further important consideration was the economic usefulness of soils covering the Continent. In the northern zone, the most fertile soils were the chernozems, developed over a loessic substrate, stretching in extensive areas from the Ardennes and Vosges as far as the foothills of the Sudety mountains and the Bohemian-Moravian highlands, from the northern and eastern foothills of the Alps, around the Carpathian range, into Ukraine. To their north, on the European Lowland, there are enclaves of equally fertile black-earths, developed in poorly drained sites. River valleys have fertile alluvial soils and, in some regions they covered extensive areas, such as on the middle Danube (Fig 2.2) and the lower course of the Rhone and the Po. Similar in origin were marshlands, stretching along the shores of the North Sea and of the Bay of Biscay. However, the greater part of the Continent is covered with less fertile, brown and podsolic soils, developed in the north chiefly on clays and sands of glacial origin. In the south, there are bronze soils, known also as cinnamon soils. In addition, some parts are totally unfit for cultivation, such as the most mountainous areas and, in the far north, the soils of the tundra.

Climate, plants and animals

An equally important element of the ecosystem is the climate. During the early medieval period, there was a continuation of the relatively wet Sub-Atlantic period which dated back a thousand years. In the western part of the Continent, the proximity of the sea was an additional influence, particularly in the case of the Atlantic Ocean; in eastern areas, the physical connection to the Asian landmass was a factor. The western and northern shores of the British Isles and Scandinavia were washed by the Gulf Stream, carrying masses of warm water from the Americas to help make the climate milder. In addition, climatologists believe that, on the European Lowland, the differences in tem-

The River Danube seen from Visegrad, Hungary (photo: M Valor).   **Fig 2.2**

perature of the seasons of the year were smaller than at present, with less harsh winters and so presumably a longer growing season for crops and vegetation. More continental conditions, and therefore greater contrasts, occurred east of the Baltic and the Carpathians. Similarly, mountainous regions were characterised by a more severe climate, a longer period of snow-cover and a shorter growing season. In the higher regions of the Alps and the Fennoscandian mountains, as well as in Iceland, there were glaciers, remnants of the once vast continental ice-sheet. Harsh climate also characterised lands lying beyond the Arctic Circle.

Climate is responsible for differences in vegetation and thus there are in Europe a number of distinctive zones (Fig 2.1). In the south, along the Mediterranean coast, we find subtropical conditions. In addition to local species of deciduous and coniferous trees, such as fig trees, stone pines and cypress, there were monocotyledonous palms, with olive trees and the vine being staples of the farming economy.

Further to the north, the uplands and lowlands were under mixed deciduous-coniferous woodland, typical for the temperate climate, usually with a rich undergrowth and forest-floor flora. On fertile soils, cleared for farming since the Neolithic, forest-cover was substantially thinner. Landscape of this kind is sometimes described as woodland-field or park-woodland. Tree species included primarily, oak, lime, beech, birch, alder and willow. On poorer soils, the prevailing tree species were coniferous: pine, fir and larch. River valleys have meadow vegetation or, locally, bog vegetation.

Plant-cover alters with rising altitude: mountains have coniferous forest, growing in tiers, primarily composed of spruce and fir, with, higher up, dwarf mountain pine, and even higher, Alpine meadows. Only on the younger massifs, such as the Pyrenees, Alps and Carpathians, were the highest craggy summits bare of all vegetation.

In the north, across the centre of the Scandinavian Peninsula, along the north coast of the Gulf of Finland and onwards through the upper Volga basin, ran the southern range of the taiga. These dense northern forests were composed mainly of coniferous species such as spruce, fir, pine and larch, with an admixture of broad-leaved birch, alder and willow. Beyond the Arctic Circle started the tundra, covered by vegetation adapted to the inhospitable conditions of the boreal zone: lichens, mosses, shrubs, dwarf birch and willow.

In South-East Europe, there is a zone associated with a dry continental climate, namely, the steppe. This is formed from grassy vegetation with an admixture of perennial plants. On its western and northern reaches, it passes into forest steppe, with tree stands established in wetter locations. The westernmost enclave of this landscape occurs on the Hungarian Plain. From the lower Danube and areas to the east of the Carpathian range, the steppe continues along the coast of the Black and Azov Seas as far as the Caspian, deep into Central Asia. In the north, the forest-steppe extended as far as the watershed of the Pripyat, Desna and Oka, and of rivers draining south to the Black Sea (i.e. the Dnestr, Bug, lower Dnepr and Don). To the north, there stretched dense forest, in many places established on boggy ground, formed by stands of mixed woodland, pine forest and marshy alluvial forest.

The animal world is an element of the biotope of equal importance to vegetation. Species domesticated by man are not discussed here, although their upkeep had consequences for the natural environment. In the forests of the temperate zone, there would have been numerous species of mammals, both carnivorous and herbivorous. The former included, for example, bear, lynx, wild cat, fox, marten and wolf, the latter such as bison, aurochs, red deer and wild pig, with elk in wetter areas. In the far north, the tundra and the adjacent taiga were the domain of the reindeer. In the northern forest, there were squirrels, prized for their fur, as well as beavers and otters, dwellers on river and lake margins. Forest margins were inhabited by, for example, roe deer, wild horse and hare.

Bird life was equally rich. In addition to predatory eagles, hawks, falcons and buzzards, there was black grouse, capercaillie, jay and raven; wetland species included wild ducks and geese, cormorants and other divers. Meadows and marshes harboured the crane; more open areas were preferred by partridges and the great bustard; species associated with areas inhabited by man included stork, crow and jackdaw. On the sea-coasts, as well as deeper inland, are to be found various species of gulls. The northern forest was also home to industrious wild bees, the producers of honey and wax.

Waters teemed with numerous species of fish. Rivers and lakes held pike, carp, sturgeon, sheatfish, perch and many others. In the seas were herring, cod and flatfish, as also mammals such as the seal; sub-Arctic regions teemed with whales and walrus. In many coastal areas there was also an abundance of edible shellfish. Only species encountered in the archaeological record have been mentioned here, although sometimes also mentioned in written sources.

For humans, wild fauna provided not only a source of additional food and valuable raw materials, but also a source of inspiration for many customs and beliefs. It was also most important for the preservation of the biocentric balance of the natural world surrounding man.

The function of the North, Baltic and Mediterranean Seas in inter-regional contacts

In describing the natural landscape of early medieval Europe, it is important to enlarge on the role played by the seas and rivers, given that they were more than just a source of food and, in some areas, of sea-salt. They also formed important communication routes, with the consequent exchange of goods and information (see Chapters 9 & 10).

The collapse of the unity of the Mediterranean world marked the onset of the Middle Ages. The conquest of the south Mediterranean by the Muslims signified the definitive break in the uniformity created by the Roman Empire, with the progressive introduction of an oriental civilisation into these territories. This process began in the middle of the seventh century and affected also the borders of the northern Mediterranean, in the case of the conquest of the Iberian Peninsula (711-16), Sicily (827), Malta (829) and the Balearic islands (903). Thus, during the ninth and the tenth centuries the Mediterranean was firmly dominated by the Muslims, coming from Egypt, Africa or al-Andalus (the name of the territories in the Iberian Peninsula occupied by the Muslims). Probably as a consequence of this fact, the political and economic centre of Europe experienced a tendency to move northwards, thanks to the Carolingian Empire and later to the German Empire.

The process of Arabicisation in the south-western part of Europe that was conquered by the Muslims can be clearly detected archaeologically, as also to some extent that of Islamisation. The territory in question was known as al-Andalus (see Box 2.3), where an Islamic state persisted for 800 years, although with a gradual reduction in extent. The most populated areas were around the major rivers, such as the Ebro and the Guadalquivir, but also the Tagus and the Guadiana.

The northern seas (the North Sea, with the English Channel, and the Baltic) gained in importance, as did the great rivers flowing into them. The major river in Britain was the Thames with, on the Continent, the Seine, Meuse, Rhine, Weser and Elbe; further to the east, the Odra, Vistula, Neman and Western Dvina were of significance. In Scandinavia, maritime communication was facilitated, in the west, by the fjords that penetrated deeply inland; in the east, the inland lakes of Vänern, Vättern and Mälaren served the same purpose. Across the Baltic, similarly favourable conditions were offered by the Finnish Lakeland. A comparable role was played in Eastern Europe by the Danube, Dnestr and Dnepr, which drain southwards to the Black Sea, as well as the Volga, emptying into the Caspian Sea. It is striking that the Emperor Charlemagne, towards the end of the eighth century, endeavoured to link the upper drainage basin of the Rhine with the Danube by means of a canal, so as to create a water-route that would connect the North Sea with the Black Sea, but technological problems prevented completion of the project (p 263).

The North Sea linked the countries of mainland Europe with the British Isles and Scandinavia. During the seventh and eighth centuries, this facilitated the exchange of

BOX 2.1   THE NORSE EXPANSION ACROSS THE NORTH ATLANTIC

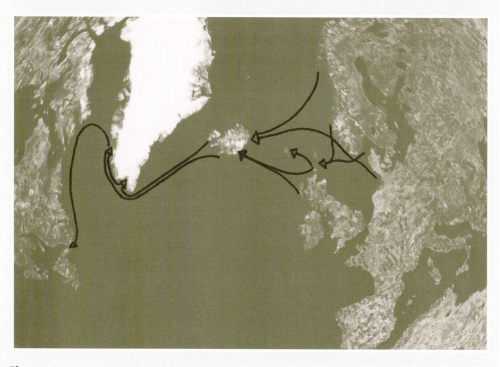

Fig 1

The Norse expansion across the North Atlantic.

Although the Vikings are remembered primarily for their raiding and military conquests, and to a lesser degree for their far-flung trading networks, a significant aspect of Scandinavian expansion in the ninth and tenth centuries took the form of overseas settlements of ordinary farming people. Scandinavians settled in England, Ireland, Normandy, the eastern side of the Baltic and in Russia, but in those areas it is difficult to gauge the extent or intensity of the Scandinavian settlements and the newcomers' culture was quickly subsumed by the pre-existing ones, leaving traces primarily in the place-names of those regions. A much more permanent impact was felt in the Northern Isles of Scotland, where the pre-existing culture was obliterated by the Scandinavian settlers and a Scandinavian language was spoken into early modern times. The Scandinavians also sailed into the North Atlantic and established settlements in previously uninhabited lands: the Faroes, Iceland and Greenland. They even visited the eastern shores of North America and established a short-lived base-camp at the northern tip of Newfoundland, presumably for the exploitation of 'Vinland' (Fig 1).

This expansion was a technological achievement; never before in the history of Europe had people sailed repeatedly over open seas, for days and even weeks, without sight of land. It was, by all accounts, a risky business with a high chance of failure, but nevertheless, from at least the late ninth century onwards, Scandinavian seafarers maintained regular contact with the Faroese and Icelandic settlements. The Greenland settlements were established towards the end of the tenth century and shortly afterwards the east coast of America was being explored. There is limited evidence for continued contacts between the Greenlanders and the American coast, but Greenland represented the western limit of sustainable settlement by the Scandinavians during the medieval period (Fig 2). They briefly flourished, evidenced by fine church architecture in the thirteenth century, but in the late Middle Ages the Greenland settlements went into decline and had become extinct by the end of the fifteenth century.

The precise dating and sequence of this expansion into the North Atlantic is not well understood. It is normally assumed that it began in the early ninth century with the occupation of Shetland, then the Orkneys, Caithness and the Hebrides. From there the Scandinavians explored and settled the Faroes, followed by Iceland and then Greenland. There is, however, limited dating evidence for the first Scandinavian presence in the Northern Isles of Scotland, or in the Faroes, and all that can be said at present is that it began in the ninth century. In Iceland, however, there is firm archaeological evidence that people were there before 870 and that the colonisation of the whole island proceeded at a very rapid pace during the following decades.

The reasons for the expansion are even less well understood. Population pressure is normally cited as the main reason, but there is no positive evidence for this, and it may be that social and ideological factors played a greater part.

In Iceland, evidence is emerging for a largely planned settlement, suggesting a degree of centralised control. The apparent ethnic diversity of the settlers may also suggest that the settlement of the North Atlantic from northern Europe was not so much a matter of people being pushed by unfavourable circumstances back home, but more of them being pulled by the prospect of a better life or, perhaps, by unscrupulous entrepreneurs.

Sources: Jones 1986; Fitzhugh & Ward 2000; Wawn & Sigurðardóttir 2001; Lewis-Simpson 2003.

By Orri Vésteinsson

Fig 2

One of three complete walrus tusks found in a 10th-century hall in Reykjavík (Iceland). One of the reasons why Norse navigators sought out places like Iceland and Greenland may have been to hunt walrus for this expensive commodity, paving the way for later permanent settlement based on animal husbandry (photo: Minjasafn Reykjavíkur/ Reykjavík Municipal Museum).

diverse cultural models between the Insular area, on the one hand, and the Merovingian and subsequent Carolingian area, on the other, together with the Scandinavian world. In later centuries, the North Sea provided the route by which the Vikings were able to leave their burning imprint on various post-Roman countries; however, as contacts took on a more peaceful aspect, it helped bring the inhabitants of the North into the sphere of Latin civilisation. In addition, the fact of the North Sea opening out into the North Atlantic lead to the Norse settlement of Iceland and Greenland, allowing access to Vinland in North America (Box 2.1).

At the same time, the Baltic became something like a 'Mediterranean Sea' of northern Europe (Herrmann 1982). From the eighth century onwards, there was an intensification of contacts with the European West. A shorter, partly overland, route running along the border between Danish and Saxon lands replaced the much longer sea-route around the Jutland Peninsula, which was anyway hazardous because of the dangerous shallows on its western coast. Another route led south along great rivers, through Lake Ladoga and up the Volkhov, running up the Western Dvina and partly overland, to the Dnepr, all the way to the Black Sea and Byzantium. An alternative route followed the Volga, to the Caspian Sea and beyond, to the countries of Islam. The Baltic thus formed the crossroads of two major communication routes of medieval Europe – western and eastern – which helped to bring closer the communities living in the region. Armed excursions of the so-called 'Varangians' did not have such negative consequences as those of the Vikings in the West, and commercial exchange assumed a greater importance than armed conflict. A closer look at the ethnic and cultural divisions that can be traced in this part of the Continent will help in understanding why this was so.

Ethnography and Archaeology

To what extent were the opportunities created by the natural landscape utilised by the inhabitants of medieval Europe? To what extent did ecological conditions affect the shape of their cultures? Any answers to these questions must take into account the origin of these cultures, their earlier achievements, the diversity and direction of social and culture change. During the Middle Ages the role of humans in the transformation of the natural environment increased rapidly, leading to changes in many regions, the consequences of which are felt to this day.

First of all, it must be borne in mind that behind Mediterranean Europe lay many centuries of transformation resulting from the development of Classical civilisation, both Greek and Roman. Despite the collapse of the Roman Empire and the decay of civilisation, in the western provinces around the middle of the first millennium AD, the human factor to a great extent continued to determine the appearance of the natural environment. Those countries situated on the North Sea and the Baltic, which had never formed part of the Roman Empire, were less affected, given that the culture of primitive societies depends to a higher degree than that of civilized societies on opportunities offered by ecological conditions.

ICELAND

NORTH CAPE

BORG

SAAMI

ATLANTIC
OCEAN

SKIRINGESHEAL   BIRKA

PICTS

SCOTS

Limfjord   SCANDINAVIANS

W.Divina

IRISH   NORTH SEA   RIBE

BALTIC   Neman

YORK   HEDEBY

BALTS

ANGLO SAXONS   RERIC   TRUSO

Thames   Elbe   Vistula

DORESTAD   Weser

LONDON   MAGDEBURG   WESTERN SLAVS

Meuse   Rhine   Odra

BRITTANY   PARIS   AACHEN

Seine

Loire   REGENSBURG

CAROLINGIAN EMPIRE

AVARS

ATLANTIC OCEAN

KINGDOM OF   TOULOUSE   Rhône   AQUILEIA

ASTURIAS   LYONS   PAVIA

Minho   OVIEDO   Po   SOUTHERN SLAVS

Douro   PATRIMONIUM

Ebro   MARSEILLES   S. PETRI   SPLIT

Tagus   AL-ANDALUS   BARCELONA   Tiber

Guadiana   ROME

SEVILLE   Guadalquivir   BENEVENTO

CORDOBA   BYZANTINE

EMPIRE

SICILY

MEDITERRANEAN SEA

0   500

■ A   ■ B

- - - C   - - - - D - - - E

············ F   - - - - G

Western Europe about 800 (after Leciejewicz 2004). [For explanation of key, see map p 47].   **Fig 2.3**

Fig 2.4 *Irish grasslands well-suited for stock breeding surround the early medieval ring-fort at Danesfort, Co Kilkenny (photo: T Barry).*

North-West Europe

The following description commences with the countries of North-West Europe. Some of these had been Roman provinces, such as Gaul and Britain, whereas others, such as Ireland and most of modern Scotland (inhabited by the Picts), had lain beyond the Roman *limes*. Most of the population living in these territories belonged originally to the Celtic ethnic community of Indo-European stock. Following the Roman conquest, the inhabitants of Gaul and Britain had rapidly succumbed to Romanisation during the first centuries AD. Invasions of Germanic peoples (the Franks, Alamans, Vandals, Burgundians, and eventually also the Goths) led Gaul to a crisis in its Classical culture during the fifth century, and similar consequences resulted from the invasion of Britain by Angles and Saxons, as well as Jutes and some Frisians. Even so, the Roman legacy continued to be felt, and this process was greatly assisted by the assimilation of the new-comers into the native populations (Wilson 1980; Ó Cróinin 1995; Rouche 2003).

Those ethnic groups that adhered longest to the Celtic cultural model were the ones beyond the *limes*, principally the inhabitants of Ireland. These were communities occupied chiefly with stock breeding and, to a lesser extent, cereal farming (Fig 2.4). They were ruled by local kings or chiefs and had not developed a political organisation higher than a tribal one. Celtic social traditions were maintained by the inhabitants of Wales and (for a period) Cornwall, as well as by those who had fled Anglo-Saxon pressure and settled across the English Channel in Roman Armorica, from then on known as Brittany.

For their part, the inhabitants of Ireland did not remain on the sidelines of the changes taking place in Britain and Gaul. As a result of the activity of dedicated missionaries, St Patrick in particular, the Irish adopted Christianity in the fifth century. They went on to create original monastic communities and soon set forth to spread the new faith. The religious and artistic culture of the Irish first made an impression on their nearest neighbours, the Scots of Dalriada (in western Scotland), who were of Irish origin themselves, and the Anglo-Saxon kingdom of Northumbria, but later also on the Merovingian and Carolingian countries on the European mainland.

In the area of former Roman provinces not all the Germanic arrivals succumbed to Romanisation; for example, the Anglo-Saxons in Britain retained their native language. On the Continent, the newcomers assimilated the remaining inhabitants of the Roman border provinces. Those Franks who settled on the lower Rhine remained ethnically German; areas of the upper Rhine and Danube were under Alamannic control. Further east, the lands of the Danube, at the foot of the Alps, were occupied by Bavarians. Only Alpine valleys continued to harbour enclaves of Romance population, to this day having speakers of Rhaetian dialects. The result of these processes was, from the onset of the medieval period, the formation of a boundary between Romance and Germanic languages that runs across the territories of modern Belgium, eastern France, Switzerland and northern Italy. The economic mainstay of these Germanic communities, from beyond the *limes*, was animal husbandry, although they also cultivated cereals and other plants for food.

The Merovingian rulers of Francia persistently attempted to bring the Thuringians (who lived in the foothills of the Thuringian forest) as well as the Bavarians under their authority. Only the Frisians on the North Sea and, deeper inland, the Saxons (on the Weser and the lower Elbe) continued to resist. The Frisians were nevertheless connected to the Frankish state by trading relations, and their lands around the mouth of the Meuse and the Rhine were finally subordinated. The Saxons managed to withstand Frankish pressure for a longer period, doggedly defending the tribal organisation of their society with its pagan religious practices. Only the armed campaigns of Charlemagne, in 772-804, often involving bloody pacification and the resettlement of the local population, ultimately led to the incorporation of this region within the sphere of Christian civilisation.

Conquest went hand in hand with Christianisation. During the eighth century the cultural landscape changed in Bavaria, Hesse and Thuringia, and finally also in Frisia and Saxony. The Carolingian Empire set the frontiers of the civilised world on the Elbe, Saale, the mountain ranges of the Bohemian Forest and along the eastern foothills of the Alps. Differences, in comparison with the post-Roman territories, continued to be apparent for a long time; however, with ongoing social and political change, the standards of living levelled out. In the lands of the former *Barbaricum*, we begin to see the construction of stone churches and abbeys, the rise of the first non-agrarian settlements of early urban type, and also a slow but steady change in the countryside. Ecclesiastical centres not only introduced the principles of Christian religion, but also literacy, education and new forms of elite artistic culture.

BOX 2.2   CENTRAL AND NORTHERN EUROPE AS SEEN BY EARLY MEDIEVAL

The incorporation of the peoples in the lands outside the former Roman Empire into the sphere of European civilisation triggered a growing interest in the post-Roman countries in Central and Northern Europe. Information drawn from second-hand sources no longer sufficed and there are now original reports by travellers and accounts by geographers who used them as their source. These reports transmit much valuable ethnographic information, which can be most useful in the interpretation of the archaeological record.

One of the most interesting examples of this type of initiative is the new version of Orosius's 'World History' from the fifth century, commissioned by the English king, Alfred the Great (872-99). This enlightened monarch not only included many new details about Central Europe in the introductory description of the world, or chorography, but he also added the reports of two travellers. One of them, a Norwegian chieftain, Ohthere, had his lands in a region close to the Arctic Circle (Fig 1) and ventured in pursuit of whale and walrus far beyond the North Cape, into the White Sea. There he maintained numerous contacts with the Finno-Ugrian peoples of that region, as well as travelling in the opposite direction, south, to the market-place of Skiringesheal, most probably Kaupang in the south-east of Norway and then on to Hedeby, at the base of the Jutland peninsula. Alfred's other source, Wulfstan, was commissioned by him to sail into the Baltic Sea. He navigated by sailing along its southern shore and reached the mouth of the Vistula, and the nearby Prussian market-centre of Truso. Wulfstan eventually brought back a detailed account of the customs of the Prussians living in the area.

Slightly later, around 965/6, knowledge of Central Europe was gained at first hand by a Jewish merchant from the Spanish Tortosa, Ibrahim ibn Jakub. His account is known to us from excerpts included in the works of later Arabic geographers. The aim of Ibrahim's journey is unclear to us. He reached the court of Emperor Otto I at Magdeburg, before travelling on to the land of the Obodrites (on the Baltic), and to Bohemia where he visited Prague. Ibrahim ibn Jakub's account also contains a valuable description of the state of the Polanian prince Mieszko, and some interesting details concerning the neighbouring Old Prussians. From information surviving elsewhere we know that the same traveller had journeyed in France and the Rhineland, visiting Fulda and Hedeby. Ibrahim ibn Jakub is distinguished by his broad interests, in politics as well as economics, local customs, natural phenomena, questions of geography and medicine. All of this makes his account an exceptionally valuable source for understanding the living conditions among the Slavs of Central Europe during the tenth century. It is worth adding that for reasons of climate, the traveller treated this part of the continent as the north.

The first comprehensive study of the ethnic geography of Northern Europe was given in the next century by Adam, canon and master of the Cathedral school in Bremen. His book, *Gesta Hammaburgensis ecclesiae pontificum*, written in 1070-80, contains much information, drawn from his own experience and obtained from Adalbert, Archbishop of Hamburg, the Danish king Sven Estridsson and from merchants and other travellers in the region of interest. Adam recorded many important details on Scandinavian peoples, Western Slavs, Balts, Finns, their customs and beliefs, and the progress of Christian missionary works in their countries, as well as describing the early towns and even some of the merchants' itinerar-

Fig 1

Borg at Vestvågøy (northern Norway), with recon-struction of the 83m long main building of a chief-tain's farm, next to the excavation site; this was built in a commanding position in the landscape, probably in the 7th or early 8th century AD, and functioned until sometime in the 10th. The home of Ohthere, which was located elsewhere in the same region, was doubtless similar (photo: DM Wilson).

ies. The last volume (no IV), entitled *Descriptio insularum aquilonis*, gives a methodical descrip-tion of the Baltic and North Sea countries, as well as of Iceland, Greenland and Vinland, identified with the north-east coast of North America, pen-etrated by the Norsemen (see Box 2.1). The wealth of ethnographic detail makes the work by Adam of Bremen an invaluable record of the changing civilisation of Northern Europe in the tenth to eleventh centuries. At the same time, it testifies to the rapid expansion of geographic horizons of the inhabitants of early medieval Europe.

The strengthening of the ties binding the countries of Northern Europe with Latin civi-lisation in the twelfth century helped to bring them closer still and promoted greater familiarity between different nations. Even so, several cen-turies still had to pass before the knowledge of the central and northern reaches of the continent found appropriate expression in European trea-tises on geography.

Sources: Foote & Wilson 1980; Lund 1984; Leciejewicz 1991; Blomkvist 2005; Bately & Englert 2007.

By Lech Leciejewicz

The cultural situation of the Germanic peoples living on Jutland and the Scandinavian Peninsula, with their neighbouring islands, was different (Foote & Wilson 1980; Roesdahl & Wilson 1992; Graham-Campbell 1994). A harsher environment than that of the Central European Lowland favoured animal husbandry as the main means of food production. Areas of good cultivable soil were few and, from a slightly later period, there is sound evidence that corn was in short supply, with Scandinavia having to make up its requirements with imports. Adverse natural conditions were compensated for, in part, by the presence in Scandinavia of high quality iron and copper ores (particularly in central Sweden). This led to a high level of development in metallurgy. In addition, Scandinavia's extensive coastline, with numerous fjords cutting deeply into the rocky mountain massifs in the west, and its vast lakes in the east, made water the main means of communication. This resulted in the development among the Scandinavians of high navigational skills (as witnessed by the North Atlantic voyages of the Vikings; Box 2.1); their diverse links with the sea also found expression in their daily customs and even their funerary practices.

The Germanic societies inhabiting the area of Scandinavia (or Norsemen, as they are sometimes known) were divided into four main groups. The lands to the north of the lower Elbe, formerly occupied by the Angles and the Jutes, were for some time sparsely populated. The Jutland Peninsula, with its neighbouring islands, and the southernmost part of the Scandinavian Peninsula were occupied by the Danes. Further north, the lands around lakes Vänern and Vättern, together with the islands of Öland and Gotland, were the homeland of the Goths. It was presumably from this area that groups of the same name had, during the first centuries AD, penetrated southwards to the Black Sea. Around Lake Mälar lived the Svear, as known to Tacitus, writing at the close of the first century. It is to them that Sweden owes its origins. In the mountainous valleys of Norway there were local communities whose various names were recorded by Jordanes in the sixth century. Later, during the medieval period, they acquired the name of Norwegians because of their location along the 'Northern Way'. During the early part of the Middle Ages, the Norsemen gradually drifted apart from their continental brethren, as in their language, remaining for some centuries in the Late Iron Age of prehistory.

At the beginning of the Middle Ages, however, the inhabitants of Scandinavia were in close contact with the Merovingian cultural sphere and, because of this, the period from around 550 until the second half of the eighth century has been classified as the Merovingian period. Only Sweden does not follow this classification and, owing to the importance of the finds from a cemetery at Vendel, in Uppland, the same period is known there as the Vendel period. From the end of the eighth century, the phenomenon of the Viking raids and the Norse settlements overseas not only influenced the cultural development of Scandinavia, but has also found its expression in historical terminology. The beginning of the Viking period is traditionally marked by the well-documented raid on the Holy Island of Lindisfarne in 793 (off the coast of Northumbria) and many – in the West, at least – consider it to have come to an end with the Norman conquest of England, following the Battle of Hastings in 1066.

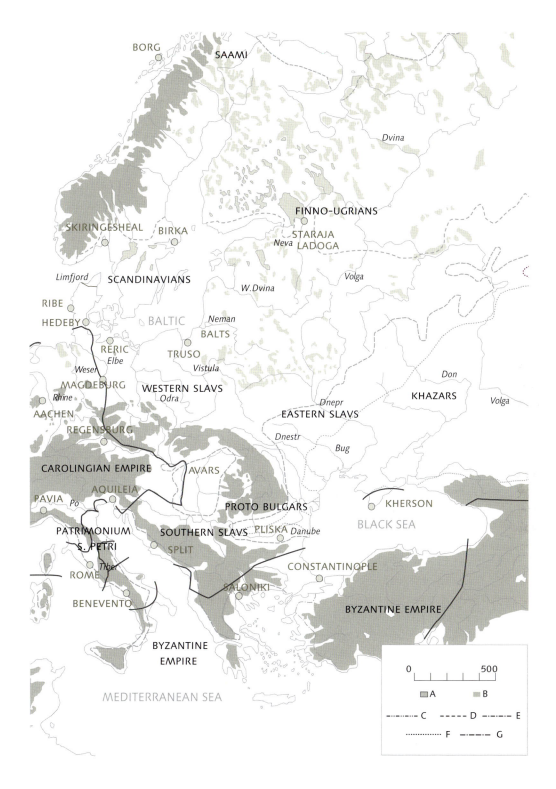

Eastern Europe about 800 (after Leciejewicz 2004). [For explanation of key, see map p 47].

Fig 2.5

Fig 2.6 *Forests and fields in the vicinity of the Slavic stronghold at Grodziec (Opole region), dating from the 7th-10th centuries (photo: W Gorgolewski).*

North-East Europe

The Slavs, who inhabited Central and Eastern Europe, were different in many respects from the Germanic peoples, although they also belonged to the Indo-European language family and were farmers and stock-breeders (Hensel 1964; Váňa 1983; Herrmann 1986; Leciejewicz 1991). In contrast to the Germanic peoples, however, they were land-bound in character; for example, the ratio of coastline to land-surface area among the Western Slavs was thirty times less than the same ratio calculated for Scandinavia. The fertility of the Slav lands at the foot of the Central European mountain ranges and of the Lowland to the north favoured cereal farming, and the Slavs were perceived as the most agricultural people of medieval Europe. Failure of the cereal harvest, or its destruction, frequently caused the disaster of famine. The cycle of farming activities was deeply rooted in the rhythm of Slav life, and their world-view, making their culture seem more conservative in comparison, for example, with Germanic culture, and their contacts with other peoples were less developed. This was to change only with the breakthrough represented by the coming of Christian civilisation.

The groups of Slavs settled on the territories that drained into the North Sea and the Baltic (by way of the Elbe, Odra and Vistula), and as far as the upper Danube, are referred to as the Western Slavs. To their east, in the drainage basin of the Black Sea (on the Dnestr, middle Dnepr and the Don), lived the related peoples known as the Eastern Slavs. The latter mainly inhabited areas of the forest-steppe and adjacent areas of woodland, but they sometimes also penetrated into the steppe zone. During the early part of the medieval period, the culture of the Eastern Slavs spread to the peoples already settled in the upper drainage basin of the rivers Neman, Western Dvina and Dnepr, in time reaching as far as Lake Ladoga and the lands of the upper Volga. Those Slavs who, during the early medieval period, penetrated the former Roman *limes* to settle in the Balkans, are known as the Southern Slavs. As late as the ninth century, they still retained their linguistic unity and only drifted apart during subsequent centuries, as a result of the differences in their political, cultural and social development.

At the outset of the Middle Ages, the groups of Western Slavs occupying the fertile lands at the foot of the Ore, Sudety and Carpathian mountain ranges are distinguished in archaeological terminology as the 'Prague Culture'. In the more wooded areas of the Central European Lowland, during the eighth century, there emerged a number of distinct ethnographic regions, differentiated by their material culture and forms of settlement (e.g. fortifications): on the Baltic, the Feldberg-Kędrzyno; in the Lowland, Tornow-Klenica and Rössen-Chodlik; and on the Danube, in the contact area with the Avars, Devinska Nova Ves. The tribes were referred to in Carolingian sources of the eighth and ninth centuries as Obodrites, Veletians, Serbs, Czechs and Moravians. Later, and further to the east, historical accounts start to mention Pomeranians, Polanians, Mazovians, Silesians, Vistulanians and others.

In Eastern Europe, in the open forest and forest-steppe zone, on the sub-stratum of the 'Prague Culture', there emerged regional societies which were similar in many respects. Slavs also exerted their influence on the Balts and, in the north, on the Finno-Ugrians settled in the woodland zone. The Russian 'Primary Chronicle' refers to the tribes living in the lands that stretch from Lake Ilmen in the north to the boundary of the steppes in the south, during the ninth and tenth centuries, as Slavs.

On the western margin, from the Baltic as far as the eastern foothills of the Alps, during the eighth and ninth centuries, Slavs became the immediate neighbours of the Carolingian Empire, although they continued to represent a barbarian tribal sphere, with their traditional world-view and patterns of everyday life. Attempts made by Carolingian rulers to bring Slavs under their influence were largely unsuccessful. Only about the mid-ninth century, on the Morava river (at the intersection of the routes linking the Baltic with the Adriatic) and along the Danube (linking the Carolingian Empire with the Black Sea), do we see the rise of a state which was the first to bring the Slavs of the region into the world of Christian civilisation, in both its western (Latin) and eastern (Byzantine) variants. This was the state of Great Moravia. It was during the following century that both Bohemia of the Premyslids and Poland of the Piasts finally associated themselves, in a lasting manner, with western civilisation.

The Baltic peoples who inhabited the south-western shores of the Baltic were closely related ethnically to the Slavs (Gimbutas 1963). Linguists believe that, at an earlier period, these two groups of Indo-European stock had formed a Balto-Slav language community. However, by the close of Classical Antiquity, differences between these two ethnic groups had become apparent, with the line dividing them being the southern range of dense forest covering Eastern Europe. The disintegration of this Balto-Slav community may consequently have been influenced by environmental factors. The study of place-names suggests that, at the beginning of the Middle Ages, the Balts were settled deeply within the wooded zone, as far as the upper Neman, Dvina and Dnepr rivers. During the ninth and tenth centuries they became Slavicised there, but their older substrata continued to be evident in their material culture.

The Baltic peoples who settled closer to the Baltic Sea stemmed from communities known already during the Roman period and even retained their old names. During the eighth to tenth centuries, Old Prussians settled among them to the east of the mouth of the Vistula, Jatvings on the upper Narew, in modern Poland, with Lithuanian and Latvian groups between the lower Neman and the Dvina. In the forest environment, agriculture could not prosper and stock breeding became the main occupation and source of food. Close contacts were maintained with Scandinavia and, despite the restricted supplies of raw material, metallurgy was well developed. The process of Western European civilisation was delayed for many reasons and so for a long time, until the thirteenth century, the Balts resisted attempts at Christianisation.

Northern and north-eastern areas of the Continent were inhabited by Finno-Ugrians, members of the great non-Indo-European family of Uralic languages that stretched, by way of northern Europe, to northern Asia (Kivikoski 1967; Roesdahl & Wilson 1992). Their culture evolved in an environment of mixed forest and taiga, extensive bogs and lakes, and the tundra of the sub-Arctic north. Soils favourable for cultivation were rare, such as those found on the Gulf of Finland, the mainstay of their existence was thus animal husbandry (in the north, reindeer), together with hunting and fishing as well as primitive slash-and-burn agriculture. Scandinavian influences contributed to their development of metallurgy, including that of iron-working.

The areas furthest to the west, on the northern periphery of the Scandinavian Peninsula, were inhabited by the Lapps or Saami. Linguists believe that these people were assimilated relatively late by the Finno-Ugrians. Lands on both sides of the Gulf of Finland were settled by Western Finns, and further to the east, in the drainage basin of the upper Volga, lived the Volga Finns; further east still, on the Kama, were the Kama Finns. They mainly inhabited the boundary zone between the mixed forest and taiga. From this area they penetrated into the Finnish lakelands, as far as the White Sea, and the drainage basin of the Northern Dvina, all the way to the Barents Sea. Their southern margins, on Lakes Peipus and Ilmen, were Slavicised during the early medieval period. Scandinavian penetration from the west and Russian penetration from the south brought models of Christian civilisation to the Finno-Ugrians, but until the close of the Middle Ages they remained, for the most part, faithful to the traditions of their tribal culture and their particular world-outlook.

The ecological conditions to be encountered on the steppes, stretching along the Black and Caspian Seas, were entirely different from the rest of Europe, with its westernmost enclave on the Hungarian Plain. People arrived in this region in waves from Central Asia: Huns, Avars, proto-Bulgars, Khazars, Magyars, Pechenegs and Polovci, all of whom led a nomadic life (Bálint 1989). Pastoralism was the mainstay of their economy, as was raiding their neighbours. To a great extent, the steppe environment determined the form of their culture and their system of values. Even so, their contacts with their sedentary agriculturalist neighbours, together with their participation in wide-ranging trade, promoted frequent culture change and even led, as in the case of the steppe peoples on the Volga, to the emergence of early towns. On occasion, this eventually resulted in their loss of ethnic identity, as in the case of the proto-Bulgars on the lower Danube, or in the formation of their own state, as that of the Khazars and Kama Bulgars. It also happened that some of these peoples vanished entirely, destroyed or assimilated by their more powerful neighbours.

As far as the peoples of the steppe are concerned who settled on the middle Danube and Tisa, it was the Avars who made the most significant impact on the history of Europe; these were a people of probably Turkic stock, who occupied the Pannonian Lowland from 568. After a period of armed confrontation with both Slav farmers and the Byzantine Empire, they lost their military impetus following an unsuccessful siege of Constantinople in 626. In time, the Avars even began to establish, here and there, permanent settlements and took up agriculture. A major development for them occurred during the second half of the seventh century when, in metallurgy, the technique of forging was supplanted by the technology of casting. Changes which took place during this period are linked by some historians with an influx of new groups of nomads from the east (proto-Bulgars?). After a period of stagnation in the eighth century, the final blow was dealt to the Avars by Charlemagne who (in 791-805) destroyed their state and captured a gold hoard of legendary size.

The Magyars, or Hungarians, were the next wave of nomads to enter the Pannonian Lowland. They came to the area at the close of the ninth century and, until about 950, posed a real threat to the inhabitants of Europe. These people of the Finno-Ugrian language family, despite adopting a sedentary lifestyle, retained their ethnic identity. In the second half of the tenth century, the Hungarian rulers adopted Christianity and brought their people into the sphere of European civilisation, in its Latin variant. An archaeological expression of the process of integration of the ethnically mixed peoples of the region is the Bijelo Brdo Culture. At a later stage, other nomads found shelter for a time within the boundaries of the Hungarian state, including the Pechenegs and the Polovci, pushed out of their lands on the Black Sea.

The nomads made a lasting contribution to European cultural legacy. It is to the Avars that we owe the introduction of the solid saddle and stirrups, which together made it possible to use the horse for transport and in war, as also of new types of helmet and armour. The same people probably also introduced an improved method of harnessing draft animals in which the strain was taken on the chest rather than its neck, thus enabling the horse to be used efficiently for hauling wheeled transport and for ploughing.

The next genuine threat to the inhabitants of Europe came only in the thirteenth century, with the Mongol incursions that led to the collapse of Kievan Russia, bringing destruction to Poland and Hungary.

Southern Europe

The development of the South is substantially different from that of the rest of Europe during the early medieval period, the reason being the deep Romanisation that these territories had experienced. Some Germanic peoples invaded these areas, such as the Goths, Suevi and Lombards, but (with the exception of the Lombards in Italy) the final result was the integration of these new settlers. The legacy of Rome is basic to an understanding of the history of the Mediterranean (Müller-Wille & Schneider 1993; Rouche 2003).

The most significant change was the Muslim conquest of much of the Iberian Peninsula and the establishment of al-Andalus. The invasion took place at the beginning of the eighth century by groups of Berbers and an Arab military elite (see Box 2.3). The peninsula then began to be both Arabicised and Islamised, both processes with a variable rhythm. Arabicisation was the most intensive at first and influenced not only the population living in al-Andalus, but also the Christian kingdoms in the north. Conversion to Islam (Islamisation) was a slower process that only seems to have been completed in the tenth century.

Al-Andalus was part of the Islamic world on the same terms as many other territories, such as North Africa or the Near East. In this way it was profoundly influenced by the Umayyad and Abbasid Caliphates, but at the same time created a most original Islamic culture of its own under the dynasties of the Umayyads (756-1010) and the Almohads (1147-1248).

Socio-Political Transformation and Economic Progress: the Environmental Consequences

Socio-political transformation

The period from the eighth to twelfth centuries saw the formation of the foundations of European civilisation, referred to as Latin civilisation from its language of learning and literature. The process was advanced by the Carolingian Empire, which united within its borders almost all the post-Roman Christian territories, acknowledging the Bishop of Rome as the highest authority of the Church (Braunfels 1966-68). Only the inhabitants of the British Isles, Brittany and the northern part of the Iberian Peninsula remained independent of the Frankish rulers, but shared with them many of their cultural models (Hodges 1989; Rouche 2003). At this time, the frontiers of the civilised world reached beyond the former Roman *limes*, to the Elbe, Saale and the heights of the Bohemian Forest, only on the middle Danube corresponding with the ancient imperial frontier.

The Carolingian Empire disintegrated during the ninth century and was succeeded by the kingdoms of France, Italy and Germany. The latter continued the tradition of universal imperial rule, from the second half of the tenth century, but it extended only over Germany and some of the neighbouring countries, reaching, not without difficulty, as far as Italy. Sovereign monarchies were also consolidated in the British Isles and beyond the Pyrenees. Over time these states gave rise to the nations that were to form the subject of European history during the later medieval period.

Within the Carolingian Empire and its successors, there can be seen the rise of a new society, organized along principles described in more recent historiography as 'feudal'. The main form of social tie binding the highest ranking members of those societies to the other classes was the relationship between the lord and his vassal. The duty of the former was to offer his vassal political and material protection; the latter, in return, was to serve his lord with council and assistance, *consilio et auxilio*. The relationship of the lord to the common village people was defined by the economic obligations of the latter. In time, an independent status was won by townspeople, organised by merchants with support from artisans. In the eleventh-twelfth centuries, the society that emerged in Latin Europe was perceived as being divided into three estates: *oratores, bellatores et laboratores*, the clergy, warriors and workers (the rest of the population engaged in production).

Al-Andalus emerged as a centralised state, governed by emirs, caliphs or kings, with a non-feudal structure based on the control of territories by governors and in the marches (border territories) by local families dependent on the ruler. The dominant group were those of Arab origins, who in time mixed with the local population and were named 'Andalusies'. In certain areas, the Berbers were predominant.

The tribal structure of the pre-Islamic civilisation in the Arabian Peninsula was initially established in al-Andalus, as in the rest of Dar al-Islam. Groups can be recognised as having colonised specific geographical areas from place-names and chronicles, but these different origins cannot be detected archaeologically, despite current research.

During the ninth-eleventh centuries the sphere of Western European civilisation was joined by some of the societies of the former *Barbaricum*. Christian missionaries were active both among the Slav inhabitants of Central and Eastern Europe, and the Germanic peoples of the North. These efforts could hope for permanent success only where new forms of political organisation (i.e. the state) had already emerged (Herrmann 1986; Urbańczyk 2000; Wieczorek & Hinz 2000). Among Western Slavs, as already mentioned, the first of these was Great Moravia in the ninth century which was nevertheless to founder early in the tenth century. It was soon succeeded by the state of the Premyslids, formed in the Bohemian Basin, and the state of the Polanian Piasts, to the north of the Sudety and Carpathian Mountains. The Hungarian kingdom of the Arpads, on the Hungarian Plain, was similar, although it retained certain features recalling its nomadic roots. The conversion to Christianity of the Czech (883), Polish (966) and Hungarian (973) rulers brought the inhabitants of their lands into the mainstream of Latin civilisation. During the same period, Christianity also took root in the young Scandinavian states: Denmark (960) and Norway, with Iceland (c1000), although in Sweden there was a major pagan centre at Uppsala as late as c1070 (Foote & Wilson 1980; Roesdahl 1991; Graham-Campbell 2001). It should also be noted that Russia embraced Christianity in 988, but in its Byzantine Orthodox form, the influence of which extended to the Baltic.

Greater resistance to the new religion and to Western European models of civilisation was put up by the Slavs on the Elbe and the Baltic coast. They were under constant German, Polish and Danish political pressure, but it was only in the twelfth century,

BOX 2.3 ARABS AND BERBERS IN AL-ANDALUS

It was supposedly in 711 that, according to Arabic sources, a group of Berbers, under the leadership of Tariq b. Ziyad, landed in the Iberian Peninsula, after crossing the Straits of Gibraltar (Fig 1). This was the final step in the movement of expansion that had carried Islamic armies from the Arabian deserts to the conquest of western Mediterranean lands. Today, the memory of this crucial event is still preserved in the name of the mountain above the place where Tariq and his followers landed: Gibraltar, meaning 'Mountain of Tariq' (Jabal Tariq).

Tariq was a Berber, but the Islamic governor of North Africa, the man responsible for military expeditions such as Tariq's, was an Arab, Musa b. Nusayr, who followed himself with a group of Arabic warriors. Thus, Berbers and Arabs participated jointly in the conquest of what Arabic sources called 'al-Andalus', a new addition to the Dar al-islam in the eighth century, where it was to remain until the fall of the Nasrid kingdom of Granada in 1492.

From 711 onwards, according to the ups and downs that marked political and social conditions, Arabs and Berbers continued to arrive in al-Andalus. It is, however, impossible to quantify the number of individuals who moved from the Middle East and North Africa to the Iberian Peninsula. Arabic documents, the only sources of relevance, are either mute or untrustworthy in this respect and, in any case, many were written centuries after the events they describe. Nevertheless, one can be sure that the early history of al-Andalus, following the Arab-Berber conquest, is that of a double process of acculturation: cultural, through Arabicisation; and religious, through Islamisation.

Berbers, the original inhabitants of the North African regions, arrived easily on the Iberian Peninsula after the conquest. They transferred themselves either as mixed groups of different tribal origins, or as tight kin-related groups, although this is a much debated question in contemporary research. During the first two centuries of Andalusian history, Berber settlements are documented in the frontier regions of al-Andalus, in the northern and central parts, as in some areas of the east and the south (north of Cordoba, Algeciras and Ronda). In this early period, the Berbers who became established in al-Andalus were themselves recent converts to Islam and were not fluent in Arabic, if they knew it at all, the Berber language having no relation to it. It is of note that, in this early period, there are references to several revolts by Berbers against the Arab governors of al-Andalus.

However, once incorporated into the new Islamic religious and social order, the Berbers experienced a slow but steady process of Arabicisation, and in some cases, they became part of the administration of al-Andalus, and of the urban elites. High officials, army commanders and renowned scholars of Berber origin occupied a social space in which their ancestry was superseded by their new Andalusian identity, shared with the other elements of the local population.

Arabs arriving with Musa b. Nusayr, and in subsequent years, represented the two main branches of the original Arabic population: Northern Arabs (Adnanids) and Southern Arabs (Qahtanids or Yemenis). Both groups had a long history of inter-ethnic struggles in the Arabian Peninsula, and they continued fighting among themselves during the early period of Andalusian history. Further arrivals of Arabic contingents are dated to 741, when the defeated army of Balj crossed the Straits, and again later, when the presence in al-Andalus of the first Umayyad prince, Abd al-Rahman b. Mu'awiya (756), attracted many of his family supporters to join him

Fig 1

The North African coast seen from Tarifa in southern Spain (photo: A Torremocha Silva).

there. Obviously, Arabs, as the overlords of the territory, played a fundamental role in the Arabicisation of society and in the establishment of the new social, religious and political order. By virtue of their ethnic origins, Arabs enjoyed a privileged situation and embodied the model of behaviour for the rest of Andalusian society.

To what extent both the Arabs and the Berbers transferred their tribal structures to al-Andalus in the early period is a matter of debate, but it seems clear that, by the tenth century, al-Andalus was a society in which tribalism had nearly disappeared

Sources: de Felipe 1997; Guichard 1977; Kennedy 1996; Manzano Moreno 2006.

By Helena de Felipe

with the consolidation of their own statehood, that they experienced this breakthrough in religion and civilisation. As late as the thirteenth century, the Balt tribes between the mouth of the Vistula and the Western Dvina were refusing to adopt the new faith, despite all the efforts that were being made from the end of the tenth century.

For some centuries there lingered a tribal legacy in the social and political systems of East-Central and Northern Europe. The authority of the monarch was based on the patrimonial principle, with support from his armed retinue from which he recruited his officials. Important support was also given by the educated clergy. Nevertheless, some regional differences may be observed. The mainstay of territorial authority in Slav states were strongholds, built on sites of importance from the point of view of communication and strategy (Fig 2.6; Box 11.2). There the rural population had to bring their

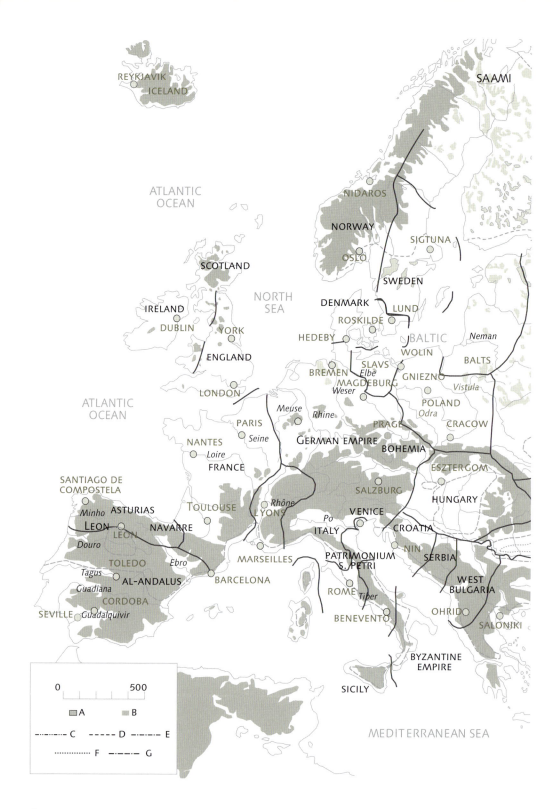

Fig 2.7 *Western Europe about 1000 (after Leciejewicz 2004). [For explanation of key, see map p 47].*

A border castle at Gormaz (al-Andalus), constructed in 963 (photo: P Españoles).

Fig 2.8

dues and render their services. Gradually, however, landed property also started to grow in importance, granted by the king to his nobles and to the Church. In Scandinavia, on the other hand, it was more difficult to exercise authority over peasant-farmers who wished to escape payment of dues and services because they might join Viking expeditions, or even leave the land with their entire families to settle abroad. Such factors played a part in the beginnings of Scandinavian settlement in Iceland towards the end of the ninth century (Box 2.1). Due to the greater independence of these farmers compared with those of mainland Europe, large estates in the Scandinavian areas never reached a size comparable to those on the Continent.

Assimilation of the models of Latin civilisation was a lengthy process in this part of Europe. The new religion was accepted most rapidly in court circles and by the inhabitants of the early towns. In rural areas, it was only in the twelfth century that the establishment of a regular parish system helped to establish the new faith more firmly. It was also not until this period that writing became more widely used as a medium of communication, for example in recording legal decisions. In addition, this was the first period when there was a widespread need felt to preserve the past of one's country and dynasty in the form of historical works. The foundation of many new abbeys, together with participation in crusades, provides strong evidence that the societies of Central and Northern Europe had lastingly linked their destinies to the Roman Catholic Church.

There is no concrete data concerning the progress of Islamisation; however, bearing in mind the construction in al-Andalus of Friday mosques, the equivalent to cathedrals in Christian cities (see pp 390-1), two important periods can be detected: the first in the mid-ninth century, and the second during the Cordoba caliphate (tenth century). The earliest Friday mosque was constructed in 786, by the first Umayyad emir of al-Andalus,

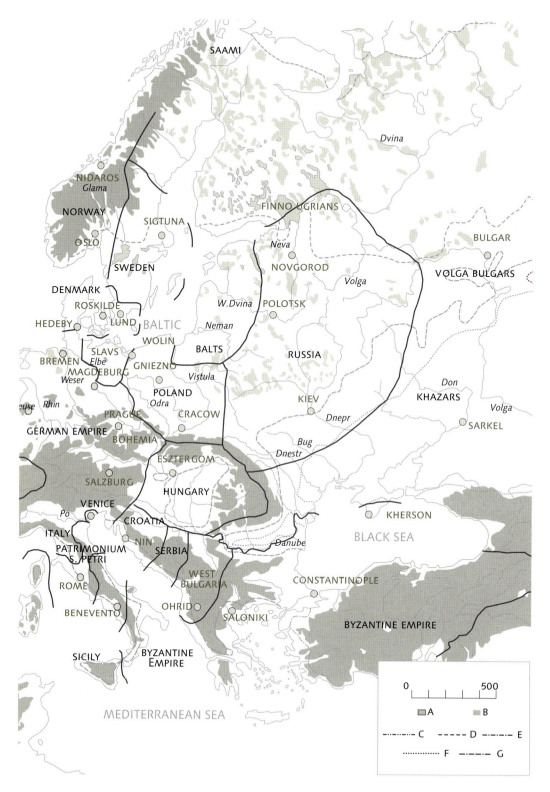

Fig 2.9 *Eastern Europe about 1000 (after Leciejewicz 2004). [For explanation of key, see map p 47].*

Abd al-Rahman I; before this, Christians and Muslims had shared the use of what was the Visigothic cathedral of Cordoba – the church of Saint Vincent – with Christians worshipping to the east and Muslims to the south. Islamisation was a slow process, as well as Arabicisation; however, both processes seem to be completed during the Umayyad caliphate in the tenth century.

Economic progress

In Western, as well as Central and Northern Europe, socio-political change was accompanied by economic progress. The result was rapid demographic growth that, in turn, fuelled demand for food, at no small cost to the natural environment.

The first consequence was the expansion of agricultural land, which encroached steadily on the forest surrounding human settlements (Böhme 1992; Roesdahl & Wilson 1992; Brather 2001). Acceleration in this process can be seen as early as the eighth/ninth century in both the Carolingian Empire and Slavic Central Europe, as well as in the Scandinavian North. Subsequently, land was opened up by means of internal colonisation within royal estates, as well as the property of the nobility and the Church. Further consequences for the landscape resulted from an improvement in the processing of grain because the spread of watermills, during the eleventh-twelfth centuries, led to the widespread damming of rivers and streams, causing serious disturbance to the hydrographic system (see pp 214-17).

Human activity also impacted on wild-life on both land (forest) and sea. The hunting of 'big game' became a privilege reserved by law for members of the elite. Hunting not only helped to secure a food supply, but also played an important role in the development of warlike skills, as well as providing entertainment. Smaller game could be hunted by the common people. In the far North, however, big-game hunting was practised generally. In newly Christianised countries, there was also an incremental increase in the consumption of fish, with the development of deep-water fishing commencing the depletion of fish-stocks (Box 6.3). An increased demand for leather was also of importance, given its use in various trades, but the greatest depredation by far was caused by the demand for the pelts of animals living in the cool northern climate. Furs became one of the most sought-after commodities on the European markets (and beyond). All these developments had painful consequences for the natural environment, although their extent cannot be readily assessed for the early Middle Ages.

The natural landscape was also greatly affected by the intensified exploitation of the natural and mineral resources required for the production of tools, weapons, ornaments and other objects of everyday use. In particular, timber was an especially significant and prized commodity in the Temperate zone of Europe. The construction of numerous defensive works led to the destruction of tree-stands in many areas, with a particularly heavy loss of oak. As a hard wood, oak was chosen, wherever possible, for such activities as ship-building and the construction of bridges. Houses and outbuildings were also made of timber, as best suited local climatic conditions (i.e. generally of pine, but occasionally birch, etc). The use of firs from Central European mountains in the construction of one of the fortresses in Jutland demonstrates that trade in prized species of timber could be far-ranging. This inevitably led to losses from which the natural environment could not readily recuperate of its own accord.

Changes in the landscape resulted not only from the increased demand for the fruits of nature. The patterns of daily life were also changing. As a result of the new organisation of society and authority, other reasons than just the necessity for adapting as best as possible to the natural environment gained in importance, such as the need for military protection and for prestigious display. The latter was served by the replacement of timber with stone in courtly, military and ecclesiastical architecture. The construction of domestic and ecclesiastical buildings in stone became a symptom of progress in the civilisation of the North. In places, the same functions started to be served by the utilisation of brick, in the twelfth century (pp 230-2), although its use had long been widespread in the South. Mediterranean Europe preserved the Roman tradition of stone building, in both town and country; so that only in northern areas are timber buildings to be found.

Further changes in the natural environment during the early Middle Ages were caused by the development of non-agrarian markets and trading-centres (i.e. towns) (Leciejewicz 2004). To a large extent in post-Roman countries use was made of the surviving remains of Late Antique towns. However, the Roman towns that survived, mostly as a bishopric or political centre, were to undergo transformation. This process began in the late Roman period and resulted partly from Christianisation (with the abandonment of former public buildings and the construction of churches) and partly from militarisation (with the construction of town walls). During the early Middle Ages this process continued, and it was only in the eighth century that there began a progressive increase in the size of these urban settlements, as a result of religious, economic or political reasons, giving rise to the development of suburbs around the old fortified centres (see Chapter 4, for 'Urban Settlement').

In the area of the former *Barbaricum*, settlements of proto-urban type were a complete novelty. A loosely-knit group of farmsteads, near a trading-place or port, might evolve during the ninth to eleventh centuries into a built-up centre in which care was taken to retain the continuity of individual settlement-plots. These had a regular network of roads and were usually surrounded by earth and timber walls, occasionally reinforced with stone. The main building material was timber. Such substantial concentrations of the population in limited areas gave rise to new problems with health conditions. Unhealthy air, polluted water, excessive noise, all became the everyday reality in towns, as occasionally mentioned in contemporary written accounts. Fires would break out and pestilence could spread easily. It was only during the later Middle Ages, at first in the West, but then in the East and North, that new methods of construction and urban planning were developed that resulted in the raising of living standards (see Vol. 2).

BIBLIOGRAPHY

Bálint, Cs (1989) *Die Archäologie der Steppe. Steppen-völker zwischen Volga und Donau vom 6. bis zum 10. Jahrhundert*, Cologne/Vienna

Bately, J and Englert, A (eds) (2007), *Ohthere's Voyages*, Roskilde

Blomkvist, N (2005) *The Discovery of the Baltic. The Reception of a Catholic World-System in the European North (AD 1075-1225)*, Leiden/Boston

Böhme, HW (ed) (1992) *Die Salier. Siedlungen und Landesausbau zur Salierzeit*,1-2, Sigmaringen

Brather, S (2001) *Archäologie der westlichen Slawen. Siedlung, Wirtschaft und Gesellschaft im früh- und hoch-mittelalterlichen Ostmitteleuropa*, Berlin/New York

Braunfels, W (ed) (1966-68, 2nd & 3rd eds) *Karl der Grosse. Lebenswerk und Nachleben*, 1-5, Düsseldorf

Caballero Zoreda, L (ed) (2001) *Visigodos y Omeyas: un debate entre la Antigüedad Tardía y la Alta Edad Media*, Madrid

Córdoba Salmerón, M (ed) (2001) *El esplendor de los Omeyas cordobeses: la civilización musulmana de Europa Occidental. Catálogo de piezas,* Granada

Chalmeta, P (1994) *Invasión e Islamización*, Madrid

Encyclopaedia of Islam (1996, new ed, compiled by PJ Bearma), Leiden

de Felipe, H (1997) *Identidad y onomástica de los bereberes de al-Andalus*, Madrid

Fitzhugh, WW and Ward, E (eds) (2000) *Vikings. The North Atlantic Saga*, Washington

Foote, PG and Wilson, DM (1980, 2nd ed) *The Viking Achievement*, London

Gimbutas, M (1963) *The Balts*, London

Glassé, C (1991) *Dictionnaire encyclopedique de l'Islam*, Paris

Graham-Campbell, J (2001, 3rd ed) *The Viking World*, London

Graham-Campbell, J (ed) (1994) *Cultural Atlas of the Viking World*, Oxford

Guichard, P (1977) *Structures sociales et occidentales dans l'Espagne musulmane*, Paris

Guichard, P and Sénac, Ph (2000) *Les relations des pays de l'Islam avec le monde Latin. Milieu X-milieu XIII,* Éditions CNED-SEDES

Hensel, W (1964) *Die Slawen im frühen Mittelalter. Ihre materielle Kultur*, Berlin

Herrmann, J (ed) (1982) *Wikinger und Slawen. Zur Frühgeschichte der Ostseevölker*, Berlin

Herrmann, J (ed) (1986) *Welt der Slawen. Geschichte, Gesellschaft, Kultur*, Leipzig/Jena/Berlin

Hodges, R (1989) *The Anglo-Saxon Achievement. Archae-ology and the Beginnings of English Society*, London

Insoll, T (1999) *The Archaeology of Islam*, Oxford

Jones, G (1986, 2nd ed) *The North Atlantic Saga*, Oxford

Kennedy, H (1996) *Muslim Spain and Portugal. A Political History of al-Andalus*, London

Kivikoski, E (1967) *Finland*, London

Leciejewicz, L (1991) *Gli slavi occidentali. Le origini delle società e delle culture feudali,* Spoleto

Leciejewicz, L (2004) *La nuova forma del mondo. La nascita della civiltà europea medievale*, Bologna

Lewis-Simpson, SM (ed) (2003) *Vinland Revisited: the Norse World at the turn of the First Millennium. Selected Papers of the Viking Millennium International Symposium, 15-24 September 2000,* St John's, NL

Lund, N (ed) (1984) *Two Voyagers at the Court of King Alfred*, York

Manzano Moreno, E (2006) *Conquistadores, emires y califas. Los Omeyas y la formación de al-Andalus*, Barcelona

Müller-Wille, M and Schneider, R (eds) (1993-94) *Ausgewählte Probleme europäischer Landnahmen des Früh- und Hochmittelalters. Methodische Grundla-gendiskussion im Grenzbereich zwischen Archäologie und Geschichte*, 1-2, Sigmaringen

Ó Cróinin, D (1995) *Early Medieval Ireland 400-1200*, London/New York

Roesdahl, E (1991) *The Vikings*, Harmondsworth

Roesdahl, E and Wilson, DM (eds) (1992) *From Viking to Crusader. Scandinavia and Europe 800-1200*, Copenhagen

Rouche, M (2003) *Les racines de l'Europe. Les sociétés du haut Moyen Age (568-888),* Paris

Urbańczyk, P (ed) (2000) *Europe around the Year 1000*, Warsaw

Váňa, Z (1983) *The World of the Ancient Slavs*, London

Vernet, J (1993) *El Islam en España*, Madrid

Viguera, MJ and Castillo Castillo, C (eds) (2001) *El esplendor de los Omeyas cordobeses: la civilización musulmana de Europa Occidental. Exposición en Madinat al-Zahra, 2001*, Granada

Viguera, MJ (1992) *Los reinos de Taifas y las invasiones magrebíes*, Madrid

Wawn, A and Sigurðardóttir, Þ (eds) (2001) *Approaches to Vínland. A conference on the written and archaeo-logical sources for the Norse settlements in the North-Atlantic region and exploration of America. The Nor-dic House, Reykjavík, 9-11 August 1999*, Reykjavík

Watt, M (1972) *The Influence of Islam on Medieval Europe,* Edinburgh

Wieczorek, A and Hinz, HM (eds) (2000) *Europas Mitte um 1000. Handbuch zur Ausstellung*, 1-3, Stuttgart

Wilson, DM (ed) (1980) *The Northern World*, London

CHAPTER 3

RURAL SETTLEMENT

Jan Klápště and Anne Nissen Jaubert

Introduction

The great majority of the population of medieval Europe lived in a rural and, at the same time, agrarian milieu. Rural settlement comprised an unusually diverse mosaic, dependent on the regionally differentiated natural environment (as described in Chapter 2), as well as on a variety of economic and social needs and necessities. The ultimate form of rural settlement was, everywhere and always, a significant part of the cultural identity ('habit'), often developing long-term traditions. The determining factors provide us with valuable cognitive opportunities. Research into rural settlement reveals the specific means by which these factors were applied, thereby opening the way to important knowledge about the Middle Ages. Information regarding the interaction of past populations with the natural environment, the economic regime, the social system of communities and the 'habit', including symbolic dealings (all of which are integral to the life of every social system), falls within this context.

Archaeology is central to research into rural settlement from the eighth to twelfth centuries, given that monuments of this category no longer survive even among the oldest standing buildings, the only exceptions being in southern Europe. Excavation is the essential method by which archaeological information can be obtained, accompanied by various types of surface survey, which can also be applied at a broader landscape level. History – the area of study, by definition, based on written sources – and architectural history, with an emphasis on rural sacral buildings, are both important partners to medieval archaeology. Many other disciplines, particularly in the natural sciences, have also grown in importance, e.g. archaeozoology, archaeobotany (including palynology or pollen analysis), etc. The methodologies applied in all of these fields can shed much light on various aspects of the past (from the immense bibliography, see at least one early item, e.g. Kossack Behre & Schmid 1984).

On a European scale, archaeological fieldwork has always been divided up into an intricacy of projects originating both in planned research and in rescue activities. In general, the tradition for the rural archaeology of the early medieval period has been surprisingly short in most European countries. During the second half of the twentieth century, it came to be generally accepted that medieval settlement had been static in character – modern settlements were supposedly superimposed on early medieval settlements, and so the former stood in the way of archaeological research. The main focus of research during that period was rural cemeteries. It was virtually only in North-West Europe that there existed a different situation because of there being a deliberate reasearch policy into early medieval settlements (see Chapter 1).

Many European countries experienced a fundamental change in research focus at the end of the twentieth century. Various activities, such as the construction of highways and railways, or opencast mining, combined with the development of cultural heritage legislation, resulted in an increase in rescue archaeology. This phase included a number of large-scale excavations that far surpassed earlier small-scale interventions, and as a result opened up a new cognitive era. Despite all these developments, European archaeological research into the early medieval village remains uneven in its coverage, and all too little is known regarding the situation across large swathes of the Continent.

The disparate nature of the questions that have formed the subject of individual research projects, together with a lack of published syntheses and bibliographical surveys concerning the progress of such research in Europe, hinders the archaeological study of rural settlement during this period. There have been few transnational studies; the important monographs by Chapelot and Fossier (1980) and Donat (1980) were both written before the spectacular development of rural archaeology, so that the more recent publication by Hamerow (2002) and the broadly-based study by Zimmermann (1998) are rare exceptions. The establishment of the Ruralia Association, with its Jean-Marie Pesez Conferences on medieval rural archaeology, was a reaction to this unfavourable situation. The biennial conferences, which have taken place since 1996, have always been thematic, and the resultant *Ruralia* proceedings (1996 onwards) reflect the current state of research in Europe.

Although rural archaeology remains embedded within each European country, the broad trends have been similar everywhere. The recent large-scale excavations have, for example, not only led to an improved knowledge of construction traditions, but also enabled research into the internal organisation of settlements. The study of the development of inter-relationships within individual settlements has proved to be an important source of information, as is now appreciated in many European regions. Such discoveries allow us to recognise that transformations of contemporary spatial behaviour provide important evidence for the character of the countryside during the medieval period. Research into the relationship of rural settlements with socially differentiated components of the medieval settlement hierarchy has also demonstrated its value. In this respect, there is a common tendency to broaden out from settlement-sites themselves to a wider interest in their surroundings, with the development of regional surveys incorporating different social aspects.

Another major change that has occured within the last few decades is the increasing use of environmental studies. Archaeological research focusing on ecofacts continues to expand, with the result that ecofacts and artefacts have become equally important pillars supporting the study of medieval rural settlement.

Rural settlement forms

Archaeology presents the medieval countryside as a system that was not static, but one that was developing and changing. The 'historical picture' of the village, as we understand it, began to stabilise at the beginning of the later Middle Ages – the period that initiated a largely continuous tradition. This observation has also had important consequences for terminology. The modern dictionary-term 'village' (*le village, das Dorf,* etc) means a communal rural settlement formed by a group of buildings and used by a number of families. In this sense it clearly differs from single isolated farmsteads.

Terminology is also used to differentiate the villages of the later Middle Ages from the inhabited places of earlier periods. Following this logic, the term village should really only be used for settlements dating to the later Middle Ages (i.e. for more stable settlements), so that the more neutral term 'rural settlement' is usually applied to the early Middle Ages.

The use of the term 'hamlet' (*le hameau, der Weiler,* etc) is even more complicated. This term has been used for small rural settlements from both the later Middle Ages and the modern period. It is, however, an inappropriate term for the early Middle Ages given that it has the same shortcomings as 'village'; its arbitrary character is a particular problem (the key can be found in an exact number of homesteads, something which makes sense only within the framework of particular regional surveys). Furthermore, it is a term that does not translate well into many languages.

It seems therefore, for the purposes of the archaeological study of the eighth to twelfth centuries, that the most suitable term for general use is 'rural settlement'. This may be refined by reference to its degree of concentration or dispersal. This supplementary definition is, however, not always available; in the case of individual farmsteads, for example, it may be difficult to prove a temporal dimension – did they exist concurrently or sequentially?

When a rural settlement is composed of several farms (as in the case of 'villages'), a number of possible models can be considered (Fig 3.1), as for example by Riddersporre (1999, 173):

(1) Live together and work together (nucleated settlement, with a farming hinterland in common); (2) live apart and work together (dispersed settlement, with a farming hinterland in common); (3) live together and work apart (nucleated settlement, with the hinterland divided into several independent parts); and (4) live apart and work apart (dispersed settlement, with sections of the farming hinterland divided commensurately).

Single farmsteads form a major part of rural settlement in several European regions, such as the so-called 'ring-forts' and 'crannogs' of Ireland (Edwards 1990; Stout 1997; see Figs 2.4 & 11.9) and also the Scandinavian settlement pattern during the Viking period in Scotland, the Faroes, Iceland and Greenland (Box 5.1). They are considered to be relatively independent socio-economic units. The fact remains that these different models are difficult to tell apart and thus to prove, and so care needs to be taken with regards to terminology and interpretation.

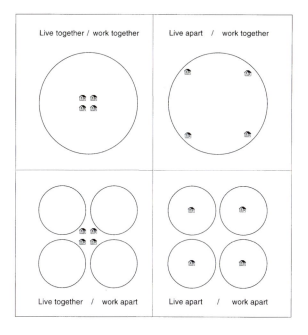

Theoretical model of four   **Fig 3.1**
types of organisation of landscape and settlement (after
Riddersporre 1999).

Continuity and change

Since the nineteenth century, the wider study of medieval archaeology has determined the division of rural settlement archaeology into periods. Traditionally, the first phase has been labelled in a manner corresponding to individual concepts of national histories (as used since Romanticism was in vogue): e.g. the Anglo-Saxon, Slavic, Carolingian, Viking periods, etc. The situation with regards to the archaeology of the later Middle Ages, however, remained different for several decades, not becoming part of such national discourses; in consequence, its cognitive potential only began to be developed consistently during the 1950s.

Given that these period-divisions originated in concepts pertaining to national history, it is not surprising that research into rural settlement began outside this framework and that the extant divisions were found to be inadequate. If one attempts a division into periods focussed specifically on medieval rural settlement, then one soon discovers the broad range of views with which modern rural archaeology evaluates the relationships between continuity and change. These evaluations are extremely inconsistent because this disparity coincides with the character of the historical reality that is being researched, into which 'continuity and change' naturally permeate (e.g. Zadora-Rio 1995).

In terms of rural settlement, to take the year c800 as a watershed is an arbitrary delimitation in itself, even if the decades around 800 do appear outstanding in political history: Vikings attacked Lindisfarne in 793, Charlemagne was crowned Emperor in Rome in 800, while his friend Offa was king of Mercia. Furthermore, the principle textual sources for continental rural history, the *Capitulare de villis* (792-3) and the *poly-*

ptyques, which detail the huge royal and monastic demesnes, mostly relate to the ninth and early tenth centuries. Turning to archaeology, fundamental economic and social changes clearly precede the year 800. Settlement patterns thus change in the late seventh century in France and c700 in southern Scandinavia and northern Germany. Even in Italy, the settlement patterns of Classical Antiquity had been progressively abandoned before 700. The main point is that both archaeological and documentary evidence suggest that the early Middle Ages can be subdivided into at least two distinctive periods, with their own characteristics. In the Roman world, the first period strongly maintained the traditions of Antiquity, whereas the second – which is the object of the following paragraphs – points forward to the central Middle Ages.

The upper temporal limit, the year 1200, is a different matter. This dividing line falls in a period in which an important change can be seen in rural settlement in the broader European context. Delimitation of this phase of change varies by region, and nowhere does it focus on any particular turning-point. This division existed within a broader period lacking in strict delimitation that seemingly represents the culmination of certain historical processes.

If we must identify a fundamental turning-point that can be documented and that corresponds to rural settlement development, then it can perhaps be seen in the more general stabilisation of rural settlement and formation of the related countryside. At a certain point, every individual region witnesses a considerable decrease in the evidence for settlement activity outside their village nuclei – a characteristic trait of later medieval and modern settlement networks. At the end of the process many (or most) of the actual villages had become 'established' in their precise locations. The temporal delimitation of the turning-point under consideration shows marked variation within a European context, but its centre of gravity clearly fell between the eleventh and thirteenth centuries; more specific determination is a task for regional research.

A critical time lag appears between the western and eastern parts of the Continent. If a given process clearly existed in Western Europe during the ninth to twelfth centuries (e.g. Nissen Jaubert 1999; Schreg 2001, 339, for northern France), then it existed in south-western Germany in the twelfth century (Schreg 2001, 337) and occurred in eastern Central Europe in the thirteenth to fourteenth centuries. An evaluation of the diminishing horizons of early medieval settlement in very large regions – northern France, south-western Germany, etc – and the results of intensive regional survey, e.g. in Picardy (Haselgrove & Scull 1995, 63), in eastern Languedoc (Durand-Dastès et al 1998), and north-western Bohemia (Klápště 1991), provide evidence to support this conclusion.

Archaeological questions, too, can be treated in radically different ways. The opinion scale ranges from narrowly framed concepts claiming a 'medieval revolution' to concepts emphasising complex connections of continuity and discontinuity, i.e. a gradual progression of transformations typical of the later Middle Ages. There are also extreme views of continuity that shed doubt on the very existence of these changes, ascribing the acknowledged differences merely to the arbitrariness of the available evidence. Even here, though, seeking a generic answer for the European setting as a whole would make no sense. Truly credible archaeological conclusions can materialise only from the exhaustive study of individual European regions. More recent research has thus been focused on exploring regional changes in the use of the medieval countryside (e.g. Bourin & Zadora-Rio 2002, 502).

An archaeological inquiry into the transformations that took place between the early and late Middle Ages has been closely related to historical research into the subject. Distinguishing between two contrasting medieval eras has for decades been typical of one branch of French medieval studies, producing the concept of the *revolution de l'an mil* or *mutation de l'an mil* that greatly influenced archaeological research in Southern and Central Europe, particularly in the 1980s-90s (in Central Europe, e.g. Klápště 1994; Schreg 2001). The extensive ongoing discussions have either corroborated this concept or pointed out its pitfalls (in the French literature, see Poly & Bournazel 1980, on one side, and Barthélemy 1997, on the other; for a more balanced assessment, see Bonnassie & Toubert 2004).

Archaeology also uses terminology borrowed from the historical discourse on the transformation of medieval Europe. The changes in the spatial organisation of the countryside related to its social restructuring, and the frequent concentration of settlement taking place during the eleventh to thirteenth centuries, are sometimes referred to (particularly in northern France) as *l'encellulement*; a loosely corresponding German term would be *die Verdorfung*. While both of these terms can serve in a fairly broad geographical context, the term *l'incastellamento* has a more restricted, territorial relevance: it refers to the concentration of settlement at strategically advantageous locations on rocky hilltops that took place in the western Mediterranean, and especially in Italy and southern France (Fig 3.2). According to the primary historical concept, this process took place in the short period from c920 to the eleventh century (Toubert 1973; Barcelo & Toubert 1998). More recent archaeological discoveries, however, suggest that this process began far earlier. Thus, several nucleated hill-top sites show early medieval occupation, currently dated to the seventh/eighth centuries, represented by wooden structures, as in Scarlino and Montarrenti, in Tuscany (Francovich 1998; Francovich & Hodges 2003), or at Casale San Donato in the Sabine mountains, east of Rome (Moreland et al 1993). Adherents of the traditional dating consider that the remains are too faint to relate them to the *incastellamento* and stress the importance of the defensive aspects in the written evidence of the tenth to eleventh centuries, where the settlements were qualified as *castella*. Anyhow, it cannot be denied that occupation dating from the seventh/eighth centuries has been observed in several hill-top villages, even if its general layout is difficult to comprehend. Furthermore, some historians stress that in most regions of Italy nothing can be concluded from the written evidence before 900 about the modalities of the settlement patterns (e.g. Wickham 1989; 1999). However, they quite often agree to designate the tenth to eleventh centuries as the 'classical' period of *incastellamento*, when most of the hill-top villages were founded. This is, for instance, the case with Rocca San Silvestro where, besides agricultural production, there was also important metalworking activity (Francovich & Wickham 1994).

Fig 3.2   *Montarrenti, Tuscany (Italy): hypothetical reconstruction of the settlement in the 8th to 9th centuries. Several hill-top sites reveal occupation from this period, indicating that a settlement shift from dispersed settlements in the valley towards nuclear settlement on rocky summits had been going on for two centuries before the classical period of* incastellamento *in the 10th to 11th centuries (after Francovich & Hodges 2003).*

Rural Settlements as Internal System

A typical rural settlement of the early Middle Ages had to satisfy two basic requirements: effective access to a water supply, and protection from the dangers posed by watery extremes. An almost infinite number of variations in adaptation to these necessities can be found in Europe, which can often be adequately identified by means of surface survey.

The archaeological classification of the internal social and economic systems of early medieval rural settlements can only result from excavation leading to the discovery of structures, artefacts and ecofacts. On a broad geographical scale, the most typical building materials throughout the early Middle Ages were wood and clay, complemented by straw or wattle, easily available almost everywhere. The use of fundamentally different building technologies, however, means that archaeological research methods differ widely by region.

Some regions, especially those along the continental coasts of North-West Europe, have more examples of relatively well-preserved sites, notably in thick water-logged sediments that have preserved the interiors of buildings: posts, stalls, walls and sometimes even indications of furnishings. In the same regions, recent agriculture was not very intense on the elevated sandy soils, especially when the late formation of hard podsols, such as at Kootwijk, in the Veluwe region of the Netherlands, seriously hampered ploughing (Heidinga 1987; Groenman-van Wateringe & Wijngaarden-Bakker 1987). This has ultimately preserved the layouts of buildings, farmsteads and settlements. These favourable conditions explain the early development of rural archaeology in these areas, and why these sites have – in the Netherlands, north-west Germany and Denmark – largely dominated our knowledge of building and settlement patterns.

Rural settlement stability

Vorbasse in Denmark, investigated as early as the 1970s-80s, may be recalled as an example of different aspects of settlement stability (Hvass 1984; 1986; 1989; Kieffer-Olsen 1987).

Several fundamentally different kinds of settlement continuity can be distinguished in the development of Vorbasse (see Box 3.1). The long-term continuity began with the early medieval settlement area; it was within this framework that there fitted several relatively short stages of local and formal continuity. Excavations near the village church have revealed settlement evidence from the twelfth century. Furthermore, the regression study of the plots – the *tofts* – in Vorbasse compared to the enclosures of the settlement from the tenth to eleventh centuries reveals a strong continuity in the modules of the plots. This observation is fundamental in a Scandinavian context because the *toft*, at least since the twelfth century and probably even earlier, served as the reference for calculating the size of the fields of each farmstead in the village (Porsmose 1993).

The careful distinction of aspects of heterogeneous stability forms one of the basic requirements for a proper understanding of rural settlement. Each of these aspects makes its own specific cognitive demands that cannot be changed.

The stability of early medieval rural settlements was therefore different from that of later medieval and early modern settlements, but most sites were occupied over several generations and often for many centuries. The exact length of occupation is often difficult to ascertain for many reasons, chief among which are the chronological problems that archaeologists have to face. In many European regions ordinary rural settlements from the medieval period tend to be poor in artefacts. Organic materials, such as wooden objects and basketry, must have accounted for the majority of artefacts, but these rarely survive and their dating is anyway often contentious. The dating of ceramics is another recurrent problem in settlement studies. There are ongoing projects attempting to improve this matter, but it must be stressed that the dating of settlements by such means is not necessarily sufficiently informative about their duration, as a result of typo-

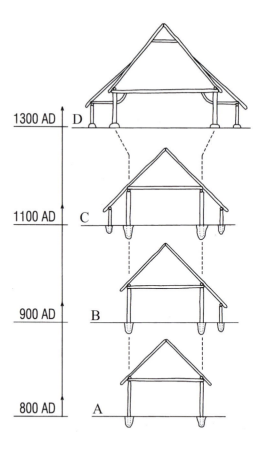

Fig 3.3 *The long-term house-building tradition in north-west Europe, with its transition from earthfast to non-earthfast vertical posts (after Zimmermann 2002).*

logical-chronological problems. This also explains why the abandonment of settlements like Serris and Villiers-le-Sec, in the Ile-de-France region, was dated to c1000 in the 1990s, whereas recent ceramic studies have revealed evidence for their occupation into the twelfth century (Mahé 2002). Nevertheless, the reconstruction and repair of the domestic buildings in many farmsteads indicates that successive houses were built and maintained on the same plot, implying long continuity of the dwelling-sites.

The shifting or the stability of a settlement is dependent on several factors. Agricultural arguments have been advanced, especially by historians or archaeologists who regard the period as one of regression in comparison to Antiquity. In their view, short-lived settlements were the inevitable result of poor agriculture, with farmers unable to improve the soil; when the latter was exhausted, the settlements had to move in order to cultivate new areas. Large-scale excavations, combined with archaeobotanical studies and the chemical analyses of soils, together with evidence for manuring, and even documentary sources, have countered these theories (e.g. Henning 1996, 779; Nissen Jaubert 2006).

The different principles at work in the later Middle Ages relate to the different legal situation, marked by the long-term retention of specific delineated plots and weighed down by long-established obligations. This legal change fundamentally influenced the general rules of spatial behaviour.

Building traditions

The interiors of early medieval rural buildings either rested on the surface of the earth or were sunk into it to varying degrees. The wooden structures that predominated over large areas of early medieval Europe were either supported by 'earthfast' vertical load-bearing systems, anchored in the subsoil, or by a system organised horizontally that did not enter the soil in any way clear enough for our recognition (Fig 3.3). The option chosen has a fundamental impact on the opportunities presented for archaeological investigation.

The early medieval building culture in the western European countryside may to a considerable extent be characterised as comprising earthfast structures, meaning that:

> … the bottom end of the roof-carrying post was dug or more rarely rammed into the soil. Non-earthfast building means either *'Ständerbau'*… with the vertical posts set on padstones and/or sills or, alternatively, corner timbering, where the roof-carrying walls are built of timber lying horizontally. (Zimmermann 1998, 207)

Earthfast constructions leave relatively good archaeological traces, although of course their state of preservation will be decided by other factors. Rural dwelling-sites are usually destroyed by erosion and ploughing over the centuries, with only the bottoms of post-holes and pits surviving. The preservation of floor-levels, hearths and internal divisions within houses is uncommon. A comparison of the houses excavated in eastern and western Denmark is instructive. Buildings in western Jutland generally have their outer walls preserved and quite often internal divisions as well as hearths. In the intensively cultivated regions in the east, an identical structure retains only the post-holes of its most deeply founded roof-supports. A quick glance might lead to the identification of different building types, whereas closer analysis of the depths of the post-holes, completed by phosphate analysis, reveals that the apparent differences are in fact solely due to the degree of erosion that has taken place.

Understanding structures in which their load-bearing system did not penetrate the earth's surface, and which were not built resting on any kind of (stone) foundations, is far more difficult. Ample examples are available in eastern Central Europe. Archaeological excavations of early medieval rural settlements in Poland, the Czech Republic, Slovakia, etc, commonly reveal, along with sunken-featured buildings, just a jumble of unclear remains that do not allow for the differentiation of individual structures, let alone any determination of their appearance (summary in Donat 1980). Wrocław-Partynice in Poland (Kolenda 2001) is one example in a long series of such essentially unassessable sites (Fig 3.4). In general, it is assumed that corner timbering (log-houses) made a considerable contribution to early medieval architecture in eastern Central Europe. These problems in interpretation require the development of new methods of excavation and their systematic application at suitable sites.

Only in some European regions were early medieval rural buildings built with the use of stone. A special position in this respect is held by some sites in north-western France of which one of the earliest examples, dating back to the sixth/seventh century, is that

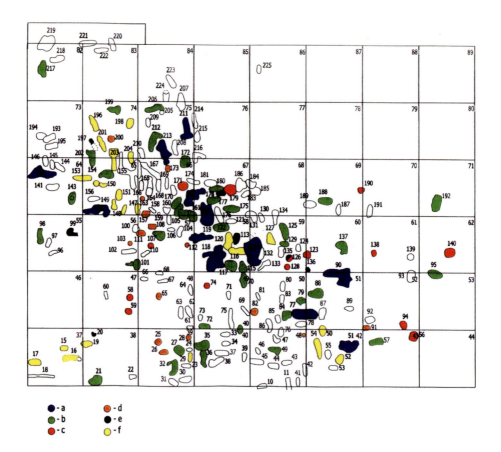

Fig 3.4   *Partynice (Poland): settlement area from the 11th-13th centuries, with a 10x10m grid, showing the remains of (a) dwellings, (b) production features, (c) grain storage-pits, with (d) & (e) subsidiary hearths (after Kolenda 2001).*

of Goudelancourt-les-Pierrepont in Picardy (Nice 1994, 29-33). This two-aisled house with earthfast roof-posts, 6x10m in plan, had wall-sills made of small stones (Fig 3.5). Remarkable examples are also known from the long-term excavations at Mondeville, south of Caen (Normandy), where a tradition of stone building, typical of the first to third centuries AD, was replaced by timber structures after the third century. Building stone began to be used again in this area during the seventh to ninth centuries. Further development is represented by slightly sunken structures, about 3.5x7m in plan, with perimeter stone sills and roofs supported by earthfast posts (Lorren 1989; 1996).

Evaluating the use of building stone in north-western France is not simple. In some cases stone formed part of buildings which had an earthfast wooden load-bearing system and which had only a short life-span (e.g. Goudelancourt-les-Pierrepont), whereas elsewhere (e.g. at Herblay) stone was used for the main buildings (Valais 1998), or merely in a complementary manner, as at Giberville (de Saint Jores & Hincker 2001) and Distré (Valais 2002).

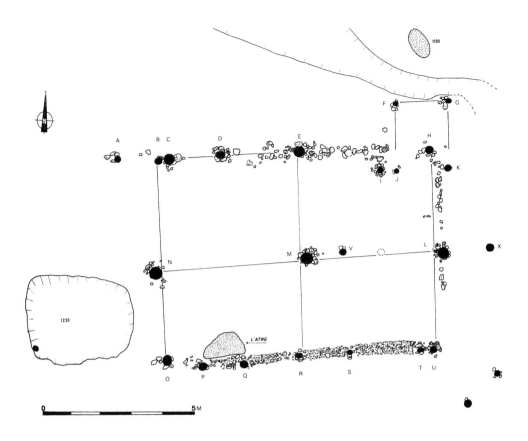

Goudelancourt-les-Pierrepont (France): building with an earthfast wooden load-bearing system combined with wall-sills made of small stones (6th/7th century); an early instance of the partial use of building stone in the medieval countryside (after Nice 1994).

Fig 3.5

An exceptional early use of stone is to be found in the alpine pastures of Switzerland. In areas above the natural tree line (that is over 1550m above sea-level), archaeology has identified dry-stone structures for seasonal use, the oldest known examples of which date from the beginning of the eleventh century. These are connected with the summer pasturing of cattle for the production and processing of milk. In the prevailing conditions stone was the only locally available building material; its use is therefore unrelated to demands for long-lasting structures, being the only possible adaptation to local conditions (Meyer 1991). Another example of such adaptation is provided by the use of turf for the walls of Icelandic buildings (p 156), given restricted access to structural timber in the North Atlantic region.

In the European temperate band above all, from the Ukraine to England (but even in Iceland), sunken-featured buildings or SFBs (sunken huts/houses, pit-houses, etc; summaries in Donat 1980; Chapelot 1980) were part of the early medieval building culture (see also Chapter 5). Their construction was relatively undemanding and thus, in suitable pedological and hydrological conditions, their use came to be extremely widespread. On a European scale, archaeology has ascribed various uses to them: in the West they were normally ancillary structures to ground-level houses (Hamerow 2002, 33; Tipper 2005); in the East they were, in the vast majority of cases, capable of serving as dwellings.

Weaving is the best documented of the activities that took place within them in Western Europe and has been demonstrated at early Anglo-Saxon sites like Mucking (Hamerow 1993), as well as in numerous SFBs in North-West Europe and southern Germany. This should not, however, obscure the fact that, in the great majority of cases, it is not possible to determine the precise function of these structures. Their use as dwellings has been much discussed and their small dimensions and lack of hearths have often been highlighted to refute this idea (e.g. Chapelot 1980; see also Meier 1994), although the pit could have been floored over (Tipper 2005). It is clearly too limiting to suggest a single interpretation for these buildings. It should also be remembered that often it is only constructed features in SFBs that leave archaeological evidence, such as the warp-weighted loom at Dalem, northern Germany (Zimmermann 1991; Fig 7.5), and most of the artefacts recovered from SFBs come from the layers that filled the pit after the structure had been abandoned. So SFBs were probably used for many different purposes: storage, shelter for small animals, as workshops and sometimes even as simple dwellings, e.g. for the slaves that were frequently present in early medieval rural societies (Bonnassie 1985).

The situation is quite different in East Central and Eastern Europe where SFBs obviously served as dwellings (Šalkovský 2001). Early rural settlements in this region were characterised by rectangular sunken huts with stone ovens, generally with a floor area of about 10m² and an estimated original depth of about 80cm (e.g. Kuna & Profantová 2005, 107). Structures of this type were undoubtedly accompanied by others on the ground surface which, with rare exceptions, have escaped detection during archaeological investigation. The principle of using sunken huts as dwellings is part of the East European building tradition, and their spread into eastern Central Europe, in areas with fundamentally different natural conditions, is clearly linked to the expansion of the Slavs as an ethnic group in the sixth to seventh centuries AD (Donat 1980). Even before the end of the first millennium, however, the proportion of structures constructed on the ground-surface had been gradually increasing, with the proportion of sunken huts in decline.

Building trends

In the vast territory stretching from the Alps to the Baltic and the North Seas, within which the primary building material during the early Middle Ages was wood, it is possible to trace the gradual transition from earthfast to non-earthfast construction. In the prehistoric period, earthfast structures predominated, although non-earthfast buildings evidently had their place as well. The European environment of the eleventh to fourteenth centuries, however, was marked by the opposite situation, with a clear predominance of non-earthfast structures. Structures of the latter type were characterised by their far greater lifespans; while the structures that had dominated previously could be expected to last for perhaps a few decades, structures not set into the ground could be used for centuries. While the majority of the early structures served their purposes for no more than 50 years, a whole series of non-earthfast structures survives to this day, and their age can be determined through dendrochronology.

Contemporary with the medieval expansion of non-earthfast structures, there was a major increase in the proportion of buildings made of stone. The choice between these technologies depended directly on the regional availability of building materials. The causes of such fundamental changes have been explained in various ways, but there can be no doubt that they were contemporary with the greater degree of stabilisation in rural settlement that, with regional variations, took place between the eleventh and fourteenth centuries.

Farmsteads as socio-economic units

A theme of primary importance is the study of early medieval farmsteads (households) that are expressed in the archaeological record as spatially distinct units consisting of functionally diverse structures. As a rule, the remains of the fences that delimited the farmyards are essential for the identification of such household units. The clearest evidence of farmsteads comes from the Continental regions along the North Sea, where good house typologies and layouts make it possible to follow the general trends in settlement evolution during the first millennium.

At the end of the second century, settlement patterns changed rather suddenly. A new type of enclosed farmstead replaced the earlier, frequently dispersed, agricultural units that were often concentrated into a single longhouse, consisting not just of accommodation but also containing a byre and storage space, etc. The new fenced household had an even more spacious longhouse, with stalls for more animals than hitherto, and even some minor outbuildings. Their 'plots' were regular, and the general layout is actually similar to 'planned' medieval villages. Vorbasse illustrates this development – which may be related to the nucleation of formerly dispersed settlement patterns – very clearly. Although it should be noted that the village of Vorbasse is exceptionally large (see Box 3.1), there are many other examples to provide confirmation of this process.

Settlements retained this appearance for several centuries, although minor differences in the details of house construction can be observed regionally. There was next a radical change about 700; however, the general layout of the settlement continues to consist of regular 'plots' of farmsteads, each with a central longhouse surrounded by several outbuildings, notably SFBs. This transition took place in northern Germany and the Netherlands, where the households and buildings of such places as Dalem and Gasselte covered much larger areas than the earlier farmsteads at Flögeln or Odoorn (Zimmermann 1991; 1992; Waterbolk & Harsema 1979; Waterbolk 1979; 1991). At the same time as the areas of both settlements and farmsteads increased, rural architecture became more varied, presenting greater regional and functional diversity than before.

The North-West European three-aisled longhouse is an outstanding example of common architectural principles applied over a large area from the Bronze Age to the fifth cen-

BOX 3.1   VORBASSE, DENMARK

Excavation of an area exceeding 26 hectares in extent at Vorbasse, in Jutland, revealed eight different settlement phases, dating from the first century BC to the eleventh century AD (Fig 1). Only then did the settlement move to the existing village of Vorbasse (8), a distance of about 500 metres (Kieffer-Olsen 1987). This final topographical adjustment was in line with developments that were then spreading steadily across Europe (see above, 'Continuity and change').

Vorbasse is located in a landscape well-suited to cattle breeding, and its layout and construction entirely suit this purpose. The way in which the settlement area was structured in each of its phases has been recovered from traces of the ditches that originally held its perimeter fences. With the help of these, it is possible to distinguish the individual farmsteads (or households), which would have been independent social and production units. In the phase dating from the eighth to tenth centuries, each farmstead had a large longhouse with a byre (see Fig 5.3). These longhouses were accompanied by other farm buildings: smaller houses, including SFBs, used mainly as weaving huts. The structures were supported on vertical posts set firmly in the ground and can be reconstructed from their post-holes (Fig 2).

One of the requisites for an informative excavation site is its potential for undertaking the spatial differentiation of its different phases. At Vorbasse, for example, it has been possible to establish that there were seven households in the final phase of its early existence, dating from the tenth to eleventh centuries (Fig 3). The fences at this site would have been lost had an additional 5cm been scraped away before excavation commenced.

The excavations at Vorbasse revealed important traits common to many early medieval set-

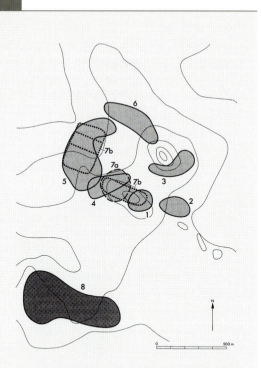

Fig 1

The eight settlement areas of Vorbasse from throughout the 1st millennium AD (after Hvass).

tlements. Its seperate phases were marked by a compact arrangement that is generally classified as 'row-settlement'. In the fourth century, for instance, there were 20 enclosed farmsteads in two well-defined rows, separated by a wide trackway (for more details, see Hvass 1986; cf. Hamerow 1995; 2002). In addition, clear-cut spatial behaviour was revealed, with each settlement site being abandoned after a certain amount of time, relocating to another area.

By Jan Klápště & Anne Nissen Jaubert

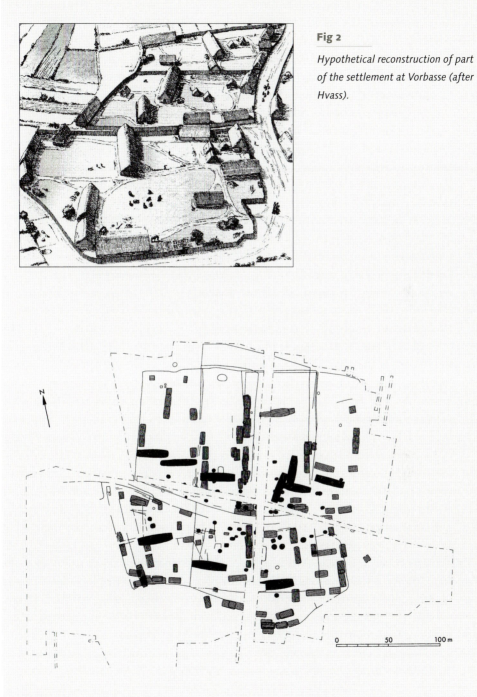

Fig 2

Hypothetical reconstruction of part of the settlement at Vorbasse (after Hvass).

Fig 3

Plan of the Viking period settlement of Vorbasse, showing its buildings and fences (after Hvass).

tury AD. The main logic behind this house-type was to group most agricultural and social functions under the same roof. Width was generally constant, at about 5-6.5m, but length varied from period to period; these farmsteads could be from 20-50m long, although the latter is somewhat exceptional, with these differences being linked to the prevailing social and economic conditions. A longhouse will always have a living-space and a byre (see Fig 5.3), but in many cases other spaces are added, such as shelters for vehicles, workshops, etc. The total length of the longhouse thus depends on the size of the byre and the number of additional functional spaces, which presumably reflected the social status of its owner.

The traditional longhouse has always two rows of posts supporting the roof. Such an arrangement is somewhat surprising, given that their widths rarely surpass those of the contemporary single-aisled houses south-west of the Rhine. As there is no reason to doubt the technical level of carpentry, the explanation for this phenomenon is probably functional and may relate to storage capacities. It is striking that storage-pits are almost absent from around three-aisled longhouses, while they are numerous in Belgium and France.

The abandonment of the traditional longhouse in the southern zone thus broke a millennium-old cultural and architectural unity (Zimmermann 1998). The new households had more buildings with specific functions, and the byre was separated from the dwelling. The northern areas, by contrast, retained the classic longhouse until the end of the tenth century, when a new type of dwelling with a large central hall arranged around a hearth served for people, with the livestock kept in separate byres.

The development and abandonment of the longhouse raises many questions and has inspired numerous hypotheses. The absence of this house-type from Anglo-Saxon settlements has intrigued numerous researchers. Some have suggested a climatic explanation for this, but this hypothesis fails to appreciate that livestock can be kept outside in many regions with much harsher winters. It also appears that animal warming is not effective in large buildings and parasites will easily find their way into living areas (Zimmermann 1999). Furthermore, this hypothesis neglects the documentary evidence: many Anglo-Saxon documents mention byres, and later the *Gerefa*, dated to the eleventh century, stresses the importance of byres and pigsties (Hughes 1984, 72; Gardiner 2006).

Building traditions are somewhat different on the other side of the Rhine. The true longhouse, combining habitation and byre, is less frequent. In northern Brabant, in Belgium, there are examples of (normally) two-aisled houses with sunken floors from the second and early third centruries AD. This type seems to disappear and, before the early Middle Ages, the identification of the byre becomes more problematic. Houses of the Merovingian period are often two-aisled, while most Carolingian buildings have a single aisle and are often 12-16m long and 5-6m broad. In addition to these buildings, small hexagonal granaries became quite frequent from the seventh/eighth century. Different sizes may relate to differing functions, such as those of barn and byre. The modesty of these buildings compared to the longhouse of the coastal regions and of Scandinavia can readily be explained by functional specialisation in a number of separate buildings, as opposed to the concentration of multiple functions under one roof. If comparisons are limited to living-areas, then the dimensions are fairly similar.

In the Netherlands region of Veluwe, where there are at least some dwellings of the seventh and eighth/ninth centuries, at Kootwijk, the latter had a separate entrance in the gable, with an opposing one leading into the habitation (Heidinga 1987, 49). The byres in northern regions are generally more spacious which can perhaps be explained by the greater importance of livestock.

The recent development of rural archaeology has been particularly significant in northern France, which includes some of the Frankish and Carolingian core regions, from both the quantitative and qualitative points of view (Chapelot 1993; Peytremann 2003). This new advance, directly linked to rescue archaeology, operates on the assumption of a 'long' early Middle Ages that includes the twelfth century (Peytremann 2003). The prolongation of the early Middle Ages can also be observed in the Rhône-Alpes region of France, where second-generation settlements dating from the tenth to thirteenth centuries are similar in layout to many early medieval settlements, while the classic Carolingian settlement patterns are scarce (Faure-Boucharlat 2001). In the Mediterranean regions, the discovery of settlements that can be dated to the seventh to tenth centuries has been infrequent.

Given the almost stereotypical architecture of the coastal regions along the North Sea, structures in France seem extremely diverse. Ground-plans and the technical solutions adopted may vary from one site to another, and even from one farmstead to another. As many of the excavations are located on good agricultural soils, and many settlements were densely occupied in the early Middle Ages, later agriculture has often badly eroded the structures, which can thus be extremely difficult to identify. The great majority of the buildings are of wattle and daub, with earthfast posts, but some structures must have been built on a kind of framework erected on a sill-beam resting on the earth, on a row of stones or on low stone walls. This is, for example, the case at Mondeville in Normandy, during the seventh-eleventh centuries (Lorren 1989; 1996).

In some settlements, the building materials and layouts are obviously dependent on the social context. At Serris, in the Ile-de-France, it was only the buildings of the manor site, and in the graveyard, that had foundations of stone, and they were larger and longer than the houses on ordinary farmsteads. The Carolingian buildings are much smaller than the longhouses of Northern Europe. Most are hardly 10m long, even if some may measure up to about 15m; it is exceptional to find a house of 20m or more. The usual width of these buildings is about 5-6m, or slightly more, even if there are many examples of larger structures, with a two-aisled plan (sometimes more). These proportions, which relate to the current techniques of carpentry and the most common sizes of timber, can be observed from excavations in all the regions that have yielded significant remains of seventh- to twelfth-century rural architecture (Faure-Boucharlat 2001).

Building size seems to increase at the end of the millennium (Peytremann 2003, figs 128-31). It is also apparent, at least in the Ile-de-France, that buildings seem to be more homogenous, following similar schemes or models (Gentili 2001, 34-5).

Some buildings may have been on two storeys, e.g. the long high-status seventh-century hall, with stone foundations, at Serris, and the tenth-century wooden building, with closely-set posts, from Villiers-le-Sec (Gentili 2001, 35-6; Foucray & Gentili 1995).

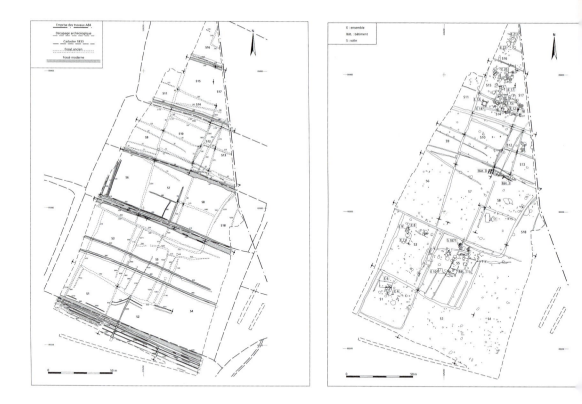

Fig 3.6   *Le Teilleul, Montours, Ille-et-Vilaine (France): the limits of the 19th-century fields follow the orienta-tion of the farm-plots from the 8th-10th centuries, stressing the impact of the early medieval period in the making of the agrarian landscape, with (right) the early medieval archaeological structures on the site (after Catteddu et al 2001).*

Sometimes the remains of a hearth may indicate that a building served as a dwelling, but in most cases it is impossible to ascribe one function rather than another. Moreover, buildings may have served several purposes, as can be seen from the storage-pits inside ninth-century dwellings at Mondeville and Distré, and perhaps also at eleventh/twelfth-century Marcé in Anjou (Lorren 1989; Valais 2002; Pétorin 1997). Single-aisled struc-tures are the most common, but two-aisled buildings also occur frequently, but three or more aisles are unusual. Plans are generally rectangular, often slightly irregular or even slightly trapezoidal, but some buildings have perpendicular wings, like the aforemen-tioned house at Mondeville, or the rather more spacious structures in the Ile-de-France from the end of the tenth to the twelfth century.

In eastern Brittany, excavations on a 3-hectare site at Montours have shown the exist-ence of two small hamlets: Louvaquint and Teilleul (Fig 3.6), associated with other farm-steads (Catteddu et al 2001). They face each other on the slopes of the valley of a little river. The first medieval farmsteads were probably established in the seventh to eighth centuries. The proximity of the two settlements and their almost identical disposition indicate a general planning of the settlements. Their proximity, and the ford crossing the river, implies some sort of common organisation of the countryside. All the buildings in the settlements were of wood and most had earthfast posts, but some structures had a sill-beam or a row of sill-stones. Nearly all were single aisled and internal divisions were rare; they ranged from about 20-50m² in area, but their width rarely exceeded 5m (ibid, 43-6, 148). Their functions have not been determined, but the abundant rubbish remains clearly indicate that some livestock was stabled. Other structures provide further information regarding activities in the settlement. Storage-pits and baking ovens have been found at several locations. Some of the ovens may have served for drying grain prior to storage, especially those surrounding an empty area where archaeobotanical evidence indicates that cereals were threshed (ibid, 163).

The building traditions of early Anglo-Saxon England are somewhat homogenous, but do not equal the extraordinarily detailed house typology of the northern regions on the Continent. Anglo-Saxon houses are rather small, measuring less than 12m in length (Marshall & Marshall 1991). As mentioned previously, the absence of the large traditional longhouses of the home regions of the Angles, Saxons and Jutes has often puzzled researchers. In the seventh century building size increased, and the first hall is to be found about 600 (Hamerow 2002, 46). Layouts were also more varied than in the earlier period, probably the result of a more specialised architecture corresponding to different functional aspects of the buildings. Dimensions and plans became even more diverse in the ninth to tenth centuries and discourage most attempts at typological classification. From a technical point-of-view, however, it may be noted that more than 75% of buildings had foundation-trenches for sill-beams or other wooden structures.

Urgent questions attend the study of the beginnings of farmsteads in eastern Central Europe, where sites from the eighth to twelfth centuries contain a remarkably small number of identifiable economic and auxiliary buildings. Traces of foundations and trenches for fences are also rare and they do not often relate to the delineation of individual settlement-units. These facts have caused some to doubt the existence of farmsteads in the western Slavic area during the early medieval period (Donat 1980; Brather 2001, 109). This would match the zoning of some settlements into functionally distinct areas. An example is provided by Bajč, in south-western Slovakia (Fig 3.7), where, on an eighth- to ninth-century settlement covering some 3.5ha, it has been possible to differentiate between residential, storage and production zones (Ruttkay 2002, 276). Even examples of this kind, however, are insufficient to provide an overall resolution of the problem. The fact that the information is so incomplete from most of the sites so far investigated also means that no firm conclusions can be justified. Individual holdings in the western Slavic area during the latter part of the early Middle Ages are otherwise attested by data from documentary sources (see Laszlovszky 1986, for a discussion of the early existence of farmsteads in Hungary).

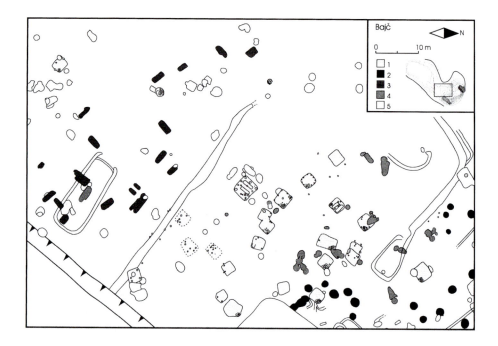

Fig 3.7   *Bajč (Slovakia): settlement from the 8th-10th centuries, with three differentiated areas: (1) residential: sunken-featured buildings; (2) storage: grain storage-pits; and (3) production: roasting pits (after Ruttkay 2002).*

Rural Territories as Economic Space

Fields

Written sources divide rural territories into three parts: *ager* (cultivated fields), *saltus* (uncultivated land and pastures), and *silva* (forest). This largely literary, tripartite division summarises the main resource zones of the countryside. In contrast to earlier Celtic field-systems and the later ridge-and-furrow of the High Middle Ages, archaeological evidence for early medieval fields is very scarce. Documentary evidence provides some information, which can sometimes be complemented by the regressive analysis of cadastral maps.

One way of organising rural territories into a clear separation of infield and out-field may be illustrated by the extended field-systems in several Norwegian and Swedish regions. In Östergötland, Sweden, phosphate analyses have complemented the mapping of extensive systems of fossilised field-boundaries, evidenced by long stone walls from the first to fifth centuries AD. Their study has revealed intensively cultivated infields near settlements that have been heavily manured, with occasionally cultivated outfields and pastures surrounding the core area (Widgren 1983). Evidence for such organisation is, however, almost entirely lacking from the last centuries of the first millennium, even where historically documented hamlets and villages had similar systems. Extended field-systems from the Viking period have been preserved in some marginal areas, such as Iceland and Greenland.

Northern landscape laws allot many passages to the building of fences, but as in later times these were constructed each year following the rotation of crops and fallow land. This may perhaps be at least one of the explanations for the poor evidence for field-boundaries in the latter part of the early Middle Ages. Fences are also mentioned frequently in old tribal laws, which were mainly written in the sixth to eighth centuries. The main function of fences was to protect the crops from livestock, the laws dealing with responsibilities if animals crossed them.

Manuring of fields was to a considerable extent dependent on the housing of cattle. The manure that accumulated in byres and sties could be returned to the fields, providing valuable nutrients (Donat 1999; Zimmermann 1999). Archaeological surveys have demonstrated that field rejuvenation was also conducted through spreading potsherds, which can be distinguished from the ceramics of habitation-sites by their extreme fragmentation and well-worn edges. In other cases, phosphate or heavy metal soil analyses have indicated high values near settlements. At some places (e.g. Montours), pit-fills have been identified containing the remains of animal waste (Catteddu et al 2001, 78), which was probably intended for use as manure. In France archaeobotanical studies have revealed the cultivation of legumes (beans, etc), which can supply the fields with nitrates. Sod-manure or *Plaggenwirtschaft* is another very elaborate system of soil improvement used on the sandy soils of the coastal regions along the North Sea. It consists of creating artificial fertile soil by mixing animal waste with sand and earth. The oldest example of sod-manure comes from excavations at Archsum, in northern Germany, where it was possible to date a layer of sod to the beginning of the first millennium AD. In Denmark, evidence for sod-manure from the eighth century has been found at Ribe, and some excavations have revealed the use of the method in northern Jutland, notably at Mors where there was a layer about a metre thick (Madsen & Vegger 1992; Lerche & Jensen 1985).

Rural technology and innovation

The Middle Ages experienced no unique fast-spreading revolutions that might be termed 'inventions' of the sort well known from the nineteenth and twentieth centuries. Instead, there was the gradual modification of practices and of artefacts that had sometimes been long known, followed by their effective and widespread use as part of a functionally unified entity, which has been referred to as the 'technological package' or 'technological complex' (e.g. Dyer 1997, 294). This process is well illustrated by the large-scale diffusion of the plough in Central and Northern Europe.

Comparative research reveals considerable differences in the functional efficiency of the ploughs for which there are surviving iron parts (Box 3.2). These are so great that they defy any definition of the plough based exclusively on the evidence for single-sided tillage. Rather, it suggests a more subtle approach, which also takes account of earlier tools, of symmetrical or slightly asymmetrical implements that are inclined to one side. The impression today is that the implement concerned was characterised by having its share set almost horizontally, the effectiveness of which was increased by the vertical cut made by a coulter. The Great Moravian shares evidently served as parts of ploughs of

BOX 3.2   THE DIFFUSION OF THE PLOUGH

The terminology in use today refers both to the structure of the plough and how it was used. The plough works asymmetrically, its share cutting and lifting the soil on one side, while the mould-board turns it on the other. A previously hidden layer of soil, richer in nutrients, is thus brought to the surface; during this process, the plough-soil is aerated and the passage of water through it is facilitated. At the same time, weeds are buried and the soil can be mixed with manure. These are the factors that influence the possible applica-tions of the plough and, on this basis, it found its place in the permanent cultivation of the damp and heavy soils of northern Europe, best suited for growing cereals. Accordingly, its use was in-effective in the warmer, drier south, which has light porous soils in which it is necessary to retain moisture.

Archaeology provides two forms of evidence: the discovery of plough parts and of traces of till-age. The former mainly consist of iron plough-shares and coulters, because the wooden struc-tures onto which these were fitted fail to survive. It is therefore not generally possible to verify the existence of the wooden mouldboard, one of the key features of a plough.

The uneven distribution of archaeological evidence for early medieval ploughing, both geo-graphically and chronologically, is a phenomenon worthy of note (Fries 1995; Reigniez 2002). There are, however, several different concentrations of evidence in Europe. Traces of tillage are con-centrated in Northern and the northern part of Central Europe (Gringmuth-Dalmer 1983). The oldest ploughing traces from the regions along the North Sea can be dated to around 400BC. At Velsen, for example, the plough replaced the ard about 300BC and there are several other ex-amples of plough tillage in Lower Saxony from the following centuries. In southern Scandinavia

the oldest evidence of plough tillage can be dated to the third/fourth century (Zimmermann 1995, 308-9, fig 6.4-5). Recent discoveries indicate that the plough was also in use between the Lower Rhine and the Danube from Late Antiquity (Henning 1985; 1996, 777-9; 2004).

The evidence of early medieval iron plough-shares and coulters indicates two further re-gions (Henning 1987). One of these, focused on southern Moravia and south-western Slovakia, is mainly associated with the 'Great Moravia' and has to date yielded over 30 shares from the eighth to tenth centuries (Fig 1). The second, even richer, region lies in the Balkans, covering the lands of the first Bulgar realm. Both regions also have discoveries of coulters. Given this evi-dence, there is not the slightest doubt that the asymmetric plough existed in the early Middle Ages, equipped with asymmetrical and sym-metrical shares. The morphology of the shares themselves is not, of course, sufficient to allow for the evaluation of this problem. Attention needs to be paid to the size and mass of the sur-viving artefacts, as these may provide some idea of the effectiveness of the ploughing implements of the period. The largest of the Great Mora-vian shares weighed close to 2kg, but most of the known examples are far smaller, only rarely exceeding 0.5kg in weight. The smaller sizes were used on one side (e.g. Poláček 2003). By contrast it is enough to mention that the major-ity of later, conspicuously asymmetrical, shares weighed around 3kg. It is only these latter shares that represent the 'heavy plough', so-called because of the demands it made for traction, given that the implement as a whole may have weighed 70–80kg (Lerche 1994).

By Jan Klápště & Anne Nissen Jaubert

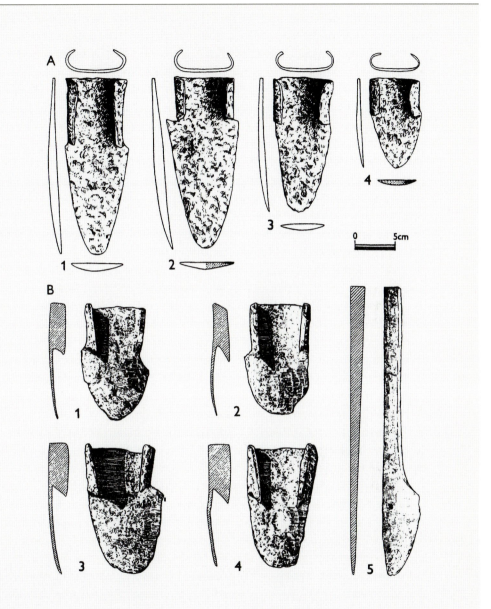

Fig 1

Iron plough-shares and a coulter (9th century) from (A) Ivanovice and (B) Pohansko u Nejdku, Moravia (Czech Republic). (A): symmetrical plough-shares weighing 514g, 558g, 370g and 178g; the smallest share (A:4) has a steel plate on its right side, i.e. this symmetrical artefact was intended for slightly asymmetrical tillage (metallographic research on the others is absent). (B): plough-shares with symmetrical or slightly asymmetrical morphology (B:1-4); with (B:5) a coulter (after Klápště 1998).

this kind. Traces of early medieval asymmetrical tillage at sites on the North Sea coast can be similarly explained; here too there is no evidence for early medieval tillage that came at all close to the late medieval plough in terms of effectiveness (Klápště 1998). One should, however, as Jean-Marie Pesez has pointed out, distinguish between the knowledge of a technical solution and its widespread adoption (Pesez 1991).

Similar testimony is afforded by other examples of medieval technology, of which harrows should at least be mentioned here. An important tool for cultivation, the harrow was used for breaking up the plough-soil, loosening and aerating it, as well as for covering seeds. Evidence for the harrow in the early Middle Ages is sporadic, but comes from both western and eastern Central Europe. The harrow of the time was a wooden grid set with wooden nails some 10cm long (Bärenfänger 1993; Schuldt 1981; Zimmermann 1995); however, even branches could be used, as modern ethnographic evidence attests. The later Middle Ages saw the introduction of far more efficient harrows, suitable for use on soils tilled using a heavy plough. Their use together with the plough is attested by, for example, the Bayeux Tapestry, embroidered before the end of the eleventh century, which also illustrates the considerable demands for pulling power that harrows, like ploughs, made. It shows a horse pulling a harrow, while the plough is drawn by an animal similar to a donkey or mule.

Any mention of increased demands for traction must lead to the consideration of horse-collars (p 65) and horse-shoes (p 254). These too have an earlier history, but their more general spread is linked to changes characteristic of the later Middle Ages; only then did horse-power begin to be seriously applied for traction, its efficiency increasing fivefold with the introduction of the horse-collar (Knittler 1999; Schmaedecke 1999).

Ever since the nineteenth century, studies of medieval agricultural technology have emphasised the importance of crop rotation. It is this method of alternating the crops grown over time in a particular area that has become a marker of agricultural maturity, comparable in this sense to the 'true plough'. There are, however, two different implications to crop rotation. Its origin is clearly related to the alternation of winter crops, spring cereals and lying fallow, carried out by individual farmers within their own holdings. This principle had evidently been known since Antiquity, and there is evidence for its use on large landholdings in Western Europe from the ninth century. Its other significance was collective and depended on rules being applied across all the fields of a settled community. The hinterland was divided into three comparable sections, and each farmer held a roughly equal part of each third, so that every year approximately the same benefits could be expected. This system has been termed 'regulated crop rotation'. The sequence of winter crops and spring cereals characteristic of both systems did not itself bring benefits, although it reduced the risk of famine. The annual spring sowing of cereals ensured the minimum of soil resting, and at the same time freed space for pasturing cattle, urgently required wherever pastures had been lost to tilled fields (Fig 6.6). The advantages of unregulated, and especially regulated, crop rotation were therefore to be found only in the type of agricultural landscape created by cereal growing. It was for this reason that regulated three-field rotation was largely diffused relatively late (in the thirteenth century), even in northern France, in 'landscapes created by the growing of cereals' (Devroey 2003, 108; Comet 1997, 29; Thoen 1997, 74).

Each of the phenomena outlined above came to be associated with a particular economic system, within which it could develop and be applied effectively. A particularly notable chapter in this story relates to milled grain. In the early Middle Ages this need was mostly met by manual querns comprising two circular grinding-stones. These are known from diverse social environments and some sites have yielded hundreds, with a combined weight of several tonnes, e.g. Mikulčice in the Czech Republic (Marek & Skopal 2003). Watermills, mentioned in many Carolingian *polyptyques*, were far more productive than hand-querns and were, indeed, the most complex pieces of technical equipment utilised during the early medieval period (Lohrmann 1996; Amouretti & Comet 2000); they are thus discussed more fully in Chapter 7 (pp 214-17). In many European regions it can be seen that the diffusion of watermills was part of a functionally linked 'technological package', which spread in the first centuries of the second millennium. The windmill, first developed in the Orient, was to spread quickly across the Occident from the twelfth century (Lohrmann 1996, 228).

Rural Settlements in Relationship to Cemeteries and Churches or Chapels

A natural element of the countryside comprised the relationship between the living and the dead. This was (and remains) a significant buttress of the cultural stability of every social system. The relationship between the two worlds is expressed spatially, the understanding of which is one of the tools of archaeological cognition. The study of the transition from the use of 'unassociated burial-grounds' to churchyards is one of the important themes of rural archaeology. At the beginning of the early Middle Ages burials were usually sited outside settlements, and the spaces of the dead and of the living were clearly separated (Fig 3.8). This location of cemeteries in the proximity of actual settlements, however, indicates territorial stability and continuity. The long-term formation of a new relationship marked by the abolition of this separation began in Western Europe in the seventh to eighth centuries, while in eastern Central Europe a similar process began at the start of the twelfth century (cf. p 432). The first step in this direction was the decline in use of burial-grounds ('row cemeteries') located on the outskirts of settlements.

In some regions, groups of burials have been identified inside settlements (e.g. Bücker & Hoeper 1999). Two types have been observed: small groups of graves actually within farmsteads, as at Kirchheim (Fig 3.9), in Bayern (Geisler 1997), and – to varying degrees – larger groups associated with a shrine, e.g. at Lauchheim in Baden-Württemberg, Germany (Stork 1997), or Serris (Foucray & Gentili 1995). The re-use for burial of barrows and of extant Roman buildings, on villas which seem generally to have been abandoned for several centuries before their conversion into Christian funeral areas (Le Maho 1994), is another matter.

Archaeological recognition of these processes is accompanied by such problems as the disappearance of artefacts from grave inventories, which seriously impedes chronological classification as well as the opportunities for social interpretation. The gradual institutionalisation of Christianity and the concurrent changes in mentality are attested

Fig 3.8   *Černice (Czech*
           Republic): a small
           hollow, surrounded
           by woods, containing
           an early medieval
           settlement area
           (on the site of the
           present village) and
           an adjacent cemetery
           (+) (after Klápště
           1991).

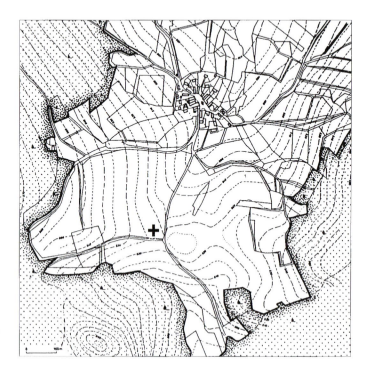

Kirchheim (Germany): settlement area from the 7th-8th centuries, with an attempt at differentiating **Fig 3.9**
the farmsteads (A-O);'plots' E, F & J have grave-groups (after R Christlein & H Geisler, in Donat 1991).

by documentary evidence during the fifth to seventh centuries (Treffort 1996; Lauwers 2005). Everywhere across Europe, the key element in these changes was the parish system, which was a relatively late development. In Western Europe, in France and England, its stabilisation came in the tenth to twelfth centuries, while eastern Central Europe underwent similar changes only in the thirteenth century. Only within parish organisations were churchyards established as the sole legitimate burial-place for the local community (Zadora-Rio 2003; 2005; Fixot & Zadora-Rio 1994).

Fig 3.10

Gasselte (Netherlands): the
excavated settlement area
from the early Middle Ages in
relation to the 19th-century
cadastral map (after Waterbolk
1991).

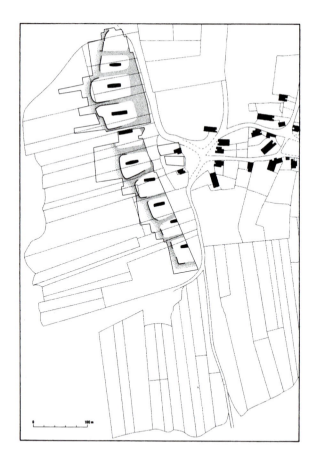

The Heritage of Early Medieval Rural Settlement

Archaeology is of particular importance for understanding the remains that have been
imposed since the early Middle Ages on the rural landscapes of various European
regions. It is the archaeological record that, by the methods associated with its study, can
distinguish demonstrable evidence from false impressions.

In what had been the Romanised world, old roads and estates often influenced ter-
ritorial organisation and settlement patterns during the first millennium and later. The
inheritance of the settlement patterns of Antiquity varies according to the degree of
Romanisation, for example often appearing rather slight in Britain in contrast with the
Mediterranean world, but even there settlement patterns changed markedly during Late
Antiquity (Raynaud 2001). This has even been observed in Italy, the core of the Roman
Empire, where during the long period of decline the traditional patterns of rural settlement, based on villas, were gradually and progressively replaced by smaller dwellings
made of wattle and daub, corresponding to a different system of agricultural organisation comprising more family-based units (Ouzoulias & Van Ossel 2001). The progressive decline in Romanised areas gives rise to the question of a supposed lack of conti-

nuity in early medieval settlement patterns when compared to Antiquity and the later Middle Ages. The fully developed 'classical' villa system did not survive Late Antiquity; on the hand, many early medieval settlements, with continuous occupation lasting centuries, were to survive for just as long as had most villas.

The impact of earlier plots on the layout of early medieval settlements has been observed in numerous excavations. At Genlis in Burgundy, for example, seventh/eighth-century buildings were strictly perpendicular to a Roman road of the early first millennium (Catteddu 1995). At Dassargues in southern France, ditches of the first centuries AD had a decisive influence on the planning of early medieval farmsteads: rows of storage structures and other features, of the seventh century and later, respected and perpetuated the ancient boundaries (Garnier et al 1995).

The retention of estate boundaries and trackways is a decisive indicator of territorial continuity. In some cases, these boundaries may simply reflect ground-relief, but in most cases they are simply transmitting artificial limits. The survival of Roman cadastral systems in many regions was only possible because the plot boundaries were passed down through the centuries and even millennia, notably during the early Middle Ages. The same applies to the transmission of place-names. This should not, however, lead to the conclusion that there was general territorial continuity. Only some estate boundaries survived, and many rural territories disappeared, with their names being definitively lost. The continual adoption and modification of existing patterns is proper to territorial organisation through time, even if the nature of inheritance and change varies greatly from one period to another – and from one region to another.

The modalities of estate and/or plot survival are rarely observable; however, the excavations at Odoorn in the northern Netherlands (Waterbolk 1991), and at Montours in Brittany (Catteddu et al 2001), have revealed part of this evolution. In both cases, the enclosures of early medieval farmsteads have determined the boundaries of modern plots. At Odoorn this can be explained by the conversion of old farmsteads into cultivable fields, as attested by the vestiges of ploughing that to some extent at least respected the limits of the former enclosures. A detailed study of the occupation of the plots has demonstrated their evolution, but ultimately it was their width that determined that of the fields shown on the Napoleonic cadastral map (Fig 3.10).

In any case, field-continuity and persistence in plot-modules are decisive arguments in favour of the continuous occupation of rural territories. In many places, this can be confirmed by palaeobotanical analysis, but it is very rarely that the true abandonment of an area can be proven.

BIBLIOGRAPHY

Amouretti, MC and Comet, G (2000) 'La meunerie antique et médiévale', *Archives internationales d'histoire des sciences* 50, 18-29

Astill, G and Langdon, J (eds) (2005) *Medieval Farming and Technology: The Impact of Agricultural Change in Northwest Europe*, Leiden/New York

Barcelo, M and Toubert, P (eds) (1998) *L'incastellamento*, Actes des rencontres de Gérone (26-27 novembre 1992) et de Rome (5-7 mai 1994), Rome

Bärenfänger, R (1993) 'Frühmittelalterliche Eggenbalken und weitere Holzfunde aus Hattersum, Kreis Wittmund/Ostfriesland', *Archäologisches Korrespondenzblatt* 23, 127-39

Barthélemy, D (1997) *La mutation de l'an mil a-t-elle eu lieu? Servage et chevalerie dans la France des Xe et XIe siècles*, Paris

Boddington, A (1996) *Raunds Furnells. The Anglo-Saxon Church and Churchyard*, London

Bonnassie, P (1985) 'Survie et extinction du régime esclavagiste dans l'Occident du haut Moyen Age (IVe-XIe s.)', *Cahiers de Civilisation médiévale* 28, 307-43

Bonnassie, P and Toubert, P (eds) (2004) *Hommes et Sociétés dans l'Europe de l'An Mil*, Toulouse

Bourin, M and Zadora-Rio, E (2002) 'Analyses de l'espace', in Schmitt, J-C and Oexle, OG (eds), *Les tendances actuelles de l'histoire du Moyen Age en France et en Allemagne*, Paris, 493-510

Brather, S (2001) *Archäologie der westlichen Slawen. Siedlung, Wirtschaft und Gesellschaft im früh- und hochmittelalterlichen Ostmitteleuropa, Ergänzungsbände zum Reallexikon der Germanischen Altertumskunde*, Bd 30, Berlin/New York

Bücker, C and Hoeper, M (1999) 'First aspects of social hierarchy of settlements in Merovingian southwest Germany', in Fabech, C and Ringtved, J (eds), *Settlement and Landscape. Proceedings of a Conference in Aarhus, Denmark, May 1998*, Højbjerg, 441-54

Catteddu, I (1995) 'L'habitat mérovingien de Genlis (Côte-d'Or)', in Lorren, C and Périn, P (eds), *L'habitat rural du haut Moyen Age (France, Pays-Bas, Danemark et Grande-Bretagne). Actes des XIVe Journées internationales d'archéologie mérovingienne*, Rouen, 185-92

Catteddu, I et al (2001) *Les habitats carolingiens de Montours et La Chapelle-Saint-Aubert (Ille-et-Vilaine)*, Documents d'archéologie française 89, Paris

Chapelot, J (1980) 'Le fond de cabane dans l'habitat rural Ouest-Européen', *Archéologie médiévale* 10, 5-57

Chapelot, J (1993) 'L'habitat rural: organisation et nature', in *L'Ile de France de Clovis à Hugues Capet du Ve siècle au Xe siècle*, Saint-Ouen-l'Aumône, 178-99

Chapelot, J and Fossier, R (1980) *Le village et la maison au Moyen Age*, Paris

Comet, G (1997) 'Technology and agricultural expansion in the Middle Ages: the example of France north of the Loire', in Astill, G and Langdon, J (eds), 11-39

Devroey, JP (2003) *Économie rurale et société dans l'Europe franque (VIe-IXe siècles), Tome 1, Fondements matériels, échanges et lien social*, Paris

Donat, P (1980) *Haus, Hof und Dorf in Mitteleuropa vom 7.-12. Jahrhundert*, Berlin

Donat, P (1991) 'Zur Entwicklung germanischer Siedlungen östlich des Rheins bis zum Ausgang der Merowingerzeit', *Zeitschrift für Archäologie* 25, 149-76

Donat, P (1999) 'Befunde aus Mittel- und Süddeutschland zur Stallhaltung im frühen und hohen Mittelalter', *Beiträge zur Mittelalterarchäologie in Österreich* 15, 35-48

Durand-Dastès, F et al (1998) *Archeomedes. Des oppida aux métropoles. Archéologues et géographes en vallée du Rhône*, Paris

Dyer, C (1997) 'Medieval farming and technology: conclusion', in Astill, G and Langdon, J (eds), 293-312

Edwards, N (1990) *The Archaeology of Early Medieval Ireland*, London

Faure-Boucharlat, E (2001) 'Les constructions rurales – l'âge du bois?', in Faure-Boucharlat, E (ed), *Vivre à la campagne au Moyen Âge. L'habitat rural du Ve au XIIe s. (Bresse, Lyonnais, Dauphiné) d'après les données archéologiques*, Lyon, 77-92

Fixot, M and Zadora-Rio, E (1994) *L'environnement des églises et la topographie religieuse des campagnes médiévales*, Documents d'archéologie française 46, Paris

Foucray, B and Gentili, F (1995) 'Le village du haut Moyen Age de Serris (Seine-et-Marne), lieu dit "Les Ruelles" (VIIe-Xe siècle)', in Lorren, C and Périn, P (eds), *L'habitat rural du haut-Moyen Age (France, Pays-Bas, Danemark et Grande-Bretagne)*, Actes des XIVe Journées internationales d'archéologie mérovingienne, Rouen, 139-43

Francovich, R (1998) 'L'incastellamento e prima dell' incastellamento', in Barcelo, M and Toubert, P (eds), *L'incastellamento*, Actes des rencontres de Gérone (26-27 novembre 1992) et de Rome (5-7 mai 1994), Rome, 13-20

Francovich, R and Hodges R (2003) *Villa to Village. The Transformation of the Roman Countryside in Italy, c. 400-1000*, London

Francovich, R and Wickham, H (1994) 'Uno scavo archeologico e il problema dello sviluppo della Sinoria territoriale: Roca San Silvestro e i rapporti di produzione minerari', *Archeologia medievale* 21, 7-30

Fries, JC (1995) *Vor- und frühgeschichtliche Agrartechnik auf den Britischen Inseln und dem Kontinent. Eine vergleichende Studie*, Internationale Archäologie 26, Espelkamp

Gardiner, M (2006) 'Implements and utensils in *Gerefa* and the organisation of seigneurial farmsteads in the High Middle Ages', *Medieval Archaeology* 50, 260-7

Garnier, B, Garnotel, A, Mercier, C and Rayand, C (1995) 'De la ferme au village: Dassargues de Ve au XIIe siècle (Lunel, Hérault)', *Archéologie du Midi Médiéval* 13, 1-78

Geisler, H (1997) 'Haus und Hof im frühmittelalterlichen Bayern nach den archäologischen Befunden', in Beck, H and Steuer, H (eds), *Haus und Hof in ur- und frühgeschichtlichen Zeit*, Abhandlungen der Akademie der Wissenschaften in Göttingen, Philologisch-historische Klasse, Dritte Folge, Nr 218, Göttingen, 461-83

Gentili, F (2001) 'Villages, maisons et annexes autour de l'an mil', in Trombetta, JP and Depraetere-Dargery, M (eds), *L'Ile-de-France médiévale*, Catalogue (2000), Paris, 36-7

Gringmuth-Dallmer, E (1983) 'Frühgeschichtliche Pflugspuren in Mitteleuropa', *Zeitschrift für Archäologie* 17, 205-21

Groenman-van Wateringe, W and van Wijngaarden-Bakker, LH (eds) (1987) *Farm Life in a Carolingian Village*, Assen

Hamerow, H (1993) *Mucking, Volume 2: The Anglo-Saxon Settlement*, London

Hamerow, H (1995) 'Shaping settlements: early medieval communities in Northwest Europe', in Bintliff, J and Hamerow, H (eds), *Europe between Late Antiquity and the Middle Ages. Recent Archaeological and Historical Research in Western and Southern Europe*, British Archaeological Reports, International Series 617, Oxford, 8-37

Hamerow, H (2002) *Early Medieval Settlements. The Archaeology of Rural Communities in Northwest Europe 400-900*, Oxford

Haselgrove, C and Scull, C (1995) 'The changing structure of rural settlement in southern Picardy during the first millennium A.D.', in Bintliff, J and Hamerow, H (eds), *Europe between Late Antiquity and the Middle Ages. Recent Archaeological and Historical Research in Western and Southern Europe*, British Archaeological Reports, International Series 617, Oxford, 58-70

Heidinga, HA (1987) *Medieval Settlement and Economy north of the Lower Rhine. Archaeology and History of Kootwijk and the Veluwe (the Netherlands)*, Assen/Maastricht

Henning, J (1985) 'Zur Datierung von Werkzeug- und Agrargerätefunden im germanischen Landnahmegebiet zwischen Rhein und oberer Donau (der Hortfund von Osterburken)', *Jahrbuch des Römisch-Germanischen Zentralmuseums Mainz* 32, 570-94

Henning, J (1987) *Südosteuropa zwischen Antike und Mittelalter. Archäologische Beiträge zur Landwirtschaft des 1. Jahrtausends u. Z*, Berlin

Henning, J (1996) 'Wirtschaft, Handel und Verkehr', in Wieczorek, A et al (eds), *Die Franken. Wegbereiter Europas* 2, Mainz, 774-85

Henning, J (2004) 'Germanisch-romanische Agrarkontinuität und -diskontinuität im nordalpinen Kontinentaleuropa – Teile eines Systemwandels? Beobachtungen aus archäologischer Sicht', in Hägermann, D et al (eds), *Akkulturation. Probleme einer germanischen-romanischen Kultursynthese in Spätantike und frühen Mittelalter*, Ergänzungsbände zum *Reallexikon der Germanischen Altertumskunde* 41, Berlin/New York, 396-435

Hughes, M (1984) 'Rural settlement and landscape in late Saxon Hampshire', in Faull, ML (ed), *Studies in Late Anglo-Saxon Settlement*, Oxford, 65-80

Hvass, S (1984) 'Wikingerzeitliche Siedlungen in Vorbasse', *Offa* 41, 97-112

Hvass, S (1986) 'Vorbasse: eine Dorfsiedlung während des 1. Jahrtausends n. Chr. in Mitteljütland, Dänemark', *Bericht der römisch-germanischen Kommission* 67, 529-42

Hvass, S (1989) 'Rural settlements in Denmark in the first millennium AD', in Randsborg, K (ed), *The Birth of Europe: Archaeology and Social Development in the First Millennium AD*, Analecta Romana Instituti Danici, Supplementum XVI, Rome, 91-9

Kieffer-Olsen, J (1987) 'Vorbasse by', *Meta* 1-2, 51-7

Klápště, J (1991) 'Studies of structural change in medieval settlement in Bohemia', *Antiquity* 65, 396-405

Klápště, J (1994) 'Změna – středověká transformace a její předpoklady' (Transformation – la transformation médiévale et ses conditions préalables), *Památky archeologické – supplementum* 2, Prague, 9-59

Klápště, J (1998) 'Les outils de la préparation du sol au Moyen Age (à propos des fouilles archéologiques tchèques)', in Feller, L, Mane, P and Piponnier, F (eds), *Le village médiéval et son environnement. Études offertes à Jean-Marie Pesez*, Paris, 359-65

Knittler, H (1999) 'Tierische Zugkräfte in der mittelalterlichen Landwirtschaft', *Beiträge zur Mittelalterarchäologie in Österreich* 15, 207-21

Kolenda, J (2001) 'Osada wczesnośredniowieczna', in Leciejewicz, L (ed) *Od neolitycznego obozowiska do średniowiecznej wsi. Badania we Wrocławiu-Partynicach*, Wratislavia antiqua 4, Wrocław 108-79

Kossack, G, Behre, K-E and Schmid, P (eds) (1984) *Archäologische und naturwissenschaftliche Untersuchungen an ländlichen und frühstädtischen Siedlungen im deutschen Küstengebiet vom 5. Jahrhundert v. Chr. bis zum 11. Jahrhundert n. Chr.*, Bd 1, Ländliche Siedlungen, Weinheim

Kuna, M and Profantová, N (2005) *Počátky raného středověku v čechách. Archeologický výzkum sídelní aglomerace kultury pražského typu v Roztokách* (The Onset of the Early Middle Ages in Bohemia. Archaeological Research at a large Settlement-site of the Prague-type Culture at Roztoky), Prague

Laszlovszky, J (1986) 'Einzelhofsiedlungen in der Arpadenzeit (Arpadenzeitliche Siedlung auf der Mark von Kengyel)', *Acta Archaeologica Academiae Scientiarum Hungaricae* 38, 227-55

Lauwers, M (2005) *Naissance du cimetière. Lieux sacrés et terre des morts dans l'Occident médiéval*, Paris

Le Maho, J (1994) 'La réutilisation funéraire des édifices antiques en Normandie au cours du haut Moyen Age', in Fixot, M and Zadora-Rio, E (eds), *L'environnement des églises et la topographie religieuse des campagnes médiévales*, Documents d'archéologie française 46, 10-17

Lefèvre, A and Mahé, N (2004) 'La céramique du haut Moyen Âge en Ile-de-France à travers la fouille des habitats ruraux (VIe-XIe siècles). État de la question et perspectives de recherches', *Revue Archéologique de la Picardie* 3-4, 105-49

Lepets, S, Matterne, V, Ruas, MP and Yvinec, JH (2002) 'Culture et élevage en France septentrionale de l'âge du fer à l'an Mil. Approche carpologique et archéozoologique', in Belmont, A (ed), *Autour d'Olivier de Serres. Pratiques agricoles et pensée agronomique du Néolithique aux enjeux actuels. Actes du Colloque de Pradel (27-29 septembre 2000)*, Bibliothèque d'Histoire Rurale 6, Rennes, 77-108

Lerche, G (1994) *Ploughing Implements and Tillage Practices in Denmark from the Viking Period to about 1800 experimentally substantiated*, Herning

Lerche, G and Jensen, S (1985) 'A note on farming practice in the Viking period: sod manure (træk)', *Tools and Tillage* 5:2, 122-5

Lohrmann, D (1996) 'Antrieb von Getreidemühlen', in Lindgren, U (ed) *Europäische Technik im Mittelalter, 800 bis 1200, Tradition und Innovation, Ein Handbuch*, Berlin, 221-32

Lorren, C (1989) 'Le village de Saint-Martin de Trainecourt à Mondeville (Calvados), de l'Antiquité au Haut Moyen Age', in Atsma, H (ed), *La Neustrie. Les pays au nord de la Loire de 650 à 850*, Beihefte der Francia 16/1 & 16/2, Sigmaringen, 439-66

Lorren, C (1996) 'Einige Beobachtungen über das frühmittelalterliche Dorf in Nordgallien', in Wieczorek, A et al (eds), *Die Franken – Wegbereiter Europas. Vor 1500 Jahren: König Chlodwig und seine Erben*, Mainz, 745-53

Madsen, HJ and Vegger, P (1992) 'Karby på Mors. En landsby fra vikingetiden' (Karby on Mors, a Viking village), *Kuml* 1990, 133-50

Mahé, N (2002) 'Un ensemble céramique du XIe siècle provenant du village des Ruelles à Serris (Seine-et-Marne)', *Archéologie médiévale* 32, 55-68

Marek, O and Skopal, R (2003) 'Die Mühlsteine von Mikulčice', in Poláček, L (ed), *Studien zum Burgwall von Mikulčice*, Bd 5, Brno, 497-589

Marshall, A and Marshall, G (1991) 'A survey and analysis of the buildings of early and middle Anglo-Saxon England', *Medieval Archaeology* 35, 29-43

Meier, D (1994) *Die wikingerzeitliche Siedlung von Kosel (Kosel-West), Kreis Rendsburg-Eckernförde*, Offa Bücher 76, Neumünster

Meyer, W (1991) 'Die hochmittelalterliche Siedlungsentwicklung in zentralen Alpenraum – die Erschliessung marginalen Landes in salischer Zeit', in Böhme, WH (ed), *Siedlungen und Landesausbau zur Salierzeit, Teil 2, In den südlichen Landschaften des Reiches*, Römisch-Germanisches Zentralmuseum, Monographien 28, Sigmaringen, 57-66

Moreland, J, Pluciennik, M, Richardsson, M, Fleming, A, Stroud, G, Patterson, H and Dunkley, J (1993) 'Excavations at Casale San Donato, Castelnuovo di Farfa (RI), Lazio, 1992', *Archeologia medievale* 20, 185-228

Nice, A (1994) 'L'habitat mérovingien de Goudelancourt-les-Pierrepont (Aisne). Aperçu provisoire d'une unité agricole et domestique des VIe et VIIe siècles', *Revue archéologique de Picardie* 1-2, 21-63

Nissen Jaubert, A (1999) 'Ruptures et continuités de l'habitat rural du haut Moyen Age dans le nord-ouest de l'Europe', in Braemer, F et al (eds), *Habitat et Société. XIXe Rencontres internationales d'Archéologie et d'Histoire d'Antibes*, Antibes, 519-33

Nissen Jaubert, A (2006) 'L'agriculture du haut Moyen Âge', in Ferdière, A et al (eds), *Histoire de l'agriculture en Gaule. Ve s. av. J.-C. – Xe s. ap. J.-C.*, Paris, 133-89

Ouzoulias, P and Van Ossel, P (2001) 'Dynamiques du peuplement et formes de l'habitat Tardif: le cas de l'Ile-de-France', in Ouzoulias, P, Pellecuer, C, Raynaud, C, Van Ossel, P and Garmy, P (eds), *Les Campagnes de la Gaule à la Fin de l'Antiquité*, Antibes, 47-72

Pesez, JM (1991) 'Outils et techniques agricoles du monde médiéval', in Guilaine, J (ed), *Pour une archéologie agraire*, Paris, 131-64

Pétorin, N (1997) 'Marcé, Bauce', *Bilan Scientifique Régional. Pays de Loire*, 38-9

Peytremann, E (2003) *Archéologie de l'habitat rural dans le Nord de la France du IVe au XIIe siècle*, 1-2, Nantes

Poláček, L (2003) 'Landwirtschaftliche Geräte aus Mikulčice', in Poláček L (ed), *Studien zum Burgwall von Mikulčice*, Bd 5, Brno, 591-709

Poly, J-P and Bournazel, É (1980) *La mutation féodale X^e – XIIe siècle*, Paris

Porsmose, E (1993) 'Rural settlement', in Hvass, S and Storgaard, B (eds), *Digging into the Past. 25 Years of Archaeology in Denmark*, Aarhus, 264-7

Raynaud, C (2001) 'Les campagnes languedocienne aux IVe et Ve siècles', in Ouzoulias, P, Pellecuer, C, Raynaud, C, Van Ossel, P and Garmy, P (eds), *Les Campagnes de la Gaule à la Fin de l'Antiquité*, Antibes, 247-74

Reigniez, P (2002) *L'outil agricole en France au Moyen Age*, Paris

Riddersporre, M (1999) 'Village and single farm. Settlement structure or landscape organisation', in Fabech, C and Ringtved, J (eds), *Settlement and Landscape. Proceedings of a Conference in Aarhus, Denmark, May 4-7 1998*, Højbjerg, 167-75

Ruralia 1-5 (1996, 1998, 2000, 2002, 2005) *Památky archeologické – supplementum* 5, 11, 14, 15, 17

Ruttkay, M (2002) 'Ländliche Siedlungen des 9. bis 11. Jahrhunderts im Mitteldonaugebiet', in Henning, J (ed), *Europa im 10. Jahrhundert. Archäologie einer Aufbruchszeit. Internationale Tagung in Vorbereitung der Austellung 'Otto der Große, Magdeburg und Europa'*, Mainz am Rhein, 267-82

de Saint Jores, JX and Hincker, V (2001) 'Les habitats mérovingien et carolingien de la "Delle sur le Marais" à Giberville', *Archéologie médiévale* 30-31, 1-38

Šalkovský, P (2001) *Häuser in der frühmittelalterlichen slawischen Welt*, Nitra

Schmaedecke, M (1999) 'Technische Innovationen im Mittelalter (11. bis 13. Jh.). Modelle zur Erfassung ihres Ablaufs und ihrer Durchsetzung', *Archäologische Informationen* 22, 203-13

Schreg, R (2001) 'Dorfgenese und histoire totale. Zur Bedeutung der histoire totale für die Archäologie des Mittelalters', in Pfrommer, J and Schreg, R (eds), *Zwischen den Zeiten, Archäologische Beiträge zur Geschichte des Mittelalters in Mitteleuropa, Festschrift für Barbara Scholkmann*, Internationale Archäologie, Studia honoraria, 15, Rahden/Westf, 333-48

Schuldt, E (1981) 'Eine Egge des 10. Jahrhunderts aus der slawischen Siedlung von Groß Raden, Kreis Sternberg', *Bodendenkmalpflege in Mecklenburg, Jahrbuch 1980*, 203-7

Stork, I (1997) 'Friedhof und Dorf, Herrenhof und Adelsgrab. Der einmalige Befund Lauchheim', in Fuchs, K et al (eds), *Die Alamannen*, Stuttgart, 290-310

Stout, M (1997) *The Irish Ringfort*, Dublin

Thoen, E (1997) 'The birth of "the Flemish husbandry": agricultural technology in medieval Flanders', in Astill, G and Langdon, J (eds), 69-88

Tipper, J (2005) *The Grubenhaus in Anglo-Saxon England: an Analysis and Interpretation of the Evidence from a most distinctive Building Type*, Landscape Research Centre Archaeological Monograph Series 2:1, Yedingham

Toubert, P (1973) *Les structures du Latium médiéval: le Latium méridional et la Sabine du IXe à la fin du XIIe siècle*, Rome

Toubert, P (2004) *L'Europe dans sa première croissance. De Charlemagne à l'an Mil*, Paris

Treffort, C (1996) *L'église carolingienne et la mort. Christianisme, rites funéraires et pratiques commémoratives*, Lyon

Valais, A (1998) 'Le site de Gaillon à Herblay (Val d'Oise). Une occupation des Ve-VIIe siècles)', in Delestre, X and Périn, P (eds), *La Datation des structures et des objets du haut Moyen Âge: méthodes et résultats*, X, Mémoires publiés par L'AFAM: Association Française d'Archéologie Mérovingienne, 207-12

Valais, A (2002) 'Le village carolingien des Murailles à Distré (49)', *Archéologia* 386 (février), 58-66

Waterbolk, HT (1979) 'Siedlungskontinuität im Küstengebiet der Nordsee zwischen Rhein und Elbe', *Probleme der Küstenforschung im südlichen Nordseegebiet* 13, 1-21

Waterbolk, HT (1991) 'Das mittelalterliche Siedlungswesen in Drenthe. Versuch einer Synthese aus archäologischer Sicht', in Böhme, WH (ed), *Siedlungen und Landesausbau zur Salierzeit, Teil 1, In den nördlichen Landschaften des Reiches*, Römisch-Germanisches Zentralmuseum, Monographien 27, Sigmaringen, 47-108

Waterbolk, HT and Harsema, OH (1979) 'Medieval farmsteads in Gasselte (Province of Drenthe)', *Palaeohistoria* 21, 227-65

Wickham, C (1989) 'Documenti scritti e archeologia per una storia dell'incastellamento in Etruria Meridionale alla luce di nuovi dati archaeologici', *Archeologia medievale* 16, 79-103

Wickham, C (1999) 'Early medieval archaeology in Italy: the last twenty years', *Archeologia medievale* 26, 7-20

Widgren, M (1983) *Settlement and Farming Systems in the Early Iron Age. A Study of Fossil Agrarian Landscape in Östergötland, Sweden*, Stockholm

Zadora-Rio, E (1995), 'Le village des historiens et le village des archéologues', in Mornet, E (ed), *Campagnes médiévales: l'Homme et son espace. Études offertes à Robert Fossier*, Paris, 145-53

Zadora-Rio, E (2003) 'The making of churchyards and parish territories in the early-medieval landscape of France and England in the 7th-12th centuries: a reconsideration', *Medieval Archaeology* 47, 1-19

Zadora-Rio, E (2005) 'Territoires paroissiaux et construction de l'espace vernaculaire', *Médiévales* 49, 105-20

Zimmermann, WH (1991) 'Die früh- bis hochmittelalterliche Wüstung Dalem, Gem. Langen-Neuenwalde, Kr. Cuxhaven. Archäologische Untersuchungen in einem Dorf des 7.-14. Jahrhunderts', in Böhme, WH (ed), *Siedlungen und Landesausbau zur Salierzeit, Teil 1, In den nördlichen Landschaften des Reiches*, Römisch-Germanisches Zentralmuseum, Monographien 27, Sigmaringen, 37-46

Zimmermann, WH (1992) 'Die Siedlungen des 1. bis 6. Jahrhunderts nach Christus von Flögeln-Eekhöltjen, Niedersachsen: Die Bauformen und ihre Funktionen', *Probleme der Küstenforschung im südlichen Nordseegebiet* 19, 7-360

Zimmermann, WH (1995) 'Ackerbau in ur- und frühgeschichtlicher Zeit auf der Geest und in der Marsch', in Dannenberg, HE and Schulze, HJ (eds), *Geschichte des Landes zwischen Elbe und Weser, Vol 1, Stade*, Schriftenreihe des Landschaftsverbandes der ehemaligen Herzogtümer Bremen und Verden Bd 7, 289-315

Zimmermann, WH (1998) 'Pfosten, Ständer und Schwelle und der Übergang vom Pfosten- zum Ständerbau. Eine Studie zu Innovation und Beharrung im Hausbau. Zu Konstruktion und Haltbarkeit prähistorischer bis neuzetlichen Holzbauten von den Nord- und Ostseeländern bis zu den Alpen', *Probleme der Küstenforschung* 25, 9-241

Zimmermann, WH (1999), 'Why was cattle-stalling introduced in prehistory? The significance of byre and stable and of outwintering', in Fabech, C and Ringtved, J (eds), *Settlement and Landscape. Proceedings of a Conference in Aarhus, Denmark, May 4-7 1998*, Højbjerg, 301-18

Zimmermann, WH (2002), 'Kontinuität und Wandel im Hausbau südlich und östlich der Nordsee vom Neolithikum bis zum Mittelalter', *Ruralia* 4, *Památky archeologické – supplementum* 15, Prague, 164-8

CHAPTER 4

URBAN SETTLEMENT

John Schofield and Heiko Steuer

PART 1: WESTERN EUROPE *by John Schofield*

Editors' note: this first part deals with urban development from the eighth to twelfth centuries in Britain and Ireland, the Low Countries, France and Spain. Part 2, by Heiko Steuer, covers the rest of Europe (for a general map, see Fig 4.1). The references are combined at the end.

Introduction

What features should we look for in studying post-Roman towns? In 1976 Martin Biddle proposed twelve criteria, which are also objectives of enquiry: (1) defences; (2) a planned street-system; (3) one or more markets; (4) a mint; (5) legal autonomy; (6) a role as a 'central-place'; (7) a relatively large and dense population; (8) a diversified economic base; (9) plots and houses of 'urban' type; (10) social differentiation; (11) a complex religious organisation; and (12) a judicial centre (Biddle 1976b, 100). The more of these a place has, the more urban it may be regarded. This approach to the archaeology of towns in the eighth to twelfth centuries was closely allied to a belief in 'continuity', a belief that a central theme was what survived, perhaps in altered form, in towns of the Roman Empire.

Since the 1970s, partly as a result of archaeological work, there is now an alternative view. Why were towns necessary at all? Perhaps people just did not need them. We should think of intermittent generations using urban spaces for their own and very varied purposes. An evolutionary model, or one in which urban character was first lost then slowly regained, is inappropriate (Astill 2000).

This part is in two sections, the first dealing with the eighth and ninth centuries, and the second with the tenth to twelfth centuries, both covering a small number of topics. It will become clear that in the eighth and ninth centuries (and in some countries, well into the tenth century), urban settlements had a limited range of functions. In the tenth to twelfth centuries, on the other hand, we can begin to measure the development of towns by the type of criteria mentioned by Biddle. Some of the more important urban settlements mentioned in this chapter are shown on the map, Fig 4.1.

Types of urban settlement

Although there are many sorts and sizes of urban settlement in these centuries, four types may be distinguished: (1) the ex-Roman towns; (2) the trading-stations around the North Sea (called *wics*); (3) new fortified places; and (4) the Muslim cities in Spain.

There are many cases in France and Flanders of Roman towns surviving as religious sites in the sixth to eighth centuries; the ex-Roman town served both as the seat of a bishop and as a place of burial, especially for the elite. Examples are Maastricht, where parts of the seventh-century manufacturing settlement have been excavated, Tours or Soissons, which had a collection of churches in Merovingian times, with hospitals and abbeys along the bank of the river Aisne. From about 750, but mostly during the ninth century, these overwhelmingly religious centres began to sprout areas of secular settlement, as at Angers, Tours, Dijon and Lyon. The same process can be detected in Italy and the Iberian Peninsula, where continuity appears to be the most common situation.

From about the middle of the seventh century, trading-stations began to appear, perhaps as deliberate royal foundations, on both sides of the English Channel and North Sea. The English examples at Hamwic (Southampton) and Lundenwic (London) were probably the largest on the British side, though there were many smaller ones. On the continental side, the larger examples are found from Dorestad (Fig 4.2) on the Rhine delta to Amiens and Rouen in the south. There were also smaller beach markets on the coasts between and beyond these centres. Two examples used here are Dorestad and Lundenwic (Box 4.1).

Dorestad (Netherlands), established by c675 near the site of a Roman fortification, was a major port, trading with Germany, Scandinavia and England (van Es 1990). Its success between the 780s and 820s was evidently in response to the increased demand for specialised goods by the Imperial courts in the Middle Rhineland; it also served Maastricht. The site, excavated in the 1960s and 1970s (Fig 4.2), included a stretch of the bank of the contemporary Rhine, at least 1km long, packed with long jetties which went out into the water, in cumulative stages over time, to reach lengths of over 200m (van Es & Verwers 1980). The port seems to have declined after c830, was attacked by the Vikings several times, and was empty by c875. A similar settlement in character and dates of foundation, flourishing and decline has been excavated since the 1980s in London, between the Roman City and Westminster: this is Lundenwic, founded by c650 (see Box 4.1).

A third type of urban settlement, especially studied in Flanders, is a fortified place, often based on a lord's stronghold, but with no clear Roman antecedent: Dinant, Huy, Liège and Namur are examples. These are first traced archaeologically in the second half of the eighth century, but their development into towns is usually up to 200 years later.

The Iberian Peninsula was conquered by Muslims (Arabs and Moors) in 711; they were halted near Poitiers in 732, but for the period considered here most of Spain was in Muslim hands, as described in Chapter 2 (al-Andalus). This invasion was directed towards existing towns, but also led to the foundation of new ones where needed. Urban archaeology in Spain has been active only since 1985 (Ministry of Culture [Spain] 1999),

Some of the more important urban settlements in Europe, 8th-12th centuries.

[For explanation of key, see map p 47].

Fig 4.1

BOX 4.1   LUNDENWIC

By c650 Lundenwic, a large trading-station, lay next to the Roman city of London but immediately upstream on the Thames. The monk Bede, writing in the 730s far away in the north of England, knew it as a port and market where people came by land and sea. The evidence includes buildings, lanes, pits, ditches and copious environmental material; imported pottery includes items from France and the Rhineland. Building and population density seem to have reached a peak around the end of the eighth century, and the settlement may have held between 5,000 and 10,000 people.

The largest investigation reported to date is that at the Royal Opera House in Covent Garden, recorded during redevelopment in 1989–99 (Malcolm & Bowsher 2003). A street and dozens of buildings, showing developments over two centuries, were seen. The variety of finds indicates many manufacturing and trading activities taking place in close proximity, with no zoning of occupations. There was a tannery and a jewellery workshop, a smithy and buildings which had housed looms. As at Dorestad, there was evidence for processing of antlers and animal

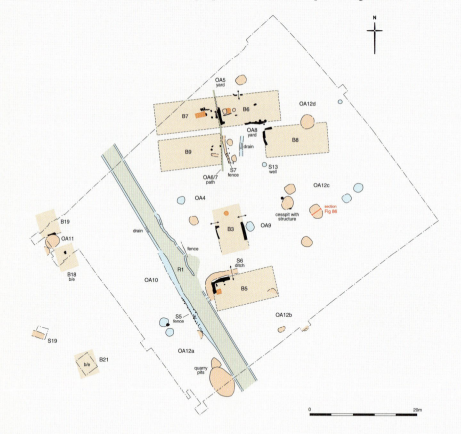

Fig 1

Lundenwic: the Royal Opera House site in Covent Garden, in the first phase of a period of development, 675–730 (Museum of London; from Malcolm & Bowsher 2003). Whether the road preceded the first buildings or could be later, which would help explain their indifferent alignment, is not clear.

bones to make objects such as combs. Coins were minted by 640; gold and silver coins from seventh-century London have been found throughout south-east England, in Scotland, and on the Continent from Denmark to south-west France, indicating the network of exchange, trade and the payment of tolls on merchandise.

The meat diet of these Londoners, with a high proportion of bones from mature cattle and sheep, was similar to that of people at Hamwic and Ipswich; but other sites in Lundenwic had higher proportions of bones from younger cattle and sheep, so perhaps there were parts of this emporium where more select meals were enjoyed. Thus some idea of wealthy and poor areas within the settlement might be gained by studying the distribution of animal bones.

During the ninth century this part of Lundenwic declined, probably both in economic activity and population. It was abandoned in the mid-ninth century, as was the rest of Lundenwic as far as we know.

By John Schofield

Fig 2

Lundenwic: the Royal Opera House site in Covent Garden, in the period 730–70. More of the buildings are on the street, several at right-angles to it, on both sides; to the rear are tanning pits which at first functioned with the nearby buildings shown in the earlier plan. By 730, for whatever reason, the street dominated the arrangement of the buildings and functions.

Fig 4.2   *Excavations at Dorestad, showing the typical lines of posts, formerly going out into the Rhine; also shown is the drill for core-sampling the underlying silts (ROB).*

but we know that continuity was most commonly the case, with Islamisation being a slow process consolidated only in the mid-ninth century. Only a few towns were established for political purposes, as was the case with Murcia in 831 and Badajoz in 875.

Patterns of public and private space

It is traditionally thought that the Roman infrastructure, and therefore many aspects of town life, survived better in Gaul, which was more Romanised, than in outer provinces such as Britain. Perhaps in France we should expect a picture like that in Italy, where towns continued to serve as centres of religious and secular administration, and as places for the secular aristocracy to have houses. What is noticeable in many ex-Roman towns from London to the northern half of the Iberian peninsula is that the post-Roman cathedral is usually in a different place from the Roman forum, often on the edge of the defended enclosure. This implies that some form of authority or different function still held sway over the forum area, or perhaps it was redolent of memories which were to be avoided. When market life flickered, it was in other places within the town: commonly along a main street between gates, ensuring the survival on roughly the same alignment of the Roman street into the medieval period, as at Winchester (Fig 4.4) and London.

Some of the *wics* were planned by an authority. Hamwic (50ha in area) and Lundenwic (at least 60ha) had several straight streets running at right-angles to the river, and at Hamwic there is probably evidence of other streets crossing these. In the main the archaeological evidence suggests that crafts did not congregate in different areas within the settlement, apart from pottery production, but there are signs that bone and antler working may have been concentrated in specific areas at Hamwic (Brisbane 1988; Morton 1992).

In the eighth century the streets of Hamwic and Lundenwic were lined with narrow properties laid out at right angles to the street. Principal buildings lay against the streets, though there might be more haphazard arrangements of lesser buildings in the plot behind, with pits along the plot boundaries and wells. Larger complexes like the courtyard houses in later European towns (in which an idea of rectilinearity extended to the rear) have not yet been identified in the *wics*; but in several ways the design of the medieval property was decided in the eighth-century trading-stations.

By c800, many towns in France and Flanders contained an urban stronghold, a combination of castle and palace: Huy, Namur, Ghent, Tournai and Cambrai are examples (Verhulst 1999). Some of these aristocratic sites were linked into the town's defences, and others fortified a weak point in the circuit. They point to the active rise to prominence of local lords, whether churchmen or secular leaders, and perhaps to the deliberate devolution of royal power for administrative purposes. So far, such aristocratic sites within towns have not been identified very much in Britain. Within some of the larger Roman towns, there may have been aristocratic compounds, with buildings in timber and occasionally in stone, as is suggested for Brook Street in Winchester, where a secular complex preceded the laying out of new streets in the late ninth century.

In al-Andalus, towns played an important role: political, economic and religious activity was centred on them, as in the Roman period (Fig 4.3). We do not yet however have adequate archaeological evidence for the appearance of the urban castle or linear markets, nor for the construction of mosques. Essentially, these three elements were central to the Islamisation of towns.

Religion in towns

Churches are often the key to explaining the revival or emergence of towns over most of Western Europe; sometimes, as in several smaller towns in Britain, the town is based on a church which had a pre-urban rural existence, before it became the kernel of urban settlement and practices. Several medieval towns in Ireland are based on small monasteries going back to the eighth century, if not before (Clarke & Simms 1985; Thomas 1992). A late seventh- or early eighth-century 'Christian building' has been excavated at

Caen, and there are probably more to find in towns which are thought to have started later. Of course, they could indicate that the town itself is much older than thought.

Where no bishop took over, an ex-Roman town was likely to die. In these towns, up to the ninth century, religious institutions multiplied: monasteries and small churches which would later become parish churches. In 700, Paris may have had 30 religious establishments. Though the cathedral or major church might be almost the only standing complex within a field of Roman ruins, surrounded by a distant wall of the former city, it clearly formed a link in a chain of civilised and cultural stations which led ultimately to Rome. This network of high-quality religious sites was not exclusively urban: in the ninth century, some spectacularly large churches were built in Carolingian Europe, both in rural areas (e.g. Volturno, in Italy (Fig 14.4), and Saint-Denis, France) and in towns, such as Auxerre (France) and Paderborn (Germany). This has been called the Carolingian Renaissance, but its chief importance was to salvage and hand on a large quantity of Latin literature from Antiquity.

From present evidence, it seems that the *wics* were places lacking monuments or elaborate religious facilities. They probably had churches (a woman living in Birka around 850 thought Dorestad had many), but excavated examples are few. A suggestion from a small number of sites in the English *wics* is that peripheral burial grounds, perhaps with small timber churches, might have been replaced during the eighth century by a central cemetery attached to the main community church (or perhaps more than one in a large place like London).

None of the churches of this time, however, was anything like the size of the hall and courtyard of the Great Mosque in Cordoba (al-Andalus) in its first phase of construction in the 780s. This was c95m square and, by 987, the prayer-hall alone was 125m long and 115m wide. This would not be matched by a Christian church in northern Europe for another 150 years. This underlines the Muslim view that great religious buildings were a public statement of the permanence of their faith and the largely urban culture that stemmed from it.

Manufacturing and trade

Dorestad had industries specialising in bone and antler objects, which it exported, and tanning of leather, which it probably imported in quantity as hides from the countryside. Hamwic had a number of industries, in a variety of metals (including the production of coins), wood and bone working, and textile and probably pottery production. Ipswich (Suffolk) had a thriving pottery production in the eighth century; Ipswich ware is the first English post-Roman pottery to be made on an industrial scale and fired in permanent kilns. It appears in London, Canterbury and York, and thus indicates the contemporary regional trading network. On the continent there were larger and technologically superior pottery industries in the Meuse valley and at sites on the Rhine, and these spread far wider over the entire economic zone of the emporia: distinctive pottery from Badorf from south of Cologne, from c725 until 900, and later Tating ware, in the shorter period 775-825 (pp 225-6). A second archaeological indicator of regional

Excavations at Cordoba, the largest city in al-Andalus (Spain): part of the rabad (quarter) of al-Saqunda, built in the 8th century and destroyed in 818, following a rebellion (after Guía Arqueológica de Córdoba, 2003).

Fig 4.3

and international trade are quern-stones of lava from Niedermendig near Mayen, which may have been finished for export in Dorestad. These everyday objects were being traded on a large scale around western Europe and into Scandinavia (see Box 10.2).

Silver coinage was introduced in France and England from the seventh century; the large value of each coin suggests they were not initially for trade, but for raising and conversion of tribute, and for regional or continental exchange (there were also short experiments with gold coins, but they were not widespread, and these even more than the silver were probably not for normal transactions). The sites where these coins are found are of royal and noble status, or churches, all centres of authority where they might be used and lost (Astill 2000). Coins were symbols of power and identity. Kings and emperors insisted that only they should control its minting. In this regard they made no distinction between ex-Roman towns and trading settlements: in 864, for instance, Charles the Bald stated that within his kingdom money would only be minted at his 'palace' (possibly Compiègne), Quentovic, Rouen and Paris, as well as a few other selected places (McKitterick 1983, 191).

By the end of the ninth century, several regional economies can be identified, such as the area between the Loire and the Rhine, or in northern Italy. Trade between these regions, and local trade, was probably more important than international trade, which took place through controlled 'gateway' places on the borders of kingdoms, whether in Britain or on the continent, where tolls were paid to the regional monarch.

In the Iberian Peninsula, al-Andalus maintained close contacts with North Africa as well as with the Near East. So, at the time of the Andalusian Umayyads (756-1010), this was an important trade and cultural route between Islam and Christianity, between East and West (Reilly 1993, 51-89; Ventura 2005, 53-97).

Towns as 'central-places'

In the sixth and seventh centuries, the 'afterglow' of Roman authority and prestige may have lingered in many Roman towns and been one attractive element to bishops and secular rulers. By the eighth century, however, this must have been but a faint memory. Roads led to towns and they were a convenient quarry, or they contained reusable defences and occasional stone buildings. Until the ninth century, monasteries both in the countryside and on the edge of old Roman towns may well have been the only important 'central-places'. These religious houses ran the industries which produced textiles, salt, wine and metals. They owned much of the land, so many people paid them rent.

In general, excavation of towns will tell us much about the policies of the ruling dynasties, who are otherwise often shadowy figures. The commercial history of Dorestad, for instance, probably mirrors the rise and decline of the Carolingian royal house. Further, when enough excavation has taken place (if ever), we will understand the royal uses of the different kinds of town. It has been suggested, at least for Hamwic and Winchester, that the two places were complementary in their urban functions in the eighth and ninth centuries: the king, bishop and powerful men lived at Winchester, but the mint, long-distance trade, intense industrial activity and relatively dense population were all at Hamwic (Biddle 1976b, 114, 120).

From the mid-ninth century, deliberate royal policies with regard to towns can be discerned. When the *wics* disappeared in the mid-ninth century, settlement was established or re-established nearby and it was these new settlements which became the later medieval town. Dorestad declined and was replaced by Deventer and Tiel in the ninth and especially late tenth centuries. Hamwic and Lundenwic apparently disappeared in the same decade, the 850s. There might have been relevant economic factors, and they had been declining for some time, but this abrupt end must have been a political decision. More specifically, the *burhs* of King Alfred in southern England, in the mid- to late ninth century, seem to be a scheme for the establishment of a whole network of towns which is without parallel in the rest of Europe. These were fortified towns, meaning that defence and military function came first, and the hoped for economic benefits came up to a century later, in times of relative peace.

It is difficult to describe the pleasures or innovations of town life in the eighth and ninth centuries at the moment. Clearly, security and religion were dominant concerns. But there was nothing distinctive about the known architecture, mostly church-es, in towns. Perhaps the urban residents had ideas about fashion and style: most of the Continental imported pottery found in English *wics* comprises items for the table.

Conclusions for the eighth and ninth centuries

Among many questions, two for archaeologists to explore in this period are the char-acter and purpose of the *wics*, and the details of the effects of the Viking raids from the late eighth century.

Some historians have thought that only the ex-Roman centres were 'real towns'; Dorestad has been dismissed as a single narrow street containing a few merchants (Duby 1974, 106). But the archaeological evidence produced during the last 30 years has forced a rethinking. The emporia were simultaneous and probably related experiments in urban-ism in several European kingdoms in the seventh to ninth centuries. They were special-ised, important, and some of them were large. Estimates of population at this time are always hazardous, but it has been suggested that Lundenwic may have contained more than 5000 people (Keene 2000, 188). We do not yet know if they were merely servants of an economy directed by kings, or whether they had internal organs and any mind of their own.

We also do not know much about how the Viking attacks influenced the development of towns. From c790 all of Northern and Western Europe, as far south as Lisbon and Muslim Spain, were subject to attacks from Scandinavian Vikings. Towns were particu-larly under pressure from the 840s (Rouen was sacked in 840, Lisbon and Seville in 844, and Paris in 845), until the threat faded in the 890s. One consequence was that towns in all north-western countries went through a phase of rebuilding their defences against the threat. The Viking raids forced the embyronic towns to assert themselves as defensible communities; they may have hastened the demise of some of the *wics*. Viking urban set-tlement which followed in several countries is primarily a feature of the tenth century.

The Tenth to Twelfth Centuries

Types of urban settlement

From the tenth century, the archaeological study of towns is on firmer ground. The *wics* had disappeared, and towns began to resemble each other more closely. The European town crystallised into its medieval form in the tenth to twelfth centuries, in two ways: the urban topography of walls, streets, churches and houses became permanent, or more so, and disparate little communities coalesced to form new towns, or the scattered set-tlement within an old Roman city wall grew together. By the end of the twelfth century, the larger towns were flexing their political and financial muscles and wanting to run themselves. They were also developing urban tastes and ways of living which were dif-ferent from those in the countryside.

In the late ninth and tenth centuries, in the towns of Flanders and what is now north-ern France, secular lords built new citadels, often on sites traditionally associated with previous royal regimes, but now with a regional or local emphasis. Far from being simple consumers, the strongholds (which were built at different times, not only to repel Viking attacks) were among the main active factors of urban development; examples are Antwerp, Ghent and Bruges. They were matched in the same spirit by towns based on one or more large churches, such as Liège, Arras, Tournai and Cambrai. Though it had been the site of a fourth-century bishopric, Tours only took post-Roman shape in the tenth century. During the eleventh century several cathedral cities sprouted new commercial suburbs, almost new towns with their own churches and other facilities, which were later incorporated into the town by defensive walls, such as at Auxerre. This timetable of increasing urban population, diversity of functions and growth in physical area is shared with many towns in Britain, though even at the larger towns such as Winchester and London, there is little archaeological evidence for concerted growth until the end of the tenth century.

Some towns were formed by the growing together of adjacent hamlets or groups of buildings, as shown by archaeological work in Douai. Here settlement was at first dispersed in the ninth and tenth centuries (Fig 4.5), and Douai is only recognisable as a town in the late twelfth century (Demolon & Louis 1994). A similar coming together of different settlements has been demonstrated by archaeology in Norwich, where neighbourhoods of the eighth and ninth century came together in the tenth. Caen was the union of three settlements, and villages came together to form Salamanca and Segovia.

In the tenth century there were important Viking towns in western Europe, at York (Hall 1994; 2004) and Dublin (Wallace 1992), and probably at Rouen (though there is far less archaeological evidence there: Le Maho 1995). On the other hand, there is virtually no trace of Viking occupation or influence at London, and probably few lasting effects. Excavations in York, Dublin and Waterford (Hurley, Scully & McCutcheon 1997) have emphatically shown that when they settled down, the Vikings knew how to make a town prosperous far more than Alfred and his immediate Saxon successors to the south. The material culture of Viking York in the tenth century is difficult to match in any other excavated town in Western Europe.

It was in al-Andalus, however, that the most vigorous urban culture in Europe at this period can be found. In the tenth century, one third of all European towns with populations of more than 10,000 were situated in this region, and Cordoba, the principal Muslim city, reached a total of more than 100,000 at this period. In 936, only 5km from Cordoba, there was founded a royal town named Madinat al-Zahra. This new town was designed to be the political capital of the Umayyad caliphate, but some administrative functions were still performed in Cordoba. As a result of recent archaeological excavations, we now know of the existence of many new residential districts built between these towns during the tenth century, most of them terraced houses.

The tenth and especially the eleventh century was the period when the network of Andalusian towns became definitively established. Enlargements, renovation of infrastructure and new town-walls were systematically built during the Almohad caliphate, after the second half of the twelfth century, and a good example of this process is provided by Seville (Valor & Tahiri 1999).

Towns have always been instruments of conquest or colonisation, and during the twelfth century this was clearly demonstrated by the spread of towns as royal policy by the Anglo-Norman kings into Wales and Ireland (Clarke & Simms 1985; Thomas 1992). Scotland acquired a network of towns in the twelfth century, its first truly urban settlements, often based on royal supply-centres. A map of these towns is a map of Scottish royal influence.

Patterns of public and private space

A feature of several major tenth-century towns which were formerly Roman cities is that their street system was replanned, usually in a rectilinear manner but only vestigially following the Roman pattern, as at London, Winchester and Rouen. Further, by the end of the tenth century, Winchester displayed a form of internal specialisation: the royal and eccesiastical compounds and buildings occupied more than a quarter of the walled area. By 970 the three important churches in this quarter were bounded by a single wall which divided them from the rest of the city and from the royal complex (Fig 4.4). Manufacturing and commercial interests began to be localised in areas of towns. Three streets in Winchester had names which derived from trades: tanners, butchers, and makers of shields (Biddle 1976a, 472-8). In France, the lower town of Chartres by the river Eure was, by 1100, a manufacturing zone of workers of leather and wool; texts mention tanners, curriers, other leatherworkers, shoemakers and saddlers (Chédeville 1980, 124). Other trades congregated together for marketing reasons: the butchers were on the main streets, and the goldsmiths were next to the cathedral or the princely residence. Markets were public spaces but sections of the main street were also used, often near gates.

Increasingly, both boundaries and building complexes of the local centre of authority were constructed in stone. Throughout the tenth to twelfth centuries there are many examples of the rebuilding of Roman defences and the containing of expanding settlements with new walls, so that the growth of a town can be shown by the lines of defence at different times. Some towns which began to flourish in the twelfth century, such as Lille, expanded thereafter in stages with new defences until the seventeenth century, and occasionally later. In Britain and Ireland the Normans introduced the castle, both as a crushing imposition on existing towns (always with the removal of all buildings and streets in its path) and as a frontier post which attempted to protect new towns. The Normans settled colonies of 'Frenchmen' in several towns, but the effect of the Norman invasion on several English towns was to decrease their population (as shown in the Domesday Book). Towns which had royal connections prospered.

From the beginning of the twelfth century there are also traces of urban government in the excavation record. Early town assemblies were often in churchyards (or, where they survived in a few cases, old Roman amphitheatres), but by the 1120s in the larger towns we know of meetings in special buildings, the ancestors of town-halls. The towns were corporately concerned about maintaining and improving the urban environment: this is the time of rebuilding in stone of many important bridges (such as at Rouen, Paris or London) and the first building regulations (in London, c1200, fire-break walls of a

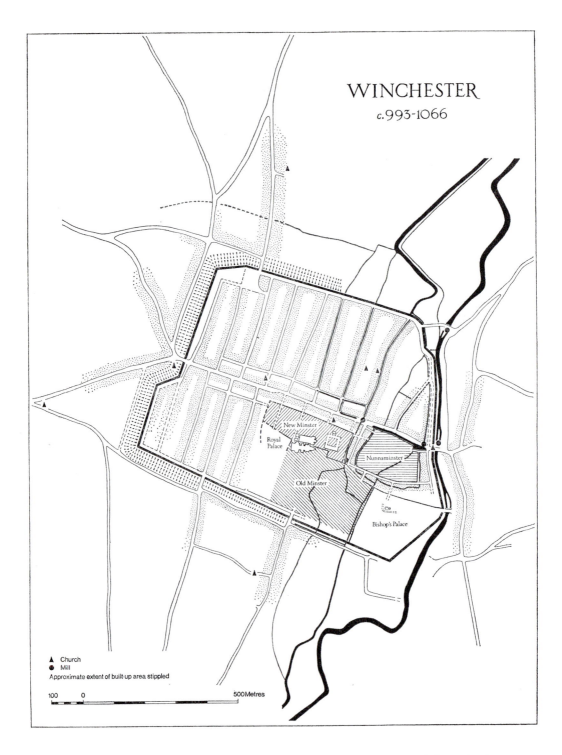

WINCHESTER
c.993-1066

New Minster

Royal
Palace

Nunnaminster

Old Minster

Bishop's Palace

▲ Church
● Mill
Approximate extent of built-up area stippled

100   0   500 Metres

Fig 4.4   *Plan of Winchester, c993-1066, showing the extent of the walled town, with the royal palace and ecclesiatical complex in the south-east quarter, and growing suburbs; note the location of the three mills (after Biddle 1976a).*

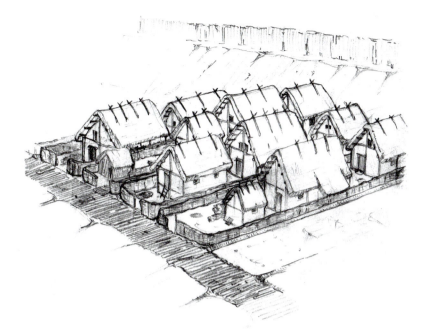

Douai (France), la Fonderie: reconstruction of four properties in the 10th century **Fig 4.5**
(E Louis, Musée de Douai).

new regulation width are excavated). Excavations in several towns confirm the impression given by the documents that town authorities concerned themselves with boundaries of properties, including the street side, but within a property the character of buildings was up to the owner or tenant. The concern with building regulations was probably hastened by frequent serious fires in towns, which shows that buildings were close together and normally built of combustible materials.

Towns grew suburbs along their approach roads, but also into the adjacent river. Waterfront archaeology has been one of the main developments in the study of post-Roman European towns since 1970. Massive amounts of artefacts, dated by dendrochronology of the timber reclamation walls, are now forming the basis of detailed typologies of pottery and all kinds of household and trade objects; the main ports which have produced archaeological reports on waterfronts before 1300 include Bergen, Dordrecht, Dublin and London (e.g. Herteig 1985; Steedman et al 1992; Schofield et al, in prep). The well-preserved timbers themselves contain much information about woodland management and carpentry, so that important aspects of vanished medieval buildings on land can be deduced, such as an increasing sophistication in the late twelfth century which allowed construction of higher buildings in towns. Fragments of timber buildings from the tenth century onwards are also found in these reclamation dumps, showing the sophistication of urban buildings in their architecture and methods of construction.

Study of documents has shown that there was a free property market in Winchester and London before the Norman Conquest, with buying, selling, and renting of properties. As the population expanded, properties were subdivided, as early as the tenth century. The typical medieval long and narrow property can be traced in many towns from this time (Fig 4.5), though as we have seen it might have been present in the *wics*. A range of house-types, nearly all in timber, is known in these larger towns (see also pp 166-9); the buildings could easily be adapted for either domestic or industrial use).

During the second half of the tenth century many towns throughout northern Europe expanded, and in both England and Germany a new form of house appeared – or rather, a large timber-lined cellar supporting a building which has otherwise been lost. Some of these cellars were at the back of courtyards. Their appearance suggests that there was a new need for subterranean storage on a large scale, presumably by traders who built these private warehouses to respond to the ups and downs of a true commercial market, taking advantage of dearth and over-supply of commodities. The town had taken on a new function, as container and redistribution centre.

From the opening of the twelfth century, stone houses appear in the major towns: one in Ghent, which still stands, has been dated to the eleventh century. This may have been part of an aristocratic compound, but it was soon followed by many others which combined storage functions with twelfth-century urban polite living. This is illustrated best by the surviving groups of buildings at Cluny or Regensburg. The houses of the urban elite now compared favourably with rural residences and standards of living within contemporary monasteries. At Cluny (Figs 5.1 & 5.8) there are whole streets of stone houses, reflecting the rich monastery in their midst, but in the great majority of towns, there was no upper-class district or street; stone houses, usually a rarity, were surrounded by timber buildings of all sizes.

In al-Andalus the traditional Mediterranean house with a central courtyard continued to be used (see Box 5.1). Sizes, decoration and shapes are very variable depending probably on the owner's economic level as well as his occupation. Normally, re-used building materials (stones and bricks) were employed. Walls and pavements were very commonly painted in dark red and white.

Religion in towns

From the second half of the eighth century, a cathedral was usually surrounded by buildings of its community and staff (canons), to make a small district which often had walls and gates. From the ninth to the twelfth centuries, rebuilding and crystallisation of a cathedral precinct was often of great topographical significance. Particularly in a small town, the church and its precinct would dominate the neighbourhood, and perhaps the town, for centuries.

Archaeology has revealed some striking early examples of church architecture in towns. In Bruges, the church of St Donatian (c950) was built by a count and modelled on the palatial chapel in Aachen, with a similar round crypt but smaller; the new church was part of an expansion of the fortress, and included all the necessary ancillary buildings in a cloister. The pilgrimage to Santiago de Compostela in north-western Spain started in the ninth century, and the main churches, dating now from the eleventh century, are found in towns on the several pilgrim-routes there (e.g. Tours, Limoges, Conques, Toulouse and Compostela itself; see also Box 13.2).

In the west of Europe, town parishes are mainly a creation of the tenth and eleventh centuries. In some towns, perhaps because the churches began life as chapels on private estates, there are many parish (i.e. public) churches by 1100: London had most of its 110 churches by then, and Winchester had perhaps 50. Whenever these small neighbourhood churches are investigated archaeologically, their origins are taken back two centuries before they first appear in documents, but hardly ever before 900. Cemeteries accompany the parish churches, and study of human skeletons can tell us much about the health of the population (e.g. White 1988). When large groups of burials from tenth/twelfth-century sites in towns and the countryside have been excavated and analysed, it may be possible to see if town people had a better diet, were healthier and lived longer than those in the countryside.

Mosques were still being constructed or renovated in al-Andalus to meet the requirements of the Almohads. This process has been recognised from archaeological remains at (e.g.) Seville and Almeria, or Mertola in Portugal, and occasionally from documentary sources.

Manufacturing and trade

Industries that functioned mainly in towns are likely to have been those which required extensive facilities, such as tanning of leather and dyeing of cloth. The leather would have been readily available given that much of the town's meat supply arrived on the hoof, live to the market. In 1148, at least 50 different trades are known in Winchester, a medium-sized town. It seems also that trades which required a high level of competence, such as weaving with the new horizontal looms (see pp 218-20 & Fig 7.8) and dyeing, became concentrated in towns especially in the twelfth century.

During the eleventh and twelfth centuries craft-guilds (co-operative associations of specific trades, such as goldsmiths or weavers) are heard of in a number of towns. The degree of control of the manufacturing guilds might be ascertainable by a study of manufacturing techniques of objects found on archaeological sites in towns, particularly of metalwork. Waste from manufacturing is commonly found, for the bone, antler, and leather preparation industries, and from the making of wooden implements or shoes (Vince 1991, for London). The urban economy was becoming truly diversified.

From the tenth century, control of trade was no longer a royal monopoly. The general picture is shown by towns in Flanders, where markets were usually local, outside the gate of the lord's castle. Some towns had little international contact and prospered as regional centres, such as Lincoln and Thetford (Norfolk), away from the coast. The use of coins was spreading, but only for expensive items or transactions; there must still have been much bartering at a local level, for food and other essentials.

Towards the end of the tenth century some towns began to participate in international trade, a development made possible by their local and regional experience. A short list of tolls on imports of c1000 survives for the harbour of Billingsgate in London:

it mentions merchants from Rouen and Ponthieu in Normandy, Huy (where compa-rable levels have been recently excavated), Liège and Nivelles in Flanders, and from the Holy Roman Empire (Robertson 1925, 73). Excavation on the contemporary water-front nearby has found embankments and what may be the supports for a jetty out into the river. The transport system, both by road and river, was greatly improved by 1200; bridges were rebuilt, some in stone, and ships were redesigned for carrying bulk com-modities across the sea (see Chapter 9). The nodes of this transport system were towns, and those where major roads crossed rivers or met the sea were particularly fortunate. In the towns Jewish communities which specialised in overland trade were numerous by 1200, all over Europe; the Jews are one of the very few ethnic groups in towns which can be traced by their buildings, places of worship and material culture (see Chapter 13), as for example in Muslim Spain (Mann et al 1992).

Seville seems to become the most important centre in international trade after the sec-ond half of the twelfth century. Gold and ivory came from southern Africa and were re-distributed throughout Europe from the Iberian Peninsula. At the same time Andalusian products, such as olive oil, ceramics and silk, were also included in this commerce.

Towns as 'central-places'

In the campaign of foundation of new towns from the eleventh century, the lords encouraged trade and coinage spread into regions which had formerly lived without it. But the new towns only succeeded as business ventures when they developed a sound economic base which would give them independence from the lord's castle. To do this a town had to establish itself as a market-centre over a region. Archaeology still has to work out how to study this, especially since documents which illuminate this topic (or most other urban topics) are not numerous until the thirteenth century.

Medieval states were created around the towns which had preceded their formation, often by hundreds of years. It did not follow, however, that kings always made the big-gest town, or any town, into the capital; in the eleventh century the English kings and William the Conqueror settled on Westminster, not the City of London, and the capital of France was not immediately Paris. At Westminster a strong association with the abbey associated with the previous royal house, and therefore a seat of traditional authority, was more important. And in any case, until the later thirteenth century, a king and his court roved around the kingdom; the seat of government was where the king happened to be. The idea that a ruler should occupy the largest city was not yet widespread.

In the tenth century, as far as we know, there were few civic buildings and no differ-ences between churches or monasteries in towns and those in the countryside. By the end of the twelfth century, however, the most splendid and architecturally innovative Romanesque buildings were on balance to be found in or near towns, and probably for several reasons. One was pilgrimage which brought a lot of money to a few towns; but, more generally, the town was becoming a living pattern-book for architectural sponsors. As noted above, it was also establishing standards of construction, safety and hygiene in

ordinary building work such as houses. There were also, by 1200, special urban buildings such as market-halls, and the majority of hospitals were in or near towns.

Conclusions for the tenth to twelfth centuries

In this second part of the period, archaeologists can begin to study the many interlocking features of towns according to lists like that of Biddle, above (p 111). Urban archaeology remains fundamental to this study, for documents are not available for much of
the period under discussion.

By the end of the twelfth century, towns had become 'central-places' for many functions besides the religious. A town also began to look more like other towns than like
the villages and farms of its region. In towns, archaeology is beginning to demonstrate
urban ways of living, with higher houses, urban diseases, but probably a better diet than
was had in the countryside.

Towns were spreading everywhere, giving Europe economic and cultural unity. Towns
reflected regional differences in government, ethnicity and wealth, but they also represented a network of common aspirations and attitudes. In a town, from Ireland to Spain,
there was a recognisable formula of institutions, facilities and security. Towns transmitted power and wealth from generation to generation, and this concentration of wealth
in the hands of prominent townspeople brought about change. In the twelfth century,
urban dwellers were proud of themselves and of their towns. The West European town
as we know it today is largely a creation of the eighth to twelfth centuries

PART 2: CENTRAL, NORTHERN, EASTERN AND
SOUTHERN EUROPE *by Heiko Steuer*

Introduction

The history of Central European towns in the Middle Ages is delineated by both geo-
graphical and chronological limits. Geographically, the Rhine, formerly a border of the
Roman Empire, forms a division between different types of urban development (Clarke
& Simms 1985).

The town as an entity with a written constitution had not yet come into existence in
the period between the eighth and twelfth centuries, although the Carolingian documentary sources for such northern trading-places as Hedeby (in southern Jutland) and Birka
(in central Sweden) mention not only the king as the town's ruler, but also the existence
of a *comes vici*, which points indirectly to the existence of a rule of law. Indeed, market,
commercial and traders' rights predate urban law. The latter originated in northern Italy
and Tuscany from where the development into autonomous urban communities (i.e.
towns that appointed their own rulers) spread across the Alps into Central Europe.

For the period before 1150, therefore, instead of using the term 'town' some scholars prefer to refer to 'pre-' and 'proto-urban sites' in Central and Northern Europe,

BOX 4.2   ROME

Fig 1

Rome – view of the Fora Imperiali in the 10th century (© Ministero per i Beni e le Attivitá Culturali – Soprintendenza Archeologica di Roma – Museo Nazionale Romano – Crypta Balbi).

During the first half of the fifth century Rome was still the magnificent queen of the world, although she had not been the imperial seat for some time. Even the sackings at the hands of the Goths in 410 and the Vandals in 455 cannot have inflicted lasting damage on the city's monumental heritage, since Rome still appeared to be at the apogee of its splendour. Its population numbered in the region of hundreds of thousands (although the actual total is the subject of debate), occupying the vast area enclosed by the Aurelian Walls, that extended for 18km. Its buildings devoted to spectacular public entertainment were fully active and its baths were supplied, as also hundreds of public fountains, by fourteen aqueducts. Its pagan temples were still standing, although closed for worship, alongside the majestic new Christian basilicas. Rome's monuments still dazzled visitors.

Fleets of ships laden with grain and oil arrived every year and enormous herds of pigs were driven to Rome from southern Italy, to provide for this vast concentration of population (unparalleled again before the Industrial Revolution in the eighteenth/nineteenth century). The majority of the inhabitants lived in large four- or five-storey *insulae*; the nobility, on the other hand, resided in grandiose mansions, veritable 'cities within the city', according to Ammianus Marcellinus, with gardens and fountains, and decorated with coloured marbles.

During the last twenty years a series of major urban excavations, including the Crypta Balbi and the Fora Imperiali (Fig 1), together with preparatory work on Rome's new Museo dell'Altomedioevo, which opened in 2000, have provided new data for the transition from imperial city to medieval town. All the dwellings that were subject to stratigraphic excavations proved to have been abandoned, or deliberately buried, during the second half of the fifth or at the beginning of the sixth century. The same applies to many other buildings and public areas – often occupied by cemeteries. These latest studies also indicate that the population collapsed at about the same time, with the result that the number of inhabitants dropped by almost 90% in the space of a few decades, from several hundred thousands to 50-60,000 by the early part of the sixth century. The bloody war between the Byzantines and Goths (535-54), which saw Rome besieged and occupied by both contenders several times, must have dealt the final blow to the city's structure.

Unfortunately, the archaeological and historical data that would enable us to reconstruct the urban plan during the sixth to eighth centuries is almost nonexistent. When data is available (i.e. from the end of the eighth to the beginning of the ninth century), it provides a completely different picture. In all likelihood, the population was even smaller, stabilizing at 20-30,000 inhabitants, remaining so throughout the Middle Ages. The residential zone was restricted to less than a quarter of the area within the walls and was concentrated near the river. The rest of the imperial city was abandoned and used for agricultural purposes, creating the swathe of gardens and vineyards that characterized Rome until its major expansion at the end of the nineteenth century. In the inhabited area, the urban fabric was very sparse, also broken up by gardens and vineyards. Even the papal seat (then the Lateran Palace) remained isolated in an area that was mostly uninhabited, while the Vatican zone – completely marginal in the ancient city – became increasingly central to Rome's medieval image, due to the presence of the Basilica of

BOX 4.2 ROME

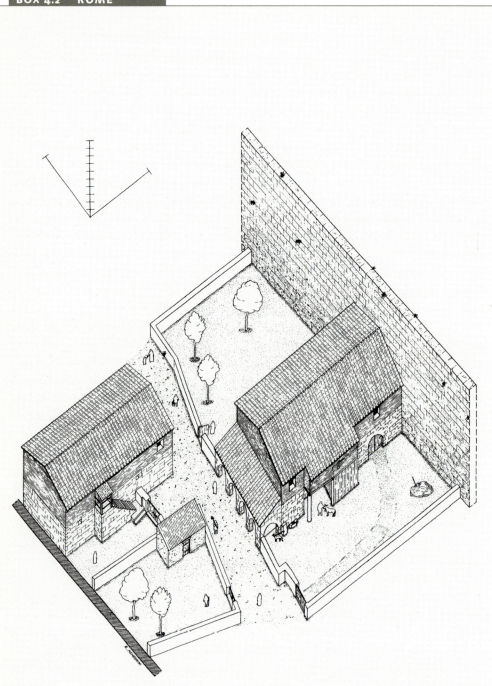

Fig 2

Rome: reconstruction of 9th/10th-century housing in the Forum of Nerva (after Santangeli Valenzani 2000).

St Peter, and was protected by new walls in the mid-ninth century. Building types also appear to have changed completely. Plebeian dwellings took the form of huts consisting of a single room measuring a few square metres, built with reused materials and clay, and grouped in small settlements inside the ruins of monumental constructions from the Imperial Age. The aristocracy, on the other hand, lived in large two-storey houses (cf. Fig. 2) that were part of complexes (referred to as *curtes* in written sources) which included stables, stores, orchards and also, in some cases, private chapels and small bathing facilities, but these were also built largely with reused material, wood and other perishable materials.

The eleventh century marked another turning-point in Rome's urban history. Excavations have revealed that this period is characterized, in all strata, by a significant rise in paving levels, and the consequent obliteration of many structures and ancient ruins. The inhabited zone is even smaller, but the occupation density of the residential buildings shows a substantial increase. It is mostly the building types that change radically. For the first time we find a typical medieval urban fabric: houses of brick or masonry, and often with two storeys, built side-by-side along the thoroughfares. Even more radical is the change in the type of building occupied by the wealthier classes: the increasing conflict within the nobility led to the militarisation of the urban landscape, most evident in the spread of fortified complexes, dominated by towers, in which the nobles resided. These towers were one of the most striking characteristics of the late medieval urban landscape in Rome, as in many other towns in central and northern Italy. An English pilgrim, Magister Gregorius, who visited Rome at the end of the twelfth or at the beginning of the thirteenth century, when first setting eyes on the city from the surrounding hills, compared the towers to ears of wheat, 'so many that no one can count them'. From the eleventh to fourteenth centuries, Rome was marked by continual strife between rival noble factions, between the populace and the aristocracy, and between the nobility and the papacy, leading to economic decline.

By Riccardo Santangeli Valenzani

depending on their situation and function, using also such terms as: 'ports-of-trade', emporia, trading-places, 'centres of wealth', markets, 'central-places' and early urban sites (Jankuhn et al 1975; *Reallexikon der Germanischen Altertumskunde*).

Medieval urbanism developed successively, spreading from the West to the North and East, developing differently from one region to another. With regard to urban sites in what was formerly the Roman Empire, in the countryside along the Rhine and south of the Danube, as well as in Italy, there always exists the question of continuity of development from Late Antiquity into the Middle Ages (Brogiolo et al 1999; 2000; Liebeschütz 2001; Witschel 2004). In every region beyond the former Roman Empire, there developed a different type of medieval urban site: in the Ottonian, Salian and Staufer empires from the Rhine to the Elbe (Steuer & Biegel 2002), and later to the Oder (Brachmann 1991); in the North Sea and Baltic regions with the kingdoms of Denmark, Norway and Sweden (Clarke & Ambrosiani 1991); in the Slavic settlement area east of the Elbe (Piekalski 2001); in the later kingdoms of Poland, Bohemia and Hungary (Gerevich 1990); and in the Russian princedoms (Mühle 1991). A remarkable urban landscape also appeared in Great Moravia during the ninth century.

Definition

Regardless of what are laid down as the hallmarks of a town in the urban laws recorded in later documentary sources, the criteria that serve to define a proto-urban site were collected by Edith Ennen in her works, 'Frühgeschichte der europäischen Stadt' (1953), and *Die europäische Stadt des Mittelalters* (1972) (Ennen 1972/87), against the background of Max Weber's essay on *Die Stadt* (1921). A town is fundamentally different from a village, but it also differs both from specialized trading settlements and from castles (Johanek & Post 2004).

The characteristics that can be identified in the archaeological record are: (1) an easily accessible location on inter-regional routes (by both land and water); (2) a concentration of trading and craft production; (3) a dense population;(4) separation from the surrounding countryside (often by means of a fortification); (5) infrastructure facilities for the inhabitants (such as a systematic layout of plots, a system of roads and paths, open squares for markets, bridges, quays and other port facilities); and (6) specialised building types to meet the needs of craftsmen and merchants (differing from the farm structures required for agricultural use). In addition, there are religious or sacred structures, which after Christianisation included churches, monasteries and convents (Fig 4.6). In the north, around the North Sea and the Baltic, the elite had a hall for festivals and ceremonies in the 'central-places', and in the Slavic east there were temples. Long-distance trading could only become significant for an urban site when its craftsmen were able to produce trade-goods in sufficient quantities, and when the neighbouring farms were capable of producing surpluses with which to supply the craftsmen.

What is archaeologically less evident, or only indirectly, is independence of thought and a self-sufficient urban life-style, although this is detectable from the materials of daily life that have been found in concentrations on urban sites. Likewise, the functions

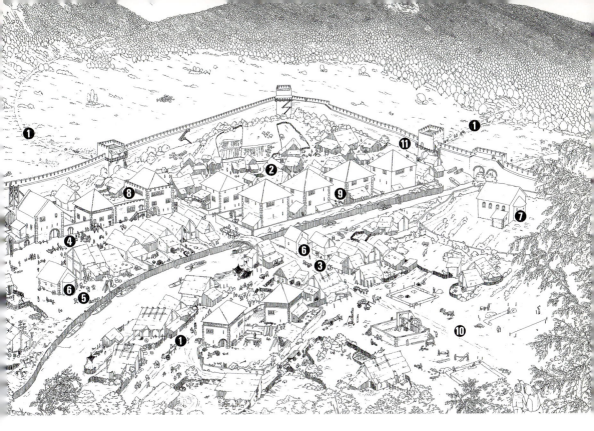

'A town about 1100' (or 1200); a hypothetical reconstruction based on excavations in Basle and Zurich: (1) old country roads; (2 & 3) craftsmen's settlements; (4) market-place; (5) hythe; (6) chapels; (7) parish church, with cemetery; (8) the first stone houses; (9) new row of housing; (10) construction sites; and (11) the town-wall (after Rippmann & Tauber 1991).

Fig 4.6

of 'central-places' can only be verified when the surrounding area has been sufficiently investigated archaeologically.

Phases of Urban Development

Archaeological research during the last few decades has not only considerably changed what we know about the appearance of early urban sites, it has also brought to light some completely new phases of development (Steuer 1990; Fehring 1996; Brachmann & Herrmann 1991; Jarnut & Johanek 1998).

The number of coastal trading-places in the Baltic region known from the eighth to ninth centuries has risen from some ten in the mid-twentieth century to about 100 in the twenty-first (Clarke & Ambrosiani 1991; Callmer 1994; Müller-Wille 2004). Studies of inland areas are still in their infancy, and so there we should expect to find further such concentrations of trade and crafts – in other words, the basic structures of an early urban settlement – as at Karlburg am Main, near Würzburg.

In contrast to Western Europe, the development of the town in the areas under discussion cannot be divided into the two periods of the eighth to ninth, and then the tenth to twelfth centuries. Rather, several different phases have emerged in a period of continuous development. In the Baltic area there was no interruption until the eleventh century, when the locations of the early urban sites were shifted: in northern Germany, there was a move from Hedeby to Schleswig, and then later, in the twelfth century, to Lübeck, whose predecessor had been Alt-Lübeck; in Sweden, from Birka via Sigtuna to Stockholm and from Uppåkra to Lund; in Poland, from Truso to Elbing/Elbląg. Only towards the end of the twelfth century did there commence a wave of new foundations, relating to internal topographical re-structuring and the expansion of existing urban sites, in parallel with the setting down of urban laws. The proto-urban castles in the Slavic settlement area east of the Elbe also underwent re-organization, acquiring further structures, in the wake of the eastern expansion of the type of urban law exemplified by Lübeck and Magdeburg.

Types of Early Urban Settlement

Early urban settlements were seldom founded 'from scratch' in the open countryside; either the older cores of settlements were expanded or settlements with other political or religious functions developed into an urban settlement. Examples of this include the *Pfalz (palatium)* constructions between the Rhine and the Elbe, which served as the king's residences while he travelled, fortified bishop's seats in areas of missionary activity, hill-top castles (*Höhenburgen*) used as military bases during the conquest of the Saxons by the Carolingian Empire, and monasteries that served also as commercial centres.

(1) The Roman towns on the Rhine and the Danube, after the decline of the third-fourth century, experienced new growth starting in the seventh century (Eck & Galsterer 1991). Continuity can be determined in the re-use of architectural structures in Cologne, Trier and Regensburg (Clemens 2003), in the continuation of the economic function of crafts and trade, of the rulers and population, of the church – the bishop's seat in a *civitas* – as well as the functions that 'central-places' performed with respect to their surrounding areas, although the dislocation between Antiquity and the early Middle Ages led to a temporary decrease in population. There is also the appearance of a new network of roads. The most recent excavations in Cologne, Mainz, Trier, Strasbourg, Basle, Constance, Regensburg, Passau and Vienna have all brought to light new evidence for continuity of settlement, trading and craft production throughout the Merovingian period.

(2) During the eighth to ninth centuries, some of the former centres of wealth and landing-places developed into merchants' emporia (Stoob's large proto-urban settlements) (Stoob 1979) or coastal trading-places and markets where long-distance trade was concentrated and where craftsmen settled (Hodges & Hobley 1988). Most of these were located on geographical, political or ethnic borders, on sea coasts

Parchim, Mecklenburg (Germany): site-plan, with wooden rampart, reconstructed house-plans (stippled) and, below the broken line, the distribution of coins, scales and weights (after Brather 2003).

Fig 4.7

or on inland borders dividing Germans and Slavs (e.g. on the Elbe, as 'ports-of-
trade'). These proto-urban sites are notable for the considerable expanse of their settled areas. In most cases, it is still unknown what types of buildings were located
within them. It can be assumed that the merchants had assembly places and storage rooms and that there were many pit-houses (SFBs) for the various production
activities, from textile production and non-ferrous metal working to bead production and even glassblowing; or the land may have been parcelled into large rural
farms with agricultural areas, as was the case at Dorestad, with extensive market-
places. Diachronically, places like Lundeborg, near Gudme on the island of Fyn,

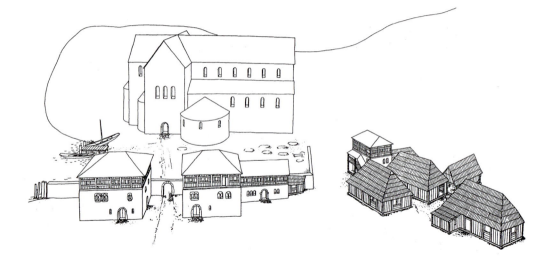

Fig 4.8   *Zurich, Münsterhof: reconstruction based on finds from the period around 1136-39, and from the late 12th century, respectively (after Steuer 1995).*

Groß Strömkendorf (*Reric*) in Mecklenburg (Tummuscheit 2003), Hedeby, near Schleswig (Box 4.3), Bardowick and Madgeburg, near the Elbe, and Karlburg am Main, near Würzburg, are examples of this type.

In the ninth to tenth centuries, these proto-urban places became early urban sites, with new forms of houses, a regular system of plots and roads (in the west, Cologne; in Norway, Kaupang (Skre 2007); in Sweden, Birka, Åhus and Uppåkra (Larsson & Hårdh 1998); on the Jutland Peninsula, Hedeby and Ribe; Tissø on Zealand (Jørgensen 2003); on the southern Baltic coast, Starigard/Oldenburg, Ralswiek and Menzlin; to the east of the Baltic, Grobin and Truso; in Russia, Staraya Ladoga and Novgorod). Examples of such places further inland are Parchim in Mecklenburg (Brather 2003) (Fig 4.7), and Karlburg am Main.

(3) The *Pfalz*, a palace-castle serving the king as a temporary residence during his travels, was made up of a core-complex (on about 1-3ha) consisting of the palace, a church, residential structures and store-houses built of wood, with later, from the tenth century, additions in stone (Aachen, Ingelheim, Duisburg, Frankfurt, Paderborn, Werla and Tilleda in the Harz region, Magdeburg, Regensburg and Zurich; Fig 4.8). Such palaces (see also Chapter 12) take on an early urban character through their size and through the development of sometimes vast outer works, built onto the core-complex and fortified with ramparts and ditches, in which there could be several hundred SFBs and other workshop constructions where craft production was focused, from textiles to non-ferrous metalworking and blacksmithing. The number of buildings attests to surplus production for the purposes of commerce and trade. Some older *Pfalz* from the Carolingian period, such as Ingelheim and Aachen, have not yet displayed the ele-

ments of an early urban site, other than their core structures, as there are no references to fortifications (cf. p 343), although the *Pfalz* of Paderborn developed differently, functioning also as the bishop's castle in the insecure border region of Saxony.

The Danish fortified complexes (circular fortresses) from the time of Harald Bluetooth, in the late tenth century, such as Aggersborg, Fyrkat and Trelleborg, apparently held a position somewhere between the *Pfalz*, the garrison town and the craftsmen's town, in being supply-centres for the royal army (see p 319, Fig 11.2).

While some of these castle-sites north of the Alps developed further, into towns, the German kings in Italy moved their castles outside the towns for fear of the urban population.

(4) From Late Antiquity and during the Merovingian period, bishop's seats (*civitates*) became the nucleus of a new and different type of urban development. In addition, with the onset of the Saxon Wars in 772 and the ensuing Christian mission, the lands reaching as far as the Elbe were organised through the founding of a network of bishop's castles that functioned as proto-urban centres (Steuer 2003). Their locations, at travel junctions and on navigable rivers, were carefully chosen. Proto-urban sites were created that later all developed into towns. Bishop's seats were zones of immunity – and thus legally and spatially enclosed units.

(5) The early monasteries of the Carolingian period were large, multi-purpose, commercial operations, with a variety of craft production, that were integrated into long-distance trade across the regions. They therefore counted several hundred residents, not including their monks and clerics. The monastery of Corvey was the first place east of the Rhine, in 833, to acquire not only market and customs rights, but also the right to issue coins. (So far, however, no coins are known from this mint, apparently because coins were not yet being used in market dealings in this region). Examples of such monastic sites include San Vincenzo al Volturno and Farfa in Italy, Müstair in South Tyrol, St Gallen and Reichenau in southern Germany, and Corvey in Lower Saxony.

(6) Extensive farmsteads, on estates documented as belonging to the king or a bishop, were enlarged in the Ottonian period. Like the *Pfalz*, they consisted of a core-complex surrounded by fortified proto-urban structures (Steuer 2001). A representative building, a church and store-houses formed the centre, surrounded by outer works in which SFBs were built for use as workshops (Donat 1999). In the Old Saxon area, the farmsteads of Gebesee and Helfta have undergone archaeological investigation.

(7) The heavily populated town-like castles of the Carolingian period in the area bordering on Saxon territory, such as Büraburg by Fritzlar, with an area of 8ha including its outer works, and the Christenberg by Marburg, with 3-4ha, were abandoned in the ninth century, and their additional functions, such as that of bishop's seat, relocated in the case of Büraburg into the valley at Fritzlar, where the town subsequently developed. The castle-building code of Henry I (919-36) led to the expansion, after

BOX 4.3 HEDEBY

From the eighth to eleventh centuries, a manufacturing and trading centre was located at Haddebyer Noor, a southerly side-arm of the River Schlei, which provided access to the Baltic. According to documentary sources, the site was known as *Sliaswich* and *Sliesthorp*, as well as *Haiðaby* (hence modern Haithabu, in German, and Hedeby in Danish/English). In 808, the Danish king – Godfred – moved traders there from Reric in Mecklenburg. After the mid-eleventh century, Hedeby was relocated to the north bank of the Schlei, where it became the town of Schleswig (Fig 9.8).

This early urban settlement was crossed by roads at right-angles along which rows of fenced plots were situated (Fig 1), containing the buildings belonging to specialised craftsmen and traders (Fig 5.2). Along over 400m of river-bank, several jetties were sited, serving as both piers for trading vessels and market-places (Fig 2). In the late tenth century, the site was fortified with a substantial bank, continued into the water in the form of a palisade. Excavations in 1897, 1930-39 and 1959-80 uncovered 5% of the 24ha area within the rampart. More recently, by means of geophysical prospecting and the use of metal-detectors, further streets with a high building density have been revealed across the entire site.

The numerous finds shed light on the lives of the town's consumers and producers, with hundreds of thousands of animal bones and plant remains enabling the living conditions to be reconstructed (Box 6.1). Quernstones and ceramics from the Rhineland, soapstone and slate whetstones from Norway, drinking-glasses and weapons from the Carolingian Empire, as well as luxury goods from the Orient, tell of the trading activity (see Chapter 10). Refuse from craft production includes 340,000 pieces from comb-making, evidence for leather-working and

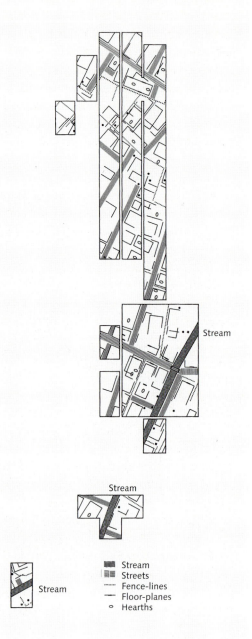

Stream

Stream

Stream

■ Stream
▤ Streets
⋯ Fence-lines
— Floor-planes
○ Hearths

Fig 1

Plan of Hedeby in the 9th century, with stream, main and secondary streets, fence-lines and floor-planes, including hearths (after Schietzel 1981).

textile production, as well as iron-working and goldsmithing, including finds of mercury from fire-gilding.

The many cemeteries surrounding the town, and the burial customs associated with them, reflect the presence of Saxon, Danish and Slavic residents, as well as travelling traders; the population in the ninth/tenth century exceeded 1,000.

Sources: Schietzel 1981; Jankuhn 1986; Elsner 1994; *Berichte über die Ausgrabungen in Haithabu* 1-35 (1969-2006)*; 'Haiðaby', in Reallexikon der Germanischen Altertumskunde* 13 (1999), 361-87.

By Heiko Steuer

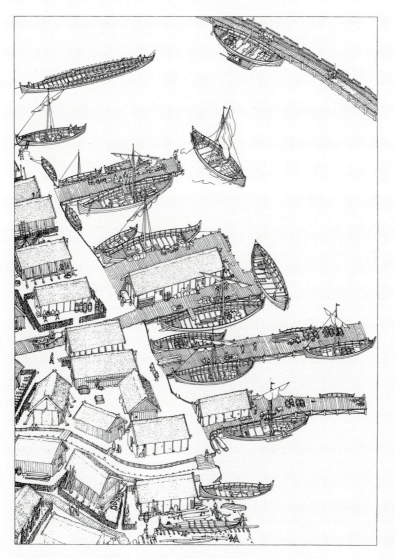

Fig 2

Reconstruction of the river-bank area of Hedeby, from the harbour excavations of 1979-80, with jetties, trading vessels and urban houses of the 9th/10th century (after Elsner 1994).

926, of fortifications as protection against the Hungarians; this was intended solely as a system of defence and did not result in the foundation of towns.

Between the Rhine and the Elbe, the development was not usually from castle to town. However, in the Slavic settlement area of eastern Central Europe, it was precisely the castle settlement that, as it was expanded with ever-larger outer works, housing specialized craft production as a so-called service to the rulers, became the core of new urban sites after the High Middle Ages. The origins of this development lie in the ninth century, however, and perhaps even as early as the eighth. Among the places that have been studied are: Kolobrzeg/Kolberg, Wolin/Wollin and Szczecin/Stettin, on the Baltic coast; farther inland, Brandenburg, Berlin-Spandau and Meissen; in Greater Poland, Ostrów Lednicki, Gnesen/Gniezno and Posen/Poznań; in Lesser Poland, Cracow (Piekalski 2001); in Bohemia, Prague; and in Hungary, Zalavar. These early urban settlements in Poland, or the eastern part of the German Empire, were re-structured beginning in the second half of the twelfth century, when the Lübeck model of urban law was adopted in the north, along the Baltic coast from Kiel to Elbing, Reval and Memel, and the Magdeburg model was adopted in the interior. The smaller urban sites founded during the land expansion east of the Elbe and the Saale extending to the Oder, or founded by *Lokatoren* (entrepreneurs), often adopted these western urban laws as well.

In Great Moravia during the ninth century, outer works were arranged around a core-castle forming the seat of the nobility, in which stood not only their own churches (with the richly furnished graves of the elite), but also workshop areas. Among these 'central-places' were Mikulčice (Fig 4.9) and Staré Město in Moravia, and Stará Kourim in Bohemia.

(8) During the Ottonian period, new towns were formed through the fusion of several separate centres, such as churches, a bishop's seat, a port or traders' settlement and a market-place. It was in this manner that Hildesheim, for example, came into being (Herzog 1964). Cologne also had polycentric roots, growing out of the combination of the new extra-mural traders' tenements, between the Roman wall and the Rhine, with the settlement-cores near the various martyrs' churches, located on former Roman cemeteries along the town's through-roads. Such multifunctional, polycentric settlement agglomerations, with their proto-urban characteristics, grew continuously until they reached the status of a town.

(9) Several market-places developed or, from the middle of the eighth century, were founded by the king or nobility as a meeting place for local and long-distance traders and for the producers of agricultural goods in the surrounding area. This development was triggered by the Merovingian kings' coinage reforms. In the area between the Rhine and the Loire, there is evidence for 200 such markets in the ninth century. After some 120 years the number of fairs had risen so steeply that Charles the Bald, in 864 in the *Edictum Pistense* (MGH Capit II no 273, pp 310f), ordered his counts to make a list of them and to determine when and by whom their market-

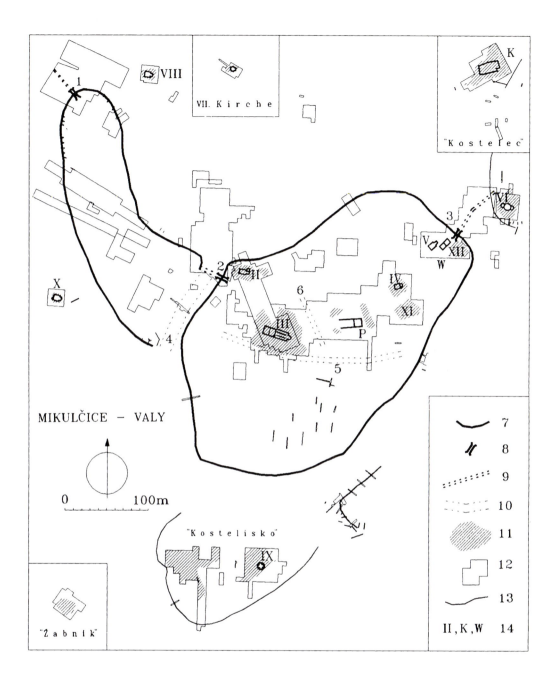

Mikulčice (Great Moravian castle-town). Areas investigated and significant discoveries: (1) north-west gate of the outer work; (2) west gate of the main castle; (3) north-east gate of the main castle; (4) ditch between the main castle and outer work; (5) ditch south of church no III; (6) ditch between church no III and the 'palace' (P); (7) defensive wall of the main castle and outer work; (8) gates; (9) bridges; (10) ditches; (11) cemeteries; (12) excavated areas; (13) well-defined ridges; (14) churches numbered II-XII, with (K) religious building on the meadow 'Kostelec', and (W) jewellery workshop beside church no V (after Poláček 2002).

Fig 4.9

rights had been granted. In Westphalia, market foundation and urban development can be illustrated by the example of Corvey, which had obtained coinage rights as early as 833 because there was no convenient market. In south-west Germany, Ulm, Villingen and Esslingen on the Neckar, for example, had markets before 1000, as well as early urban structures, including clusters of SFBs. Freiburg im Breisgau developed from a market to a town on the Upper Rhine with the grant of market-rights in 1120. Markets and market-rights repeatedly provided the starting-point for urban development from the Carolingian period until the twelfth/thirteenth century. In the Baltic area, only a few of the many emporia of which we have evidence later became towns.

(10) In areas where there were significant deposits of raw materials, industrial urban sites were formed by the establishment of production facilities. Pottery production sites, e.g. Siegburg near Cologne, only rarely became urban sites. Other pottery centres, connected to the high-quality clay deposits in the 'Vorgebirge', the hills west of the Rhine near Cologne (Badorf and Pingsdorf; see pp 225-7), did not develop into urban sites because the craft production there was organized indirectly by the urban manorial lords in Cologne who owned farms in the villages. It was also the case that a good many potters produced their wares in the towns themselves. Salt deposits constituted the basis for the urban development of Bad Nauheim, in the Taunus region (with, in this case, occupation having begun as early as the La Tène period; see p 232), for Soest in Westphalia, from the seventh/eighth century, and for Halle an der Saale (which also had prehistoric origins). Mines in the vicinity of mineral deposits, especially silver for minting coins, were the nucleus from which grew mining towns in the Black Forest and in the Vosges, Harz and Erz mountains (Erzgebirge). The Rammelsberg copper deposits in the Harz led to the establishment both of a royal palace and of the town of Goslar.

Population Estimates

None of the existing population estimates for early urban sites are satisfactory. For the trading-place of Hedeby, the population in the tenth century has been estimated at 1,000-2,000 permanent residents, based on its occupation density and the size of its cemeteries. For Dorestad, in the 'north quarter' alone (which was 1km long and 150-200m wide, with 300-400 plots containing one or two houses each), the estimate varies from 1,200-4,000 residents. But it is a question of scale. Between Rome and Trier, Hedeby and Birka, there are qualitative differences that result in quantitative differences. The farther south the location, the higher the population will have remained even after the Late Antique period, if only because urban life was more of a tradition in the Mediterranean (cf. Rome, see Box 4.2; Santangeli Valenzani 2000).

The surface area of early urban sites varied considerably, according to their type and origins: the early site of Soest was only 4.5ha (150x250m), while a settlement like

Hedeby, inside its tenth-century rampart, was significantly larger, at 24 hectares. All early emporia, like Dorestad (far exceeding 100ha of occupied space, of which 30ha have been excavated), and the border trading-places along the Elbe, named in the *Diedenhofen Capitulary* from the ninth century (Bardowick, Magdeburg, Erfurt, Hallstadt, Forchheim, Regensburg, *Lauriacum*/Lorsch and Enns) (Hübener 1989), were of huge size, being 30-90ha in extent, which is several times that of many later urban settlements. The Saxon bishop's castles, or cathedral-castles, of the ninth to tenth centuries measured on average 100-200 by 200-300m, or 2-6ha (Hammaburg/Hamburg, Bardowick, Bremen, Verden, Minden, Paderborn, Osnabrück, Münster, Hildesheim, Halberstadt and Merseburg; Wilschewski 2000); however, the extent of some bishop's castles in the empire was as much as 10ha (Constance, Bamberg, Passau and Basle). The sites of Great Moravia were also remarkably extensive: the main castle of Mikulčice, at 7.7ha, was surrounded by many extra-mural structures with a total of 40ha (Fig 4.9), with Staré Město having an area of 250 hectares. The tenth-century Ottonian palaces likewise had only a small core castle (of 0.5-2ha), but were connected to extra-mural settlements, some of which measured more than 20ha (Tilleda and Werla). The valley settlement at the base of the Karlburg was over 1km long with a width of c200m, giving it a size of 20 hectares. Almost all of the exceptionally large commercial sites were discontinued and thus abandoned before they developed into towns.

Several important urban settlements were already of considerable size in the tenth and early eleventh centuries: Cologne had an area of about 90ha during the Roman period, its measurements, within the enclosing wall of 1106, were 200ha, and within the outer wall of 1180, it even reached 400ha; Mainz had an area of 100ha; Würzburg 42ha; Speyer 60ha; Worms 40ha; Regensburg 25+30ha; Strasbourg 19ha (and later in the eleventh century, 55ha); and Augsburg 15ha. Trier was only 9-10ha in the cathedral-castle, although its ancient walls encompassed 280 hectares (Hirschmann 1998; 2005).

Patterns of Public and Private Space

The early medieval proto-urban and early urban sites were planned, roads were laid out and constructed and the plot structure was surveyed and marked out (Steuer 1988; 1995). This state remained as it was for several generations, thus in Hedeby from the early ninth to the late tenth century (Schietzel 1981; Elsner 1994; see Box 4.3), and also in Dorestad (Es & Verwers 1980; Es 1990), where the piers reaching into the Rhine (Fig 4.2), with their associated stores and dwellings, remained the same for generations until it was abandoned (p 112). A comparable plot size to that in Dorestad has been found in the trading settlement from the Merovingian period at Cologne, on the banks of the Rhine, which has pit-house complexes at regular intervals that most likely included longhouses. It was only in the eleventh/twelfth century that a new plot layout was surveyed, as recorded in the so-called *Schreinsbücher*; this plan has remained in existence until today. Such permanent plots have been demonstrated by archaeological research from Freiburg to Braunschweig, Osnabrück, Hamburg and Schleswig; they are often connected with the introduction of a new type of urban dwelling (Steuer & Biegel 2002).

Urban settlements regularly went through phases of growth that, in the High Middle Ages, were protected by new rings of fortification. The sequence of these walls has been demonstrated archaeologically for towns with Roman roots (Cologne, Strasbourg and Regensburg), but also for Braunschweig, Freiburg and Basle, which were enclosed from about 1100 (Isenberg & Scholkmann 1997; Porsche 2000).

For every urban settlement, the system of roads leading to and through it, as well as the streets within the town itself, had to be built and maintained, otherwise there could be no inter-regional trading operations. Excavations have revealed superimposed layers of roads made of timber or paving stone that have been renovated several times.

Urban sites on major rivers, lakes or the coast required harbour facilities (i.e. jetties, quays or wharfs) for docking, loading and unloading ships. Such are known in considerable numbers as far back as the seventh and eighth centuries from archaeological excavation. In the commercial centre of Hedeby there were several jetties dating from about 800 that were in use until the eleventh century (see Box 4.3), as also in its successor town of Schleswig, starting in the late eleventh century (Fig 9.8). Wooden jetties, combined with stones, were constructed in the tenth century at Birka in Sweden. Bank revetments and quay structures of wood have been identified on the Rhine in Mainz, and on Lake Constance in Constance, as well as in Venice as far back as the Merovingian period.

The urban water-supply was organized in the public arena. Wells were available on the plots of land, with running water being channelled through the town in a complex system of streams to provide water for craftsmen's workshops and waste disposal. Stream systems supplying the entire urban area have been established for twelfth-century Freiburg, as well as in neighbouring towns like Staufen, as also in Lower Saxony (e.g. Goslar). Urban settlements situated on rivers possessed water-mills (pp 214-17) to grind grain, for tanning and cloth-fulling, and to drive forges and stamping-mills (Fig 4.4). Before public mills were introduced, each household needed quernstones to grind grain for bread; these were traded, notably the basalt from Mayen, in the Eifel, found in the territories on the North Sea and the Baltic (see Box 10.2).

It seems that market-places were usually located on the periphery of early urban settlements; they were not generally provided for in the original building plan but were, as a rule, set up later within the town itself (e.g. after fire destruction). In almost all urban settlements, from Schleswig in the north, to Cologne, Osnabrück and Braunschweig, and as far south as Freiburg, as well as in the newly-established urban sites in the East, excavations have revealed that below seemingly early market-places there are older structures from the first stages of settlement. It was in the twelfth century when private land within urban sites started being systematically transferred to public ownership that buildings were torn down to create the new market-places that had become essential for trading. Excavation has demonstrated that the 'old markets' in Magdeburg, Braunschweig and Cologne are all secondary markets, with earlier dwellings beneath them. The surveying of space for traders' stands has been demonstrated for the market-squares of Lübeck, Duisburg and Cologne.

In many places, urban development during the late twelfth century required extensive works involving the movement of massive amounts of earth. Lübeck enlarged its settlement area to the west and east by reclaiming land from the river-plains. Braunschweig, which was founded as an urban settlement c1065 and enclosed with a rampart and ditch in c1100, almost doubled in size during the second half of the twelfth century, by infilling the river-plain of the Oker. In Constance, towards the end of the twelfth century, the bank of Lake Constance was built out to create space for new buildings and a market.

Churches, with their graveyards, as also fortifications, were structures that existed for the benefit of the community as a whole; later, in the High Middle Ages, an assembly hall or town-hall was required and public fountains and bake-houses (in addition to mills) were constructed for communal use. In building cathedrals, monasteries and convents, the Church made use of the economic advantages of early urban sites. To protect a town, the urban lord erected a castle inside the settlement, usually to one side or at a corner. Archaeological evidence for this practice is, however, confined to the late eleventh and twelfth centuries. The organization of towns into parishes began in the tenth/eleventh century.

The construction of stone bridges over rivers began late in this period, the first being in 1133 at Würzburg, although older Roman bridges may still have been intact, as in Trier and Verdun; by contrast, in Cologne, the Roman bridge supports had been torn down by the archbishop, in the tenth century, with royal permission.

Fortifications for the defence of early urban sites were constructed at all stages of their development. The bishop's castles in the Saxon missionary area were surrounded by ramparts and ditches in the ninth century. Many early urban sites, throughout the area from Cologne to Hedeby (and beyond), were fortified in the tenth century. Stone walls were erected c1100 in Basle and, somewhat later, in Freiburg. The stone wall did not, however, become the norm until 1200, even in the most affluent settlements (Porsche 2000). In this connection, private plots had to become public property, as is evident from walls and sentry-paths constructed over demolished houses (e.g. in Basle and Freiburg). Indeed, it is evident from differently constructed sections that individual noblemen or urban patrician families were each responsible for building part of the fortification. The transfer of urban wall-building rights to the jurisdiction of the town is documented, in writing, for Cologne in 1106; in Basle, it has been demonstrated archaeologically for the period c1100.

As noted above, some palaces like Ingelheim were apparently not fortified, whereas the border castles on the Büraburg and the *Pfalz* Paderborn were defended by ramparts, walls and ditches. Magdeburg already had three or more concentric defensive ditches in the Carolingian period. At the turn of the twelfth century, many urban settlements were major construction-sites, due to the expansion of cathedrals and the increase in infrastructure facilities, such as the often enlarged rings of defences.

The private sphere in every urban settlement included individual construction on the merchants' and craftsmen's plots. These dwellings, stores and cellars were ones that reflected an urban life-style. Urban buildings north of the Alps were customarily constructed of wood and clay, in the timber-frame technique. These wooden houses are considerably smaller than rural constructions, as shown by such examples at Hedeby in the ninth century (Fig 5.2) or in Schleswig and Lübeck (Fig 4.10) in the eleventh/

Fig 4.10 *Lübeck: reconstruction of a timber house, with cellar and several storeys, from the last quarter of the 12th century (after Legant-Kalau 1994); see also Fig 5.7.*

twelfth century, Basle in the tenth, and Zurich in the twelfth century. Beginning c1100, in the south, cellars were renovated in stone and ground-level rooms raised with stone walls, while in the north wooden construction remained predominant, until the brick was introduced as a building material in the twelfth to thirteenth centuries (see pp 230-2). However, the dating remains unclear as to when the use of stone for domestic building became prevalent in the southern regions of Central Europe. The idealised reconstruction of a town (Fig 4.6), incorporating evidence from Basle and Zurich, shows not only craftsmen's wooden houses, but also some multi-storey stone buildings belonging to the wealthier urban residents, in the period c1100, although these probably only became prevalent c1200.

Stone construction was well known by this time, however, as cathedrals and ordinary churches had long been built in this material. It was the development of the basement or ground-level sections of houses in stone, or stone construction extending for several storeys – as high as a tower-house – that was innovative at the onset of the High Middle Ages. Thus, in Regensburg, Basle and Zurich, the urban elite lived like their counterparts in Italy, in multi-storey stone towers, although here they were only erected from the thirteenth century. This custom of building castle-like stone towers inside urban walls was initiated by urban patricians, wealthy merchant families and officials of the landed nobility in the twelfth century. These new developments resulted in the simple timber-framed house becoming a multi-structure building complex, with varied types of stone work, so only c1200 did there appear continuous, closed-off, facades facing the street.

In Cologne, Mainz and Regensburg, new settlements for long-distance traders developed, from the seventh to tenth centuries, between the Roman walls and the river. Further new settlement-foci sprung up next to the martyrs' churches in a wide ring around the old Roman settlement, in the Roman road-side cemeteries. Only later were the spaces between settlements filled in, when these isolated settlement-cores grew together to form an urban site, in a similar manner to that in which towns developed east of the Rhine: from several churches, a centre of authority (such as a bishop's castle), and the commercial streets that had evolved to connect them. In their ground-plan, such polycentric settlements are comparable to the early, multi-partite, urban settlements of Great Moravia, or to the later towns east of the Elbe in the settlement area of the Slavs, consisting of a castle with attached tenements for craftsmen.

Towns as 'Central-Places'

'Central-places', as precursors to early urban settlements, existed in the post-Roman period, well before the eighth century, and have been excavated, in particular, in the Baltic area and Denmark. These places are evidence of a hierarchically organized society in which the elite held their position not least because of their control of long-distance trade (besides their military and religious leadership roles), giving them a monopoly in the redistribution of valuable and rare imported goods.

During the Vendel period, 'central-places' of the Gudme or Helgö type had developed in the Baltic area, complemented by many 'ports-of-trade' along the coasts, where long-distance traders could land and spend the night. Some of these ports existed continuously until the Viking period. New coastal trading-places were constantly springing up, but not all of these continued to exist into the Middle Ages, although some of them did become proto-urban settlements, like Hedeby or Birka and Lund. In turn, some of these were abandoned or simply shifted, whereas others became towns that still exist today. The internal dynamics and the causes of the rise and fall of 'central-places' cannot always be explained; however, the increasingly detailed nature of the archaeological evidence becoming available permits a description of the process as a whole.

Those who held political power controlled religion, manufacturing and trade, meaning that authority was created by developing and extending such monopolies. The proto-urban site was a place with several central functions, not all of which are visible in the archaeological record; it was a political and religious (or church) centre, the site of regular market-activity and, as of the tenth century, it often had coinage rights. The grant of privileges like market, coinage and customs rights can only be known from documentary sources, although urban minting is evident from coin-finds, both from the Merovingian and Carolingian periods, and from the tenth century onwards (Fig 10.5).

The urban site did not exist independently of its surroundings. It was, in the first place, the top of a hierarchical settlement structure, resting on the settlements of its rural hinterland; it regulated the relationships between centre and periphery in a territory that was geographically delimited, or connected by a road-system. The connection of the 'central-place' with its rural surroundings has been established through archaeological research at Hedeby, Ribe and Birka, where not only the early urban site itself, but also its surrounding rural settlements have been excavated. Long-distance trade-goods spread out from the 'central-place' into these rural settlements, which in turn provided the centre not only with agricultural products but also with other goods, such as textiles.

An individual town is but a link in a network of urban sites; that is, a town is only conceivable in terms of its relations and its relationship to other towns, which in turn are also hierarchically organised with regard to their economic and political functions, and more generally their function as 'central-places'. In the German Empire, the king needed a wide network of palaces, many of which became towns in due course. The Church developed a close network of *civitates* in the missionary territories (the bishop's castles), almost all of which became urban sites. Along the coasts, trading-places sprung up at regular distances that corresponded to a day's journey, as well as along the major inland routes, which together formed a network of stopping-points along the way. The large ecclesiastical properties (monasteries and convents), in urban sites, sometimes had hundreds of often quite distant farms at their disposal during the eleventh and twelfth centuries, some even located in other proto-urban settlements. In a sense, such networks formed 'virtual' towns, bringing together a greater population engaged in various production trades and in local and long-distance trading; i.e. a convent in Cologne might possess farms in another market-place such as Dorestad, in order to secure its involvement in overseas trade, in a pottery producing settlement beside the Rhine, to obtain goods for trading, and in a rural settlement in the Wetterau region, to obtain wine and other agricultural products.

Conclusions

Every urban settlement of the medieval period had its individual characteristics and an independent history of development, resulting from the particular decisions of its residents and those in power at the time. And yet local history was always mixed with more widespread and systematic developments that all urban settlements received in parallel and engaged with at the same time. It was the mobile merchants who played the decisive role in carrying information and disseminating new ideas. Street lay-outs and plots were similar in size on urban sites in both the Lower and the Upper Rhine, new walls were built everywhere starting c1100, market-places in urban sites were universally established from 1200 onwards, urban rights were formulated and citizens began revolting against urban lords in the late eleventh century, as in Cologne in 1074.

The decline of urban settlements and their reduction in size during Late Antiquity was not caused by the raids of Germanic tribes; similarly, the attacks and threats on urban settlements during the Viking period, from the end of the eighth up to the tenth century, were not factors that led to their abandonment. Towns were always rebuilt after destruction in warfare; abandonment was the result of economic and political changes. They were either moved to a different site or other towns took over their functions.

On the one hand, the concentration of royal power in select towns and, on the other, the need to have networks of urban sites a day's travel apart, were opposing tendencies, which in the end led their citizens, merchants and craftsmen to strive for independence. The wave of town-foundation beginning in the twelfth century has been described above, as also how towns already in existence were then renovated to such an extent that this was often equivalent to a new foundation. It was not therefore until c1200 that there had come into existence what we now think of as the typical picture of a medieval European landscape densely covered with urban settlements, governed by autonomous citizens under town laws.

BIBLIOGRAPHY

Astill, GG (2000) 'General survey 600-1300', in Palliser, DM (ed), *The Cambridge Urban History of Britain, 1: 600-1540,* Cambridge, 27-49

Biddle, M (ed) (1976a) *Winchester in the Early Middle Ages: an Edition and Discussion of the Winton Domesday,* Winchester Studies 1, Oxford

Biddle, M (1976b) 'Towns', in Wilson, DM (ed), *The Archaeology of Anglo-Saxon England,* Cambridge, 99-150

Brachmann, H (ed) (1991) *Burg – Burgstadt – Stadt. Zur Genese mittelalterlicher nichtagrarischer Zentren in Ostmitteleuropa,* Berlin

Brachmann, H and Herrmann, J (eds) (1991) *Frühgeschichte der europäischen Stadt. Voraussetzungen und Grundlagen,* Berlin

Brather, S (2003) 'Parchim', in *Reallexikon der Germanischen Altertumskunde 22*

Brisbane, M (1988) 'Hamwic (Saxon Southampton): an eighth-century port and production centre' in Hodges, R and Hobley, B (eds), *The Rebirth of Towns in the West AD 700-1050,* Council for British Archaeology Research Report 68, London, 61-8

Brogiolo, GP and Ward-Perkins, B (eds) (1999) *The Idea and Ideal of the Town between Late Antiquity and the Early Middle Ages,* The Transformation of the Roman World 4, Leiden/Boston/Cologne

Brogiolo, GP, Gauthier, N and Christie, N (eds) (2000) *Towns and their Territories between Late Antiquity and the Early Middle Ages,* The Transformation of the Roman World 9, Leiden/Boston/Cologne

Callmer, J (1994) 'Urbanization in Scandinavia and the Baltic Region c.AD 700-1100: trading places, centres and early urban sites', in Ambrosiani, B and Clarke, H (eds), *Birka Studies* 3, Stockholm, 50-90

Chédeville, A (1980) 'De la cité à la ville', in Le Goff, J (ed), *Histoire de la France urbaine, 2: des Carolingiens à la Renaissance,* Paris, 31-181

Clarke, H and Ambrosiani, B (1991) *Towns in the Viking Age,* Leicester/London

Clarke, HB and Simms, A (eds) (1985) *The Comparative History of Urban Origins in Non-Roman Europe,* British Archaeological Reports, International Series 255 (2 vols), Oxford

Clemens, L (ed) (2003) *Tempore Romanorum constructa. Zur Nutzung und Wahrnehmung antiker Überreste nördlich der Alpen während des Mittelalters,* Stuttgart

Cressier, P and García-Arenal, M (eds) (1998) *Genèse de la ville islamique en al-Andalus et au Maghreb occidentale,* Madrid

Demolon, P & Louis, E (1994) 'Naissance d'une cité médiévale flamande: l'exemple de Douai', in Demolon, P, Galinié, H and Verhaeghe, F (eds), *Archéologie des villes dans le Nord-Ouest de l'Europe (VIIe - XIIIe siècle),* Douai, 47-58

Donat, P (1999) *Gebesee – Klosterhof und königliche Reisestation des 10.-12. Jahrhunderts,* Weimarer Monographien zur Ur- und Frühgeschichte 34, Stuttgart

Duby, G (1974) *The Early Growth of the European Economy* (trans HB Clarke), New York

Eck, W and Galsterer, H (eds) (1991) *Die Stadt in Oberitalien und in den nordwestlichen Provinzen des Römischen Reiches*, Mainz am Rhein

Elsner, H (1994) *Wikingermuseum Haithabu: Schaufenster einer frühen Stadt*, Neumünster

Ennen, E (1972; 1987, 4th ed) *Die europäische Stadt des Mittelalters*, Göttingen

Es, WA van (1990) 'Dorestad centred', in Besteman, JC, Bos, JM and Heidinga, HA (eds), *Medieval Archaeology in the Netherlands. Studies presented to HH van Rgeteren Altena*, Assen/Maastricht, 151-82

Es, WA van and Verwers, WJH (1980) *Excavations at Dorestad 1, the Harbour: Hoogstraat I*, Nederlandse Oudheden 9, Amersfoort

Fehring, GP (1996) *Stadtarchäologie in Deutschland*, Archäologie in Deutschland Sonderheft 1996, Stuttgart, 23-31

Gerevich, L (1990) *Towns in Medieval Hungary*, Budapest

Hall, RA (1994) *Viking Age York*, London

Hall, RA (2004) *Aspects of Anglo-Scandinavian York*, Archaeology of York 8/4, York

Herteig, A (ed) (1985) *Conference on Waterfront Archaeology in North European Towns No. 2, Bergen 1983*, Bergen

Herzog, E (1964) *Die ottonische Stadt. Die Anfänge der mittelalterlichen Stadtbaukunst in Deutschland*, Berlin

Hill, D and Cowie, R (eds) (2001) *Wics: the Early Mediaeval Trading Centres of Northern Europe*, Sheffield

Hirschmann, FG (1998) *Stadtplanung, Bauprojekte und Großbaustellen im 10. und 11. Jahrhunderts. Vergleichende Studien zu den Kathedralstädten westlich des Rheins*, Stuttgart

Hirschmann, FG (2005) *Die Bischofssitze im Reich und ihre Urbanisierung bis ins 12. Jahrhundert*, Stuttgart

Hodges, R and Hobley, B (eds) (1988) *The Rebirth of Towns in the West, AD700-1050*, Council for British Archaeology Research Report 68, Oxford

Hübener, W (1989) *Die Orte des Diedenhofer Capitulars von 805 in archäologischer Sicht*, Jahresschrift für mitteldeutsche Vorgeschichte 72, Halle, 251-66

Hurley, MF, Scully, OMB and McCutcheon, SWJ (eds) (1997) *Late Viking Age and Medieval Waterford*, Waterford

Isenberg, G and Scholkmann, B (eds) (1997) *Die Befestigung der mittelalterlichen Stadt*, Städteforschung A 45, Cologne/Weimar/Vienna

Jankuhn, H (1986, 8th ed) *Haithabu. Ein Handelsplatz der Wikingerzeit*, Neumünster

Jankuhn, H, Schlesinger, W and Steuer, H (eds) (1975) *Vor- und Frühformen der europäischen Stadt im Mittelalter*, Göttingen

Jarnut, J and Johanek, P (eds) (1998) *Die Frügeschichte der europäischen Stadt im 11. Jahrhundert*, Städteforschung A 43, Cologne/Weimar/Vienna

Johanek, P and Post, F-J (eds) (2004) *Vielerlei Städte. Der Stadtbegriff*, Städteforschung A 61, Cologne/Weimar/Vienna

Jørgensen, L (2003) 'Manor and market at Lake Tissø in the sixth to eleventh centuries: the Danish "productive" sites', in Pestell, T and Ulmschneider, K (eds), *Markets in Early Medieval Europe: Trading and 'Productive' Sites, 650-850*, Macclesfield, 175-207

Keene, D (2000) 'London from the post-Roman period to 1300', in Palliser, DM (ed), *The Cambridge Urban History of Britain, I: 600-1540*, Cambridge, 187-216

Larsson, L and Hårdh, B (eds) (1998) *Centrala Platser – Centrala Frågor. Samhällsstrukturer under Järnalderen. En Vänbok till Berta Stjernquist*, Uppåkrastudier 1, Stockholm

Legant-Kalau, G (1994) 'Mittelalterlicher Holzbau in Lübeck an der Schwelle vom ländlichen zum städtischen Siedlungsgefüge', *Archäologisches Korrespondenzblatt* 24, 333-45

Le Maho, J (1995) 'Rouen à l'époque des incursions vikings (841-911)', *Bulletin de la Commission des Antiquités de la Seine Maritime* 42 (1994), 143-202

Liebeschütz, JHWG (2001) *The Decline and Fall of the Roman City*, Oxford

Malcolm, G and Bowsher, D with Cowie, R (2003) *Middle Saxon London: Excavations at the Royal Opera House 1989-99*, MOLAS Mono 15, London

Mann, VB, Glick, TF and Dodds, JD (eds) (1992) *Convivencia: Jews, Muslims and Christians in Medieval Spain*, New York

Mazzoli-Guintard, Ch (1996) *Villes d'al-Andalus. L'Espagne et le Portugal à l'époque musulmane (VIII-XV siècles)*, Rennes

McKitterick, R (1983) *The Frankish Kingdoms under the Carolingians, 751-98*, London

Morton, A (1992) *Excavations at Hamwic: Volume 1*, Council for British Archaeology Research Report 84, London

Mühle, E (1991) *Die städtischen Handelszentren der nordwestlichen Ruś. Anfänge und frühe Entwicklung altrussischer Städte (bis gegen Ende des 12. Jahrhunderts)*, Stuttgart

Müller-Wille, M (2004) 'Zwischen Gudme und Reric. Frühgeschichtliche Zentralplätze Südskandinaviens und benachbarter Gebiete', *Bodendenkmalpflege in Mecklenburg-Vorpommern Jahrbuch* 51 (2003), 267-94

Nicholas, D (1997) *The Growth of the Medieval City: from Late Antiquity to the Early Fourteenth Century*, London

Nicholas, D (2003) *Urban Europe, 1100-1700*, Houndsmills

Patronato de la Alhambra y. Generalife (1990) *La Casa Hispano-Musulmana*. Aportaciones de la Arqueología, Granada

Piekalski, J (2001) *Von Köln nach Krakau. Der topographische Wandel früher Städte*, Zeitschrift für Archäologie des Mittelalters 13, Bonn

Poláček, L (2002) 'Mikulčice', in *Reallexikon der Germanischen Altertumskunde* 14

Porsche, M (2000) *Stadtmauer und Stadtentstehung im mittelalterlichen deutschen Reich*, Freiburg

Reallexikon der Germanischen Altertumskunde, 'A-Z' , vols 1-35 (1973-2007): see 'Handel', 'Handelsplätze', 'Ports of Trade', 'Reichtumszentrum', 'Seehandelsplatz', 'Stadt' and 'Zentralorte', Berlin/New York

Reilly, BF (1993) *The Medieval Spains*, Cambridge

Rippmann, D and Tauber, J (eds) (1991) *Eine Stadt um 1100. Spurensuche und Einladung zur Stadtbesichtigung*, Sigmaringen

Robertson, AJ (ed) (1925) *The Laws of the Kings of England from Edmund to Henry I*, Cambridge

Santangeli Valenzani, R (2000) 'Residential building in early medieval Rome', in Smith, JMH (ed), *Early Medieval Rome and the Christian West: Essays in Honour of Donald A Bullough*, Leiden/Boston/Cologne, 101-12

Schietzel, K (1981) 'Stand der siedlungsarchäologischen Forschung in Haithabu. Ergebnisse und Probleme', *Berichte über die Ausgrabungen in Haithabu* 16, Neumünster

Schofield, J, Dyson, T and Blackmore, L (in preparation) *London Waterfront Tenements 1100–1750: I*

Skre, D (ed) (2007) *Kaupang in Skiringssal*, Kaupang Publication Series 1, Norsk Oldfunn 22, Aarhus

Steedman, K, Dyson, T, and Schofield, J (1992) *Aspects of Saxo-Norman London, III: the Bridgehead and Billingsgate to 1200*, London & Middlesex Archaeological Society Special Paper 14, London

Steuer, H (1988) 'Urban archaeology in Germany and the study of topographic, functional and social structures', in Denecke, H and Shaw, G (eds), *Urban Historical Geography: Recent Progress in Britain and Germany*, Cambridge, 81-92, 356-63

Steuer, H (1990) 'Die Handelsstätten des frühen Mittelalters im Nord- und Ostseeraum', in *La genèse et les premiers siècles des villes médiévales dans les Pays-Bas meridionaux. Un problème arch. et hist. 14e Colloque International, Spa*, Brussels, 75-116

Steuer, H (1995) 'Freiburg und das Bild der Städte um 1100 im Spiegel der Archäologie', in Schadek, H and Zotz, Th (eds), *Freiburg 1091-1120. Neue Forschungen zu den Anfängen der Stadt. Archäologie und Geschichte*, Freiburger Forschungen zum ersten Jahrtausend in Südwestdeutschland 7, Sigmaringen, 79-123

Steuer, H (2001) 'Das Leben in Sachsen zur Zeit der Ottonen', in Puhle, M (ed), *Otto der Große. Magdeburg und Europa. Bd. I Essays*, Mainz, 89-107

Steuer, H (2003) 'The beginnings of urban economies among the Saxons', in Green, DH and Siegmund, F (eds) *The Continental Saxons from Migration Period to the Tenth Century: an Ethnographic Perspective*, Woodbridge, 159-81

Steuer, H and Biegel, G (eds) (2002) *Stadtarchäologie in Norddeutschland westlich der Elbe*, Zeitschrift für Archäologie des Mittelalters Beiheft 14, Bonn

Stoob, H (1979) 'Die hochmittelalterliche Städtebildung im Okzident', in Stoob, H (1979), *Die Stadt. Gestalt und Wandel bis zum industriellen Zeitalter*, Cologne/Vienna, 131-56

Thomas, A (1992) *The Walled Towns of Ireland*, 2 vols, Dublin

Tummuscheit, A (2003) 'Groß Strömkendorf: a market site of the eighth century on the Baltic sea coast', in Pestell, T and Ulmschneider, K (eds), *Markets in Early Medieval Europe: Trading and 'Productive' Sites, 650-850*, Macclesfield, 208-220

Valor, M and Tahiri, A (eds) (1999) *Sevilla Almohade*, Madrid (with English translation)

Ventura, JM (2005) *An Illustrated History of Cordoba*, Cordoba

Verhulst, A (1999) *The Rise of Cities in North-West Europe*, Cambridge

Vince, A (ed) (1991) *Aspects of Saxo-Norman London: 2, Finds and Environmental Evidence*, London

Wallace, PF (1992) *The Viking Age Buildings of Dublin*, Dublin

White, W (1988) *The Cemetery of St Nicholas Shambles*, LAMAS Special Paper 9, London

Wilschewski, F (2000) 'Die karolingischen Domburgen in Nordwestdeutschland und die ältesten dänischen Bischofsitze. Eine vergleichende Darstellung', *Offa* 56 (1999), 481-93

Witschel, Chr (2004) 'Rom und die Städte Italiens in Spätantike und Frühmittelalter', *Bonner Jahrbücher* 201 (2001), 113-62

CHAPTER 5

HOUSING CULTURE

Else Roesdahl and Barbara Scholkmann

Introduction

A sheltered space, 'a roof over one's head', is a basic necessity of human life in Europe. This led to the emergence and development of houses – buildings for living in. Different concepts of housing developed in order to meet the basic needs, such as shelter from the climatic and seasonal conditions, for the preparation of food and other housebound work, for separate zones reserved for rest or communication within the household, and for some degree of safety. The efforts made to improve housing conditions resulted in the formation of specific housing cultures for specific social and economic groups, such as peasants, craftsmen and tradesmen, monks and aristocrats. As a result, very different solutions were developed for the spatial organization of daily life, for heating systems and other technology, for the use of furniture and other facilities for the sake of comfort, and so on. Housing culture, then, depended on practical as well as socio-economic and cultural aspects. During all periods it has covered the whole range between basic necessities and extravagant comforts (Pounds 1989, 95-6).

The natural environment was of crucial importance, especially the varied climatic conditions – which in Europe stretch from the Arctic to the Mediterranean, from coastal to continental climate and from lowland to high altitudes – as well as the availability of building materials. In some regions there continued to be abundant timber, and in some it became scarce; some regions had good building stone, while others started to produce bricks or re-used brick from deserted Roman buildings (pp 230-2). Regional and ethnic cultural concepts might also be implemented. Also of great importance were the context (rural, urban or religious community), the size of the household and concepts of gender, the state of technology and regional cultural traditions. All these factors were the cause of different architectural and technical solutions.

Right from the beginning of the period under consideration the transmission and transformation of the Roman inheritance was of crucial importance, also for the development of housing culture. This was helped by the economic rise over much of Europe, by the spread of Christian institutions and by rapidly growing networks and communication. The cultural setting was, however, to a large extent determined by the different courses of history during Late Antiquity. Roman housing traditions lingered on in parts of the former Roman Empire (particularly in the Mediterranean zone), where some Roman houses continued to be lived in, while other traditions were effective beyond the imperial frontiers. But by the eighth century houses throughout most of Europe had a rectangular or sub-rectangular ground-plan and they might, according to the social and economic status of the people who lived in them, be divided into rooms which fulfilled different functions. Only on the fringes of Europe, on the Scottish islands, in Ireland and the Isle of Man, for example, people still built round houses in the prehistoric tradition, but this did not last long.

Variety and diversity are, then, major characteristics of housing during the eighth-twelfth centuries (see Box 5.1). There was, however, a growing physical division in the use of house space, and much new technology was adopted. Numerous elements of housing culture can be found in similar form throughout much of Europe, especially from the twelfth century onwards and particularly in monastic, urban and aristocratic contexts (see Vol 2). They reflect the rapidly growing communications within Europe and its development towards a more coherent cultural area.

The Archaeology of Housing Culture

Since the 1980s there has been a growing interest in the archaeological study of standards for, and variations in, the spatial structure of houses, their interior fittings and their inter-relationship with other structures on the plot and in the community (e.g. Wood 1965; Hillier & Hanson 1984; Chapelot & Fossier 1985; Johnson 1993; Grandchamp 1994; Price 1995; Grenville 1997; *Lexikon des Mittelalters* 7-8, 1997-98; Bazzana & Hubert 2000; Klápště 2002; Roesdahl 2003). All this relates to how houses were lived in.

Many demands on a house required architectural solutions, and many domestic activities have left material traces. The main archaeological features of a building to be studied in relation to its function and to the housing culture are the following (although traces of all features are rarely preserved): the size, plan and number of storeys; the occurrence of room divisions, cellars, cooking and heating facilities, other built-in fittings (e.g. benches), access to rooms (doorways and stairs), lighting, arrangements for special functions of rooms (e.g. stables, workshops or shops), the distribution of certain types of artefact (e.g. women's tools, or cooking utensils, or decorative or symbolic artefacts) and of waste and ecofacts. Also important is the relation of the building to other buildings on the plot and their particular function, the relation to neighbouring plots and the street (or road or path), and the general organisation of plots in the area. Waste-disposal and water-supply must also be considered, as well as the surroundings of a house: were there gardens, for example?

Such features might be structured and formed in very different ways, and the study of them is sometimes labelled 'feature analyses'. Many houses would have different activity zones, sometimes in separate rooms and sometimes related to gender, age or status within the household, or to formal gatherings. But the basic requirements would be space for sleeping and eating, cooking and storage, domestic work, some recreation and

BOX 5.1   THE ICELANDIC HOUSE

Iceland was settled in the late ninth and early tenth centuries by people from North-West Europe (Box 2.1). The first generations of settlers established farmsteads, consisting normally of one to five sunken-featured buildings (*Gruben-häuser* or SFBs) and a hall. The halls, typically 15-20m long and 5-6m wide, had curved long-walls, a central hearth and a main entrance towards the end of one long-wall. They were three-aisled, with raised 'benches' and/or sleeping areas on either side of the hearth. Towards the ends of these buildings wooden partitions defined often elaborate entrances and separate spaces for storage, food processing and even iron-working. These houses were built on a timber frame inside 1-1.5m-thick turf walls; it is believed that the roof was also covered with turf, although evidence for this is rarely found (Fig 1).

Unlike South Scandinavian halls, the early Icelandic ones were never attached to byres, which were separate buildings often located at some distance from the hall. The SFBs are generally sub-rectangular, 15-25m² in size, with an oven. They have been interpreted as workshops, although in some cases it is clear that people lived in them.

At one early site, the farm consisted only of SFBs for almost a century; then a small hall was built. In general SFBs seem to belong to the earliest phase of settlement and they are not known after the Viking period. By the late Viking period, houses had become more elaborate, with separate rooms (typically kitchens and pantries) added to the hall. It was only in the thirteenth/fourteenth century that a major change occurred, when the rooms began to be arranged around a central corridor, together with the appearance of a small room at the back with a heat source, which in time became the main living-room.

Sources: Price 1995; Roberts et al 2003; Vésteinsson 2004; Milek 2006.

By Orri Vésteinsson

Fig 1

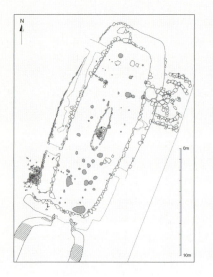

Plan of a 10th-century hall in Aðalstræti, Reykjavík; it is 17m long, with a large central hearth. A few animals were stabled in the northern end, but the actual byre was elsewhere; the porch is later (© Fornleifastofnun Íslands). The digital reconstruction of the Aðalstræti hall shows one possible interpretation of its internal organisation. There is no positive evidence for wattle in Icelandic buildings and its partitions could have been of wood. There was a wooden floor or platform along one side; the floor-layers that had accumulated on the other side indicate that various activities, including food preparation, had taken place there (© Gagarín).

BOX 5.1   THE ANDALUSIAN HOUSE

The house-type in al-Andalus has the same structure as in other Muslim areas during the medieval period. Its elements were conditioned by two factors: climate and religion. Good examples are to be found in Siyasa or Cieza (Murcia), in Bezmiliana (Málaga), and in Saltés (Huelva).

The Muslim house was essentially private, closed off from the outside world, for the protection of the household's women and family honour. The building was constructed from stone, bricks or *tabiya* (earth walls), according to local tradition, and was isolated from the street by walls without openings, other than a single door (Fig 1). This gave access to (1) a small hall (*zaguán*), which opened onto (2) a courtyard (*patio*), but which also further isolated the house from the street. The courtyard was the central element of the house, essential for the admission of light and air. On its north and south sides were (3) the living-rooms, where family and social life took place, with (4) separate alcoves (*alhanías*), so that they could be adapted for use as bedrooms. The main rooms were entered through a portico, creating a transition from the courtyard, which contained a pool, cistern or well, depending on the size of the house; in some cases, evidence for gardens has been found.

The courtyard and living-rooms were the most decorated spaces: their walls were painted with a low border, in colours such as dark red, white and yellow, in geometric or foliate (*ataurique*) patterns. There was a separate kitchen (5), recognisable by its earth floor, with sometimes an oven and an adjacent food-store (6). In urban houses, it is usual to find latrines (7) connected to sewage pipes or cess-pits, placed in the street. Excavated latrines have produced ceramics such as water-jugs and earthenware bowls used for sanitary purposes. Some houses had two floors, the upper storey (*algorfa*) being accessed by means of a staircase from the courtyard.

Sources: Bermúdez & Bazzana 1990; Bazzana & Bedia 2005.

by Pilar Lafuente

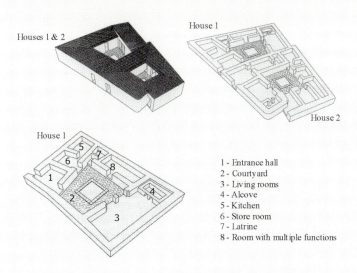

Houses 1 & 2

House 1

House 2

House 1

1 - Entrance hall
2 - Courtyard
3 - Living rooms
4 - Alcove
5 - Kitchen
6 - Store room
7 - Latrine
8 - Room with multiple functions

Fig 1

Saltés, Huelva (Spain). Above: plan and reconstruction of two 12th-century urban houses; although two separate dwellings, the houses are conjoined in a recognisably urban arrangement. Below: the architecture of the houses features the same main elements, although they may be arranged slightly differently (after Bermúdez & Bazzana 1990).

Fig 5.1   *Three houses at Cluny (France), on the south side of the Main Street, near the original market-place. Left: chemist shop with a façade of c1800, fronting a long early 13th-century building. Centre: disused shop with a clairvoie at the top from c1140/60, a replacement window from c1350, and a rebuilt ground floor from the 17th century; the building behind is 12th century. Right: shop with a timber-framed upper storey from the 16th century; the first floor is probably 15th century, and the ground floor late 16th (photo: P Dixon).*

leisure activities, communication within the household and heating facilities. The spatial organisation of all this, including access to rooms, is of major importance for the understanding of housing culture. Indeed, access-analysis has been discussed as a possible major method for the understanding of housing cultures, based on the idea that certain 'laws' govern the interrelation between accessibility and function. However, many other factors are at play here, including the size and fittings of rooms, and in archaeology the often fragmentary state of evidence in any case reduces the potential of the method (see e.g. Grenville 1997, 17-22).

However, housing culture kept changing. During the period in question many technological innovations spread over large parts of Europe, such as stoves replacing open fireplaces, which caused profound changes to the interior design of houses and consequently to life within them. There was also a growing specialisation in the use of space for particular purposes; consequently, houses might be divided into more rooms, including, for example, a separate living-room (see below). On the other hand, ancient traditions for interior arrangements of a house might be maintained by the elite in order to signal legitimacy and roots, and to maintain ancient ways of formal communication, as (e.g.) in the chieftain's farm at Borg in Lofoten, northern Norway (see Fig in Box 2.2), and in Westminster Hall, London (Näsman & Roesdahl 2003; Steane 1993, 71-9). Changing concepts of household versus family (in the modern sense) and of private life would also have profound influences on houses and how they were lived in. The various housing cultures were part of the non-verbal communication within society. They reflect both practical needs and ideas, some of which are sometimes difficult to identify from sources other than archaeology. One of the many challenges to archaeology is to define the reasons for, and routes to, the changes in housing culture, and why it hardly changed in some places.

The following deals in particular with the spatial use and the fittings of houses in relation to social contexts and evolving technology in Northern and Central Europe.

Sources

For the period and regions considered here, archaeological remains preserved in the ground are by far the most important sources for housing culture. In Central Europe, standing remains of residential buildings earlier than the ninth century are unknown, and only a few go back to the ninth-tenth centuries, all from aristocratic or monastic contexts. More are preserved from the eleventh, and especially the twelfth, century; from the twelfth century, there are also a few town houses. All of these are built in stone. Standing remains of rural houses do not survive and, in Scandinavia, there are no standing buildings at all from this period, other than churches.

The houses remaining from this period have mostly been in continuous use, and they have therefore been repaired and altered many times. This includes modern restoration which is sometimes based more on the architect's idea as to what such a building might have looked like, conditioned by the ideas prevailing at the date of restoration, than on any archaeological evidence. Modern buildings archaeology may, however, reveal the original parts of the structure and also indicate functions, even if all or most of the early interior arrangements have disappeared. There are no comprehensive descriptions of houses or rooms in documentary sources or pictorial representations.

The archaeological evidence depends on the formation processes. For excavated houses, the plans are particularly important, for they provide information not only as to the form of the house, but also its building materials and construction techniques, and

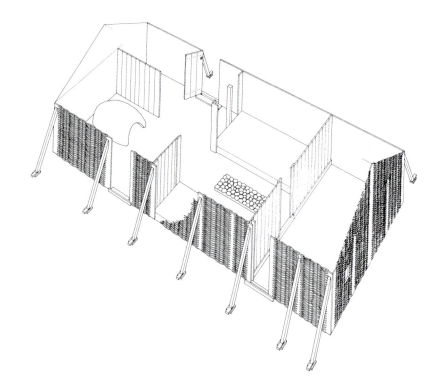

Fig 5.2   *Reconstruction of a house in the town of Hedeby (Schleswig, N Germany), based on well-preserved excavated evidence (see Box 4.3). Built of wattle-and-daub on timber posts, it measured 5x12m; the roof was supported by sloping outer posts. It was divided into three rooms: a main central room with open fire-place and raised platforms, and two gable-rooms, with either one or two outer doors, both having access to the central room. There would have been little furniture: some chests and boxes for storage, some stools, a loom, perhaps a narrow bench and table. One gable-room had a domed oven/ stove (see Box 5.2) and would have functioned as scullery/kitchen and for food storage; the function of the other is unknown (workshop?). According to dendrochronology, the house was built in 870 and was repaired and slightly altered 12 years later, when the stove was replaced by a trough. It is discussed whether one of the gable-rooms was, at some stage, used for animals (drawing: Stiftung Schleswig-Holsteinische Landesmuseen Schloss Gottorf; cf. Schietzel 1984).*

sometimes also on entrances and internal organization, such as room divisions. Walls are normally gone, but the remains of roofing, walls or (rarely) floor or roof timbers may be found in demolition debris. If erected on the ground-surface, remains of permanent fixtures are sometimes preserved, such as open fireplaces, hearths or stoves, or facilities for water-supply, and there may be remains of wall-benches and other built-in furniture. Underground features, such as cellars may also be found (e.g. Schietzel 1984; Untermann 1995; Svart Kristiansen 2005, 48-52, 163-280). Distribution patterns of artefacts and ecofacts may provide information on spatially distinct activities within a house, but such patterns must be carefully evaluated in relation to their context: *in situ* finds are important sources, while finds from later infillings must be avoided in the interpretation of the house in question. An 'ideal' excavation find is a house destroyed by sudden disaster, such as a violent fire, which would not allow the rescue of furnishings but provide a solid protective layer of debris.

The conditions for the preservation of timber-framed buildings and buildings made entirely of wood are, in general, much worse than for stone buildings. Timber would normally have been either re-used in other structures or as fuel, or would have rotted away. But in damp and wet environments the lower part of walls and other features may have survived, as for example in the Viking period town of Hedeby, in present north Germany (Schietzel 1984). Elsewhere, informative house-plans may be revealed from the setting of post-holes or from floor remains or wear-traces on former surfaces (e.g. Schmidt 1994; Svart Kristiansen 2005).

The movable furnishings of a house were also largely reused and recycled. Larger household utensils of metal are therefore exceptions in the archaeological record. The same is true of household objects and furniture of organic materials such as wood, which was commonly used. Most would have ended as fire-wood or rotted away, but some have survived in wet environments. The most common items found are those made of fired clay, especially potsherds and other small objects used in the preparation and consumption of food, in textile production or for leisure activities. Domestic utensils and movable furniture may, however, also be found in precious-metal hoards (especially vessels) and particularly as grave-goods in richly furnished burials from Merovingian Central Europe and Viking period Scandinavia. They provide some information on what was used by the upper classes and, as opposed to settlement finds, these are often complete or near complete, and sometimes well preserved. A few surviving examples of such artefacts are also known from aristocratic residences and churches (e.g. Mercer 1969; Paulsen & Schach-Dörges 1972; Appuhn 1986; Roesdahl & Wilson 1992, 136-43, nos 43-81, 123-7, 154-67, 457-9 & passim; Egan 1998).

The eighth- to twelfth-century pictorial records contain many illustrations of buildings and furnishing, but they follow strict conventions and are far from naturalistic. Nearly all appear in religious manuscripts, or mural paintings in churches, and thus have religious motifs. But these are often set in vernacular contexts and show near-contemporary form. Their main information in relation to housing culture concerns formal aristocratic dining, the form and function of beds, chairs and benches, and the extensive use of textiles. The Bayeux Tapestry, from c1070, is a unique source with its pictures of contemporary historical events, some of which are set in houses (Mercer 1969; Kluge-Pinsker 1998, 217-19; Wilson 1985).

Written records of this period only yield sporadic information concerning housing culture. A little may be found in wills, charters, chronicles and legal texts, such as the tribal/regional laws of many parts of Europe, which give names and functions of buildings as well as indirect information on construction techniques (Hoff 1997, 44-122; Kilian 1998, 17-18).

Rural Housing

In large parts of Europe rural housing (see also Chapter 3) did not change much during the eighth to twelfth centuries (Chapelot & Fossier 1985; Kilian 1998). Household communities lived on single farms or in villages, which were usually small. Stone buildings are known from southern Europe and the western British Isles, but elsewhere all buildings on a farm were normally timbered, the walls often completed with clay or organic materials. In coastal regions of north-western Continental Europe and in the North Atlantic lands and Greenland, however, timber walls were often insulated on the outside with turf, or walls might be built entirely of turf or of a combination of turf and stone (Box 5.1). The majority of rural buildings had load-bearing posts dug into the ground.

Farmsteads were enclosed by a fence and comprised several buildings with distinct functions. The main building either had living-quarters at one end and space for animals at the other, the two parts normally being separated by a wall or screen, or it was a house exclusively reserved for humans. In much of Scandinavia, for example, the accommodation for animals often became separated from the main farmhouse during the ninth to eleventh centuries. Room divisions of rural houses (or the living-quarters in them) are not found in Central Europe until the late Middle Ages (Kluge-Pinsker 1998, 88-92), while sub-divisions of the living-space are known in Scandinavia throughout the period covered by this volume. Almost all houses were one-storeyed with an open roof over the living-space and a vent allowing smoke from the hearth to escape into the open air (Heidinga 1987; Waterbolk 1991; Hvass 1993; Schmidt 1994; Klápště 2002).

Additional farm-buildings were used as byres and stables, for the storage of food for men and animals, and to protect agricultural tools and goods, while some were perhaps living-quarters for farm-hands and slaves. The exact function is often difficult to identify from excavated evidence. But bakeries and bath-houses are mentioned in written sources. In North-West Europe such outbuildings were often placed against the fence, but in Central and East Europe in particular many were dug into the ground – the so-called *Grubenhäuser* or 'sunken-featured buildings' (SFBs).

These are also well-known in North-West Europe and parts of Scandinavia, where the ground is not too hard and the water-level not too high. They were easy to build and

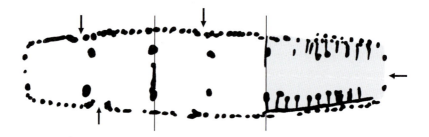

Fig 5.3 *Plan of the 9th-century main building of a farm at Vorbasse (Denmark), for which see Box 3.1. It has a byre at one end (right) and living-rooms at the other; entrances and room partitions are indicated (after Roesdahl 2003, based on Hvass 1993).*

often measured about 3-5 by 2-4 metres. In Scandinavia (as in the village of Vorbasse, Denmark; Box 3.1), there was often one or two of them within a farmstead, together with the above-ground buildings. Archaeology shows that SFBs were often equipped with an upright loom and therefore were used for textile production (Fig 7.5), but particularly in Eastern Europe and in the eastern parts of Central Europe they often had a stove and were used to live in (pp 87-8). Experimental archaeology adds strength to the idea that this particular type of building had the advantage, compared to buildings on ground-level, of being warmer in winter and cooler in hot summers. Everywhere, they would therefore have presumably also served as general retreats in times of extreme heat or cold. During the period considered in this book they began to be replaced by cellars in Central Europe and went out of use in England. In Scandinavia they went out of general use in the eleventh century, while in Eastern Europe they were in use much longer (see *Reallexikon*, for 'Hütte'; Roesdahl 1982, 59; for SFBs in England and their different interpretation, see Tipper 2004).

The living-space in houses was used for many purposes such as cooking, eating, sleeping, pastimes, some storage and the reception of guests. So far, the archaeological record provides limited information on the actual interior design of houses and of the living conditions there (Kilian 1998, 58-65), partly because of the conditions of preservation, but also because traditional research has focused on construction, rather than on function. However, information is building up (e.g. Roesdahl 1982, 110-18): keys found during excavation show that front doors could be locked. There were few and small openings in order to keep the warmth inside and perhaps also for security reasons. Windows were known, allowing some daylight into the otherwise fairly dark interior. The floor was often simply earth but might be covered by sods or loam. The focus of the living-space was a multi-purpose open hearth, which provided heat, light and cooking facilities; sometimes a hand-quern was placed next to it. However, some houses had a stove with its back against an outer wall or in a corner instead of an open hearth. Other fixtures are rarely documented, but in Viking period Scandinavia and elsewhere in the Viking world, such as Dublin and Waterford (Hurley, Scully & McCutcheon 1992), there is evidence for well-defined platforms along outer walls, often c1.5m wide. They were probably slightly raised – and therefore helped against drafts in the lower levels of the room and could be kept clear of dirt from the floor and fire-place. These platforms would have been the living and sleeping areas of the house, while the floor itself was simply for passage (see Box 5.1 & Fig 5.2). These platforms seem to disappear in the eleventh century.

Evidence for movable furniture is rare, save for small stools and the remains of chests and boxes for storage; other furniture would have been extremely infrequent, except in aristocratic circles (see below), but there would have been many textiles. It was probably normal to sit on a flat surface in a crouched position as is still common in many parts of the world. Most evidence of domestic work relates to women and textile production, such as loom-weights and spindle-whorls. Small oil lamps are also known from rural contexts, as well as gaming pieces and other items for leisure activities. Items for the preparation and consumption of food are the most commonly found household appliances. Numerous finds of pottery, as well as utensils of wood, iron and stone, show that the range of household items was limited. Pots were multi-purpose vessels used for cooking, serving and storage, etc, and there were hand-querns, roasting spits and ladles, and also beakers and small bowls which might be used for the consumption of food, as well as various containers such as baskets, wooden buckets and barrels (e.g. Graham-Campbell 1980, nos 25-107; Roesdahl 1982, 110-26, see Chapter 8). However, all these items are normally found out of their exact context and therefore rarely provide information on the activity zones of a house.

Most rural settlements were situated next to a watercourse in order to ensure water supply for people and livestock, but sometimes wells were dug to tap ground-water (Scholkmann 1999). In the semi-arid climate in parts of southern Europe more elaborate constructions for water-supply, such as cisterns, were required. There is no evidence of constructions for waste-disposal. Distribution patterns show that household waste was deposited in the immediate surroundings of the house. Latrines have not been identified. People would have relieved themselves in the stable or in the open, as was common in rural regions until modern times.

The construction of the houses and the basic necessities of farming communities, and tradition, restricted the development of housing culture in rural settlements with regard to comfort – in the modern understanding of the word. There were social and regional differences, but in many parts of Europe households continued to live close to the live-stock, with the smell of animals, with the limited heat emission of an open hearth, with smoke escaping through the room, with little lighting, thin walls and waste disposal just outside. Further, the relationship between house and household must have been limited by the short life-span of timber buildings. Their posts were normally dug into the ground and because of rot at ground-level they would not have lasted very long, in some places only about 30 years. Houses therefore needed to be repaired and rebuilt over and over again. The site of entire farms and villages might also change. A rural house was normally an unstable and changing frame for living.

Monastic Housing

Monastic life was carried on in entirely different architectural settings, developed in early medieval Benedictine monasteries. These partly adopted and continued Roman technologies, which had profound influences on the monasteries founded during the eleventh and twelfth centuries. The ideas of religious housing were based on concepts of the ideal life according to the principle *ora et labora*, being one of prayer, devotion and labour. Their realisation led to architectural solutions that were to have major impacts on secular housing culture.

Remains of residential monastic buildings from the eighth to tenth centuries are known from archaeological excavations in, for example, Italy (e.g. San Vincenzo al Volturno), Germany (e.g. Reichenau, in Lake Constance) and Switzerland (Sennhauser 1996), while standing buildings from the eleventh and, especially, the twelfth centuries are known in many parts of Europe. The monastic concept of housing is, however, particularly well illustrated in the plan of St Gall (Fig 14.5), the ground-plan of a monas-

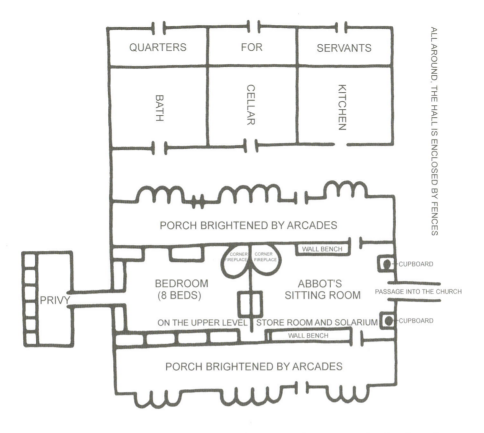

QUARTERS   FOR   SERVANTS

BATH

CELLAR

KITCHEN

ALL AROUND, THE HALL IS ENCLOSED BY FENCES

PORCH BRIGHTENED BY ARCADES

WALL BENCH

CORNER FIREPLACE   CORNER FIREPLACE

CUPBOARD

PRIVY

BEDROOM (8 BEDS)

ABBOT'S SITTING ROOM

PASSAGE INTO THE CHURCH

ON THE UPPER LEVEL   STORE ROOM AND SOLARIUM   CUPBOARD

WALL BENCH

PORCH BRIGHTENED BY ARCADES

The abbot's residence (aula) from the plan of St Gall (c825), with its text translated (redrawn by A Frey, after Kluge-Pinsker 1998; text from Horn & Born 1979).

Fig 5.4

tery drawn c825-30 and still in the library of St Gall monastery, Switzerland (Horn & Born 1979; Hecht 1999). It shows an idealised plan of a Benedictine monastery. The Cistercian order, founded in 1098, even developed a strict plan to be used in all its monasteries, but their economic means did not always allow this to be realised until centuries after the foundation of a monastery, and all rules were not always followed.

For monastic communities, the accommodation had to meet functional as well as religious requirements. As shown by the St Gall plan, the different aspects of living such as sleeping, cooking, eating, meeting and prayer took place in distinct spaces. This is true for the enclosure as well as for the abbot's residence (Fig 5.4) and the guesthouses, and there were specific buildings for health services, as well as for crafts and other economic activities. The residential buildings had fine facilities, and the plan shows several heating systems: sub-floor heating in the monastic buildings, domed stoves in the living spaces and open hearths in the industrial buildings, which served as workshops, as well as stables and accommodation for servants. Further, the enclosure, the abbot's residence and the guesthouses all had toilet systems. Not shown on the plan, but known from other monasteries, are constructions for water-supply and sewage (Kosch 1991; Bond 2001).

The ideas of functional partitions of houses as well as the innovative technological solutions were gradually adopted in aristocratic and urban housing in most of Europe, especially from the eleventh century onwards. The abbot's house on the St Gall plan (Fig 5.4), for example, is of the same general type as the aristocratic residences that became common in the eleventh and twelfth centuries (Kluge-Pinsker 1998, 194-5).

Urban Housing

Housing conditions in towns (see also Chapter 4) differed significantly from those in rural settlements. Specific architectural solutions were required because the size of the houses and other buildings was restricted by the dimensions and the organisation of the plot. The size of a house also depended on the size of the household, which would normally be considerably smaller in a town than on a farm, and little space was required for domestic animals; instead space might be needed for crafts, trade, and storage of supplies and goods. The internal organisation of a plot was much dependant on the functional topography of the town with its streets and open spaces, and on the closeness of neighbours. In many towns in Northern and Western Europe, such as Trondheim in Norway (Fig 5.5), Dublin in Ireland and York in England, the plots were long and narrow, and buildings were aligned in rows, one behind the other, while there was hardly any distance between neighbours (cf. Fig 4.5). In Central Europe, however, plots were often broader and shorter.

These conditions, together with other aspects of urban life, such as steady communication with people from other communities, led to the beginnings of urban (as opposed to rural) identities and to urban ways of living (Pounds 1989, 251-88). However, the situation varied significantly among the various types of urban and proto-urban settlements of this period, for example the early Scandinavian and Slavonic towns of the ninth to tenth centuries, the episcopal cities of Central and Southern Europe rooted in early medieval or late Roman times, craftsmen's settlements adjacent to aristocratic or royal estates, and twelfth-century burghers' towns. Further, the inhabitants of an urban community usually did not form a socially homogenous group. The nobility, the merchants, the craftsmen and others had different requirements and means for housing. But some features and developments are especially characteristic of urban housing cultures, although they were sometimes also seen in aristocratic and monastic houses situated in the countryside, and although there was much regional variation (for houses in many North and North-West European towns, see Gläser 2001a).

Houses of timber construction, often in combination with other materials, continued to dominate throughout the Middle Ages, but more elaborate timber-framing was developed during this period and replaced the traditional load-bearing posts dug into the earth. Increasingly, the timber-frameworks of the walls were also set on rows of stone in order to protect their lower parts. Stone and brick houses also came into use.

The footprint of a town house was normally smaller than that of a farmhouse and was often divided into more than one room in order to provide separate spaces for different activities. Early examples of two- and (rarely) three-roomed houses are known

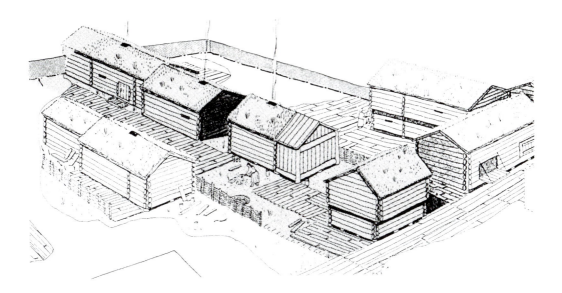

Reconstruction of buildings on a long narrow plot in Trondheim (N Norway), c1150-75; shops often faced the street. All buildings were of timber; streets and yards were laid with timber (after Christophersen & Nordeide 1994).

Fig 5.5

from the ninth century in the Viking town of Hedeby (Fig 5.2). These houses had a central open hearth (Schietzel 1984, 135-58). Similar houses from the eleventh century are known in the episcopal town of Basel, in Switzerland (Berger 1963); these are interpreted as craftsmen's houses. In Norway, standard town-houses from the eleventh century onwards were built entirely of timber; they were fairly small and normally consisted of two rooms: a smaller entrance and a room with a corner-stove (sometimes a central hearth) and narrow benches for sitting along two or three walls (Fig 5.6). It has been argued that they expressed a rural housing culture in an urban context, since similarly organised houses are known from rural sites (Christophersen 1989; Christophersen & Nordeide 1994). The commercial settlements of dependent craftsmen adjacent to tenth/ twelfth-century palatinates and royal estates, e.g. in the palatinate of Tilleda, in the Harz Mountains, Germany, had an entirely different structure (Kluge-Pinsker 1998, 164-7). They consisted of numerous SFBs, some of which had hearths. Finds indicate that they were used as workshops, but some may also have been for habitation.

The medieval burghers' town of the twelfth century saw important innovations in house construction. Within Germany this is especially noticeable in newly established towns, such as Freiburg im Breisgau, Brunswick and Lübeck (Untermann 1995; Rötting 1997; Gläser 2001b). The most important innovation was houses of several storeys encompassing many functions under one roof, including living, storage and formal gathering, and this was applied at least in the houses of the upper classes of the urban bourgeoisie. Their increasingly elaborate timber-frameworks were based on stone foun-

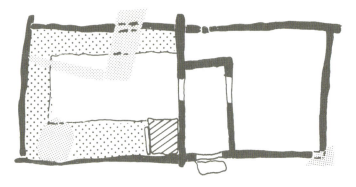

Fig 5.6   *Plan of a small 11th-century house in Trondheim (N Norway). Entrance is through a small room into a 'living-room', with corner fireplace and wall benches (left), or (right) into a possible store-room (after Christophersen & Nordeide 1994).*

dations or on a stone-built ground-floor, or the entire building was of stone. Tower houses (stone-built multi-storeyed residences of urban nobility) existed even earlier in episcopal cities in Central Europe. These are the oldest urban houses preserved in Central and Northern Europe and are known from the eleventh and twelfth centuries, e.g. in Trier (Wiedenau 1984) and Regensburg (Schnieringer 1997). Stone-built houses from the twelfth century are also preserved in Lincoln (England) and Cluny (France; Fig. 5.8), as well as other places (e.g. Wood 1965, 1-15; Grandchamp 1994; Grandchamp et al 1997).

Another important innovation, which became known in large parts of Europe during the eleventh to twelfth centuries, especially in the central and northern parts of the Continent – and became extremely popular in the following centuries – was a moderate-sized, comfortable and heated 'living-room', with sitting facilities (often as built-in benches). Particularly in the southern parts of Central Europe it is called *Stube* (for definitions, see 'Stube' in *Lexikon des Mittelalters*). Its walls and ceiling were panelled with boards, and it was smoke-free, being heated by a stove fired from an adjacent room (see Box 5.2). However, rooms of similar arrangement might also be built of other materials or entirely of wood (e.g. Krongaard Kristensen 1999, 73f), and if such a 'living-room' had an open hearth or an oven fired from the room itself, the German term is *Rauchstube*. The main room of the Norwegian town-houses mentioned above would be of this category.

Important achievements relating to housing culture during this period were, then, the development, over most of Europe, of town-houses – types of houses and arrangements of buildings on a plot – which met the special urban needs. There were many varieties but a general move towards greater permanency of buildings due to new methods of construction, and also the beginnings of assembling many functions under one roof but assigned to distinct floors, and the division of house-space into separate rooms with specific purposes (Schofield & Vince 1994, 63-98; Gläser 2001a; cf. Box 5.1). These achievements formed the basis for late medieval and early modern urban houses.

All this had a strong impact on the architectural organisation of domestic infrastructure and housing culture. There were innovations (discussed below) concerning heat-

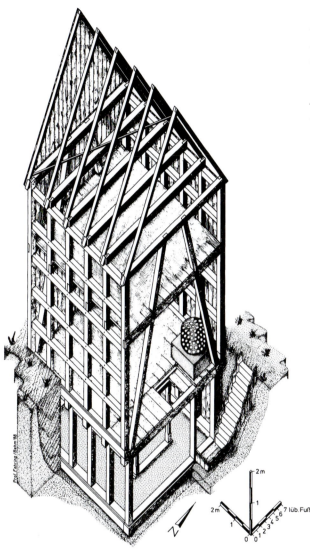

Fig 5.7

Reconstruction of a two-storeyed house with cellar in Alfstrasse, Lübeck; late 12th century. There is a tiled stove on the ground-floor (after Fehring 1989); see also Fig. 4.10.

ing, lighting, interior design, furnishing, disposal facilities, etc. Similar innovations were developed in the context of aristocratic housing during the eleventh and twelfth centuries. All this made life much more comfortable, while its adoption in urban dwellings shows that the bourgeoisie, or at least its upper classes, strived for a more elaborate housing culture comparable to that of the aristocracy.

Aristocratic Housing

The residences of the aristocracy (see also Chapter 12) changed significantly during the period. Until the tenth century or later the farms of the rural upper-classes or aristocracy were normally situated within or next to rural settlements, and neither the build-

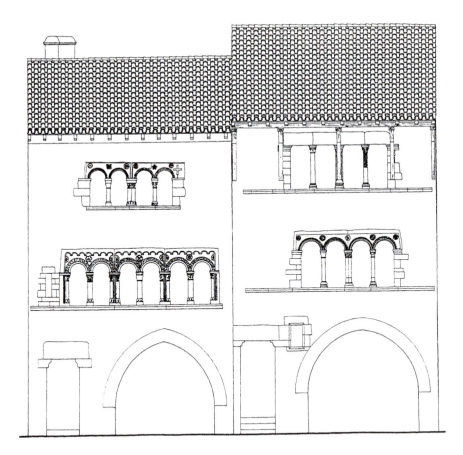

Fig 5.8   *Reconstruction of two stone-built, 12th-century urban houses at Cluny (France); cf. Fig 5.1 (after Grandchamp et al 1997).*

ing types, nor the applied construction techniques differed from the peasants' farm-steads. They were distinguished by larger plots, grander houses and more buildings of various kinds (Kilian 1998, 66-7). But already then, princely and royal palatinates and estates were isolated from other settlements. They would comprise churches and chapels (in Christian lands), a hall for official business and entertainment, residences and numerous other buildings, and the main buildings would often be of stone, particularly from the twelfth century onwards. While some churches, chapels and halls are preserved, e.g. in Ingelheim, near Frankfurt am Main (Grewe 1999), the residences are largely unknown. From the tenth century onwards, significant structural changes within the aristocracy also led to the separation of their residences from other settlements and to the development of the medieval castle – although the chronology of these developments varies greatly within Europe. They may be seen as spatial manifestations of the aristocracy's social segregation from the peasantry, and as matters of status and security. There are no standing aristocratic residences or castles from before the tenth century, and neither buildings archaeology nor excavations offers comprehensive information on

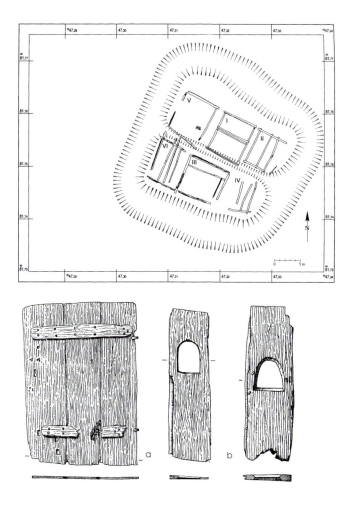

'Haus Meer', at Meerbusch, Lkr. Neuss (Germany); plan of the 11th-century manor which had six timber buildings, within a fortified enclosure; (a) door (height: c155cm) and (b) two wall-planks with window-openings (after Janssen & Janssen 1999).

Fig 5.9

aristocratic domestic spaces and housing culture before the eleventh to twelfth centuries, although many plans are known, e.g. Borg in Lofoten, Norway (see Fig in Box 2.2), Tissø in Denmark (Fig 13.5), and Cheddar in England (Kaldal Mikkelsen & Herschend 2003; Jørgensen 2003; Meirion-Jones & Jones 1993).

Buildings of both timber and stone (or brick) are often found at the same site – although secular stone and brick buildings were probably unknown in Scandinavia and the West Slav lands before the twelfth century. There might be two- to four-storeyed lived-in towers or several buildings of distinct function within a fortified enclosure. 'Haus Meer', in south-west Germany (Fig 5.9) is a good example of such a residence from the tenth/eleventh century (Janssen & Janssen 1999). It comprised six fairly small houses set on horizontal timbers; these were used as residences, but also for agricultural purposes and crafts. During the eleventh/twelfth century, the largely stone-built types of royal and high-aristocratic castles developed, and from the late eleventh century a keep or donjon might be the central architectural component of a great castle and the core of its fortification and formal functions including feasts – it therefore often had good toilet facilities close to the hall – while private living-quarters were usually still in a different building, which was often timbered (see also Chapter 11). But separate halls continued to be fashionable, now sometimes with serving facilities, and by the end of our period the main chamber-block also began to be integrated into the halls of the mighty (Wood 1965; Meirion-Jones & Jones 1993; Böhme 1999).

Aristocratic housing in these centuries is thus characterised by a growing spatial separation from other settlements, by a growing functional differentiation of architecture, by vertical and horizontal partition of housing, and by growing formality and little privacy. In some parts of Europe fortification came to play a dominant role, and domestic life would sometimes have been quite uncomfortable despite the provision of various modern facilities in a building. A vital component of all aristocratic residences was the hall where assemblies and feasts were held, legal and administrative decisions taken and power and prestige demonstrated.

Warm, Bright, Safe and Formal in Castles and Towns

These new house-types in aristocratic residences and urban settlements were accompanied by important changes and technological innovations of facilities within the houses and, subsequently, by changes in housing culture and new concepts of living – particularly in castles and towns. During this period significant steps were taken in the development of housing from merely the satisfaction of basic needs towards a more comfortable daily life – in the modern sense (Wood 1965; Kluge-Pinsker 1998, 199-226; Roesdahl 1999).

Heating and lighting

With the improvement in timber construction, as well as the more extensive use of stone for building purposes, a house might last much longer. This allowed for longer lasting housing in one and the same building and intensified ties between household and house, especially if this was passed on through generations within the same family. Further, the partition of houses into rooms with specific functions gave new opportunities for the unfolding of a private life. The search for a heated but smoke-free room was also central to the development, and several new heating technologies appeared: stoves, open fireplaces with outlet for the smoke through the wall, and sub-floor heating systems (see Box 5.2). The fundamental innovation in this was the separation of cooking and heating facilities which both used to be provided by a central hearth. Cooking was removed from the 'living-room' which (in Central and parts of Northern Europe) often got a stove placed along a wall, or in a corner, instead of the open fire. This completely changed the interior design of the room. In Northern Europe the platforms along the walls also disappeared; instead, narrow wall-benches were often built for sitting, and an open and larger floor space emerged. All this would make more room for furniture (see below).

Another consequence of the demise of the open hearth and the introduction of stoves – which enclosed the fire – was a need for more light. This might come from larger windows, which could be closed or protected with semi-transparent materials and shutters.

(a) Chair with lathe-turned posts and details in Urnes Church (W Norway); probably 12th century. Such chairs, and also beds, with lathe-turned elements are well known from pictorial evidence and parts are occasionally found in excavation, e.g. at 'Haus Meer': Fig 8.4 (photo: DM Wilson).

Fig 5.10

(b) Decorated gable of a cradle (height: 53cm), excavated in the town of Schleswig (N Germany); 12th century (photo: Stiftung Schleswig-Holsteinische Landesmuseum Schloss Gottorf).

By the twelfth century window-glass was widely available and much used in churches; it was probably also known in aristocratic residences in castles and towns. There is also much evidence for an increasing use of artificial light from various types of portable oil-lamps and candlesticks made of iron, ceramics or other materials, and of many forms and qualities. All this would provide a fairly dim light but allow a range of activities within the house. And there were candelabras and chandeliers in the houses of the rich. Iron holders for pinewood chips also start to appear among the finds and would have provided a brief, but cheap, source of light (e.g. Roesdahl 1999; see also pp 256-7).

BOX 5.2   HEATING SYSTEMS

An open fireplace would normally have had a frame and been slightly raised above the floor; it always had a foundation, often of clay-covered stones. The early type of stove was fuelled via an opening from the room itself; smoke would escape from the same opening into the room and then into the open air. An example of such a stove is known from an early urban house at Hedeby (Fig 1), built in 870, which also had an open hearth in its central room (Fig 5.2). This type of stove could be used for purposes other than heating (e.g. as an oven for cooking, baking or industrial processes).

From the eleventh century onwards a new type of stove is known from castles in Switzerland and southern Germany and its use soon spread to towns; there is archaeological evidence from (e.g.) Zurich in Switzerland, Ulm and Lübeck in Germany, and Viborg in Denmark (Tauber 1980; Krongaard Kristensen 1999, 73f). Such stoves (Fig 2) allowed for a heated and smoke-free 'sitting-room'. They were placed against (or in) the wall towards the kitchen and were fuelled from the kitchen-fireplace, from where the smoke also escaped. They were normally domed structures of clay or stone and might be tiled. No stove from this period survives, but excavations show that stove-tiles were usually vessel-shaped in order to provide a larger surface for heat emission, and probably also for embellishment. In the period under consideration, tiles remain simple. It was in the late Middle Ages and the Renaissance that they became elaborate and highly decorated, when tiled stoves became important markers of status and ideologies. In the late Middle Ages this stove-type also spread to rural houses, remaining common in many regions of Europe until modern times.

From the tenth century onwards, there is good evidence for fireplaces placed against walls, or in corners, with outlets for smoke through the wall. During our period they are known from stone and brick-built aristocratic residences and were part of the furnishing of a formal room.

Fig 1

Simple stove ('smoke-stove') as known (e.g.) from a house built in 870 in the town of Hedeby (Fig 5.2); smoke escapes through the fuelling opening into the room in which the stove is situated (after Roesdahl 1999/2004).

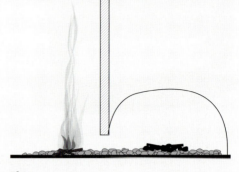

Fig 2

Schematic drawing of a simple stove fuelled from an adjacent room, providing a smoke-free 'sitting-room' – a type much developed during the Middle Ages (drawing: L Hilmar, Moesgaard, 2006).

The oldest example identified in Europe is from the tenth century, in the first-phase hall at Doué-la-Fontaine, in south-western France. Such fireplaces subsequently spread to town houses and later to rural houses, particularly in the western parts of northern Europe. There are fairly distinct regional differences for the use of either stoves or fireplaces, particularly outside aristocratic circles.

More sophisticated heating systems with sub-floor channels, based on Roman traditions (hypocausts), are known from Carolingian monasteries, such as Reichenau; they are also shown on the plan of St Gall (Fig 14.5). These were fuelled from outside and provided permanent, smoke-free room-heating. During the ninth and tenth centuries this technology was adopted in great royal halls. As opposed to this, the sub-floor storage-heating system (Fig 3) was a genuine Central European innovation (the term 'hypocaust' is often also used for this type); however, this did not provide permanent heating. During the eleventh and twelfth centuries it is to be found both in the calefactories (heated rooms) of monasteries and in the formal rooms of castles (Bingenheimer 1998; Zettler 1988; Hertz 1975).

by Else Roesdahl & Barbara Scholkmann

Fig 3

Sub-floor storage-heating system ('hypocaust'). Left: a heap of stones is heated from below; the damper is open in order to allow the smoke to escape into the open air, while vents in the floor above are closed. Right: heat is emitted from the hot stones into the room above through the open vents in the floor; the damper is closed (drawing: J Hertz, 1990).

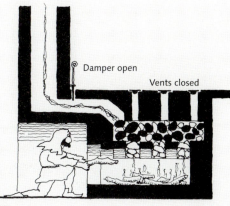

Damper open
Vents closed

Firing

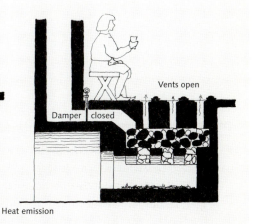

Vents open
Damper closed

Heat emission

The horizontal and vertical division of houses gave new opportunities for interior design. Floors of mortar or stamped clay are frequently found, while floors of glazed and decorated tiles are almost exclusively known from monasteries and churches (Kluge-Pinsker 1998, 216-17). Coloured walls and mural paintings are known especially from eleventh- and twelfth-century aristocratic residences, but well-to-do houses would also have been fitted with textile wall-hangings, while other hangings would have separated spaces within a house. Textiles in general, such as bedding, cushions, blankets, table-cloths and other coverings, would have played a major role in the furnishing of a house. All this is known from pictures; very little is preserved (Mercer 1969; Andersson 1970, 389-93).

The furnishing of a house would include various built-in features, which might be for heating, storage, sitting, eating and sleeping. Such furnishings are lost with the house itself, but sometimes traces can be identified by excavation and an occasional survival in stone and brick buildings – such as benches along walls, and wall niches. Compared with modern times there was little movable furniture, although all basic types were known in aristocratic circles and increasingly used in towns. In most European languages the word itself (*Möbel, meuble, møbel*, etc) is fairly recent and means 'movable', ultimately deriving from Latin *mobilis* (mobile). The quality and quantity of furniture depended on social status.

Furniture was quite varied and can be divided into functional types. There were boxes, chests, cupboards and shelves for storage; stools, chairs and benches for sitting; tables; beds; and furniture for children. Examples of all are preserved, and the general form of most is also known from illustrations and, in the case of chairs, from sculpture. Most surviving furniture from this period is now (or was) in churches – Norway and Sweden in particular have some that are convincingly dated to the twelfth century (Fig 5.10a) – while other pieces have been preserved in castles or other residences of the upper-classes. A few pieces (such as beds, chairs, stools, chests and tables) are also known from richly-furnished Merovingian graves in Central Europe (Paulsen & Schach-Dörges 1972, 23-57); from the ninth and tenth centuries, there are chests, beds, a chair and a small table known from pagan aristocratic graves in Scandinavia, in particular the Norwegian Oseberg burial, from 834 (Grieg 1928). But with the introduction of Christianity the rite of furnished burial came to an end and thus also this source of information. Settlement finds include many iron mounts and keys for boxes and chests, with some planks from them, and some stools; indeed, for practical reasons, such furniture must have been by far the most common types. Chairs from excavations are rare. An eleventh-century baby-chair and the ornamented gable of a twelfth-century cradle are the oldest known examples of specialised children's furniture in Scandinavia (Fig 5.10b). All other furniture types had been known in most of Europe for centuries, except cupboards, which came into use north of the Alps c1200, probably first in churches to safeguard books (Karlson 1928; Mercer 1969; Anker 1968; Appuhn 1986; Roesdahl & Wilson 1992: 136-43, nos 67-70, 161-7, 457-9 & 551-66).

Technically, all furniture was solid carpentry work, but there are several types of construction. It might be embellished with decorative carvings, colours or painted motifs, or with lathe-turned or sculpted details (Figs 5.10 & 8.4), or with iron mounts – which would also strengthen the construction (as with doors). Without a good context furniture is often difficult to date, particularly because some constructions are simple (e.g. chairs and chests cut from a log) and because traditions in certain regions were strong. Old furniture traditions might also be revived. So far only a few pieces of medieval furniture are dated by dendrochronology, but this method is certainly the way forward; at the same time the origin of the timber could be established and the exchange within Europe of furniture or timber as raw material illuminated.

Not a single room in Europe from this period is preserved with its furnishing, nor do pictures illustrate how rooms were furnished. But with knowledge of the lay-out and function of a room in a house, of its size, doors, windows and heating system, and the range of built-in features and furniture known at the date in question, it is possible to reconstruct a room in a fairly convincing way. A basic principle would be to place as much as possible along walls in order not to crowd the space for moving.

Food, water and waste

Food preparation did not change much during this period. The archaeological record shows that meals continued to be cooked on an open hearth or in a stove (cf. pp 191-2). Simple pots remained the most common cooking vessels till the late Middle Ages, although cauldrons of iron and bronze were also known. High quality ceramics from the Rhineland and Flanders were exported as far as Scandinavia and were obviously of some significance (see pp 225-6), and the range of utensils grew. Fine tableware, and particularly drinking vessels, was important for formal feasting. Most vessels were of pottery and wood (Fig 8.4), but glass and precious metal were also used, although probably only by the very rich (see Chapters 8 & 12). Ornamented hand-washing basins, jugs and animal-shaped 'aquamaniles' (pouring vessels) of copper-alloy (Figs 8.3 & 12.6) are interesting evidence of the hygienic standards and formal dining culture of the upper classes. Most examples date from the twelfth century onwards, although hand-basins also occur in Merovingian graves and in tenth-century Scandinavian graves (e.g. Graham-Campbell 1980, passim; Roesdahl & Wilson 1992, passim).

With regard to the supply of water, the increasing number of private wells in early urban settlements is remarkable. They were dug in open parts of the plots (e.g. Fig 10.6), but the vicinity of wells and cess-pits on the same or neighbouring plots probably caused some hygienic problems (Scholkmann 1999). In castles built on heights, it was particularly difficult to secure sufficient supplies of fresh water, and most of these had cisterns. Some also had pipes carrying water from outlying springs into the castle (Kluge-Pinsker 1998, 204-7). Latrines were also an important innovation. Castles were furnished with toilet oriels or chutes in the outer walls, and from the twelfth century onwards, cess-pits are frequently found in towns. They were usually situated in the rear part of plots and probably often covered by some building. When out of use, the pits were usually filled with domestic waste, just like other pits on a plot. Waste disposal was obviously managed privately.

Leisure

Leisure activities are reflected in the archaeological record by numerous finds from aristocratic as well as urban and rural contexts. Gaming-pieces of many materials and qualities show, together with boards and dice, that chess, tric-trac, dice and other games were played (see pp 257-8 & 357, Figs 8.9 & 12.8). Musical instruments are less frequently found. Flutes are the most common of these, but fragments of stringed instruments also occur, such as harp pegs at Waterford, Ireland (Hurley et al 1992, 581-2), and there are many pictures in manuscripts. Children's toys, such as miniature horses, boats or weapons, date mostly from the eleventh century onwards. All this helps to understand life within a house, and the housing culture.

Concluding Remarks

During the eighth to twelfth centuries housing ranges from the very simple to the elaborate and comfortable. Innovations are closely linked to the growing differentiation of society and the development of specific concepts of housing for specific groups. Interaction between these groups with regard to housing is easily observed, especially between the aristocracy and the urban bourgeoisie. Housing concepts and technical solutions were developed in particular within monastic housing, which served as models. Much work remains to be done in order to explain how these spread to lay society, as also to determine when and why (and sometimes why not) particular innovations were adopted in the various European regions, and yet why rural housing in many other areas remained largely untouched.

Acknowledgements

We would like to thank Uwe Meyerdirks (Tübingen), Søren Sindbæk (Aarhus), David M Wilson (Castletown), and Philip Dixon (Newark), for discussion and comments on various aspects of this chapter.

BIBLIOGRAPHY

Andersson, A (1970) *The Art of Scandinavia*, Vol 2, London/New York

Anker, P (1968) *Norske Møbler i Fortid og Nåtid*, Bergen/Oslo/Trondheim

Appuhn, H (1986) 'Einige Möbel aus der zeit um 1200', in Steuer, H (ed), *Zur Lebensweise in der Stadt um 1200*, Cologne, 11-128

Bazzana, A and Bedia, J (2005) *Excavationes en la Isla de Saltés (Huelva) 1988-2001*, Seville

Bazzana, A and Hubert, E (2000) *Maison et Espaces domestiques dans le Monde Méditerranéen au Moyen Age*, Paris

Berger, L (1963) *Die Ausgrabungen am Petersberg in Basel*, Basel

Bermúdez, J and Bazzana, A (eds) (1990) *La Casa Hispano-musulmana. Aportaciones de la Arqueología*, Granada

Bingenheimer, K (1998) *Die Luftheizungen des Mittelalters*, Hamburg

Bond, J (2001) 'Monastic water management in Great Britain', in Keevill, G, Aston, M and Hall, T (eds), *Monastic Archaeology*, Oxford, 88-136

Böhme, W (1999) *Burgen in Mitteleuropa: ein Hand-buch*, Stuttgart

Christophersen, A (1989) 'Dwellings houses, workshops and storehouses. Functional aspects of the development of wooden urban buildings in Trondheim from c. AD 1000 to AD 1400', *Acta Archaeologica* 60, 101-29

Christophersen, A and Nordeide, S (1994) *Kaupangen ved Nidelva*, Trondheim (English summary)

Chapelot, J and Fossier, R (1985) *The Village and House in the Middle Ages*, London

Egan, G (1998) *The Medieval Household. Daily Living c.1150-c.1450*, London

Fehring, GP (1989) 'Domus lignea cum caminata – hölzerne, turmartige Kemenaten des späten 12. Jahrhunderts in Lübeck und ihre Stellung in der Architekturgeschichte', in Lüdtke, H, Lüth, F and Lauth, F (eds), *Festschrift für Wolfgang Hübener. Hammaburg* NF 9, 271-83

Gläser, M (ed) (2001a) *Lübecker Kolloquium zur Stadtarchäologie im Hanseraum III. Der Hausbau*, Lübeck

Gläser, M (2001b) 'Archäologisch erfasste mittel-alterliche Hausbauten in Lübeck', in Gläser, M (ed), *Lübecker Kolloquium zur Stadtarchäologie im Hanseraum III. Der Hausbau*, Lübeck, 277-306

Graham-Campbell, J (1980) *Viking Artefacts: a Select Catalogue*, London

Grandchamp, PG (1994, 2nd ed) *Demeures Médiévales. Coeur de la Cité*, Paris

Grandchamp, PG et al (1997) *La Ville de Cluny et ses Maisons: XIe-XVe Siècles*, Paris

Grenville, J (1997 & reprints) *Medieval Housing*, London

Grewe, K (1999) 'Die Königspfalz zu Ingelheim am Rhein', in Stiegemann, C and Wemhoff, M (eds), *799 – Kunst und Kultur der Karolingerzeit*, Mainz, 142-51

Grieg, S (1928) *Osebergfundet*, II, Oslo

Hecht, K (1999), *Der St. Galler Klosterplan*, Wiesbaden

Heidinga, HA (1987) *Medieval Settlement and Economy North of the Lower Rhine*, Assen/Maastricht

Hertz, J (1975) 'Some examples of medieval hypocausts in Denmark', *Chateau Gaillard* VII, 127-39

Hillier, B and Hanson, J (1984) *The Social Logic of Space*, Cambridge

Hoff, A (1997) *Lov og Landskab*, Aarhus (English summary)

Horn, W and Born, E (1979) *The Plan of St. Gall. A Study of the Architecture and Economy of and Life in a Paradigmatic Carolingian Monastery*, I-III, University of California

Hurley, MF, Scully, OMB and McCutcheon, SWJ (eds) (1992) *Late Viking Age and Medieval Waterford*, Waterford

Hvass, S (1993) 'Settlement', in Hvass, S and Storgaard, B (eds), *Digging into the Past. 25 Years of Archaeology in Denmark*, Copenhagen, 187-94

Janssen, W and Janssen, B (1999) *Die frühmittelalter-liche Niederungsburg bei Haus Meer, Kreis Neuss*, Cologne

Johnson, M (1993) *Housing Culture. Traditional Archi-tecture in an English Landscape*, Washington DC

Jørgensen, L (2003) 'Manor and market at Lake Tissø in the sixth to eleventh centuries: the Danish "produc-tive" sites', in Pestell, T and Ulmschneider K (eds), *Markets in Early Medieval Europe: Trading and 'Pro-ductive' Sites, 650-850*, Macclesfield, 175-207

Kaldal Mikkelsen, D and Herschend, F (2003) 'The main building at Borg (I:1)', in Stamsø Munch, G, Johansen, OS and Roesdahl, E (eds), *Borg in Lofoten. A Chieftain's Farm in North Norway*, Trondheim, 41-76

Karlson, W (1928) *Studier i Sveriges Medeltida Möbelkunst*, Lund

Kilian, I (1998) 'Wohnen im frühen Mittelalter (5.-10. Jahrhundert)', in Dirlmeier, U (ed), *Geschichte des Wohnens*, Vol 2, Stuttgart, 11-84

Klápště, J (ed) (2002) *The Rural House from Migration Period to the Oldest Still Standing Buildings* (= *Ruralia* 4), Prague

Kluge-Pinsker, A (1998) 'Wohnen im hohen Mittelalter (10.-12. Jahrhundert, mit Ausblicken in das 13. Jahrhundert)', in Dirlmeier, U (ed), *Geschichte des Wohnens*, Vol 2, Stuttgart, 85-228

Kosch, C (1991) 'Wasserbaueinrichtungen in hochmit-telalterlichen Konventanlagen', in Frontius-Gesell-schaft, V (ed), *Die Wasserversorgung im Mittelalter*, Mainz, 89-146

Krongaard Kristensen, H (1999) 'Land, by og bygnin-ger', in Roesdahl, E (ed), *Dagligliv i Danmarks Mid-delalder. En arkæologisk kulturhistorie*, Copenhagen, 55-81

Lexikon des Mittelalters 8 (1997), 'Stube'; ibid 9 (1998), 'Wohnen, Wohnkultur, Wohnformen', Munich/Zurich

Meirion-Jones, G and Jones, M (eds) (1993) *Manorial Domestic Buildings in England and Northern France*, London

Mercer, E (1969) *Furniture 700-1700*, London

Milek, KB (2006) *Houses and Households in Early Ice-landic Society: Geoarchaeology and the Interpretation of Social Space*, unpublished PhD thesis, University of Cambridge

Näsman, U and Roesdahl, E (2003) 'Scandinavian and European perspectives', in Stamsø Munch, G et al (eds), *Borg in Lofoten. A Chieftain's Farm in North Norway*, Trondheim, 283-299

Paulsen, P and Schach-Dörges, H (1972) *Holzhandwerk der Alemannen*, Stuttgart

Pounds, NJG (1989) *Hearth & Home*, Bloomington/Indianapolis

Price, N (1995) 'House and home in Viking Age Ice-land: cultural expression in Scandinavian colonial architecture', in Benjamin, DN (ed), *The Home. Words, Interpretations, Meanings and Environments*, Aldershot, 109-29

Reallexikon der Germanischen Altertumskunde (1968ff), Bech, H et al (eds), 'Hütte', Berlin/New York

Roberts, HM, Snæsdóttir, M, Vésteinsson, O and Mehler, N (2003) 'Skáli frá víkingaöld í Reykavík', *Árbók hins íslenzka fornleifafélags* 2000-01, 219-334 (English summary)

Roesdahl, E (1982) *Viking Age Denmark*, London

Roesdahl, E (1999; 2004, 2nd ed) 'Boligernes indret-ning og udstyr', in Roesdahl, E (ed), *Dagligliv i Danmarks middelalder. En arkæologisk kulturhistorie*, Aarhus, 82-109

Roesdahl, E (ed) (2003) *Bolig og Familie i Danmarks Middelalder*, Højbjerg (English summaries)

Roesdahl, E and Wilson, DM (eds) (1992) *From Viking to Crusader. Scandinavia and Europe 800-1200*, Copenhagen

Rötting, H (1997) *Stadtarchäologie in Braunschweig*, Hannover

Schietzel, K (1984) 'Die Baubefunde in Haithabu' and 'Die Topographie von Haithabu', in Jankuhn, H et al (eds), *Archäologische und Naturwissenschaftliche Untersuchungen an Ländliche und Frühstädtischen Siedlungen in Deutschen Küstengebiet*, Bonn, 135-62

Schmidt, H (1994) *Building Customs in Viking Age Den-mark*, Herning

Schnieringer, K (1997) 'Das mittelalterliche Bürger-haus in Regensburg', in Borgmeyer, A, Hubel, A, Tillmann, A, and Wellnhofer, A (eds), *Denkmäler in Bayern III.37: Stadt Regensburg*, Regensburg, lxxxviii-cxii

Schofield, J and Vince, A (1994) *Medieval Towns*, London

Scholkmann, B (1999) 'Öffentliche und private Wasserversorgung als Forschungsproblem der Mittelalterarchäologie', in Paulus, H-E, Reidel, H and Winkler, PW (eds), *Wasser – Lebensquelle und Bedeutungsträger*, Regensburg, 65-76

Sennhauser, HRS (1996) *Wohn- und Wirtschaftsbauten frühmittelalterlicher Klöster*, Zürich

Steane, J (1993) *The Archaeology of the Medieval English Monarchy*, London/New York

Svart Kristiansen, M (2005) *Tårnby. Gård og Landsby Gennem 1000 år*, Højbjerg (English summary and captions)

Tauber, J (1980) *Herd und Ofen im Mittelalter*, Olten

Tipper, J (2004) *The Grubenhaus in Anglo-Saxon England*, Yeddingham

Untermann, M (1995) *Das 'Harmonie'-Gelände in Freiburg im Breisgau*, Stuttgart

Waterbolk, HT (1991) 'Das mittelalterliche Siedlungs-wesen in Drenthe. Versuch einer Synthese aus archäologischer sicht', in Böhme, HW (ed), *Siedlungen und Landesausbau zur Salierzeit, Teil 1: in den nördlichen Landschaften des Reiches*, Sigmaringen, 47-108

Vésteinsson, O (2004) 'Icelandic farmhouse excava-tions. Field methods and site choice', *Archaeologia Islandica* 3, 71-100

Wiedenau, A (1984) *Katalog der Romanischen Wohn-bauten in Westdeutschen Städten und Siedlungen*, Tübingen

Wilson, DM (1985) *The Bayeux Tapestry*, London

Wood, M (1965, and reprints) *The English Medieval House*, London

Zettler, A (1988) *Die Frühe Klosterbauten der Reichenau*, Sigmaringen

CHAPTER 6

FOOD

Sabine Karg and Pilar Lafuente

PART 1: THE SOUTH *by Pilar Lafuente*

Editors' note: this first part introduces the subject of medieval food from a Mediterranean perspective, with special reference to the Iberian Peninsula. In Part 2, Sabine Karg examines the evidence from a northern viewpoint, and the chapter closes with a Box, by James Barrett, on the development of sea-fishing in North-West Europe, followed by the combined bibliography. Further aspects of the preparation and consumption of food and drink are covered in Chapters 5 and 8.

Introduction

Knowledge of food among Southern European societies during the Middle Ages can be obtained in various ways: from documentary sources, such as agricultural treatises, historical and geographical texts, culinary treatises, medical books, or *hadices* (documents describing Islamic traditions) and *hisba* texts (including guidelines to proper behaviour in the market-place and the moral principles behind customs); from iconography, in the form of representations in miniatures and calendars; and from archaeology, especially through archaeozoology and archaeobotany.

A combination of environmental influences affected the availability of nutritional resources, such as soil fertility, climate, land-ownership and farming methods, access to markets, etc. So too did subsistence strategies, meaning that, semi-nomadic groups, who tended towards temporary agricultural techniques, cannot be expected to have had the same nutritional regime as sedentary agriculturalists. Both these approaches differed also from the situation in urbanised al-Andalus, where it was necessary to ensure adequate supplies of foodstuffs for the town-dwellers and their animals. In the first group, agricultural produce and livestock were exploited at the subsistence level, consumed within the group, but the produce of the settled farmers was often concentrated in the hands of powerful individuals, landlords and the aristocracy, who used the surplus for their own ends. In al-Andalus, food production was organised to meet the needs of a developing market-economy (Figs 6.1 & 2).

Fig 6.1 *Land conditions and water supply are determining factors in agricultural production; as in the hilly areas of al-Andalus, a common solution was terracing (after Quesada 1995).*

Cultural and religious influences were also dividing factors. Certain foods were forbidden or had limited consumption, such as pork for Muslims and Jews, wine among Muslims, meat during Lent for Christians, along with prescriptions during the slaughter of animals, or deep-rooted dietary customs when preparing and eating foods.

Foods of Animal Origin

The analysis of animal remains uncovered at archaeological sites poses several dilemmas. To carry out an acceptable evaluation of the remains along with the resulting statistical research, values such as the number of remains (NR), the minimum number of individuals (MNI), or the weight and sizes of bones, must be taken into account.

However, individual circumstances at each site influence research, and it is not always possible to collect all the specific data required for precise interpretation. For example, the study of the contents of a deliberately deposited midden, providing a wide spectrum of stratified food-remains along with other elements that can be associated with the corresponding cultural levels, cannot be compared with the analysis of the scattered remains found on a habitation site where samples are usually scant and the depositional characteristics more varied.

In addition, account must be taken of the fact that the quantity of bones does not necessarily correspond to the quantity of animals eaten, given that there is a wide difference between living, dead and buried specimens (following the division of the carcass

In repopulated areas, self-sufficiency was achieved by cultivating small plots of land and raising sheep and cattle (photo: F Andrés).

Fig 6.2

for consumption, use of bones for manufacture, methods of food-preservation for later use, by salting, smoking, drying, etc). The meat-yield must also be considered when dealing with each different species, taking into account the biomass of each animal – the meat-yield from a cow is different from that of a sheep – and in the case of shell-deposits of molluscs and land snails, it is necessary to ascertain whether the specimen had grown sufficiently for human consumption and whether there are traces of handling which indicate that they had been eaten.

Which animals were used?

Some general considerations may be arrived at, with due precaution, from the analysis of published data on research carried out on faunal remains recovered from medieval sites prior to the twelfth century.

Within both Christian and Muslim contexts, the main sources of meat were domestic animals. These were usually smaller in size and weight than the present-day species. In Christian areas, the most commonly used species were cattle and ovicaprids (sheep & goats), followed by pigs. Meanwhile, among Muslims, consumption was mainly concentrated on ovicaprids, cattle and avian species, in that order of importance. In the Islamic context, hunting was not a supplementary practice and, except for animals that were habitually eaten, such as hares, rabbits and partridges, only the most common wild animals were hunted. This may be due to the fact that the Islamic population preferred

BOX 6.1   ARCHAEOBOTANY AND ARCHAEOZOOLOGY

Archaeobotany and archaeozoology are inter-disciplinary subjects within the research area of environmental archaeology (Jones 2002).

Plant remains from archaeological excavations are the main archaeobotanical source material, which are analysed in a laboratory with special equipment. First though, soil samples have to be taken from well-defined, and well-recorded, contexts or layers during the course of the exca-vation. In the laboratory, each sample is washed separately through sieves with mesh sizes down to 0.25mm, from which both small artefacts, such as beads, and ecofacts, such as fish-bones, seeds and fruits, will normally be recovered (Fig 1). With the help of a binocular microscope, all morphological features, even the finest cell-structure of the seeds can be seen which can then be identified by comparison with a modern refer-ence collection. The state of preservation of plant remains is strongly dependent on their location in the archaeological deposit (Jacomet & Kreuz 1999). If the layer in question is situated below the modern water-table (meaning that it is per-manently wet), and if no oxygen or micro-organ-ism has decomposed the layer, uncarbonized organic material can be preserved.

If the archaeological layers are above the water-table, only charred and mineralised plant remains are preserved. Desiccated plant remains are known in Europe from graves and from building materials dating to the late medieval and post-medieval periods (see Vol 2).

Bones, teeth and antlers from domestic and wild animals are commonly found during exca-vations. For the most part, these finds are recov-ered and sampled by the excavators. Again, in order to identify the often fragmented material, a modern reference collection is needed.

Plant and bone remains from archaeological excavations provide information about many

Fig 1

Seeds and fruits from the Viking period town of Hedeby (Box 4.3), in northern Germany (photo: Stiftung Schleswig-Holsteinische Landesmuseen Schloss Gottorf).

aspects of the everyday life of medieval popula-tions. Which foods were staples in the daily diet? Which crops were cultivated? Which domestic animals were kept? Were wild plants and game animals important to supplement the diet? Were plants used to dye textiles (Hall, in Kroll & Pasternak 1995)? Were plants and animals used for ceremonial purposes? With the help of plant remains the environmental condition and the vegetation cover around sites can be recon-structed. Was the surrounding area covered with woodland? Or was there an open landscape dur-ing the occupation of the site? How was the land-scape modified by the population? Within the settlement itself, plant and animal remains can help to reconstruct and define activity areas, e.g. stores, threshing areas, stables, ovens, latrines, etc. Functional analyses of the distribution of plant remains and dung residues from domestic animals within individual buildings can help to reconstruct the interior organisation of farm-steads (Viklund 1998; Karg et al 2004). Medieval land-use systems and crop-processing methods can also be illuminated (see also Vol 2).

By Sabine Karg

tender meats and tended to avoid the strong-flavoured flesh of deer and wild goats. In Christian areas, there are no certain indications of wild mammals having been consumed in the countryside. However, in urban and elite areas, where such was a sign of social status, there is plenty of evidence for game hunting, especially deer.

In coastal areas and near rivers or lakes, various types of fish were eaten (and were an important element in the Christian diet, particularly in Lent). These were mainly caught using shallow-water or coastal fishing methods and it does not seem likely that deep-sea fishing took place at this period. There are also signs of fishing in places such as the canals made for powering water-mills, where a reserve or hatchery could be kept. The consumption of molluscs and crustaceans is recorded, along with land snails.

The main species that were consumed are:

- SHEEP AND GOATS: (*Ovis aries* – *Capra hircus*): these need to be treated as a single species because, on most sites, it has not been possible to differentiate between the two. The animals were eaten whilst still young, aged two years at the most. It was also common to butcher animals younger than six months. Where it has been possible to distinguish between the two species, it has been established that there was a predominance of goat over sheep in the Mediterranean subsistence systems, with this ratio reversed when moving away from the region. It is likely that sheep were used for wool as well as meat, whereas goat-rearing was mainly done for milk production.

- CATTLE: (*Bos taurus*). The consumption of cows, bulls and oxen has been widely recorded on both Christian and Islamic sites, although there is one important difference: on the former, the consumption was of adult and older animals, which had already been used for work, milk production or reproduction; whereas on the latter, it was mostly young animals that were slaughtered, signifying their use solely for consumption.

- PIGS/BOARS: (*Sus scrofa*): it is difficult to ascertain whether the remains recovered from different sites are those of domestic pigs, boars, wild pigs or pigs reared in semi-wild conditions. Within the Christian context, the pig was a main source of meat supply and its use is recorded in documentary sources, in iconographic representations, in literature and, of course, on archaeological sites. The presence of pork in the Islamic context is, however, a more complex issue to approach because of the Koran forbidding its consumption. Nevertheless, archaeological finds (e.g. from Lisbon, Seville and Mértola) repeatedly suggest that pig-meat was quite frequently eaten in such places, indicating the presence of Christian communities that were not affected by this prohibition.

- RABBITS: (*Oryctolagus cuniculus*): there are almost always remains of rabbit present on Mediterranean sites, becoming virtually non-existent when moving northwards. It has not been determined whether this species had been domesticated prior to the twelfth century, whether it was reared in semi-wild conditions or whether they were wild rabbits obtained by hunting. This animal was commonly eaten in Islamic areas.

- CHICKENS: (*Gallus domesticus*): these birds were widely eaten, both as adults and young. The consumption of eggs was also important, as indicated by frequent finds of egg-shells and bones from egg-laying hens.

- GAME: the main hunted species were hares (*Lepus granatensis*) and partridges (*Alectorys rufa*), and to a lesser extent red deer (*Cervus elaphus*) and other deer species.

- OTHER MEATS: there is some evidence for the consumption of horse (*Equus caballus*) and also donkey (*Equus asinus*), although it was minor and supplementary food-source, given that these animals were bred for work, war and leisure.

- FISH: fishing was carried out near the coast, on river estuaries and on lakes and inland waterways; tuna, sturgeon, grey mullet, cuttlefish, mullet, carp, eel, etc, were caught.

- MOLLUSCS, CRUSTACEANS AND LAND SNAILS: were gathered from their habitats.

How were they eaten?

The bones of animals eaten by humans have traces of whatever methods were used to butcher and bone the meat once the animal had been slaughtered. The resultant cut-marks are a sign of how the meat was prepared for consumption. First of all the areas which cannot be eaten were removed – horns, antlers, skin, lower parts of limbs; however, these parts were often useful as raw materials. This work was usually done at the place where the animal was slaughtered; subsequently, the animal was butchered, using specific cuts through joints and along the shafts of long bones, with the intention of dividing the meat up so as to make it easier to transport to another place, for selling or for further butchery before cooking. The last step in the process was boning the meat, which took place either when the meal was being prepared or when it was eaten.

The most common method of preparation was to cut the meat into small pieces for cooking, accompanied possibly by vegetables and pulses. This can be deduced from an analysis of the bones and by studying the various surviving recipes. This method provided a better way of obtaining nourishment than roasting a complete animal, or large pieces of meat, which seems to have been less popular. Butchery traditions (cut-marks) and methods of cooking and eating are cultural characteristics that may serve as distinguishing traits between communities, or to differentiate between periods within the same community (Bertrand 2001).

Other foods of animal origin were also consumed in addition to the basic meat products, especially milk and its secondary products, but also beef and pork lard, and honey.

Honey was used mainly as a sweetener, although it served also as a seasoning, preservative and medicine. The apiculture industry was significant, particularly in al-Andalus, where large quantities of honey were produced for selling, although the nests of wild bees were also exploited.

Food of Vegetable Origin

During the early Middle Ages, it seems that people had a varied diet based on food of vegetable origin – cereals, pulses and other vegetables – supplemented by animal products. These eating habits were common across the board, both in Muslim and Christian communities, but in some areas these need to be studied more closely. This is because different factors, such as climate, soil fertility, agricultural techniques and land-ownership, etc, had considerable influence on the production and consumption of vegetable species. In areas with a Mediterranean climate, the main crops were cereals, olives, figs and grapes.

Which vegetables were eaten?

- CEREALS: mainly wheat and barley in the warmer areas, and rye in colder areas towards the north; of lesser importance were: oats, sorghum, millet and emmer.

- GARDEN PRODUCE, VEGETABLES AND LEGUMES: Andalusian garden produce was most varied, the following all being grown: pumpkins, aubergines, watermelons, cucumber, melons, garlic, parsnips, cabbage, carrots, leeks, beetroot, spinach, artichokes, etc. Several species of legume were in use (e.g. broad beans, peas, chick peas, lentils, kidney beans, etc). Produce from suburban gardens was mainly for market purposes, while there were also some experimental gardens, such as Arruzafa, in the eighth century, and Madinat al-Zahara, in the tenth century, in Cordoba, where species such as date-palms, rice and sugar-cane were acclimatised.

- FRUITS: the principle species of the Mediterranean region were olives, grapes and figs. In areas which were not suitable for the growing these trees, other species became more important: apple, walnut, hazel and wild fruits, such as blackberries. A wide variety of fruit trees was cultivated in Andalusian gardens: apples, pears, plums, apricots, quince, cherry and also some nuts, such as walnuts, almonds and pine.

- HERBS AND SPICES: spices were not used for preserving and were expensive for seasoning, so that they not available to most people; hence the use of herbs, such as thyme, marjoram, fennel, coriander, saffron, cumin, etc, was more common for both seasoning and preservative purposes.

How were they used?

Cereals, mostly wheat and rye, were used for making bread as well as *plumenta*, a porridge-like mixture made from rye, oats or millet. Some pulses and nuts, such as chestnuts, were also used for making flour used in soups and stews, and even bread-making.

Wine was a highly-regarded drink with food, but it was also associated with Christian worship. A revered beverage, it was even taken by Muslims who ignored the Koran's proscription. Known as *cervioisse* or *cervogia*, at that time, beer was a cloudy liquid made from fermented cereals. It was mainly consumed in the outermost regions of the Mediterranean basin.

Olives, grapes and figs were eaten in their natural state, but when converted into trade products they became commercially significant. Olive oil from al-Andalus was held in high esteem, being exported to both Christian and Islamic lands, along with dried grapes and figs. Freshly-picked fruit was eaten mainly in warm regions, but it was also transformed into preserves, jams, syrups and liquid refreshments.

Food of Mineral Origin

Water and salt were and remain basic necessities. Even though water was plentiful in its natural state, there were significant difficulties relating to its availability and portability. It had to be sought out and routed through canals and wells, stored in cisterns and domestic vessels, such as earthenware storage jars. Water was blessed and disinfectant products, such as *almagra* (red earth containing high levels of iron), were used, in the hope of maintaining a steady clean supply (Fig 6.3).

Salt is essential to the human diet: it provides sodium and other basic minerals, and enhances food's natural flavour. It is also widely used as a preservative. There is not much known about salt production in this region (cf. pp 232-3). It was extracted by means of evaporation, using sea-water to form coastal salt-pans, or from saltwater taken from streams or underground currents at inland salt mines, this latter being the most common form (Fig 6.4). In warm areas, evaporation was natural, while in colder, damp regions, the water had to be heated, which made the end product more expensive.

Preservation and Storage

The different techniques and methods used to preserve and store food are a means of solving the problem of what to do with surplus supplies, to be kept for a variety of reasons and for different lengths of time. It was necessary to store food so that times of

Fig 6.3   *Storage and shipping jars for the red ochre used for disinfecting water in el-Andalus (photo: M. Valor).*

Traditional inland evaporating ponds for salt, at Cortijo de la Salina, Montejácar, Granada, Spain **Fig 6.4**
(after Quesada 1995).

need could be endured without hunger. Seeds were preserved for sowing, surpluses were stored for domestic use, and stores could be laid up in case of siege. All kinds of food-stuffs were stored, using different preservation techniques to lengthen the period that they would remain edible.

Cereals were the mainstay of both Christian and Muslim diets. Consequently, their storage in suitable surroundings and conditions, to ensure their preservation over long periods, was of utmost importance.

Silos are underground structures, built in a globular, truncated cone or sack shape, having a relatively narrow opening at ground-level, covered by a lid (Fig 6.5). Stone lids have been found inside abandoned silos, some of which are rotary querns that have been re-cycled as covers. Urban silos have been located under the floors of dwellings, as well as in series, connected by underground corridors or by their side walls.

Although there was no fixed design for this type of structure, when choosing the location for installing a silo, temperature and humidity had to be taken into account to avoid spoiling the stored goods (e.g. germination, bacterial growth or fungus). Also, the silo had to be well protected from invasion by insects and rodents. Where possible the silo was carved from rock, but the most common form was dug into the ground, in which case the walls were covered with mortar or mud, or were hardened by lighting a fire inside the structure.

Within the Christian context, groups of silos have been studied, and it is possi-ble to differentiate large, pear-shaped silos from other smaller and shallower construc-

Fig 6.5 *Silos such as these (pre-12th-century), excavated at Plaza de Ramales, Madrid (Spain), were used to store cereals for long periods (photo: A Fernández).*

tions. The former were used to store a village's harvest, while the smaller versions were used to store seed corn for sowing the following year. Often, these groups of silos were connected to a religious centre and/or a cemetery (Reyes Téllez 1986), and their fall into disuse coincides with the extension of the place of worship and the building of a new church. Another theory (Fernández Ugalde 1994) relates the assemblages of silos to social forms of tribal origin, connected to family or joint property ownership, and the quantities they needed to store, with their later decline and disuse being due to the adoption of a feudal system, with the landlord taking possession of the surplus crops.

The existence of granaries is not completely recognised, although some specific areas near domestic structures, where large post-hole patterns have been detected, may have been used for the purpose of grain storage.

Other methods for keeping food include smoking and salting, for meat and fish, the drying of certain fruits, such as grapes and figs, and the domestic manufacture of preserves, of which there are several types mentioned in written sources, using fat, vinegar or brine as preservatives. Other methods of preservation and manipulation of foodstuffs, to produce a longer life, include milk being made into butter or cheese.

These foodstuffs were stored in ceramic vessels – storage jars and jugs, or in plant-based containers – baskets, panniers, nets and wooden recipients, such as barrels, associated with the production and sale of wine. The stored goods had to be protected from animals, keeping them off the floor and using natural deterrents, or by using processes or products such as smoke, ashes, aromatic plants or dried animal excrement.

It was necessary to build structures for collecting, routing and storing a permanent and clean water-supply. Within dwellings wells were dug and small tanks were used to collect rain water. Also, large earthenware jars were used to store water brought in from rivers and fountains. However, when it was necessary to have a plentiful supply available over a long period of time, large water cisterns were built, called *aljibes*.

Aqueducts were used to collect and transport water to towns which might be several kilometres away from the source. This system became the basis for a singular agricultural landscape where vegetable gardens and irrigation systems were the norm, as well as water-mills. Another method used in the Andalusian area was underground channels, known as *qanats*, which could convey water over several kilometres.

Preparation and Consumption of Food

Some foodstuffs were eaten raw, but they were mostly cooked. There are broad distinctions to be made between common nourishment, directly related to local supply and customs and the richer and more diverse diet of the aristocracy where more elaborate and varied dishes were prepared, including rare and expensive products, especially spices.

The most popular dish was *olla* or *cocido* (hotpot or stew), made from broth with meat and vegetables, to which lard and bread was added. Roast meats were not a very common dish, pertaining mainly to the nobility.

Preparation and cooking of food required a specific place to set and keep a fire under control. The most common place was a hearth, a worked structure which is easily recognised on an archaeological site because of the remains of fire and ashes.

In Islamic houses there is evidence for the hearth being located in a space dedicated to cooking (see Box 5.1). There are various types which divide into two categories:

- Basic hearths made by just digging a pit in the ground; pot-sherds may be included and/or a small brick or stone surround. This was the commonest form.

- Brick-built hearths. These were not common and co-existed with the above-mentioned hearths, being found in the same locations. They were used in urban dwellings and are well-documented in Cordoba, but are practically non-existent in rural areas.

Bread-ovens are rare and thus not well documented. They are found as an additional element in the cooking area, e.g. at Madinat al-Zahara, Cordoba (Vallejo Triano 1990), alongside hearths, e.g. Castillo Viejo Alcoutim, Portugal (Catarino 2004).

Other fireplaces used for cooking foods that have been documented in al-Andalus are *tannur* and *anafe* (braziers), both made of ceramic. The *tannur* has a truncated cone or cylindrical shape, open on both sides, with air-vents underneath. It was used both as a stove and for baking bread. The *anafe* is another kind of portable brazier, divided into two sections by a central grill. Cooking pots were placed in the upper section, using knobs or prongs to prevent them from coming into direct contact with the fire, with the lower section being used for collecting ashes and providing ventilation.

In Christian areas, hearths and stoves were likewise basic necessities of daily-life. Used for both heating and cooking, they might be located in the kitchen area and were sometimes just pits in the ground. Alternatively, some previously-used construction that had fallen into disuse could be restored, or, particularly in the case of ovens, be purpose-made outside the dwelling. On sites in the Iberian Peninsula, their identification is somewhat difficult, their traces not being very evident, perhaps due to a semi-nomadic life-style resulting in the use of temporary or ephemeral construction techniques. However, the large quantity of pots and other narrow-mouthed forms, showing signs of having been used for cooking, implies the existence of such hearths.

Food was prepared and eaten using containers made from a variety of different materials, mainly ceramic and wood, although metal and glass were also used for more luxurious items. The study of ceramic production, not just forms and techniques, but also matters such as function, diffusion and influences, all contribute to a better understanding of Andalusian culture, eating habits and relationships with nearby cultures. In Southern Europe, from the eighth-twelfth centuries two large regions became defined: a southern area, very advanced and open to influences coming from the Eastern Mediterranean, consisting of the southern and central regions of Italy and al-Andalus on the Iberian Peninsula; and another area, with less-developed ceramic technologies, some clearly relict and resistant to change, and of inferior technical quality, which, broadly speaking, included the remaining territories considered in this study.

A general overview of the development of the different areas reveals that the northern region had ceramics produced at a lower technical level, with little variety in forms, made by hand or on a slow-wheel – the fast-wheel was not common until the eleventh or twelfth century depending on the region – and mainly using reduced firing. The decoration consisted of simple motifs, and there was a predominance of narrow-mouthed shapes, such as pots and jugs. In contrast, in the southern region, rough-textured ceramics for everyday use, such as cooking and storage, existed alongside fine-quality tableware. Both were made using the fast-wheel, with oxidised firing and a variety of clays, depending on the intended use of the item. Glaze began to be used and would eventually become a common feature (see Box 8.1), both as an impermeable surface layer and as a decorative technique. The basic assemblage of forms became more varied, having different shapes for specific usage: pots and casseroles for cooking; shallow forms for the table; small mugs for drinking; jars and jugs for storing water; oil lamps for lighting; and so forth.

PART 2: THE REST OF EUROPE *by Sabine Karg*

Food from Fields

During the High Middle Ages, the spread of urbanism across Europe removed more and more people from the primary agricultural sector who had to be supported with food. This fact led to a change within the land-use system from subsistence farming to surplus production. The two-field rotation system was replaced by three-field rotation (Henning

1994). The arable land around villages was divided into the summer-crop area, the winter-crop field and fallow land (Karg & Pfrommer 2003), as illustrated in Fig 6.6 (see also p 100). According to Rösener (1987), this system of land-use emerged during the High Middle Ages, first in the huge agrarian regions of Northern France, the Netherlands and Western Germany, before it spread with different speed to the neighbouring areas.

New crops were introduced, as shown by many archaeobotanical studies, but regional differences existed in the preference for specific crops (van Zeist et al 1991). To give an example (Fig 6.7), during the eighth-tenth centuries in Southern Germany spelt wheat (*Triticum spelta*), oats (*Avena sativa*), naked wheat (*Triticum aestivum*), barley (*Hordeum vulgare*) and einkorn wheat (*Triticum monococcum*) were the dominant species. Rye (*Secale cereale*) seems to have spread from the North and East into the Alamannic region, whereas spelt and einkorn were still were common in Northern Switzerland (Rösch et al 1992). In the coastal regions of Northern Germany, barley and oats were mostly cultivated. Spelt wheat and rye did not play an important role, as did horse bean (*Vicia faba*) and flax (*Linum usitatissimum*). At trading-places, such as Hedeby, naked wheat and a wide variety of fruits and imported goods have been found (Behre 1983). In the Slavonic settlements in Central Germany, barley and rye were the most appreciated crops (Willerding, in Benecke et al 2003).

These regional preferences are connected with different soil types and soil fertility, but probably also with regional food preferences and traditions. Rye is a very modest but high yielding crop that therefore was – and still is today – cultivated in many areas with sandy soils. Oats are also easy to cultivate on poor soils. Kroll (1987) could even show that in the coastal areas of Northern Germany a special oat species, naked oat (*Avena strigosa*), was planted. Oats played an important role in the areas formerly under Roman control. It was probably mostly used as animal fodder for horses (Rösch et al 1992).

Millet (*Panicum miliaceum* & *Setaria italica*) is rarely found and was more widespread in the southern regions of Europe and the Slavonic parts of Central/Northern Europe. The evidence for legumes within archaeological layers is very rare during all periods. The question as to 'why should this be case?' has often been discussed. Most authors tend to the hypothesis that legumes would not have been roasted before being consumed and therefore the chances of them being preserved by burning are very small; in uncarbonised condition, their remains are not easy to recognize. Most of the medieval evidence is derived from charred storage finds dating from the late Middle Ages (see Vol 2).

As highly important oil- and fibre-plants, flax (*Linum usitatissimum*) and hemp (*Cannabis sativa*) must be named, being also important for the production of textiles and ropes. From many Scandinavian settlements dated to the Viking period, linseeds and seed capsules are recorded (Karg 2007).

Food from Gardens

The centuries between 800 and 1200 are marked by the foundation of villages and monasteries all across Europe. In the regions that had been occupied by the Romans, it

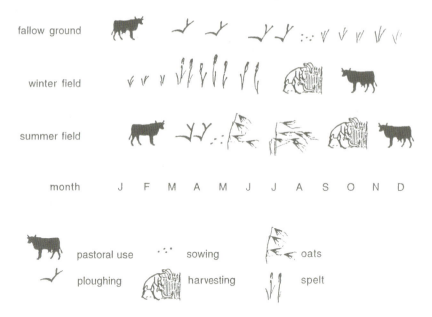

The three-field rotation system

fallow ground

winter field

summer field

month   J   F   M   A   M   J   J   A   S   O   N   D

pastoral use   sowing   oats

ploughing   harvesting   spelt

Fig 6.6   *Reconstruction of the medieval 3-field rotation system in the region of Laufen (Switzerland), adapted from Abel 1978 (from Karg 1994; by permission of Springer Science & Business Media).*

seems that the tradition of cultivating vegetables, herbs, spices and fruit, had been carried on continuously. In this connection, the archaeobotanical results of Knörzer, in the German Rhineland, must be mentioned (Knörzer, in van Zeist et al 1991). The documentary sources provide information about the setting up, organisation and plant spectrum in monastery gardens, such as the well-known *Capitulare de villis* of Charlemagne, dated to 812, and the monastery plan of St Gall (Fig 14.5). In these ideal plans for a Carolingian Benedictine monastery, three different garden types are mentioned: a vegetable garden, a spice- and medicinal garden, as well as an orchard, which was often situated on the same ground as the graveyard (Fischer-Benzon 1894).

To be accompanied by the spread of monasteries towards the Northern and Eastern parts of Europe, these garden concepts were introduced by monks all over the region and later taken over by the local peasants. The systematic creation of gardens is first documented in Europe in connection with the foundation of the monasteries. The garden culture seems to have been very advanced, at least within the Carolingian Empire, as is demonstrated by archaeobotanical studies in southern France (Ruas 1996). Depending on their location, the gardens were divided into monastery gardens, castle gardens, peasant gardens, and citizen or tradesman's gardens. Archaeobotanical studies from the English medieval towns of Norwich, York and London show that several spices and medical plants had been cultivated in the citizen's gardens, such as dill (*Anethum graveolens*) and celery (*Apium graveolens*), as well as coriander (*Coriandrum sativum*) (Dickson, in Moe 1994).

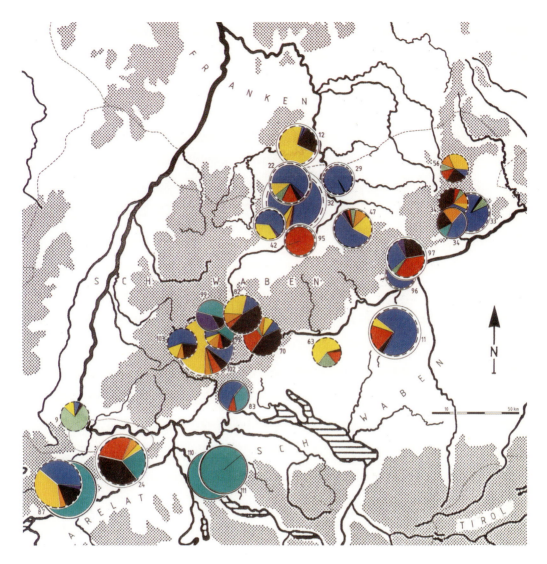

Percentage of cereal grains from sites of the High Middle Ages (11th-13th centuries). Yellow: Triticum **Fig 6.7**
spelta (spelt wheat); Blue: Secale cereale (rye); Violet: varia; Blue/Green: Panicum miliaceum (millet); Black: Avena spec (oats); Red: Hordeum vulgare (barley); Green: Triticum aestivum/durum (naked wheats); Orange: Triticum monococcum (Einkorn); for further details, see Rösch et al 1992, fig 7 (reproduced with permission of Springer Science & Business Media).

Not many analyses for the Viking period have yet been undertaken in the Nordic countries, with the important exception of Hedeby (summary in Elsner 1994). The reviews given by Eggen (in Moe 1994) and by Robinson (1994) indicate the presence of typical Nordic plant species, such as angelica (*Angelica archangelica*) besides the widespread, and obviously much appreciated, coriander. With the foundation of the monasteries and the first towns, the diversity of species increased (Karg 2007). Fig 6.8 illustrates a range of vegetables that was found in archaeological excavations in Denmark dating from 1050-1300. In the samples from the twenty-three sites that were analysed, it is dill (*Anethum graveolens*), cabbage (*Brassica species*), carrot (*Daucus carota*), celery (*Apium graveolens*) and chicory (*Cichorium intybus*) that dominate the spectrum.

It is still not clear what role vegetables and spices played in the daily diet of the European population during the early and High Middle Ages. According to archaeobotanical results there must have been considerable regional differences. The new cultivars were introduced into the areas outside *Germania Romana* but did not reach, or were not accepted, in the regions occupied by the Slavonic tribes and the Scandinavians of the Viking period (Willerding, in Benecke et al 2003; Karg & Robinson 2002). In eastern Germany, as well as in Scandinavia, it has been shown that cultivated fruits, for example, were spread by the Cistercian order from the twelfth century onwards (Fig 6.9). In Hungary and south-western Germany it seems that there was a continuity in cultivating fruit trees from the Roman period onwards, as shown by archaeobotanical evidence (Wasylikowa et al, in van Zeist et al 1991). Huge quantities of fruit-stones have been found in the deposits of the early urban settlements all over temperate Europe and the fruit-tree assortment seems to be largely the same as that of Roman period (Knörzer, in van Zeist et al 1991). The following species are frequently found: sour cherry (*Prunus cerasus*), wild cherry (*Prunus avium*), plum (*Prunus domestica*), pear (*Pyrus* sp) and apple (*Malus* sp). Peach (*Prunus persica*) and walnuts (*Juglans regia*), for example, are recorded at the trading-place of Hedeby (Behre 1983), and later in early towns like Oslo, in Norway (Griffin 1979), but are rarely found. Figs (*Ficus carica*) are first recorded again outside the Mediterranean regions from the twelfth century onwards, having been present all over the Roman Empire, as were many other Mediterranean products, until the fourth century AD (Bakels & Jacomet, in van der Veen 2003). Not all the products found their way back to the regions north of the Alps and then mostly for the first time during the twelfth/thirteenth century, as was the case with the figs (see Vol 2).

Food from Hedges and Forests

In nearly every archaeological excavation of this period the remains of oil- and vitamin-rich plants collected from the wild are recorded (Karg & Jacomet 1991; Karg & Robinson 2002). Fig 6.9 shows the spectrum of fruits and nuts from the same twenty-three archaeologically investigated sites in Denmark dating from 1050-1300. It is obvious that collected wild fruits and berries dominate the spectrum. The most frequently found berries are common elder (*Sambucus nigra*) and wild strawberry (*Fragaria vesca*), beside hazelnuts (*Corylus avellana*). These species were collected all over Europe because they were important vitamin and oil suppliers and could be easily preserved and stored for the winter months. At least for the less rich population, wild collected vegetables, fruits, nuts and berries played an essential part in daily nutrition. It is worth mentioning that there was most probably trade in wild berries between the rural population and the urban inhabitants, as shown by finds of the very tasty cloudberry (*Rubus chamaemorus*; Karg 2007). In the late medieval period this sort of trading can be detected for other wild fruit species (see Vol 2).

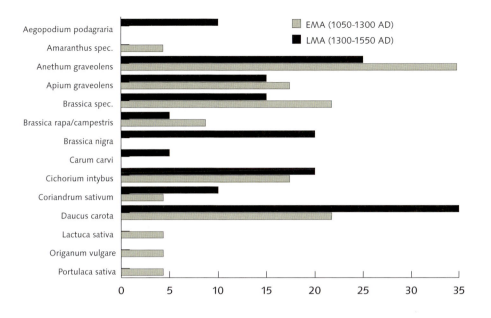

Spectrum of the vegetables and herbs from medieval sites in Denmark (after Karg & Robinson 2002).   **Fig 6.8**

Alcoholic Beverages

Important raw products for the most common alcoholic beverages were honey, barley and grapes. Honey was used for making mead, as described by ancient authors. Beer played an important role in the life of the Vikings, but also for the inhabitants of the early towns all over Europe. The ingredients for the production of beer were water, cereal crops (especially barley), and spices to flavour and preserve the beer (Box 6.2). In places where the consumption of fresh water was dangerous for health, people preferred to drink beer whenever it was affordable. Wine played an indispensable role in the Church. It seems that the spread of grapes to Northern and Western Europe was closely connected with the newly-founded monasteries (Karg 2007). The favourable climatic conditions during this part of the medieval period made the cultivation of grapes possible in regions that later became unsuited (Glaser 2001). Wine was certainly also imported from the South. Wine was transported in barrels that have been found in archaeological excavations; at Ribe, barrels made from staves of oak are interpreted as wine-casks imported from the Rhine valley (Daly 2007); see also those from Hedeby (p 308, Fig 10.6).

Food from Domestic Animals

During the early and High Middle Ages animal husbandry was based on nearly the same domestic species as those of the previous centuries: cattle, pigs, sheep, goats, horses, hens and geese. However, many domestic animals diminished in size during the early medieval period compared to the Roman period (Benecke et al 2003).

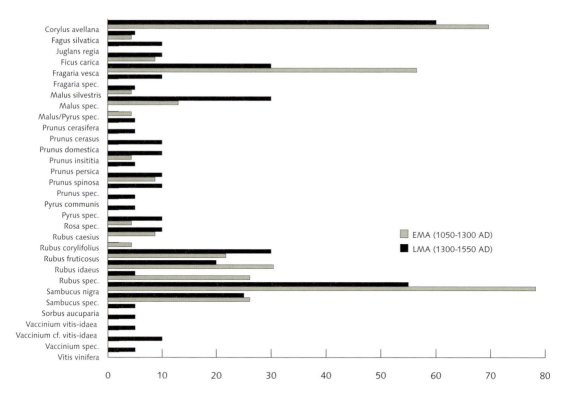

Fig 6.9　*Spectrum of the fruits and nuts from medieval sites in Denmark (after Karg & Robinson 2002).*

Dogs and cats, donkeys and doves were introduced to the northern parts of Central Europe. It has been suggested that the spread of rabbit is attributable to the Vikings, but this is not proved. Pig-rearing can be seen to become more intensive in many parts of the landlocked countryside of Central Europe during the sixth-tenth centuries, whereas in earlier centuries cattle-bones dominate in the archaeozoological record. A reason for this increase in pig-rearing might be the consequences of a re-structuring of the agrarian landscape. According to Benecke et al (2003), it is much more efficient to keep pigs than cattle, because the former deliver more fat and meat in a considerably shorter period of time than cattle. It is interesting to note that the increase in pigs is contemporaneous with an increase in human population. Poultry farming (most probably geese) also seems to have become more important.

As with the cereal crop spectrum, regional preferences for specific animal species can be seen in the archaeozoological material; in the coastal areas of northern Germany, cattle and sheep were still the preferred animals. Horses may have been eaten in Eastern Europe, given the high percentage of their bones found in archaeological excavations (Benecke et al 2003).

Regarding age at slaughtering, it is clear that the population of domestic animals was reduced in autumn, and during the winter months, because of the shortage of fodder, but then meat could also be stored more easily in the colder weather. It was the meat,

BOX 6.2   BEER & WINE

Fig 1

Sweet gale growing at a lakeshore in southern Sweden (photo: S Karg), and a fruit from the medieval site of Næstved, Denmark (photo: JA Harild).

Fig 2

A hop plant growing in Lejre, Denmark (photo: S Karg), and a hop seed from the medieval site of Næstved on Zealand, Denmark (photo: JA Harild).

Whenever affordable, beer was the preferred beverage during the Middle Ages. The kind of beer brewed was not at all comparable to modern beers. It was much lighter and often spiced with different kinds of herb, but the principles of beer brewing were the same then as now. The main ingredient is cereal, whether barley, rye or wheat does not matter. The corn has to be moistened so that it starts to germinate, but the germination is then arrested by careful drying. During this process, known as malting, the starch in the cereal grains is converted into soluble sugar. The malt is then ground and hot water is added to it, dissolving the sugar. The so-called 'stone-beer' got its name, because hot stones were used to heat the water in wooden barrels. The sprouted grains are then removed, and yeast is added to begin fermentation. In Northern Europe the leaves of sweet gale (*Myrica gale*) were added to the fermenting liquid to give a special taste, but also as a preservative (Fig 1). During the late medieval period, sweet gale (in Danish, *porse*) was forbidden, because it was said to make people blind. The wild growing bushes were replaced by hops (*Humulus lupulus*) that had to be cultivated in special hop-gardens (Fig 2). The female flowers are still used today as a beer additive. It is said that hopped beer was an invention of the Carolingians, when the profession of beer brewer was already in existence (Behre 1999).

Wine was much appreciated by the Romans who introduced the cultivation of grapes to the favourable regions within the Roman Empire. It is not known whether these vines survived during the Dark Ages. With the spread of Christianity in Europe, wine played an important role in religious ceremonies, but also again in daily-life. Not only did it symbolise the blood of Christ during the Mass, but many heathen festivals, such as spring rituals, were replaced by ceremonies connected with wine-saints. Already in the ninth century, 'urban customs' were strongly connected to Christian life in the wine-growing areas of Germany, Austria and Northern Italy (Graff 1988).

Thanks to the climatic optimum during the Middle Ages, vines could be cultivated in regions of Europe that became less favourable, e.g. along the south coast of the Baltic Sea. Wine was certainly an important trade commodity, but this commerce is difficult to detect in archaeobotanical finds. Seeds from grapes found in archaeological layers may derive from raisins that were also traded during the medieval period.

By Sabine Karg

milk and eggs that were the most appreciated products of domestic animals, but their skin and hair (wool), feathers, bones, horns and teeth also had value.

It must be remembered that domestic animals were also an important provider of locomotion for transporting goods and humans. Archaeological finds and illustrations show the use of large animals, such as horses, as draft animals. Castrated cattle were also used as working animals. Oxen were traded on a large scale in Northern Europe (Enemark 2003). The available osteological information indicates that cattle were different to modern breeds, being mostly a small and slim variation of the short-horned form (Benecke et al 2003).

Pigs also looked very different from today. They were smaller, with longer feet, and the head, with its tapered shape and small ears, resembled the wild pig more closely than modern pigs. They were mostly coloured black and had more hair (at least on their backs), as pictorial sources show (Benecke et al 2003, 182, fig 66). Metrical differences in the size of sheep bones demonstrate that different breeds existed in Europe. Their size varied from 57-67cm in height at the withers. Documentary sources from the end of the ninth century describe the use (amongst the Saami) of tame/domestic reindeer for milk and packing/carrying purposes (Benecke 1994).

Horses seem to have varied in size and form. In most of the regions they were no longer used as meat producers as among the Germanic tribes during the first centuries AD. In Central Europe, horse-skeletons began often to be found in human graves, indicating a closer relationship between mankind and horse; riding-horses are likewise to be found in Viking period pagan graves from Scandinavia to Iceland.

Variation in dogs is already obvious during the early medieval period. In the countryside, the remains of large dogs have been found, well suited for the protection of men and their domestic animals. Whereas in towns, castles and trading-places small breeds dominated which were probably also used, alongside cats, for hunting rats (Benecke et al 2003). The skins of the cats were appreciated for use as fur, as is indicated by the presence of cut-marks on the skulls.

Food from Wild Animals

Archaeozoological analyses reveal that considerable regional differences existed in the percentages of hunted animals present within the bone material. In general, it seems that hunted animals played little or no part in daily diet. 'Big-game' hunting became reserved for the elite (see pp 350-1 & 354), although in the North hunting for food (and furs) was more generally practised. It would have been profitable to hunt those animals that reduced the crops and garden plants, as for example roe deer, wild pigs and hare. Birds were certainly also hunted, when other food supplies were meagre.

As a result of the progressive introduction of Christianity, fish became a more important element in the diet across the whole of Europe. Within the Christian calendar, there were 100 days when the consumption of meat was forbidden, and so the flesh of mammals and birds was often replaced by fish (see Box 6.3).

BOX 6.3   SEA FISHING AND LONG-TERM SOCIO-ECONOMIC

The importance of sea fishing varied tremendously through space and time in medieval North-West Europe. This has long been suspected from historical sources, but these mostly postdate the eleventh century (e.g. Holm et al 1996; Starkey et al 2000; Campbell 2002). Archaeology now allows us to trace the 'history' of sea fishing further back in time and thus to begin to interpret its ebb and flow in the context of wider socio-economic developments. This is possible due to the zooarchaeological study of fish bones (Barrett et al 1999; Enghoff 1999; 2000; Perdikaris 1999; Van Neer & Ervynck 2003; Makowiecki 2003,

195; Barrett et al 2004), and to the stable-isotope analysis of human bone (Barrett et al 2001;

Fig 1

Boxplots (a-c) showing the percentages of common marine species in English fish-bone assemblages from AD600-1300 (based on the number of identified bones); (d) for comparison, the percentage of freshwater and migratory taxa, based on cyprinids, pike, perch, eel, smelt, salmonids and flatfish (many of which are probably flounder, which enters freshwater) (after Barrett et al 2004).

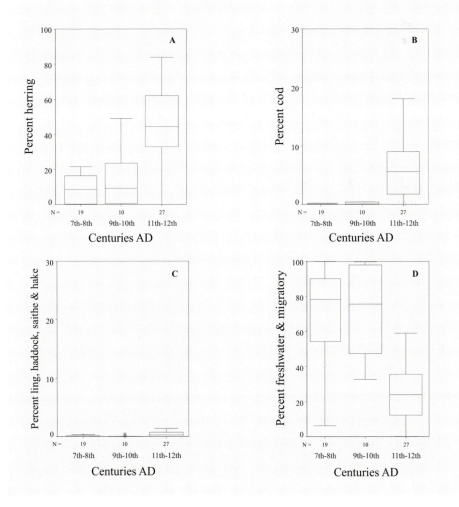

BOX 6.3   SEA FISHING AND LONG-TERM SOCIO-ECONOMIC

Müldner & Richards 2005; Barrett & Richards 2004). The former can tell us which sea fish were being caught and the latter how much marine food was being eaten.

A surprising result of this work has been the recognition of a major increase in the importance of fishing around, or shortly after, the end of the first millennium AD. This 'fish-event horizon' involved a major increase in catches of cod, herring and related species. Many of these were probably cured for long-range trade, as was the norm in

Fig 2

δ¹³C values and 2δ radiocarbon (or grave-good) date-ranges for Pictish to Viking period burials from Westness, Orkney. Each bar represents one skeleton: solid = females; open = males; hatched = child (after Barrett & Richards 2004).

subsequent centuries. This is earlier than the first surviving historical evidence for commercial fishing and may mark the development of trade in high bulk, low value, staple goods.

Although a widespread phenomenon, the specific chronology of the fish-event horizon varied from region to region; its causes are thus equally variable. A general trend has been overwritten by the environmental and historical contingencies of time and place. In some extremely maritime environments, such as coastal Arctic Norway, fish (cod in particular) was important throughout the first millennium, becoming more so at the beginning of the second as this region entered a pan-European fish trade (Christensen & Nielssen 1996; Perdikaris 1999). In contexts with greater agricultural potential, such as England, the transition was more dramatic (Fig 1). Within a few decades of 1000, the catch of herring prob-

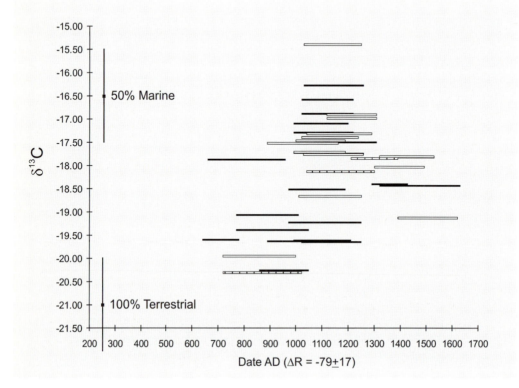

ably increased fourfold and cod were landed on a meaningful scale for the first time (Barrett et al 2004). Here the transition may have been driven by population growth (particularly in towns; see Dyer 2002), changes in Christian fasting practices (e.g. following the Benedictine reform of c970; Barrett et al 2004, 628-30), and human impacts on freshwater ecosystems (reducing the availability of freshwater fish; Hoffmann 1996).

Orkney, an archipelago off northern Scotland, provides an example between these extremes. It was part of the Pictish kingdom during the mid-first millennium, before being settled from Scandinavia, c850 (Graham-Campbell & Batey 1998). Here marine fishing was probably intensified in two stages: first, by the introduction of Norwegian food-ways during the Viking period (Barrett et al 1999; 2001; Cerón-Carrasco 2002); and, second, in response to the growing export market for dried fish in the eleventh-twelfth centuries (Barrett 1997; Barrett et al 2000, 15-19). These trends emerge from the analysis of fish bones from both domestic middens and semi-specialised 'fish middens' derived from dried cod production. They are also implied, however, by analyses of stable carbon and nitrogen isotope ratios in human bone that show increases in the dietary importance of fish through time (Figs 2-3).

By James H Barrett

Fig 3

$\delta^{13}C$ values and 2δ radiocarbon date ranges for Viking period to late medieval burials from Newark Bay, Orkney. Each bar represents one skeleton: solid = females; open = males; hatched = indeterminate (after Barrett & Richards 2004).

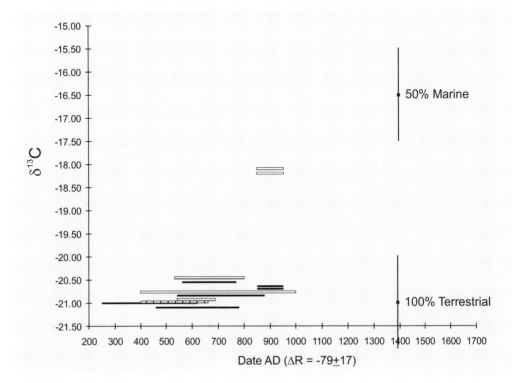

BIBLIOGRAPHY

Arellano Hernandez, OL et al (1994) 'El monasterio de San Vicente de Alcozar (Soria): aproximación arqueológica a su realidad histórica', *Numantia* 5 (1991/92), 167-79

Arié, R (1975) 'Remarques sur l'alimentation des musulmans d'espagne au cours du bas moyen age', in *Cuaderno de estudios medievales II-III*, Granada, 299-312

Arranz Minguez, JA et al (1994) 'El yacimiento romano-medieval de La Ermita en Melgar de Ariba (Valladolid)', *Numantia* 5 (1991/92), 127-38

Bakels, CC and Jacomet, S (2003) 'Access to luxury foods in Central Europe during the Roman period', *World Archaeology* 34:3, 542-57

Barrett, JH (1997) 'Fish trade in Norse Orkney and Caithness: a zooarchaeological approach', *Antiquity* 71, 616-38

Barrett, JH, Nicholson, RA and Cerón-Carrasco, R (1999) 'Archaeo-ichthyological evidence for long-term socioeconomic trends in northern Scotland: 3500BC to AD1500', *Journal of Archaeological Science* 26, 353-88

Barrett, J, Beukens, R, Simpson, I, Ashmore, P, Poaps, S and Huntley, J (2000) 'What was the Viking Age and when did it happen? A view from Orkney', *Norwegian Archaeological Review* 33, 1-39

Barrett, JH, Beukens, RP and Nicholson RA (2001) 'Diet and ethnicity during the Viking colonisation of northern Scotland: evidence from fish bones and stable carbon isotopes', *Antiquity* 75, 145-54.

Barrett, JH, Locker, AM and Roberts, CM (2004) '"Dark Age Economics" revisited: the English fish bone evidence AD600-1600', *Antiquity* 78, 618-36

Barrett, JH and Richards, MP (2004) 'Identity, gender, religion and economy: new isotope and radiocarbon evidence for marine resource intensification in early historic Orkney, Scotland', *European Journal of Archaeology* 7, 249-71

Barris Duran, J and Templado Lázaro, AM (1986) 'Primeras aportaciones al estudio del hábitat medieval de la cueva 'La Caula II' Boadella d'Empordá, Girona', in *Congreso de Arqueología Medieval Española* 5, Huesca, 599-613

Bate, M (1983) 'Los huesos de fauna en San Baudelio de Casillas de Berlanga', in Banks, P et al, 'Excavaciones en S. Baudelio de Casillas de Berlanga (Soria)', *Noticiario Arqueológico Hispánico*, 16, 433-34

Behre, K-E (1983) *Ernährung und Umwelt der wikingerzeitlichen Siedlung Haithabu*, Ausgrabungen Haithabu 8, Neumünster

Behre, K-E (1999) 'The history of beer additives in Europe – a review', *Vegetation History and Archaeobotany* 8, 35-48

Benecke, N (1994) *Der Mensch und seine Haustiere. Die Geschichte einer Jahrtausendalten Beziehung*, Stuttgart

Benecke N, Donat P, Gringmuth-Dallmer E and Willerding, U (2003) *Frühgeschichte der Landwirtschaft in Deutschland*, Beiträge zur Ur- und Frühgeschichte Mitteleuropas 14

Benavides Barajas, L (1992) *Al-Andalus. La cocina y su historia*, Motril

Benito Iborra, M (1989) 'La fauna de la rábita califal de las dunas de Guardamar', in Azuar, R et al (eds), *La rábita califal de las dunas de Guardamar (Alicante)*, Alicante, 153-61

Benito Iborra, M (1990) *Fauna medieval: el valle Sur del Vinalopó Medio*, Alicante

Bermúdez López, J. y Bazzana, A. (eds) (1990) *La casa hispano-musulmana. Aportaciones de la Arqueología – La maison hispano-musulmane. Apports de l'Archeologie*, Granada

Bernáldez Sánchez, E and Bernáldez Sánchez, M (2002) 'El subsuelo de la Catedral de los siglos XI al XVIII: de vertedero a cantera', in Hernán Ruiz, A (ed) *Magna Hispalenses (I) Recuperación de la aljama almohade*, Seville, 429-72

Bernáldez Sánchez, E and Bernáldez Sánchez, M (1997) 'Basureros y desechos haciendo historia. Restos paleobiológicos de la actividad urbana en las Reales Atarazanas de Sevilla', *P H (Revista del Instituto Andaluz de Patrimonio Histórico) nº 19 junio 1997*, Seville, 58-65

Bernáldez Sánchez, E and Bernáldez Sánchez, M (1998) 'Muladares y basureros de ayer, historia de hoy', *P H (Revista del Instituto Andaluz de Patrimonio Histórico) nº 22 marzo 1998*, Seville, 29-44

Bernáldez Sánchez, E and Bernáldez Sánchez, M (2005) 'Clambakes en la antigua villa romana de la Almagra (Huelva)? Tafonomía de basureros islámicos', *P H (Revista del Instituto Andaluz de Patrimonio Histórico) nº 53 Especial Criterios, abril 2005*, Seville, 35-43

Bernáldez Sánchez, E and Bernáldez Sánchez, M (2003) 'El vertedero islámico del Hospital de las Cinco Llagas. Historias orgánicas en la basura', in Vázquez Labourdette, A and Angel Tabales, M (eds), *Arqueología y rehabilitación en el Parlamento de Andalucía. Investigaciones arqueológicas en el Antiguo Hospital de las Cinco Llagas de Sevilla*, Seville, 288-318

Bertrand, M and Sánchez Viciana, JR (2001) 'Poblamiento y explotación del territorio en la región de Guadix/Baza durante la Edad Media', *Anuario Arqueológico de Andalucía'97-II*, Seville, 98-104

Bertrand, M, Sánchez Viciana, JR and Garrido García, JA (2001) 'Poblamiento y explotación del territorio en la región de Guadix-Baza durante la época medieval', *Anuario Arqueológico de Andalucía'98-II*, Seville, 56-67

Bolens, L (1992) *La cocina andaluza, un arte de vivir. Siglos XI-XIII*, Madrid

Campbell, J (2002) 'The millennium herring', in Harper-Bill, C, Rawcliffe, C and Wilson, RG (eds), *East Anglia's History*, Woodbridge, 5-17

Cartledge, J (1978) 'Le ossa animale dell'area Sud del Chiostro di San Silvestro a Genova, 1977', *Archeologia medievale* 5, 437-51

Castaños, P.M. (1986) 'Estudio conjunto de la muestra faunística', in Domínguez A et al 'Un nuevo yacimiento arqueológico en el Alto Sobrarbe (Huesca)', in *I Congreso de Arqueología Medieval Española* 5, Zaragoza/Huesca, 529-52

Catarino, H (2004) *Castelo Velho de Alcoutim. As ruinas de una fortificação islâmica*, Loulé.

Cerón-Carrasco, R (2002) *Of Fish and Men, De Iasg agus Dhaoine: aspects of the utilization of marine resources as recovered from selected Hebridean archaeological sites*, unpublished PhD thesis, University of Edinburgh

Christensen, P and Nielssen, AR (1996) 'Norwegian fisheries 1100-1970: main developments', in Holm, P, Starkey, DJ and Thor, J (eds) *The North Atlantic Fisheries, 1100-1976: National Perspectives on a Common Resource*, Esbjerg, 145-76

Cuisenier J and Guadagnin R (dir) (1988) *Un village au temps de Charlemagne. Moines et paysans de l'abbaye de Saint-Denis du VIIᵉ siècle à l'An Mil*, Paris

Daly, A (2007) *Timber, Trade and Tree-rings. A dendrochonological analysis of structural oak timber in Northern Europe, cAD1000 to cAD1650*, unpublished PhD thesis, University of Southern Denmark

Démians d'Archimbaud, G. (ed) (1997) *La céramique médiévale en Méditerranée. Actes du VIᵉ Congrès de L'AIECM2*, Aix-en-Provence

Dickson, C (1994) 'Macroscopic fossils of garden plants fromBritish Roman and medieval deposits', in Moe, D (ed), *Garden History: Garden Plant, Species, Forms and Varieties from Pompeii to 1800*, PACT 42, Court-St-Étienne, 47-72

Dyer, C (2002) *Making a Living in the Middle Ages*, London

Eggen, M (1994) 'The plants used in a Viking Age garden AD800-1050', in Moe, D (ed), *Garden History, Garden Plants, Species, Forms and Varieties from Pompeii to 1800*, PACT 42, Court-Saint-Étienne, 45-6

Elsner, H (1994) *Wikingermuseum Haithabu: Schaufenster einer frühen Stadt*, Neumünster

Enemark, P (2003) *Danske oksehandel 1450-1550: fra efterårsmarkeder til forårsdrivning*, Aarhus

Enghoff, IB (1999) 'Fishing in the Baltic region from the 5th century BC to the 16th century AD: evidence from fish bones', *Archaeofauna* 8, 41-85

Enghoff, IB (2000) 'Fishing in the southern North Sea region from the 1st to the 16th century AD: evidence from fish bones', *Archaeofauna* 9, 59-132

Fernandez Ugalde, A (1994) 'El fenómeno del relleno de silos y la implantación del feudalismo en Madrid y en el reino de Toledo', in *IV Congreso de Arqueología Medieval Española* 3, Alicante, 611-17

Fischer-Benzon, R (1894) *Altdeutsche Gartenflora. Untersuchungen über die Nutzpflanzen des deutschen Mittelalters, ihre Wanderung und ihre Vorgeschichte im klassischen Altertum*, Kiel

Flandrin, J-L and Montanari, M (eds) (2004) *Historia de la alimentación*, Gijón

Francesc Cariana, J et al (1986) 'Datos para el estudio del poblamiento rural altomedieval del Maresme (Barcelona)', in *I Congreso de Arqueología Medieval Española* 4, Zaragoza/Huesca, 569-85

Gallart, J, Giralt, J and Miró JM (1986) 'Excavaciones en el lado norte de la iglesia de Sant Martí (Lleida). Época andalusí y medieval', in *I Congreso de Arqueología Medieval Española* 4, Zaragoza/Huesca, 313-30

Garcia Gomez, E and Lévi Provençal, E (1992) *Sevilla a comienzos del siglo XII. El tratado de Ibn Abdun*, Seville

Garcia Sánchez, E (1983) 'La alimentación en la Andalucía islámica. Estudio histórico y bromatológico I. Cereales y leguminosas', *Andalucía Islámica* 2-3 (1981-82), Granada

Garcia Sánchez, E (1986) 'La alimentación en la Andalucía islámica. Estudio histórico y bromatológico II. Carne, pescado, huevos, leche y productos lácteos', *Andalucía Islámica* 4-5, (1983-86), Granada

Garcia Sánchez, E (1986) 'Fuentes para el estudio de la alimentación en la Andalucía islámica', *Actas del XII congreso de la Union Européenne d'Arabisants et d'Islamisants*, Madrid, 269-88

Garcia Sánchez, E (ed) (1992) *Kitab al-agdiya. (Tratado de los alimentos) por abu Marwan abd al-Malik B Zuhr*, Madrid

Garcia Sánchez, E (1994) 'La conservación de los productos vegetales en las fuentes agronómicas andalusíes', in Marin, M and Waines, D (eds), *La alimentación en las culturas islámicas*, Madrid, 251-93

Garcia Sánchez, E (1995) 'Los cultivos en Al-Andalus', in Malpicas Cuello, A, García Sánchez, E and Quesada T (eds), *El agua en la agricultura de Al-Andalus*, Barcelona, 41-55

Gil Zubillaga, L (2001) 'Seguimiento arqueológico de las obras del regadío de la Sonsierra. Excavación de los yacimientos de Las Sepulturas y San Pablo', *Estrato* 13, 93-101

Ginatempo, M (1984) 'Per la storia degli ecosistemi e dell'Alimentazione Medievali: recenti studi di archeozoologia in Italia', *Archeologia medievale* 11, 35-61

Glaser, R (2001) *Klimageschichte Mitteleuropas. 1000 Jahre Wetter, Klima, Katastrophen*, Paderborn

Graff, D (1988) *Weinheilige und Rebenpatrone*, Saarbrücken

Graham-Campbell, J and Batey, CE (1998) *Vikings in Scotland: an Archaeological Survey*. Edinburgh

Griffin, K (1979) 'Fossil records of fig, grape and walnut in Norway from medieval time', *Archaeo-Physica* 8, 57-67

Gutierrez González, JA and Bohigas Roldán, R (eds) (1989) *La cerámica medieval en el norte y noroeste de la peninsula iberica. Aproximación a su studio*, León

Gutierrez Lloret, S (1996) *La cora de Tudmir de la Antigüedad tardía al mundo islámico. Poblamiento y cultura materia*, Madrid/Alicante

Hagen, A (2006) *Anglo-Saxon Food and Drink: Production, Processing, Distribution and Consumption*, Swaffham

Henning, F-W (1994) *Deutsche Agrargeschichte des Mittelalters: 9. bis 15. Jahrhundert*, Stuttgart

Heras Fernandez, E (1999) 'Actividades Arqueológicas. Soria', *Numantia* 7 (1995/96), 295-312

Hernandez Carrasquilla, F (1991) 'Las aves del yacimiento de Angosta de los Mancebos (Madrid)', *Boletín de Arqueología Medieval* 5, 181-91

Hoffmann, RC (1996) 'Economic development and aquatic ecosystems in medieval Europe', *The American Historical Review* 101, 631-69

Holm, P, Starkey, DJ and Thor, J (eds) (1996) *The North Atlantic Fisheries, 1100-1976: National Perspectives on a Common Resource*, Esbjerg

Huici Miranda, A (1966) *Traducción española de un manuscrito anónimo del siglo XIII sobre la cocina hispano magrebí*, Madrid

Jacomet, S and Kreuz, A (1999) *Archäobotanik*, Stuttgart

Jones, DM (2002) *Environmental Archaeology. A guide to the theory and practice of methods, from sampling and recovery to post-excavation*, English Heritage Publications, London

Karg, S (1994) 'Plant diversity in late medieval cornfields of northern Switzerland', *Vegetation History and Archaeobotany* 4:1, 41-50

Karg, S (ed) (2007) *Medieval Food Traditions in Northern Europe*, PNM Studies in Archaeology and History 12, Copenhagen

Karg, S and Jacomet, S (1991) 'Pflanzliche Makroreste als Informationsquellen zur Ernährungsgeschichte des Mittelalters in der Schweiz und Süddeutschland', *Archäologie und Museum* 20, 121-43

Karg, S and Pfrommer J (2003) 'Eine Kulturlandschaft soweit das Auge reicht! Die spätmittelalterliche Stadt Laufen (CH) im Fokus der Disziplinen Archäologie und Botanik', *Ethnographisch-Archäologische Zeitschrift* 44, 255-64

Karg, S and Robinson, DE (2002) 'Secondary food plants from medieval sites in Denmark: fruits, nuts, vegetables, herbs and spices', in Viklund, K and Engelmark, R (eds), *Nordic Archaeobotany – NAG 2000*, Umeå Archaeology and Environment 15, 133-42

Karg S, Henriksen PS, Ethelberg P and Sørensen, AB (2004) 'Gården og markerne i jernalderen. Fosfatanalyser og forkullet korn fortæller om gårdenes indretning og om agerbrug fra yngre romersk og ældre germansk jernalder i Sønderjylland', *Nationalmuseets Arbeidsmark*, 139-51

Knörzer, K-H (1991) 'Deutschland nördlich der Donau', in van Zeist, W, Wasilykowa, K and Behre, K-E (eds), *Progress in Old World Palaeoethnobotany. A Retrospective View on the Occasion of 20 Years of the International Work Group for Palaeoethnobotany*, Rotterdam, 189-206

Kroll, H (1987) 'Vor- und frühgeschichtlicher Ackerbau in Archsum auf Sylt. Eine botanische Grossrestanalyse', *Römisch-Germanische Forschungen* 44, 51-158

Kroll, H and Pasternak, R (eds) (1995) *Res archaeobotanicae – Symposium Kiel*, International Workgroup for Palaeoethnobotany, Proceedings of the 9th Symposium, Kiel 1992, Kiel

Lopez Mullor, A, Caixal, A, Fiero, J, Domingo, R and Juan, M (1986) 'Excavaciones en la iglesia de Santa Càndia d'Orpí (Barcelona)', in *I Congreso de Arqueología Medieval Española* 5, Zaragoza/Huesca, 95-109

Macías, S and Torres, C (1998) 'Consumo Alimentar e Utensilios de Cocinha', *Actas das 2ª Jornadas de Cerâmica Medieval e Pós-Medieval*, Porto, 67-79

Makowiecki, D (2003) *Historia Ryb I Rybołówstwa W Holocenie Na Nizu Polskim W Swietle Badan Archeoichtiologicznych*, Poznan

Mariezkurrena, K and Altuna, J (1981) 'Alimentación de origen animal de los habitantes del Castillo de Aitzorrotz (Escoriaza, Guipuzcoa)', *Munibe* 33:3-4, 199-229

Moe, D (ed) (1994) *Garden History: Garden Plants, Species, Forms and Varieties from Pompeii to 1800*, PACT 42, Court-Saint-Étienne

Montanari, M (1993) *El hambre y la abundancia. Historia y cultura de la alimentación en Europa*, Barcelona

Moreno-García, M and Davis, S (2001) 'Estudio de las asociaciones faunísticas recuperadas en Alcácer do Sal; convento de São Francisco, Santarém; y Sé de Lisboa', in *GARB Sítios Islâmicos do Sul Peninsular/*

Sitios Islámicos del Sur Peninsular, Lisbon/ Mérida, 231-55

Moro i Garcia, A and Roig i Buxo, J (1994) 'El conjunt de sitges alt-medievals de Sta Maria d'Egara per a l'emmagatzematge de cereal', in *IV Congreso de Arqueología Medieval Española* 3, Alicante, 619-24

Müldner, G and Richards, MP (2005) 'Fast or feast: reconstructing diet in late medieval England by stable isotope analysis', *Journal of Archaeological Science* 32, 39-48

Navarro Palazón, J and Jiménez Castillo, P (eds) (2005) *Historia de Cieza II: Siyasa*, Estudio arqueológico del despoblado andalusí (Siglos XI-XIII), Murcia

Navarro Saez, R and Mauri i Martí, A (1986) 'La escavación de un silo medieval en Santa Margarida (Martorell, Barcelona)', in *Actas del I Congreso de Arqueología Medieval Española* 5, Zaragoza/Huesca, 435-52

Ollich i Castanyer, I; Reynolds, PJ and Rocafiguera i Espona, M (1994) 'Agricultura medieval i arqueología experimental. El projecte de L'Esquerda', in *IV Congreso de Arqueología Medieval Española* 3, Alicante

Perdikaris, S (1999) 'From chiefly provisioning to commercial fishery: long-term economic change in Arctic Norway', *World Archaeology* 30, 388-402

Porras Crevillen, AI (2003) 'El medio natural antropizado en el yacimiento de Cote (Montellano, Sevilla): Análisis geo-arqueológico', in Valor, M (ed) *Un enclave en la Banda Morisca: Cote (Montellano, Sevilla) y su entorno*, Seville, 46-60

Quesada, T (1995) 'El agua salada y las salinas', in Malpicas Cuello, A, García Sánchez, E and Quesada, T (eds), *El agua en la agricultura de Al-Andalus*, Barcelona, 57-80

Ramalho, MM, Lopes, C, Custodio, J and Valente, MJ (2001) 'Vestigios da Santarem islâmica – um silo no convento de S. Francisco', *Arqueología Medieval* 7, 147-83

Reyes Tellez, F (1986) 'Excavaciones en la ermita de Santa, Cruz (Valdezate, Burgos)', in *Actas del I Congreso de Arqueología Medieval Española* 5, Zaragoza, 7-27

Riquelme Cantal, JA (1991) 'Estudio faunístico del yacimiento medieval de 'El Maraute' (Torrenueva, municipio de Motril, Granada), *Boletín de Arqueología Medieval* 5, 93-111

Riquelme Cantal, JA (1992) 'La fauna de época califal procedente de la catedral de Granada', *Boletín de Arqueología Medieval* 6, 193-207

Robinson, DE (1994) 'Plants and Vikings: everyday life in Viking Age Denmark', *Botanical Journal of Scotland* 46, 542-51

Rösch M, Jacomet S and Karg, S (1992) 'The history of cereals in the region of the former Duchy of Swabia (Herzogtum Schwaben) from the Roman to the post-medieval period: results of archaeobotanical research', *Vegetation History and Archaeobotany* 1:4, 193-231

Rösener, W (1987) *Bauern im Mittelalter*, Munich

Ruas, M-P (1996) 'Eléments pour une histoire de la fructiculture en France: données archéobotaniques de l'antiquité au XVIIe siècle', in Colardelle, M (ed), *L'homme et la nature au moyen Age*, Actes du Ve Congrès International d'archéologie médiévale (Grenoble, 6-9 October 1993), Paris, 92-105

Ruiz Gil, Jose A and López Amador, JJ (2001) 'Excavaciones en Pocito Chico (El Puerto de Santa María). Campaña de 1998', *Anuario Arqueológico de Andalucía '98* 3:2, Seville, 79-92

Ruiz Montejo, I (1998) 'La vida campesina en el siglo XII a través de los calendarios agrícolas', in Aguilera Castro, M del C (ed), *La Vida Cotidiana en la España Medieval. Actas del VI Curso de Cultura Medieval*, Madrid, 107-23

Sayers, W (2002) 'Some fishy etymologies: Eng. *Cod*, Norse *Porskr*, Du. *Kabeljauw*, Sp. *Bacalao*', *North-Western European Language Evolution* 41, 17-30

Sénac, P (1994) 'El yacimiento musulmán de Marcén (Huesca)', *Arqueología Aragonesa* 17 (1991), 181-5

Sénac, P (ed) (2006) *Del al Tarraconaise à la marche Supèrieure d'Al-Andalus (IV-XI siécle): les habitats ruraux*, Toulouse

Starkey, DJ, Reid, C and Ashcroft, N (2000) *England's Sea Fisheries … since 1300*, London

Vallvé, J (1982) 'La agricultura en al-Andalus', *Al-Qantara* 3:1-2, 261-97

van der Veen, M (ed) (2003) 'Luxury Foods', *World Archaeology* 34:3

van Neer, W and Ervynck, A (2003) 'The late mediaeval heyday of the Flemish marine fishery: a fish-eye view', in Pieters, M, Verhaeghe, F, Gevaert, G, Mees, J and Seys, J (eds), *Colloquium: Fishery, Trade and Piracy – Fishermen and Fishermen's Settlements in and around the North Sea*, Ostend, 40-3

van Zeist, W, Wasilykowa K and Behre, K-E (eds) (1991) *Progress in Old World Palaeoethnobotany. A Retrospective View*, Rotterdam

Viklund, K (1998) *Cereals, Weeds and Crop Processing in Iron Age Sweden. Methodological and Interpretative Aspects of Archaeobotanical Evidence*, Archaeology and Environment 14, Umeå

Wasylikowa, K, Cârciumaru, M, Hajnalová, E, Hartyányi, BP, Pashkevich, GA and Yanushevich, ZV (1991) 'East-Central Europe', in van Zeist, W, Wasilykowa, K and Behre, K-E (eds), *Progress in Old World Palaeoethnobotany. A Retrospective View*, Rotterdam, 151-240.

Willerding, U (2003) 'Die Landwirtschaft im frühen Mittelalter', in Benecke, N, Donat, P, Gringmuth-Dallmer, E and Willerding, U (eds), *Frühgeschichte der Landwirtschaft in Deutschland*, Beiträge zur Ur- und Frügeschichte Mitteleuropas 14, 151-240

CHAPTER 7

TECHNOLOGY, CRAFT AND INDUSTRY

Ricardo Córdoba, with Jan Klápště, Anne Nissen Jaubert, James Graham-Campbell, Jerzy Maik, Radomír Pleiner, Sabine Felgenhauer-Schmiedt, Hans Krongaard Kristensen and Jens Vellev

Introduction

Archaeological research into the industrial activities of the early Middle Ages is still in its infancy. Up to now, one of the best studied aspects has been the work tools and farming implements, which have been excavated on many early medieval rural sites, relating to daily life in the countryside at this period (see Chapter 3). On the other hand, far less is known about industrial sites because most of those so far investigated date from the late Middle Ages. There is therefore much work still to be done with regard to studying medieval production sites and to reconstructing techniques and manufacturing processes from archaeological evidence, as well as in establishing the distribution routes of products and the trading networks maintained during the early Middle Ages.

Editors' note: this chapter commences with an overview of various medieval crafts from a West European perspective, by Ricardo Córdoba. It is followed by a discussion of watermills (Jan Klápště et al), with additional northern perspectives on textiles (Jerzy Maik) and iron production (Radomír Pleiner). The chapter is completed by studies of Continental ceramics (Sabine Felgenhauer-Schmiedt) and the beginnings of brick production (Hans Krongaard Kristensen), with a final contribution on 'Salt' (Jens Vellev). There is a combined bibliography at the end which includes a greater range of references than those cited in the texts.

Textiles

The activity for which there exists the best archaeological evidence from eighth/twelfth-century Europe is the textile industry (see also, pp 217-20). In Anglo-Saxon England and Scandinavia, fragments of combs used to comb or card wool and flax have been studied, but especially common finds are spindle-whorls, the perforated weights of baked clay, stone or antler/bone, which were placed at the bottom of the wooden spindle so as to set it spinning and thus wind the yarn onto it (e.g. Graham-Campbell 1980, nos 66-73, with refs; Wilson 1976, 271). Spindle-whorls are abundant on all Germanic, Scandinavian and Slavonic sites of the seventh to eleventh centuries – and they have also frequently been found in al-Andalus. The wooden rods known as 'distaffs', cylindrical-shaped pieces of bone or wood turned on a lathe, on which was placed the raw wool to be spun, rarely survive in the North. However, distaffs have often been found throughout the Islamic Mediterranean, especially in Morocco and al-Andalus, where they are sometimes decorated with linear or anthropomorphic designs (Torres 1986).

Loom-weights are frequently found. These weights of clay or stone are much larger than those used on spindles. Bunches of warp yarns were tied to them on the upright or vertical loom (thus also sometimes known as the 'warp-weighted loom'; Fig 7.5); their existence is thus evidence for the use of the vertical loom all over early medieval Europe. Two kilns for firing loom-weights, dating from the twelfth century, have been excavated in England, at Rochester, Kent (Clarke 1986, 231). Two different types of weight have been identified in early medieval England: a ring-shaped one used up until the seventh century, and a bun-shaped one used during the eighth to eleventh centuries (Wilson 1976, 271). From the twelfth century onwards, the use of the vertical loom was abandoned in favour of the horizontal or treadle-loom (Fig 7.8). This was still in use at the end of the Middle Ages for certain types of cloth. The horizontal loom did not require weights, their function having been replaced by a wooden bar; in general, therefore, loom-weights do not appear on archaeological sites after the twelfth century.

Indeed, from the eleventh century onwards, there is growing evidence for the dissemination of the horizontal loom across Europe. Manuel Retuerce has studied a *templen*, a piece of iron from a horizontal loom found in an eleventh-century Andalusian context, demonstrating that such looms were already in use in the Iberian Peninsula from the tenth century (Retuerce 1987). This discovery, together with excavated evidence from places such as Hedeby (Germany) and Lund (Sweden), dating from the late Viking period, shows that this type of loom was in use across Europe at least from the eleventh century (see also, below).

Finally, in some places, deposits have been found which could have been employed in the dyeing and finishing processes of cloth. The Swan Lane excavations in London revealed several hearths surrounded by fulling clay, while dyeing places have been documented in Bristol, Winchester and at Fountains Abbey (Clarke 1986, 135).

Tanning

Tanneries usually had running water and a series of tanks or pits in which the hides were immersed during the processes of hair-removal and of tanning in mixtures of water and plant products. The tanks used for removing hair were square or rectangular, like small ponds, whereas those for tanning were usually circular and half-buried in the ground. Stones for rubbing the hair-side of hides and the remains of the plant matter used as tanning agents are usually found associated with tanneries. Excavations in England at

Lower Brook Street, Winchester (called Tanner Street in the twelfth century), brought to light several pits with wood remains dating from the eleventh century (Clarke 1986, 137). The tenth-century tanning pits reported from York have, however, been re-identified as sunken-floored buildings (Mould et al 2003, 3227-8). In el-Andalus, several small tanneries have been recorded, such as those of Vascos, Toledo, dating from the eleventh century (Izquierdo 1996).

Other archaeological evidence that can be used to detect the presence of a tannery is provided by deposits of bones from certain parts of an animal (feet and tails) because these were only removed by the tanners from the hide at the moment of tanning; the abundance of sheep and goat bones on some excavation sites in France has been interpreted by Isabelle Rodet, Claude Olive and Vianney Forest (2002) as indicating the existence of a tanner's workshop.

Other elements related to leatherworking are metal needles for sewing, shoemaker's knives and thimbles. The latter, of cast bronze, have been widely recorded in al-Andalus; they usually have small circular grooves on the outside (to hold the needle) and have the manufacturer's name engraved on top (Córdoba & Hernández 1994).

Bone, Antler and Horn

Bone, antler and horn were much worked during the early Middle Ages and are present in abundance on Anglo-Saxon, Scandinavian and Slavonic sites (see e.g. MacGregor 1985; MacGregor et al 1999; Ulbricht 1978). A wide variety of everyday objects could be made from these materials, including combs, brooches, needles and pins (cf. Schwarz-Mackensen 1976). The workshops where bone and antler were carved may be recognized from the discovery of the waste material, resulting from the cutting down of the raw materials during the fashioning of the end-products.

Ironworking

The metal most used in the early Middle Ages was iron and the facilities required for its preparation and forging are those most documented by archaeological research (see also, below). The furnaces used for the initial roasting process were usually relatively broad, rectangular structures, surrounded by low dry-stone walls; the smelting furnaces were generally circular structures of smaller dimensions (cosm diameter, and 50cm deep), lined inside with clay, and with a channel for tapping the slag. The heat of the furnace was raised with bellows, which had their nozzles protected with clay sheaths (*tuyères*), the remains of which are frequently found on these sites.

An iron-smelting 'shaft' furnace excavated in Stamford, Lincolnshire (and dated to the eleventh century by archaeomagnetic means), was clay-built on a base measuring 35x25cm and had its slag basin surviving (Wilson 1976, 262). Marta Sancho (1996) dates one at the Catalonian site of La Fabregada to the tenth century; half-buried in the rock and partly built with limestone, it was an oval structure measuring 80x40cm, with a depth of 60cm. It had side platforms and a central channel for evacuating the slag; the

Andalusian 'bar-kiln' **Fig 7.1**
for pottery production
(after Mostalac 1990).

air-injection channel had a double entry-hole for the bellows, situated on a tilted shelf in the rock. In England, forges have been excavated at Waltham Abbey, Essex, and Winchcombe, Gloucestershire (Clarke 1986, 163; J Geddes, in Blair & Ramsey 1991).

Pottery

Two types of kiln are known from early medieval potteries: one with a single chamber in which the fire was in direct contact with the vessels; and the other with two superimposed chambers, usually separated by a grating which let through the heat and some of the flame. Single-chamber kilns have been recorded in many places, including England (Hurst 1976, fig 7.32), France, Italy and the Iberian Peninsula. Good examples are provided by the Carolingian kilns of Meudon, in Vannes, studied by François Fichet (1996). These are circular in shape with an unexcavated diameter of 1-1.20m, provided with a horizontal floor lined with a layer of clay 2cm thick, either directly on the ground or resting on a bed of stones.

In the Iberian Peninsula, numerous examples have been found of the so-called 'bar-kilns', which have a cylindrical structure with no grating to separate the chambers (Fig

7.1). Inside them was an open space, which was usually divided up by two or three platforms at the bottom of the kiln, where the heavier vessels were fired. Then there were three to five rows of holes in the walls in which the potter placed bars (hence the name) to form a sort of shelf on which further vessels were stood during the firing process. This type of kiln is characteristic of al-Andalus: a group of kilns in Zaragoza, dating from the eleventh century, has been studied by Mostalac (1990), and Fernando Amores (1995) has described several twelfth-century Almuwahid kilns in La Cartuja, Seville.

As noted above, the second type of kiln used during this period throughout the Mediterranean area had two superimposed chambers, the lower one contained the heating material for combustion, and an upper firing-chamber where the artefacts were placed and which was covered by a dome-shaped 'cupola', built of bricks. These chambers were separated by a perforated floor or grating which let the heat and flames through, held up by brick arches resting on the walls of the firing-chamber. The roof was usually provided with a central chimney and the base of the lower chamber was finished with a fine layer of clay. There was only one entrance into this chamber, opening to the outside of the kiln at the level of the grating, through which the fuel was fed. The outside of the kiln was given a protective covering, in the form of a thick layer of clay incorporating pieces of adobe, which enabled the heat to be maintained inside. These kilns could be either circular or square in ground-plan; an example of the first type is the kiln in the calle Montgó in Denia (Gisbert 1990), and of the second type, the three kilns on the farming estate del Cura in Cordoba, dating from the tenth century (Córdoba & Castillo, in press).

The most important technique for finishing pottery was glazing, consisting of coating the surface of the vessel with a transparent vitreous film. In the Mediterranean, from the tenth century onwards, this coating was obtained by mixing lead oxide with sand. This mixture could be applied to the surface of earthenware vessels in various ways: by immersing it in the mixture; by decorating it with brush-strokes or just with drops, so that the glaze could cover either the whole vessel or only part of it, such as the inside or the neck. Once the lead oxide was applied, the vessel was given a second firing, during which the mixture became vitrified, forming a waterproof, transparent and shiny coating. If no other oxide was added, the vessel remained the colour that the clay had acquired during the first firing. If, however, it was desired to vary that colouring or to obtain different tones, it was necessary to add another metal oxide to the mixture. The colours that could be achieved in this way were ochre and reddish tones (iron oxide), green tones (copper oxide), yellow (antimony oxide), and blue (cobalt oxide).

The glazing on the vessels was often monochrome, although possibly alternating colours towards the inside and outside of the container; in some cases, two tones were combined, generally using one as a background and the other for decoration, such as geometrical or floral motifs, e.g. black on honey colour, or yellow on ochre (see also Box 8.1). Up to the twelfth century, lead glazing was used in the Islamic and Byzantine worlds. In the Christian Western Mediterranean it began to be used during the thirteenth century, as a direct result of Islamic influence, together with tin glazing, only spreading throughout Central and Northern Europe during the late Middle Ages.

Glass

Glass was used in Europe during the Middle Ages for tableware (Figs 8.1 & 8.2) and for glazing windows, but also for the manufacture of beads. Already in the seventh century, the use of stained (flat) glass in churches and monasteries has been reported.

The kilns used for glass production in the Middle Ages were of two types, usually called the 'Southern' (or meridional) and 'Northern' (or septentrional). The Southern kiln was circular and covered by a vault, on which two or three superimposed chambers were placed: in the bottom chamber, provided with a front opening, combustion took place and the firing crucibles (or glass-pots) were placed, while a perforated floor permitted the heat to rise to the upper chamber which had a series of openings to the outside coinciding with the same number of work-stations (Fig 7.2). The Northern kiln was characterized by the horizontal positioning of its three chambers; its floor-plan was rectangular and the chambers were located close to each other, joined by a transverse tunnel situated under the floor where the combustion took place, and from which, through diverse openings, the heat was radiated. However, archaeological research in recent years has provided evidence that, in the same glass workshop, kilns with a circular floor-plan can be found next to rectangular ones, so these were presumably being used for different phases in the process (firing, annealing and blowing).

Once the glass-paste was prepared, the making of the objects could begin by means of some simple tools. A cane, iron tube or hollow bone blow-pipe, equipped with a wooden mouthpiece, was needed for blowing the glass, with pincers and shears for cut-

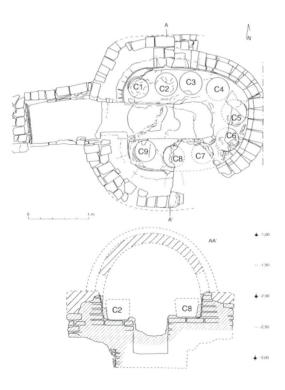

Andalusian glass-kiln from Belluga plaza, Murcia (after Jiménez et al 2000). **Fig 7.2**

ting the glass and helping with the process, and a 'pontil', a solid iron rod which held an item while it was being shaped.

The only glass-firing kilns to have been excavated in an Anglo-Saxon context were found at Glastonbury Abbey, in Somerset, dating from the ninth to tenth centuries (Wilson 1976, 269). In York, mid-tenth/eleventh-century crucibles containing remains of high-lead glass form part of the evidence for manufacture there, doubtless for beads (see J Bayley & R Doonan, in Mainman & Rogers 2000). The use of glass beads was common among Scandinavians during the Viking period (Callmer 1977) and their production has been widely documented in excavations (e.g. Graham-Campbell 1980, nos 462-4). One of the oldest medieval glassworks excavated in Mediterranean Europe is that of Torcello, in Venice, dating from the eighth century (Leciejewicz et al 1977); two kilns were found, one with a circular ground-plan and the other with a rectangular plan, the former was probably used for the annealing of the glass-paste and the latter for its blowing. In el-Andalus, the kilns that have been most studied are those in Puxmarina street and Belluga plaza in Murcia, dating from the eleventh to twelfth centuries, the latter still showing the marks of the crucibles on the inside platform where the glass was heated up for blowing (Jiménez et al 2000).

Watermills
by Jan Klápště, Anne Nissen Jaubert and Ricardo Córdoba,
with James Graham-Campbell

As noted in Chapter 3, watermills were far more productive for grinding purposes than hand-querns and were, indeed, the most complex pieces of technical equipment utilized at this period in both town and country (Lohrman 1996; Amouretti & Comet 2000). Early medieval watermills built on the traditions of Antiquity, and the most recent analyses of documentary sources have traced their diffusion to the period immediately after the fall of the Roman Empire, meaning that their beginnings are no longer to be linked to the great landholdings of the Carolingian period (e.g. Claude 1981, 230-3; Devroey 2003, 134-40). However, from a modern perspective, the path to their being in common use was a particularly long one. Evidence for the existence of early medieval watermills does not by itself answer the question as to whether or not they were in general use. In any case, considerable regional differences may be assumed.

At least three types of early medieval watermill can be distinguished: those with vertical or horizontal wheels, and the ship-mill (e.g. Höckmann 1996). Around the Mediterranean, in particular, there were also mills operated by animal traction. A large millstone (diameter: 80cm) found in a storage-pit at Dassargues, in southern France, was probably used in this way (Garnier et al 1995, 44, 56, fig 38). The windmill, first developed in the Orient, was to diffuse quickly across the Occident from the twelfth century (Lohrmann 1996, 228).

The watermill with a horizontal wheel is quite simple and can readily be constructed for use with a small current. The mill with a vertical wheel can grind a greater volume of grain, but its construction is more complicated. Unlike with the horizontal type, a cog-

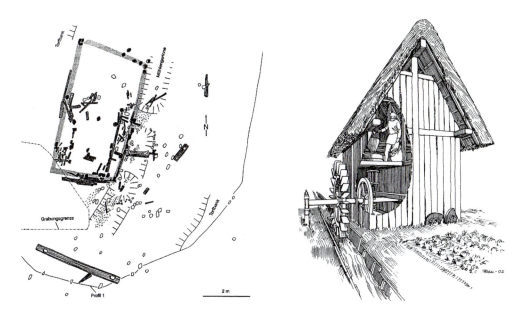

Dasing (Germany): archaeological remains of a watermill powered by a vertical wheel (7th-8th
centuries), with a hypothetical reconstruction (after Czysz 1998).

Fig 7.3

wheel system was required to convert the power of the vertical wheel into the horizontal rotation of the millstone. At the same time, modifications were necessary to the hydrological surroundings: the stream and its strength required regulation by the digging of mill- and tail-races, while mill-ponds needed to be excavated to ensure the supply of water (all features that allow the locations of abandoned mills to be identified).

Remnants of watermills have been studied in France at Belle-Église in Picardy (ninth/tenth century), and at Audun-le-Tiche (Moselle) where huge posts supported the mill; wooden features in the bank of the latter have been dated to c840 (Lorquet 1994; Rohmer 1996). The archaeological evidence from Ireland demonstrates that both horizontal and vertical watermills were in use there from the seventh century (Rynne 1989). In Denmark during the Viking period, there is a mill known at the rural settlement of Omgård, Jutland (Nielsen 1987). One of the earliest watermills to be have been excavated in England is an eighth-century horizontal mill at Tamworth, Staffordshire (Rahtz & Meeson 1992). A major mill-leat (3.7m deep) off the River Thames, which held three vertical wheels, has been investigated (but not published) at the site of the Late Saxon royal palace at Old Windsor, Berkshire (Hope-Taylor 1958-59); its construction has been dated dendrochronologically to the mid/late seventh century (Hillam 1981, 42). On the occasion of the Norman compilation of the 'Domesday Book' (1086), some 6,000 watermills were recorded in the area of England covered by the survey.

The excavations of Dasing in Bavaria have made an exceptional contribution to our knowledge of early medieval mills. They revealed the remains of a mill powered by a vertical water-wheel (1.6m in diameter) made from wood felled between the years 696/7

(Fig 7.3). The original mill, built on a plan measuring 2x3.2m, was marked out by its technical complexity. The intensity of its use is attested by more than 300 pieces of worn-out millstones. Several repairs made to the wooden structure in the eighth century have been identified with the aid of dendrochronology. After about a century, floods changed the course of the local river and this remarkable mill was abandoned (Henning 1994; Czysz 1998; Böhme 1999).

The normal type of watermill found throughout the Mediterranean world during the early Middle Ages used the vertical wheel. In the Iberian Peninsula, a particular technology was utilized given the absence of abundant and powerful flows of water to enable the water-supply to be regulated so as to deliver it with the necessary speed onto the wheel. Whereas most medieval European mills used sloping conduits of decreasing size for this purpose, the structure used in Andalusian and Christian Spain was in the form of a vertical cylinder of considerable height, which acted as a chute for the water and was called *cubo* (or pond). The *cubo* was known in Arabic as *masabb*, meaning 'funnel', given the way in which the water was conducted onto the water-wheel. This represents a technology imported from the East after the Muslim conquest (Fig 7.4).

It has generally been supposed that this type of vertical mill-pond was the system used most extensively in the Iberian Peninsula; however, hardly any excavations of medieval watermills have been carried out in the Mediterranean area. The only truly Andalusian watermill excavated so far is a tenth-century mill in Valencia (Arnau & Martí 2000). It has confirmed the belief that this was the type of mill most used in Muslim Spain, given that it has the same characteristics as those described in documentary sources: a

Fig 7.4 *Andalusian cubo-type watermill.*

horizontal wheel set within a horseshoe-shaped double vault with walls and flooring of ashlar masonry. At the flag-stoned base of the vault, there was an opening for the beam used to raise and lower the mechanism. Also found were: four quartzite blocks to support the shaft; the corroded remains of the tip of the shaft itself; and a millstone (1.10m in diameter and 12cm thick), with an opening for the dowel. Remains of other such Islamic pond-mills have been described near the town of Planes (Alicante) and Caravaca (Murcia), and some elements of the mechanism of a hydraulic mill, a dowel and some *sonajas* (a set of small irons which warned the miller of the absence of wheat during the grinding), form part of a collection of eleventh-century Andalusian objects found in the town of Liétor (Córdoba 2003).

Cloth Production
by Jerzy Maik

At the beginning of the Middle Ages the basic weaving tool was the vertical loom – either warp-weighted or tubular. The two methods leave distinctive signatures in the finished cloth: a starting border is essential when using the warp-weighted loom, as are the loop-endings of textiles woven on the tubular loom.

Vertical looms are also documented by archaeological finds. Remains of a burnt loom of eighth- to tenth-century date have been found in northern Germany, at Dalem (Fig 7.5) and Midlum Northum, near Cuxhaven (Zimmermann 1982, 113-15), and parts of a tubular loom came to light in the ninth-century Viking ship-burial at Oseberg, in Norway (Hoffmann 1974, 330-1, fig 137).

Vertical looms are also represented in iconographical sources, e.g. a warp-weighted loom in a thirteenth-century manuscript from Rein, near Graz, in Austria (Stærmose Nielsen 1999, 80, fig 44), and a tubular loom in the eleventh-century manuscript of Rabanus Maurus from Monte Cassino (Hoffmann 1974, 329, fig 136).

At the close of Antiquity and the beginning of the Middle Ages the most popular weave used in the production of woollen cloth was the 2/2 twill (Fig 7.6). It was used to produce simple unfelted textiles for everyday clothing. These have been recovered on many archaeological sites, such as York and London in England (Walton 1989; Crawfoot, Pritchard & Staniland 1992), Elisenhof in northern Germany (Hundt 1981), the Viking town at Hedeby in Schleswig-Holstein (Hägg 1984), and Wolin in Pomerania, Poland (Maik 1988, 162-86).

However, some of the textiles in 2/2 twill, and particularly in 2/2 diamond twill, are of very high quality, with thread counts of over 50 per cm. Bender Jørgensen has called them the 'Birka type', after the Viking period cemetery in Sweden where they occurred in great quantity (Bender Jørgensen 1992, 138-40). The origin of these luxurious textiles is not yet fully understood. According to one of the most interesting hypotheses, they should be identified with the Frisian cloth called *pallium fresonicum*, such as was given by Charlemagne to Harun al-Rashid, the caliph of Baghdad (Geijer 1938, 40-7). According to other scholars they may have originated in England where they would be known as 'haberget' cloth (Carus-Wilson 1969, 148-66), or in western Norway where

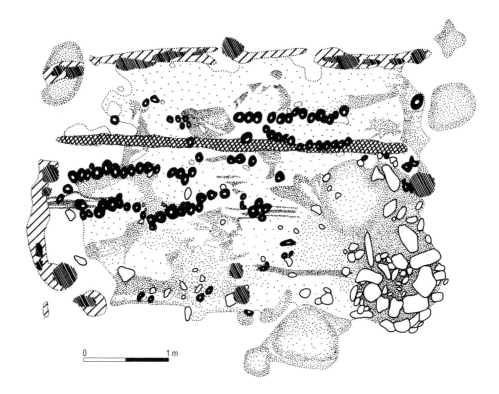

Fig 7.5　*Warp-weighted (vertical loom) from Dalem (Germany); 8th/10th century (after Zimmerman 1982).*

they have often been found in excavations (Bender Jørgensen 1992, 138-40). These textiles have also been discovered in Novgorod, Russia, where the Polish scholar, A Nahlik, has identified them as being of English origin on the basis of their raw material (Nahlik 1964, 37-46).

In addition to the 2/2 twill in its numerous varieties, tabby weave and 2/1 twill were also used in the production of wool textiles. From the eleventh century onwards, the number of fabrics in 2/1 twill grows considerably, this being particularly noticeable in the collections from such towns as Schleswig (Germany), Lund (Sweden), Gdańsk and Opole (Poland; Maik 2005, 84-92). These textiles were sometimes felted and a certain standardization in their production is observable. After the early thirteenth century, a further change in the weaving technique can be detected: 2/1 twill is more and more frequently replaced with tabby weave, and the felted textiles increase in number (Fig 7.7). Thus, there was an increasing standardisation of woollen cloth taking place (Maik 2005, 84-92).

The manufacture of fabrics in 2/1 twill is linked with the change from the vertical loom to the horizontal form (Nahlik 1965, 59-88; Maik 1988a, 160-7), although fabric in this weave, provided with a starting border, can still be encountered in the thirteenth century, e.g. at Emden, northern Germany (Tidow 1990, 416, fig 9A).

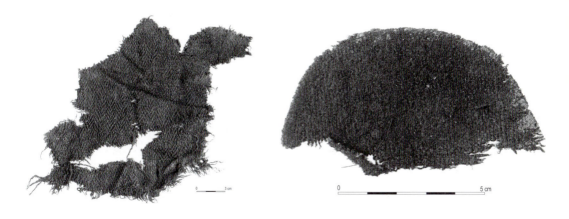

Left: 2/2 broken twill woollen textile from Wolin (Poland); 9th century (photo: K Karpińska). **Fig 7.6**

Right: felted cloth in tabby weave from Elbląg (Poland); 13th/15th century (photo: K Karpińska). **Fig 7.7**

In view of the large number of archaeological finds of horizontal looms dating from the tenth to thirteenth centuries, it is possible to assume that this type of loom became popular in the whole of Northern Europe in this period (see also p 209). The finds come from Hedeby, Lund, Gdańsk (Fig 7.8), Opole, and from Novgorod and Novoe Toropickoe Gorodische in Russia, as well as Koknese and Riga in Latvia (Cardon 1999, 400-7, fig 145).

On the basis of these finds, supported by contemporary depictions in documentary sources, such as a manuscript from St Albans, from c1250, and the Mendel Book from Nuremberg, 1389 (Carus-Wilson 1969, 163; Cardon 1999, 195), it seems reasonable to suppose that the weavers now had an up-to-date tool at their disposal, which was not to change until the eighteenth century, even surviving in household weaving in Central and Eastern Europe until the twentieth century.

Experiments conductd by Nahlik have shown that the productive capacity of the horizontal loom was at least nine times greater than that of the vertical loom, and so it is possible to suggest that its use contributed to the emergence and development of a professional textile industry (Nahlik 1965, 59-88).

The selvedges of certain woollen textiles from the eleventh-thirteenth centuries (e.g. at Gdańsk and Opole) and the preserved width of one fabric from Opole, indicate that a broad loom, operated by two weavers and producing high-quality cloth, may already have been in use at that time (Kamińska & Nahlik 1958, 90-2; Maik 1991, 82-3).

A similar loom is also shown in West European iconographic material, e.g. in the stained glass windows of the cathedrals of Bourges (1195-1209) and Amiens (1240-50), in France, and in the Kuerboek manuscript (1363) from Ypres, in Belgium (Cardon 1999, figs 179, 185 & 131).

Cloth manufacture developed on a large scale particularly in Flanders and England. The great quantity of high-quality cloth produced there was exported to many European

Fig 7.8 *Parts of a horizontal loom from Gdańsk (Poland) and its reconstruction; 11/12th century (after Kamińska & Nahlik 1958).*

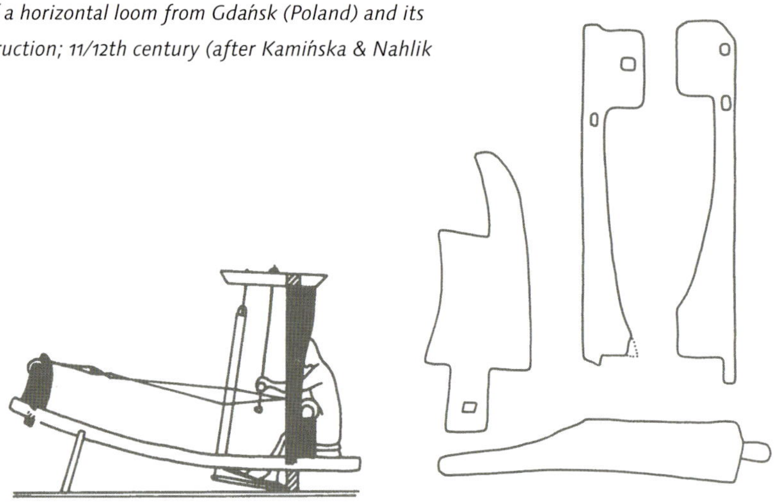

countries. This export provided the strongest stimulus to the flourishing Hanseatic trade. West European cloth has been excavated in both Poland, at Gdańsk and Elbląg (Maik 1997, 23-36), and Russia, at Novgorod (Nahlik 1964, 18-64), where it can be identified by its raw material. English and Spanish wool was of much higher quality than the wool from Central and Eastern Europe.

Western European colonists, mainly from Germany, who settled in Polish and Teutonic Prussian towns, were responsible for introducing western weaving techniques into Central Europe. In addition, the Hanseatic trade (see Vol 2) brought luxurious (and thus expensive) Flemish cloth to the region, as well as a good quality, but cheaper, cloth from England. In order to compete successfully, the local weavers had to adopt the new techniques themselves and cut their production costs. This was probably the reason for the increasing standardisation, mentioned above, and for the simplification of weaving technology through replacing 2/1 twill with tabby weave.

Iron and Ironworking

by Radomír Pleiner

From the beginning of the late Bronze Age, the smelting of iron was achieved by means of the bloomery process until the introduction of the first medieval blast-furnaces; these produced carburized iron/steel in the solid state and liquid slag as waste (cf. Pleiner 2000). During the early Middle Ages, the production of iron did not exceed middle-scale parameters, although some major iron-production areas can be traced. The most important of these were Carinthia and Styria (Austria), and the Amberg-Sulzbach region to the east of Nuremberg – and (from the tenth-eleventh centuries) the Kelheim area (Bavaria), in the Bergisches Land, east of Cologne, and around Schwäbisch Hall, north-east of Stuttgart. During this period, activity commenced in a most important region in the Lahn-Dill tract of north-western Germany. In France, there was Morvan (Burgundy); in England, the Forest of Dean (Gloucestershire) and the Sussex Weald. Iron was also produced in Italy; in Tuscany, ores from the Elbe region were in use during the twelfth century, and there was also activity in the Italian Alps, centred around Brescia and Bergamo. An increase in production can also be detected in Northern Europe, around Trondheim (Norway), and Dalarna in Sweden (which was called *Järnberaland*: an 'iron-bearing country'). This iron-production was based on both Roman and non-Roman (native) traditions.

Documentary sources from the ninth-twelfth centuries mention the mining of iron ore, under the control of feudal lords and clergy. Iron was the subject of tributes and taxes collected by monasteries (Fulda 912, Lorsch 1187, and St Gall, in Switzerland, during the ninth century). The Cistercian and Carthusian monastic orders were particularly prominent in this respect, especially during the twelfth century, influencing both England and Scandinavia.

In eastern Central Europe, it was the Slavs who influenced iron-working from the sixth century onwards. Important discoveries concerning iron-metallurgy during the eighth to ninth centuries have been made, particularly in Great Moravia, where metallurgists have discovered considerable quantities of iron, given that iron was an important factor in trade, serving as a means of exchange (e.g. Slavic axe-shaped iron bars). Slavic iron-working followed different traditions: those of the Cimmerians and Scythians.

The bloomery furnaces (*fornacia*) were, in most parts of Europe, built as vertical-shaft structures of clay or stone, with a refractory inner lining. They were some 1-1.5m high and 30-60cm in internal diameter, with the air supplied by bellows, and were adapted for tapping the slag. The thickness of the walls depended on the material used, with clay ones being up to several centimetres, and stone ones up to 40cm thick (Fig 7.9, nos 2 & 3). A charge of charcoal and iron ore (oxides like haematite, limonite including bog ore, siderites, containing around 60% Fe_2O_3, normally roasted) must have been ignited and the temperature in the hearth reached about 1400°C (i.e. below the melting point of iron). The smelt lasted 6-7 hours; the liquid slag was tapped out and the iron was smelted as a sponge, or more compact bloom with adhering slag, which would have necessitated the product being reheated in a special open hearth and forged to expel the slag. This heating, connected with re-oxidation processes and the creation of hammer-scale, caused a loss of more than 50% of the already reduced iron/steel.

A specific type of bloomery furnace was introduced temporarily by the colonising Slavs: these were underground types dug into the soil and lined with refractory clay (e.g. Fig 7.9, no 1). The most advanced variety is exemplified by the ninth-century furnaces discovered forming a battery at Želechovice in northern Moravia. Behind the shaft and an oblique air-inlet for the bellows, there was a chamber into which the smelted iron was pushed, reheated and secondarily carburized to steel (this has been verified experimentally). Recently, similar batteries have been discovered in the smelting region in the Moravian Karst.

During the seventh to twelfth centuries iron was a metal in common use, but at the same time, however, it was a very valuable material. About 100 different types of

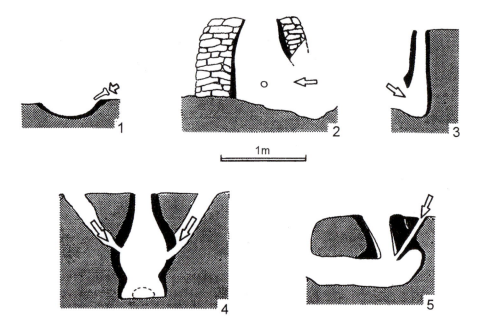

Fig 7.9   *Early medieval bloomery furnaces: (1-3) bowl and shaft structures; (1) Žerotín (Moravia), 10th century; Ludres (France), 8th century; and (3) Imola (Hungary), 11th/12th century; (4-5) underground furnaces; (4) Yutanovka (Ukraine); and (5) Želechovice (Moravia), c800 (after Pleiner 2000).*

iron artefact were in use: weapons, armour, tools, agricultural implements and domestic utensils. The weaponry included swords, sometimes of a renowned quality (e.g. the inscribed *Ulfberht* blades, as well as their imitators, and those from the workshops of other swordsmiths), spear- and arrow-heads, as also armour, mostly in the form of chain-mail shirts, each consisting of about 20,000 riveted and welded rings.

Certain smelters, and definitely certain experienced blacksmiths, were able to recognize empirically (by sound, type of sparks, etc) the softer wrought iron and harder as well hardenable steel (above 0.3% carbon) which was used in the construction of tools, as several hundred samples have shown from metallographic investigation. The proportion of inferior (soft) iron tools decreased in comparison with those manufactured by sophisticated methods, especially the combination of soft iron and hard steel (Fig 7.10). A crucial development is to be observed in the manufacture of knife blades: a lustrous phosphoric iron was combined by welding with phosphorus-poor iron and hard steel, appearing dark after having been exposed to atmospheric influences. The main blade construction methods were: the three-layered 'sandwich' system with a central plate of steel and wrought side plates; this was the most effective – the hard sharp cutting-edge could not be worn away by abrasive grinding; however, it required considerable quantities of steel. This resulted in the introduction of more economical construction methods, i.e. scarf- or butt-welding of steel cutting-edges (Fig 7.10, nos 1-5).

The ultimate technique observed through archaeology is pattern-welding, which was applied above all in the making of blades (England, Bohemia, Poland, Belarus and Russia, but rarely Germany). The knives and swords consisted of a hard-steel cutting-edge, a central rod of twisted iron and steel wires, and a wrought iron back. Enormous skill was required in the manufacture of these blades by experienced smiths, with natural etching developing a permanent effect of light-and-dark zones. Pattern-welded knives are to be regarded as expensive items, worn for display and prestige (Fig 7.10, no 6 & Fig 7.11).

The High Middle Ages saw a further development of ironworking influenced by the increasing production of iron in high bloomeries, often driven by water-wheels, and with the introduction of hammer-mills. What had been labour-intensive techniques were gradually replaced by working methods that concentrated labour and consequently reduced the costs of iron- and steel-making.

Sources: Pleiner 2000; 2006

Iron-working techniques: (1) three-layered 'sandwich'; (2) scarf-welded steel cutting-edge; (3) butt-welded cutting-edge; (4 & 5) striped scheme; and (6) pattern-welded knife (after Pleiner 2006). **Fig 7.10**

Pattern-welding: (2) from Mutějovice (Bohemia); 12th century (after Pleiner 2006). **Fig 7.11**

Continental Ceramics

by Sabine Felgenhauer-Schmiedt (translated by Paul Mitchell)

Introduction

Fundamentally, in terms of pottery the European area in the early Middle Ages, after the collapse of the Roman Empire, was again divided into two great complexes. In the Frankish Empire of the Merovingians, built on the basis of the Roman economic and administrative system, the potters' workshops continued to work with Roman forms. One of the most active potteries of this type was Mayen in the Eifel, the products of which enjoyed a wide distribution. Roman formal traditions were also continued for a lengthy period in the products of the 'rough wheel-thrown ware' of southern Germany in the Upper Rhine area. The retention of the potter's fast-wheel, a sophisticated firing technique and a broad range of forms, which included not only ceramics for the kitchen and storage purposes, but also tableware, are characteristic of the workshops working in the late Roman tradition. The wealth of forms was, however, gradually lost (particularly with regard to tableware). However, a new form of pottery vessel was created in the form of the spouted pitcher (or jug), the distribution of which, in the early and High Middle Ages, clearly demonstrates the eastwards transmission of pottery, which accompanied the comprehensive expansion over the centuries. In the southern and eastern Alpine area, which had also been part of the Roman Empire, the range of local pottery was reduced to hand-made pots and bowls, after its collapse. That means that the once highly-developed Latin potteries, and their accompanying economic foundations, did not persist. In the Italic area there was continuity, but also a gradual reduction in late Roman forms during the early Middle Ages. In many areas east of the Rhine and north of the Danube, as well as in the entire Alpine area, a hand-made turned, but not wheel-thrown, unevenly fired earthenware, confined almost exclusively to the kitchen and storage sphere, was dominant in the later early Middle Ages. With the expansion of the Frankish Empire into the territory of the Alamanns, on the right bank of the Rhine, a lightly-coloured wheel-thrown ware spread into the Upper Rhine area. The main forms were pots and spouted pitchers.

During the Carolingian period there was a decisive change in economic life. Landed estates with their respective centres – these could be halls (*Höfe – curtes*), and also royal halls or palaces – dominated the life of the economy. As a result of the *Capitulare de villis*, the court-property ordnance of Charlemagne, we know about craft activities in the respective centres that were intended to secure the independence of each estate. Due to the famous St Gall monastery plan (Fig 14.5), we also know of the important role of monasteries as craft-centres. Archaeological finds around secular and ecclesiastical centres of the Carolingian period confirm and strengthen this picture. Analysis of the archaeological remains also conveys further important aspects. These concern formal and technical conditions, and the influences which shaped the product, contributing in depth and breadth to the historicisation of the material objects. New insights are being gained in this way into the organisation of economic life and into production, as well as trade and distribution.

Tableware

During the eighth and ninth centuries in those places within the Carolingian Empire, which combined suitable clay deposits with the necessary demand, trans-regionally active workshops can be recognised that supplied buyers through the markets which were increasingly shaping economic life. West of the Rhine, in the area around the Cologne heights, between Bonn and Cologne, a particular ceramic landscape blossomed in this way, the controlling figures of which are thought to have been large clerical landlords in the Cologne area. Among other wares, the so-called 'Badorf ware' – to name the best-known Carolingian Rhenish pottery – was produced there until c900, a light yellowish, wheel-thrown, finely-tempered earthenware, which is often decorated in the 'roller-stamped' technique. The main forms are tall pots, spouted pitchers, bowls, and 'relief-band' amphorae (Fig 7.13). This was not mainly a matter of earthen vessels for cooking or storage purposes, but of vessels for use at table (or crockery). A particular importance of this ware is that it was continuously brought/traded to the north and north-east (see p 308). A similar pottery was also produced in northern France, around Rouen, and similarly traded through markets to a wide area.

In the southern German area, in the distribution area of the yellow wheel-thrown ware, that is in Alsace and on the Upper Rhine, a red-painted tableware also emerged during the late eighth century; its distribution is, however, largely regional. A similar type of earthenware has also been found in the Paris basin.

As well as the pottery types that are to be considered as mass-produced wares, from the Rhenish, Belgian and northern French production areas, there is also archaeological evidence from these same areas during the Carolingian period for the manufacture

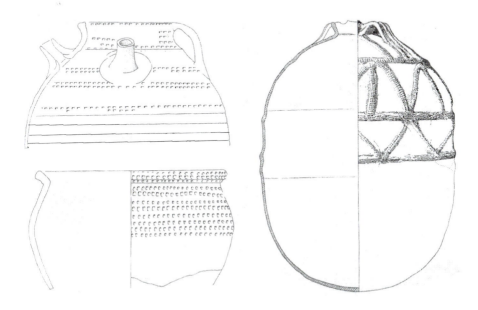

Badorf ware: (left) bowl and pitcher (Lüdtke 2002); (right) 'relief-band' amphora (not to scale). **Fig 7.12**

of earthenware for the most elevated tastes. This is the so-called 'Tating ware' (Fig 7.13), a jug manufactured in a black glossy ceramic and sometimes lavishly decorated with tin foil. Its production centres are assumed to have been in the Eifel (Mayen) and/or in northern France. The rarity of this pottery from widely-separated find-places shows that was not a mass-produced ware, but rather it represents an instance of individually valuable objects that occur as presents or articles of exchange, or trade, in the elite circles of the period and which were therefore regarded as status-symbols.

From the tenth century onwards the so-called Pingsdorf ware was produced by the same workshops that had earlier produced the Badorf pottery. There is evidence for potteries spread from Koblenz across to the Dutch border region of South Limbourg. The ware is well-fired and characterised by red or brown paint. It was traded in even greater quantities than Badorf pottery, to the north, to the north-east and increasingly to the south also (p 308). Its significance in the importing areas – as was earlier the case with the Badorf ware – is that it influenced the local pottery both in form and technique. The increasing demand then led to the establishment of so-called 'subsidiary workshops', which in their turn influenced the traditional local manufacture of ceramics. Pingsdorf pottery is once again not a matter of cooking vessels, but for the most part tableware, the main forms being amphorae, bowls and slim or rounded beakers (Fig 7.14). From Pingsdorf pottery there is a direct line to forms in proto-stoneware, which began at the end of the twelfth century, continuing a characteristic formal detail, the 'waved flat foot'.

A method of finishing ceramics in a special way, which had already been practised by the Romans, is the use of glaze. The *renovatio imperii* of the Carolingian period stim-

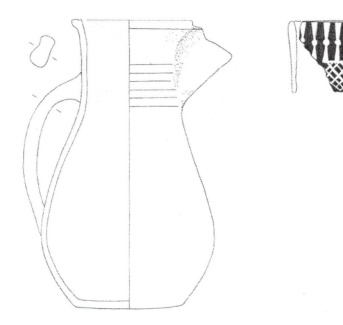

Fig 7.13   *Tating-ware jug; scale 1:3 (Lüdtke 2002).*

ulated this aspect also. In Italy, with the floruit of Rome at this period (Box 4.2), there was a blossoming of pottery with thick lead glaze, known as Forum ware (Fig 7.15); this is found above all as spouted pitchers for use at table. During the eleventh and twelfth centuries, however, glaze was no longer much used, but in the High Middle Ages coloured, enamelled and glazed vessels from Byzantium and different parts of the Arabic world (cf. Box 8.1) are found in the Italic area. In France (e.g. St Denis) and Belgium there is an increasing number of finds indicative of a local production of glazed, mostly light olive-coloured, pottery as early as the late ninth and tenth centuries, but the number of finds is very few in comparison with the unglazed wares. This is also tableware in the form of spouted pitchers, among other things. In Central Europe there are only a few traces of glazed earthenware in the early Middle Ages, so that one can only speak of a very sporadic use of this decorative technique. During the late eleventh and twelfth centuries, the potteries of Andenne (Belgium) and Schinfeld (South Limbourg), which were active in trans-regional trade, take up the decoration of vessels with yellow and orange-coloured lead glaze in a big way, making a great range of products. It was not until the thirteenth century that urban potters in Central Europe followed the demand emerging there and began to manufacture tableware with external glazing (see Vol 2).

Another type of crockery emerged in those parts of eastern Central Europe that had come into contact with the Carolingian Empire, but without having any long-term influence on the future range of types in the region. In the production of this so-called 'Feldberg luxury pottery', in the power-centres of the north-western Slavs, a relationship can be presumed with the so-called 'serving bowls' in the Badorf tradition – that

Pingsdorf ware; scale 1:3 (Schenk 2002).

Fig 7.14

Fig 7.15 *Forum ware (Kunst und Kultur der Karolingerzeit).*

is an attempt to imitate Carolingian table-culture. Fine pottery in the Byzantine style, presumably from the Pannonian area, is found in the centres of the so-called Great Moravian Empire, reflecting an orientation of this area to the south-east (as was also the case with jewellery design), which was otherwise strongly connected to the Carolingian Empire (as with weapons and riding equipment). In those areas of what was later to become Hungary that had also become Carolingian, one finds fine tableware that is again attributed to workshops continuing to work in a Late Antique tradition. This was not mass production, but vessels for a (probably short-lived) elite.

Kitchenware

In contrast to the technically high-quality tableware, produced at first only in the West, earthenware vessels for cooking and storage (i.e. for kitchen-use) were more simply fashioned. It was not thrown on the foot-driven potter's wheel, but hand-made and turned afterwards; for the most part it was not even well fired. The spectrum of types is narrow, simply being a range of pots in different sizes that were used for cooking and storage purposes. The range of forms was, however, soon extended as a result of the influence of the important pottery regions in the Rhineland and east of the Rhine, with liquid containers being produced in the form of spouted pitchers.

Spouted pitcher from Lower Austria; 12th century (photo: S Felgenhauer-Schmiedt).   **Fig 7.16**

Generally speaking the design of cooking vessels during the period 800-1200, over a broad geographical area, can be categorised on the basis of where the vessel was positioned in the fireplace. While the so-called 'globular' pot, a vessel with a fully rounded base, is typical for the northern part of Central Europe, a pot with only a slightly rounded base (a 'lens base') was used in northern France and the northern Rhineland, while in the southern German area and further eastwards, a pot with a flat base was normal. In northern Italy, a particular type of pot was developed for cooking: a vessel with a device allowing it to be hung over the fire. In Hungary, which at the millennium had turned (under Stephen I) to Christian Europe, the earthenware cauldron, which had been popularised by the land-grabbing Magyars in the tenth century, could also be hung over an open fire and existed alongside the flat-based vessel until the thirteenth century. In parts of the southern German area, the eastern border regions of the Empire and among the neighbouring Slavs, a characteristic pottery type was used (the so-called 'Danube type'), a pot that was decorated with wavy lines and, in some areas, a combed decoration. The variety of form and the quality of the pottery improved in those places where particularly powerful ruling centres were built, often in opposition to the Carolingian Empire, such as among the north-west Slavic Abrodrites or in the centres of Great Moravia.

In the lower Austrian Danube area, which was absorbed into the Carolingian Empire as Bavaria's eastern territory, after the victory of Charlemagne, a type of pottery emerged during the ninth century that can be described as of high quality because of the clay employed, despite being hand-made, not always turned afterwards, and betraying no particular skill in its production. Around the millennium, however, improved production techniques and formal influences from the West can be recognised. The clay had special qualities, it was heat-resistant graphite clay, which occurs in particular deposits north and south of the Danube. Vessels from this deliberately selected material were manufactured into the twelfth century and were distributed over a wide area. While it was mainly pots that had been produced in the ninth and tenth centuries, the range of types was extended in the south-east of the Salian Empire during the eleventh and twelfth by the introduction of the spouted pitcher, that pottery type which, in its basic form, was created in the Carolingian West before spreading at differing speeds into the areas newly won for the Empire (Fig 7.16).

Finally, a clear restructuring of the pottery sector took place with the floruit of the town, and urban crafts, during the late twelfth and thirteenth centuries. This clearly demonstrates how a broad base, in the form of a newly-created population group striving for its own lifestyle, is necessary before demand is stimulated and new standards in production and consumption can be achieved.

Sources: Brather 2001; Felgenhauer-Schmiedt 1995; Gross 1991; Heege 1995, Losert 1993; Schenk 2000; Lüdtke & Schietzel 2002; Mannoni 1975; Takács 1986; see also the exhibition catalogues listed in Chapter 8.

The Production and Use of Bricks

by Hans Krongaard Kristensen

Brick was widely used in the Roman Empire; however, after this period, the production of bricks stopped. Instead, there was a widespread re-use of bricks taken from Roman ruins, a practice which continued, where the material was abundant, well into the Middle Ages, as for instance with the building of the large abbey church of St Albans in England (1077-1115).

Through archaeology, we can detect a revival of brick production in Lombardy, shortly before the middle of the twelfth century. This new production was probably initiated by the great Cistercian abbeys situated on the plains of the Po valley, an area which lacked both quarried stone and Roman ruins. In the middle of the century, the use of this technique spread to Northern Europe, to both Germany and Denmark. The technology then spread quickly to many other parts of Europe, particularly to places which lacked good building stone. The fire-resistance of brick was appreciated and its use for hearths, etc, often preceded its more general adoption for building purposes.

Exactly how this technology was spread has been the subject of much discussion, but many commentators have proposed a rather direct transmission once the idea was rediscovered. In any case, the process of burning clay to create a ceramic product is relatively simple, and pottery production was well understood by the twelfth century (as described above). Most agree that other ceramic building products (floor and roofing tiles) had been in production before medieval brick manufacture began. The remarkable thing, however, is the scale of production – the enormous quantities of bricks that had to be fabricated in order to build large medieval churches.

South side of the presbytery of St Nicholas church **Fig 7.17**
in Svenborg (Fyn, Denmark), from c1200, demon-
strating the possibilities for making friezes with
bricks (photo: HK Kristensen).

The bricks were produced by pressing well-kneaded clay, sand and water into a form (a frame of wood) and thus, with the removal of surplus clay, a regular block was produced. Afterwards the raw brick was knocked out of the form and transported to a drying ground. Whilst there, passing animals often left their imprints on the soft pieces of clay, before they had hardened ready for firing.

In Denmark, traces of several hundred medieval kilns have been found, indicating that brick production was a decentralised industry. The material for production, clay and perhaps a little sand for meagring, could be found nearly everywhere. Acquiring wood for fuel was, in some localities, perhaps a greater problem. Most kilns were quite simple, no more than clamps, shaped as a square box without permanent covering. Usually, they were dug into a slope so that only the front side (i.e. the fire opening) was visible. The dried bricks were then stacked carefully, leaving channels for air circulation during firing, as well as exhaust outlets.

In some places, there will have been a more permanent production of brick. The brick-yard St Petri in Lübeck, for example, of which the exact position is not known, exported roof tiles (stamped with a mark of the letters SP) to many areas around the Baltic Sea.

Brick does not have the same strength as the best quarried stone, but this factor was not so important in the construction of Romanesque churches (Fig 7.17). On the other hand, it later became a problem with Gothic architecture. This is the reason why one finds in the west, for example in the Low Countries, that bricks and ashlar are mixed so that the load-bearing elements, as also the decorative mouldings, are made of ashlar, whereas the in-filling is of brick. In this way, the architecture appears close to the norm for church-building at that period.

In the Baltic, on the other hand, the Gothic idiom was transformed to take advantage of the new material, using its qualities to create a refined architecture seen in such Hanseatic towns as Lübeck, Wismar, Rostock and Stralsund. Old Lübeck, with many great churches and enormous numbers of townhouses, almost all of brick, is the most important example of a brick-built town from the Middle Ages (see Vol 2).

Sources: Hansen 1985; Kristensen 2003.

Salt

by Jens Vellev

Along with drying and smoking, salt has played a central role in the preservation of foodstuffs. The word for salt has the same root in several European languages: *sal* (Latin), *sel* (French), *salt* (Danish), *Salz* (German) and not least *Hall* (Old High German). And the many place-names which contain the word 'salt' often designate localities where salt production occurred in the Middle Ages. At the seaside in southern Europe, salt was extracted by means of evaporation in large flat basins, whereas the inland production was normally carried out through evaporation in metal containers over an open fire (but cf. Fig 6.4). The raw material for the inland production was gathered from saline springs which in many cases run several metres underground.

Archaeological studies have been carried out in a number of localities. In about 1960, a study exposed traces of large-scale 'salt' production from c650-900 at Nauheim in Hessen (Germany). Protected by an earthwork c75m in diameter, the evaporation process took place out in the open over oblong stone-built kilns, after the brine had been purified through filters of straw. At this site lead pans were used to evaporate the brine – as opposed to earlier when production took place in remarkably small clay bowls in many of the areas studied by archaeologists. The lead pans in Nauheim were cast in flat clay forms up to 2m long (Fig 7.18).

In Lüneburg, south of Hamburg, salt extraction is mentioned for the first time in an official record issued by King Otto I in 956. The document shows that even then the production of salt was considerable. The almost saturated brine (crystallization occurs when the salt content reaches about 25%) was raised manually from the mine-shafts, which descended c15m to the underground springs. The production conditions had hardly changed much before the medieval method of production was reorganized c1800. Until then the evaporation process took place in c50 boiling huts (Fig 7.19), which were each equipped with four lead pans measuring c1m^2.

On the small island of Læsø, situated between Denmark and Sweden, large scale salt production was carried out until 1652, made possible due to a very favourable natural situation. The shallow salt meadows in the southern areas of the island were often flooded, but a couple of metres below ground, massive clay strata stopped the downward percolation, and the salt concentration in the sea-water then increased from about 3% to up to 15 %, in connection with the natural evaporation caused by the sun and wind. The brine was then evaporated in iron pans over rectangular kilns in small boiling huts. The

'Mould' for lead pan from Bad Nauheim, Germany (after Süss 1978). **Fig 7.18**

The interior of a boiling hut in Lüneberg, Germany (drawing by LA Gebhardi, late 18thC). **Fig 7.19**

production of salt there is known from written sources from the beginning of the four-teenth century, but its start should certainly be looked for a couple hundred years earl-ier, when the Danish king transferred ownership of the island to the Chapter of Viborg Cathedral. Extensive archaeological studies carried out since 1990 have provided useful insights into the construction of the boiling huts. The roof was supported by wall posts dug into the ground and four large central posts, which were positioned around the cen-tral kiln. The huts, which measured 10x10m, were protected against flooding by a low peat bank.

The high percentage of salt in the natural brine which was exploited in Lüneburg and on Læsø could rarely be obtained. In Nauheim, the spring-water contained merely 2-3% salt. But the demand was great and the price often very high. Salt was called white gold. Almost everywhere where salt springs occurred, small extraction industries arose. Many were only in operation for a short time, others for centuries.

Sources: Emons & Hans-Henning 1988; Lamschus 1989; Süss 1978; Vellev 2002.

BIBLIOGRAPHY

Amores, F (1995) 'Las alfarerías almohades de La Cartuja', in Valor Piechotta, M (ed), *El Ultimo Siglo de la Sevilla islámica*, Seville, 303-6.

Amouretti, MC and Comet, G (2000) 'La meunerie antique et médiévale', *Archives internationales d'histoire des sciences* 50, 18-29

Arnau, B and Martí, J (2000) 'Aigüa i desenvolupa-ment urbà a Madinat Balansiya (València). L'excavació d'un molí hidràulic de l'època califal', in Glick, TF (ed), *Els molins hidràulics valencians*, Valencia, 168-70

Bender Jørgensen, L (1992) *North European Textiles until AD 1000*, Aarhus

Biddle, M (ed) (1990) *Object and Economy in Medieval Winchester*, Winchester Studies 7, Oxford, 2 vols

Blair, J and Ramsay, N (eds) (1991), *English Medieval Industries*, London/Rio Grande

Böhme, HW (1999) 'Wassermühlen im frühen Mit-telalter', in Böhme, A (ed), *Die Regnersche Mühle in Bretzenheim*, Beiträge zur Geschichte Wasser-mühle, Bretzenheimer Beiträge zur Geschichte 1, Mainz, 26-55

Brather, S (2001) *Archäologie der westlichen Slawen. Siedlung, Wirtschaft und Gesellschaft im früh- und hochmittelalterlichen Osteuropa*, Berlin/New York

Callmer, J (1977) *Trade Beads and Bead Trade in Scan-dinavia, ca. 800-1000 AD*, Acta Archaeologica Lundensia, series in 4° 11, Bonn/Lund

Carus-Wilson, E (1969) 'Haberget: a medieval textile conundrum', *Medieval Archaeology* 13, 148-66

Clarke, H (1986) 'Craft and industry', in Clarke, H (1986) *The Archaeology of Medieval England*, Oxford, 129-65

Claude, D (1981) 'Die Handwerker der Merowing-erzeit nach der erzählenden und urkundlichen Quellen', in Jankuhn, H et al (eds), *Das Handwerk in vor- und frügeschichtlicher Zeit*, Teil I, Abhand-lungen der Akademie der Wissenschaften in Göttingen, Philologisch-historische Klasse Dritte Folge 122, Göttingen, 204-66

Córdoba, R (1996), 'Arqueología de las instalaciones industriales de época medieval en la Península Ibérica. Estado de la cuestión', *Medievalismo* 6, 193-212.

Córdoba, R (2003), 'Some reflections on the use of water power in al-Andalus', in Cavaciocchi, S (ed), *Economia ed energia, seccoli XIII-XVIII*, Florence, 931-54

Córdoba, R and Castillo, F, 'Los hornos califales de cerámica del Cortijo del Cura, Córdoba', *Arqueología y Territorio Medieval* (in press)

Córdoba, R and Hernández, P (1994) 'Dedales hispano-musulmanes de la provincia de Córdoba', in Azuar, R and Martí, J (eds), *IV Congreso de Arqueología Medieval Española, Alicante*, Vol 3, 919-25

Cressier, P (ed) (2000) *El vidrio en al-Andalus*, Madrid

Crossley, DW (ed) (1981) *Medieval Industry*, Council for British Archaeology Research Report 40, London

Crowfoot, E, Pritchard, F and Staniland, K (1992) *Textiles and Clothing c.1150-c.1450*, Medieval Finds from Excavations in London 4, London

Czysz, W (1998) *Die ältesten Wassermühlen. Archäologische Entdeckungen im Paartal bei Dasing*, Thierhaupten

Emons, H-H and Hans-Henning, W (1988) *Alte Salinen in Mitteleuropa. Zur Geschichte der Salzerzeugung vom Mittelalter bis zur Gegenwart*, Leipzig

Felgenhauer-Schmiedt, S (1995) *Die Sachkultur des Mittelalters im Lichte der archäologischen Funde*, Frankfurt am Main/Berlin/Bern/New York/Paris/Vienna

Fichet, F (ed) (1996) *Ateliers de potiers médiévaux en Bretagne*, Paris

Francovich, R (ed) (1993) *Archeologia delle attivitá estrattive e metallurgiche*, Florence

Garnier, B, Garnotel, A, Mercier, C and Raynaud, C (1995) 'De la ferme au village: Dassargues du Ve au XIIe siècle (Lunel, Hérault)', *Archéologie du Midi médiévale* 13, 1-78

Geijer, A (1938) *Die Textilfunde aus den Gräbern = Birka*, Vol 3, Uppsala

Gisbert, J. A. (1990), 'Los hornos del alfar islámico de la Avda. Montgó ', *Fours de potiers et "testares" médiévaux en Méditerranée Occidentale*, Madrid, 75-91

Graham-Campbell, J (1980) *Viking Artefacts: a Select Catalogue*, London

Gross, U (1991) *Mittelalterliche Keramik zwischen Neckarmündung und Schwäbischer Alb*, Forschungen und Berichte der Archäologie des Mittelalters in Baden-Württemburg 12

Hägg, I (1984) *Die Textilfunde aus dem Hafen von Haithabu*, Berichte über die ausgrabungen in Haithabu 20, Neumünster

Hansen, BA (1985) 'Middelalderlige teglovne med udgangspunkt I de senere års fund', *Bygningsarkæologiske Studier*, 7-16

Heege, A (1995) *Die Keramik des frühen und hohen Mittelalters aus dem Rheinland*, Bonn

Henning, J (1994) 'Mühlentechnologie und Ökonomiewandel zwischen Römerzeit und Frühmittelalter. Fragen aus archäologischer Sicht', *Saalburg-Jahrbuch* 47, 5-18

Hillam, J (1981) 'An English tree-ring chronology, A.D. 404-1216', *Medieval Archaeology* 25, 31-44

Höckmann, O (1996) 'Eine Schiffmühle aus Gimbsheim (Kreis Alzey-Worms), in *Die Franken. Wegbereiter Europas* (catalogue), Mainz, 786-8

Hoffmann, M (1974) *The Warp-Weighted Loom*, Oslo

Hope-Taylor, B (1958-59) 'Old Windsor', *Medieval Archaeology* 2, 183-5, & 3, 288-90

Hundt, HJ (1981) *Die textil- und schnurreste aus der frühgeschichtlichen wurt Elisenhof*, Studien zur Küstenarchäologie Schleswig-Holsteins, Serie A, Frankfurt am Main

Hurst, JG (1976) 'The pottery', in Wilson, DM (ed), *The Archaeology of Anglo-Saxon England*, London, 283-348

Izquierdo, R (1996), 'Unas tenerías excavadas en la ciudad hispano-musulmana de Vascos', *Arqueología y Territorio Medieval*, 3, 149-165

Jiménez, P, Muñoz, F and Thiriot, J (2000) 'Les ateliers urbains de verriers de Murcia au XIIe siècle', in Pétrequin, P, Fluzin, P, Thiriot, J and Benoit, P (eds), *Arts du feu et productions artisanales*, Antibes, 433-52

Kamińska, J and Nahlik, A (1958) *Włókiennictwo gdańskie X-XIII wieku*, Łódź

Kristensen, HK (2003) 'Backsteinarchitektur in Dänemark bis zur Mitte des 13. Jahrhunderts', in Gläser, M, Mührenberg, D and Hansen, PB (eds), *Dänen in Lübeck 1203-2003*, Lübeck, 94-103

Lamschus, C (1989) 'Die Bergwerke der Saline Lüneburg. Arbeit und Technik in Mittelalter und Neuzeit', in Lamschus, C (ed), *Salz – Arbeit und Technik – Produktion und Distribution in Mittelalter und Früher Neuzeit,* Lüneburg, 83-92

Leciejewicz, L, Tabaczynska, E and Tabaczynski, S (eds) *Torcello: scavi 1961-62*, Venice

Lohrmann, D (1996) 'Antrieb von Getreidemühlen', in Lindgren, U (ed), *Europäische Technik im Mittelalter, 800 bis 1200, Tradition und Innovation, Ein Handbuch*, Berlin, 221-32

Lorquet, P (1994) 'Découverte d'un moulin carolingien à Belle-Eglise "Le Pré des Paillards" (Oise)', *Revue archéologique de Picardie* 3-4, 51-7

Losert, H (1993) *Die früh- und hochmittelalterliche Keramik in Oberfranken*, Zeitschrift für Archäologie des Mittelalters 8, Bonn/Cologne

Lüdtke, H and Schietzel, K (2002) *Handbuch zur mittelalterlichen Keramik in Nordeuropa*, Neumünster

MacGregor, A (1985) *Bone, Antler, Ivory & Horn. The Technology of Skeletal Materials since the Roman Period*, London

MacGregor, A, Mainman, AJ and Rogers, NSH (1999) *Bone, Antler, Ivory and Horn from Anglo-Scandinavian and Medieval York*, The Archaeology of York 17/2, York

Mannoni, T (1975) *La ceramica medievale a Genova e nella Liguria*, Studi Genuensi 7

Maik, J (1988) 'Frühmittelalterlichen textilwaren in Wolin', in Bender Jørgensen, L Magnus, B and Munksgaard, E (eds), *Archaeological Textiles: Report from the Second NESAT Symposium, 1-4 May 1984*, Arkeologiske Skrifter 2, Copenhagen, 162-87

Maik, J (1988) *Wyroby włókiennicze na Pomorzu z okresu rzymskiego i ze średniowiecza*, Acta Archeologica Lodziensia 34, Łódź

Maik, J (1991) *Tekstylia wczesnośredniowieczne z wykopalisk w Opolu*, Warsaw/ Łódź

Maik, J (1997) *Sukiennictwo elbląskie w średniowieczu*, Łódź

Maik, J (2005) 'Stand und notwendigkeit der forschungen über die mittelalterliche wollweberei auf dem südlichen Ostseegebiet', in Pritchard, F and Wild, JP (eds), *Northern Archaeological Textiles*, NESAT VII, Textile Symposium in Edinburgh, May 1999, Oxford, 84-92.

Mainman, AJ and Rogers, NSH (2000) *Craft, Industry and Daily Life: Finds from Anglo-Scandinavian York*, The Archaeology of York 17/14, York

Mannoni, T (1975) *La ceramica medievale a Genova e nelo Liguria*, Studi Genuensi 7

Mannoni, T and Gianichedda, E (1996) *Archeologia della Produzione*, Turin

Mostalac, A. (1990), 'Los hornos islámicos de Zaragoza', *Fours de potiers et "testares" médiévaux en Méditerranée Occidentale*, Madrid, 63-74

Mould, Q, Carlisle, I and Cameron, E (2003) *Leather and Leatherworking in Anglo-Scandinavian and Medieval York*, The Archaeology of York 17/16, York

Nahlik, A (1964) *Tkaniny wełniane importowane i miejscowe Nowogrodu Wielkiego X-XV wieku*, Wrocław/ Warsaw/Krakow (French summary)

Nahlik, A (1965) *Tkaniny wsi wschodnioeuropejskiej X-XIII wieku*, Łódź

Nielsen, LC (1987) 'Omgård. The Viking Age watermill complex. A provisional report on the 1986 excavations', *Acta Archaeologica* 57, 177-210

Ottaway, P (1992) *Anglo-Scandinavian Ironwork from Coppergate*, The Archaeology of York 17/6, York

Pleiner, R (2000) *Iron in Archaeology. Early European Blacksmiths*, Prague

Pleiner, R (2006) *Iron in Archaeology. The European Bloomery Smelters*, Prague

Rahtz, PA and Meeson, R (1992) *An Anglo-Saxon Watermill at Tamworth*, London

Retuerce, M. (1987), 'El templén, primer testimonio del telar horizontal en Europa?', *Boletín de Arqueología Medieval*, 1, 71-77

Rodet, I, Olive, C and Forest, V (2002) 'Dépôts archéologiques de pieds de mouton et de chèvre: s'agit-il toujours d'un artisanat de la peau?', in Audouin-Rouzeau, F and Beyres, S (eds), *Le Travail du Cuir de la Préhistoire à nos Jours*, Antibes, 314-49

Rohmer, P (1996), 'Le moulin carolingien d'Audun – le Tiche', *L'Archéologie* 22, 6-8

Rynne, C (1989) 'The introduction of the vertical watermill into Ireland: some recent archaeological evidence', *Medieval Archaeology* 33, 21-31

Sancho, M (1996) 'Aportaciones de la arqueología para el estudio de la producción de hierro en la Cataluña medieval', in La Hullera, V-L (ed), *Actas de las I Jornadas sobre Minería y Tecnología en la Edad Media Peninsular*, Madrid, 436-50

Schenk, H (2000) 'Zu Chronologie und Gefäßtypologie der Pingsdorfer Ware', *Bonner Jahrbücher* 200, 329-405

Schwarz-Mackensen, G (1976) 'Die Knochennadeln von Haithabu', in Schietzel, K (ed), *Berichte über die Ausgrabungen in Haithabu* 9, Neumünster, 1-94

Singer, C et al (eds) (1956) *A History of Technology*, II, *The Mediterranean Civilizations and the Middle Ages, c.700BC to c.AD1500*, Oxford

Stærmose Nielsen, KH (1999) *Kirkes væv. Opstadvævens historie og nutidige brug*, Lejre

Süss, L (1978) *Die frühmittelalterliche Saline in Bad Nauheim*, Frankfurt am Main

Takács, M (1986) *Die arpadenzeitlichen Tonkessel im Karpatenbecken*, Varia Archaeologica Hungarica

Torres, C (1986) 'Uma proposta de interpretaçao funcional para os conhecidos cabos de faca', *Actas I CAME* 1, Huesca, 331-41

Ulbricht, I (1978) *Die Geweihverarbeitung in Haithabu*, Berichte über die Ausgrabungen in Haithabu 7, Neumünster

Vellev, J (2002) 'Salt and the island of Læsø in Denmark. Archaeological explorations from 1990 to 2000', in Wirth, H (ed), *Investitionen im Salinenwesen und Salzbergbau. Globale Rahmenbedingungen, regionale Auswirkung, verbliebene Monumente*, Weimar, 118-35

Walton, P (1989) *Textiles, Cordage and Raw Fibre from 16-22 Coppergate*, The Archaeology of York 17/5, York

Wilson, DM (1976) 'Craft and industry', in Wilson, DM (ed), *The Archaeology of Anglo-Saxon England*, London, 253-81

Zimmerman, WH (1982) 'Archäologische Befunde frühmittelalterlicher Webhäuser', in Bender Jørgensen, L and Tidow, K (eds), *Textilsymposium Neumünster*, Neumünster, 109-34

CHAPTER 8

MATERIAL CULTURE AND DAILY LIFE

Sabine Felgenhauer-Schmiedt (translated by Paul Mitchell),
with James Graham-Campbell

Political and Economic Foundations

During the tenth century, there began the gradual development and strengthening of the so-called 'nation-states' that were to shape the rest of the medieval period and have continued to the present day. Economically and socially, through the increasing division of labour, through the establishment of the feudal order and of an urban bourgeoisie, a generally strongly-ordered society arose in the secular sphere with each class having distinct needs and living conditions that found expression in material culture (see also Chapters 5 & 12). In consequence, the ethnic aspects of material culture were increasingly displaced by material culture that was socially and economically determined.

Archaeologically, the period after the collapse of the Roman Empire can be divided into two, defined by archaeological features: the first period being that of burial with grave-goods; and the subsequent one when this rich source of information for material culture (admittedly not the culture of the living, but that considered by the living to be appropriate for their dead) is no longer present because of the influence of Christianity. In what had once been the core areas of the Roman Empire, the practice of grave-goods generally came to an end during the eighth century, so that some objects of contemporary material culture (such as glass vessels) are in fact better known from burials containing imported grave-goods in Northern Europe. Subsequently, only highly important people were buried with symbols of their worldly authority (or with the help of comparatively cheap imitations), e.g. the members of the Salian ruling-house, in the cathedral at Speyer (see p 437 & Box 12.2). The higher clergy, notably bishops, also continued to be buried with the insignia of their rank. On the eastern fringes of the old Empire, however, and in some other areas with the beginning of rudimentary Christianity, people were still sometimes furnished with jewellery into the twelfth century, and even beyond (see Box 8.3). The main focus of archaeological work on the period 800-1200 lies clearly in the area of settlements, whereby 'central-places' and other power centres, such as castles (Chapter 11), palaces (Chapter 12) and towns, have generally so far been better analysed than rural settlements (cf. Chapters 3 & 4).

Generally speaking, one can characterise the state of research into the archaeology of material culture in this period as acceptable, but there is still need for much further work, even with regard to basic typological and chronological questions. As far as ceramics are concerned, the differing fabrics (or wares) can readily be dealt with because of their developed production techniques, and their repertoire of forms is known to a considerable extent, even if there remains scope for improvement. Our knowledge is best concerning the products of the trans-regional potteries active in the Rhineland and North-West Europe (pp 225-7). The hand-made ceramics of northern Central Europe have also been well published, but there are still several research gaps in southern Central Europe, in Bavaria and south of the Alps. The pottery of the Slavic area in eastern Central Europe, which was in touch with the Carolingian Empire from the ninth century onwards, has been thoroughly researched.

Turning to glass objects, finds have increased in recent decades, so that today it is possible (particularly through the increased use of the analysis of the chemical composition of the glass) to draw a rounded picture of the use of what was still an elite material. Individual discoveries can, however, still lead to surprising new developments in this area.

As far as metalwork is concerned, the state of play varies: weapons and riding equipment, but also artistically significant non-ferrous metal artefacts, enjoy rather more attention than the simple tools of daily life. Wooden objects are rarely found across much of Europe and one must therefore presume that the full spectrum of objects in this material is not nearly known as yet. Bone as a raw material is important throughout the medieval period, despite regional differences: the state of publication is in parts very good, particularly regarding the finds from York, Hedeby and Schleswig in the North, but also, in the case of ivory carving as far as artistic craftwork is concerned.

Vessels and Life-Styles

Ceramics for table and kitchen

Because of their indestructibility, and because they occur almost everywhere, ceramics are a decisively important artefact-type for archaeologists. They allow an insight into the respective regional spectra of forms and also, because of their methods of manufacture, an increasingly formal and functional differentiation, the extent of their distribution-patterns and the respective milieus in which they were used, provide important information about the particular life-styles of the users and both general and particular economic and social frameworks and conditions. It is, therefore, particularly important to examine contexts when not only simple cooking vessels occur, but also more elaborate ceramic forms because together they reveal not just how a household was equipped, but also the refinement of the householder's tastes (cf. Chapter 5). The production and use of the clay vessels that can be characterised as tableware provides therefore a definite signal for differentiation in the furnishing of a household, depending of course on there being workshops to satisfy the demands, as well as a corresponding circle of buyers. The question of the symbolism of certain household objects for particular social classes can also be analysed with the help of ceramics (see Box 8.1).

In the case, for example, of the well-known 'Badorf ware', produced in the Carolingian Rhineland, the main forms are tall pots, spouted pitchers, bowls, and 'relief-band' amphorae (Fig 7.12). This was not mainly a matter of earthen vessels for cooking or storage purposes, but of vessels for use at table (or crockery). The use of such vessels indicates a differentiated pattern in household furnishing – an aspect of social and cultural life, which cannot be shown east of the Carolingian Empire – at least as far as the material clay is concerned.

In contrast to the technically high-quality tableware, produced at first only in the West, earthenware vessels for cooking and storage (i.e. for kitchen-use) were more simply fashioned (see pp 228-9). The spectrum of types is narrow, simply being a range of pots in different sizes, which were used for cooking and storage purposes. The range of forms was, however, soon extended as a result of the influence of the important pottery regions in the Rhineland and east of the Rhine, with liquid containers being produced in the form of spouted pitchers (Fig 7.16).

Glass vessels

During the Roman period, glass vessels were manufactured in many diverse forms both for general use and as a luxury product, and traded throughout the Roman Empire. During the Merovingian Empire in the west of Continental Europe, where Late Antique structures survived for some time, glass vessels continued to be used in a reduced formal spectrum and manufacturers slowly conformed formally to their new clients' taste. Important changes, in the range of designs as well as in composition, are not felt until the Carolingian period: the import of soda from Italy as flux in the manufacture of glass was gradually ended and a slow switch to the use of local wood ash took place. From both documentary sources and archaeological finds (e.g. glass workshops in the monasteries of San Vincenzo near Rome, St Ulrich and Afra (Augsburg), Lorsch and Fulda), we know that the art of glass-blowing was primarily kept going by the Church during the Carolingian period. Glass vessels from settlements can be found around ecclesiastical and secular power-centres in Western Europe during this period They indicate a particular life-style, one reserved for the upper classes, with drinking vessels, such as the tapered 'funnel-beakers' (Fig 8.1), being mostly found during the ninth and tenth centuries. A particular style of decoration took place with the application of transparent rods of coloured glass, the so-called *reticella* technique, which can be found on shallow bowls, bag-shaped beakers and funnel-beakers. Exceptionally luxurious glasses were produced with gold-leaf decoration.

Apart from hollow glass, window glass has also been found in the vicinity of the elite and the Church. It is clear, however, in contrast to the Roman period, that the use of

BOX 8.1   GREEN-AND-BROWN DECORATED POTTERY

In the Andalusian town of Madinat al-Zahara (now Cordoba), built during the second half of the tenth century by order of the Umayyad caliph Abderraman III, fine pottery was produced featuring green and black/purple decoration on a white base. This has become known as *verde y manganeso* (green-and-brown) decorated pottery.

The colour combinations were white used as the background, black to outline the design and for filling in some areas, and green to fill in the main motifs. To achieve the opaque white slip, tin was used in combination with other elements, while the other colours, green and black/purple, were made respectively with copper oxide and manganese dioxide. This colour choice was not accidental, given that in the Islamic world these colours were of great symbolic significance. One of the commonest interpretations is that which identifies white as the colour of the Umayyads, green as the colour of Islam, and black as em-

blematic of power and dignity, combining to represent the Cordoban Umayyad's power – ceramics as a means of communication.

The commonest ceramics were shallow open forms made for use as tableware, such as *ataifores* (large serving-bowls; Fig 1) and smaller bowls (*jofainas*). Jugs, bottles (Fig 2), vases, pitchers and cups were also made. The clay used was of good quality: beige, orange or pink in colour, and less frequently red. When making open forms the outer surface was usually given a transparent amber or yellowish coloured glaze, with sometimes green or white being used, whereas narrow-mouthed shapes normally had an impermeable coating on the inside made from highly diluted glaze. Another method of lesser quality was also used, in which the items were totally coated in an amber-coloured glaze beneath which the decorative motifs could be seen – usually of a very simple nature – made with *verde-manganeso* (green-and-brown).

Fig 1

The designs used on verde y manganeso *(green-and-brown) fineware were rich and varied; this* ataifor *(serving-bowl) is decorated with a horse motif (after Caviró 1991; Museo Arqueológico Provincial de Cordóba).*

The decorative motifs were varied and usually based on architectural designs or textile patterns which were reinterpreted by the potters for their own use. These motifs originated in a learned environment and consequently their symbolic significance was of great importance. The basic motifs are:

- **GEOMETRIC**: lines, stripes filled with solid colours or dots, circles and semi-circles and checkerboard patterns.
- **INTERLACE:** using two or three strands, denoting immortality.
- **FLORAL:** palmettes (Fig 2), leaves, stems, pines and flowers.
- **CALLIGRAPHIC:** using Cufic script, but also Roman; the commonest phrase was *al-Mulk* (power), referring both to divine power and that of the ruler.
- **ANIMAL:** horses (Fig 1), lions, hares, gazelles, peacocks, birds of prey, etc, with abstraction replacing naturalism in order to enhance symbolism and ornamentation.
- **HUMAN:** uncommon, usually depicting images from the court.

These green-and-brown decorated items, obviously luxurious, became status-symbols and spread all over the territory of al-Andalus, reaching Christian areas as gifts, booty and through the commercial exchange of luxury items. After its preliminary success, this type of pottery was produced in other Andalusian areas, such as Madina Elbira, Granada, where variations on the originals were produced which differentiated these products from the Cordoban ceramics.

After the *fitna* (399-422/1009-31), the caliphate was divided into petty kingdoms called *taifas*, whose rulers were intent on having poets, artists and craftsmen at their courts to establish their prestige. Consequently, potters who specialized in the green-and-brown technique were welcomed to establish workshops in Toledo, Saragossa, Murcia and Seville. In these centres, the green-and-brown technique was continued with local differences which help to determine the origins of a piece.

Source: Caviró 1991.

By Pilar Lafuente

Fig 2

Ceramic bottles (limetas), *such as this one with palmette decoration, were used to contain or serve liquids; their shapes were based on metal or glass examples (photo: P Lafuente; Municipal History Museum of Écija, Seville).*

Fig 8.1   *'Funnel-beakers' depicted in Prudentius, Psychomachia: 'Representation of Luxury'; late 9th century (Paris, Bibliothéque Nationale, lat 8085, ſ61v, after Kunst und Kultur der Karolingerzeit).*

glass products was more and more reserved for the elite, which had begun to distance itself, as also in this respect, from the mass of the population. Hollow glass was not produced east of the Frankish Empire, but workshops for glass beads or small glass rings have been excavated in many places such as Hedeby and York, as also in the 'central-places' of the Slavs. When glass 'funnel-beakers' are found at Mikulčice, the centre of

Great Moravia, it is because they symbolised a western world in which the Slav elite wanted to participate, at least in part. This was alongside the fine pottery and jewellery that demonstrate another important influence on their life-style: the Byzantine-influenced areas to the south-east.

During the eleventh and twelfth centuries, the range of local glass forms was significantly diminished and altered. An important written source from the early twelfth century, the *Schedula Diversarum Artium* by the monk Theophilus, makes it clear that the art of glass production in the High Middle Ages, as in the preceding centuries, was still being borne by the Church. There are few finds from this period, however, because among other things the normal composition of glass at that time (using local wood ash, after the import of soda had ended) does not lead to any great durability. The few local hollow-glass forms known to us are conservatively decorated bottle and beaker-type vessels (Fig 8.2), as well as rounded forms with applied glass threads of which several date from the late twelfth century. These already come from an urban context – evidence of the burgher-class now being formed, which oriented its daily life towards that which had formerly been reserved for the nobility. The major part of local glass production was, however, devoted to making flat glass for church windows, or even by this time glass for windows in castles.

High quality glass-ware, which is definitely be classified as luxury goods, eventually came to Europe during the eleventh and twelfth centuries, as a result of the more intensive contacts with Byzantium and the Near East resulting from the Crusades. Among these are the thick-walled 'Hedwig beakers', with their characteristic cut decoration, of which several examples remain in Treasure Cabinets, having been used in aristocratic circles. More common, although still rare, are blue glasses with gold paint, which are thought to be Byzantine products.

Metal vessels

There is little archaeological evidence for metal vessels from the period 800-1200, but fragments of both non-ferrous metal and iron are frequently found which had most probably formed part of metal vessels. As written sources confirm, vessels of precious metal were in use among the elite, but are rare as archaeological finds, although sometimes known from hoards (e.g. Fig 10.4). Chalices and patens can sometimes be found in the graves of bishops, however, as symbols of their ecclesiastical office, at a time when there are normally no longer any grave-goods.

Shallow engraved bronze bowls (so-called 'Hanseatic bowls') are particularly widespread, serving both as precious table vessels and for ritual hand-washing (Fig 12.7). They were used in the Christian liturgy, but also in secular contexts, often together with animal-shaped or other pouring vessels, to demonstrate courtly table-manners (see Chapter 12).

Fig 8.3 Aquamanile, *12th century (after Hütt 1993).*

An important type of pouring vessel is the so-called *aquamanile* (Fig 8.3), which became established in secular table manners through their use in ecclesiastical liturgy. It thus demonstrates the incorporation of initially Christian objects into the profane rituals of an upper class in need of self-definition. Hand-washing is not only a sensible hygienic measure, but it is also, in both courtly ceremony and the liturgy of the Mass, a way of achieving moral purity. These non-ferrous metal vessels were cast in animal shapes (see also Fig 12.6). From the late twelfth century, such vessels were increasingly made from clay. They show how, during the period of the Crusades, the Islamic world was nevertheless able to formally influence courtly society.

Wooden artefacts

Over much of Europe, medieval wooden vessels rarely survive in any quantity because of the seasonly low water-table, although there are a number of northern, mostly urban, sites with good wood preservation, e.g. Dublin (Lang 1988), York (Morris 2000), Hedeby (Schietzel 1970; Elsner 1994) and Lund (Blomqvist & Mårtensson 1963). Although outside the geographical scope of this book, attention must be drawn to the great number of medieval wooden artefacts of all types known from the Novgorod excavations (Kolchin 1989; see above, p 21). The material increases again in the late Middle Ages thanks to finds in wells and cesspits in urban or monastic environments.

The Oseberg ship (from Vestfold, Norway) was sealed in a burial mound of clay, in 834, which resulted in a remarkable degree of preservation of the aristocratic lady's possessions (Grieg 1928). As already noted above, these included her wooden furniture, sledges and a wagon (Fig 9.3), as well as an abundant supply of household equipment. The early medieval wooden objects from the Oberflacht cemetery of the Alamanni, in Southern Germany, also survived because of uniquely favourable ground conditions. Their variety displays both the important role and the outstanding quality of the wooden objects in the life of medieval people. Turned and coopered vessels demonstrate mature craftsmanship (see Box 8.2) and allow us to appreciate that, despite the lack of relevant finds before the High Middle Ages, there was considerable continuity of form in the production of certain vessels. Bowls, plates and pilgrims' bottles (as well as furniture parts) were turned, as continue to be found in late medieval contextst. The same is true of stave-built buckets and pails, and small coopered beakers, which were extensively used as drinking vessels in the towns of the High to late Middle Ages (Fig 8.4).

Clothing and Jewellery

Clothing is the most intimate component of daily-life and it communicates a picture of the contemporary norms to which the wearer is subject, whether consciously or not. It can express a particular regional identity and/or emphasise the rank or social status of the wearer. The medieval archaeologist can hardly get to grips with the respective costumes or fashions, given that the items were made from cloth or other perishable materials. One has largely to be satisfied with the metal components of clothing and draw

BOX 8.2   WOODEN ARTEFACTS

The preservation of wood on medieval sites is often poor, with only materials resistant to decay surviving. However, on a few sites (particularly in Northern Europe) waterlogging has caused anaerobic conditions in which decay is sufficiently slowed down for wood and other organic remains to survive, often very well. Such sites are invaluable in assessing the role that wood played as a material in medieval societies. Analysis of a broad range of remains from important urban sites such as York (Morris 2000), Dublin (Lang 1988), Hedeby (Schietzel 1970), Lund (Blomqvist & Mårtensson 1963) and Novgorod (Kolchin 1989) has answered vital questions concerning woodworking technologies, species selection and craftsmanship, and the relationship between the use of wood and other materials in the manufacture of objects for both domestic and economic aspects of society.

In most areas of Europe access to woodland was within the reach of most societies, presenting a range of resources from large timber to wood from smaller trees and bushes. All households would have had access to at least the simplest of woodworking tools, an axe and knife, and so the potential for each household to manufacture its own wooden objects is clear. The vast range of wooden objects recovered from sites such as Viking period York and Dublin show that many were produced by the conversion of timber in the round by an axe and then by whittling with a knife. Such household objects include small items of furniture, carved boxes and bowls, spoons, children's toys, and pins and needles. Identification of the wood species of these objects reveals a deep knowledge of the different qualities of each species: ash (*Fraxinus excelsior*) used for the flexibility required for tool handles; oak (*Quercus spp*), where strength and durability are required; and the very dense and fine grained wood of yew (*Taxus baccata*) and box (*Buxus sempervirens*) for small objects such as combs and needles.

Though it is clear that the household was responsible for the production of many of the objects used in everyday life the development of two important woodworking technologies took the manufacture of domestic objects to the level of the specialist craftsman. A specialist craft industry defined not simply by a knowledge and ability in manufacture, but also in the tools required. The woodworking technologies of turning and cooperage, both with origins in the early Iron Age in Europe, became in the medieval period essential industries providing objects for both domestic use and for the local economy. For example, the evidence of the turning industry from York suggests the thriving production of bowls and plates for domestic use (Fig 1), while the cooperage industry supplied households, farms and industries with a vast range of stave-built containers from beakers (Fig 8.4) and buckets to bath-tubs.

Beyond supplying the needs of domestic households and the local economy, the cooperage industry played a vital role in providing trade with containers that could easily be transported by land or sea (as illustrated in the Bayeux Tapestry). Stave-built kegs and casks could carry wet or dry goods and could be reused over and over again - and when not in use could be 'knocked down' or disassembled for easy transport. On the other hand, the excavations at Hedeby have revealed imported Rhenish wine-casks (Fig 10.6), reused as the linings for wells (Roesdahl 1982, 122; also see p 197).

The role of wood in providing for both domestic and economic needs, and the degree to which these needs were provided for by unspecialised craft workers within the household, or by more specialised craft industries, would have varied. Naturally enough, the local environment will have provided differently in terms of its wood resource from region to region, but craftspeople with their specialist knowledge were not necessarily always available, and the cultural requirement for wood over other materials, if these were available, is also likely to have differed. Wood is only preserved archaeologically under specific anaerobic conditions and where these conditions do not prevail the role of wood cannot be addressed. It is important therefore to guard against constructing too broad an interpretation from the relatively few, though often rich, urban waterlogged sites that have been excavated.

By Jon Hather

Fig 1

A selection of turned and carved vessels and implements from Anglo-Scandinavian York (photo: York Archaeological Trust).

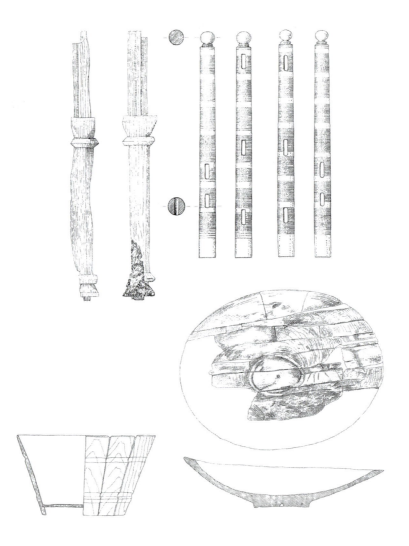

Fig 8.4   *Wooden vessels: stave-built beaker from Strasburg (after Gross 1991), and turned bowl from Haus Meer (Janssen 1999), both scale 1:3; with furniture parts from Haus Meer (ibid), scale 1:10.*

conclusions from these, in conjunction with an analysis of pictorial sources. The latter demonstrate that changes in clothing can be perceived every twenty years or so - that clothes are subjected to a permanent shifting of fashions. A rich source for the early Middle Ages, the grave-goods and clothing components in graves start to dry up in the Carolingian period. Grave-goods and clothing can still be found in Saxon graves up to c850, but from the late ninth century onwards, they can be found only in the eastern and south-eastern parts of the Empire (and beyond; see Box 8.3). However, settlement and workshop finds are increasingly adding to our picture. One interesting observation is that during the Carolingian period, and then with the expansion of the Holy Roman

Empire eastwards under the Ottonians and the Salians in the tenth and eleventh centuries, a type of brooch began to become accepted that indicates a standardisation of clothing to that of an originally Christian-Mediterranean style. Differences in traditional dress between different tribes, as during the early Middle Ages, can no longer be followed through these clothing components. Archaeological finds thus indicate, as far as clothing is concerned, a trend towards overcoming regionalisation by means of a standardised style of dress. Older traditions were longer-lived only in peripheral areas, with Slavic dress being a different matter. Here the main component of Carolingian clothing, the brooch, was absent, but particularly rich neck and head jewellery ('temple-rings') survived until well into the High Middle Ages.

The trend for dress to be organised around a single brooch was already clear by the late Merovingian period. From those ninth-century graves that still included grave-goods, we know that – with the exception of the area conquered by Charlemagne from the Avars in the south-east - only women were buried with a brooch, on the middle of their breast. This is evidence for the cloak (*palla* or *tunica*) known from illustrations, which was closed at the front with the help of such a brooch. Men also wear brooches in the illustrations, which close a cloak over the tunic on the right-hand side. This can sometimes be regarded as a *topos*, however, and it need not be understood as men's everyday dress, for from written sources (Einhard) we learn that Charlemagne, for example, wore a cloak only on formal occasions, held together by a golden clasp.

There is a wide range of brooch forms known from the ninth century and their find-spots, with their different milieus, demonstrate that brooches represented a mass-produced item as an essential clothing accessory during the Carolingian and Ottonian periods, which were worn in rural settlements, early towns and castles alike. The form of, or images on, some brooches let us draw conclusions about the beliefs on display. The symbolic, identity-building, content of dress is particularly clear in the case of those brooches that can be connected to Christian iconography, whether they are cross-shaped or the popular enamelled disc brooches with relevant designs. The so-called 'Saints' brooches' testify to a growing popular devoutness through veneration of the saints (Fig 8.5). Coin brooches, with 'portraits' of ninth-century Carolingian rulers, demonstrate the existence of a close relationship with the expanding Carolingian order. Rectangular (or square) brooches, as well as equal-arm brooches, are also common. During the later ninth and tenth centuries, enamelled disc brooches with animal-motifs became more and more popular (Fig 8.6). In the south-east, a so-called Ottonian-early Salian 'imperial culture' emerged as far as clothing is concerned. This can be deduced from the escalating popularity of the increasingly standardised brooches of the tenth to eleventh centuries, which make clear the orientation of the wearer.

In the late tenth and eleventh centuries, a strong influence over jewellery design can be discerned from the Byzantine-Fatimid region, probably helped by the union of the Ottonian imperial house with a Byzantine princess, as far as brooches and also ear ornaments are concerned, half-moon-shaped ear-rings enjoying particular popularity. The Empress Kunigunde wore such ear-rings as late as 1020, but they seem to have gone out of fashion in the course of the eleventh century.

BOX 8.3 WOMEN'S COSTUME IN SOUTH-WESTERN FINLAND

Under Christian influence, inhumation burials became more common in Finland from the eleventh century, displacing cremation. Although the practice of burying the dead in festive dress,

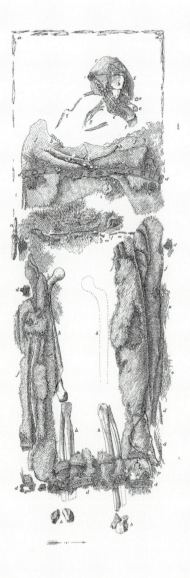

Fig 1

A 12th-century grave with well-preserved textiles (after Appelgren-Kivalo 1907).

with tools, utensils and weapons, was of pagan origin, it continued in use until the end of the twelfth century.

Dress details have been preserved in graves because of the use of bronze jewellery and bronze spiral ornaments sewn onto some garments, with the copper oxides preserving an effigy of the textile. Spirals were used less frequently on men's clothes, and that is why most reconstructions are of women's clothing. Only the wealthiest women were buried wearing such splendid costumes.

The use of spiral ornamentation on clothes is typical of the Finnish people and the Balts and had its heyday during the eleventh and twelfth centuries. Spirals and ornaments made from them were easy to transport and sell. Spiral-decorated garments replaced shimmering gold fabrics and bands, which were fashionable in Europe and Byzantium at that time. The designs of spiral ornaments and tablet-woven bands may perhaps have carried a language of signs and symbols that would have been readily understood by contemporary people (if no longer by us).

Because Finnish soil is poor in lime, preserved textiles are mostly of wool, which resists acidic soils better than vegetal fibres. The fabrics were woven on warp-weighted looms. The identified items of female dress are: a shirt or undergarment, a dress, an apron, a mantle, a head-dress/veil, puttees and mittens.

Only small fragments of shirts, made of linen or hemp, have been discovered. The preserved undergarments are often of wool. Bracelets were worn over the sleeves and sometimes sleeve fragments are found inside the arm-ring. A popular ornament was a necklace made from colourful beads, often together with silver coins and pendants.

The mantle dress, fastened with brooches on the shoulders, has been compared to the Greek *peplos*. During the late Viking period (1025-50), heavy, convex circular bronze brooches dominated, and the richest women used a chain arrangement with the brooches. Later, small penannular brooches made of bronze or silver became the fashion. Given that shoulder brooches appear only in a few graves, there must have been various different types of garment in use.

The apron was edged with a bronze spiral line, and there were sometimes separate spiral figures or a broad spiral lattice sewn on to the cloth. The apron was worn only by sexually mature women and also had magical significance. A large, bronze-plated sheath, with a small knife inside, was suspended from the waistband of the apron, and appears to have hung horizontally. It may have been worn across the stomach, like a great amulet to protect its wearer.

Under the dress and spiral-decorated apron hem, fragments of puttees are sometimes preserved, fastened with plaited woollen braids. The shoes were carefully made of leather.

The finest mantles were large in size, often blue in colour and decorated with spirals and tablet-woven patterned braids. The decoration was influenced by the depiction of the Madonna's mantle in Byzantine art. The head-dress was made of a single piece of fabric, as were many of the other garments. Temple decorations made of plaited woollen threads and bronze spirals were worn with the head-dress.

A tradition of putting mittens into the graves is typical of the Balt-Finnish peoples. Fragments of mittens are sometimes found on finger-rings, but the deceased did not necessarily wear the mittens. They functioned, perhaps, more like an amulet giving magical protection on the way to the after-life.

Sources: Appelgren-Kivalo 1907; Lehtosalo-Hilander 1984; Peets 1987.

By Jaana Riikonen

Fig 2

President Tarja Halonen wore the Eura costume at the Independence Day celebration of Finland in 2001; her dress reconstruction is based on a rich grave dating from the early 11th century (Office of the President of the Republic of Finland).

Fig 8.5 *Saints' brooches in Europe, 9th century (after Spiong 2000).*

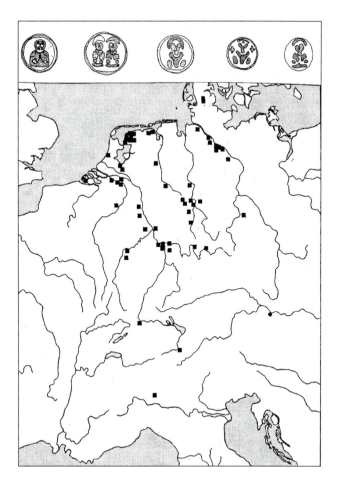

Disc brooches were used into the first half of the twelfth century, but then as part of a change in clothing fashions – clothes became tighter – ring-brooches gradually appeared towards the end of the century; they were then produced in many diverse varieties until the fourteenth century. We also find evidence of a new fastening technique: the button (although this had been in use in eastern Central Europe for some time).

We have concentrated on the use of a single brooch for clothing solutions as an identity-building element within the expanding Empire in the ninth and tenth centuries, but in the eleventh and twelfth centuries above all, the social component of this clothing accessory and embellishment came to the fore – as an expression of the layered society, with its clear division of labour, then establishing itself, with knights, peasants and the first urban burghers, all of whom were recognisable apart through their clothes and jewellery. It is conspicuous that brooches of silver and gold, but now also of tin/pewter, from the eleventh and twelfth centuries, come overwhelmingly from castles and towns. This means that peasants were no longer equipped with more or less expensive objects of this kind. Social differentiation, previously largely expressed through high-production quality, using expensive materials, was now visible through the use of the

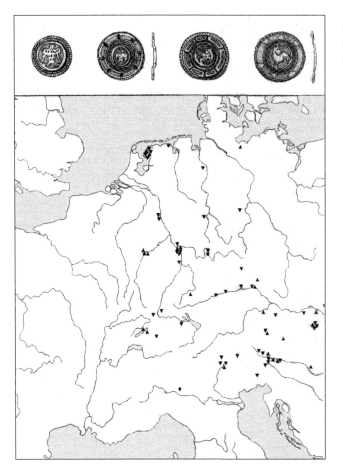

Animal brooches, 10th/11th century (after Spiong 2000).

Fig 8.6

object in the first place – a sign that the gap between people had widened. On the other hand, the rarity of such finds indicates that life was increasingly running along organised and controlled lines; the re-cycling of all kinds of metals was apparently spreading.

Horse and Rider

The use of iron in the daily life of medieval people during the period 800-1200 differed considerably according to social status. Because of burial finds the archaeological sources are considerably more informative for the ninth and tenth centuries than for the eleventh/twelfth-century period, from which only stray finds are known. As far as weapons, tools and other equipment were concerned, the demand for iron grew particularly in the eighth century. This had to do with the increasing importance, from the Carolingian period onwards, of the heavily-armed equestrian warrior, or cavalryman, with both sword and lance; the need for so much of this expensive metal has been seen as one of the grounds for the development of the system of vassalage in this period. The sword, the most important weapon of the Carolingian warrior was spread widely across Europe – despite repeated

banning of the arms-trade – probably from production centres on the Lower Rhine which were of more than local importance. A chain-mail tunic, shield, helmet, spurs (the item most readily accessible to archaeologists) and stirrups, which became more common from the Carolingian period onwards (e.g. Fig 9.2), were also part of military equipment. Spurs went through periodic changes from 800-1200, including their goads becoming longer. During the eleventh century, the goad began to turn upwards and, towards the end of the twelfth century, the arms also became curved so as to fit better around the foot. Gilding or silvering on a few examples makes it clear how important spurs were for a knight's appearance. Apart from buckling on the sword, the putting-on of spurs was an important component of the rituals involved with joining the knighthood.

The quality of Frankish weaponry led to the development of an increasingly unified standard of weaponry in the Central and Western European areas. The increasing expense of this equipment increased the gulf between the knight and the land-working population. At the same time it led to closer relations between the respective upper classes, a development also expressed among other things in increasingly similar weaponry. As in other areas of material culture in the High Middle Ages after the Second Crusade (1147-49), there was an oriental influence on the appearance of a knight through the introduction of rounded helmets curved in a horned fashion, but this is, however, known only from pictorial evidence.

An important innovation took place in the tenth century when horseshoes were introduced, which are found, especially from the eleventh century onwards (see p 271), in knightly contexts, above all in castles, where the first iron horse-combs have also been found, demonstrating particular effort in caring for valuable mounts.

Archaeology has revealed the existence of pendants of non-ferrous metal that decorated horse's bridles. They were often gilt and thus demonstrate the importance of a magnificent appearance on the part of horse and rider in the High Middle Ages. These pendants are decorated in open-work and serve as a medium for motifs that are also known from Romanesque churches and manuscript illustrations and which partly reflect a world of the imagination, spread by the *Physiologus* and the Bestiaries (Fig 8.7). This is an interpretation of the animal world with references to Christ, the Church and the devil, however naive they may seem to us today. In this way, a mystical-sacral note was conferred upon a knight whose horse was decorated in this manner.

Tools

Everyday iron objects from the period 800-1200 are better known from the surroundings of the high-status, castle-dwelling social strata, or the early urban settlements (e.g. York; Ottaway 1992), than they are from the purely peasant sphere. This shows, among other things, that castles were often organised to perform multiple functions and were not simply power-centres, but also economic centres and land-owning businesses. The general low frequency of metal tools, above all in the High medieval urban environment, is conspicuous. This can be interpreted as an indication that iron objects were increasingly part of organised re-cycling.

On the other hand, during the Viking period in North-West Europe, the Scandinavian practice of depositing grave-goods has ensured the survival of a wide range of tools and equipment connected with agriculture, hunting and fishing, blacksmithing and daily life in general (Petersen 1951; Graham-Campbell 1980; Roesdahl & Wilson 1992). A remarkable discovery at Mästermyr, on the Swedish island of Gotland, was a complete tool-chest containing sets of metalworking and carpentry tools (Fig 8.8), together with a steelyard, three bells and a firegrid (Arwidsson & Berg 1983).

The most common tool was without doubt the knife, which could be produced in differing qualities, with expensive knives being pattern welded into the twelfth century (see pp 222-3, Figs 7.10 & 7.11). In the High Middle Ages, there were knives with curved backs; in this way a point was created with which one could skewer pieces of meat. Iconographic evidence shows that such knives were used at the dining-table.

Apart from picks and axes, which were used for land clearance and woodworking, objects to do with agricultural activities, such as sickles, shears or pruning knives, can be found in High Medieval contexts, mostly in castles. Only rarely do component parts of ploughs survive, such as the iron ploughshare or coulter (see Box 3.2). Some tools, such as those used in woodworking, were already so functionally designed that no more changes were necessary, but others for work in the fields, particularly the plough underwent changes during the medieval period, demonstrating technological progress.

Private Space

Little archaeological material illuminates the private sphere of life, with the exception of pottery. Hardly any wooden furniture is left, but the fragments show production of high quality, in which the craft of turning was employed (cf. Figs 5.10 & 8.4). Small boxes and

Fig 8.8   *Selection of metalworking and carpentry tools found in the Viking period tool-chest from Mästermyr, Gotland (photo: Iwar Anderson, ATA, National Heritage Board, Stockholm).*

chests (e.g. Fig 8.8) were provided with iron locks – keys are part of the archaeological inventory above all in early medieval palaces and 'central-places', and then in the castles of the nobility in the eleventh and twelfth centuries. The frequency of finds suggests an increase in private property in upper-class circles.

Archaeological material culture also indicates an improvement in living standards in the private sphere (Chapter 5). However, this is connected to particular social status and cannot be observed among all levels. Clearly the source of warmth played an important role in the creation of a comfortable living environment. The open fire brought smoke with it and thus diminished the quality of living space. Through the increasing construction of hot-air heating systems in monasteries and castles, an attempt was made to reach a level of comfort which had last been known during the Roman period. The tiled 'storage' stove was, on the other hand, a genuinely new invention of the Middle Ages, offering smoke-free living comfort (see Box 5.2).

Light also contributes to well-being in living-rooms (see pp 172-3). The best effect in this regard was achieved by window glass, which has been proven for the ninth century in monasteries (e.g. Corvey, Brunshausen and Lorsch), but also in important secular buildings. Window glass is known from a few examples in the urban environment of the eleventh and twelfth centuries, but towards the end of the High Middle Ages glass windows are likely to have become common in the heated castle-chambers mostly reserved for women, as is known from the literature of the period. For artificial light in specific rooms, iron candlesticks were employed and there were also specially designed candlesticks, which were manufactured in the production centres of non-ferrous metals between the Rhine and the Meuse and in the Harz area - just as the aquamaniles had been. Chandeliers have also been archaeologically proven in the High Middle Ages – presumably the most expensive source of light in the highest social circles. In the peasant sphere, however, the stove fire remained the most important source of light until the end of the Middle Ages.

Family life is illuminated through children's toys, among other things, which appear during the medieval period in various forms (see also p 178), including small earthenware animal and human figures. This is a sign that childhood was seen in the upper class as a separate period of life with its own needs, different from the adult state of being, and that children were also becoming part of the increasing interaction between consumption and production, which in the later High Middle Ages was being boosted through a re-structuring of the craft industries (see Vol 2).

Reading and Writing

It is generally known that during the early Middle Ages the art of reading and writing was exercised and passed on above all by the Church. With the expansion of the Carolingian Empire eastwards and the Christianisation which accompanied it, new religious centres were created in which these skills were practised. This process can be followed archaeologically through two material objects: the stylus, as a writing instrument, and the book, or rather its metal fittings. The finds and the environment in which they are found are, above all, a visible sign that Christianisation had been taken up by the upper classes. In the eleventh and twelfth centuries, book-fittings or book-clasps, with animal and vegetal ornament, are increasingly found in castles, a sign that literacy was slowly becoming common among the castle-dwelling noble milieu.

A characteristic type of stylus, usually made from non-ferrous metal, is known archaeologically from twelfth/thirteenth-century castles and towns. Their special feature is an eye at the upper end. This means that they could be hung from a belt, like keys; that is to say that they could be used anywhere at any time. They prove, on the threshold of the late Middle Ages, that there was already a widespread, if in some sectors expected, use of notepads in the form of wax tablets. These are therefore no longer simply to be understood as an expression of the elite activity of an educated upper class, but as the use of writing instruments in daily life, for economic-mercantile purposes.

Gaming

An archaeologically noticeable aspect of life in upper-class circles, during the tenth, but above all the eleventh and twelfth centuries, is the remains of board-games in the form of gaming-pieces, mostly made of deer antler or bone (Fig 8.9). The individual pieces are often decorated with realistic or fantastic faunal motifs, as known also from the decoration of Romanesque churches and the Bestiaries. In secular life, they served as picto-

Fig 8.9 *Bone gaming-pieces decorated with birds and beasts, 11th century (after Scholkmann 1982).*

rial conveyors of a world of the imagination with which medieval people were much preoccupied. Apart from the figurative pieces, there are also less lavishly decorated examples with geometric patterns. The great number of figurative pieces, especially from castles, demonstrates the socio-cultural component of board-games – as an artistically and lavishly-staged leisure activity, in which the nobility, now a self-contained layer of society, took part, among other things, in order to demonstrate both their separateness and a general sense of belonging together. This attempt to fashion daily life in a particular way was communicated more clearly still through chess, which during the eleventh and twelfth centuries was also played with enthusiasm in elite circles and even became part of a knight's training and instruction. Contacts with the East were responsible for the knowledge of this demanding game, the oriental influence being visible, at least initially, in the abstract design of chess-pieces during the eleventh century. Chess-pieces could be made from many different materials – from wood, deer antler, bone, ivory and also from expensive stone, such as rock crystal. Chess-pieces are found above all in castles, but a most remarkable find was that of a 'hoard' of twelfth-century, walrus ivory, chessmen on the island of Lewis, in north-west Scotland, which are representational figures in Romanesque style (Fig 12.8).

Summary

During the period 800-1200, decisive political, economic and social changes took place throughout Europe. The expansion of the Carolingian Empire (and subsequently those of the Ottonians, Salians and Hohenstaufens) eastwards brought with it a visible trend in the material culture to unify standards in different areas of life, particularly among the upper classes. This can be seen on the one hand in the sphere of weaponry and the appearance of horse and rider, but also in the management of life generally. As regards clothing, the increasing spread eastwards and south-eastwards of dress organised around a single brooch, during the Carolingian and Ottonian periods, suggests the increasing consciousness of a unified whole. The equipping of a household with specially designed ceramic tableware, as known from archaeology, is a socio-cultural phenomenon of which the beginnings can be identified in Western Europe during the early Middle Ages. Its gradual adoption throughout large parts of Central Europe signifies a degree of standardisation, in the sense of an Europeanisation. This is again particularly clear for the upper classes, which was forming in the eleventh and twelfth centuries in the castle, and then also increasingly in the town, and who documented their striving for common symbolic, ritualised actions through the observance of particular table-manners – archaeologically tangible through vessels for hand-washing. Leisure activity belongs in the same way to the common behaviour of an upper class and is indicated by chess or other board-games, played with expensively crafted gaming-pieces – and also by objects such as styli or book-fittings, which provide evidence for literacy.

Economic life went through enormous changes during the period 800-1200. Production, which at first remained located around the estate-centres, in castles and monasteries, was subsequently concentrated in the High Medieval town with its market and developed money economy. The emporia, that is merchants' and craftsmen's settlements in the North, but also the early urban conurbations with their markets, in particular connected with former Roman settlements, such as Cologne or Trier, were forerunners of these developments. Structural change in the eleventh and twelfth centuries brought to mass-produced pottery an improved technology moving from West to East, and also formal stimuli, prompted by more sophisticated requirements and the significantly increased market in the blossoming towns. Growing production and consumption reinforced each other.

The deep changes are also clear in the finds material from the different social layers. The separateness of the upper class increased, which eventually even removed itself physically from the rest of the population through the construction of castles (Chapter 11). This is also visible archaeologically in artefacts, through the special furnishing of the living area and of the table, and through the increase of leisure activities such as demanding games. In the town, the burghers were increasingly able to get closer to this upper class and consequently, through the use of particular material objects, to adopt its habits and needs. A type of Europeanisation, which at first was reserved for the nobility, spread in this way to broader layers of the population and strengthened the trend to a unified standard of life within particular layers of society. In rural society, improved standards were more visible in improved agricultural techniques than in the organisation of daily life in the household. Archaeologically, and in terms of the surviving material objects, no attempt appears to have been made to conform to the behaviour patterns of the upper class which became so clearly separate during the High Middle Ages.

BIBLIOGRAPHY

Exhibition catalogues:

Die Zeit der Staufer, I-III (1977), Stuttgart

Viking Artefacts: a Select Catalogue (1980), London

Das Reich der Salier (1992), Sigmaringen

From Viking to Crusader. Scandinavia and Europe 800-1200 (1992), Copenhagen

Bernward von Hildesheim und das Zeitalter der Ottonen, 2 vols (1993), Hildesheim *799.*

Kunst und Kultur der Karolingerzeit, 2 vols (1999), Mainz

Europas Mitte um 1000, 2 vols & cat. (2000), Stuttgart

Appelgren-Kivalo, H (1907) *Suomalaisia pukuja myöhemmältä rautakaudelta – Finnische Trachten aus jüngeren Eisenzeitt*, Helsinki

Arwidsson, G and Berg, G (1983) *The Mästermyr Find. A Viking Age Tool Chest from Gotland*, Stockholm

Baumgartner, E and Krueger, I (1988) *Phönix aus Sand und Asche. Glas des Mittelalters*, Munich

Blair, J and Ramsay, N (eds) (1991) *English Medieval Industries*, London

Blomqvist, R and Mårtensson, AW (1963) *Thule grävningen 1961*, Archaeologia Lundensia 2, Lund

Brather, S (2001) *Archäologie der westlichen Slawen. Siedlung, Wirtschaft und Gesellschaft im früh- und hochmittelalterlichen Osteuropa*, Berlin/New York

Caviró, BM (1991) *Cerámica hispanomusulmana: andalusí y mudéjar*, Madrid

Elsner, H (1994) *Wikingermuseum Haithabu: Schaufenster einer frühen Stadt*, Neumünster

Felgenhauer-Schmiedt, S (1995) *Die Sachkultur des Mittelalters im Lichte der archäologischen Funde*, Frankfurt am Main/Berlin/Bern/New York/Paris/Vienna

Giesler, J (1997) *Der Ostalpenraum vom 8–11 Jahrhundert*, Studien zu archäologischen und schriftlichen Zeugnissen 2

Graham-Campbell, J (1980) *Viking Artefacts: a Select Catalogue*, London

Grieg, S (1928) *Osebergfunnet*, II, Oslo

Kolchin, BA (1989) *Wooden Artefacts from Medieval Novgorod*, British Archaeological Reports, International Series 495, 2 vols, London

Krüger, K (2002) *Archäologische Zeugnisse zum mittelalterlichen Buch- und Schriftwesen nordwärts der Mittelgebirge*, Universitätsforschungen zur prähistorischen Archäologie 91

Hodges, R (1995) *San Vincenzo al Volturno 2: the 1980-86 Excavations*, London

Hütt, M (1993) *Aquamanilien. Gebrauch und Form*, Mainz

Janssen, W and Janssen, B (1999) *Die frühmittelalterliche Niederungsburg bei Haus Meer, Kreis Neuss*, Rheinische Ausgrabungen 46

Kulturhistorisk leksikon for nordisk middelalder 1-22 (1956-78), Copenhagen

Lehtosalo-Hilander, P-L (1984) *Ancient Finnish Costumes*, Vammala

Lexikon des Mittelalters (1977-99), Munich

Mainman, AJ and Rogers, NSH (2000) *Craft, Industry and Everyday Life: Finds from Anglo-Scandinavian York*, The Archaeology of York 17/4, York

Lang, JT (1988) *Viking Age Decorated Wood*, Dublin

Margeson, S (1985) *Norwich Households: the Medieval and Post-Medieval Finds from Norwich Survey Excavations 1971-78*, East Anglian Archaeology 58

Morris, C (2000) *Wood and Woodworking in Anglo-Scandinavian and Medieval York*, The Archaeology of York 17/13, York

Ottaway, P (1992) *Anglo-Scandinavian Ironworking from Coppergate*, The Archaeology of York 17/6, York

Peets, J (1987) 'Totenhandschuhe in Bestattungsbrauchtum der Esten und anderer Ostseefinnen', *Fennoscandia archaeologica* 4, 105-16

Petersen, J (1951) *Vikingetidens redskaper*, Oslo (with English summary)

Prohaska-Gross, Ch (1991) 'Die Glas- und Schmelztiegelfunde aus dem gemauerten Schacht bei St. Peter und Paul', in *Hirsau St. Peter und Paul 1091-1991, Teil I. Zur Archäologie und Kunstgeschichte*, Forschungen und Berichte der Archäologie des Mittelalters in Baden Württemberg 10/1, 179-98

Roesdahl, E (1982) *Viking Age Denmark*, London

Roesdahl, E (ed) (1999) *Dagligliv i Danmarks middelalder – en arkæologisk kulturhistorie*, Copenhagen

Roesdahl, E and Wilson, DM (eds) (1992) *From Viking to Crusader. Scandinavia and Europe 800-1200*, Copenhagen

Schietzel, K (1970) 'Hölzerne Kleinfunde aus Haithabu (Ausgrabungen 1963-64)', in Schietzel, K (ed), *Berichte uber die Ausgrabungen in Haithabu 4. Das Archaeologische Fundmaterial I*, Neumünster, 77-91

Scholkmann, B (1982) *Burg Baldenstein*, Sigmaringen

Spiong, S (2000) 'Fibeln und Gewandnadeln des 8.-12. Jahrhunderts in Zentraleuropa', *Zeitschrift für Archäologie des Mittelalters* 12, Bonn

Theophilus, *On Divers Arts*, trans (with intro & notes) by JG Hawthorne and CS Smith (2nd ed, 1979), New York

Wedepohl, KH (1998) *Mittelalterliches Glas in Mitteleuropa: Zusammensetzung, Herstellung, Rohstoffe*, Nachrichten der Akademie der Wissenschaften in Göttingen II, Mathematisch-Physikalische Klasse 1

CHAPTER 9

TRAVEL AND TRANSPORT

Jan Bill and Else Roesdahl

Introduction

The area which constituted medieval Latin Europe (see Introduction & Chapter 2) was bound together internally, and to its neighbours, by travel and transport – by sea, rivers and roads. Compared to Asia and Africa, medieval Europe was a small area, much of which (except for the Alpine regions and northern Scandinavia) was fertile lowland, easy to travel through. Rivers, and in some places fjords, penetrated deep into the land, so too did the Baltic Sea. To the west it was bordered by the Atlantic Ocean and to the south by the Mediterranean Sea. The Alps and the Pyrenees were serious obstacles to travel and transport, but routes through mountain passes were well established from Roman times; they could also be circumvented by land and sea. There were no huge dividing deserts, as in Africa and Asia. Being an area of great diversity due to climatic variations and differing resources, there was considerable impetus for communication and exchange within this area. This was facilitated by a common language among the learned, Latin, following the spread of Christianity, as well as by the common religion itself.

Travel, Transport and Society

Travel and transport (see e.g. Leighton 1972, for a general survey) was the basis for trade and towns, the Church, the spread of technology and culture and much else. It connected the varied and rapidly growing networks within Europe and was also the basis for the creation of larger political units – the beginnings of 'nation states'. There were networks of trade, of religion (monastic orders, the Church in general, with its archbishoprics and bishoprics dependent on papal Rome), and of social occasions. There was also travel and transport in relation to aristocratic and royal networks, to wars, crusades, pilgrimage, conquest and migration (such as Scandinavian settlement in England), to education (at schools, monasteries or courts), to the discovery and colonisation of wilderness and of new land (as in the Faroes, Iceland and Greenland), and to exploration (as with the 'Vinland voyages' from Greenland to North America around 1000). Some kinds of travel and transport involved large numbers of people, like crusades, pilgrimage and some Viking raids, while others were undertaken individually or in small groups.

Transport took place on different levels. Local transport related to food production and collection, to housing and other practical needs, and to local religious, social, legal or administrative activities, while regional transport connected local areas with wider distribution and social systems, and inter-regional/international transport linked major centres and nodal points. With the growing importance of such systems the amount and importance of transport itself increased, and it has been suggested that the transportation industry was – or, perhaps rather, became – the largest employer of hired labour in medieval Europe (Hunt & Murray 1999, 47).

All transport was dependent on the interaction of some common factors, which may be summarised as: (i) the friction of space (the resistance which landscape and other circumstances forced the traveller to overcome); and (ii) the technology of transport (the equipment available to the traveller to overcome this friction). The friction of space depended on natural hindrances and possibilities, such as mountains, swamps and rivers, but also on cultural products like political borders and safety issues. The friction of space could be significantly reduced by, for example, the construction of roads, bridges and hospices, and by the organisation of security, but it could also be increased, e.g. by establishing toll-stations, by piracy or by simple everyday constructions like mills and fishing weirs in rivers.

Transport routes and equipment developed, or were created, when and where there was a need for them, together with political and practical possibilities. They were selected according to the character of the transport and an estimate of the friction of space. For riverine or maritime routes, vessels suitable for the particular cargo and for the expected navigational and safety conditions needed to be chosen; for land routes, there were similar criteria for choices between horses, wagons or pack-animals, etc. Political conditions and security were of major importance. The state of confrontation between Christian and Muslim states throughout long periods of the Middle Ages had direct influence on routes, and possibly even delayed the restoration of sea traffic between the Mediterranean and northern Europe, which had virtually fallen out of use with the collapse of the western Roman Empire (see also Chapter 10).

Transport technologies varied greatly within Europe, especially in the first part of the period. This was partly due to the physical terrains and waters, partly to the natural resources available and partly to cultural conditions. In regions which had been part of the Roman Empire there were still, by the eighth century, ancient but functioning stone roads and bridges – for example, the bridge at Rochester, England, which had been built in the first or second century AD, continued to be maintained and used until it collapsed in 1381, and there are still existing but inevitably repaired bridges in Rome, Cordoba, Trier and other places (Brooks 1997, with refs; Harrison 2004). The construction of new stone bridges continued in southern parts of Europe. Sails also continued to be used in the South, while in Scandinavia, for example, sails for ships were not introduced before the seventh/eighth centuries and the earliest known bridges in the North were built just before AD1000. The late introduction to this region of such useful transport tools, which would have been learnt from foreign travels, must be due to changing demands on travel and transport technologies – undoubtedly based on the growth of trade and of the ambitions of political powers. New technology might have wide consequences – without sailing ships there could hardly have been a Viking period – and major constructions may be viewed in relation to changing concepts of state power (Brooks 1997). In general, improvements in transport technology were quickly exploited for military purposes, and some probably spread to certain countries for military reasons. Transport technologies were dynamic. Most developed during this period, finally spreading to nearly the whole of medieval Europe.

There are some basic distinctions between waterborne and land transport. In general, the friction of space for land transport increases much more rapidly per transported weight unit than for waterborne transport. Therefore, heavy cargo transport sought to use rivers and seas whenever possible and may have needed to travel considerably further than the direct geographical distance to its destination. This becomes particularly clear with the distribution of stone building materials in relation to their place of origin. Sea journeys would, however, have depended heavily on weather conditions, and transport time would be unpredictable, while river journeys often were possible only during part of the year. In contrast, personal transport and transport of goods with a high value-to-weight ratio often prefer the swifter land routes, especially in densely settled areas where a general need for local transport had already produced a good infrastructure (although such travel was of course also dependent on weather conditions). In northern Scandinavia and in Eastern Europe much travel and transport took place in winter, on snow and ice, with equipment specialised for this purpose. Written sources, such as travel accounts and twelfth-century pilgrims' itineraries, provide information on average travel times for certain distances (30-40km per day was normal), and on facilities and obstacles for personal transport. These sources include accounts of travel throughout Europe, from Scandinavia to the Holy Land (Friedman & Figg 2000, 613-16; Møller Jensen 2004). It is also clear that travel might be uncomfortable and even highly dangerous due to conditions of weather and terrain, of robbery, the break-down of wagons or problems with horses and accommodation, and so forth.

Large construction works might be carried out in order to overcome land obstacles to waterborne transport (canals) and water obstacles to land transport (fords and bridges). In 726, a canal was constructed across a peninsula on the island of Samsø, situated at the northern entrance to the waterways connecting the North Sea and the Baltic through the Danish archipelago. This, the Kanhave canal, was 500m long, 11m wide, 1.25m deep, and was lined with oak boards; it would have allowed the swift movement of long-ships from one side of the island to the other, making Samsø a very effective naval base for the control of large parts of the inner Danish waters. The canal, however, fell out of use after a few decades (Nørgård Jørgensen 2002, 135-7, 143-5).

In 793, Charlemagne initiated large-scale construction works in order to connect the rivers Main and Donau by means of a canal, the *Fossa Carolina*, but in vain (Spindler 1998); in this case, the work was probably also military in purpose (Hausen 2000). The citizens of Milan were more successful when they started, in 1187, to connect their land-bound city to the major rivers of the Po valley via canals in order to strengthen their city's trade. Slightly earlier, between 1134 and 1180, the town of Bruges, in Flanders, built a 5km long canal to re-establish access to the North Sea (De Witte 1999). Some Roman infrastructure was also still functioning – in England the Roman canal, Foss Dyke, near Lincoln, is reported in use in the eleventh century and was dredged by Henry I in 1121 (Priestley 1831).

Fords and bridges were situated where natural conditions made crossings most convenient, and settlements and nodal points for trade and other communication grew up in many places where important waterways and land-routes met. The same is true of places where rivers met the sea and provided good harbour facilities, and where both winter and summer routes met, such as at Birka in central Sweden. The construction of a new bridge might also cause restructuring within a town – as when London bridge was rebuilt c1000 (it succeeded a Roman bridge which had fallen out of use in the fourth century); this resulted in a rearrangement of the entire waterfront (Milne 2003, 55-62). The relationship between settlement and transport is thus a dynamic one. The better the communication possibilities, the more attractive it is to exploit the natural resources in a given area; the more settlement there is, the greater is the incentive for investment in transport infrastructure. Transport itself also creates a need for services, which in turn increases or even creates an economic basis for settlement.

Travel and transport relied on facilities. Among these were information, accommodation, harbours, storage space, landmarks, agreements between political powers for the safety of travellers and goods, and mundane objects to facilitate travel itself. These included tents, mobile fireplaces for cooking (as seen in use on the Bayeux Tapestry) and folding utensils for hanging cooking-pots over a fire (as found in the ninth-century Oseberg grave in Norway). Textiles were also important, and the variety of specialised textiles known archaeologically includes materials for travelling clothes and tents, for packing and covering goods, and for sails, etc (e.g. Pritchard & Wild 2005).

The creation and maintenance of major travel facilities during this period demonstrates an awareness of the importance of communication for economic, military and social reasons, as also spiritual ones. Kings and emperors, who almost constantly travelled with retinues within their lands, had rights of support from local inhabitants; monastic houses were obliged to provide accommodation and food for all travellers, and written sources have many examples of individuals donating means for travel. This was considered a good Christian deed, and many facilities were therefore available on important ecclesiastical routes and on pilgrims' roads, in particular, such as those to Rome and to Santiago de Compostela in north-western Spain (*Lexikon des Mittelalters*, 'Brücke'; Blanco et al 1989). At the same time the provision of transport facilities and also personal transport equipment might be prestigious symbols for the donor or owner. They appear in a variety of qualities, and it is clear from archaeological finds (e.g. beautifully executed ships, carved wagons and sledges and precious riding gear) that to travel in splendour was an important issue for the mighty.

Transport archaeology, then, deals with much more than the physical reflections of communication and trade. Transport was an active and decisive agent in the formation, life and development of medieval Europe, and the equipment used is decisive for the understanding of this. One must, however, be aware that some aspects of travel and transport are only documented in either archaeological or written or pictorial sources, and some are hardly documented at all. There is, for example, little archaeological evidence for the most common way of travel and transport in this period – on human feet with the simplest of equipment, although ethnological evidence from recent centuries can offer some insight into this matter.

Land Transport

The study of early medieval European land transport is fragmented. Not only is it fragmented according to region, but contextual studies within individual regions are also rare, the focus usually being on individual types of artefacts or structures, and sometimes even these are sparse. It is, however, increasingly clear that the period from the seventh to the twelfth century saw a revolution within land-transport technologies (e.g. Friedman & Figg 2000, 607-13).

Roads, fords and bridges

Most medieval roads (Schou Jørgensen 1988; Brink 2000; Hindle 2002; *Reallexikon*, 'Wege') were simple dirt tracks, often in the form of several near-parallel tracks. They were wear-traces in the landscape, not constructions, although hollow roads were sometimes dug into steep inclines in order to ease wagon traffic in particular. According to 'the law of dry feet' roads tended to follow water-shed lines and avoid rivers. Such roads

An ancient road in Södermanland (Sweden), lined with burial mounds and standing stones (from an 18th-century lithograph); some of these were probably rune-stones from the Viking period, one of which survives (photo: Sörmlands Museum, Nyköping). **Fig 9.1**

had existed since the Neolithic and continued in use right through the Middle Ages; however, some stone-paved roads still survived within the former Roman Empire, and urban streets all over Europe might be paved with stone, timber or brush-wood, or even animal bones and other stable rubbish, for the sake of comfort.

Villages and towns, churches and monasteries, castles and major estates were linked by roads. With the growing interest in communication during the early Middle Ages more roads would have appeared, and there would also have been a vast network of narrow riding and foot-paths linking local societies. Landscape conditions provided general frames for the more important road-lines; ancient monuments might line them; place-names may also help trace them. Examples which can be dated specifically to this period are, however, rare, except in towns. But in some cases road-markers and memorials – e.g. in tenth/eleventh-century Scandinavia, rune-stones or other standing stones (Fig 9.1) – demonstrate that a certain road did indeed function during this period, and sometimes nature would force roads of all periods through narrow corridors, such as Alpine passes, dry passages through wetland or good natural river and sea crossings – where also tolls might be taken, facilities found and settlement develop. On the other hand, man-made obstacles or facilities, or the lack of maintenance, might change the course of a land-route.

By far the most common way of crossing a river was by ferry or ford, as in ancient times and for a long time to follow. Some fords were built for the passage of wagons, but many just consisted of a row of stones allowing passage of men and horses. Important crossings were marked in the landscape; where tracks lead down to river crossings – or had to pass through a wet and swampy area elsewhere – this might be stabilised with stone, timber or brush-wood, or a dam or causeway might be built to lift the travel surface above the surrounding ground. Many such 'roads' have been investigated.

Dry passage across a brook might be provided by a couple of planks, and across a river by a bridge of timber or stone, or a combination of these materials. In practical terms, bridges were particularly important for the passage of wagons and pack-animals, but naturally made all sorts of travel safer and more comfortable; they were also important for the movement of armies (on bridges in general, see e.g. *Lexikon des Mittelalters*, 'Brücke'; Brooks 1997; Wilke 2000; Harrison 2004, with refs; see also Box 9.1). As mentioned above, some Roman stone bridges continued to be repaired and used, and new stone bridges were also built in southern parts of Europe – in Christian Spain, for example. But it was in this period that bridges were introduced or re-introduced to the rest of Europe. Major bridges were grand investments, and individual bridges may be mentioned in written sources; sometimes the construction and maintenance is known to have been a public obligation, and it might take several years to build a bridge (e.g. in Regensburg it took ten years from 1135, and in Avignon eight years from 1177).

Riding, driving, carrying, walking – and animals

Animals were crucial for travel and transport, and all were considerably smaller than their modern equivalents. They were used for riding (horses), for carrying goods (pack-horses) or as draft animals for pulling wagons and other vehicles that carried goods or

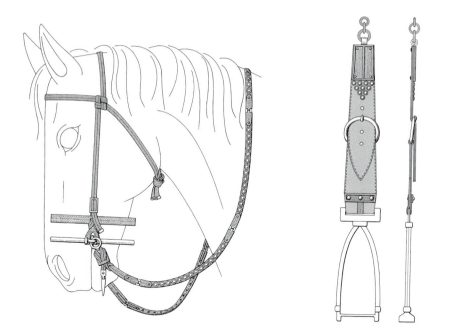

Reconstruction drawings of a well-preserved bridle and stirrup in a male Viking grave (mid-10th century), from Thumby-Bienebek, Schleswig, North Germany (after Müller-Wille 1987, no 37A).

Fig 9.2

people (oxen or horses); in Spain, donkeys and mules often fulfilled the same functions. Larger households had many horses, specialised for different purposes, some of which were very costly. This is obvious from written sources, including the many different words used for horses, and it may also be observed on contemporary pictures. Osteological investigations provide physical information on the animals themselves.

The most prestigious animals were riding horses. They were for travel, transport and display, and warhorses were always stallions. Equipment for horse and rider became increasingly sophisticated during this period (Fig 9.2). More types were introduced, and became more efficient for controlling the animal, and materials, execution and decorative mounts (Fig 8.7) demonstrate that this equipment also had display functions (on horses and equipment see, e.g. *Reallexikon*, 'Hufeisen', 'Pferdegeschirr', 'Sporen und Sporn', 'Steigbügel'; Langdon 1986; Felgenhauer-Schmiedt 1993, 201-8; Hyland 1999; Clark 2004). There is much archaeological evidence for such equipment in Europe, mostly of metal and normally as single-finds of individual components, but whole sets are known from pagan male graves in Central Europe and in Scandinavia. Much riding equipment would, however, have been simple and made of organic materials, and little of this survives. It is of interest how the various types of equipment spread to different parts of Europe at different times, e.g. to Viking period Scandinavia and Anglo-Saxon England (cf. Roesdahl 1982, 40-2; Pedersen 1999; with Graham-Campbell 1992).

Metal horse-bits were known from ancient times in most of Europe. There were two main types: snaffle-bits and curb-bits, each with a number of sub-types; curb-bits

BOX 9.1 BRIDGES

Fig 1

The Romanesque stone bridge at Puente la Reina in Navarra (northern Spain) is on the pilgrims' route to Santiago de Compostela, crossing the river Arga; it was constructed in the 11th century (before c1090, when first recorded), but has some later repairs (photo: HJ Frederiksen, University of Aarhus).

There has been considerable interest in medieval bridges, to a large extent based on surviving ones, all of which are of stone (Fig 1). However, due to archaeological techniques developed during the latter part of the twentieth century, many timber bridges have now been excavated, often in connection with modern bridge building, and dated precisely. Much constructional detail is now known about both stone and timber bridges, and sometimes the long and varied history of a river crossing is revealed, e.g. with fords succeeded by timber bridges, followed by a stone bridge (such as the one built in London 1176-1209) – or perhaps again by a ford.

Timber bridges are large-scale examples of carpentry, and they need almost constant maintenance. In many parts of Europe they were surely much more common than stone bridges during most of the Middle Ages, and when the first bridges were constructed in northern Germany, Scandinavia and the Slavic lands, stone-building techniques were unknown there. Bridge engineering itself was a challenge. It was with great

difficulty that Charlemagne managed to have a timber bridge constructed across the Rhine; sadly, this wonder was destroyed by fire in 812, shortly after completion. Early bridge-building is probably also a mark of new concepts of state power (Brooks 1997); for example, the earliest known bridge in Scandinavia, the 760m long and at least 5m wide Ravning Enge bridge in Denmark, dating from c980 (Schou Jørgensen 1988; 1997), must have been built by King Harald Bluetooth as part of a major monumental and military plan, but it was never repaired and soon fell into disuse – probably in tandem with the collapse of his power. A few smaller timber bridges were built elsewhere in the country around the same time (Fig 2), after which bridges are unknown there for more than a century.

Bridges all over Europe could also have other symbolic meanings. They were for the common good; donations for bridges were Christian deeds, and according to written sources, including runestones (Gräslund 1989), some were built to benefit the souls of dead relatives. Some stone bridges also bore a chapel. Further, many river bridges, particularly in towns, would have defensive functions: to prevent access by river-borne enemies and to stop them passing (cf. p 322); there are many accounts of bridge fighting.

Among the most impressive and best investigated bridges of the period are those built in the

Fig 2

River crossing at Risby in Zealand (Denmark), from c1000, with a stone-paved road (2.5m wide); it was a timber construction on top of a large stone and discarded wooden objects, including a primitive sledge (photo: M Schou Jørgensen, National Museum of Denmark).

Slavic lands south of the Baltic Sea. Many were part of fortifications and gave access to timber fortresses in lakes or rivers, but bridges to unfortified settlements and across rivers are also well known. Dendrochronology has revised some of the earlier dates advanced and, although examples from the eighth century are known, most of these bridges were built in the tenth or later centuries. Some bridges crossed deep water, e.g. 10-12m at Ostrów Lednicki, and some bridges were very long – three successive bridges leading to the Teterow fortress were 600-750m long (Fig 3), while the Oberueckersee bridge measured 2.2km (Schuldt 1975; Bleile 1998; Wilke 2000).

By Else Roesdahl

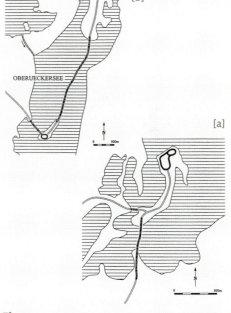

Fig 3

Reconstruction of a 750m Slavic timber bridge leading to the Teterow fortress, with schematic drawings of the locations of the bridges to Teterow (a) and to Fergitz in Oberueckersee (b), both in northeast Germany (after Wilke 2000).

Fig 9.3   *Above: One of the sledges from the 9th-century Oseberg ship burial in southern Norway; and below: the wagon from the same burial (photos: EJ Johnsen, Museum of Cultural History, University of Oslo).*

allowed for better control of the horse. Spurs were known from Roman times but now became more solid, the shape better fitted to riders' feet and footwear, and the goad (with which to control the horse) more prominent. Iron stirrups are known in central parts of Continental Europe from the sixth/seventh century, probably inspired from the Avars. They spread to North-Western and Northern Europe during the second half of the eighth century, probably through Frankish influence. In England, however, spurs were still rare during the Anglo-Saxon period, and stirrups seem to be introduced there as late as c1000, from Scandinavia. Stirrups eventually became all-important for fighting on horseback, which again relates to developments of the medieval warrior aristocracy (White 1965, chapter 1). But nothing suggests that cavalry techniques were used as early as this in either Scandinavia or Anglo-Saxon England; such horse equipment was prestigious in itself, and in relation to fighting, horses were at this time used for transport to the battle-field, while fighting itself was done on foot. The horseshoe is a late invention; examples formerly thought to be of Roman origin are probably misdated. Horseshoes are known in Central Europe from the late ninth/tenth century, in England from the tenth/eleventh century, and in Scandinavia from the late eleventh/twelfth century onwards (and there is a chronologically based typology of shoes and nails). Horseshoes protected hooves against wear on hard surfaces and gave safer footing on slippery and icy ground.

Haulage became much more efficient during the Middle Ages as a result of the introduction of the padded horse-collar, and improvements in harnessing, with the result that the use of oxen for farm-use and wagon hauling was to a large extent replaced by horse hauling during the twelfth to thirteenth centuries (Langdon 1986; Friedman & Figg 2000, 261f, 608f). On the other hand, archaeological evidence shows that horses were indeed used for haulage in ninth- and tenth-century Scandinavia, at least for personal transport in wagons (e.g. Roesdahl 1982, 44).

Archaeology has revealed many broken wheels and axles from wagons, as well as wheel tracks, remains of wagon bodies, iron draught chains, gilt-bronze harness-bows and bits for the horses. There are also pictures of wagons, but only one wagon survives from this period, that from the Oseberg mound in southern Norway, which was buried with an aristocratic woman and many other grave-goods in 834 (Fig 9.3). It has four wheels and was hauled by two horses – an embroidered textile from the same grave shows harness for wagon-horses – and it had a 2m long carved wagon body which was removable. This wagon was for personal transport, and wagon transport in general was predominantly for women, while men rode. Wagons of related construction were used for transporting goods (Grieg 1928, 3-65; Berg 1935; Roesdahl 1982, 42-4; Schovsbo 1987).

Some other types of equipment for transporting goods and materials are known. Simple sledges would also have been used in summer on easy surfaces for moving heavy loads, such as stones, over short distances (Fig 2, Box 9.1), and there were hand-barrows carried by two persons (Roesdahl 1982, 44). Goods were also carried by pack-animals, which in difficult terrain, unsuitable for wagons, was the only means of such transport other than human portage. Nevertheless, a lot of portable goods would have been carried by humans in bundles and baskets, etc, of which hardly any evidence survives (cf. Fenton et al 1973, for ethnological evidence), and the greatest proportion of travel was achieved on foot with simple equipment such as shoes, walking-stick, cloak, hat, bag and water-flask – as known from pilgrim pictures, but rarely identified in archaeological finds.

Winter transport

In the northern parts of Europe – in Norway, Sweden and Finland, in particular – the climate meant that much travel and transport would have taken place during the long and cold winters, when land, rivers, lakes and (in the east) the sea were covered with snow and ice, which nevertheless provided stable and even surfaces. Winter hunting, especially for good furs, was also important. This led to the development of special facilities for winter transport. Most of these were known also in southern Scandinavia, where winters can occasionally be very cold, as of course in Russia. The history of some of the necessary equipment, such as skis, can be traced back to the Stone Age, and they were presumably to a large extent developed by Saami people (cf. Edgren 1992).

Three finely carved sledges for personal transport, to be hauled by horses, are known from the ninth-century Oseberg burial (Fig 9.3), which also had a small simple sledge for transport of goods. Sledge fragments are increasingly identified, with specialised types of sledge being used for hunting and other purposes (Grieg 1928, 3-65; Berg 1935; Kolchin 1989). Many ancient skis are known, some of them carefully decorated; there was a rich variety of types including regional ones, and some have been dated to this period. The word itself is Norwegian (*Reallexikon*, 'Ski'). Snowshoes were also known. Skates were much used and are often found, both within and outside Scandinavia. They consisted simply of long bones of elk, cattle or horse, which might be tied to the feet but often were not; a pointed stick was used for moving. This type continued until recent centuries. For good footing on ice and snow, horses in Scandinavia might be provided with iron crampons with a short, solid spike; they went out of use in the eleventh or twelfth century, perhaps because of the introduction of horseshoes. Other forms of crampons were used by men (Graham-Campbell 1980, 298-300; Roesdahl 1982, 39f). Some special equipment for transport on ice and snow must also have been used in the various high altitude regions elsewhere in Europe.

Sea and River Transport

Organisation and routes in the Mediterranean area

The organisation of maritime transport in the Mediterranean area reflects the political situation. Byzantium held the north-eastern part of the area, including the Bosporus with the entrance to the Black Sea. The Arabs controlled the entire coastal region from Spain over North Africa to Palestine, including, during parts of the eighth and ninth centuries, Cyprus, Crete, Sicily and other islands. The Straits of Gibraltar and therefore access to the Atlantic coast were under Muslim control. Frankish control was exercised over the coasts of southern France and northern Italy. In the eleventh and twelfth centuries southern Italy and Sicily, which had belonged to Byzantium, became the seat of Norman power (see also Chapter 10).

Frequent wars between the various political powers was a hindrance to trade, but did not prevent it. Venice, situated on the fringe of the Byzantine Empire, was already from the eighth century able to develop as an independent middleman in the trade between Byzantium and the Franks. That the Franks, already in 840, entrusted the Venetian navy with the defence of the Adriatic demonstrates the importance of sea-routes to the Venetians and their potent presence at sea (Feldbauer & Morrissey 2002).

Coastal routes, such as that between Constantinople and Venice, must have connected other urban centres along the coasts of modern Italy and France. Ship-finds from Bozborun, in Turkey, and off Mljet, in Croatia, show the export of wine from the Crimea into the eastern Mediterranean area in the tenth century (Doorninck 2002). Likewise, Arab seamen travelled along the coasts of Spain, North Africa and Palestine.

Evidence for routes between the Muslim and the Christian sides of the sea is limited. One year between 797 and 802 the Abbasid caliph, Harun al' Rashid, sent an elephant by ship from Egypt to Pisa as a gift to Charlemagne, which may indicate that this route was also used for the transport of more ordinary cargo. Carolingian written sources point to the existence of a trade-route between North African ports, such as Sousse, to Gaeta, Naples and Salerno, but after the 830s this seems to have fallen out of use (Hodges 1997). Venice traded wood – illegally – to the Arabs, demonstrating that the exchange involved bulk cargoes (Unger 1980, 99-100). A number of ninth/tenth-century Arab ship-finds along the coasts of southern France attest seaborne trade and contacts between there and Muslim Spain and North Africa. The Serçe Limani ship, which sank with its cargo of Muslim scrap glass in Byzantine waters off Turkey, c1024, indeed attests to seaborne trade between the Fatimid Caliphate in Egypt and the Byzantine Empire at this time, as does the import of Muslim ceramics to Pisa, among other places, in the eleventh to thirteenth centuries.

The Arabs, who had an extensive eastward maritime trade up until the fourteenth century, reaching as far as China, undoubtedly also sailed along the Atlantic coast of the Iberian Peninsula. A few Viking and crusade expeditions through the Straits of Gibraltar into the Mediterranean are recorded, but there is no evidence of sea-routes facilitating trade between Northern and Southern Europe at this time.

Towns were the engines behind the growth in seafaring on the Mediterranean in the eighth to eleventh centuries. Around 1000, urban ports in both northern and southern Italy had built up sufficient maritime capacity to become significant players in both economic and military respects. Indeed, piracy in a lawless Mediterranean region was partly the basis for their growth, and the same ships were often used both as warships and cargo vessels. The major players were, however, the political powers: the Byzantine Empire with its imperial fleet, as well as various provincial fleets; the fleets of the various Arab rulers, which were, however, declining at this time; and, of increasing importance towards the end of the early Middle Ages, the Western powers (Christides 2002; Odetallah 2002).

Mediterranean shipbuilding traditions

Basic shipbuilding traditions appear to have been relatively homogeneous throughout the Mediterranean before the thirteenth century, perhaps thereby reflecting the earlier maritime dominance exerted by Rome. Ships were built primarily from pine and cedar, for which purpose the latter had especially splendid qualities. Oak and elm were, due to their mechanical strength, preferred for certain elements like the keel, wales (longitudinal reinforcements in the shape of extra thick planks), framing timbers and the like, when available in sufficient quantities (Guibal & Pomey 2003). Shipbuilding was based on the carvel technique, where the planks were laid edge against edge, producing a hull

Fig 9.4   *St Mark is shown rescuing a ship from wreckage, in this mosaic from the first half of the 12th century, in St Clement's Chapel (south vault), St Mark's, Venice; it depicts a fine example of a Mediterranean 3-masted ship, with quarter rudders and a castle at the stern (reproduced with the kind permission of Procuratoria di San Marco, Venezia).*

with a smooth surface. Seagoing vessels had a strong keel, stem and stern, which served as a backbone in the construction. The concept of the watertight deck, as well as that of cabins and galleys for the convenience of crew and passengers, was in place long before 700. On vessels meant for transport alone, sail provided the propulsion, with the triangular lateen rig dominating during this period. On the other hand, ships serving both military and civil purposes had numerous oars to supplement or replace the sail. Ships could have one, two or even three masts, each with one sail (Fig 9.4). Two side rudders aft, mounted one on each side of the vessel, provided steering.

Shipbuilding techniques, however, changed continuously, and there was plenty of regional variance in the way this development took place, also in the Mediterranean. An important alteration in the century before and around 700, was the transition from a shell-based to a partially skeleton-based building technique. Classic Greco-Roman shipbuilding was based on joining the edges of the planks together with mortises and tenons. They would, together with keel, stem and stern, form a shell, which was afterwards reinforced with frames and other internal timbers. Already c600, however, the Byzantine Yassi Ada ship (Fig 10.2) shows a shipbuilding industry in which the edge-fastenings are only of temporary importance during the building process, and in which the upper part of the hull is constructed by nailing planks and wales directly to framing timbers protruding over that part of the hull that has already been built (Steffy 1993). The Dor D wreck, from c650, is another example using mortise-and-tenon joints only as temporary fasteners (Kahanov 2003; Kingsley 2004). The change meant saving labour during construction, which thus seems to have been a priority in early medieval shipbuilding in this area.

There are few ship-finds from the period that have been thoroughly analysed. The early ninth-century wreck Tantura B (believed to have been c23m long) is an early, but not yet fully studied, example of a larger vessel built entirely without mortise-and-tenon joints (Kahanov 2000). Analysis of the Byzantine Serçe Limani vessel, sunk c1025, presents a detailed picture of how such a construction was carried out (Steffy 1993, 85-91). After the keel, stem and stern of this (15.6m long) vessel had been set up, the central frames were designed according to simple geometrical principles and erected, defining the shape of the mid-ship area. Temporary supports for the planking fore and aft were established, and the fairly flat bottom was planked simply by nailing the planks to the frames, the temporary supports and the stem and stern. Next, the framing and the side planking, including wales, progressed more or less simultaneously, and at some point the turn of the bilge – the transition between bottom and sides – was closed with a patchwork of planks. The internal longitudinal timbers – keelson, stringers and clamps – were added when feasible during the construction process.

With few deviations, the same building process can be observed in the Bozborun wreck, which was of the same size as the Serçe Limani vessel, but built from timber felled 874 in south-eastern Greece or north-western Anatolia (Hocker 2004). An interesting detail in the Bozborun vessel is that a rudiment of the mortise-and-tenon joints is still found, in the shape of dowels inserted in the plank edges to align these during construction.

Little is known about the changes in Mediterranean shipbuilding during the eleventh and twelfth centuries, and its interaction with more northern shipbuilding traditions. The Port Berteau II wreck, built c600 in south-west France and excavated during the 1990s in the river Charente, gives an early, but also unique archaeological indication that the Mediterranean building style was applied outside the Mediterranean in the early Middle Ages. The vessel, which was only c14m long and suited for coastal and riverine use, was carvel-built in the skeleton-first fashion (Rieth 2003).

Performance and transport capacity

The complete dominance of the lateen rig in the early medieval Mediterranean is to be seen against the background of a more heterogeneous picture during the preceding centuries. The lateen rig is more difficult to manoeuvre and requires a larger crew than the square sail, which was the preferred type for larger vessels in Roman times. That the lateen rig took over may be related to the fact that it is a more efficient rig for tacking (advancing against the wind). At a time when the scale of seafaring was reduced and the risk of piracy had increased, the change to the lateen rig may have been seen as an adequate response.

Ship sizes were probably also reduced in the early Middle Ages, compared with the Roman period, although some large vessels were still being built. Two Arabic eleventh-century *bacini* (glazed ceramic discs popular in Italy for decorating buildings), from S Piero a Grado near Pisa, show large three-masted vessels with stern castles (Pryor & Bellabarba 1990). Also, a three-masted Apulian ship from the late eleventh century is reported by the Byzantine princess Anna Comnena; archaeological evidence for such large ships is, however, limited (Pryor 1994).

It is not possible give exact figures for the development of tonnage throughout the period. The presence of trade in bulk commodities demonstrates clearly, as do the written and pictorial sources, that ships existed which were considerably larger than those that have so far been studied archaeologically. But, as in almost any period, the archaeological material suggests that it was small ships, of less than 100 tonnes capacity, that carried a great deal of the maritime commerce.

Mediterranean harbours

At the beginning of the eighth century, a Mediterranean harbour did not necessarily include anything other than the most basic necessity: an advantageous point for the transfer of goods between ship and land. As in preceding centuries, constructed harbours with quays and breakwaters were more the exception than the rule, and goods were often carried between ship and land on smaller vessels. Still, the changes in political power during the seventh and eighth centuries, and the disruptions of trade, led to a reduction in the number of harbours, in the maintenance and dredging of existing structures, and apparently also to a loss of knowledge concerning harbour construction (Kingsley 2004). There seems to be archaeological evidence of harbours falling out of use during the seventh century, such as Ephesus in western Turkey and some of the harbour areas of Constantinople itself (Dark 2004). Also the thriving Roman and Byzantine ports of Dor and Caesarea in Israel appear to have lost their economic significance in the early Arab period (Kingsley & Raveh 1996), as did the port of Ravenna. Many harbours continued in use, however, and new ones were established (see map, Fig 10.1). The growing new urban ports, like Venice and Pisa, had to build facilities to accommodate their trading enterprises. As the volume of trade grew, good harbour services that allowed for the swift and safe loading and unloading of commodities became increasingly important in the competition between towns, but the military aspects of these towns' seafaring also resulted in harbour construction. The construction in 1104 of Venice's first arsenal (as a protected naval base and storage for naval armoury and equipment) is a spectacular example of this, and the Venetian arsenal was even to become an important producer of galleys for the Byzantine fleet later in the twelfth century (Bondiolo 2003).

Organisation and routes in Northern Europe

The web of waterborne transport routes in Northern Europe expanded vastly during the eighth-twelfth centuries. Following the Slav colonisation of the southern Baltic coast and the Scandinavian expansion to the east, the Baltic quickly became a much travelled sea, but communications with the North Sea region were predominantly by way of the land-route across the neck of the Jutland Peninsula (via Hedeby), or by boat through the Limfjord. The sea route around the Skaw, the northern tip of Jutland, was used by cargo ships from the North Sea region at the latest around the mid-twelfth century. The Channel region saw extensive seafaring between the mainland and the British Isles, especially where large rivers gave access to the interior or where the sea-crossing was particularly short. During the ninth-eleventh centuries the Scandinavians extended their seafaring to the Faroes, Iceland and Greenland and, sporadically, to North America.

Piracy was a well-known phenomenon throughout the period, both in the Baltic and in the North Sea region. The rich kingdoms around the North Sea especially attracted the attention of Scandinavian raiders whenever they showed signs of political weakness and were no longer able to maintain sufficient coastal defences.

Northern shipbuilding traditions

North European shipbuilding was less homogeneous than that of the Mediterranean. The dominant tradition was that of the clinker-built, keeled vessel. The keel had its origin in the north German and Scandinavian areas and was brought to other parts of Europe by the migrations of the fifth/sixth and tenth/eleventh centuries. During the Middle Ages, keels were constructed in Scandinavia, Frisia, Anglo-Saxon England, Scotland, Ireland and Normandy, all the way around the Baltic and along the Russian waterways.

The keels were, as all other North European ships of the period, built shell-first (Fig. 9.5). Oak was the preferred material, but was replaced with other materials, primarily pine, when supply was limited. The building process started with the joining of keel, stem and stern to form a backbone for the vessel. Next, the bottom of the hull was constructed from planks placed with overlapping edges, held together (clenched) with nails. This technique – also called 'lapstrake' – produced the characteristic, stepped surface of the clinker-built ships. Iron clench nails, or rivets, were dominant in Viking shipbuilding, be it in Scandinavia or abroad, while small treenails were used in Slavic and to some extent also in Frisian shipbuilding (Fig 9.6). Anglo-Saxon shipbuilders developed a peculiar technology including the use of 'rawlplugs', pre-inserted wooden pegs of hazel, through which thin, square-shanked iron nails were hammered and riveted.

When the construction of the plank shell had advanced sufficiently, framing timbers were inserted to provide transverse stiffness to the hull. In Scandinavian vessels, a strict frame design was used. The lower part of the frame consisted of a symmetrical floor timber, which was fastened to the bottom planks of the vessel. On top of this rested a beam, kept in place by vertical knees that also supported the ship's sides. When necessary, additional beams were placed higher up in the ship, and longitudinal reinforcements, stringers, could either be joggled from the inside over the frames or integrated in the planking. The vessels could have deck-planks laid or mounted between the beams, but there were no watertight decks or accommodation facilities. A single side-rudder, mounted on the starboard aft quarter, provided steering. Propulsion was delivered by oars and by a single square sail – the only type of rigging found in Northern Europe during the eighth to twelfth centuries.

There are plenty of examples of clinker-built, keeled vessels from this period (Fig 9.7). The Oseberg, Tune and Gokstad ships (see Box 9.2) together with the Ladby ship exemplify Scandinavian shipbuilding in the ninth and early tenth centuries, while the

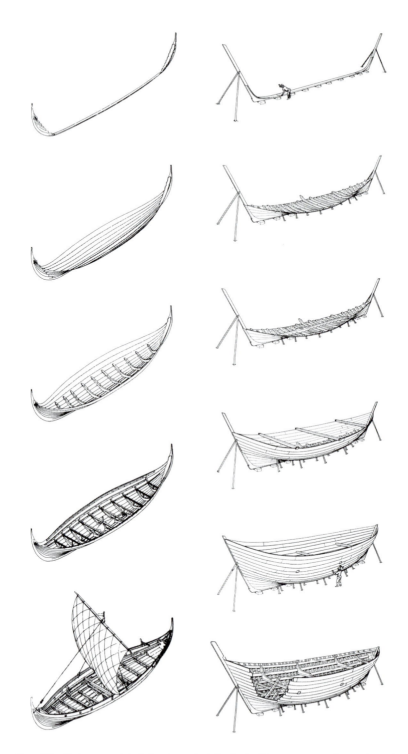

Fig 9.5   *Construction of North European 'shell-first' vessels: left, the building sequence of a Nordic 11th-century 'lapstrake' vessel; and right, of a late 12th- to 14th-century cog (drawings: The Viking Ship Museum, Roskilde, & Museum voor Scheepsarcheologie, Netherlands).*

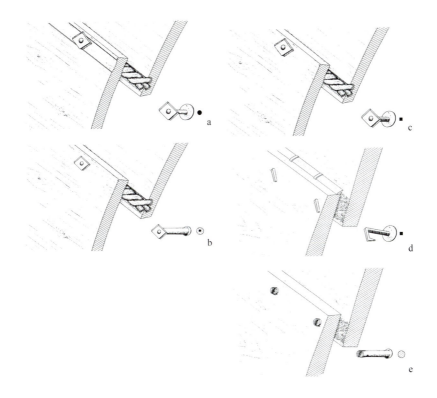

Various types of fastener used in clinker shipbuilding in Northern Europe during the Middle Ages: **Fig 9.6**
(a) round-shanked iron clench nail, as normal in Scandinavian shipbuilding until the 12th century;
(b) square-shanked iron clench nail, in wooden dowel, as used in late Anglo-Saxon shipbuilding;
(c) square-shanked iron clench nail, as used in lapstrake shipbuilding over the greater part of
Northern Europe, after the 12th century; (d) square-shanked, double-clenched nail, as used in
lapstrake planking in (e.g.) cogs; and (e) small treenails, as used in (e.g.) Slavic lapstrake
shipbuilding (drawings: W Karrasch & J Bill, The Viking Ship Museum, Roskilde).

Hedeby and Skuldelev ships represent the late tenth and first half of the eleventh century (Crumlin-Pedersen 1997; Crumlin-Pedersen et al 2002; Sørensen 2001). Large cargo carriers known from the twelfth century include the Lynæs 1 and Karschau ships, as well as the fragmentarily preserved, but highly important, 'Big Ship' from Bergen in western Norway (Christensen 1985; Englert 2000). The tenth-century Graveney find is the best preserved example of an Anglo-Saxon vessel, while the Ralswiek boats from Rügen, in northern Germany, give a good impression of Slavic boatbuilding in the tenth century (Fenwick 1978; Herfert 1968; Herrmann 1998).

With its origin probably in the area of the Rhine mouth, and with roots in Gallo-Roman shipbuilding, bottom-based shipbuilding developed among the Frisians gave rise to the cog (Fig 9.5). The oldest known examples of this type of ship were built in the second half of the twelfth century in south-western Denmark and were used both in the North Sea and the Baltic. A carvel-constructed bottom was formed around a

BOX 9.2   THE GOKSTAD SHIP

This ship was the main artefact in a rich Viking period grave excavated in 1880 at Gokstad, on the Oslo Fjord, in southern Norway (Fig 1). The remains of a male skeleton show that the person buried was a tall man, aged c60, who had been badly troubled by rheumatism. The grave had been plundered and the set of weapons usually found in male Viking graves was missing. Wooden artefacts were evidently of less interest to the robbers, and the grave still contained a rich suite of equipment, including three small boats and a sledge, which had been broken up as part of the burial rites, several beds, wooden buckets, fragments of textiles, a large copper cauldron with iron chain, etc. The subsoil in this part of Norway is blue clay and the mound was built from the same material; this had preserved the organic materials unusually well.

The Gokstad ship was larger and better preserved than the Tune ship, which had been excavated in 1867, and was for a long time seen as *the* Viking vessel. The excavator published the find in 1882, in a bilingual English-Norwegian book, which made the ship well known worldwide (Nicolaisen 1882). A number of models built for maritime and historic museums added to its fame. Bronze mounts in the Jellinge and Borre styles of Viking art indicated a tenth-century date, which has recently been refined by dendrochronology (Bonde 1993). The ship was built shortly before AD900 and was buried in the early tenth century.

The ship is c24m long, 5m wide and c2m high amidships. It has 16 clinker-laid planks on each side, fastened with iron rivets. The framing system consists of floor timbers reaching to strake 10. The floor timbers are not fastened to the keel and sheerstrake, but lashed to cleats left standing on strakes 2 to 8, and treenailed to strake 9. A crossbeam rests on each floor timber. Knees standing on the crossbeams are treenailed to strakes 11 to 14, while top timbers at every second frame support strakes 12 to 16. The crossbeams are rabbetted for loose deck-boards. Strake 14 has oar-ports for 16 rowers on each side. There are no permanent seats for the rowers, and it has been suggested that each man used his sea-chest as a rowing bench. Amidships is a sturdy mast support, consisting of a keelson spanning four floor timbers and a mast partner resting on six crossbeams. The mast partner has a long slit, enabling the mast to be raised or lowered from aft. Fragments of woollen cloth, believed to be from either the sail or tent covering, were also found. Three belaying cleats on each side aft are in all probability for securing running rigging. The ship would have carried one square sail on

Fig 1

The Gokstad ship during excavation in 1880 (photo: Museum of Cultural History, University of Oslo).

the mast amidships; apart from this, little definite proof of sail or rigging was found.

From the time of its excavation until 1930, the ship stood as it came from the burial mound, exhibited in a shed by the University buildings in Oslo; it was then moved to its present location in the Viking Ship Museum, part of the Museum of Cultural History, University of Oslo (Fig 2). The ship was dismantled and re-built, using some new wood where the original material was missing or too decayed for use.

Altogether eight replicas or near replicas have been built; the first one crossed the North Atlantic in 1893 to be part of the Norwegian stand at the World Exhibition in Chicago. These have demonstrated that the ship was fast and seaworthy. They have been rigged using evidence from the open, square-rigged fishing boats of northern and western Norway, which were in use until the beginning of the twentieth century, and from Viking-age iconographic material. Most replicas have had a sail of c100m².

Until the 1962 excavation of the Skuldelev ships near Roskilde (Denmark), the Gokstad ship remained the prototype Viking ship. It is probably the youngest representative of the all-purpose vessels from the Iron Age, equally well suited for carrying men to battle or for bringing a cargo of luxury goods from one chieftain to another. It is also, together with the near-contemporary Tune ship, the youngest example known where the strakes and frames are lashed together. It has been suggested that the Gokstad ship (as also those from Tune and Oseberg) is representative of a type known in medieval written sources as *karve* or *karfi*. These were the personal travelling vessels of kings or nobility. The three small Gokstad boats have also been reconstructed and are 6.5m, c8m and c10m long, being for two, four and five rowers.

By Arne Emil Christensen

Fig 2

The Gokstad ship restored in the Viking Ship Museum, Oslo (photo: EJ Johnson, Museum of Cultural History, University of Oslo).

Fig 9.7 *Reconstructions (right) of the 30m-long Skuldelev 2 long-ship, and (left) the 16m-long Skuldelev 1 cargo ship, on Roskilde Fjord, where the original ships were excavated. Both ships date from the first half of the 11th century. Norwegian-built Skuldelev 1 had a cargo capacity of 24 tons and was an ocean-going vessel; Skuldelev 2 was built in Ireland, equipped with 60 oars, for a crew of 65 (photo: W Karrasch, The Viking Ship Museum, Roskilde).*

keel plank, the ends of which were joined with knee-shaped transition timbers to the stem- and sternposts. The planks were temporarily held together by means of clamps, which were removed as massive floor-timbers were put into place. The sides of the vessel were, however, constructed in clinker technique, joined with double-bent iron nails. All seams were made watertight with moss, inserted after assembly, and held in place by laths secured with iron staples (sintels; see Fig 9.6d). The cogs were much more massively built than the keels and were well suited for the transport of heavy cargoes in a tidal environment, where the goods could be loaded and unloaded when the ship settled on the seabed at low tide. For propulsion, the twelfth-century and later cogs relied entirely on their single square sails; oars were not used. Examples of cogs, from before 1200, are those from Kollerup and Kolding (Hocker & Dokkedal 2001; Kohrtz Andersen 1983). Both were manoeuvred with a stern-rudder, and the Kollerup cog, from c1150, is the oldest known example of a Northern European vessel carrying a stern-rudder. A text indicates that, in the Rhineland, ships in the early ninth century might already be equipped with cabins; indeed, the Kollerup cog had a closed space under the fore-deck which may have been used by the seamen for accommodation (Ellmers 1984, 169).

Towards the end of the twelfth century an important development can be observed in the frame construction of both cogs and clinker-built keels. At some frame stations, including the mast frame, one or more beams were inserted that penetrate, and interlock with, the planking. The beams, which are situated above the waterline, facilitate the construction of higher, more spacious, seagoing and easily defensible hulls. The earliest examples of through-beams are the Kolding cog and the Bergen ship.

Flat-bottomed barges were constructed in a similar tradition as cogs for the important navigation of rivers, for use as ferries and for transport between ship and land in non-tidal harbours without quays. Ninth-century examples are known from Kalkar and Bremen in Germany, tenth- and eleventh-century examples from Tiel, Deventer and Utrecht, in the Netherlands, and twelfth-century examples from Egernsund and Hedeby, on the south-east coast of the Jutland Peninsula (Bill & Hocker 2004; Hoffman & Ellmers 1991; Kühn 2004; van Holk 2004). Barges were punted or hauled and probably also sailed, although this has not yet been archaeologically documented for this period.

The Utrecht ship (17.45m long), built shortly after 1000 in the lower Rhine area, represents a third shipbuilding tradition in Northern Europe at this time (van de Moortel 2003). Its bottom consists of a 14m long and 1.9m wide expanded logboat, made of oak. Following the expansion of the log, it was stabilised by inserting framing timbers covering only the width of the logboat base. Next, extension pieces were added to both ends of the base and a clinker strake was fastened to its sides. Then a second set of framing timbers, encompassing both the logboat base and the clinker strake, was inserted. A wale, semicircular in section, was fastened to the sides, followed by a plank and another wale forming the rubbing strakes. All elements were assembled with treenails.

Three other smaller vessels built in this tradition are known from the Lower Rhine area, and one from London. All date from the late tenth to the twelfth century, and it is debated whether they might represent the 'hulk', a ship-type known from written sources from the late tenth century onwards in use for cross-Channel trade. The hulk was to become one of the dominant ship-types in Northern European seafaring, but so far it has not been proven archaeologically.

The smaller vessels of the Utrecht-type were not seagoing, but were built primarily for use on sheltered waterways. This is true also for the large number of ordinary logboats found along river-systems in most parts of Europe (McGrail 2001, 172-80, with refs). Oak was preferred when available, but many other wood species were used as well. In spite of their limited capacity, logboats were used for a variety of purposes, including fishing, ferrying and transport.

Performance and transport capacity of North European ships

Experiments with reconstructions of Scandinavian and Slavic vessels from the ninth to eleventh centuries have shown that these were well capable of tacking, but that advancing directly against the wind seldom exceeds 2-3km per hour (1-1.5 knots). With favourable winds, distances of 150-250km can be covered within a 24-hour period (Crumlin-Pedersen & Vinner 1993). Given that these results are representative for other contemporary North European vessels, ships were in general able to stay clear of a lee shore, but seafarers would tend to wait for favourable winds before setting out on a voyage. This complies well with written evidence from the period (Ohler 1989, 98-9). Oared vessels, which were used for warfare and for the voyages of the aristocracy, were able to advance over longer distances with a speed of 9-10km per hour (5 knots). This figure would be reduced by contrary winds or by large waves, but the sail would be used whenever possible.

Roman Northern Europe saw the construction of ships up to at least 50 tons of cargo capacity like the Blackfriars 1 ship (Marsden 1994, 33-96), but there is no indication that vessels of this size were constructed during the fifth-seventh centuries. During the eighth-twelfth centuries, however, there can be seen a renewed increase in the size of the largest vessels and adaptation to cargo transport. Although being oared vessels, the ninth-century Norwegian Oseberg, Tune and Gokstad ships are relatively beamy. They have a cargo capacity of less than 10 tons, when the weight of the large crew has been accounted for. Around 1000, however, a marked increase in the size of the Scandinavian finds can be seen, at the same time as specialised cargo ships (vessels for propulsion by sail only) are first found. The Skuldelev 1 ship (c1030) could carry up to 24 tons of cargo, the Hedeby 3 (c1025) and Lynæs 1 (c1140) both c60 tons, and the Bergen ship (1187/88) at least 120 tons (Crumlin-Pedersen 1999).

The evidence from other parts of Northern Europe is less extensive, but we may assume that the general pattern of growth was the same, albeit starting earlier than in Scandinavia. The tenth-century Graveney boat, from England, with a cargo capacity of c7 tons, was apparently a specialised cargo vessel. Documentary evidence about wine ships from Ghent and Ypres, arrested in Sandwich and Winchelsea in 1217, shows that these reached sizes similar to the Bergen ship (Bill 2002).

Harbours in Northern Europe

As in the Mediterranean, most harbours in the North did not show any extensive hydraulic constructions, if any at all. Many harbours were situated in river mouths or as far upstream as it was practical to sail with a seagoing vessel. Even small rivers could, through their scour channels in the seabed, facilitate the ships' approach to the coast, and anchoring in fresh water was attractive to seamen as it helped to reduce the growth of marine organisms on the ships' hulls.

Harbour structures are found only at the most important nodal points in the trade networks of the time. They may consist of nothing more than 'hards', reinforced sur-

Fig 9.8   *Artistic reconstruction of the Schleswig waterfront, seen from the south, in the first half of the 12th century (drawing: Stiftung Schleswig-Holsteinische Landesmuseum Schloss Gottorf).*

faces that facilitated the access to ships that were lying dry on the foreshore at low tide. Several are known, for example, from the early phases of Trondheim and Anglo-Saxon London (Christophersen 2000; Milne 2003). Birka and Hedeby in the non-tidal Baltic had landing bridges (Box 4.3): pole-built constructions that allowed for mooring vessels directly at the bridge (Crumlin-Pedersen 1997; Nakoinz 2002). Schleswig, the successor of Hedeby, built in the late eleventh-twelfth century, had wood-lined, earth-filled quays (Fig 9.8), situated close together and mostly at right-angles to the coast (Vogel 1999). It is likely that such constructions were primarily meant for the loading and unloading of smaller vessels plying between land and the ships lying further out in the harbour. The same system is seen in Slavonic Ralswiek, on Rügen, and in the outskirts of seventh- and eighth-century Dorestad (Herrmann 1997; van Es & Verwers 2002; see above, Fig 4.2). In the latter case, however, its use may be related to land reclamation rather than to facilitating the unloading and loading of the ships involved in the international trade of this emporium. The most important harbour towns developed continuous stretches of quays. Examples are known from the tenth century onwards in London, from mid-twelfth-century Lübeck, and from late twelfth-century Bergen, in Norway (Herteig 1991; Gläser 1999; Milne 2003). Simple types of harbour crane, similar to the sweeps used at wells, apparently came into use, at the latest, in the twelfth century (Ellmers 1984, 169).

BIBLIOGRAPHY

Berg, G (1935) *Sledges and Wheeled Vehicles: Ethnological Studies from the View-Point of Sweden*, Stockholm

Bill, J (2002), 'The cargo vessels', in Berggren, L, Hybel, N and Landen, A (eds), *Cogs, Cargoes, and Commerce. Maritime Bulk Trade in Northern Europe 1150-1400*, Toronto, 92-112

Bill, J and Hocker, FM (2004) 'Haithabu 4 seen in the context of contemporary shipbuilding in southern Scandinavia', in Brandt, K und Kühn, HJ (eds), *Der Prahm aus dem Hafen von Haithabu. Beiträge zu antiken und mittelalterlichen Flachbodenschiffen*, Neumünster, 43-54

Blanco, A, Fuentes, DM and Ortiz, NC (1989) *Puentes Historicos de Galicia*, Xunta de Galicia

Bleile, R (1998) 'Slawische Brücken in Mecklenburg-Vorpommern', *Bodendenkmalpflege in Mecklenburg-Vorpommern Jahrbuch* 46, 127-69

Bonde, N (1993) 'Dendrochronological dating of the Viking-age ship burials at Oseberg, Gokstad and Tune, Norway', *Antiquity* 67, no 256, 575-83

Bondiolo, M (2003) 'The Arsenal of Venice and the art of building ships', in Beltrame, C (ed), *Boats, Ships and Shipyards. Proceedings of the Ninth International Symposium on Boat and Ship Archaeology, Venice 2000*, Oxford, 10-13

Brink, S (2000) 'Forntida vägar', *Bebyggelseshistorisk tidsskrift* 39 (Vägar och vägmiljöer), 23-64 (English summary)

Brooks, N (1997) 'Medieval bridges: a window onto changing concepts of state power', *The Haskins Society Journal* 8 (1995), 11-29 & figs 1-15

Christensen, AE (1985) 'Boat finds from Bryggen', in Herteig, AE (ed), *The Archaeological Excavations at Bryggen, 'The German Wharf', in Bergen 1955-68*, Vol 1, Bergen, 47-278

Christides, V (2002) 'Arab-Byzantine struggle in the sea: naval tactics (7th-11th centuries AD): theory and practice', in Al-Hijji, YY and Christides, V (eds), *Aspects of Arab Seafaring. An Attempt to Fill in the Gaps of Maritime History*, Athens, 87-106

Christophersen, A (2000) 'I brygge, bod og strete', in *Havn og handel i 1000 år. Karmøyseminaret 1997*, Stavanger, 41-68

Clark, J (ed) (2004, 2nd ed) *The Medieval Horse and its Equipment c.1150-c.1450*, Woodbridge

Crumlin-Pedersen, O (1997) *Viking-Age Ships and Shipbuilding in Hedeby/Haithabu and Schleswig*, Ships and Boats of the North 2, Roskilde

Crumlin-Pedersen, O (1999) 'Ships as indicators of trade in Northern Europe 600-1200', in Bill, J and Clausen, B (eds), *Maritime Topography and the Medieval Town*, Copenhagen, 11-21.

Crumlin-Pedersen, O, Olsen, O, Bondesen, E, Jensen, P, Petersen, AH and Strætkvern, K (2002) *The Skuldelev Ships I. Topography, Archaeology, History, Conservation and Display*, Ships and Boats of the North 4.1, Roskilde

Crumlin-Pedersen, O and Vinner, M (1993) 'Roar og Helge af Roskilde – om at bygge og sejle med vikingeskibe', *Nationalmuseets Arbejdsmark* 1993, 11-29 (English summary)

Dark, KR (2004) 'The new Post Office site in Istanbul and the north-eastern harbour of Byzantine Constantinople', *International Journal of Nautical Archaeology* 33:2, 315-19

De Witte, H (1999) 'The maritime topography of medieval Bruges', in Bill, J and Clausen, B (eds), *Maritime Topography and the Medieval Town*, Copenhagen, 137-144

Doorninck, Jr Fv (2002) 'Byzantine shipwrecks', in Laiou, AE (ed), *The Economic History of Byzantium: From the Seventh through the Fifteenth Century*, Washington, 899-905

Edgren, T (1992) 'Winter transport', in Roesdahl, E and Wilson, DM (eds), *From Viking to Crusader. Scandinavia and Europe 800-1200*, Copenhagen, 50-1

Ellmers, D (1984, 2nd ed) *Frühmittelalterliche Handelsschiffahrt in Mittel- und Nordeuropa*, Offa-Bücher 28, Neumünster

Englert, A (2000) 'Large cargo vessels in Danish waters 1000-1250. Archaeological evidence for professional merchant seafaring before the Hanseatic period', in Beltrame, C (ed), *Boats, Ships and Shipyards. Proceedings of the Ninth International Symposium on Boat and Ship Archaeology*, Oxford, 273-280

Es, WA van and Verwers, WJH (2002) 'Aufstieg, blüte und niedergang der frühmittelalterlichen Handelsmetropole Dorestad', in Brandt, K, Müller-Wille, M and Radtke, C (eds), *Haithabu und die frühe Stadtentwicklung im nördlichen Europa*, Neumünster, 281-302

Feldbauer, P and Morrissey, J (2002) *Venedig 800-1600. Wasservögel als Weltmacht*, Vienna

Felgenhauer-Schmiedt, S (1993) *Die Sachkultur des Mittelalters im Lichte der Archäologischen Funde*, Frankfurt am Main/Berlin, etc

Fenton, A, Podolák, J and Rasmussen, H (eds) (1973) *Land Transport in Europe*, Studies of Folklife 4, Copenhagen

Fenwick, V (ed) (1978) *The Graveney Boat: a Tenth-Century Find from Kent*, British Archaeological Reports, British Series 53, Oxford

Friedman, JB and Figg, KM (eds) (2000) *Trade, Travel and Exploration in the Middle Ages. An Encyclopedia*, New York/London

Gläser, M (1999) 'The development of the harbours and market places of Lübeck', in Bill, J and Clausen, B (eds), *Maritime Topography and the Medieval Town*, Copenhagen, 79-86

Graham-Campbell, J (1980) *Viking Artefacts: a Select Catalogue*, London

Graham-Campbell, J (1992) 'Anglo-Scandinavian equestrian equipment in eleventh-century England', *Anglo-Norman Studies* 14, 77-89

Grieg, S (1928) *Osebergfundet*, II, Oslo

Gräslund, A-S (1989) "Gud hjälpe nu väl hennes själ", *Tor* 22, 223-44 (English summary)

Guibal, F and Pomey, P (2003) 'Timber supply and ancient naval architecture', in Beltrame, C (ed), *Boats, Ships and Shipyards. Proceedings of the Ninth International Symposium on Boat and Ship Archaeology*, Oxford, 35-48

Harrison, D (2004) *The Bridges of Medieval England. Transport and Society 400-1800*, Oxford

Hausen, J (2000) 'Shipping between Danube and Rhine from medieval to modern times (Canal of Charlemagne, Canal of King Luis of Bavaria, Rhine-Danube-Canal)', in Litwin, J (ed), *Down the River to the Sea. Proceedings of the Eighth International Symposium on Boat and Ship Archaeology, Gdansk 1997*, Oxford, 21-6

Herfert, P (1968) 'Frühmittelalterliche bootsfunde in Ralswiek, Kr. Rügen (zweiter grabungsbericht)', *Ausgrabungen und Funde. Nachrichtenblatt für Vor- und Frühgeschichte* 13:4, 211-22

Herrmann, J (1997) *Ralswiek auf Rügen. Die slawisch-wikingischen Siedlungen und deren Hinterland. Teil I - Die Hauptsiedlung*, Beiträge zur Ur- und Frühgeschichte Mecklenburg-Vorpommerns 32, Lübstorf

Herrmann, J (1998) *Ralswiek auf Rügen. Die slawisch-wikingischen Siedlungen und deren Hinterland. Teil II - Kultplatz, Boot 4, Hof, Propstei, Mühlenberg, Schlossberg und Rugard*, Beiträge zur Ur- und Frühgeschichte Mecklenburg-Vorpommerns 33, Lübstorf

Herteig, AE (1991) *The Buildings at Bryggen - their Topographical and Chronological Development*, The Bryggen Papers, Main Series 3:2, Bergen

Hindle, P (2002) *Medieval Roads and Tracks*, Shire Archaeology 26, Princes Risborough

Hocker FM (2004) 'The Bozborun Byzantine ship-wreck', in Kingsley, S (ed), *Barbarian Seas. Late Rome to Islam*, London, 61-4

Hocker, FM and Dokkedal, L (2001) 'News from the Kolding cog', *Maritime Archaeology Newsletter from Roskilde, Denmark* 16, 16-17

Hodges, R (1997) 'Trade routes of the Carolingian Empire', in Mackay, A and Ditchburn, D (eds), *Atlas of Medieval Europe*, London and New York, 61-2

Hoffman, P and Ellmers, D (1991) 'Ein Frachter aus der Zeit Karls des Großen', *Bremer Archäologische Blätter Neue Folge* 90/91, 33-7

Holk, AFL van (2004) 'Some remarks on flat-bottomed boat-finds from the Netherlands', in Brandt, K and Kühn, HJ (eds), *Der Prahm aus dem Hafen von Haithabu. Beiträge zu antiken und mittel-lalterlichen Flachbodenschiffen*, Neumünster, 105-24

Hunt, ES and Murray, JM (1999) *A History of Business in Medieval Europe 1200-1550*, Cambridge

Hyland, A (1999) *The Horse in the Middle Ages*, Cambridge

Kahanov Y (2000) 'The Tantura B shipwreck. Tantoura Lagoon, Israel. Preliminary hull construciton report', in Litwin, J (ed), *Down the River to the Sea. Proceedings of the Eighth International Symposium on Boat and Ship Archaeology, Gdansk 1997*, Gdansk, 151-4

Kahanov, Y (2003) 'Dor D wreck, Tantura Lagoon, Israel', in Beltrame, C (ed), *Boats, Ships and Shipyards. Proceedings of the Ninth International Symposium on Boat and Ship Archaeology*, Oxford, 49-56

Kingsley, S and Raveh, K (1996) *The Ancient Harbour and Anchorage at Dor, Israel. Results of the Underwater Surveys 1976-1991*, British Archaeological Reports, International Series 626, Oxford

Kingsley, S (ed) (2004) *Barbarian Seas. Late Rome to Islam*, Encyclopaedia of Underwater Archaeology 4, London

Kohrtz Andersen, P (1983) *Kollerupkoggen*, Thisted

Kolchin, BA (1989) *Wooden Artefacts from Novgorod*, British Archaeological Reports, International Series 495, Oxford

Kühn, HJ (2004) 'Ein hochmittelalterlicher Fähr-prahm im Haddebyer Noor (Haithabu Wrack IV)', in Brandt, K and Kühn, HJ (eds), *Der Prahm aus dem Hafen von Haithabu. Beiträge zu antiken und mittelalterlichen Flachbodenschiffen*, Neumünster, 9-16

Langdon, J (1986) *Horses, Oxen and Technological Innovation. The Use of Draught Animals in English Farming from 1066 to 1500*, Cambridge

Leighton, AC (1972) *Transport and Communication in Early Medieval Europe AD500-1100*, Newton Abbot

Lexikon des Mittelalters, Vol 2 (1981-83), 'Brücke', Munich/Zürich

Marsden, P (1994) *Ships of the Port of London, First to Eleventh Centuries AD*, London

McGrail, S (2001) *Boats of the World from the Stone Age to Medieval Times*, Oxford

Milne, G (2003) *The Port of Medieval London*, Gloucestershire

Moortel, A de van (2003) 'A new look at the Utrecht ship', in Beltrame, C (ed), *Boats, Ships and Shipyards. Proceedings of the Ninth International Symposium on Boat and Ship Archaeology*, Oxford, 183-9

Møller Jensen, J (2004) 'Vejen til Jerusalem. Danmark og pilgrimsvejen til det Hellige Land i det 12. år-hundrede: En islandsk vejviser', in Carelli, P et al (eds), *Ett annat 1100-tal*, Lund, 284-337 (English summary)

Müller-Wille, M (1987) *Das wikingerzeitliche Gräberfeld von Thumby-Bienebek (Kr. Rendsburg-Eckernförde)*, Neumünster

Nakoinz, O (2002) 'Archäologische Untersuchungen im Hafen von Haithabu', *Archäologie in Schleswig* 7, 59-64

Nicolaisen, N (1882) *The Viking Ship discovered at Gokstad in Norway* (facsimile reprint, Oslo 2003)

Nørgård Jørgensen, A (2002) 'Naval bases in Southern Scandinavia from the 7th to the 12th century', in Nørgård Jørgensen, A, Pind, J and Clausen, B (eds), *Maritime Warfare in Northern Europe. Technology, Organisation, Logistics and Administration 500BC-1500AD*, Copenhagen, 125-52

Odetallah, RK (2002) 'Salah al-Din and the sea. The case of 'Akka', in Al-Hijji, YY and Christides, V (eds), *Aspects of Arab Seafaring. An Attempt to Fill in the Gaps of Maritime History*, Athens, 213-16

Ohler, N (1989) *The Medieval Traveller*, Woodbridge

Pedersen, A (1999) 'Riding gear from late Viking-age Denmark', *Journal of Danish Archaeology* 13 (1996-97), 133-60

Priestley, J (1831) *Historical Account of the Navigable Rivers, Canals and Railways of Great Britain*, London

Pritchard, F and Wild, JP (eds) (2005) *Northern Archaeological Textiles*, Nesat 7, Oxford

Pryor, JH (1994) 'The Mediterranean round ship', in Unger, RW (ed), *Cogs, Caravels and Galleons. The Sailing Ship 1000-1650*, London, 59-76

Pryor, JH and Bellabarba, S (1990) 'The medieval Muslim ships of the Pisan Bacini', *Mariner's Mirror* 76, 99-113

Reallexikon der Germanischen Altertumskunde (1968f), Bech, H et al (eds), 'Hufeisen'; 'Pferdegeschirr'; 'Ski'; 'Sporen und sporn'; 'Steigbügel'; 'Wege', Berlin/New York

Rieth, É (2003) 'Essay to restore the operating process of a shipyard in the early medieval period: the example of the Port Berteau II Wreck, Charente-Maritime, France', in Beltrame, C (ed), *Boats, Ships and Shipyards. Proceedings of the Ninth International Symposium on Boat and Ship Archaeology*, Oxford, 113-23

Roesdahl, E (1982) *Viking Age Denmark*, London

Schou Jørgensen, M (1988) 'Vej, vejstrøg og vejspærring. Jernalderens landfærdsel / Roads and road blocks. Land communication in the Iron Age', in Rasmussen, B and Mortensen, P (eds), *Fra Stamme til Stat i Danmark 1. Jernalderens stammesamfund*, Højbjerg, 101-16 (English summary)

Schou Jørgensen, M (1997) 'Vikingetidsbroen i Ravning Enge – nye undersøgelser', *Nationalmuseets Arbejdsmark*, 74-87 (English summary)

Schovsbo, PO (1987) *Oldtidens Vogne i Danmark*, Frederikshavn (German Summary)

Schuldt, E (1975) *Burgen, Brücken und Strassen des frühen Mittelalters in Mecklenburg*, Schwerin

Spindler, K (1998) 'Der Kanalbau Karls des Großen', *Nearchos* 2, 47-99

Steffy, JR (1993) *Wooden Shipbuilding and the Interpretation of Shipwrecks*, College Station, Texas

Sørensen, AC (2001) *Ladby. A Danish Ship-Grave from the Viking Age*, Ships and Boats of the North 3, Roskilde

Unger, RW (1980) *The Ship in the Medieval Economy 600-1600*, London/Montreal

Vogel, V (1999) 'Der Schleswiger Hafen im hohen und späten Mittelalter', in Bill, J and Clausen, B (eds), *Maritime Topography and the Medieval Town*, Copenhagen, 187-97

White, L (1962) *Medieval Technology and Social Change*, Oxford

Wilke, G (2000) 'Brücken und Brückenbau im Östlichen Mitteleuropa um 1000', in *Europas Mitte um 1000. Beiträge zur Geschichte, Kunst und Archäologie*, Vol 1 (exhibition catalogue), Stuttgart, 142-5

CHAPTER 10

TRADE AND EXCHANGE

Paul Arthur and Søren M Sindbæk

PART 1: THE MEDITERRANEAN REGION *by Paul Arthur*

Introduction

It can hardly be doubted that the Roman world, contracting since the fifth century, had finally come to an end by the late sixth. Archaeology has shown as much, and whatever one may claim for more lingering continuity in an evermore anachronistic Byzantine East, whatever residuality there was, was but a token in reshaping the Mediterranean Sea, adjusting to new political and economic constraints. This does not mean that entirely new forms of commerce began to appear. Indeed, the variety of forms and means of exchange, through coin or barter, periodic markets, *dirigisme* (state-controlled supply), redistribution, contracts, donatives and gift-exchange, had all been seen already in Classical times and were all to continue through the Middle Ages. What was to change were the relative proportions of the diverse forms, as separate regions of what had once been a unified empire changed hands and allegiances, and the geographical distribution of both supply and demand was radically transformed. Thus, the old Roman commercial network broke up and new nodes of exchange gradually came to be recognised.

The upheaval of the old order led to a diminishing output of agrarian produce, which does not seem, however, to have adequately covered the overall demand of the declining population. Perhaps the total aggregate surplus was not wanting, but the uneven political and geographical distribution of resources, as well as the difficulty in maintaining the Mediterranean-wide connectivity of earlier times, did not permit adequate redistribution. This was possibly the main causative factor in a generalised drop in living-standards, when compared to the Roman period, and was certainly one of the main factors in migrations, invasions, piracy and pillage.

Of course, the change charted above was gradual, stretching back to mid-Imperial times. The late Roman Empire already seems to have seen an increase in state-controlled trade or *dirigisme*, which favoured some areas of substantial agricultural potential and output and some consumer sites. Thus, the Tunisian and Sicilian granaries on the one hand, and the Egyptian granary on the other, supplied the major consumer cities of Rome and Constantinople respectively. Both cities, in the fourth century, had pop-

Fig 10.1   *Key-sites in the Mediterranean referred to in Part 1 (P Arthur).*

ulations that still ran into the hundreds of thousands. Tunisia also supplied much of the Western Empire with olive oil, supplemented by that from the region of Antioch in Syria, which also supplied vast tracts of the Eastern Empire. Wine came preferentially from the developing Palestinian heart-lands, including Gaza, Askelon and Caesarea, stimulated by the growth of major monasteries. Much of this immense movement of goods is witnessed archaeologically by the tens of thousands of fragments of commercial amphorae (see Box 10.1) and late Roman tableware found on archaeological sites. Such pottery often rode piggyback on ships that crossed the Mediterranean Sea and ventured, occasionally, into the waters of the Atlantic.

Ceramics

Ever since the publication of John Hayes's ground-breaking study on *Late Roman Pottery* (1972), and the studies on transport amphorae by scholars such as Clementina Panella and John Riley in the 1970s (Riley 1979; cf. Panella 1993), ancient ceramics have become a fundamental instrument for the reconstruction of Roman trade. The extent to which goods circulated throughout the Mediterranean in Late Antiquity can now be clearly seen, as can the sudden recession that took place during the course of the sixth century. For instance, a study of African Red Slip Ware gathered during surveys in Italy, Sicily, Spain and Algeria shows a gradual drop in quantities from the end of the fourth century to a virtual disappearance after c600 (Fentress & Perkins 1988). Sufficient literary texts exist to indicate that merchants, often from the East, were still important during the sixth century and that they continued to ply their wares even later. The *Vita* of John of

BOX 10.1   COMMERCIAL AMPHORAE

During Classical Antiquity, wine, olive oil and fish sauces were shipped around the Mediterranean, and further afield, in ceramic transport containers commonly known as *amphorae*; Italian vintages were thus enjoyed in such disparate places as Scotland and India. The recent study of ancient amphorae has revolutionised archaeological views of the ancient economy because, if the types of amphorae and clays employed in their manufacture are correctly identified, the provenance and distribution of amphorae can often be well defined. Furthermore, the analysis of lipids entrapped in the porous clay fabrics of the vessels can also aid in the identification of their contents. The combined use of analytical techniques, distribution studies, quantification of potsherds and minimum vessel numbers, as well as calculations based on container sizes and volumes, can lead to significant deductions concerning past patterns of commerce and consumption. The archaeology of large consumer sites, such as towns, can yield hundreds of fragments of these vessels dating well into the sixth century. Later their quantities declined, as maritime commerce waned, although amphorae continued to be produced around the Mediterranean even into the later Middle Ages, when they were gradually supplanted by wooden barrels as the preferred means of transport for liquid products.

Until the early 1990s there existed little awareness amongst scholars that production and use of amphorae had survived Classical Antiquity. Now it can be shown that, although the scale of trans-Mediterranean commerce declined severely after the sixth century, some areas continued to produce surplus agricultural products to be shipped abroad, preferentially to centres of substantial populations or privileged consumer sites, such as large monasteries or *castra*. By the year 1000, amphorae began picking-up again in quantity, although production sites appear to have been concentrated in areas under Byzantine domination. At present, much of the best archaeological evidence for growth in production and trade at the end of the first millennium comes from in and around the Sea of Marmara, at Ganos, where both kiln-sites and shipwrecks stacked with amphorae have been found. The industry was probably established largely to meet the needs of the growing population of Constantinople. However, vessels manufactured in the workshops along the coast at Ganos were not only used to ship wine to the eastern capital, they were also (from the tenth century) reaching Sweden in the north, both western and central Asia Minor, as well as Italy in the west (including Naples and Venice). Wine amphorae produced near Corinth or in southern Apulia also reached Venice, as well as Genoa.

[1]

[2]

By Paul Arthur

Fig 1

Wine amphora from Ganos, on the Sea of Marmara (photo: N Gunsenin).

Fig 2

Commercial amphora from Gaza (photo: P Arthur).

Cyprus (Bishop of Alexandria, 610-19), for instance, tells of a grain ship that sailed from Alexandria to Britain to return with gold and tin.

Although African Red Slip Ware vanishes from smaller towns and rural sites throughout the Mediterranean during the course of the sixth century, it continued to be exported to an increasingly select number of areas up until the invasion of Tunisia by the Arabs at the end of the seventh century. The recent excavations at the Crypta Balbi site, in the heart of Rome, have shown that imports from North Africa arrived until the area fell to the Arabs (Saguì & Manacorda 1995), but the Arab conquest does not seem to have been the causal factor, as the same Rome excavations have also yielded late seventh-century imports from the Arab Levant. Indeed, a similarly striking diminution of trade may be witnessed by the distribution of amphorae produced around various parts of the Mediterranean basin, even those not conquered by the Arabs.

Perhaps even more significantly in the context of tied-trade is the number of privileged consumer sites that are coming to light outside of the major towns, including some really minor ones. The excavations of the Byzantine *castrum* of S. Antonino di Perti, near the Ligurian coast, are telling (Mannoni & Murialdo 2001). The fort was built to safeguard Byzantine territorial possessions from the Lombards, who had invaded Italy in 578. The garrison needed to be supplied with goods which, archaeology shows, came principally from North Africa, including small amphorae or *spatheia* and African Red Slip Ware. The very specific pattern of supply appears to be replicated at other strategic sites like Ostrakine in northern Sinai, soon to be lost to the Arabs, or the hilltop site at Emporio, on the Aegean island of Chios. Even the fortified hill-top site of Vranje in Slovenia was supplied with goods in *spatheia*, whilst other pottery was of local manufacture (Knific 1994).

If we turn to the evidence of smaller ceramic industries with regional distributions, quite another picture emerges. After the sixth century, professional ateliers survived only near large settlements, where substantial populations guaranteed demand. In many parts of the Mediterranean they were replaced by minor ceramic productions, perhaps in the hands of part-time potters serving the needs of small communities at subsistence level. In parts of Cyprus, for instance, there was even a return to hand-made pottery (Rautmann 1998).

Shipwrecks

These were all signs of a changing age, to which we are gradually adding data from underwater archaeology. Mediterranean commercial shipping declined and transformed between Late Antiquity and the early Middle Ages (McCormick 2001, 103-14). Work on shipwrecks can contrast the massive transporters of the late Republic and early Empire to the *caboteurs* of the early Middle Ages, that tramped the coasts from harbour to harbour. The ship of late Republican date found at Madrague de Giens, off the southern shore of France, with its cargo of c7,500 standardised wine amphorae, was 40m long. It was twice as long as the seventh-century Byzantine ship, found at Yassi Ada, near Bodrum, Turkey (Bass & Van Doorninck, 1982), which sank c625 containing some 800

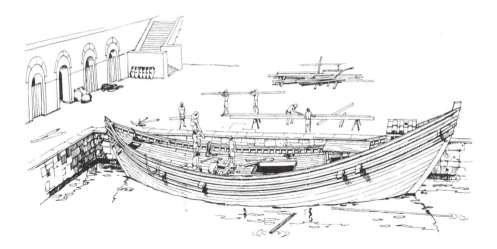

Reconstruction of the Yassi Ada ship, wrecked (c625) near Bodrum, Turkey (after Bass & Van Doorninck 1982).

Fig 10.2

amphorae (Fig 10.2). Their respective cargo-weights have been calculated as 375 and 40 tons. The early eleventh-century Arab shipwreck of Serçe Liman, also found off the south-west coast of Turkey, was only 15m long. It contained a mixed cargo, comprising Byzantine wine amphorae from the Sea of Marmara, quernstones of volcanic rock from the island of Melos, and a most astounding assortment of broken glass from the Near East. These last two shipwrecks evoke the idea of traders tramping the Mediterranean coasts, over a period of 500 years.

Coinage

A further nuance to the tale may be added by an examination of coin finds (Hendy 1985; Ward-Perkins 2005). The transformation of commerce and exchange is echoed by the ups and downs of monetary output and circulation. Quite substantial quantities of bronze coins continued to be produced well into the fifth century, from a variety of mints scattered throughout the Empire. Numbers of coins found by archaeologists drop quite rapidly in the sixth century, to all but disappear by the seventh. Coinage was never replaced by the successor states to the Western Roman Empire in sufficient quantities for everyday use and was generally limited to gold and silver. Indeed, in some Mediterranean areas coins were even employed in jewellery as a form of wealth-display. Byzantine bronze coinage gradually began to circulate once again under the Emperor Theophilus (829-42), although its distribution appears to have been limited mainly to areas of effective Byzantine control. In much of the Mediterranean, debased silver or bronze only seeped into everyday life after the year 1000. It can hardly be doubted that most daily exchange in the second half of the first millennium was carried out through barter, with coins of noble metals used primarily for the sale of property or political bargaining. This penury of coinage will not have helped the problematic issue of tax collection, adding to the difficulties in obtaining the wealth necessary to run a state as large and complex as was Byzantium.

Collapse and Revival

The aggregate sum of the material evidence, supported by written sources, thus points to an almost total collapse of large-scale Mediterranean-wide commerce through the course of the sixth century, particularly in the latter half. The seventh century saw the Byzantine Empire struggling to maintain footholds and influence across the old Roman provinces through directed trade to allies and to military or quasi-military garrisons. The greater part of the Mediterranean population, instead, reverted to regional economies of self-sufficiency, with limited access to a wider market.

The upper end of the social strata continued to practise gift-exchange, which had its roots in such practices as Imperial donatives, church foundation gifts and covenant payments to potentially hostile populations that lay outside of the Empire.

Accumulating archaeological discoveries, as at the Crypta Balbi in Rome (see Box 4.2), are now shining beams of light through the oppressive darkness of the eighth century, which appears ever more to have marked a turning-point in what had seemed an inexorable decline of Antiquity. With some innovative historical revisionism, a picture is now emerging of a far more dynamic early medieval Mediterranean, often taking its place as intermediary between the Frankish West and the Islamic East. Even though Byzantium continued to keep a tenuous hold on its far-flung possessions, new markets were gradually developing in the wake of new and autonomous states that grew largely on former Roman territory.

The Arabs

The Arabs represented one of the principal new protagonists in the Mediterranean, setting up a series of emirates from east to west. By the early eighth century, the entire southern seaboard of the Mediterranean was in Arab hands, as well as its eastern and western extremities (see Chapter 2). In many of the newly-conquered territories, agricultural production appears to have continued unabated, despite the economic difficulties that had characterised the sixth and seventh centuries. In the Palestinian strip and the Nile valley, for instance, Roman-style amphorae were continuously produced under the Arabs for the exportation of wine. Some of this production may have remained in the hands of Christian communities, as archaeology shows the use of churches and monasteries well into the eighth century, such as the church at Um Er-Rasas, where one Byzantine-style mosaic bears the date of 756 (Piccirillo 1986). Re-examination of discoveries at the old Roman town of Lepcis Magna, in Libya, with the identification of an olive press and a kiln producing transport amphorae, shows that even the Aghlabid Magreb was participating in Islamic economic development by the ninth century. Amphorae were likewise produced and exported from Djerba. Though archaeology still does not tell us where the amphorae were exported to, it would seem that much of the agricultural surplus produced under the Arabs was redistributed within their own territories. The not-so gradual economic expansion that had been hastened by the Arabs appears to have met a shortage of manpower that could only be replenished through the supply of slave labour. This was particularly so following the establishment of the capital of the Abbasid dynasty at Baghdad by al-Mansur in 762, which provided a key node for exchange between the Mediterranean and the Far East. According to literary sources, slaves were also much required in Egypt, across the Maghreb and in Spain, giving rise to a brisk trade that was underway by the eighth century. Much of the need was filled through Arab raids on Europe, as has been so eloquently illustrated through the excavations of the Benedictine monastery of San Vincenzo al Volturno (Fig 14.4). Tucked away in the hills of south-central Italy, the entire complex was sacked and burnt to the ground by an Arab raiding party on 10 October 881, creating destruction levels that have survived until this day (Hodges & Mitchell 1985).

Major towns of the Mediterranean seaboard quickly took advantage of the demand for manpower, helping to boost their own economic development. Thus Venice became a leading market for slaves from Slavic territories, supplying even Rome; Marseilles helped tap the human reserves of North-West Europe; Naples sold slaves captured in Lombard areas; and Taranto served as a base for exporting prisoners from its own hinterland.

Markets and Trading-Sites

So where did trade in slaves, as well as agrarian produce and manufactured items, take place and through what mechanisms? Aside from everyday exchange between individuals, perhaps often outside specific market environments, a new set of places gradually substituted many of the markets of Roman times. Of course, many old towns continued to function as local 'central-places', even if in a severely reduced capacity. However, archaeology is now showing how some major towns, particularly those accessible by sea, continued to witness a flow of goods. In early medieval times such settlements were to become the key nodes, or emporia, in interlocking regional exchange networks. They include such sites as Marseille and Naples, Corinth, Ephesus and Alexandria, and some substantially new foundations like Amalfi and Venice, which were to develop into powerful city-states through the course of the eighth and ninth centuries.

It is chastening to consider the plentiful archaeological evidence now available from Rome, much of which has come from the Crypta Balbi (Panella & Saguì 2001). In the early eighth century, imports appear to have almost stopped and most objects were locally produced, from pottery to metalwork. The few imports identified are ceramics from southern Italy or Sicily, perhaps from papal possessions. Documentary evidence, however, appears to show rapidly expanding exchange by the mid-eighth century and, from the later eighth and ninth centuries, silver coins from Carolingian mints in northern Italy appear in excavations.

Combined historical and archaeological data are now showing how successive sites on the Venetian lagoon, for instance, developed to link Northern Europe with the

Mediterranean world, effectively replacing Rome's gateway-port of Aquileia, once the southern terminal of the amber route from the Baltic. The seeds of the success of Venice in the Middle Ages had been sown through immigration to the lagoon from the main-land during the troubled times of Late Antiquity.

The redating of old excavations at Torcello, in the lagoon, the site known as *emporion mega* to Emperor Constantine Porphyrogenitus in the tenth century (*De Administrando Imperio*, 27-8), appears to illustrate the birth of glassworks in the ninth, presaging what was to become Venice's renowned production (first documented in 982). Excavations at nearby Comacchio, a short-lived rival of Venice, have yielded Byzantine transport amphorae dating from the eighth century. Perhaps they date around the time when the disputed Pact of Comacchio was drawn up, a text that stipulates duties to be paid at sites along the Po valley. They may be testimony to more significant commerce in salt, which reached the heartland of the Carolingian Empire, as well as in slaves and other goods (see Gelichi 2006).

Amalfi, where research excavations are needed, was another extremely successful emporium, fading away only with the onset of a liberal trans-Mediterranean trade after the year 1000. Exploiting the rich produce of Campania, with its timber-laden slopes that dropped down to the sea and its inhabitants' prowess in seafaring, Amalfi was already recognised as a significant trading post by the late eighth century. What appears to link such distant sites as Venice, Genoa and Amalfi was their readiness to do business with all, acting as middlemen between the Byzantine Empire, Islam and the West, cutting across trade restrictions that inhibited the freedom of movement of Byzantine and other merchants. Genoa, together with Pisa, also looked towards Spain.

But such trading-sites were not confined to Italy. Chersonesos, on the northern coast of the Black Sea, appears to have played a similar role. Though nominally a Byzantine town, it may have sought autonomy in the eighth century, when Byzantine power was at an all-time low. Its economic development was based on a position that was able to tap the grain fields of the southern Ukraine and handle the goods from the far North and the Baltic, through the Dnepr valley. It was this position as gateway-port that brought the Vikings as mercenaries to the court of Constantinople, and channelled wealth northwards to help create the state of the Rus based on Kiev. Archaeology has revealed an extraordinary development of Chersonesos, particularly between the tenth and thir-teenth centuries, with the construction of numerous houses and churches (Sedikova et al 2003). Artefacts from the town range from slate spindle-whorls from Ovruč, near Kiev, turquoise frit-ware from the Islamic world and, of course, a wealth of other items from around the Aegean. By the end of the tenth century, stone buildings, such as the Desiatinnaia church, were being erected in Kiev, clearly with the aid of Byzantine crafts-men who had travelled through Chersonesos.

Unfortunately for archaeology, the Mediterranean emporia were not generally short-lived sites like the Northern European ones, and most developed into major modern towns. Material evidence for their character and development is thus slow to come out of the ground.

Recent excavations in Naples have, however, provided a glimpse of the commercial facilities available during the 'Dark Ages'. A large seventh-century storage building has been unearthed at Piazza Bovio, near the medieval port. It appears to have continued in use until the tenth century and has yielded locally produced amphorae for the exportation of Campanian wine. In its vicinity were glass and metal workshops, whilst the written sources inform us of flourishing local shipyards, a necessary corollary to trade (Arthur 2002). At Otranto, the eighth-century amphora kiln-site was located close to the port, for ready packaging and shipping of local wines.

Thus it can be seen that, to some extent, such gateway-ports paralleled the thriving northern emporia known on the Baltic and Atlantic coasts in early medieval times, where craftsmanship and exchange were closely related (see below). Save perhaps Venice, new towns of this kind were not often founded in the Mediterranean, perhaps because there was a more pronounced urban survival, particularly amongst port-towns that had served Mediterranean-wide connectivity during the Roman period.

Maritime movement between these major gateway-ports depended upon a system of smaller ports and havens, aiding cabotage and tramping, where limited exchange almost certainly took place. Some of the latter are mentioned in later medieval *portulans* or sea charts, as stations along the principal maritime routes. Others appear in occasional early medieval writings such as the *Hodoeporicon* of St Willibald, which recounts the monk's travels from the English emporium of Hamwic (Southampton) to Jerusalem, during the eighth century (Tobler 1874). Not only does the 'Life of Willibald' mention such small havens as the island fortress of Monemvasia, on a southern tip of the Peleponnesos, but it also provides fascinating glimpses into the way in which sea-voyages were carried out, as well as the activities that took place at various stations along his route.

Fairs

Market exchange in inland areas is less well documented. Surviving urban centres must have continued to play a role, though supplemented by, often very large, rural fairs or periodic markets. These had already started to become frequent in Late Antiquity with the decline of towns, and were often managed under the aegis of the Church and under the protection of local saints. The best-known such fair in the Mediterranean was cited by Cassiodorus in the first half of the sixth century. It took place by the sacred spring of Leucothea, near the old Roman town of *Consilinum*, in southern Italy. He tells us that 'for all the notable exports of industrious Campania, or wealthy Bruttium, or Calabria rich in cattle, or prosperous Apulia, with the products of Lucania itself, are displayed to the glory of that most admirable commerce', including children being sold into slavery (Cass. *Var* VIII; Barnish 1991, 109-10). Dedicated to St Cyprian, the fair stressed the link between these commercial events and holy feasts. Thus, in the eleventh century, the bishop of *Euchaita* in Asia Minor, claimed that the fair of St Theodore, attracted people 'from every nation', transforming the city from a 'wasteland to a populous city with markets and stoas' (Haldon 1990; see also Hendy 1985, 141-2). The fair of St Denis in France, established by the seventh century, soon attracted Italian Lombards and others, laying the foundations for local wealth as a node in international trade. The cave sanctuary of St Michael Archangel, in southern Adriatic Italy, must have been the site of an important international fair. Not only has it yielded many coins, though with a hiatus between the sixth and ninth centuries, it has yielded runic inscriptions scratched on its walls (Arcamone 1994). This was the site at which, according to legend, the Norman conquest of southern Italy was first conceived.

Gift-Exchange and Holy Relics

Much information about items of long-distance commerce prior to the tenth century concerns high-status gift-exchange, that included silk, fur, gold, silver, jewellery and semi-precious stones, ivory, relics, books, papyrus, spices, drugs and wine. Silk, spices and various semi-precious stones, and even technological and medical knowledge, came from the Islamic world which also acted as intermediary for items from the Far East, including China. A bronze figure of Buddha found in excavations at Helgö, in Sweden, appears to be from Kashmir. Silks from the tombs of figures such as King Edward the Confessor, in England, could have come from Constantinople or Persia, whilst eastern silks were already attested in the Carolingian Empire. Byzantine wall-paintings in Otranto made use of crushed lapis lazuli from Afghanistan, whilst the hinterland of the town has yielded a tenth-century silver *dirham* from al-Ma'dan in Panjir. Papyrus came from the Nile valley and gold from Nubia, all of which had helped to under-

Fig 10.3 *A Byzantine white lava quernstone, probably made on the Aegean island of Melos, found at Chersonesos, Crimea (photo: P Arthur).*

pin the wealth of Fatimid Egypt. Apart from the documentary evidence of the Cairo Geniza papyri, which detail wide-ranging commercial connections from the tenth century (Goitien 1967), European trade with Egypt is attested most eloquently by the tale of two Venetian merchants in Alexandria, in 828 (*Translatio S Marci, BHL* 5283-3). They took advantage of their stay to steal away the body of St Mark to Venice, so as to support its primacy over the old see of Aquileia.

Indeed, particular note should be made of the importance of holy relics, from saints' bones to splinters of the Holy Cross, in medieval trade. They pandered to the need of churches and communities to establish their position in an ever more exacting Christian milieu. Michael McCormick's (2001) study of relic-tags, small certificates that identified the relics and sometimes provided their provenance, shows the remarkable extent to which relics could travel.

All these goods, presumably often travelling with merchants and clergy through the emporia, were far from being items of daily exchange. They were linked to the Church and to elite aristocracies, who had become gradually poorer since Late Antiquity but who began to show signs of economic revival by the ninth century, with the gradual accumulation of landed wealth.

Trade-Goods

Most exchange through the early Middle Ages probably consisted of small-scale barter within or between largely self-sufficient agricultural communities. Indeed, more mundane objects of exchange are gradually surfacing in the archaeological record. Excavation of villages in southern Apulia appears to show that very few goods imported from afar were available to such rural communities prior to the tenth century; these often consisted of fundamental items such as lava rotary querns or ironwork necessary to agriculture (Arthur 2000). Querns for milling grain came from both Mount Etna in Sicily and the Aegean island of Melos (Fig 10.3). They were distributed afar, those from Melos appearing at Chersonesos in the Crimea, and suggest a parallel to the Merovingian and Carolingian trade in querns from Mayen in the Rhineland (see Box 10.2). Lathe-turned soapstone vases were cut from quarries in the southern Alpine regions and were distributed as far as the heel of Italy, and doubtless elsewhere. Pottery, above all, remains a fundamental archaeological indicator of trade patterns for wine and other foodstuffs.

Alongside wine, Norman Sicily may also have acted as a vector for the diffusion of cane sugar from the eleventh century. Ribbed amphorae of Fatimid type, produced between Marsala and Palermo in Sicily, may have been used for transporting the sugar; they have been found distributed up the Tyrrhenian coast, as far as southern France. Sugar cane (*Saccharum officinarum*), native to New Guinea, was imported to the Mediterranean by the Arabs (cf. p 187), to be regularly cultivated and processed by the Latin states in the Holy Land and on Cyprus, where archaeological evidence for sugar production is now forthcoming (von Wartburg 1995).

The story of the spread of lead-glazed pottery is an even more eloquent example of the expanding scale of commerce. For centuries lead glazing was practised to decorate pottery in and around Constantinople and in the Arab states. Examples of Byzantine glazed white-ware, from near Constantinople, begin to appear on Western Mediterranean sites in the tenth century. These are followed by more substantive quantities of imports, particularly to Venice and Genoa, of glazed sgraffito-wares from various manufacturing areas by the mid-twelfth century. The ceramic basins of Arabic manufacture found embedded in the facades of churches in Pisa, as embellishments, demonstrate that pottery was being exported to Italy from North Africa and Sicily by the early eleventh century. By the later twelfth century, imitations of glazed pottery from the Maghreb and Sicily were being produced in Naples. The style and technique of lead-glazed pottery quickly spread throughout the peninsula and soon influenced the production of pottery in Northern Europe (cf. pp 227-8). All this amounts to both conspicuous commercial activity and the transference of technology that may be summed-up as a veritable revolution in the production of medieval ceramics – an archaeological indicator of considerable change that has been summed-up in the concept of a 'twelfth-century renaissance' (cf. Berti & Gelichi 1995).

At the beginning of the new millennium, a plethora of villages in France and Italy seem to have possessed their own blacksmiths, which fact suggests an increasing production of agricultural surplus. These smithies, in turn, imply a blossoming trade in iron or iron ores, a resource that was unequally distributed through the Mediterranean. By the twelfth century, settlements had developed around the mining of metals, as has been so well illustrated through the archaeology of Rocca San Silvestro or the island of Elba in Tuscany (Francovich 1991).

Coins, in silver and bronze, were struck in ever-increasing numbers. The distribution of coins and pottery mirrors the movement of such archaeologically invisible goods as salt and spices, cereals, wood, textiles, wines and meat, honey and sugar.

At the same time, the generalised reappearance of stone architecture presupposes the re-activation of quarries, the use of extraction and building techniques, more organised communal activity and trade in stone, not seen since Roman times. The new craftsmen, stimulated particularly by the growth in spending in the ecclesiastical and monastic sphere, may be seen through architecture, sculpture and wall-painting; such, in turn, presupposes the movement and exchange of specialists, knowledge and materials. This new phase is marked by the emergence of Romanesque architecture throughout Latin Christendom.

Development and Change

So it can be seen that the turn of the millennium marks an increment in the speed of change in both economic and social conditions throughout the Mediterranean and Europe. A complex series of interrelated factors led to the change in the nature and scale of commerce. We may enumerate, amongst these, population expansion, with more mouths to feed, though more hands with which to produce, the appearance of a wealthy and demanding bourgeoisie strongly linked to an evermore ennobled merchant class, and all within the context of a developing urban network. It is sufficient to examine the state of French and north Italian towns, to see how they had progressed since the early Middle Ages. To these factors, we should perhaps add climatic amelio-ration, helping to extend the areas available to prized Mediterranean crops such as the olive and the vine, as well as the opening up to the plough of newly-drained or deforest-ed land in the Mediterranean. Political change, particularly in the eleventh-twelfth cen-turies, was also responsible for the development of commercial activity not only with-in the Mediterranean, but also in forging an interlocking system of exchange between Northern Europe and the South, with rulers, like the Romans and Carolingians before them, who bridged the boundaries of the Alps and Pyrenees. The new supreme authori-ties not only carved out larger territories, but also created safer routes and havens for the movement of commercial shipping. The Norman invasions ousted the Arabs from Sicily and smashed remaining Byzantine power in southern Italy. Norman power and wealth may be seen to flourish under King Roger II of Sicily, whose court in Palermo was such as to illustrate the increasing internationalisation of the Mediterranean. In northern Italy, power passed into the hands of the able Emperor Frederick I Barbarossa. Further to the west, pilgrimages to Compostela and the Christian reconquest of the Iberian Peninsula had got under way. The changing political scene around the Mediterranean basin had broken Byzantine and Arab domination of the sea and allowed for freer and more articulated movement of new traders and their wares. Despite this, the well-trav-elled twelfth-century pilgrim, Benjamin of Tudela, still regarded Constantinople to be the second city of the world for commercial activity after Baghdad.

As Richard Hodges has noted (1988, 20), archaeology witnesses the development of ranked regional markets that succeeded the early medieval monopolistic emporia, and which were in place by the twelfth century. In fact, the process was already well under-way by the tenth century, as towns had developed a certain measure of autonomy from the state and could mediate directly between the income from their agricultural terri-tories and the goods available from external markets. As the population of the agrarian landscape grew, the ranked regional markets comprised the few major towns and fairs, as well as the plethora of smaller towns that housed landowners, merchants and urban craftsmen, and a developing nobility. In some towns, mints became available, as well as the capital needed to underpin large-scale investment in international commerce, lead-ing eventually to the creation of a banking system.

It is now recognised that the changes that the ancient world underwent in Late Antiquity and the early Middle Ages were in large measure due to the disappearance of the Mediterranean world-system that had gained shape under the control of Rome. Henri Pirenne's stimulating thesis on the decline of Antiquity, brought about by an Islamic wedge driven into the heart of the Mediterranean (Pirenne 1937), has now also succumbed to the eloquence of archaeological data. Archaeology has shown that, although interna-tional exchange was restricted to ever more elite classes through the sixth and seventh cen-turies, Mediterranean connectivity was never totally severed. The so-called commercial revolution, expounded by the historian Raymond Lopez (1976) amongst others, can now be seen as a rather gradual process beginning around the eighth century, growing in pace until it was in full swing by the tenth. The development of towns and lands created greater supply and demand and permitted more direct access to the market. The results are clear after the year 1000 because of the greater number of documentary sources and a more visible material culture than before. The four tendencies that Lopez saw as characterising European economic expansion during the course of the tenth century are:

(1) The redistribution of the rural population so as to eliminate opposing excesses of overpopulation and depopulation, of saturation and waste;

(2) A greater regard for the profession of merchant than in the past, thus being able to attract and conserve capital and energy;

(3) The importance and utility of machines and techniques beginning to be recognised in practice, if not in theory; and

(4) The extreme political fragmentation and the weakness of governments favouring local and private initiatives.

The new millennium had got off to a splendid start. The twelfth century closed with the fall of Byzantine Constantinople to the western states, in 1204, and the consolidation of a Mediterranean-wide Venetian trade-empire (see also pp 451-2). Within a generation, Marco Polo was able to look to new horizons.

PART 2: NORTHERN EUROPE *by Søren M Sindbæk*

If the history of Mediterranean trade during the period c800-1200 is one of decline and reluctant recovery that of Northern Europe is decidedly one of growth. One reason for this is the different points of departure. By c700, Europe's northern seas had never witnessed a system of exchange on the scale and complexity of that in the Mediterranean during Antiquity. During the following centuries, however, the development of commerce in the North corresponded ever closer to that of the Mediterranean, resulting in a twelfth-century economy no less advanced or extensive than that of Imperial Rome, but within an even wider geographical frame. Intriguingly, and hardly by accident, this process was set in motion at the very moment when the Late Antique economy ceased in the Mediterranean, in the closing decades of the seventh century. Throughout much of the period concerned here, trade remained a modest appendage to traditional forms of exchange. Its key historical importance was as a steady motor of social change and innovation.

The Emporia Network

Silver coins, sailing ships and towns, the bench-marks of early market exchange, appear in earnest on and around the northern seas of Europe, beyond the old Imperial frontier, during the seventh and eighth centuries. Being the means, vessels and locations of an exchange, which had grown beyond gift-exchange, plunder and tribute, to include the focused, calculated and nominally impersonal relationships of trade, they signal the beginning of a commercial economy.

The ships of this age are still unknown to us, except for images on Gotlandic picture-stones; the coins, however, are familiar. The so-called *sceattas*, struck since the last quarter of the seventh century, were a light silver-denomination on the model of earlier Merovingian gold *tremisses*, but effectively the first coinage in post-Roman Northern Europe suited to the transactions of a rural small-holding economy (Abramson 2006, xi). The distribution of *sceattas* clusters along the Rhine, in England and around the North Sea coast into south-east Denmark, with sporadic finds in the rest of Scandinavia and the Baltic Sea region. This distribution is echoed by a number of Frankish products, such as quernstones, pitchers, glass vessels and textiles (Gabriel 1988). They mark the main arteries of a long-distance exchange that had attained a level of intensity and regularity not found elsewhere in Northern Europe at this period.

The hub of this network was Dorestad in the Frisian Rhine delta, also one of the most prolific mints of *sceattas* (van Es & Verwers 2002). From Dorestad merchants commuted to a small group of strategically located ports, including Quentovic in France, Hamwic and Lundenwic in England, Ribe in Denmark, and Birka in Sweden (see Chapter 4). These *wics* or 'emporia' were undefended landing-sites, mostly placed at political boundaries or topographical barriers, consisting of modestly-sized permanent settlements that swelled seasonally into large markets (Callmer 1994; Hodges 2006, with refs). They differ archaeologically from more local markets through finds that include items brought by foreigners for their personal use (e.g. domestic pottery), and by the regular practice of crafts that consumed imported raw materials, such as bead-making or bronze-casting.

Towards the end of the eighth century, Arabic silver coins (*dirhams*) appear first in Russia, then in the Baltic Sea region, along with mass-produced glass beads and other items (Callmer 1995; Noonan 1998). Staraya Ladoga (in north-west Russia) and possibly Truso (east Poland) became critical links to the Near Eastern economy through trade in fur and probably slaves. The Oriental beads arrived in sufficient quantities to oust the local production of glass beads at sites like Ribe within few years. The influx of silver was probably no less significant, and it also found its way through the Mediterranean (McCormick 2001, 369). In 793/4 it provided Charlemagne with the means to introduce a larger and heavier penny, weighing 1.7 grams. This Carolingian reform-coinage was soon matched by King Offa, in England, as also by the so-called 'Hedeby' coins in Denmark.

These new currencies, as well as an increasing body of trade legislation, point to the growing volume of exchange and to the ambition of rulers to control it (Verhulst 2002, 87f). The period saw intensified conflicts over attempts to monopolise the emporia, whose locations suggest that they had originally acted as neutral zones. In the early ninth century, Hedeby (Box 4.3) was founded at the base of Jutland as a Danish response to Frankish advance (Carnap-Bornheim & Hilbert 2007, with refs). While Dorestad became strangled between Carolingian and Viking ambitions, Hedeby took over its role as the hub for sea-trade in Northern Europe (Theuws 2004). Bridging the Baltic and the North Sea, it opened routes for a new set of satellites, including Kaupang in southern Norway, Århus in Jutland, and Ralswiek in north-eastern Germany. In spite of this

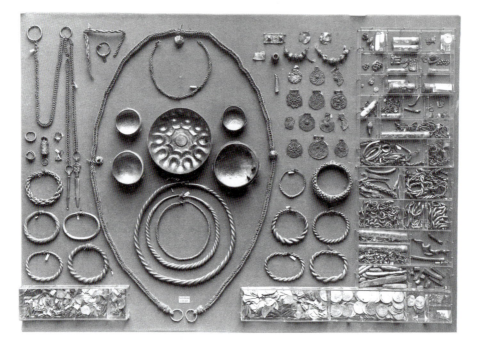

Fig 10.4 *Hack-silver hoards are evidence of the bullion-based 'weight-money' exchange practised over large parts of North and Central Europe during the 10th-12th centuries; many, such as this hoard from Terslev (Denmark), contain a large number of coins, but their fragmentation, as well as their test-marks, demonstrate that they were not being exchanged at face-value, but for their content of silver (photo: National Museum, Copenhagen).*

expansion, however, the nature of harbour facilities indicates that most ships still had a sufficiently shallow draught to be landed and loaded on the beach.

During the second half of the ninth century, many sites that had previously transmitted long-distance exchange in the North Sea area were either extinguished or substantially reduced. Traditionally, this has been linked to the disintegration of the Carolingian Empire and the escalation of Viking raids, but the evidence is more complex (Hall 2000). Interestingly, this is also the period when sources first indicate a shift in trade-routes from coastal hugging to blue-water sailing. This critically different maritime culture, which was re-introduced into the Mediterranean at the same period, would have rendered many smaller landing-sites useless (McCormick 2001, 494).

The most thriving sites of this period were those engaged with the eastern connections; these culminated during the period 930-70, when the influx of Arabic silver was at its peak. These connections are also reflected along the Dnepr and Volga river-routes, where Scandinavian finds occur regularly in the new trading-stations that were established there in the second half of the ninth century (Nosov 1993).

The most distinctive economic feature of this network was 'weight-money', a bullion-based exchange-system reflected in a large number of hoards containing hack-silver (e.g. Fig 10.4), often including whole or fragmented coins, found across Scandinavia and East Europe (Brather 1996; Hårdh 1996). With no central authority to define the value of coins, 'weight-money' exchange was facilitated by Oriental types of scales and weights introduced in the late ninth century (Steuer et al 2002; Graham-Campbell & Williams 2007). Unlike the nominal coinage in a monetarised economy, bullion did not lose its value over time and could therefore be saved by hoarding. This explains the existence of so many Northern hoards as compared with Western Europe; however, silver was used as more than a means of storage. The great fragmentation present in many hoards shows that 'weight-money' was being used even for trivial transactions.

The Urban Revival

Up until the tenth century, all ship-wrecks known from the Northern seas belong to all-purpose vessels, designed to carry a large crew and a modest cargo; however, a division then took place into slender warships and bulky transport-vessels (see Chapter 9). The latter were plainly dependent on organised protection and on the availability of proper landing facilities. Their appearance therefore marks an important threshold in both the volume of exchange and its organisation.

A similar tendency towards more proficient regulation is reflected in coinage. The influx of Arabic *dirhams* dried up in the late tenth century, probably together with the Central Asian mines which had supplied the silver for them. Within the 'weight-money' zone of Northern and Eastern Europe, they were initially replaced by coins from Western Europe, in particular north German issues – the *Sachsenpfennige* – struck in increasing numbers after the opening of the Rammelsberg silver mines, in the Harz mountains (Steuer 2005). More importantly, however, the system of exchange based on intrinsic value was receding. In England, King Edgar's reform in 973 established the first uniform, nominal coinage to circulate in all England. Domestic coins were increasingly minted in Norway and Denmark in the eleventh century and, from the 1070s, Denmark maintained a regulated, nominal currency (cf. Fig 10.5). The Slavic lands, on the other hand, mostly stuck to the bullion economy and only produced limited numbers of domestic coins as prestige issues (Spufford 1988; cf. also Kilger 2000).

This new structure of exchange was supported by an increase in new urban foundations, which appeared during the tenth century. The *burhs* in England, *Burgstädte* in Germany, and similar places throughout Northern Europe, show a different organization to that of the earlier emporia. They combined regional administrative centres and trading-places within one, usually fortified site. Some important centres changed locations in this process. From the mid-eleventh century, activities at Hedeby (Box 4.3) shifted to nearby Schleswig, which was able to receive ships with a deeper draught (Fig 9.8); in Russia, the port of Staraja Ladoga became just an appendix to the budding Novgorod, the new centre of power in a settled region.

Such centres were established in much greater numbers than the rare long-distance ports which had preceded them, and also in formerly non-urbanised areas. Towns like Dublin in Ireland, Cracow or Prague in Central Europe, and Lund or Trondheim in

Fig 10.5 *Four silver pennies struck in the later 11th century, from left to right, with obverse at top and reverse below: (1) Germany, Siegfried I, archbishop of Mainz (1060-84); (2) Low Countries, William of Pont, bishop of Utrecht (1054-76); (3) Anglo-Saxon England, Edward the Confessor (1042-66), minted at Lewes (Sussex); and (4) Denmark, Sven Estridsson (1047-76), minted at Roskilde (Zealand), with a runic inscription reading 'Suen reo tano[ru]m', for 'Sven rex danorum' (© Fitzwilliam Museum, Cambridge).*

Scandinavia, all rose to importance during the tenth and eleventh centuries. Through centres such as these Norse settlers in the North Atlantic supplied Arctic exotica, such as walrus-ivory (Box 2.1), while Slavs in Bohemia or Moravia began to receive amber from the Baltic (Roesdahl 2003; Krumphanzlová 1992).

The use of regulated nominal coinage consolidated throughout most of Europe during the twelfth century, as witnessed by the use of increasingly debased coins. The monopoly of coins was certainly of great value to lords, who could order recurring substitutions at exchange rates in their favour. It was less conducive to international trade, which continued in consequence to rely heavily on bullion silver. By accident, it was also to terminate the use of coins in the regions where exchange still relied on metal value. In Novgorod, fewer and fewer coins were available after the eleventh century, when they were replaced by an exchange almost entirely based on furs and other payments in kind (Martin 1986; Rybina 1999).

In 1143, Lübeck was founded in the south-western corner of the Baltic as part of the German colonisation east of the Elbe, the *Ostsiedlung*. Complemented by some other new foundations, it was to eclipse Schleswig as the main port of the Baltic Sea in the early thirteenth century. Along with Lübeck, Visby (Gotland) and Bergen (western Norway), all grew into ports of prime importance. About the same time, the cog developed and gradually displaced the Nordic clinker-built ships as the principal trading-vessels of the Northern seas (see Chapter 9), although perhaps not, as once claimed, for the simple reason of scale: the huge thirteenth-century wreck from Bryggen, in Bergen, shows that a late Nordic clinker-built vessel could easily compete with the capacity of contemporary cogs (Berggren et al 2002). Rather, the new ships, towns and currencies were the furnishings of a new set of actors and a new network, one that was to develop into the Hanseatic League (see Vol 2).

Places, Networks and Organisation

Early medieval trade was as much an instance of communication as one of economy. 'Trade-routes' were journeys taken on a regular basis, defined by the knowledge and experience of travellers. Details in the development and arrangement of connections were decisive for the robustness of systems and for the possibility of their control, and thus for the historical development of exchange and communication.

In the emporia network, long-distance exchange mostly took place in bulk between specific localities, situated to act as spatial and temporal buffers between traffics. Local markets communicated with the emporia, but not with the long-distance traffic between them. While this network was sometimes remarkably effective, it was also extremely vulnerable. Successful emporia could be deserted within a few years if connections failed or reconfigured (Sindbæk 2007).

The urban network established from the tenth century onwards was far more robust, but entailed a different problem. The eighth-century network of emporia had been socially a small world, in which a merchant from Dorestad was probably personally acquainted with his partner in Birka. The need for formal institutions and enforcement was therefore less pronounced than later.

By contrast, the mature urban network of the High Middle Ages, which linked large numbers of towns with crowds of strangers, required an increasingly elaborate body of regulation, institutional sanction and coercive force to buttress peaceful and lawful cooperation. Even during the Carolingian period, the elite presided over markets and collected tolls. Merchants, for their part, formed partnerships, companies and guilds. Yet, the formation of towns allowed both for a more efficient monopoly of coins and markets, and for better possibilities of commercial organisation.

The shift from emporia to towns also held implications for local exchange. The few international emporia of the Carolingian period were a clearly distinct orbit from the regional distribution that took place in fairs and markets. In Western Europe these have a documented, or assumed, connection to monasteries or other great estates, as in the case of Flixborough, in northern England (Loveluck 1998). Their equivalents in Scandinavia appear similarly associated with lordly residences or 'central-places', such as the complex at Uppåkra, in southern Sweden (Näsman 2000; Pestell & Ulmschneider 2003). As towns were established from the tenth century onwards, local exchange became assigned to them, while other types of market gradually lost importance or were prohibited (Ulriksen 1994; Naylor 2004)

Archaeologically, the search for local markets is often directed towards the metal-rich 'productive sites', discovered in recent years by metal-detectorists. The social character of local markets remains little known, but it is likely that many were held in asso-

Fig 10.6 *This barrel of silver fir, which grew in the upper reaches of the Rhine, probably contained wine before it was reused as a well in Hedeby. It is almost 2m long and testifies to a scale of commerce well beyond the exchange of occasional luxury items (photo: Stiftung Schleswig-Holsteinische Landesmuseen Schloß Gottorf, Schleswig).*

ciation with periodical general-assemblies. Some interesting cultural variations stand out: in England, 'productive sites' reveal a remarkable level of coin circulation (and loss), during the eighth and ninth centuries, whereas in Scandinavia (by contrast) exchange appears to have been conducted as barter, except in emporia.

It would be false to think that local exchange was organised along the same lines in every region. Within the Seine area, from the Carolingian period, exchange was centred on the annual wine-market at St Denis, creating a regular, cyclical pattern. In the Rhine area, by contrast, markets were continuously established on the occasion of the great assemblies held, in changing towns, by the itinerant Carolingian court. In consequence, no *locus* or similar event to St Denis existed there (McCormick 2001, 647f).

Trade-Goods

Ceramics are less enlightening for the study of early medieval trade in Northern Europe than in the Mediterranean area (see Box 10.1). Amphorae were rarely used, as wine and other liquids were transported in barrels (Fig 10.6), and few fine-wares were exchanged for their own merit. Only a few wares had a regular, supra-regional distribution (cf. Lüdtke & Schietzel 2001). The Rhenish Badorf and later Pingsdorf wares (see pp 225-7), produced in the Vorgebirge, south of Cologne, were used throughout the Rhine area and are regularly found in ports in the North Sea region. An exceptional Frankish product, the eighth/ninth-century Tating-ware pitchers, black burnished and decorated with tin-foil applications (see p 226 & Fig 7.13), occurs even further afield, having been found in Russia and at Borg, in Lofoten (northern Norway); it may either have been an admired (Christian?) souvenir or traded as a fine-ware.

Stone objects provide some of the best archaeological evidence for long-distance trade in Northern Europe: Viking period steatite vessels found on the shore at Hals Barre, Jutland, and a Mayen quernstone from the 10th-century fortress at Trelleborg, Denmark (photo: National Museum, Copenhagen).

Fig 10.7

Apart from this, pottery was mostly produced for local consumption and is rarely found outside its region of production. Only ports regularly present pottery of a mixed origin, undoubtedly used by foreigners residing there. Ceramics of more remote derivation are exceptional; among more than 100,000 sherds from Hedeby, there is only one piece of a Byzantine amphora and a few fragments of Central Asian mercury-flagons to point to contacts beyond Northern Europe (Helm 1997; Steuer 2002, 160).

In contrast to ceramics, many things that did hold significance in exchange are elusive as archaeological objects. In general, for a thing to become a regular object of trade or exchange requires that there exists an imbalance between availability and demand, and that a way can be found of overcoming this imbalance. In medieval trade, the last was often the decisive moment. For objects like furs, spices, or semi-precious stones, which were obtained from very distant sources, the limited access (and hence rarity) probably even raised the demand for them as objects of gift-exchange.

For some items the incentive for exchange was created by geographically restricted occurrence. This is true for stone tools and utensils (Fig 10.7 & Box 10.2), minerals including salt, indispensable as a foodstuff and preservative (see pp 232-4), or for iron and other metals, which were extracted only in certain regions (Magnusson 1995). In other cases, it was the production techniques that had limited availability. The secrets of making silk-cloth, swords or glass vessels, and other applied arts, were carefully guarded

BOX 10.2   STONE-TRADE

Northern Europe comprises a broad band of fertile lowland set between two mineral-rich mountain ranges – in Central Europe and along the Atlantic rim. From early on, this economic situation created important incentives for trade and exchange. Stone objects are the most durable form of archaeological evidence from the resulting relationships. Moreover, they can often be traced by petrological analysis to a specific place of origin.

Quernstones were utilitarian objects of essential value for an agrarian economy (Fig 10.7). One of the finest materials for querns in Europe, the porous basalt found in the Mayen region, south of Cologne, became a major export during the Carolingian period (Parkhouse 1997). Its distribution along the Rhine and the coastlands of the North Sea emphasises the same 'Frisian' trade-zone as the *sceattas* (Fig 1). The heavy querns were rarely transported long distances overland and are found in inland areas only along major, navigable rivers. Their virtual absence in the Baltic

Sea area is an indication that Carolingian trade was transhipped across the foot of Jutland, rather than being sailed on the risky route around the north of the peninsula.

Another characteristic material for querns was garnet-muscovite slate from Hyllestad, in western Norway. Hyllestad querns were exported from the tenth century over large parts of Northern Europe. The combination of soft slate and hard garnets gave an excellent wearing surface, which was appreciated into the twentieth century. In the Baltic Sea area, querns were often made of sandstone, which did not, however, become objects of long-distance export (Carelli & Kresten 1997).

Cooking vessels carved out of the easily workable but robust and heat-resistant steatite were in use since the Iron Age in many parts of Norway and in the Shetlands, where the stone occurs naturally. From the early decades of the ninth century, however, they were also traded on a significant scale into Denmark and southern Sweden,

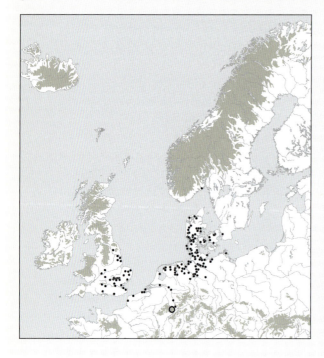

Fig 1

Quernstones of Mayen basalt found their way into the orbit of North Sea emporia during the 8th-10th centuries; their distribution traces an outline of the main coastal sailing routes of the Carolingian period, in particular (data from Parkhouse 1997; Sindbæk 2005; and personal research).

where no natural sources exist (Fig 10.7). When Norse colonists settled in the British and North Atlantic Islands in the ninth-tenth centuries, steatite bowls were also brought into these regions (Fig 2). Outside the area of Scandinavian settlement they are found only in ports, such as Ralswiek or Wolin on the South Baltic coast, presumably brought by Scandinavian sailors. The close association of steatite vessels with Scandinavians, together with the considerable effort put into transporting them over long distances, suggests that they had a significance related to cultural identity (Forster & Bond 2004). Unfortunately, no technique has yet been developed that can trace products to individual quarries.

Hones were another stone product traded in quantity. From the eighth century onwards, good quality schist hones from sources in Central Europe, the British Isles and Scandinavia increasingly replaced local stones in the lowland regions. Pet-

rological studies have identified the source of several products (e.g. Mitchell et al 1984; Resi 1990). The most characteristic type is the fine grained, and almost white, schist from Eidsborg in Telemark (southern Norway), widely distributed since the tenth century at latest (Myrvoll 1985).

A prominent example of stone-trade in the Slavic world is the spindle-whorls made of scarlet slate from the Ovruč region, north-west of Kiev (Gabriel 1988). Unlike querns, the whorls did not pose restrictions on land transport and are found across the entire Slavic world from the Volga to the Elbe, and occasionally in Scandinavia.

Even building stones were exchanged over long distances, in particular exotic stones for ornamental details: examples include the well-known 'black stones' discussed in letters between Charlemagne and King Offa (see Box 15.3).

By Søren M Sindbæk

Fig 2

Steatite vessels were traded on a significant scale during the 9th-11th centuries into Denmark and the newly-founded Norse settlements in the North Atlantic islands, but were not adopted among other groups; the dotted line encloses the area of natural occurrence (data from Resi 1979; Foster & Bond 2004, with refs; Sindbæk 2005; and personal research).

Fig 10.8 *Iron leg-shackles are rare material evidence of an important commodity in early medieval Northern Europe: slaves; this 11th-century example is from Brest, Mecklenburg, NE Germany (photo: Landesmuseum in Schwerin).*

by the workshops and the powers that possessed them. The high value of these things relative to their weight would merit transport even in small-scale cargoes, and all were exchanged throughout the Middle Ages.

Debates about the complexity of medieval economics often focus on things that were exchanged as a way of organizing production. Agrarian surplus was traded early in the form of high-value, labour-intensive products like textiles. But when did basic products like grain or wine become commodities? Both were certainly redistributed locally and were sometimes moved over long distances between the scattered holdings of Carolingian monasteries and estates (McCormick 2001, 698f). But evidence is still inconclusive as to whether an extensive grain-trade existed before the establishment of urban centres in the tenth century. The evolution of bulk cargo in particular raises discussions about a possible 'commercial revolution'.

One low-value staple product the history of which, as a commodity, is now being studied in some detail is fish (see Box 6.3). The evidence of fish-bone from archaeological sites in England shows that marine fish rapidly became available inland in the decades around 1000. The 'fish-event' may, however, be connected specifically to the introduction of preservation by salting, rather than showing a general development in the organisation of exchange.

A related class of products was manufactured goods like combs, textiles, shoes, iron objects or pottery. The raw-materials for these, and the skills for producing them, could be acquired virtually anywhere, whence their transformation into manufactured goods was motivated only as a division of labour. This signals an important step for local trade. Comb-making is widely evidenced as a pre-urban specialisation practised in local markets from the Carolingian period (Ashby 2006). Textiles were produced mostly within households, but according to standardized norms, which established certain fabrics as commodities (Jørgensen 1992; and see Chapter 7).

One final commodity of key importance in medieval trade was slaves. Slaves might be considered a higher form of agrarian surplus, yet the uncommon agency of the product, and the complexities introduced by Christian ethics, favoured procurement from distant sources, and hence long-distance trade. Although possibly the most significant European export of the early medieval period, hinted at in many written sources, the slave-trade is virtually invisible in the archaeological record (cf. Fig 10.8). The history of this aspect of early medieval European trade may yet be uncovered by future genetic studies.

BIBLIOGRAPHY

Abramson, T (2006) *Sceattas – An Illustrated Guide: Anglo-Saxon Coins and Icons,* King's Lynn

Arcamone, MG (1994) 'Una nuova iscrizione runica da Monte Sant'Angelo', in Carletti, C and Otranto, G (eds), *Culto e insediamento micaelici nell'Italia meridionale fra tarda antichità e medioevo,* Bari, 185-9

Arthur, P (2000) 'Macine intorno al Mille: Aspetti del commercio dalla Grecia e dalla Sicilia in età medievale, in Brogiolo, GP (ed), *II Congresso Nazionale di Archeologia Medievale,* Florence, 485-9.

Arthur, P (2002) *Naples from Roman Town to City-State: an Archaeological Perspective,* The British School at Rome Monograph Series 12

Ashby, SP (2006) 'Trade in Viking Age Britain: identity and the production and distribution of bone and antler combs', in Arneborg, J and Grönnow, B (eds), *Dynamics of Northern Societies,* Copenhagen, 273-9

Barnish, SJB (1991) *Cassiodorus, Variae,* Liverpool

Bass, G and Van Doorninck, FH (1982) *Yassi Ada, A Seventh Century Byzantine Shipwreck,* Texas

Berggren L, Hybel, N and Landen, A (eds) (2002) *Cogs, Cargoes, and Commerce: Maritime Bulk Trade in Northern Europe, 1150-1400,* Papers in Mediaeval Studies 15, Toronto

Berti, G and Gelichi, S (1995) 'Ceramiche, ceramisti e trasmissioni tecnologiche tra XII e XIII secolo nell'Italia centro settentrionale', in *Miscellanea in memoria di Giuliano Cremonesi,* Dipartimento di Scienze archeologiche dell'Università di Pisa, 409-45

Brather, S (1996) 'Frühmittelalterliche Dirham-Schatzfunde in Europa. Probleme ihrer wirtschaftsgeschichtlichen Interpretation aus archäologischer Perspektive', *Zeitschrift für Archäologie des Mittelalters* 23/24, 73-153

Callmer, J (1994) 'Urbanization in Scandinavia and the Baltic region c. AD 700-1100', in Ambrosiani, B and Clarke, H (eds), *Developments around the Baltic and the North Sea in the Viking Age. The Twelfth Viking Congress,* Stockholm, 50-90

Callmer, J (1995) 'The influx of oriental beads into Europe during the 8th century', in Rasmussen, M et al (eds), *Glass beads - Cultural History, Technology, Experiment and Analogy,* Lejre, 49-54

Carelli, P and Kresten, P (1997) 'Give us today our daily bread. A study of late Viking Age and medieval quernstones in South Scandinavia', *Acta Archaeologica* 68, 109-37

Carnap-Bornheim, C and Hilbert, V (2007) 'Recent archaeological research in Haithabu', in Henning, J (ed), *Post-Roman Towns, Trade and Settlement in Europe and Byzantium, Vol 1. The Heirs of the Roman West,* Berlin/New York

Es, WA van and Verwers, WHJ (2002) 'Aufstieg, Blüte und Niedergang der frühmittelalterlichen Handelsmetropole Dorestad', in Brandt, K, Müller-Wille, M and Radtke, C (eds), *Haithabu und die frühe Stadtentwicklung im nördlichen Europa,* Neumünster, 281-302

Fentress, E and Perkins, P (1988) 'Counting African Red Slip Ware', *Africa Romana* 5, 205-14

Forster, AK and Bond, JM (2004) 'North Atlantic networks: preliminary research into the trade of steatite in the Viking and Norse periods', in Housley, RA and Coles, G (eds), *Atlantic Connections and Adaptations. Economies, Environments and Subsistence in Lands bordering the North Atlantic',* Oxford, 218-29

Francovich, R (ed) (1993) *Archeologia delle attività estrattive e metallurgiche,* Florence

Gabriel, I (1988) 'Hof- und Sakralkultur sowie Gebrauchs- und Handelsgut im Spiegel der Kleinfunde von Starigard/Oldenburg', *Bericht der Römisch-Germanischen Kommission* 69, 103-291

Gelichi, S (2006) 'Venezia tra archeologia e storia: la costruzione di un'identità urbana', in Augenti, A (ed), *Le città italiane tra la tarda antichità e l'alto medioevo. Atti del convegno (Ravenna, 26-28 febbraio 2004),* Florence, 151-83

Goitien, SD (1967) *A Mediterranean Society, The Jewish Communities of the Arab World as portrayed in the Documents of the Cairo Geniza,* Vol 1, Berkeley/Los Angeles

Graham-Campbell, J and Williams, G (eds) (2007) *Silver Economy in the Viking Age,* Walnut Creek, CA

Haldon, JF (1990) *Byzantium in the Seventh Century. The Transformation of a Culture,* Cambridge

Hall RA (2000) 'The decline of the Wic?', in Slater, TR (ed), *Towns in Decline, AD 100-1600,* Ashgate, 120-136

Hayes, JW (1972) *Late Roman Pottery,* London

Helm, R (1997) 'Eine byzantinische Amphorenscherbe aus Haithabu', *Archäologisches Korrespondenzblatt* 27, 185-8

Hendy, MF (1985) *Studies in the Byzantine Monetary Economy c. 300-1450,* Cambridge

Hodges, R (1988) *Primitive and Peasant Markets,* London

Hodges, R (2006) *Goodbye to the Vikings? Re-reading Early Medieval Archaeology,* London

Hodges, R and Mitchell, J (1985) *San Vincenzo al Volturno. The Archaeology, Art and Territory of an Early Medieval Monastery,* Oxford

Hårdh, B (1996) *Silver in the Viking Age. A Regional-Economic Study,* Acta Archaeologica Lundensia, series in 8°, 25, Stockholm

Jørgensen, LB (1992) *North European Textiles until AD 1000*, Aarhus

Kilger, C (2000) *Pfennigmärkte und Währungsland-schaften. Monetarisierungen im sächsisch-slawischen Grenzland ca. 965-1120*, Commentationes de nummis saeculorum IX-XI in Suecia repertis, Nova series 15, Stockholm

Knific, T (1994) 'Vranje near Sevnica: a late Roman settlement in the light of certain pottery finds', *ArhVest* 45, 211-37

Krumphanzlová, Z (1992) 'Amber, its significance in the early middle ages', *Památky Archeologické* 83, 350-71

Lopez, RS (1976) *The Commercial Revolution of the Middle Ages, 950-1350*, Cambridge

Loveluck, C (1998) 'A high status Anglo-Saxon settle-ment at Flixborough, Lincolnshire', *Antiquity* 72, 146-61

Lüdtke, H and Schietzel, K (eds) (2001) *Handbuch zur mittelalterlichen Keramik in Nordeuropa*, Vols 1-3, Neumünster

Magnusson, G (1995) 'Iron production, smithing and iron trade in the Baltic during the late Iron Age and early Middle Ages (c.5th-13th Centuries)', in Jansson, I (ed), *Archaeology East and West of the Baltic. Papers from the Second Estonian - Swedish Archaeological Symposium. Sigtuna, May 1991*, Stockholm, 61-70

Mannoni, T and Murialdo, G (eds) (2001) *S. Antonino: un insediamento fortificato nella Liguria Bizantina*, 2 vols, Istituto Internazionale di Studi Liguri, Collezione di monografie preistoriche ed archeo-logiche 12, Bordighera

Martin, J (1986) *Treasure of the Land of Darkness. The Fur Trade and its Significance for Medieval Russia*, Cambridge

McCormick, M (2001) *The Origins of the European Economy: Communications and Commerce, c.300-c.900*, Cambridge

Mitchell, JG, Asvik, H and Resi, HG (1984) 'Potas-sium-argon ages of schist honestones from the Viking Age sites at Kaupang (Norway), Aggersborg (Denmark), Hedeby (West Germany) and Wolin (Poland), and their archaeological implications', *Journal of Archaeological Science* 11, 171-6

Myrvoll, S (1985) 'The trade in Eidsborg hones over Skien in the medieval period', *Iskos* 5, 31-47

Naylor, J (2004) *An Archaeology of Trade in Middle Saxon England*, British Archaeological Research Reports, British Series 376, Oxford

Noonan, TS (1998) *The Islamic World, Russia and the Vikings, 750-900: the Numismatic Evidence*, Aldershot/Brookfield

Nosov, EN (1993) 'The problem of the emergence of early urban centres in Northern Russia', in Chapman, J and Dolukhanov, PM (eds), *Cultural Transformations and Interactions in Eastern Europe*, Aldershot, 236-56

Näsman, U (2000) 'Exchange and politics: the eighth-early ninth century in Denmark', in Wickham, C and Lyse Hansen, I (eds), *The Long Eighth Century. Production, Distribution and Demand*, The Trans-formation of the Roman World 11, Leiden, 35-68

Panella, C (1993) 'Merci e scambi nel Mediterraneo tardoantico', in *Storia di Roma 3, L'Età tardoantica, II. I luoghi e le culture*, Turin, 613-97

Panella, C and Saguì, L (2001) 'Consumo e produzione a Roma tra tardoantico e altomedioevo: le merci, i contesti', in *Roma nell'Alto Medioevo, XLVIII Setti-mane di Studio del Centro italiano di Studi sull'Alto Medioevo*, Spoleto, 757-820

Parkhouse, J (1997) 'The distribution and exchange of Mayen lava quernstones in early medieval North-west Europe', in Boe, G de and Verhaeghe, F (eds), *Exchange and Trade in Medieval Europe. Papers of the 'Medieval Europe Brugge 1997' Conference*, Vol 3, Zellik, 97-106

Pestell, T and Ulmschneider, K (eds) (2003) *Markets in Early Medieval Europe. Trading and 'Productive' sites, 650-850*, Macclesfield

Piccirillo, M (1986) *Um Er-Rasas Kastron Mefaa*, Jerusalem

Pirenne, H (1937) *Mahomet et Charlemagne*, Brussels

Rautman, M (1998) 'Hand-made pottery and social change: the view from Late Roman Cyprus', *Journal of Mediterranean Archaeology* 11, 81-104

Resi, HG (1979) *Die Specksteinfunde aus Haithabu*, Berichte über die Ausgrabungen in Haithabu 14, Neumünster

Resi, HG (1990) *Die Wetz- und Schleifsteine aus Haithabu*, Berichte über die Ausgrabungen in Haithabu 28, Neumünster

Riley, JA (1979) 'The Coarse Pottery from Berenice', in Lloyd, J (ed), *Excavations at Sidi Khrebish, Beng-hazi (Berenice) II, Supp. to Libya Antiqua* 5, 91-467

Roesdahl, E (2003) 'Walrus ivory and other northern luxuries: their importance for Norse voyages and settlements in Greenland and America', in Lewis-Simpson, S (ed), *Vínland Revisited: the Norse World at the Turn of the First Millennium*, St Johns, 145-52

Rybina, EA (1999) 'Trade of Novgorod in the 10th-15th centuries established through archaeological data', in Gläser, M (ed), *Lübecker Kolloquium zur Stad-tarchäologie im Hanseraum II: Der Handel*, Lübeck, 447-56

Saguì, L and Manacorda, D (1995) 'L'esedra della Crypta Balbi e il Monastero di S. Lorenzo in Pallacinis', *Archeologia Laziale* 12:1, 121-34

Sedikova, L, Arthur, P, Yashaeva, T and Carter, JC (2003) 'Medieval Chersonesos', in Mack, G and Carter, JC (eds), *Crimean Chersonesos, City, Chora, Museum, and Environs*, Texas, 29-40

Sindbæk, SM (2005) *Ruter og rutinisering. Vikingetidens fjernhandel i Nordeuropa,* Copenhagen.

Sindbæk, SM (2007) 'Networks and nodal points: the emergence of towns in Early Viking Age Scandinavia', *Antiquity* 81, 119-32

Spufford, P (1988) *Money and its Use in Medieval Europe*, Cambridge

Steuer, H, Stern, WB and Goldberg, G (2002) 'Der Wechsel von der Münzgeld- zur Gewichtsgeldwirtschaft um 900 und die Herkunft des Münzsilbers im 9. und 10. Jahrhundert', in Brandt, K, Müller-Wille, M and Radtke, C (eds), *Haithabu und die frühe Stadtentwicklung im nördlichen Europa*, Neumünster, 133-67

Steuer, H (2005) 'Minting, silver routes and mining in Europe: economic expansion and technical innovation', in Heitzmann, J and Schenkluhn, W (eds), *The World in the Year 1000*, Lanham/New York/Oxford, 105-17

Theuws, F (2004) 'Exchange, religion, identity and central places in the early Middle Ages', *Archaeological Dialogues* 10:2, 121-38

Tobler, T (ed) (1874) *Vita seu potius hodoeporicon sancti Willibaldi - Commemoratorium de casis Dei vel monasteriis - Itinerarium Bernardi, monachi franci. Descriptiones terrae sanctae: ex saeculo VIII, IX, XII et XV,* Leipzig (reprinted 1974; Hildesheim/New York)

Ulriksen, J (1994) 'Danish sites and settlements with a maritime context, AD 200-1200', *Antiquity* 67, 797-811

Verhulst, A (2002) *The Carolingian Economy*, Cambridge

Ward-Perkins, B (2005) *The Fall of Rome and the End of Civilisation*, Oxford

Wartburg, M-L von (1995) 'Production du sucre de canne à Chypre: un chapitre de technologie médiévale', in Balard, M and Ducellier, A (eds), *Coloniser au moyen âge*, Paris, 126-31

CHAPTER 11

FORTIFICATIONS

Johnny De Meulemeester and Kieran O'Conor

Introduction

This chapter examines the evidence for fortifications in Europe from c700 to c1200. This is an important period in the development of fortifications, as castles evolve during this period as a result of the fragmentation of the centralised Carolingian Empire in the middle years of the ninth century, along with the parallel and subsequent development of feudalism. However, it must be stated that this chapter also looks at other forms of fortification during these five centuries, such as refuge-sites, princely residences, linear territorial defences and defended, early town walls rural sites.

Comprehensive publications dealing with the broad subject of fortifications in Europe during the period under review are few. It is clear that the evidence for this topic could be covered by a full book in order to do the subject proper justice. However, it is hoped, within the limited space available, to give an overview of the main types of fortification in use from the early eighth century through to the late twelfth century across large areas of the Continent – with particularly emphasis on North-West and Central Europe.

In general, a thematic approach is taken in this chapter, rather than a chronological one. Different types of fortification are discussed under broad headings, but this also has its problems. Many types of fortification had overlapping functions or could evolve over time into something different from their original role, e.g. the distinction between private defence (i.e. castles) and public defence (i.e. royal fortifications designed to defend or hold territories) is often blurred. It must also be said that various types of castles are not the only fortified private residences in use during the whole period under review. This can cause confusion as it is sometimes difficult to ascertain exactly when a fortified residence should be described as a castle or not. Again, many refuge-sites designed for communal defence eventually became private residential castles.

Communal Fortifications

Refuge-sites

Refuge-sites are forts that were not usually designed for permanent habitation but instead functioned, across Europe primarily as places temporarily occupied by local

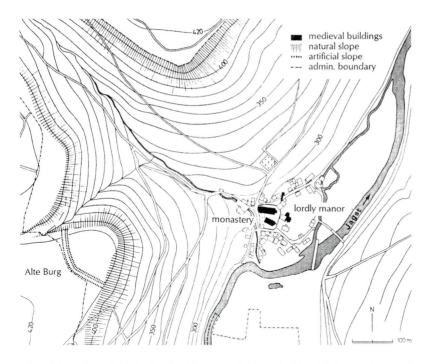

Plan of the refuge-site (Alte Burg) at Unterregenbach, Kreis Schwäbisch Hall (Germany), showing its topographical location (after Fehring 1991).

Fig 11.1

populations and their livestock in times of war and strife. Refuge-sites can be varied in terms of their morphology: some can effectively be hill-forts, while others are large circular enclosures on relatively level ground, or can be inland or coastal promontory-forts. Most have earth-and-timber defences and can have a large internal area. Some refuge-sites re-use older Roman and even pre- and protohistoric sites.

The promontory-fort at Unterregenbach (Stadt Langenburg, Kreis Schwäbisch Hall, Germany) is an example of a refuge-site (Fig 11.1). Like many such places, it is located in a remote position away from major route-ways. This site came into existence during the eighth or ninth century as a protection for local people against raiding. It continued to function as a defence against Magyar attack in the tenth century and seems to have been abandoned in the eleventh century. Excavation at the site found little evidence for buildings or finds, and this is a common feature of refuge-sites (Fehring 1991, 137-9).

The ninth century in France, the Benelux and western Germany was the period of the Viking invasions. Initially, the authorities were slow to react to this new threat. Towards the end of the century, however, defence against the Vikings is clearly coordinated in these areas by local territorial princes and lords. From texts, we know that by the end of the ninth century some hill-forts were constructed to act as refuges. For example, when the Vikings invaded the area between the Rhine and the Meuse in 883, the monks of Stavelot Abbey in the Belgian Ardennes found refuge in a fortification at Logne (De Meulemeester 1995, 37; D'Haenens 1967, 110-21, 312-5; Hoffsummer, Hoffsummer-

Bosson & Wery 1987). In the Ardennes, as in several other areas between the Loire and the Rhine and beyond, excavation has demonstrated that many prehistoric sites and late Roman forts were reoccupied as refuges from the seventh century onwards. Some of these sites were clearly re-fortified during the late ninth and tenth centuries as a precaution, initially, against Viking raids and later to counter the threat of Magyar attacks (which actually never came).

A specific type of refuge fortification developed in coastal areas from northern France to Holland from the late ninth century onwards to counter Viking attacks and general raiding. This type of refuge-site consisted of a large circular ditched and banked enclosure. Such circular enclosures were relatively simple to design, as only a pole and rope were needed to trace their layout. It might be added that large circular earthwork fortifications such as this were also common in northern Germany and further eastwards, in Slavic territory, from the sixth and seventh centuries onwards. Anyway, along the whole North Sea coast, territorial princes and local authorities began to build such circular fortresses to protect local people against Viking raids, e.g the series of circular-shaped fortresses, defined by wide ramparts and great ditches, built as refuge-sites along the Flemish and Zeeland coasts at this time. These camps are large in size, being 140-265m in diameter (Janssen 1990, 220-6; van Heeringen 1998).

Historical research, and the evidence from the excavation of some of these sites in Belgium and the Netherlands, suggests that many of these fortifications were never permanently occupied (van Heeringen 1998, 246-7), functioning purely as refuges for local populations. However, excavations at Vourne (west Belgian coast) and Oost-Souburg (Zeeland) suggest that these sites were seemingly continuously occupied from the tenth century through to the twelfth century. Indeed, some coastal refuge-sites, such as the latter site, eventually became towns.

Early State Fortifications

Garrisoned fortresses

These are defined as fortifications built in rural areas as places designed to house garrisons whose function was to defend or hold the territories of their rulers and which were not intended to have any private residential function.

The traditional view amongst scholars was that the Carolingians built little in the way of fixed fortifications, particularly Charlemagne (742-814) during his long 46-year reign. It was always believed that other methods, both political and military, were used by the latter to control his empire and defend its borders, as well as settling newly-conquered territories (e.g. Anderson 1970, 37). Nevertheless, recent historical and archaeological research has shown that this view is only partly correct, as there is evidence to suggest that Charlemagne did build fortifications to defend his lands, particularly his borders. For example, possibly following Roman precedents, it appears that he ordered the building of fortified guard-posts along the coast of the Low Countries, particularly beside harbours and river mouths, to watch out for Viking raiders (van Heeringen 1998,

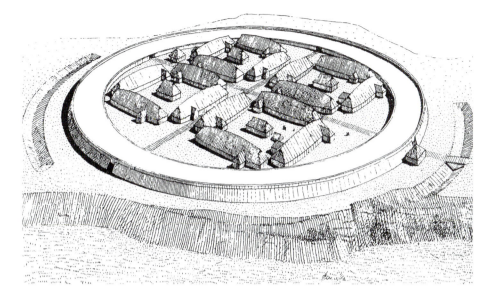

A reconstruction of the circular 'Trelleborg fortress' at Fyrkat, Jutland, Denmark (drawing: H Schmidt). **Fig 11.2**

243; Nicholson 2004, 75). In what is now Germany, Charlemagne and his successors also used fortifications to keep down the Saxons and control the Slavs. These included rectangular, banked and ditched, enclosures in West Saxony. Smaller, circular enclosures, defined by a bank, ditch and palisade, were used by the Carolingians east of the Weser (Anderson 1970, 37). The Saxons themselves had similar 'ring-fort' type fortifications, as did the Slavs (Anderson 1970, 37). It is clear that powerful monarchs at this early date, like Charlemagne, saw the importance of strong fortifications as border defences.

Among the best known fortifications of this type are the Danish circular, banked and ditched, enclosures; these were 120-240m in diameter and are known as the 'geometrical fortresses' because planned with astonishing exactness (Fig 11.2). On the evidence of dendrochronology, they were built by King Harald Bluetooth in the late tenth century and their main purpose was to house garrisons whose primary function was to enforce the king's rule during a period of unrest. Notably, these fortresses are located on important inland routes, which would have given their garrisons easy access to all parts of Denmark (Roesdahl 1987; 1991, 136-40), but they had already fallen out of use by the beginning of the eleventh century. It is clear that these 'Trelleborg fortresses' bear close similarity in size and design to the earlier refuge-sites mentioned above as being built along the French, Belgium and Dutch coasts to counter the threat of Viking attacks.

Linear fortifications and territorial defences

There is a long tradition in Europe, which stretches back into prehistory, of tribal groups and early states building great linear lines of defence in order to protect their territories against attack and to mark the boundaries of their lands. The defences of these frontier fortifications mostly consisted of earthen banks, palisades and ditches, but in the Roman period mortared stone walls were used as well (Anderson 1970, 22-4; Nicholson 2004, 71-3).

Linear earthworks defending territories and early kingdoms were also built between the eighth and late twelfth century. The best studied examples of this form of fortification from this period are the Danevirke, in Schleswig-Holstein in northern Germany, which marked the frontier of the old Danish kingdom, and Offa's Dyke, along the border of England with Wales, which was largely built in the late eighth century (Andersen 2001; Hill 2000; 2001; Roesdahl 1991, 132-6). The evidence from these linear earthworks, both of which stretch for many kilometres, shows that rulers and early kingdoms had the organisational ability to construct major territorial defences as early as the seventh-ninth centuries.

Proto-urban and urban fortifications

One function of fortification around towns was obviously to protect the inhabitants of these places from attack and to safeguard their wealth. It is also clear that many fortified towns acted as temporary refuges for people from the surrounding countryside during periods of war and unrest. Increasingly, however, particularly from the eleventh century onwards when there was a revival of urban life, town walls of stone or timber also marked judicial boundaries, within which their inhabitants had control over much of their legal and economic affairs.

Proto-urban or urban defences in use during the period from c700-1200 can arguably be divided into three types: (1) old Roman town walls that were repaired and rebuilt; (2) urban and proto-urban settlements that had always had earth and timber defences; and (3) towns that had stone walls built around them, either for the first time, or to completely replace older fortifications of timber or late Roman masonry.

Many Roman towns throughout Western Europe were fortified in the aftermath of the third-century barbarian invasions, particularly during the reign of the Emperor Constantine in the early fourth century. Clearly influenced by the earlier fortifications of Greece and the Middle East, late Roman urban fortifications had many of the main defensive features that were to be associated with the apogee of medieval castles and town defences during the thirteenth century. These Roman defences included high curtain walls with crenellations, and these often had round or D-shaped towers jutting out from them to offer flanking defence. Twin-towered gatehouses with portcullises and heavy wooden gateways in their passages were also known (Anderson 1970, 20-8; Nicholson 2004, 69-71). For example, the Porta Nigra at Trier (in modern Germany), built c300, is a well-known example of a late Roman urban gate-house that is still standing (Anderson 1970, 27).

During the fourth- to sixth-century decline in urban life, towns were often reduced both in size and importance until c1000, after which there was a recovery (see Chapter 4). Gregory of Tours, writing at the end of the sixth century, clearly shows that many of the towns and cities of Gaul still had functioning Roman walls (Nicholson 2004, 70). This situation remained, as it is clear that Roman town walls continued to be used and repaired throughout the medieval period across Europe, although possibly allowed to fall into disuse during times of peace. It is held (e.g. Nicholson 2004, 74-75) that the defences of many Roman towns fell into decay during the long, relatively peaceful reign of Charlemagne (771-814). The fortifications around these towns were then repaired, from the early ninth century onwards, as a defence against the Vikings and to counter the instability created by the break-up of the Carolingian Empire. In England, for example, King Alfred of Wessex re-established his rule after 878 partly by building fortified *burhs* in strategic places in order to counter the Viking threat. Many of these *burhs* were founded as, or grew into, fortified towns (Nicholson 2004, 76). Despite the strong Anglo-Saxon tradition of building in timber, many of the *burhs* built by Alfred and his successors were former Roman towns, with their old masonry defences being reused (ibid). Roman towns across southern France, Spain and Italy also upgraded their defences during the course of the eighth century to counter Moorish raids and invasions from North Africa. The decline in size and population of many Roman towns after the fourth century meant that these were sometimes so reduced by the eighth century and later to smaller nuclei that they only utilised a corner of the late Roman defences, requiring new walls to be erected in these places using robbed stones from abandoned buildings.

The archaeological and historical evidence also makes it clear, however, that many early towns and quasi-urban settlements during the whole period under discussion (and far later) were defended by earth-and-timber fortifications – most often a bank, palisade and external ditch. Mostly these defences were not superceded by masonry fortifications and could be rebuilt in earth and timber again and again for centuries. The surviving Viking period defences of Hedeby, at the eastern end of the Danevirke, are still impressive today, consisting of a 1,400m long, 4-5m high and 5-10m wide earthen bank, with an external ditch, which defends a semi-circular area 24ha in extent (Box 4.3). This tenth-century fortification was the result of a number of periods of construction, with its final phase seemingly built by King Harald Bluetooth, mentioned above (Jankuhn 1986; Roesdahl 1991, 120-3).

By the eighth century, many early monasteries had begun to take on proto-urban status, especially in the parts of Europe that lay outside the bounds of the old Roman Empire. The growth in warfare and raiding from the ninth century onwards led to many of these places becoming fortified. In Ireland, for example, the supposedly tenth-century fortifications around what was the monastic town of Seirkieran, Co Offaly, enclose an area of 12ha and consist of two banks, 7-10m wide and 2m high, which were presumably originally surmounted by a substantial palisade, and two 3m-deep ditches (Bradley 1995, 8). Such monasteries presumably also acted as refuges during times of trouble for ordinary lay-folk who lived in their vicinities. In all, the evidence suggests that many towns (and some agricultural villages) across Europe possessed timber fortifications from the eighth century onwards.

Purpose-built masonry walls around towns were also constructed during the period under review, e.g. in England, Aethelred II founded a town about 1010 within the defences of a deserted Iron-age hill-fort at Cadbury Castle, Somerset (Alcock 1994). The original earthen perimeter bank of this site (which had been refortified and briefly reoccupied during the late fifth and early sixth centuries) was faced externally with a substantial mortared masonry wall, with arched gateways. The defences of the town of Avila, Spain, which consisted of a high masonry wall with 88 circular towers projecting from its length, may be as early as the 1090s, although this is a matter of some debate (Bevan 1950, 176).

The gradual revival in urban life from c1000 was partly due to greater stability in society and this led in turn to increased economic productivity, a growth in trade and a rise in population. This demographic and economic growth allowed many towns across Europe to replace their old Roman fortifications, or timber defences from the Viking period, with new stone walls. In many cases, this was due to a need to protect new suburbs that had grown up beyond the line of the old walls, e.g. Paris replaced its old Roman defences in the years 1190-1215, during the reign of Philip Augustus, who was an innovative military architect in his own right (Mesqui 1991, 225). A new town wall was built that included massive round towers along its length. Dublin replaced its earth-and-timber defences, which were originally built by the Vikings (in c925; re-built and extended c1000), with a 3.5m-high stone wall during the period 1100-30, enclosing an area of 12ha (Bradley 1985, 10).

The new stone walls put up around towns across Europe, during the course of the twelfth century or earlier (e.g. Dublin), were not in any way as defensively complex as Avila, the fortifications of which stand out as being extremely innovative for the time (but may have been incorrectly dated). Nevertheless, these towns protected by relatively simple masonry defences and, indeed, ones fortified in timber as well were capable of resisting attack, if their walls were adequately and, just as importantly, stoutly manned; e.g. Dublin was besieged for two months in 1171, successfully holding out (Otway-Ruthven 1968, 47). Such sieges demonstrate that town defences were not just for show or built only for the sake of civic prestige; they were also capable of being defended against serious attack.

Other communal or early state fortifications

Sea and river barriers were also erected as fortifications during this period, a well-known example of this being documented in the (864) *Capitulary of Pîtres*, when Charles the Bald ordered the construction of fortified bridges on the Seine and Marne. These barriers were intended to block the Viking fleets trying to make their way up these rivers (Anderson 1970, 38; Nicholson 2004, 75).

The Vikings themselves also built strong temporary and permanent fortifications known as *longphorts*, erected to protect them and their ships from attack and to act as fortified bases from which to raid surrounding territories. Recent research, however, suggests that these places also functioned as trading-centres from the beginning and were not just erected for raiding purposes. These Viking forts were often located on estuaries and beside safe harbours, or on coastal, riverine and lacustrine islands (Anderson 1970,

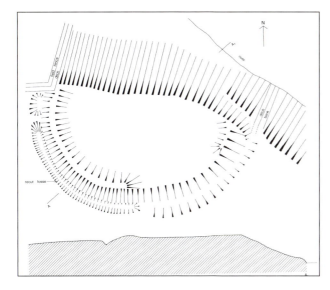

Plan of the cliff-edge fort at Linns, Annagassan, Ireland (after Buckley & Sweetman 1991). **Fig 11.3**

38-9; Nicholson 2004, 76-7). Viking fortifications were also often located on the borders of territories and kingdoms, e.g. the *longphort* established in 841 at Linn Duachaill (modern Annagassan, Co Louth) in Ireland, beside a monastery, was located on the border between two territories; it was in permanent use at least into the 920s. This *longphort* is traditionally associated with the cliff-edge fort at Linns, Annagassan, above the estuary of the River Glyde, on the southern side of Dundalk Bay (Fig 11.3; Buckley & Sweetman 1991, 95, 97-8).

As noted above, some monasteries during this period had taken on semi-urban status and some at least of these places carried defences. Stone churches and their surrounding cemeteries could readily be turned into fortifications and used as refuges for their congregations, e.g. Lisbon Cathedral was built in the twelfth century as a fortified building, like a number of other cathedrals in Portugal (Lepage 2002, 33). Likewise, the masonry church at Saintes-Maries-de-la-Mer, in the Camargue region of southern France, was built and fortified against the Moors in 1144. It included a bell-tower built rather like a keep, and the main body of the church, with its thick walls and narrow openings, was also capable of defence (ibid, 31).

Private Fortifications

Castles

The accepted definition of a castle is that it was the defended residence of a lord, who could range in rank from a king or high aristocrat to a minor knight. Simply, a castle (which could be constructed of earth and timber as well as stone) was the defended home of someone of lordly status (e.g. Anderson 1970, 17; King 1988, 1-13). The authors of this chapter feel that this definition is essentially correct, but still in need of further explanation in the light of recent research.

The origins of castles are connected to the rise of a new aristocracy, whose wealth and position were based on the control of land, who came to power in the area between the Loire and the Rhine during the course of the late ninth and tenth centuries (Anderson 1970, 17-18; McNeill 2001, 43). This period saw the genesis of the social structure known to historians from the nineteenth century onwards as feudalism – a term that is still valid but, nevertheless, unpopular with certain modern historians (e.g. EAR Brown and S Reynolds), if only because it was never used during the Middle Ages. These new men came to prominence at a local level due to the instability caused by Viking attacks and, especially, to the linked collapse of the centralised Carolingian Empire in the years after the death of Louis the Pious in 841. Such men needed castles to hold their lands and protect their families and retainers. It must be stated, however, that the first definite archaeological evidence for structures that scholars accept as castles only comes in the second half of the tenth and early eleventh centuries. At this time castles (in their various forms) seem to have been built exclusively by kings and members of the high aristocracy. Lesser lords, including comparatively humble knights, copying their social superiors, only began to build castles in great numbers during the second half of the eleventh and throughout the twelfth century (see Higham & Barker 1992, 78-111). This was the period of the 'castral revolution' that transformed the landscape of large parts of Europe (ibid, 96). There seems to be a link at this time between castle building in regions such as Normandy and the adoption of primogeniture by knightly families and the concomitant growth of landed estates (ibid, 100).

This is the accepted view of castle origins and development that still holds. However, as will be shown below, fortified residences, lived in by kings, nobles of all ranks and freemen, that are not defined as castles, despite having had many similar social and political functions to them, existed across Europe throughout this period, as well as before and after it. It is argued here that castles were, in some way, fortified private homes, but that not all defended private residences were castles. Private fortification and feudalism do not necessarily go hand in hand, as was once considered axiomatic by scholars of the medieval period. Private fortified residences can exist in kin-based societies (e.g. Ireland) from an early period, long before the ninth-tenth centuries (Edwards 1990, 6-68; Stout 1997).

What then were the essential differences between various types of castle and other forms of earlier or contemporary fortified residences? The present writers believe that the main features of castles (including timber ones) relate to the fact that the combined literary, historical, pictorial and archaeological evidence from across Europe suggests that they carried more serious defences and were more structurally complex than other types of defended residence. This becomes particularly apparent after c1100, but it is visible earlier. Overall, it is felt that castles were potentially capable of resisting sustained attack in a way that other defended residences were not. Perhaps a better, but still similar definition of a castle, to the one outlined above, is that it was the seriously-defended residence of a man of lordly rank.

The fact that castles were lordly residences meant that they were the administrative centres of their owners' estates, but so too were other private fortresses. It is also clear that castles were an important means by which the medieval lordly class displayed their status and wealth to the world (cf. Chapter 12). It might be added that recent research, especially in England, has questioned the defensibility of many castles. This new view is that castles were primarily erected as vehicles for social display, rather than for defence, and were often surrounded by landscapes designed to reinforce this impression (e.g. Coulson 2003; Creighton 2002; Liddiard 2000). This observation is clearly important and helps to explain why castles (including timber ones) tend to be more complex in terms of the size and number of buildings within them when compared with other forms of private defended residence. Nevertheless, the present writers feel that this argument has tended to be over-emphasised at times and only suits certain areas of Europe. The majority of castles were designed to defend their inhabitants against attack, and it must be admitted that even the less-fortified examples had greater defences in comparison with other forms of fortified private residence, such as *crannógs* or moated sites.

Castles can be divided into two basic types during the period under discussion: masonry castles and earthwork castles, a simple division based on the materials used to build these fortresses – and not on function. There are two major types of earthwork castle: the motte and the ring-work.

Motte castles and ring-work castles

Mottes appear in the landscape today as mounds of earth, on average c5m in height above ground level and usually, but not always, circular in shape, with flat summits and surrounded by deep ditches around their bases. Often a ditched and embanked enclosure known as a bailey was attached to the base of the motte, being rectangular or crescentic in shape, although other forms also exist (Fig 11.4). Most ring-works appear today as circular areas, c30-60m in diameter, which are defined by an earthen bank and ditch (Fig 11.5; e.g. Higham & Barker 1992, 194-243; King 1988, 42-61). Some ring-works also had baileys associated with them, e.g. that at Cefn Bryntalch, in Wales (Higham & Barker 1992, 209). Some ring-works, however, were located on sites imbued with strong natural defences, such as ridge-ends, along cliff-tops or on coastal or inland promontories. Such sites only required strong artificial defences on their landward sides (i.e. an earthen bank, palisade and ditch). These are known as partial ring-works (King 1988, 57). The original defences and buildings associated with mottes and ring-works were made of timber or clay and wood (e.g. Higham & Barker 1992, 244-325; 2000; O'Conor 2002, 175-80).

Ring-works are clearly related in terms of their morphology to the earlier refuge-sites and 'Trelleborg-type' fortresses discussed above, and also to the earlier and, indeed, contemporary 'ring-fort' type enclosures to be discussed below. What were the differences between ring-works and these other forms of fortification? Certainly ring-works were far smaller in size to most refuge-sites and were not designed for communal defence, being the homes of individual lords, their families and trusted retainers. Other types of private fortified residences, such as ring-forts in Ireland (Fig. 2.4), existed that look similar to ring-works but were not regarded as castles (O'Conor 2002, 177). In this

Fig 11.4   *Elsdon motte-and-bailey castle, Northumberland, England (photo: Museum of Antiquities, University of Newcastle upon Tyne).*

respect, as castles, ring-works were often located in defensive locations and their earth-works are generally more massive in comparison to other types of circular enclosure that housed private residences. Most importantly, excavated evidence from across Western Europe, backed up by historical research, suggests that the timber defences seen on ring-works were more complex than those seen on other forms of defended enclosure. Simply, being castles, ring-works were better defended in comparison to different types of ring-fort. It is felt that that the main defensive elements associated with ring-works were its timber gate-towers and possibly wooden keeps (Kenyon 1990, 23-9). Even quite ordinary-looking ring-works, built and occupied by relatively lowly lords, could be quite defensive, as shown by the excavation of one at Heinstert (Belgium) which produced evidence for a possible two- (if not three-) storeyed wooden keep within its defences (De Meulemeester & Dhaeze 2006).

Pictorial and historical evidence, as well as excavation, suggest that many mottes carried serious defences, such as wooden towers on their summits and along the bai-ley, with strong palisades looped for archery (O'Conor 2002, 175-80). For example, the long-term research excavation of the motte-and-bailey castle of Hen Domen (Wales) produced evidence for complex timber defences (Higham & Barker 1992, 326-47; 2000). These included towers at intervals along the line of its reinforced bailey pali-sade and an internal line of defence built across the latter enclosure; evidence for succes-sive timber towers was found on the summit of the motte (see Box 11.1). In some cases (e.g. Clough Castle, Ireland), the peripheral defences around motte summits consisted of thick cob walls with a post-and-wattle frame instead of straightforward timber pali-sades (Higham & Barker 1992, 318-19). It would also appear that some mottes were com-

326 *Medieval Archaeology*

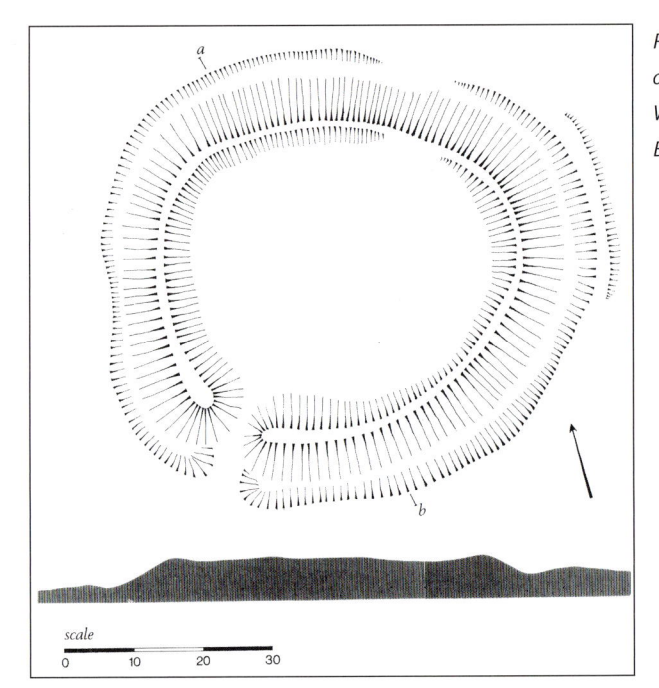

Plan of the ring-work castle at Y Gaer, Glamorgan, Wales (after Higham & Barker 1992).

Fig 11.5

pletely reveted with vertical timbers, giving them a drum-like appearance; this would have added greatly to their defensibility (Kenyon 1990, 11 & 22). The motte at South Mimms, Hertfordshire, England, built in the mid-twelfth century, was such a motte and its mound was reveted with timber shuttering (Fig 11.6; Kent 1968). Even unimportant mottes, lived in by relatively humble lords, could have quite strong defences, e.g. the excavated evidence from the motte at Lismahon (Ireland) shows that the edges of the mound summit had a palisade, with arrow-loops, and at least one tower (but possibly more) along its length (O'Conor 2002, 178-9).

Mottes seem to have been the most popular form of earthwork castle. For example, there are four times as many mottes to be seen in England and Wales today than ring-works (King 1988, 42), although this statement needs to be qualified somewhat. Excavation shows that some mottes and masonry castles had ring-work precursors – strongly suggesting that there were once more examples of the latter form of castle than it now appears (Kenyon 1990, 29). Nevertheless, despite this caveat, the overall evidence still suggests that far more mottes were erected than ring-works.

Exactly why mottes were more popular than ring-works is unclear. It has been suggested that the choice of one type of earthwork castle over another may simply have been a matter of personal preference (King 1988, 42-3). In this respect, lesser lords may have decided to copy the form of castle lived in by their immediate social superiors (ibid). Mottes took longer to build and were therefore more costly than ring-works, simply because their erection took far more effort in terms of skill and earth moving (Kenyon 1990, 7). This fact may have led many lords to choose the ring-work as their choice of earthwork castle. Also, certain sites with very strong natural defences may have

BOX 11.1   HEN DOMEN, WALES

Hen Domen is the site of the first Montgomery castle, built by Roger de Montgomery, the Norman earl of Shrewsbury. He established it during his economic revival of the western fringe of his English territory and as a base for conquests in Wales beyond the river Severn. It was mentioned in Domesday Book (1086) as the centre of a border castlery, and was held by the Montgomery family until the early twelfth century, when all their estates were confiscated by King Henry I. Thereafter, until 1207, it was the focus of a small marcher lordship held by the de Boulers, a family of Flemish origin, to whom Henry I gave the castle and its territory. This family died out in 1207, after which the castle was in royal hands, then briefly occupied by a conquering Welsh prince. In 1223, King Henry III replaced it with a new castle, a mile away, where a new town was soon founded,

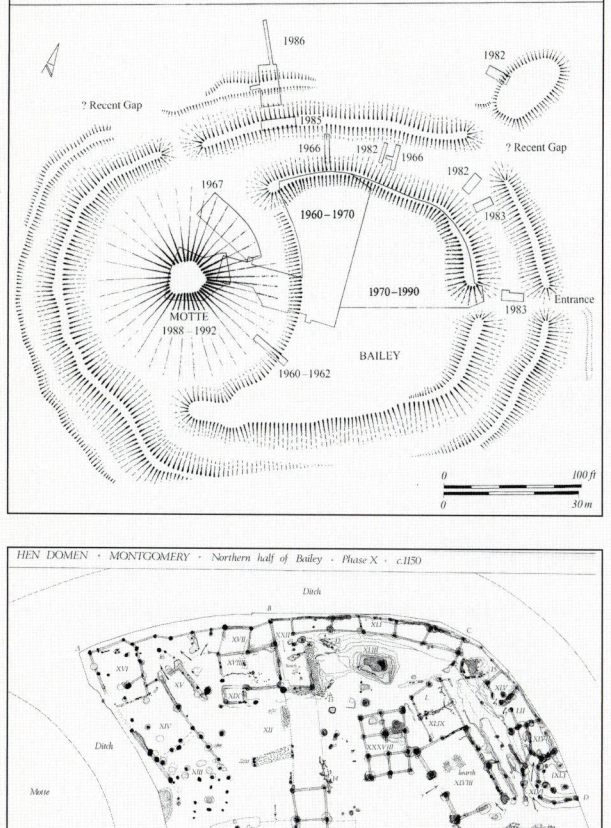

Fig 1

Plan of Hen Domen, showing areas excavated (as published by Higham & Barker 2000).

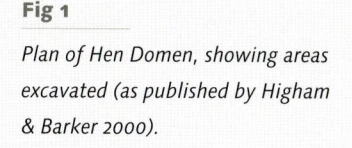

Fig 2

Plan of structures excavated in the bailey, of broadly 12th-century date (as published by Higham & Barker 2000).

which became known as Montgomery. The first castle was still occupied as an outpost for a further 50 years, eventually acquiring the Welsh name of Hen Domen meaning 'old mound'. It was never re-occupied and suffered very little damage.

Hen Domen is a motte and bailey, small in area but strongly defended by double ramparts and ditches (Fig 1). It is built on a ridge of boulder clay which made excellent earthworks and foundations for timber buildings. Throughout its 200-year occupation, it was constructed wholly of timber, undergoing a regular process of renewal and re-construction. In its early years, when it was a mainly military establishment, its buildings were simple and massive: a hall and lesser buildings (including a granary) in the bailey, and a residential tower on the motte. In the twelfth century, when it was a more domestic castle, as the centre of a small lordship, its buildings were more numerous and sometimes less sophisticated in construction method. They included rebuilds of the motte tower, main hall and granary, and the addition of a lesser hall, chapel and minor structures (Figs 2 & 3). In the thirteenth century, as an outpost of the new castle, its occupation shrank, with fewer buildings, concentrated at one end of the bailey.

Hen Domen was excavated in annual seasons of work stretching from 1960-92, becoming the type-site for this category of castle in the British Isles, perhaps in Europe. The excavations included half the interior of the bailey and its rampart, the top and sides of the motte, and various parts of the outer defences. In addition, the landscape and settlement pattern which developed around this castle were subject to much study. Several major lessons emerged from this long campaign of research. First, timber could be a choice of building material for richer castle-builders as well as more modest ones. Second, building in timber was not necessarily a prelude to re-building in stone: it could be a distinct cultural and technological choice in its own right. Third, the interior and defences of a timber castle could display all the features and functions with which we are familiar in better preserved stone castles. The work carried out at Hen Domen was crucial to re-habilitating timber castles in the wider framework of medieval defensive sites.

Source: Higham & Barker 2000.

By Robert Higham

Fig 3

Artist's reconstruction (by Peter Scholefield) of the same 12th-century evidence.

Fig 11.6 *Reconstruction of the motte castle at South Mimms, Herts, England (after Davison 1986)*

had ring-works erected on them simply because the castle-builders at these places real-ised that a simple enclosure-type earthwork castle was all that was needed to create first-class fortifications at these locations. Overall, the natural defences of some sites may have favoured the erection of ring-works (ibid).

A study of the distribution of earthwork castles in Glamorgan (Wales) has thrown interesting light on this subject, with geology having clearly influenced the distribution of ring-works and mottes. Ring-works only occur in the southern part of the county and are associated with areas of shallow soil above natural rock. As mottes need large quan-tities of soil to construct the castle mound, it would have been difficult to erect them in these conditions. Instead, they are to be found in the north of Glamorgan in districts associated with deep, glacially-derived soils (Spurgeon 1987, 206-7).

Another possible reason why mottes were far more popular than ring-works is that the former, with its division into mound and bailey, was stronger from a defensive point of view. A motte mound, with its steep sides and surmounted by a high timber tower, was possibly regarded as a more physically and psychologically daunting prospect to capture in comparison to the lower ring-work. Furthermore, in an age when lordly display was important, a high motte mound with a tall tower on it was visually more impressive than a ring-work.

On present evidence, ring-works appear to be the earliest form of earthwork castle, i.e. the first phase of the Heinstert ring-work could date as early as the late tenth century (De Meulemeester & Dhaeze 2005). It was once believed that mottes first started to be built in northern France in the later tenth century, as suggested by the excavated evi-dence from the motte at Boves (Racinet 2002); however, other research across North-Western Europe, including France, indicates that the earliest mottes date to the first half of the eleventh century and that they only began to be built regularly during its second half (Higham & Barker 1992, 93-111). Indeed, it would appear that mottes were only erected in great numbers across much of North-West Europe, as the castle of choice, during the twelfth century (ibid, 106-11). At the same time, ring-works continued to be built as an alternative, but less popular choice, throughout the twelfth and thirteenth centuries, being occupied in places well into the fourteenth century, and possibly later. Mottes continued to be built in certain parts of Europe (such as Scotland, Denmark, Poland and maybe Ireland) into the fourteenth century (ibid, 67 & 83-8).

One last point needing to be made about ring-works is especially relevant to the British Isles, but is applicable elsewhere. It was once widely believed that mottes were an ideal form of fortification in an invasion-context because they were thought quick to erect. Research in Britain since the 1960s has, however, indicated that mottes could have well taken several months to build and were therefore not suitable as campaign fort-resses, which needed to be erected rapidly (Kenyon 1990, 7); instead, motte-and-bailey castles belong to the consolidation of conquest, after the initial military phase. In effect, the first mottes in England (as also in Ireland) belong to the period when Norman lords were seeking to establish themselves in their new territories and they were usually con-structed (along with many ring-works) as permanent, defended centres from which their new lands could be administered and economically exploited. On the other hand, it has been shown that large earthwork enclosures were far more efficient in an inva-sion/campaign scenario, because they were not only easily and quickly built but also, owing to their size, were able to house and protect the large numbers of troops need-ed to subdue any given territory in a way that even large motte-and-bailey castles could not (Kenyon 1990, 7). It could be argued that such enclosures (e.g. the period II earth-works at Castles Neroche, Somerset, England) should be classified as large ring-works, but arguably these sites are not proper castles and are really temporary fortifications designed to hold a field force (e.g. Davison 1971-72).

Excavations at earthwork castles such as Hen Domen (Box 11.1), along with infor-mation gleaned from surviving historical and literary sources, demonstrate that many mottes and ring-works were covered with imposing (timber and cob) domestic, admin-istrative and agricultural buildings (Higham & Barker 2000; O'Conor 2002, 175). The existence of these buildings, together with their often serious defences, makes it easy to understand why contemporaries regarded these earthwork fortifications as castles in much the same way as masonry ones.

Masonry castles

The first definite archaeological and historical evidence for masonry castles comes in the second half of the tenth century from different parts of Western Europe and invar-iably these were built by kings, princes and great magnates (Higham & Barker 1992, 171; Fehring 1991, 111-12; McNeill 2001, 43). The extant remains at Doué-La-Fontaine (France) contain one of the earliest examples of a stone castle in Europe. An undefended ground-floor hall, built c900, was converted into a fortified first-floor hall c950, with a first-floor entrance; an earthen mound was later piled up around its base in the eleventh

Fig 11.7   *The Tower of London (photo: K O'Conor).*

century (De Boüard 1973-74). Rectangular keeps were the principal buildings in early masonry castles throughout northern France, England and Wales (and later Ireland). These early keeps can be divided into two architectural types. The first type usually consisted of a two-storey rectangular building with a first-floor entrance. Normally the solar (the lord's private chamber and inner sanctum) was located on the first floor of such a keep, separated from the hall (where public business took place and where the lord's retainers were entertained and slept) by a cross-wall or wooden partition; the ground floor was used for storage. Doué-La-Fontaine itself, Castle Rising, England (built c1150) and Chepstow, in Wales (built c1080), are extant examples of this type (King 1988, 69). The second early type of keep has the solar placed above the hall, hence these buildings tended to be three, if not four or five, storeys high. They generally look more impressive than the first type of keep and appear square-like, e.g. William the Conqueror's 'White Tower', in the Tower of London (Fig 11.7), and those extant at Rochester, England (begun c1126), and Loches, France (1035) (ibid).

A tall, slender, square tower, known as the *Bergfried*, was the central strong-point in the early masonry castles seen throughout German-speaking lands, as well as northern Italy and southern France. These multi-storeyed towers were often, but not always, free-standing, and it has been suggested that they were not used for accommodation and public business, like the keeps in northern France and England, but functioned instead as places of refuge and watchtowers (Anderson 1970, 65; McNeill 2001, 44). However,

Fehring (1991, 113) has shown that many of these towers were also residential, e.g. the tall, exactly square, tower at Turmberg (Germany), dating to c1050 (ibid).

King (1988, 62-7 & 77) has outlined the basic defensive features associated with early Norman masonry castles in England and south Wales, built before the second half of the twelfth century. As noted, the keep was the central strongpoint and residential core of these places. Other features are also common. These castles usually consist of only one ward, with low curtain walls by later standards, and tend to follow irregular or curvilinear lines. Mural towers are rare and are square or rectangular in plan, offering little in the way of flanking defence. Gatehouses usually consist of a single square or rectangular tower, with the entrance passages blocked by single wooden doorways; portcullises were few. Arrow-loops rarely occur anywhere in these early castles. It could be argued that this description of the defences of early masonry castles in England and south Wales is also applicable, in a broad sense, to contemporary stone castles elsewhere in Europe, leaving aside the differences between rectangular keeps and *Bergfrieds* (see Anderson 1970, 68-9; Fehring 1991, 111-30). There are naturally some local differences, e.g. castles in German-speaking lands tend to be more dramatically sited than elsewhere, often being located on mountain tops and crags (Anderson 1970, 68-9; Fehring 1991, 113).

Methods of besieging castles became far more efficient during the course of the twelfth century and warfare in general became more professional (King 1988, 90 & 93-6; McNeill 2001, 44-5; Nicholson 2004, 94-5). The design of masonry castles built by men of the first rank began to change from c1150 onwards, partly in response to this increase in military professionalism. The rectangular keep, for example, had disadvantages from a military point-of-view because its angled corners could be attacked by miners using a bore or ram and made to collapse (Anderson 1970, 112). Another military defect associated with this form of keep lay in the 'dead ground' at its angles. It was difficult for defenders to see what the enemy was doing at these points without having to lean out over the battlements and thus become dangerously exposed to enemy shot, probably emanating from cross-bows (King 1988, 98). Increasingly, as the twelfth century progressed, new forms of keep were experimented with by kings and magnates, especially in France but to a lesser extent in England. The round keep eventually became a popular design choice by the end of the century in France, and this fashion had spread to other places by c1200, such as Wales and Ireland (Anderson 1970, 112-27; King 1988, 97-103). Yet it must also be accepted that the appearance of these new forms of keep was as much due to social developments, linked to expanded and changing aristocratic accommodation requirements, as it was to increased military pressures and developing siege-craft (e.g. McNeill 1992, 22-7; 2001, 45).

Probably more important from a military point-of-view during the second half of the twelfth century was the gradual move of the defensive emphasis in castles away from keeps to curtain walls and entranceways (McNeill 2001, 45). This was to become a major feature of castle design throughout the thirteenth century, but the beginnings of this change are to be seen in late twelfth-century castles, such as Dover (England), Château Gaillard (France) and Chepstow (Wales), as a response to this increased efficiency in siege-craft (e.g. Anderson 1970, 121-2; Avent 2002; King 1988, 91-2; Goodall

Fig 11.8   *The gatehouse at Chepstow Castle, Gwent, Wales, dating to the 1190s (photo: K O'Conor).*

1999). King (1988, 77-8) has outlined the various new characteristics and developments that occurred in castle design by c1200, in England and Wales (but also other parts of Europe, such as France and Ireland), that became standard in important castles during the thirteenth century. These new defensive features, seen on castles of the first rank from then onwards, included higher and straighter curtain walls, the merlons of which were now often pierced by arrow-loops. Projecting towers, also looped for archery and offering flanking defence, started to be built along the sides and at the angles of these curtain walls; such towers were usually round or half-round in plan, given that this shape was, as noted, less susceptible to attack by besiegers. Twin-towered gatehouses, likewise well endowed with arrow-loops, also started to appear at this time (Fig 11.8). The passage between the two half-round towers of this new type of gateway was defended not just by a wooden gateway, but also by at least one portcullis (King 1988, 78). This all demonstrates that masonry castles had become more defensive by the beginning of the thirteenth century in comparison to earlier castles, but it must also be remembered that the new towers and gatehouses provided the extra room needed for increased aristocratic accommodation, as mentioned above (McNeill 1992, 22-7; 2001, 45).

Palaces, Carolingian Villas, Strongholds and Defended Farmsteads

This next category of fortification for examination are those defended residences that are not to be classified as castles, although it is true that many of the fortifications to be discussed had at least some of the functions of castles, if only because many of them were the homes of men of royal or aristocratic rank. Nevertheless, they are not classified as castles for two main reasons: (1) some of these fortifications are too early in date to be considered as castles; and (2), more importantly, regardless of their date, it is believed that these sites had less elaborate defences than castles, even timber ones.

Palaces and Carolingian villas

As stated above, the traditional view was for many years that both Merovingian and Carolingian society lacked fortifications, even if some fortifications were built by imperial decree to protect the borders of the Carolingian Empire. It was believed that palaces and elite residences of nobles were not fortified and the (supposed) contrast between them and the castles of their immediate descendants and successors was constantly made.

It certainly appears, on current evidence, that many of Charlemagne's great palaces, such as Ingelheim, were not fortified during his reign (but see pp 342-3). The evidence from certain of his other palaces and residences, however, does suggest that at least some of them were defended at this time, e.g. the palace at Paderborn (Germany), which included a great hall, chapel and royal residential quarters, was initially defended by earth and timber fortifications that were destroyed in 778, soon to be replaced with a substantial stone wall. This masonry rampart enclosed an area that measured 250x280m (Fehring 1991, 132). Thionville (France) was another of Charlemagne's residences. This D-shaped site was located on the Moselle, with the river bounding it on one side. Evidence from the medieval street pattern, still to be seen in the modern town of Thionville, suggests that that the original enclosure was defended on its landward sides by a curving bank, palisade and wet ditch – the latter being fed by the waters of the Moselle (De Meulemeester 1995; De Meulemeester & Zimmer 1993). Furthermore, historical and archaeological research would suggest that the Carolingian palaces at Aachen, Frankfurt and possibly Ingelheim had fortifications placed around them during the reign of Charlemagne's son and successor, Louis the Pious (814-40).

Defended palaces continue into the Ottonian period in Germany, e.g. the site at Tilleda, Pfingstberg, which began as a defended Frankish farmstead in the eighth century, is essentially located on an inland promontory where an Ottonian palace was established in the second half of the tenth century. This fortress was divided into a main upper enclosure (0.75ha in area) and a lower enclosure (4ha) downhill from it. The former enclosure was defended by banks, ditches and palisades and had within it a large hall, chapel and living-quarters for the king and his family; pit-houses (SFBs) within this enclosure may have been occupied by retainers. The lower enclosure was full of SFBs and also granaries, clearly functioning as some sort of village and manufacturing centre (Fehring 1991, 133-5). Such a bipartite, rectangular-shaped fortress is known at Höfe, near Dreihausen (Germany), and also at the ninth-century Carolingian royal or noble villa at Petegem, Belgium (ibid, 98-9). It is uncertain whether the villa at Petegem was the centre of a royal estate, but it may well have been because the surviving sources indicate that Louis the Pious stayed there on at least three occasions. Petegem, at the very least, was the home of a high-ranking member of the Carolingian elite. The site consists of two

BOX 11.2 EARLY MEDIEVAL SLAVIC STRONGHOLDS

Early medieval Slavic strongholds form a striking part of the cultural landscape in East Central Europe (cf. Fig 2.6); in eastern Germany, Poland, the Czech Republic and Slovakia more than 3,000 are now known, generally dating from the eighth to thirteenth centuries (Fig 1). Their investigation has been a key theme in regional archaeology since the nineteenth century, and in several Central European countries the early Middle Ages are consequently referred to as the 'hill-fort' or 'stronghold' period. Slavic strongholds were not, however, a culturally uniform phenomenon: in their size, internal division and fortification techniques employed, there are pronounced differences, stemming both from their various social functions and cultural contexts and from their dissimilar natural environments (from geomorphology to building materials).

Despite being of archaeological interest for so long, the beginnings of the early medieval Slavic strongholds remain a subject of controversy. For-

tified sites dating to the eighth century (when the rise of the early elites is also evident) are, however, very rare and have only the simplest defences, comprising palisades and shallow ditches.

Dendrochronology is now of fundamental importance for dating the strongholds and, since the 1990s, has significantly corrected earlier dating, but suitable wood samples occur mainly in the northern range of these sites, in eastern Germany and Poland; in the drier Czech lands and Slovakia, the chronology remains largely dependent on artefact dating.

One of the most important periods in the development of Slavic strongholds was during the ninth century in southern Moravia and south-west Slovakia, where, the foremost centres, particularly Mikulčice (Fig 4.9) and the agglomeration near Uherské Hradiště, stand out for their highly concentrated social and economic potential. Several of these centres included closed-off areas with residential, economic and sacral functions, e.g.

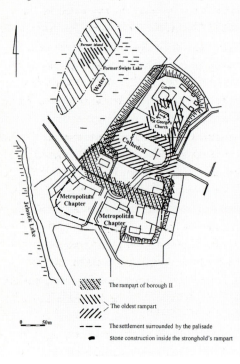

Fig 1

Gniezno (Poland): spatial development of the early medieval stronghold complex. The beginning of the stronghold on Lech Hill has been dated to c940, using dendrochronology; these oldest ramparts enclosed Cathedral Hill (borough I), with the first extension taking place probably in the 970s-80s. The stronghold at Gniezno played the crucial role in the process of the construction of the Piast (Polish) state (after T Sawicki).

Pohansko near Břeclav (Czech Republic).

During the ninth century, timber-laced clay ramparts began to appear, with their outer faces secured with a facing made of stone held together by clay (Fig 2); their breadth ranged from 4-6m, with heights estimated as between 3.5-4.5m. Such ramparts are known in a broad band stretching from Moravia and Slovakia across Bohemia to the floodplain of the Saale, in eastern Germany. In the East Central Europe, of course, not even these timber-laced ramparts with stone retaining walls, or facings, formed a closed area of distribution; they became one of the traditions. During the ninth-eleventh centuries, the number of Slavic strongholds grew markedly, and these fortified settlements became a conspicuous cultural phenomenon.

The fortified settlements themselves are seen as an expression of social complexity and structural skill, and for archaeology this instrument of government over people and land is a first-class indicator of social development. Systems of strongholds based on the eastern Central European traditions became a decisive buttress for the early medieval states. The foremost strongholds gradually developed into polycentric agglomerations generally featuring a fortified 'acropolis', a fortified *suburbium* and a mosaic of variable size of either unfortified or fortified settlement components, in the immediate area. It was within these features that specialised manufacturing and exchange concentrated, within which the contribution of market exchange gradually increased alongside the dominant redistribution function. It was on some of these agglomerations that some communal towns were to be founded in the thirteenth century.

Sources: Brather 2001; Henning & Ruttkay 1998; Urbańczyk 2004.

By Jan Klápště

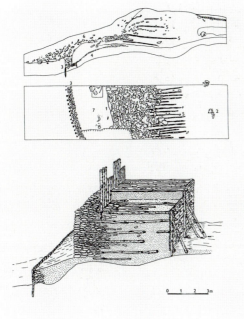

Fig 2

Mikulčice (Czech republic): the timber-laced clay rampart with stone retaining wall, from the 9th century, as excavated and with the suggested reconstruction (after R Procházka).

conjoined enclosures (giving it an '8' shape), that shared a deep, wet ditch supplied with water from the Scheldt. The main enclosure contained a large hall, with an attached *camera* or bedchamber. A chapel and cemetery lay within the second enclosure. The site at Herstal, Belgium, which was the residence of high-ranking Carolingian nobility or mayors, seems to have been morphologically similar to Thionville, consisting of a D-shaped enclosure located on the banks of the Meuse (De Meulemeester 1995, 377).

Strongholds and defended farmsteads

The site at Tilleda, already mentioned, began as a defended Frankish farmstead in the eighth century (Fehring 1991, 98-9). Phase 1 at Der Husterknupp, near Frimmersdorf (Germany), comprises a late Carolingian fortified farmstead, dated by excavation to the late ninth/early tenth century. This more-or-less circular enclosure was defended by a ditch and palisade, containing a timber-built farmstead and outbuildings. Phase 2 dates to the second half of the tenth century, when it was turned into two lightly-defended enclosures: a lower *Vorburg* and a higher *Hauptburg*, the interior of which was merely 1m higher than the former (Herrnbrodt 1958; Fehring 1991, 116-17). It is probably correct to suggest that the earliest phases of sites such as Der Husterknupp represent the homes and estate-centres of minor nobility. There are also hints in the historical sources from this period that such semi-fortified estate-centres and farmsteads may have been quite common. Other evidence from Germany and further east suggests that the Saxon and Slavic nobility (see Box 11.2) also built defended circular enclosures around their residences from the eighth century onwards (Fehring 1991, 119-20).

Fig 11.9   *Reconstruction of a crannog at Craggaunowen, Co Limerick, Ireland (photo: J O'Brien, after O'Brien & Harbison 1996).*

Ireland also displays extensive evidence for what was essentially private fortification from the fifth and sixth centuries onwards. Thousands of circular earthen ring-forts, defended by banks, ditches and light palisades, and their dry-stone walled equivalents, known as cashels (concentrated in the west), were built throughout the period under review, and even later (Fig 2.4). They are seen as being the defended farmsteads of men of noble rank, as well as freemen (Edwards 1990, 6-35; Stout 1997). Crannogs were also built and inhabited in Ireland and Scotland during this period, with one example recorded from Wales. A crannog can be described as an artificially-constructed island in a lake, created by dumping material into some shallow area so as to create a platform suitable for habitation. Crannogs were defended by simple plank-built or post-and-wattle palisades, which contained ordinary wooden houses (Fig 11.9). They are traditionally interpreted as representing the fortified homes of kings and nobility (Edwards 1990, 35-41).

It was for long presumed that the Anglo-Saxons only built communal fortifications in England and that private defence did not really exist there before the Norman Conquest (1066), but research since the 1960s has seriously questioned this view. There is now at least some historical and archaeological evidence for private fortification in England during the late Saxon period (c800-1066) (Higham & Barker 1992, 38-61), such as at Goltho in Lincolnshire (Beresford 1987). It should also be added that moated sites make their first appearance in countries such as England during the second half of the twelfth century, although the vast majority of these sites across North-West Europe were built in the thirteenth and fourteenth centuries (Wilson 1985).

Conclusions

This chapter has demonstrated the diverse range of fortifications across Europe, erected for different purposes during the eighth to twelfth centuries. It must be remembered, however, that the technology behind these fortifications had its roots deep in prehistory, as well as in the walled towns and military fortresses built by the Romans – in particular during the late Roman period.

The difficult issues of the origins, definition and early development of castles have also been discussed, with the assistance of Robert Higham and Philip Barker's book, *Timber Castles* (1992), as well as the *Château Gaillard* volumes, given that their articles are written by castle experts from across Europe. Another useful source has been William Anderson's *Castles of Europe* (1970); this volume was excellent for its day, trying to examine all types of castle from a pan-European (albeit English-speaking) perspective, in a way that has not been done since. Jean Lepage's *Castles and Fortified Cities of Medieval Europe* (2002), is a brave attempt to do the same; it is valuable in places, but lacks academic depth – being particularly weak on the subjects of earthwork castles and of castles as vehicles for social display. McNeill's *Castles* (1992) is an excellent source for castles in England and Wales, and to a lesser extent Ireland and Scotland. This all shows that Anderson's 1970 volume has never really achieved the recognition that it deserved, and it is time for a modern scholar to follow in his footsteps. Some other general sources for further reading are: Wilson (1985); Sweetman (1999); Roesdahl (2001); Goodall (2000); and Bevan (1950).

BIBLIOGRAPHY

Alcock, L (1994) *Cadbury Castle, Somerset: the Early Medieval Archaeology*, Cardiff

Andersen, H (2001) 'The Danevirke', in Crabtree, P (ed), *Medieval Archaeology – an Encyclopedia*, New York/London, 71-4

Anderson, W (1970) *Castles of Europe,* London

Avent, R (2002) 'The late twelfth century gatehouse at Chepstow Castle', *Château Gaillard* 20, 27-40

Avent, R (2003) 'William Marshal's building works at Chepstow Castle', in Kenyon, J and O'Conor, K (eds), *The Medieval Castle in Ireland and Wales*, Dublin, 50-71

Beresford, G (1987) *Goltho: the Development of an Early Medieval Manor c. 850-1150*, London

Bevan, B (1950) *Historia de la Arquitectura Española*, Barcelona

Bradley, J (1995) *Walled Towns in Ireland*, Dublin

Brather, S (2001) *Archäologie der westlichen Slawen. Siedlung, Wirtschft und Gesellschaft im früh- und hochmittelalterlichen Ostmitteleuropa,* Ergänzungsbände zum *Reallexikon der Germanischen Altertumskunde* 30, Berlin/New York

Buckley, V and Sweetman, PD (1991) *Archaeological Survey of County Louth*, Dublin

Davison, BK (1971-2) 'Castle Neroche: an abandoned Norman fortress in south Somerset', *Proceedings of the Somerset Archaeological and Natural History Society* 116, 16-58.

Davison, BK (1986, 2nd ed) *The New Observer's Book of Castles*, Harmondsworth

De Boüard, M (1973-4) 'De l'Aula au Donjon. Les fouilles de la Motte de la Chapelle à Douè–la-Fontaine', *Archéologie Médiévale* 3-4, 5-110

De Meulemeester, J (1995) 'Comment s'est-on défendu au IX siecle ...?', in Lodewijckx, M (ed), *Archaeological and Historical Aspects of West-European Societies. Album Amicorum Andre Van Doorselaer*, Acta Archaeologica Lovaniensia Monographiae 8, Leuven, 371-87

De Meulemeester, J and Dhaeze, W (2005) 'Châteaux de terre et de bois du type "petite enceinte circu-laire" en Belgique. Une approche par les fouilles', in Poklewski-Koziell, T (ed), *Architecture et Guerre. Fasciculi Archaeologiae Historicae*, Institut d'Ar-chéologie et d'Ethnologie del'Académie Polonaise des Sciences, Département de Łódź, Fasciculus XVI-XVII, Łódź, 79-86

De Meulemeester, J and Zimmer, J (1993) 'Bourgs castraux et abbatiaux de l'ancien duché de Luxembourg. Analyse archeologique des exemples d'Esch-sur-Sure, Larochette, Vianden, Echternach, Arlon, Thionville et Luxembourg-ville', *Aux Origines Du Second Réseau Urbain. Les Peuplement Castraux, Collogue de Nancy 1992*, Nancy, 321-49

D'Haenens, A (1967) *Les Invasiens Normandes en Belgique au IXe Siècle*, Louvain

Coulson, C (2003) *Castles in Medieval Society*, Oxford

Creighton, O (2002) *Castles and Landscapes*, London/New York

Edwards, N (1990) *The Archaeology of Early Medieval Ireland*, London

Fehring, GP (1991) *The Archaeology of Medieval Germany*, London

Goodall, J (1999) 'Dover Castle', *Country Life* 113:11, 44-7, 110-13

Goodall, J (2000) 'Dover Castle and the Great Siege of 1216', *Château Gaillard* 19, 91-102

Heeringen, RM van (1998) 'The construction of Frankish circular fortresses in the province of Zeeland (SW Netherlands) at the end of the 9th century', *Château Gaillard* 13, 203-26

Henning, J and Ruttkay, AT (eds) (1998) *Frühmittelalterlicher Burgenbau in Mittel- und Osteuropa. Tagung Nitra vom 7. bis 10. Oktober 1996*, Bonn

Herrnbrodt, A (1958) *Der Husterknupp; eine Niederreinische Burganlage des frühen Mittelalters*, Bonn

Higham, R and Barker, P (1992) *Timber Castles*, London

Higham, R and Barker, P (2000) *Hen Domen, Montgomery. A Timber Castle on the English-Welsh Border: a Final Report*, Exeter

Hill, D (2000) 'Offa's Dyke: pattern and purpose', *Antiquaries Journal* 80, 195-206

Hill, D (2001) 'Offa's Dyke', in Crabtree, P (ed), *Medieval Archaeology – an Encyclopedia*, New York/London, 243

Hoffsummer, P, Hoffsummer-Bosson, A and Wery, B (1987) 'Naissance, transformations et aban-don de trois places-fortes des environs de Liège: Charlemont, Franchimont et Logne', *Château Gaillard* 13, 63-80

Jankuhn, H (1986) *Haithabu, ein Handelsplatz der Wikingerseit*, Neumünster

Janssen, HL (1990) 'The archaeology of the medieval castle in the Netherlands. Results and prospects for future research', in Besteman, JC, Bos, JM and Heidinga, HA (eds), *Medieval Archaeology in the Netherlands: Studies presented to H.H. van Regteren Altena*, Assen/Maastricht, 219-64

Kent, JPC (1968) 'Excavation of the motte and bailey castle of South Mimms, Herts., 1960-1967', *Barnet District Local History Society Bulletin* 15

Kenyon, JR (1990) *Medieval Fortifications*, Leicester

King, DJC (1988) *The Castle in England and Wales*, London/New York

Lepage, J (2002) *Castles and Fortified Cities of Medieval Europe*, Jefferson/London

Liddiard, R (2000) '*Landscapes of Lordship': Norman Castles and the Countryside in Medieval Norfolk, 1066-1200*, British Archaeological Reports, British Series 309, Oxford

McNeill, TE (1992) *Castles*, London

McNeill, TE (2001) 'Castles', in Crabtree, P (ed), *Medieval Archaeology – an Encyclopedia*, New York/London, 43-6

Mesqui, J (1991) *Châteaux et Enceintes de la France Médiévale. De la Défense à la Résidence, T.1 Les Organes de la Défense*, Paris

Nicholson, H (2004) *Medieval Warfare*, Basingstoke/New York

O'Brien, J and Harbison P (1996) *Ancient Ireland: From Prehistory to the Middle Ages*, London

O'Conor, K (2002) 'Motte castles in Ireland', *Château Gaillard* 20, 173-82

Otway-Ruthven, AJ (1968) *A History of Medieval Ireland*, London

Racinet, P (2002) *Le site castral et prioral de Boves du Xe au XVIIe siècle, bilan des recherches 1996-2000*, Revue Archéologique de Picardie (special edition)

Roesdahl, E (1987) 'The Danish geometrical Viking fortresses and their context', *Anglo-Norman Studies* 9, 108-26

Roesdahl, E (1991) *The Vikings*, London

Roesdahl, E (2001) 'Trelleborg fortresses', in Crabtree, P (ed), *Medieval Archaeology – an Encyclopedia*, New York/London, 344-7

Spurgeon, CJ (1987) 'The castles of Glamorgan: some sites and theories of general interest', *Château Gaillard* 13, 203-26

Stout, M (1997) *The Irish Ringfort*, Dublin

Sweetman, PD (1999) *The Medieval Castles of Ireland*, Cork

Urbańczyk, P (ed) (2004) *Polish Lands at the Turn of the First and the Second Millennia*, Warsaw

Wilson, D (1985) *Moated Sites*, Princes Risborough

CHAPTER 12

THE DISPLAY OF SECULAR POWER

James Graham-Campbell and Matthias Untermann

PART 1: PALACES *by Matthias Untermann*

Introduction

In the realms of eighth-century Europe, there were places where the ruling dynasty reigned continuously or recurrently, and where they distinguished their seat of power with special buildings. An important precursor of these buildings was provided by the palaces of the Byzantine emperors, although their sophistication was nowhere reproduced in the early medieval period (Francescini 1999). The origin of the medieval Latin term *palatium* (secular or ecclesiastical palace) can be traced to the Palatine Hill in Rome, the seat of the Emperor in the ancient city. Long after the hill had lost its political function, its former eminence still affected terminology relevant to the estates of ruling dynasties without fixed residences. These ruling dynasties regularly frequented different estate-centres, which in time came to be known as royal palaces. The architectural form of the most important palace in early medieval Rome, the residence of the Pope on the Lateran Hill, is recorded in building plans of the Baroque period; buildings erected between the pontificates of Zacharius I and Nicholas I (i.e. 741-867) include clear references to some of the significant elements of the palace of Constantinople, particularly *tricliniums*, halls with numerous apses and long connecting corridors (Luchterhandt 1999).

Merovingian and Carolingian Palaces

The Merovingian palaces of the early eighth century are barely known archaeologically, as the sites of the most important, Paris and Attigny, lie beneath later buildings (Renoux 1994; 2002, 25-50). At numerous other important places, the late Roman palaces, such as that in Cologne, were retained in continual use (Brühl 1975; 1990).

Some of the important sites of the Frankish kings have been excavated archaeologically. In Francia, as in the later German Empire, there was no single capital, but several places described as 'king's courts' (Latin *curtis*, *villa*), which served the court as temporary residences (Zotz et al 1983). Few of these could accommodate the king and his retinue for long periods. The palaces in the heartland of the Frankish realm seem to have lacked defences, though places near the eastern border, such as at Paderborn and Frankfurt, were provided with defensive walls, and ditches served at some others, such as Duisburg (see also p 335). The Zurich palace was built within an older Roman fortification and archaeological traces of an early moat were recently discovered in Aachen (Koch 1997). The incursions of the Vikings and the Hungarians, in the ninth and tenth centuries, made fortification systems for royal places a necessity (e.g. Saint-Denis, near Paris, was fortified in 867).

The Frankish palaces of eighth- and ninth-century date featured a rectangular building for the accommodation of the king, the upper storey holding the assembly-hall (the *aula* or *sala regalis*). The chapel, living-quarters and storehouses were either annexed or freestanding. In Saint-Denis, which, in the eighth century, served as the burial-place for the Frankish kings, a 50m long and 14m wide two-storey building, complete with a corner tower, was erected on the edge of the cemetery. This complex has been linked to the lavish *regia domus* that was built for Charlemagne by Abbot Fardulf (796-806), which is mentioned in a twelfth-century document (Wyss 1996, 114-15; 2001, 175-92).

Two further Frankish palaces, of Quierzy (Oise) and Samoussy (near Laon), which were uncovered during World War I by the Germans, are still inadequately researched (Renoux 1994, 85-6, 89-90). In Samoussy, there was a 50x22m assembly-hall and an enclosed semi-circular courtyard, though the dating of this complex to the ninth or to the eleventh century remains a matter of dispute. Another important palatial complex at Compiègne has been published only in preliminary form (Petitjean 1996).

After 768, Charlemagne had the palace of Aachen lavishly reconstructed and after 794/95 this habitation, with its Roman thermal baths, became his permanent winter residence (Binding 1996, 72-98; Untermann 1999; for the Roman period, see Cüppers et al 1982). Many noblemen and bishops in his entourage established their permanent domiciles here. Two main buildings framed the complex: to the north, the *aula regia*, a monumental reception-hall; and to the south, the Church of Our Lady (Fig 12.1). The assembly-hall, the foundations of which are buried beneath the Gothic city-hall, was 44m long and 17m wide. Its single space was provided with three apses and its Roman-style exterior was emphasised by pilaster strips. Adjacent to the *aula*, the tower containing the treasure-chamber is still intact. From here a long, two-storeyed corridor led southward to the church. Between church and *aula*, it passed through a rectangular building with several storeys, which might have contained the king's living-quarters. The Church of Our Lady of Aachen has survived, despite later architectural additions and alterations (Fig 12.2). With its 16-sided central structure, two-storeyed ambulatory and octagonal core, the church is of a highly distinctive form and was taken as a proto-type for many later buildings. Luxurious bronze doors and screens, which were cast in Aachen, as well as columns, capitals, marble *spolia* and other precious objects brought from Italy, decorated the Church of Our Lady and set it apart from all the other churches of the Frankish realm. Partially excavated, two-storeyed annexes provided a meeting-place and administrative facilities for the Emperor. The Aachen complex was intended to emulate Hagia Sophia and the residence of the Byzantine Emperor. Until the twelfth century, Aachen remained one of the most important palaces of the German Empire; most significantly, the German kings were crowned in its church, a tradition that persisted until 1531.

Fig 12.1 *Ground-plan of the imperial palace at Aachen, showing the early 9th-century buildings overlying the Roman baths (M Untermann).*

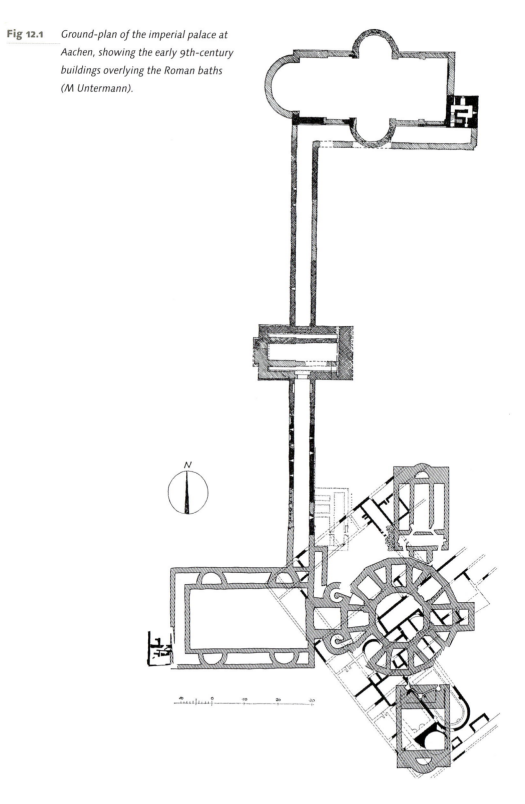

The raised throne of Charlemagne in the west gallery of the Church of Our Lady at Aachen; the marble columns, in front, form part of the 'spolia' from Italy (© akg-images, Berlin). **Fig 12.2**

An altogether different architectural model provided the inspiration for Charlemagne's construction of the Ingelheim palace (near Mainz), where excavation has recovered considerable architectural data (Grewe 2001; Jacobi & Rauch 1976; Sage 1976). The courtyard was framed by a 90m wide semi-circular building (cf. Samoussy), which contained the main entrance and frontal round towers. The *aula regia* was 40.5m long and 16.5m wide and included only a single apse. Nevertheless, it was apparently richly decorated with murals (Lammers 1972). While the semi-circular building imitated the Roman imperial forums, its small rooms were used only for secondary purposes; the main functional rooms were in other buildings to the north of the *aula*. The frontal towers similarly emulated Roman city-walls, but their ground floors merely housed latrines. The cruciform church standing on the site originates from the re-establishment of the palace in the tenth century, but the royal church, which was in use during the eighth and ninth centuries, has recently been discovered (Grewe 2006). The later buildings on the site, from the reign of Frederick Barbarossa (1152-90) have not been detected archaeologically.

The third great palace of Charlemagne, at Nijmegen on the Waal, in the Netherlands, has had no archaeological investigation.

Distinguished by numerous *karst* (limestone) springs, the site of the Paderborn palace, which was established by Charlemagne in 776/77 in the newly-conquered Saxon region has been systematically excavated (Gai & Mecke 2004). Above the springs, a 31x10m, two-storeyed building with *aula* and adjacent church were erected. A tower and a narrow perpendicular wing were replaced in the ninth century by a series of annexes – at the time, the palace already served as residence to the bishop. Evidence for rich murals cannot be assigned to any particular rooms of the palace, but these murals were destroyed

Fig 12.3 *Gable-end view of the two-storied hall of the 9th-century palace at Naranco, near Oviedo (Spain); the altar in the first-floor 'solarium' was added following its conversion for use as a church (photo: M Valor).*

c800 (Preissler 2004). A similar long hall with adjacent tower served as the main building of the palace in Zurich during the Carolingian period (Kaiser 1996; Vogt 1948).

The residences of the bishops of the eighth and ninth centuries were integrated into structures that reflected the architectural form of the cloister. This is true of the monastery at Müstair, in Switzerland, where the bishop of Chur is thought to have resided in a large three-aisled northern wing of the excavated monastery complex (Sennhauser 2002). In Rouen, Normandy, archaeological research on buildings of the southern cloister of the cathedral indicates that the bishop's residence was sited there, with a second cloister for the canons (Le Maho 2001).

Some other European Palaces

The only substantially intact king's palace of the ninth century stands on Mount Naranco, near Oviedo, in northern Spain. It was built by the Asturian king, Ramiro I (842-50), and after the tenth century it was used as a substitute for the nearby church of San Miguel de Liño, which had collapsed (Fig 12.3). The palace is composed of a barrel-vaulted, multi-chambered ground floor, in which there are the remains of baths. The upper floor includes a large, richly-decorated, barrel-vaulted hall, opening into a *solarium* at either end (Fig 12.4). The siting of the building is unusual for a medieval palace, and its architecture and ornament have no immediate parallels (Noack-Haley & Arbeiter 1994, 115-42).

In south-west England, a palace of the late ninth or early tenth century has been excavated at Cheddar, in Somerset. The main building consisted of a large timber hall,

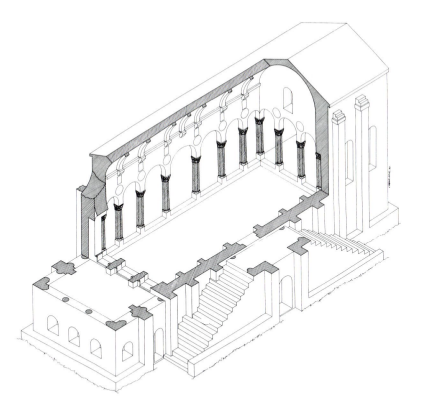

Isometric view of the upper floor of the 9th-century palace at Naranco, entered by a double flight of external stairs; the colonnaded and barrel-vaulted hall opens to a 'solarium' at either end (after Arbeiter & Noack-Haley 1999).

Fig 12.4

24m long and 6m wide, of post construction. Domestic buildings and a gatehouse were also present. In the tenth century, the complex was fully rebuilt, with the addition of a new stone chapel (17x9m). In the eleventh century, both buildings were twice renewed and in 1100/20 they were replaced by a large three-aisled hall, again of post construction. King Henry I visited this palace in 1121 and again in 1130. The living-quarters and public and legislative rooms at Cheddar were constructed of stone from the thirteenth century onwards (Rahtz 1979).

Westminster Hall in London is the oldest survival of that great medieval palace; although it was extensively rebuilt by Richard II in 1394-9, it was originally built for William II in 1097-9 (Colvin 1963, 47, fig 10; Steane 1993, 71-9). It did, however, have had a timber predecessor (depicted in the Bayeux Tapestry), and it has been proposed that the arrangement of its buttresses and the inward curvature of its stone walls suggest that it may have been built around a pre-Conquest bow-sided timber hall, c75m long (Rahtz 1976, 68, 426, fig 2.8).

The archaeology of timber royal residences in Scandinavia has, until recently, been largely missing (cf. Nissen Jaubert 1996), although a royal seat from the Viking period, and earlier, has been excavated at Lejre, near Roskilde, in Denmark (Jørgensen 2003, 181-2; Niles 2007; see also p 373). The 'magnate's complex' excavated beside Lake Tissø, also in Zealand (Fig 13.5), provides further information as to the range of timber buildings to be expected on such a site, in southern Scandinavia, during the seventh to eleventh centuries (ibid, 183-204). Indeed, Tissø has been interpreted as a possible royal residence, for a peripatetic king, with comparisons even being drawn with contemporary Carolingian imperial *Pfalz* (ibid, 204-7). The chieftain's hall at Borg, Lofoten (Box 2.3 & Fig), in northern Norway, has already been noted (Munch et al 2003).

Later Palaces and High-Status Architecture

In the eastern Frankish realm, during the tenth and eleventh centuries, many new palaces were founded on the ecclesiastical framework of monasteries and bishops' churches. A large, exquisitely-furnished hall beside the monastery of Reichenau, on Lake Constance, which Abbot Witigowo (985-97) had built for royal visits, has been excavated archaeologically (Maurer 2003). In Paderborn, Bishop Meinwerk (1009-36) returned land to the king on the north of the cathedral, which had been in the possession of the diocese since the Carolingian period. Building over one of the *karst* springs, Meinwerk erected a new two-storeyed hall, with two balconies and an adjacent chapel (Gai 2007). One of the wings housed living-quarters and led to the remarkable vaulted chapel of St Bartholomew, said to have been constructed by Greek workmen. For himself, Meinwerk constructed a second large hall to the south-west of the cathedral.

Excavation of a monumental building complex to the north of the cathedral of Magdeburg exposed a long hall, 44m long and 15m wide, with unusual double apses between stair-towers. The site has been assumed to be the easternmost *palatium* of Otto I (Lehmann 1983; Meckseper 1986), who had his capital built on the border of his Empire in 929. In 937 and 955, a monastery and the episcopal seat were established. Further excavation has revealed two phases of construction. The second phase was built during the twelfth century and was left incomplete, and roofless, in the thirteenth (Ludovici 2003). The earlier Ottonian structure also featured a double apse and reached 41m in length. These structures are interpreted as the Ottonian and pre-Gothic cathedrals of Magdeburg (Kuhn et al 2005), but there are chronological, and indeed typological, problems with this interpretation (Untermann 2006, 186-7). The structure could be a palace.

In Zurich, the royal palace was reconstructed in the tenth century as a larger complex, which required the demolition of the late Roman defensive walls (Fig 4.8). In Saxony, new palaces developed on the outskirts of towns. These had individual fortification systems and large outer fortresses, which housed retainers. Initially, the halls were large wooden structures, but building in stone became common in the eleventh century (Dapper 2002, 265-6; Grimm 1968; 1990).

In the Ottonian period, not only kings, but also the German bishops took part in palace building. The archbishops of Cologne had a series of important palaces built at the episcopal centres c955-1000. Next to the collegiate churches of Neuss, Xanten and Soest, large four-storeyed stone houses, measuring between 27x22m and 30x30m, dominated the landscape (Borger & Oediger 1969, 167-93; Lumpe 2000, 66-72). While these buildings were equal in volume to early Norman keeps, they entirely lacked any fortifications; their walls were relatively thin and the entrances were situated at ground level. A similar episcopal tower is situated at the northern side of the monastic church of Müstair, having survived the Gothic renovations there intact.

Episcopal seats were often provided with stone curtain-walls. At Hildesheim, Bishop Bernward (933-1022) erected a wall with regularly-spaced round towers that were purely ornamental, in imitation of the Ingelheim palace. In Halberstadt, the new wall constructed under Bishop Arnulf (996-1023) seems to have lacked such towers (Porsche 2000). The purpose of these walls was the demonstration of episcopal power, and not defence.

During the eleventh century high-status architecture diverged; as well as palaces, castles were being built (see also Chapter 11). Belonging to the second category, the multiple-storeyed keep, with its thick walls and small windows, spread throughout Normandy, and later through other regions of France and England. In many cases, the *aula* was now built within a larger multi-functional fortress. At the same time, palaces that were entirely without defences continued to exist in towns. Bishops and noblemen progressively adopted both building-types for their residences (Renoux 2007). For the early medieval period, documentary sources provide no clue as to the function of the various elements of these structures, but archaeological evidence suggests that they were diverse. The ground floor of the main building of the palace of Locronan, in Brittany, for example, was used for casting gold objects (Guigon 1995).

In the German realm, the *aulae* were usually two- or three-storeyed constructions with the domestic quarters, kitchen and storage rooms, being situated above a large ground-floor hall with open arcades, which could only be used in fine weather. These arcades traditionally denote palaces of the High Middle Ages, but by 830 the plan of the abbot's house at St Gall was distinguished by such arcades (Fig 5.4). An abbot's palace with arcades is still intact at the German monastery of Komburg, near Schwäbisch Hall. The twelfth-century German royal palaces at Goslar, Gelnhausen, Seligenstadt and Wimpfen, with their monumental *aulae* are well researched (Atzbach 1998; Binding 1996; Frontzek et al 1996; Arens 1967; Hölscher 1927). Palaces of noblemen, similar in appearance to royal palaces exist in Braunschweig and Wartburg (Schuchardt 2001). The chapels associated with these palaces were significant elements in the display of power, whereas the actual living-quarters must have been situated in other, less diagnostic buildings. Most palaces of the Staufian kings display massive defensive walls and up to three free-standing keeps, i.e. Wimpfen (Untermann 1991). Another unusual palace is Kaiserwerth, near Dusseldorf, which features a monumental stairway and corridors between the hall, living-quarters and the keep (Biller 1998).

Another extraordinary structure is Bishop Norpert's residence in Müstair. The two-storeyed main building lies to the west of the monastic church, to which it is connected by a four-winged atrium. The atrium also surrounds a two-storeyed chapel. About 1160, Bishop Egino had a new conventional bishop's residence built north of the church (Boschetti-Maradi 2005). Urban episcopal palaces in France and Italy consisted of towers, halls and courts, resembling the palaces of the nobility (Miller 2000; Esquieu & Pradalier 1996).

The suburban palaces of the Norman kings, William I and William II, in Palermo, Sicily, resemble Arabic residences (Meier 1994; Bellafiori 1990). These tall rectangular buildings with few windows concealed their inner structure. The main cruciform reception-hall of the Ziza palace was furnished with a fountain and a free-flowing water main. The hall was framed by long corridors, rooms that were accessed through winding routes, two stairwells and a bath. A similar hall (*triclinium*), with a baldachin of columns, was situated on the top floor. Arabic *muqqarna*-vaulted ceilings (with stalactite-like decoration) and Kufic inscriptions gave the building its unique design. The nearby garden-palace of Scibene, belonging to the archbishop of Palermo, is distinguished by its fountain, *muqqarna* ceilings and decorated hall. A large central cupola, supported on slender columns, characterises another royal garden-palace, Cuba (from the Arabic *Qubba*), where the main room was accompanied by a *triclinium*. These palaces did not serve as permanent residences, but rather were used for receptions or celebrations. In the Norman urban palace in Palermo, a huge tower, *Sala de Ruggero* (Roger's Hall), housed lavishly decorated halls. The adjacent *Capella palatina* displays walls richly decorated with mosaics and *muqqarna* ceilings. Further palaces in Palermo (e.g. Favara) and elsewhere in Sicily (e.g. Caronia) are difficult to reconstruct.

PART 2: ELITE ACTIVITIES AND SYMBOLS OF POWER
by James Graham-Campbell

Elite Activities

Two activities, above all, helped to distinguish the elite, whether in palace, castle or hall, from the peasantry: hunting (beyond that required for survival), and feasting. Both of these activities involved considerable expenditure and provided opportunities for ostentatious display, as did the tournament which had its origins in the twelfth century. Amongst other aristocratic entertainments were sports and games, such as chess.

Hunting

At the Carolingian court, as elsewhere in Western Europe during the Middle Ages, hunting occupied a great part of the autumn and winter. Hunting for sport, rather than as a necessity for food, or to obtain furs (as in Northern Europe), was by definition an elite activity, for those with leisure (Cummins 1988). It was a pursuit for the wealthy, requiring not only the ownership of large estates, but also the maintenance of forests and deer-parks, as well as the expense of training dogs and falcons by specialised huntsmen. On the other hand, hunting secured a supply of fresh meat during the winter months. Not to be forgotten, however, is that the hunt also provided a form of combat training, a preparation for the greatest hunt of all – warfare.

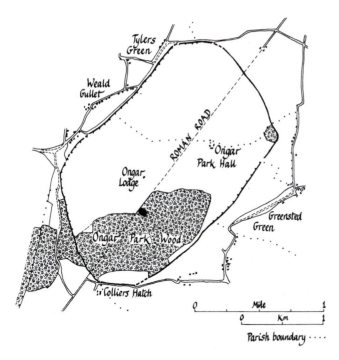

Ongar Great Park, Essex (England), as it survived until c1950. This deer-park is recorded in both 1045 and 1068. Like other early parks, it has a compact outline with rounded corners, suggesting economy in fencing; parish boundaries deviate to follow its outline (after Rackham 1990).

Fig 12.5

According to Ermold, Charlemagne had an enclosed park near the palace at Aachen where he went, in company, to hunt deer and to engage in falconry (Riché 1978, 96), but serious hunting expeditions took place in the forests of the Vosges, the Ardennes or Franconia. The deer and other wild beasts of the forest was at liberty to stray, but those in parks were confined by a deer-proof boundary, which was expensive to maintain. The tradition of enclosing animals for hunting purposes goes back to Antiquity and was well developed by the Romans, but doubtless their parks did not survive the Empire. In England, parks proliferated during the twelfth century, as a result of the Norman interest in deer-hunting, reaching their greatest extent c1300, when c3,200 parks are recorded, but many of these were small in size and would have served as deer-farms, rather than for the chase. In contrast, there are only 35 parks recorded in Domesday Book (1086), including that at Ongar, in Essex, first mentioned in an Anglo-Saxon will dated 1045 (Fig 12.5). These eleventh-century parks were for red and roe deer because the Anglo-Saxons had no fallow deer (Rackham 1986; 1990).

Fallow deer were the most important beast of the medieval chase because they are easier than the European native species to keep in a confined space. In origin an oriental beast, fallow deer were kept by the Romans and thus known to the Normans in Sicily. The Normans introduced fallow deer to England where they prospered. The problem was, however, that 'fallow deer are as strong as pigs and more agile than goats; they were confined by a *park pale*, a special palisade of cleft-oak stakes, whose maintenance was very expensive in labour and in the best timber. An alternative might be a hedge, or a stone wall – even where the stone had to be brought some miles.' (Rackham 1990, 153).

BOX 12.1   SECULAR POWER IN THE LANDSCAPE

Fig 1

Thingvellir (Iceland): site of the national assembly, or Althing (photo: A Reynolds).

Rulers have left impressive physical remains of their residences. In Ireland, multivallate ring-forts were seemingly the residences of local kings (p 339), while secular strongholds inside new or re-furbished hill-forts, or other defensible Iron-age sites, are attested across Europe (e.g. Lane & Campbell 2000; Alcock 2003). From Scotland to southern Europe and Spain, and to the east in Poland and the Baltic Sea region, such re-occupation is most common from the fifth/sixth century until the seventh-eighth centuries (Edwards 1990; Foster 2004; Castellanos & Martin Viso 2005; Kobyliński 1990). In the latter part of the first millennium, monumental stone buildings became a feature of secular residences at the highest level, as in the case of Charlemagne's palace at Aachen (see above, Figs 12.1 & 2) and that of Sta Maria de Naranco, near Oviedo, Spain (Figs 12.3 & 4).

Archaeology, however, has much to tell about other aspects of secular power including judicial activity, social organisation and civil defence. In early medieval England, for example, written laws are known from c600, although historians have doubted whether their prescriptions actually translated into judicial events. Archaeology has revealed a series of cemeteries best interpreted as the burial-places of executed felons; these appear in the later seventh/eighth century and can be seen to develop into the eleventh-twelfth centuries, as at Staines (Surrey), and Sutton Hoo in Suffolk (Hayman & Reynolds 2005; Carver 2005). Burials display signs of decapitation or amputation of limbs; corpses with the hands tied indicate death by hanging (Fig 2). Such cemeteries re-use earlier burial mounds, perhaps owing to their supernatural associations, and are placed at the limits of judicial territories.

A key mechanism for the articulation of supra-local communities throughout much of early medieval Europe was public assembly (Pantos & Semple 2004). Regular meetings served various roles including judicial courts, places of arbitration and transaction, and also, in certain regions, for competitive sports. The study of public assembly is well developed in Iceland, Ireland and Scandinavia, and to some extent in Britain, with the best known assembly-place being Thingvellir, in Iceland. There the national assembly (or *Althing*) met to settle disputes and other matters (Fig 1); it was focussed on the so-called *Lögberg* (law-rock), from which the assembly was formally opened and major announcements were made. Courts serving more specialised functions met in the vicinity. Rectangular booths for those in attendance were roofed on a temporary basis during meetings. Local assemblies in Scandinavia and the British Isles met either at pre-existing archaeological features, such as barrows and standing stones, or at fords and bridges. In Sweden, a series of assembly-places are marked by runestones. At Kjula (Södermanland), in central Sweden, a large Iron-age burial mound had a runestone erected at its base, with standing stones lining the approach (Brink 2004). In England, judicial districts often took their names from their meeting-places.

Secular power is also evident in defensive linear earthworks, such as the Danevirke (see pp 319-20), and Offa's Dyke, separating England from Wales (Hill 2000). The scale of such frontier works is a striking reflection of the ability of early medieval states to enforce obligations on local populations. More mundane indications of the administrative capabilities of secular authorities include building and maintaining roads and

Fig 2

A decapitated skeleton buried with a decapitated dog (perhaps on account of bestiality) in the late Anglo-Saxon execution-cemetery at Stockbridge Down, Hampshire (after Hill 1937).

bridges (e.g. at Hamwic, in southern England (see p 117), the regular re-surfacing of roads using carefully selected gravel has been recorded).

By Andrew Reynolds

Although the larger parks were valued for the pleasure of hunting, including the entertainment of guests (in other words, as status symbols), they were not solely a cause of expenditure given that they would yield profit from wood and could be used for grazing (in addition to providing the household with venson for consumption and as a source of gifts).

Even if the hunting of deer and wild boar provided the most common sport, other 'big-game' was to be had. Charlemagne took ambassadors from Baghdad to hunt auroch (wild ox), which apparently terrified them, whereas Louis the Pious took the Danish prince, Harald, bear-hunting during his visit to Ingelheim (Riché 1978, 95).

Feasting

Feasting had an essential role in the life of the elite, and not just because it provided the opportunity for consuming the venison and game from the hunt. A lavish table was an essential aspect of hospitality, with status displayed throughout the feast not only by the

Fig 12.6 Gilt-bronze ewer (German, c1150), decorated with silver and niello, in the form of a griffin (a fabulous beast combining the attributes of an eagle and a lion), used for hand-washing (© Victoria & Albert Museum).

quality and quantity of the food and drink, but also through the excellence of the table-ware. Entertainment was provided by musicians and mimes, with poetry and recitation in northern halls.

Courtly table-manners are exemplified archaeologically by the survival of lavish vessels used for the ritual of hand-washing. Water was poured from spouted vessels, some in the form of animals, known as *aquamanile* (Fig 12.6; see also Fig 8.3), into bowls, such as the mis-named 'Hanseatic' bowls, noted above (p 244). These twelfth-century bowls were manufactured in northern France, the Rhine-Meuse area and in the vicinity of the Harz Mountains in northern Germany, but they were distributed far beyond their production centres, having been found not only in France and Germany, but also in Italy, the Low Countries and England. These, and other such bowls, demonstrate a widespread demand across a large area of Europe for an elite symbol of table-culture, whether noble or urban patrician. Many of the 'Hanseatic' bowls are engraved with motifs drawn from Antique myths (e.g. Fig 12.7), biblical scenes and saints' legends. One particular group, the so-called 'Virtue and Vice' bowls, displays positive and negative human behavioural patterns, combined with explanatory inscriptions, thus purvey-

Shallow bronze bowl from Gloucester (England), 12th century, of 'Hansa' type, engraved with myth- **Fig 12.7**
ological scenes of King Cadmus of Thebes and the Birth and Labours of Hercules (© The Trustees of the British Museum).

ing religious instruction. Many of these bowls have been recovered from rivers, further revealing their ritual background and providing a glimpse into the medieval merging of pagan and Christian religious practices.

Feasting is depicted in contemporary manuscripts (e.g. Temple 1976, pls 158, 166, 197 & 205) and in two well-known scenes in the Bayeux Tapestry, although it is notable that the participants are characteristically depicted as drinking. Praiseworthy hospitality necessitated an unlimited supply of drink, and it was a privilege to drink from the king's own cup. The Anglo-Saxons shown drinking in the Bayeux Tapestry do so from both a pair of finely-decorated horns and a bowl (cup), the Normans from bowls alone (Wilson 1985, pls 3 & 48). Silver drinking-bowls and glass vessels (cf. Fig 8.1) were the elite choice for the consumption of wine, the noblest drink available. Written sources and rare survivals (e.g. an Irish horn, from c1100, which was preserved in use as a reliquary in the Belgian city of Tongres/Tongeren; Ryan 1988), as well as mounts from others, further demonstrate the importance of large drinking-horns to the northern aristocracy, whose ale might have been brought to table in fine buckets. The products of distillation only became available in Europe from the twelfth century, the introduction of the alembic being a further debt to the Arab world (Gwei-Djen et al 1972; Moorhouse 1972).

For the Carolingian kings, as others, great feasts were of central importance in the politics of prestige, notably in the reception of foreign emissaries, who came bearing gifts. Embassies came to Charlemagne's court from the Rus, the Emperor in Byzantium and the Caliph of Baghdad (who sent him an elephant in 802), from Anglo-Saxon kings and the rulers of al-Andalus, as also many other parts of Europe. The ambassadors and their suites were held in high regard, but according to the king's biographer 'constituted a heavy charge not only on the palace but on the whole realm' (from Riché 1978, 94).

Sports, games and tournaments

The twelfth-century Earl Rognvald of Orkney, born Kali Kolsson in Norway, composed a verse recording his nine skills (as translated by Judith Jesch):

> I am quick at playing chess, I have nine skills, I hardly forget runes, I am often at either a book or craftsmanship. I am able to glide on skis, I shoot and row so it makes a difference, I understand both the playing of the harp and poetry.

This literate northern aristocrat was thus both poet himself and patron of the arts, but also an athlete. Athleticism was naturally of importance for a warrior, alongside the skills with weaponry and of horsemanship, learnt from boyhood and practised during the hunt. Charlemagne was clearly fond of swimming when at Aachen, as Einhard recorded:

> Whenever there was bathing, the society was numerous; aside from his sons, he bade his magnates, his friends, and sometimes even his crowd of bodyguards to share his frolics. It sometimes happened that he had as many as a hundred or more people in the water with him. (from Riché 1978, 95)

Walrus ivory chess-pieces carved in Norway (12th century), found on the Isle of Lewis (Scotland), depict naturalistic figures including crowned and enthroned kings and queens (foreground); the king holds his 'sword of state' across his knees (© The Trustees of the British Museum).

Fig 12.8

The medieval tournament was clearly a development of the desire to display a combination of horsemanship and military skills. Although the tournament was supposedly invented in France during the mid-eleventh century, it was essentially a twelfth-century development (to become popular even later); the adoption of armorial bearings seems to have been closely connected with its increasing popularity (see below).

As with Earl Rognvald of Orkney, skill at chess was an expected elite achievement, but then board-games are battles in miniature (see pp 257-8). No game was more appropriate for playing at court than chess itself, with its cast of kings and queens, bishops and knights, as well as foot-soldiers (Fig 12.8), at least in its new western version.

Symbols of Power

The most important symbols of secular power were obviously those associated with kingship, particularly royal regalia and notably the royal or imperial crown used at a coronation and for display on state occasions (see Box 12.2). Elite display, particularly on the battle-field, focussed increasingly on the use of heraldic devices, in addition to the use of weapons and armour of superior quality to those of the common foot-soldier.

Heraldry also had its part to play in the use of personal seals, which the elite utilised as further symbols of power.

Regalia

A well-known ninth-century equestrian figure from Metz (Fig 12.9) is generally considered to depict Charlemagne himself, although this has been disputed (the alternative identification being Charles the Bald), as has the date of the horse (see Lasko 1972, 18-20, for the arguments). It is a superb product of the Carolingian 'renaissance' and depicts royal regalia in the form of a crown and an orb.

The evidence for crowns is considered in Box 12.2, thus orbs and sceptres are discussed here. The orb, normally associated with a cross, as depicted in the Coronation of Harold in the Bayeux Tapestry (ibid, Fig 1), is seen for the first time in England on the mid-eleventh-century seal and coinage of his predecessor, Edward the Confessor (English 2004, pls 5 & 8), and can be traced back to Roman roots. 'The orb and the cross represented the world over which, with the aid of Christ, the ruler held power' (ibid, 369). Continental depictions include that of Charles the Bald, in his Psalter of 842/69 (ibid, pl 16), who is shown also holding a sceptre, as are both Edward and Harold. The earliest orb known to have survived is that found in the grave of Emperor Henry III (who died in 1056), at Speyer (ibid, 371, pl 18, with refs).

Fig 12.9   *This small bronze statuette (height: 29cm), of an equestrian figure of Charlemagne(?), shows a crowned ruler, holding an orb in his left hand, with his sword at his side (© Louvre, Paris).*

Various forms of sceptre are depicted on coinage (e.g. Fig 10.5,3) and seals, and in manuscript illuminations, although they characteristically have a *fleur-de-lis* or trefoil terminal (as is the case with Charles the Bald, mentioned above). Harold's coronation sceptre is far more elaborate in its foliate elements and may thus relate to the much later identification of some sceptres with Aaron's Rod, which budded overnight into leaves and flowers (English 2004, 367).

Thrones are better known from depictions (including those on royal seals and coinage), rather than from actual survival, although that of Charlemagne, raised up in the west gallery at Aachen (Fig 12.2), has solid back and sides of stone. An ivory-inlaid wooden throne in St Peter's (Rome) has an arcaded back with a pediment (English 2004, pl 9). This is believed to have belonged to Charles the Bald who may have presented it to the Pope on the occasion of his imperial coronation (875), but it is unlike the curtained high-backed throne on which he is shown seated in the Vivian Bible, completed 845/6 (Dodwell 1973, pl 38). Such would not, however, have been so well suited for travelling purposes, for this folding-stools were even more convenient, such as that found at Pavia (Bullough 1980, fig 19), and that in Paris attributed to Dagobert (Wilson 1957; Lasko 1972, 20-1; cf. Temple 1976, pl 275, for one depicted in use in a late Anglo-Saxon manuscript). Later Ottonian emperors are also depicted seated on curtained high-backed thrones, some decorated with animal heads (e.g. Otto III in the Munich Gospels (983/1002): Dodwell 1973, pl 50; English 2004, pl 3). The thrones of the sixteen kings and queens that form part of the twelfth-century Lewis chessmen all have highly-decorated backs and sides, but no arms (Fig 12.8; Robinson 2004).

There appears to have been a distinction between the throne used for coronation purposes and that in which the king sat in state in his hall. The Bayeux Tapestry, for example, depicts the throne on which Harold is crowned (Box 12.2, Fig 1) as loftier, and thus grander, than that in which he is subsequently shown seated while receiving a messenger, although this is likewise ornately decorated (Wilson 1985, pls 31 & 32-3; English 2004, pls 1 & 6). In contrast, the seats of Count Guy and Duke William, in Normandy, are depicted as backless, although otherwise ornate (Wilson 1985, pls 10, 13, 16 & 25), but then so are those of King Edward the Confessor, even when he is shown seated in state (ibid, pls 1 & 28).

If we are dependent mostly on pictures as evidence for thrones and high-status seating, we are all the more so for coronation mantles, royal robes and aristocratic dress in general (cf. Renaudeau 2004; English 2004, 373), although fragments are known from the eleventh-century graves of Ottonian and Salian emperors (Schramm & Mütherich 1981, figs 158 & 166). On the other hand, two large early eleventh-century copes, embroidered in gold on silk, which were presented to Bamberg Cathedral by Henry II and (traditionally) by the Empress Kunigunde, are of such splendour that we can at least begin to imagine the richness of what has otherwise been lost to us. An inscription on Henry's so-called *Sternenmantel* (star-cloak) shows that it had first been commissioned as a gift to the Emperor by Duke Ishmahel of Apulia, who died in 1020 (Lasko 1972, 131-2, pl 133); it is one of four early copes preserved in the Bamberg Treasury (Schramm & Mütherich 1981, nos 130-3).

BOX 12.2   CROWNED HEADS

The most splendid European crown to have survived from the eighth-twelfth centuries is that in
the Imperial Treasury in Vienna which is thought
to have been made for the imperial coronation, in
962, of Otto the Great, founder of the Ottonian
dynasty. It does, however, have later additions,
including an inscribed arch added after the imperial coronation of Conrad II in 1027. It consists of
eight linked plates of which four are set in gold
with pearls and precious stones, and the other four
are decorated with large enamel plaques; it may
have been made in Italy (Lasko 1972, 83-7, pl 75).
At any rate, it differs somewhat in form and decoration from many of the northern crowns that are
familiar from depictions on coins (e.g. Fig 10.5)
and in sculpture (e.g. Figs 12.8 & 9), as well as in
contemporary manuscript illustrations (as above).

A well-known scene in the Bayeux Tapestry
(Fig 1) depicts the coronation of King Harold of
England (in 1066) – or, at any rate, it displays
him crowned 'in majesty', with all the attributes
of his rule, being proclaimed king by Archbishop
Stigand. The sword of state is being offered to the
enthroned king, who is holding the orb and sceptre (discussed above). Harold's crown has projecting trefoils, which is the form most commonly
depicted, although King Athelstan's crown was
shown (c934) as topped by balls (English 2004,
pl 10). Subsequently (c966), Edgar was depicted
with a trefoil crown, as was Cnut (ibid, pl 12). At
this date, it seems that, in England at any rate,
ownership of crowns was personal; Cnut left one
to the New Minster in Winchester. By c1059,
Edward the Confessor is depicted on his coins
wearing an imperial-style, arched crown, yet in the
Bayeux Tapestry his crown is shown with upstand-
ing trefoils, like Harold's. These trefoil crowns are
frequently depicted as 'open', but are sometimes
'covered' (e.g. ibid, pl 13; Wilson 1985, pl 31).

When Edward's tomb was opened in 1102, it

Fig 1

*The coronation of King Harold (1066), in the
Bayeux Tapestry (Municipale de Bayeux).*

is said to have contained a crown; if so, it had
already gone missing in the twelfth century. In
any case, it would probably have been a funerary crown, made for the occasion as a royal
symbol. Such simple crowns of copper gilt have
been found in the graves of Ottonian emperors
in the cathedral at Speyer (cf. Box 15.2); those
of Conrad II (†1039) and Henry II (†1056),
with their trefoil projections, certainly resemble
the ones depicted on the heads of Edward and
Harold (English 2004, 364-5, pl 14); that below
(Fig 2) is from the grave of Henry IV (†1106),
with imperial bows. The use of funerary crowns
appears to have been widespread because another
example is known from the shrine of St Erik in
Uppsala Cathedral, presumably dating from 1160
(Roesdahl & Wilson 1992, no 535).

By James Graham-Campbell

Fig 2

*The funerary crown of
Emperor Henry IV (†1106),
at Speyer (Bayerische
Akademie der Wissen-
schaften, Munich).*

Heraldry

Heraldry is conveniently defined as 'the systematic hereditary use of an arrangement of charges or devices on a shield', a usage that 'emerged at about the same moment in the mid-twelfth century over a wide area of Europe. Between 1135 and 1155 seals show the general adoption of heraldic devices in England, France, Germany, Spain and Italy (Woodcock & Robinson 1988, 1).

As armour became more fully encompassing of the body, men in battle became harder to recognise. The designs displayed on shields and banners in the eleventh century, as at the Battle of Hastings (1066) and during the First Crusade (1096), may perhaps already have been hereditary, but these proto-heraldic devices were too simple and similar to be practical, as is demonstrated in the Bayeux Tapestry where Duke William, at Hastings, is shown having to raise his helmet in order to dispel the rumour that he had been killed (Wilson 1985, pl 68.

An alternative suggestion to heraldry having had purely military origins, while not denying its strong military associations, is that it developed from seal devices adopted by families descended from Charlemagne. There is, however, no doubt that the sudden and widespread development of heraldry across Europe was associated with the Crusades and the rise of tournaments, which brought together knights from all over Latin Christendom, and emphasized the universality of western civilization (Woodcock & Robinson 1988, 14). After its immediate origins in the twelfth century, heraldry was to develop in complexity and elaboration in the later Middle Ages (see Vol 2).

Seals

The two essential features of the medieval seal were the central pictorial symbol and the legend around the edge identifying the owner (Fig 12.10). The widespread fashion for sealing documents, with impressed wax, took off in the late twelfth century (see Vol 2), although its origins were much earlier. In the mid-ninth century, Pope Nicholas I wrote to the ecclesiastical and secular elite insisting that they seal their correspondence and, indeed, seals were primarily used for correspondence until c1100 (Cherry 1997).

Some of the earliest seal matrices in Northern Europe were made of ivory, as well as metal, but their increasing use in the twelfth century doubtless resulted in the switch to metal, under the influence of both Byzantine and Southern European practices. In fact, lead was much used for sealing in the south, particularly by the Papacy. The papal seals, known as *bullae* were double-sided and hung from the document (or 'bull') to which they were attached. They were conservative in design, usually depicting the heads of the apostles Peter and Paul on one side, with the name of the pope on the other, in the form introduced by Pope Paschal II (1088-1118).

The 'Great Seal' or 'Seal of Majesty' (a circular seal depicting the seated ruler with his royal insignia) first appeared in Europe with Emperor Henry II of Germany (1002-24), in France with Henry I (1031-60) and England with Edward the Confessor (1042-66), the latter being double-sided (Cherry 1997, 126). William, as both King of England and Duke of Normandy, had himself depicted on the obverse as enthroned (for England)

Fig 12.10 *The silver seal matrix (height: 9.6cm) of Isabella of Hainault, Queen of France (1180–90), from her coffin in Notre-Dame, Paris; she is depicted standing, crowned and holding both a sceptre and a lily, symbol of the Virgin Mary and purity (© The Trustees of the British Museum).*

and, on the reverse, on horseback (for Normandy). The seals of the twelfth-century nobility often favoured the equestrian figure. Whereas the seals of male royalty and nobility were circular in form, seals for ladies of similar status were usually pointed, or vesica shaped, and depicted them as standing (Fig 12.10)

As already noted, seals provide more than just evidence for administrative practices, given that they depict regalia, changing fashions in armour and the development of heraldic devices (see Vol 2).

Acknowledgements

James Graham-Campbell is most grateful to Sabine Felgenhauer-Schmiedt, Oliver Rackham and James Robinson for their information and advice in the preparation of Part 2, and to David M Wilson for assistance with its completion.

BIBLIOGRAPHY

Alcock, L (2003) *Kings & Warriors, Craftsmen & Priests in Northern Britain AD 550-850*, Edinburgh

Arbeiter, A and Noack-Haley, S (1999) *Denkmäler des frühen Mittelalters vom 8. bis 11. Jahrhundert. Hispania Antiqua*, Mainz

Arens, F (1967) *Die Königspfalz Wimpfen*, Berlin

Atzbach, R (1998) 'Das Palatium in Seligenstadt: ein "Schloß" Friedrichs I. und Friedrichs II', in *Schloss Tirol. Saalbauten und Burgen des 12. Jahrhunderts in Mitteleuropa*, Forschungen zu Burgen und Schlössern 4, Munich/Berlin, 189-96

Bellafiori, G (1990) *Architettura in Sicilia nelle età islamica e normanna (827-1194)*, La civiltà siciliana 1, Milan

Beuckers, KG, Cramer, J and Imhof, M (eds) (2002) *Die Ottonen,* Petersberg

Biller, T (1998) 'Die Pfalz Friedrichs I. in Kaiserswerth, zu ihrer Rekonstruktion und Interpretation', in *Schloss Tirol. Saalbauten und Burgen des 12. Jahrhunderts in Mitteleuropa,* Forschungen zu Burgen und Schlössern 4, Munich/Berlin, 173-88

Binding, G (1996) *Deutsche Königspfalzen. Von Karl dem Großen bis Friedrich II. (765-1240),* Darmstadt

Bolognesi Recchi Franceschini, E (1999) 'Der byzantinische Kaiserpalast im 8. Jahrhundert', in Stiegemann & Wemhoff (eds), Vol 3, 123-9

Borger, H and Oediger, FW (1969) *Beiträge zur Frühgeschichte des Xantener Viktorstiftes.* Rheinische Ausgrabungen 6, Düsseldorf

Boschetti-Maradi, A (2005) 'Eginoturm und Wirtschaftsbauten im Oberen Garten', in *Müstair, Kloster St. Johann* 3, Veröffentlichungen des Instituts für Denkmalpflege der ETH Zürich 16, Zürich, 11-122

De Bouard, M (1973/4) 'De l'*aula* au donjon. Les fouilles de la motte de La Chapelle à Doué-la-Fontaine (IXe-XIe s.)', *Archéologie médiévale* 3/4, 4-110

Bouet, P, Levy, B and Neveux, F (eds) (2004) *The Bayeux Tapestry: Embroidering the Facts of History,* Caen

Brink, S (2004) 'Legal assembly sites in early Scandinavia', in Pantos, A and Semple, S (eds), *Assembly Places and Practices in Medieval Europe,* Dublin, 205-16

Brühl, C (1975/90) *Palatium und Civitas. Studien zur Profantopographie spätantiker Civitates vom 3. bis zum 13. Jahrhundert*: 1, *Gallien*; 2, *Germanien,* Cologne/Vienna

Bullough, D (1980, 2nd ed) *The Age of Charlemagne,* London

Campbell, J (2003) 'Anglo-Saxon courts', in Cubitt (ed), 55-169

Carver, MOH (2005) *Sutton Hoo: a Seventh-Century Princely Burial Ground and its Context,* Research Reports of the Society of Antiquaries of London 69, London

Castellanos, C and Martin Viso, I (2005) 'The local articulation of central power in the north of the Iberian peninsula (500-1000)', *Early Medieval Europe* 13:1, 1-42

Cherry, J (1997) 'Medieval and post-medieval seals', in Collon, D (ed), *7000 Years of Seals,* London, 124-42

Colvin, HM (ed) (1963) *The History of the King's Works,* Vol 1, London

Cubitt, C (ed) (2003) *Court Culture in the Early Middle Ages. The Proceedings of the First Alcuin Conference,* Studies in the Early Middle Ages 3, Turnhout

Cummins, J (1988) *The Hound and the Hawk: the Art of Medieval Hunting,* London

Cüppers, H et al (1982) *Aquae Granni. Beiträge zur Archäologie von Aachen,* Rheinische Ausgrabungen 22, Cologne

Dapper, M (2002) 'Die ottonische Pfalz Tilleda', in Beuckers et al (eds), 265-6

Dodwell, CR (1971) *Painting in Europe: 800-1200,* Harmondsworth

Edwards, N (1990/96) *The Archaeology of Early Medieval Ireland,* London

Ehlers, C, Jarnut, J and Wemhoff, M (eds) (2007) *Zentren herrschaftlicher Repräsentation im Hochmittelalter. Geschichte, Architektur und Zeremoniell,* Deutsche Königspfalzen 11/7, Göttingen

English, B (2004) 'The coronation of Harold in the Bayeux Tapestry', in Bouet et al (eds), 347-81

Esquieu, Y and Pradalier, H (1996) 'Les palais épiscopaux dans la France méridionale', in Renoux (ed), 77-89

Fenske, L, Jarnut, J and Wemhoff, M (eds) (2001) *Splendor palatii. Neue Forschungen zu Paderborn und anderen Pfalzen der Karolingerzeit,* Deutsche Königspfalzen 11/5, Göttingen

Foster, S (2004, 2nd ed) *Picts, Gaels and Scots,* London

Frontzek, W, Memmert, T & Möhle, M (1996) *Das Goslarer Kaiserhaus. Eine baugeschichtliche Untersuchung,* Goslarer Fundus 2, Hildesheim/Zürich/New York

Gaborit-Chopen, D (1987) *Regalia. Les instruments du sacre des rois de France. Les 'honneurs de Charlemagne',* Paris

Gai, S and Mecke, B (2004) *Est locus insignis ... Die Pfalz Karls des Großen in Paderborn und ihre bauliche Entwicklung bis zum Jahr 1002,* Denkmalpflege und Forschung in Westfalen 40, Münster

Gai, S (2007) 'Zu Rekonstruktion und Zeitstellung der spätottonischen Pfalz in Paderborn', in Ehlers et al (eds), 121-50

Grewe, H (2001) 'Die Ausgrabungen in der Königspfalz zu Ingelheim am Rhein', in Fenske et al (eds), 155-74

Grewe, H (2006) 'Kontinuität – Diskontinuität. Neue Beobachtungen zur Sakraltopographie der Pfalz Ingelheim im Früh- und Hochmittelalter', *Mitteilungen der Deutschen Gesellschaft für Archäologie des Mittelalters und der Neuzeit* 17, 37-42

Grewe, H (2007) 'Die bauliche Entwicklung der Pfalz Ingelheim im Hochmittelalter am Beispiel der Sakralarchitektur', in Ehlers et al (eds), 101-20

Grimm, P (1968) *Tilleda. Eine Königspfalz am Kyffhäuser, Vol. 1: Die Hauptburg*, Deutsche Akademie der Wissenschaften zu Berlin, Schriften der Sektion Ur- und Frühgeschichte 24, Berlin

Grimm, P (1990) *Tilleda. Eine Königspfalz am Kyffhäuser, Vol. 2: Die Vorburg und Zusammenfassung*, Deutsche Akademie der Wissenschaften zu Berlin, Schriften der Sektion Ur- und Frühgeschichte 40, Berlin

Guigon, P (1995) 'La résidence palatiale de Locronan (fin IXe-début Xe siècle)', in *Saint Ronan et la Troménie*, Actes du Colloque international 1989, Brest, 71-108

Gwei-Djen, L, Needham, J and Needham, D (1972) 'The coming of ardent water', *Ambix* 19, 69-72

Hayman, GN and Reynolds, AJ (2005) 'A Saxon and Saxo-Norman execution cemetery at 42-54 London Road, Staines', *Archaeological Journal* 162, 115-57

Hill, D (2000) 'Offa's Dyke: pattern and purpose', *Antiquaries Journal* 80, 195-206

Hill, NG (1937) 'Excavations on Stockbridge Down 1935-36', *Proceedings of the Hampshire Field Club* 13, 247-59

Hölscher, U (1927) *Die Kaiserpfalz Goslar*, Die deutschen Kaiserpfalzen 1, Berlin

Jacobi, HJ and Rauch, C (1976) *Die Ausgrabungen in der Königspfalz Ingelheim 1909-1914*, Römisch-Germanisches Zentralmuseum Mainz, Mono 2; Studien zur Königspfalz Ingelheim 1, Mainz

Jørgensen, L (2003) 'Manor and market at Lake Tissø in the sixth to eleventh centuries: the Danish "productive" sites', in Pestell, T and Ulmschneider, K (eds), *Markets in Early Medieval Europe: Trading and 'Productive' Sites, 650-850*, Macclesfield, 175-207

Kaiser, R (1996) 'Castrum und Pfalz in Zürich: ein Widerstreit des archäologischen Befundes und der schriftlichen Überlieferung?', in *Deutsche Königspfalzen* 4, Veröffentlichungen des Max-Planck-Instituts für Geschichte 11/IV, Göttingen, 84-109

Kobyliński, Z (1990) 'Early medieval hillforts in Polish lands in the 6th to the 8th centuries: problems of origins, function, and spatial organization', in Austin, D and Alcock, L (eds), *From the Baltic to the Black Sea: Studies in Medieval Archaeology*, London, 147-56

Koch, WM (1997) 'Die Aachener "Barbarossamauer" und ihre Vorgänger', in *Archäologie im Rheinland 1996*, Cologne, 102-4

Kuhn, R, Brandl, H, Helten, L and Jäger, F (2005) *Aufgedeckt. Ein neuer ottonischer Kirchenbau am Magdeburger Domplatz*, Archäologie in Sachsen-Anhalt, Sonderband 3, Halle

Lasko, P (1972) *Ars Sacra: 800-1200*, Harmondsworth

Lammers, W (1972) 'Ein karolingisches Bildprogramm in der Aula regia von Ingelheim', in *Festschrift für Hermann Heimpel zum 70. Geburtstag am 19. September 1971*, Vol 3, Veröffentlichungen des Max-Planck-Instituts für Geschichte 36/III, Göttingen, 226-89

Lehmann, E (1983) 'Der Palast Ottos des Großen in Magdeburg', in Möbius, F and Schubert, E (eds), *Architektur des Mittelalters*, Weimar, 42-62

Le Maho, J (2001) 'Die erzbischöfliche Pfalz von Rouen (Frankreich) zu Beginn des 9. Jahrhunderts', in Fenske et al (eds), 193-210

Lobbedey, U (2003) 'Carolingian royal palaces: the state of research from an architectural historian's viewpoint', in Cubitt (ed), 129-54

Luchterhandt, M (1999) 'Päpstlicher Palastbau und höfisches Zeremoniell unter Leo III.', in Stiegemann & Wemhoff (eds), Vol 3, 109-22

Ludovici, B (2002) '"Die Halle des Königs". Repräsentative Profanarchitektur der ottonischen Pfalzen im Harzraum', in Beuckers et al (eds), 259-63

Ludovici, B (2003) 'Magdeburg als Hauptort des ottonischen Imperiums. Bemerkungen zum Beitrag von Archäologie und Kunstgeschichte zur Konstruktion eines Geschichtsbildes', in Hardt, M, Lübke, C and Schorkowitz, D (eds), *Inventing the Pasts in North Central Europe. The National Perception of Early Medieval History and Archaeology*, Gesellschaften und Staaten im Epochenwandel 9, Frankfurt, 111-26

Lumpe, J (2000) *Pfalz, Hospital, Pfrundhaus. Neue Ausgrabungen am St. Petri-Gemeindehaus in Soest und ihre Bedeutung für die Geschichte des Hohen Hospitals*, Soester Beiträge zur Archäologie 4, Soest

Maurer, H (2003) 'Reichenau', in Zotz et al (eds), Vol 3, 493-571

Meckseper, C (1986) 'Das Palatium Ottos des Großen in Magdeburg', *Burgen und Schlösser* 27, 101-15

Meier, H-R (1994) *Die normannischen Königspaläste von Palermo*, Manuskripte zur Kunstwissenschaft 42, Worms

de Mérindol, C (2001) 'Essai sur la distinction des espaces par le décor à l'époque médiévale: iconologie et topographie', in Renoux (ed), 63-75

Miller, MC (2000) *The Bishop's Palace. Architecture and Authority in Medieval Italy*, Ithaca/London

Munch, GS, Johansen, OS and Roesdahl, E (2003) *Borg in Lofoten. A Chieftain's Farm in North Norway*, Trondheim

Moorhouse, S (1972) 'Medieval distilling-apparatus of glass and pottery', *Medieval Archaeology* 16, 69-72

Nissen-Jaubert, A (1996) 'Sites centraux et résidences princières au Danemark avant 1250', in Renoux (ed), 197-210

Noack-Haley, S and Arbeiter, A (1994) *Asturische Königsbauten des 9. Jahrhunderts*, Madrider Beiträge 22, Mainz

Pantos, A and Semple, S (eds) (2004) *Assembly Places and Practices in Medieval Europe*, Dublin

Porsche, M (2000) *Stadtmauer und Stadtentstehung*, Hertingen

Preissler, M (2003) *Die karolingischen Malereifragmente aus Paderborn*, Denkmalpflege und Forschung in Westfalen 40/1, Mainz

Rackham, O (1986) *The History of the Countryside*, London

Rackham, O (1990, 2nd ed) *Trees and Woodland in the British Landscape*, London

Rahtz, P (1976) 'Buildings and rural settlement', in Wilson, DM (ed), *The Archaeology of Anglo-Saxon England*, London, 49-98

Rahtz, P (1979) *The Saxon and Medieval Palaces at Cheddar. Excavations 1960-62*, British Archaeological Reports 65, Oxford

Renaudeau, O (2004) 'The Bayeux tapestry and its depiction of costume: the problems of interpretation', in Bouet et al (eds), 237-59

Renoux, A (ed) (1996) *Palais royaux et princiers au Moyen Age*, Le Mans

Renoux, A (ed) (2001) *'Aux marches du palais'. Qu'est-ce-qu'un palais médiéval? Donnés historiques et archéologiques*, Le Mans

Renoux, A (2007) 'Architecture, pouvoir et répresentation en milieu royal et princier dans la France du Nord aux Xe et XIe siècles', in Ehlers et al (eds), 25-68

Riché, P (1978, trans McNamara, JA) *Daily Life in the World of Charlemagne*, Pennsylvania; from Riché, P (1973) *La Vie Quotidienne dans L'Empire Carolingien*, Paris

Robinson, J (2004) *The Lewis Chessmen*, London

Roesdahl, E and Wilson, DM (eds) (1992) *From Viking to Crusader: the Scandinavians and Europe 800-1200*, Copenhagen

Sage, W (1976) 'Die Ausgrabungen in der Pfalz zu Ingelheim am Rhein', *Francia* 4, 141-60

Schramm, PE (1954-56) *Herrschaftszeichen und Staatssymbolik*, Stuttgart

Schramm, PE and Mütherich, F (1981, 2nd ed) *Denkmäle der Deutschen Könige und Kaiser*, Munich

Schuchardt, G (ed) (2001) *Der romanische Palas der Wartburg* 1, Eisenach/Regensburg

Schürer, O (1934) *Die Kaiserpfalz Eger* [Cheb], Die deutschen Kaiserpfalzen 2, Berlin

Sennhauser, HR (2002) 'Baugeschichte und Bedeutung des Klosters St. Johann', in Wyss, A, Rutishauser, H and Nay, MA (eds), *Die mittelalterlichen Wandmalereien im Kloster Müstair*, Veröffentlichungen des Instituts für Denkmalpflege an der ETH Zürich 22, Zürich, 17-29

Steane, J (1993) *The Archaeology of the Medieval English Monarchy*, London/New York

Stiegemann, C and Wemhoff, M (eds) (1999) *799. Karl der Große und Paderborn*, 3 vols, Mainz

Temple, E (1976) *Anglo-Saxon-Manuscripts 900-1066*, London

Twining, EF (1967) *European Regalia*, London

Untermann, M (1991) 'Pfalz und Stadt [Wimpfen]', in *Heilbronn und das mittlere Neckarland zwischen Marbach und Gundelsheim*, Führer zu archäologischen Denkmälern in Deutschland 22, Stuttgart, 103-7

Untermann, M (1999) '"opere mirabili constructa". Die Aachener 'Residenz' Karls des Großen', in Stiegemann & Wemhoff (eds), Vol 3, 152-64

Untermann, M (2006) *Architektur im frühen Mittelalter*, Darmstadt

Vogt, E (1948) *Der Lindenhof in Zürich*, Zürich

Wilson, DM (1957) 'An inlaid iron folding stool in the British Museum', *Medieval Archaeology* 1, 39-56

Wilson, DM (1985) *The Bayeux Tapestry*, London

Woodcock, T and Robinson, JM (1988) *The Oxford Guide to Heraldry*, Oxford

Wyss, M (ed) (1996) *Atlas historique de Saint-Denis, des origines au XVIIe siècle*, Documents d'archéologie française 59, Paris

Wyss, M (2001) 'Die Klosterpfalz Saint-Denis im Licht der neuen Ausgrabungen', in Fenske et al (eds), 175-92

Zotz, T et al (eds) (1983; in progress) *Die deutschen Königspfalzen. Repertorium der Pfalzen, Königshöfe und übrigen Aufenthaltsorte der Könige im deutschen Reich des Mittelalters* 1: *Hessen*; 2: *Thüringen*; 3: *Baden-Württemberg*; 4: *Niedersachsen*, Göttingen

CHAPTER 13

RELIGIONS

Leszek Słupecki and Magdalena Valor

PART 1: PAGAN RELIGION IN NORTH, EAST AND CENTRAL EUROPE, AND CONVERSION TO CHRISTIANITY *by Leszek Słupecki*

Introduction

The rise of Western Europe during the Carolingian period led to the expansion of Christianity outside the borders of the former Roman Empire. This process had started in the seventh century, ranging from the peaceful Christianisation of the Anglo-Saxons to the conversion of 'Continental' Germans, especially the Saxons, achieved mostly by fire and sword at the end of the eighth century. These two events created two different models for subsequent conversions. The process continued: the Scandinavians and Slavs accepted baptism between the ninth and eleventh centuries; the Finns and the Balts between the twelfth and fourteenth. In 1386 the conversion of Europe was almost accomplished, when the Lithuanian ruler, Jagaillo, elected king of Poland, accepted baptism in the peaceful manner; however, it was not until the eighteenth century that the Saami were to be fully converted to Christianity. This development was connected to important social changes within the pagan societies of Central and East Europe (mostly Slavic), and in the North (mostly Scandinavian). As a result, post-Roman and Christian Western Europe (unified for a while under Charlemagne) expanded into the 'barbarian' territories that had never formed part of the Roman Empire. The border of this eastern expansion met up, in the eleventh century, with the corresponding expansion of the Orthodox Church in Russia (cf. Fig 13.9). Expanding eastwards and northwards, Christianity encountered the traditional religions of the Scandinavians, Slavs, Balts, Finns and Saami, all indigenous to Europe, but also with those of nomadic invaders, such as Avars, Bulgarians, Khasarians, Hungarians, etc.

Pagan beliefs consist of: mythology; religious ritual; magic and divination. Mythology provides explanations for the origins and destiny of the world and its people, and the origins and reason for the most important rituals and social customs. Religion maintains the necessary connection to the supernatural world, by performing rituals such as prayers, offerings and feasts. Rituals were held in public in sanctuaries, but also on private estates, cyclically according to the religious calendar. Ritual was also practised in other places at special events (e.g. battles), and in other forms in situations of crisis (e.g. famine or pestilence). Rituals of transition connected to family life (e.g. marriages, births and funerals) were essentially private in the case of ordinary people; however, when dealing with rulers and the elite these became public. Partly public, but to some extent secret, were ceremonies of initiation into adulthood. The outcome of religious rituals depends on the goodwill of the gods. Magic, however, when performed properly, should always be effective. Oracles and divination provided knowledge about the destiny of societies and particular men (Bauschatz 1982; Słupecki 1998), but such was usually given obliquely, without details of time or place for the events foretold. The final part of belief systems is the burial custom, with some form of afterlife as its ideological background; this aspect is omitted from this chapter (cf. Box 8.3, and Chapter 15).

Pagan Beliefs

Mythologies

Mythology could survive the processes of Christianisation (e.g. the Celtic mythology of Ireland, and Germanic traditions, both Continental and Anglo-Saxon), but often with subtle influence from the new religion. Among the pagan mythologies of early medieval Europe that survived unaltered into the ninth century, the Old Norse is perhaps the best known (de Vries 1956-57; Turville-Petre 1964; Simek 2003; Andrén et al 2006), whereas our knowledge of Old Slavic is much more limited (Gieysztor 2006). What we know about Baltic (Biezais 1975), Finnish (Haavio 1967) and Saami (Rydving 1995) comes mostly from modern sources, recorded sometimes only in the nineteenth century, as in case of the Finnish epic *Kalevala*. It is also true, however, that most of the sources for Old Norse mythology were written down after conversion. The Icelander Snorri Sturluson wrote his compendium of Norse poetry and pagan mythology, the so-called *Prose Edda*, between 1221 and 1241. Large parts of the *Poetic Edda* are considered to have been written in the twelfth century, with only a few poems (such as *Voluspa*) originating in the late pagan period. Although relatively late, both *Eddas* include motifs attested earlier in 'skaldic' verses, composed in the tenth century, which appear to be reflected on monuments, notably the numerous 'picture-stones' on the Swedish island of Gotland (dating from about the eighth century), but also on a few comparable objects from the rest of Scandinavia and North-West Europe, such as some stone crosses in England and the Isle of Man, with scenes depicting Old Norse myths. Important iconological motifs are found on small objects, e.g. pocket idols, decorated gold foils called *guldgubbar* (sixth-ninth centuries, known from across Scandinavia), and especially the earlier Germanic gold bracteates (fifth-sixth centuries). This material, like a series of snapshots, shows that the *Eddas*, though obviously influenced by Christian ideas, were nevertheless based on older narratives.

In Old Norse mythology, Odin was the god of lords, warriors, war, death, ecstasy, poetry, knowledge and magic, who according to his myth offered one eye for access to the source of wisdom. In the case of the god Thor, a hammer functioned as his symbol, as shown first on some runic stones mentioning Thor as protector and defender (Simek

Fig 13.1 *According to Norse mythology, when the god Thor caught the World Serpent on his fishing line its strength was such that his foot went through the bottom of the boat, as depicted on this rune-stone from Altuna, Sweden (Słupecki 2003; after Turville-Petre 1964).*

2003, 131-3). The popularity of Thor's hammers used as amulets seems to be partly a pagan response to the use of pendant crosses by Christians (Staecker 1997; Wamers 1997). This, and other evidence, demonstrates that Thor was the most popular Norse pagan deity. The myth of him fishing for the World Serpent is easy to identify because of a characteristic detail (Fig 13.1).

A small ithyphallic figure from Rällinge, Sweden (e.g. Graham-Campbell 1980, no 513), is commonly interpreted as an image of the fertility god Frey, especially because of Adam of Bremen's (IV, 26) account of the image of Fricco (a by-name of Frey) in the eleventh-century temple at Uppsala which was said to have a huge penis (*cum ingenti priapo*). The *guldgubbar* showing an embracing couple have been interpreted as images of Frey and Freya, or Frey and Gerd (Steinsland 1992), but this image is more convincingly explained as showing the Germanic gesture of the legal act of marriage (Simek 2002, 105-9). Some *guldgubbar* show a man with a long sceptre who might be Thor (in Uppsala, his image was sculpted *cum sceptro*); another type might show dead people. There are thus three ways to interpret *guldgubbar*, not necessarily contradictory, in connection: (1) with mythology; (2) with the law of marriage; and (3) with cult, as a form of 'temple-money' (Simek 2003, 72), offered to gods in supposed sanctuaries, as at Gudme/Lundeborg (in Denmark), and Sorte Muld on Bornholm (where more than 2,000 examples of *guldgubbar* have been found).

Offering scene on a 'picture-stone', **Fig 13.2**
Hammars I, Gotland (after Nylén &
Lamm 1991).

Turning to mythological motifs on stone objects, a cross-slab from the Isle of Man depicts Odin, with a raven, being consumed by the Fenris wolf (e.g. Graham-Campbell 1980, no 534). The riders on two Gotlandic 'picture-stones' (from Alskog and Ardre) are shown on horses with eight legs, which is described as a feature of Odin's horse, Sleipnir, but they need not be depictions of Odin himself, rather of dead warriors being conveyed to Valhalla. There are more than 300 'picture-stones' in Gotland, with an abundance of iconographical motifs (Nylén & Lamm 1991), but only in a few cases can they be confidently identified with recorded myths (Fig 13.2). In general, 'picture-stones' seem to be connected to eschatological beliefs, as suggested by the frequent motif of a (funeral?) ship, and sometimes a female figure, with drinking-horn in hand (valkyrie?) welcoming a rider (to Valhalla?). Even the special shape of 'picture-stones' has been interpreted as representing the door to the 'other-world' (Andrén 1989).

It is commonly assumed that Germanic peoples, including the pagan Scandinavians, did not erect monumental idols of their gods, a notion derived from Tacitus (*Germania* 43), with reference to the grove of the twin gods Alcis, where 'no idols' stand. Precisely the same was written about Slavic groves 1,000 years later (Helmold I, 84), with no knowledge of Tacitus. The existence of some images of pagan gods is nevertheless attested in written sources, beginning with Tacitus himself, with his mention of the 'goddess Nerthus' who was taken in ritual procession in a carriage. The same practice was later reflected in Old Norse *Thattr Gunnari helmingr*, with mention of Frey being transported in a carriage around Sweden. Saga accounts also refer to some idols of Thor (e.g. in Trondheim), not to forget Adam of Bremen's (IV, 26-7) account of the three gods at Uppsala.

More general ideas of the worlds of gods and people (Asgard and Midgard) encircled by the World-Serpent (*Midgardsorm*), lying in the ocean, seem to be evoked on numerous runic stones with images of the so-called 'runic-serpent'. The idea of there being three realms to the world (sea, earth and heaven) is well known from Germanic, including Norse, formulas, and seems to be depicted on the Altuna stone (Fig 13.1), which shows Thor fishing the *Midgardsorm* on the sea, with a rider (Frey?) on earth, and a person in heaven above (Odin or Tyr?).

In contrast to the Scandinavians, depictions by the Slavs of pagan mythological motifs are very rare. Nevertheless, there are a few scenes of possible mythological meaning on the oldest Slavic pottery, among which is a rider with a kind of zigzag above that could be interpreted as a god of thunder with lightning in his hand (Moszczyński &

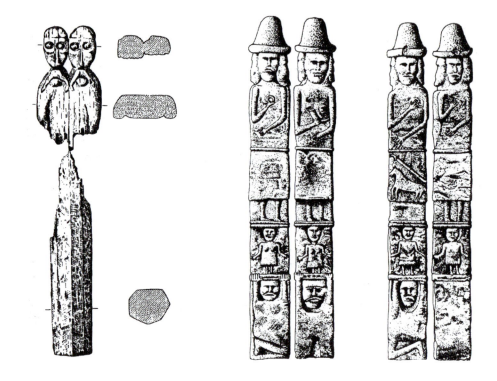

Fig 13.3 *(left) The 'Twins from Fischerinsel' (Słupecki 1994; after Gringmuth-Dallmer & Hollnagel 1971).*

Fig 13.4 *(right) Stone idol supposed to be of Svantevit from the river Zbrutsh, in southern Poland (after Słupecki 1994).*

Szymański 1987). Such a Slavic god, later known as Perun, is mentioned by Procopius of Cesarea (III, 14, 23-24), who also stressed the role of water and female water-spirits in the cult. So, the wavy motifs frequent on Slavic pottery might possibly be connected with aquatic symbolism.

As opposed to the North, monumental images of gods are well attested amongst the Slavs (cf. Váňa 1983). In addition to written accounts of the eleventh/twelfth century, the West Slavic custom of depicting gods with many heads or faces was confirmed by the discovery of the wooden statue of human size with two heads (Fig 13.3), known today as the 'Twins from Fischerinsel' (Gringhmuth-Dallmer & Hollnagel 1971). The idol of Svantevit, in his main temple at Arkona, on the island of Rügen, was described as having four heads (Saxo Grammaticus XIV, 39,3). A possible stone idol of Svantevit (almost 3m high), with four faces and holding a drinking-horn and a ring (Fig 13.4), was found in 1848 in the river Zbrutsh, then in southern Poland (modern Ukraine); the four-faced idol also appears as small figurines, e.g. from Slavic Wolin, and a recent find from Lund, Sweden (Lamm 1987; Müller-Wille 1999, 81).

Rituals

The texts of pagan prayers remain unknown, but religious language seems to be echoed in some Old Norse formulas, including oaths and magic charms. Slavic prayers referred to by Procopius of Cesarea (III, 14, 23-4), in the sixth century, ask gods for life in case of war or sickness; Ibn Rosteh recounted the Slavic custom of praying to the god of heaven and fire, for good crops; and Saxo Grammaticus (XIV, 39,5) described the appeal made by priest and people for an abundant harvest, while offering bread during the autumnal feast to Svantevit, at Arkona.

Old Norse terminology for ritual is very rich (Düwel 1970). The basic term *blot* covers ritual feasts with offerings, but in particular it refers to a sacrifice. The name of the winter festival of 'Yule' was so resistant that it has survived until the present time in the Scandinavian and Anglo-Saxon world as an alternative name for Christmas. The Old Norse religious calendar remains uncertain, although we know about feasts held in autumn and early winter, when there was a plentiful supply of food, as well as a feast at the beginning of summer, but – interestingly – nothing about midsummer, which is otherwise attested in Scandinavia in folklore and is a common festival across the whole of 'ethnic' Europe.

The etymology of the Slavic term for sacrifice, *treba* ('something you must do'), stresses the necessity for making offerings (Kahl 2004). Written sources emphasise the importance of a feast held in the autumn at Arkona, 'after harvest' (Saxo Grammaticus XIV, 39,4); spring and summer festivals are likewise attested. The other general Slavic term for a feast, *zertva*, etymologically means 'to praise the gods' (Gieysztor 1984, 251); this seems to have developed into a verb, *zrec,* denoting extreme devouring. Indeed, Saxo (XIV, 39,6) described the feast for Svantevit, at Arkona, as ending with gluttony and stuffing. To distinguish remains of such offerings from ordinary kitchen-waste is difficult, but sometimes possible. Occasionally, however, whole animals or large parts of animals were deposited as (e.g.) the parts of horses discovered around a kind of stone altar found in Starigard/Oldenburg (Gabriel 1988, 78).

In the North, various myths reveal the deep symbolic meaning of animal sacrifice (e.g. in Valhalla, the boar 'Saehrimnir' is killed and consumed every evening, but next day is always alive again). It would seem that in the North, as in Ancient Greece, the flesh of sacrificed animals was divided into two parts: some for consumption by the people, and the rest for the gods, in the hope that the sacrificed animals would return in plenty (as in comparable Finnish folk-rituals). Indeed, the Iron-age Germanic sacrificial offerings of horses consisted mostly of heads and hoofs, presumably attached to whole skins (Jankuhn 1967, 130; Simek 2003, 83).

Offerings of cattle and boars are described in the Sagas, but the most important offering was that of a horse, which included the ritual consumption of its flesh. By the eighth century, St Boniface forbade Germans to eat horse meat, and the same prohibition appears again later in Scandinavian laws following conversion, although when the Icelanders agreed to accept Christianity one of the conditions was that the consumption of horse meat should continue, so that it remained permissible to perform pagan rituals in private for a period (*Islendingabók,* 7). In Norway, when Hakon the Good attempted to introduce Christianity, the inhabitants of Trøndelag forced him firstly to taste some flesh from the horse-sacrifice before performing his royal duties (*Hakonar saga goda*, 13-17), because only then could they be sure that nothing in the previous legal order and power structure had changed (Aðalsteinsson 1998, 57-80). The ritual feast was a kind of communion uniting gods and people, to ensure good order and prosperity which was why Christians were not allowed to eat with pagans, it being equivalent to sharing a table with the devil. The Scandinavian Vikings in Britain and Ireland found a way to avoid such problems by accepting *prima signatio* in place of baptism.

In accounts of the Slavs, animal-sacrifice (mostly cattle) is only briefly noted, given that the attention of chroniclers was focused on human offerings. Evidence is concentrated in West Slavic Polabia, and mostly concerns the Lutitians. According to the earliest account from about 990, they beheaded the commander of a captured Polish stronghold on the battlefield (Thietmar IV, 13); some years later Lutitians executed two missionary monks. Finally, in 1068, at Riedegost-Rethra (the main sanctuary of the Lutitians), the Mecklemburg bishop who had been captured some months earlier, during a pagan revolt, was executed in the main square of the town (Adam of Bremen III, 51). His butchered corpse was left there, but his head, stuck on spear, was taken into the shrine and offered to the main god, Ridegost-Svarozic. This ritual was possibly a Slavic response to events in 955 when the Saxons made a display of the severed heads of the defeated Slavic king and his warriors (Widukind III, 56); the Balts may have had a similar custom.

The credibility of accounts describing human offerings varies between horror stories about barbarians and reality, but the fact of the practice is undeniable (Huldgård 2001). The sacrifice believed to be typically 'Odinic', involving hanging on a tree, is to some extent testified by iconography, as on the Oseberg 'tapestry'. On the 'picture-stone' at Store Hammars (Fig 13.2), a hanged man is shown alongside another on a kind of altar.

Convincing archaeological evidence for human offerings, although numerous in the preceding period thanks to bog-finds, is rare from 800-1200. Some depictions have survived, however, as on the so-called Kultstrand in Ralswiek, on Rügen (Herrmann 1998), and a kind of stone altar in Kaldus, near Torun, in Poland (Chudziak 2003). The evidence appears clear, at least, in funeral contexts. The custom of burying an additional person during the funerary rite is well-attested both in documentary sources (e.g. Ibn Fadlan, 481-526) and archaeologically, in some pagan Norse burials, e.g. at Oseberg (Gansum 2002, 279), and on the Isle of Man (Bersu & Wilson 1966).

Written sources never mention Slavic horse offerings and almost no archaeological remains of such have been found. Western Slavs did, however, develop the horse oracle, combined with lot-casting. Sacred horses were bred in their major sanctuaries, at Riedegost-Rethra, Szczecin and Arkona, and were used by priests for divination purposes. Casting lots was also frequently used in Scandinavian divination, as well as by the Balts, but although Scandinavian sources mention sacred horses, especially connected to Frey, there is no evidence for there having been institutionalised horse oracles.

For an oracle, in Old Norse religion, *seidr* ('magic') was used, but not exclusively for divination, but also as magic to bring bad luck and death. Although the aim of these two variants of *seidr* was different, the rituals and implements were similar. *Seidr* was a kind of ecstatic practice performed by women, professional seers called *volur* (from *volr*, 'magic staff'). Some female burials with special equipment (including staffs) have recently been interpreted as the graves of *volur* (Price 2002, 181-204). The practice performed by a seer involved contacting the spirits belonging to the 'other-world' and was to large extent similar to shamanic *séances*. It was, however, not simply a borrowing from Saami culture, as Strombäck (1935) and his followers argued, because there was usually no deep ecstasy involved and the use of shaman drums is not mentioned, except in one doubtful account (*Locasenna*, 24). Nevertheless, the practitioners are generally described as being Finns or Saami.

Among the Finns and Saami, the important cult ceremonies were performed by shamans. During the Viking period, as in earlier Germanic religion, many cult functions belonged to the head of the household or community, although some terms, such as the skaldic *olvir*, seem to suggest that there may also have been a professional priesthood during this period (Sundqvist 1996; 1998; 2003). In Iceland, both secular and religious leadership were united in the hands of the chieftain of a region, named *godi*. This term had already appeared on a few Danish runic stones (e.g. Glavendrup); although the role of *godi* seems to have been especially strong in Iceland (Aðalsteinsson 1988, 35-56), the institution of *godi* may thus have had older Scandinavian roots.

Pagan Sanctuaries and 'Central-Places'

At the beginning of the Viking period important changes in ritual and cultic geography occurred. In Northern Europe, following the decline of the great sacrificial places of the Roman Iron Age and Migration period, there came, c800, the end of such 'central-places' as Sorte Muld (on Bornholm), Gudme/Lundeborg (on Fyn) and Uppåkra (near Lund). After these archaeologically tangible holy-places (unattested in written sources), others dominated, e.g. Lejre (Denmark) and Uppsala (Sweden). Both places were rooted in the earlier period, but functioned continuously until the conversion, when they were described in written sources, but their arrangement as sanctuaries has still not been defined archaeologically. The most important information about the temple, grove and sacrificial well at Uppsala, and the great offerings held there every ninth year (during 9 days, 9 men, horses and dogs were allegedly sacrificed), and at Lejre (99 humans, dogs, horses and cocks), derives only from eleventh-century documentary sources (Thietmar I, 17; Adam of Bremen IV, 26-27). Investigations at Uppsala have discovered the remains of large halls (Hedlund 1993), with another at Lejre (Christensen 1991; Niles 2007), where a royal hall *Heort* is mentioned in *Beowulf*. Cemeteries, with monumental burial mounds at Uppsala, and ship-settings and burial mounds at Lejre, suggest links to the royal dynasties of *Ynglingar* and *Skjoldungar*, both claiming to be descended from gods (Faulkes 1978; Sundqvist 2002). Archaeological evidence of cult, in the proper sense, is still, however, lacking from both places, given that the alleged traces of the temple in Uppsala turned out to be the remains of large hall (Nordahl 1996). However, in the case of a similar place at Tissø, in Denmark (Fig 13.5), the connections of the hall to an alleged cult-enclosure and an evident sacrificial place by the lake-side are obvious

Fig 13.5 *Plan of the 9th/10th-century hall and its attached cult area(?) at Tissø, Zealand, Denmark (after Jørgensen 2002).*

(Jørgensen 2002, 215-48). In the North, during the Viking period, the halls of the elite were used as a kind of sacred place (Meulengracht Sørensen 1988), although sometimes *thing* places also served for ritual purposes, e.g. at Birka, at the time of St Anskar's mission (*Vita Anskari* 26-7), and elsewhere in Sweden, as mentioned in Adam of Bremen's

(II, 62) account of the martyrdom of Wulfrad at an assembly-place, when trying to destroy an idol of Thor.

The ritual deposit of weapons in wet places had been in decline since the Roman and Migration periods (Müller-Wille 1999, 63)), but it still continued to be practised as shown by finds from the eighth to eleventh centuries at Gudingsåkrarna, Gotland (Müller-Wille 1984, 190; Simek 2003, 80), and Tissø (Jørgensen 2002, 219). The same is true of holy groves; the many place-names that include the word *lund* (grove), now have an archaeological counterpart in recent discoveries at the place called Frösö (Frey's lake), in Jämtland (Sweden), possibly related to a sacrificial grove (Näsström 2001, 112-13). The Saami made lake-side offerings comprising animal bones, antlers and metal deposits (Zachrisson 1984; 1992, 72-3, no 242).

Around 800, the first archaeologically recognisable Slavic sanctuaries appear, but most written records and archaeological finds belong to the conversion period (late tenth-twelfth centuries). There are credible descriptions of temple buildings (Rethra-Riedegost, Szczecin and Arkona) and archaeological finds of similar structures (Gross Raden, Wolin and Ralswiek), concentrated in Polabia and Pomerania (Slupecki 1994), two regions where late pagan religion developed rapidly in the face of expanding Christianity, when the first Slavic lands were already accepting baptism. The unique Polish temple excavated at Wrocław (Moździoch 2000) is not, strictly speaking, an exception because the shrine was built at the time of heathen revolt (1033), under the clear influence of Polabian, specifically Lutitian, customs. The cult of idols in major settlements is recorded in written sources, e.g. in Pomeranian Wolin and Polabian Brandenburg. The main Slavic sanctuaries were also temples and open-air sanctuaries, with idols possibly at assembly-places or in cult-places, which might have been enclosed. Apart from a few examples in Pomerania, described in written sources in the early twelfth century, there is no evidence for halls, resembling Scandinavian halls, among the pagan Slavs, with the sole exception of one at Starigard-Oldenburg (Gabriel 1988, 75).

Prolonged debate concerning the existence and/or the role of pagan temples in Old Norse and Slavic religion has recently been resolved. It is now clear that the pagan temple was not the same as a Christian church (as earlier assumed). It was never a building large enough to house all the faithful, but rather a small shrine open for the gods (sometimes represented there in form of idols), closed to people, with even priests having limited access (Gieysztor 1984, 261), in front of which the people gathered. Such small temples undoubtedly existed among the Western Slavs during the eleventh-twelfth centuries, and possibly also among the Scandinavians. In Scandinavia, as mentioned above, the hall was the place for public activities connected to cult, especially festive banquets (Herschend 1999), e.g. that recently excavated at Borg (Box 2.2), in northern Norway (Munch et al 2003).

The Old Norse sources sometimes refer to *hörg*, seemingly a type of stone altar. In the *Poetic Edda*, a *hörg* is describe as shining with the fresh blood of sacrificed animals; such an object may possibly have been discovered recently at Sanda in Swedish Uppland (Åqvist 1995). Some concentrations of stones, interpreted as sacrificial places, are also known in Slavic archaeology. However, other sources suggest that *hörg* might have been

BOX 13.1 GROSS RADEN, GERMANY

The most impressive example of pagan religious architecture yet discovered was found at Gross Raden in Mecklenburg, north Germany. Evald Schuldt (1985; cf. Słupecki 1994, 95-105) excavated a large settlement there of ninth-tenth century date, located on a peninsula in Lake Binnen. In its first phase, the houses were built of wattle covered with clay, but in the subsequent phase of timber, using log construction. Contemporary with the second phase, there seems to have been a small stronghold in the lake, connected to the settlement by a bridge. The eastern shore of the peninsula was occupied by a large structure (12x8m), at least four times bigger than the houses in the settlement, separated from the other buildings because surrounded by a fence, close to its walls. The building also differed in its orientation and construction, consisting of two rows of wooden planks, with its exterior decorated with schematic human shapes. Many of the planks are preserved because of their secondary use as foundations for a later building. There is a path leading to the building off the main road in the settlement. There are some conflicting dendrochronological dates: both 871 and 961 (Herrmann & Heussner 1991, 271). Nevertheless, it appears to

have been built before the great pagan revolt in 983 (cf. Herrmann 1993), and quite possibly after the defeat of the Polabians, at Regnitz, in 955.

The cult function of the structure is undeniable, but the question of precisely what this was is not easy to answer. A large wooden plank, with one end resembling a human head, discovered close to the building, could be interpreted as a pillar supporting the roof, or as an idol (although no post-holes were found inside). The reconstruction of the walls as a kind of structure decorated with anthropomorphic planks, as presented by Schuldt (1985, 39 & 47), is completely convincing. A similar plank, with carved details of a human face, has been found at Ralswiek, in Mecklenburg, and others similar to Gross Raden come from nearby Parchim and Wrocław, in Poland (Słupecki 1994, 104 & 208; Moździoch 2000, 179). The reconstruction of the roof is doubtful, however, and in Schuldt's version impossible (because snow falling from the roof in winter would have destroyed the wall). The alternative reconstruction proposed by Herrmann (1993) is thus more probable. In support of his interpretation, there are documentary sources that give descriptions of decorated temple-walls

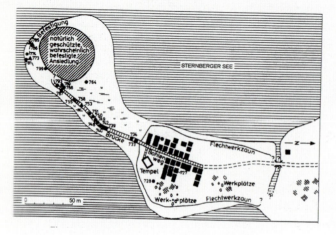

Fig 1

Plan of the settlement at Gross Raden, with its 'tempel' (Słupecki 1994; after Herrmann).

at Riedegost, Szczecin, Arkona and Gutzkow (Słupecki 1997, 299-301).

If the building was roofed, it could have been either a temple or a hall. If a temple, the building was rather large, with a size similar to the alleged Anglo-Saxon temple at Yeavering, in the north of England (Wilson 1992, 46). If a hall, it would seem to be on the small side and, anyway, it contains no trace of a hearth. If there was no roof, as suggested by Gabriel (1992) and Zoll-Adamikowa (1989), the structure could be interpreted as a kind of decorative fence (*atrium*) around a holy space, a type of construction recorded in documentary sources about the Slavs (Słupecki 1994, 97). The question then becomes how to interpret it. A fence surrounding some holy trees, for example, is precluded by its thick wooden floor. The likelihood is therefore that this was an enclosed holy or sacrificial space around idols (despite the absence of post-holes inside), or perhaps a stone altar. Such constructions around altars appear in Roman religion. In the similarly shaped, but larger building discovered at Parchim (almost certainly built without a roof), there was such a stone structure (Paddenberg 2006). There is, however, no evidence for a stone structure at Gross Raden, but an altar might just as well have been made of wood, like a table. In addition to this cult-place in the settlement (be it temple or *atrium*), the small stronghold on the island could also have served for cult purposes.

By Leszek Słupecki

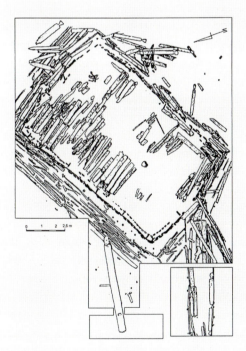

Fig 2

Plan of the excavations of the temple at Gross Raden (Słupecki 1994; after Schuldt 1985).

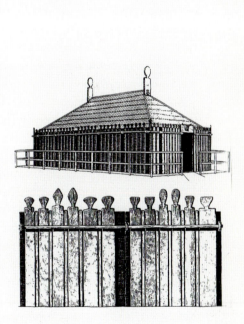

Fig 3

Reconstructions of the wall and temple (Słupecki 1994; after Schuldt 1985).

a wooden structure, but this apparent contradiction could be explained by the hypothesis that *hörg*, originally an altar, later came to be a kind of shrine with a wooden roof over an altar or idol (Olsen 1966, 103-12). Saxo Grammaticus (XIV, 39,39) describes such a construction built over an idol of Rugievit, on the island of Rügen (Słupecki 2001).

In Slavic lands, a nature-cult is recorded in written sources (Słupecki 2002, 25-9), mostly performed in holy groves: e.g. at Zutibure, the 'holy-grove' mentioned by Thietmar (VI, 38); at Prove grove, described in detail by Helmold (I, 84); on the holy mountain, Sleza (Thietmar VII, 59); and once in wetland, around the holy spring Glomac (Thietmar I, 3). Among the Balts, holy-places in natural places, generally called *alkas* (cf. Germanic *alhs*), seem to dominate completely (Vaitkevicius 2004; Daugudis 1995). It was the case also among the Finns and Saami, whose sacrificial places survived until modern times, co-existing with churches (Rydving 1995, 96-137; cf. Backman & Hultkranz 1983).

Place-names provide evidence for pagan cult-activity throughout Scandinavia, as also in England, although it is infrequent on the Continent, especially in Slavic areas (Udolph & Insley 2001); indeed, many names of Scandinavian parishes are derived from Old Norse gods. Concerning the Slavs, the situation is completely different, although some names derived from names of gods, sanctuaries, idols and notions of holiness do exist. The reason is probably the different way in which cultural landscapes developed in Scandinavian and Slavic countries (possibly on the Continent as a whole). Slavic territories were spatially reorganized in the twelfth to fifteenth centuries, during the so-called 'German colonization', when old structures of villages, fields, local roads, etc, were dramatically changed. At the same time, the network of parish churches was established, and the coincidence of these two factors caused the old cultic toponymy to be almost completely erased, before being recorded in charters. In Scandinavia, the original topography and toponymy was not significantly modified after the end of the Viking period, until modern times (Słupecki 2002, 39).

Pagan sanctuaries were hierarchical and connected to territorial organisation. Among the Lutitians, as Thietmar (VI, 25) explicitly stated, 'there are as many temples in this country as regions ... among them the above mentioned stronghold [Riedegost] is considered as superior'. This organisation was probably more rigid than elsewhere, as each of the four main Lutitian tribes had its own sanctuary (Słupecki 1994, 64-6). Saxo Grammaticus (XIV, 39,9), writing about the cult of Svantevit on Rügen stated that, apart from the main shrine at Arkona, 'this deity had other temples in various places which were ruled with almost equal dignity but with lesser power of the priests'. The main shrines thus enjoyed higher status than other cult-places. Some of them supported oracles (Riedegost, Szczecin and Arkona, for the Slavs; Uppsala for the Swedes), some contained treasures used as a public purse, well attested not only in case of West Slavic temples, but also in the Saxon sanctuary at Eresburg, which housed the holy pillar, *Irminsul*, and plentiful gold and silver when Charlemagne conquered and despoiled the place in 772 (*Annales regni Francorum* 772; cf. Modzelewski 2004, 400).

Conversion

Continuity between pagan and Christian cult-places, which is suggested in the well-known letter of Gregory the Great to Mellitus, with instructions to convert pagan Anglo-Saxon shrines into Christian churches (Bede, *Historia Ecclesiastica* I, 30), was not necessarily followed (Wilson 1992, 28-43). Converting Pomerania, St Otto of Bamberg met inhabitants of Gützkow who were seeking to convert their pagan temple into a church and offering much money to keep the building intact; the bishop, however, ordered it to be pulled down (Ebo III, 9; Herbord III, 7; cf. Słupecki 1994, 93), implying, perhaps, that there was some controversy over this aspect of the process of conversion. Archaeological evidence for the continuity of pagan sanctuaries into Christian churches is rare.

Conversion of pagan societies between 800-1200 started with rulers and elites, and, from that level, Christianity spread down to ordinary people, as had been the case among the Anglo-Saxons (e.g. Carver 2003). The first Scandinavian known to have become Christian was the Danish king, Harald Klak, baptized with his retinue at Ingelheim, in 826 (Adam of Bremen I, 15), after which there followed the mission of Ansgar to Sweden. This first phase of conversion, contemporary with the Viking expansion, brought no lasting results. Only in the tenth to eleventh centuries did the Scandinavia kingdoms become Christian, at least formally. The first was Denmark, under the rule of Harald (Gormsson), who on his famous rune-stone at Jelling stressed, that he was the king who 'made the Danes Christian' (Fig 15.9); Norway and Sweden were converted later. In Iceland, in 999 or 1000, the *Althing* decided on conversion, but under obvious pressure from the Norwegian king, Olaf Tryggvason (Aðalsteinsson 1978; Grønlie 2006).

The first major Slavic state, namely Great Moravia, was both organized and Christianised under Western influence; the rulers, however, requested Slavic-speaking clergy from Constantinople. Subsequently, Sts Cyril and Methodius created both the Slavic liturgy and alphabet, which, after the fall of Great Moravia, passed to Bulgaria and later to the Rus (already belonging to the Orthodox faith). During the tenth century, Bohemia and then Poland were converted from the West, and the Rus from the East, with Polabia and Pomerania remaining pagan until the twelfth century.

Large areas of newly-Christianised Europe were, however, converted only officially, and so mixed or syncretic beliefs and superstitions developed. More worrying for the Church, however, were the numerous revolts and uprisings caused by the association of the change of religion with the growing power of oppressive rulers and elites. The most successful was that of the Polabian Slavs in 983, who, after some years of Christianisation (which they perceived as conquest), erased the new faith. For more than a century, the old tribal structures developed (especially by the Lutitians) into a kind of heathen theocracy. The real Christianisation of the Slavs followed formal conversion only in the twelfth and thirteenth centuries (or even the fourteenth), when a network of parishes was finally established, with numerous churches being built in the countryside.

Introduction

In early medieval Europe, Christianity was the most influential factor in the integration of different ethnic groups, cultures and territories. In addition, it has certainly been the most transcendental legacy from the late Roman period. If we analyse the significance of Christianity and the Church during the period between the eighth and twelfth centuries, it could be described as one of formation in many important respects, such as:

(1) The establishment of close links with political hierarchies; (2) consolidation of the Church's administrative framework and construction of a representative range of buildings; (3) introduction of monasticism under Benedictine rule; (4) expansion of Christianity into partly Romanised or non-Romanised areas; and (5) transformation of settlement patterns in towns and countryside.

All these important elements have provided a variety of evidence that can be analysed using archaeological methods, making a broad range of information available on aspects that are not necessarily recorded in written sources. This is the case in the study of churches (cathedrals, parish churches and chapels), monasteries and convents, bishops' palaces and ecclesiastical districts. This information should be studied from an architectural and archaeological point-of-view, where the reconstruction of different aspects is possible, such as daily-life, environmental, economic and social information. It is important to remember that religious buildings, being well preserved, are the most common structures that survive from the Middle Ages, as also the fact that religious institutions are often in possession of complete archives. It is obvious that churches constitute the most complete surviving type of archaeological monument (Rodwell 1989, 46).

When we analyse churches we have to bear in mind the impact that these buildings had on pre-medieval towns and on the countryside. The existence of churches in towns is commonly mentioned in the literature. Their appearance in Romanised areas since the fourth century is one of two basic elements present in the transformation from Roman to medieval towns, the second being defence (see Chapter 4). The study of the foundation of cathedrals, parish churches and chapels is essential to understanding the evolution of urban settlement in the early Middle Ages. A noteworthy example is Tours (France), studied by Henri Galinié (1978).

In rural areas, Christianisation came about at a much slower pace, being linked to the construction of both churches and monasteries together with their cemeteries. These are the most significant traces of this definitive transformation of the landscape. The role of the churches and cemeteries in the development of a village is known not only through written sources but also through archaeology where the material evidence can be studied to provide concrete data (see Chapter 3).

The archaeology of medieval churches, monasteries and convents, began in the mid-nineteenth century. From that time until the 1950s and later, the sole interest was architectural analysis of buildings and, in some cases, the study of tombs. Most excavations were carried out because of restoration work, but not in an archaeological context. In any event, most of this activity was never recorded.

More attention was paid to archaeological aspects in the 1960s, along with, in exceptional cases, the study of the surrounding areas of churches. An example of this is Winchester Cathedral, England, studied by Martin Biddle (1975). Another significant case is the parish church of St Martin at Wharram Percy (England), excavated by John Hurst and Maurice Beresford (Hurst 1976; Thorn 1987). A further important development was the application of the stratigraphic method to the study of standing buildings (cf. Fig 1.4).

With regard to archaeological research on monasteries, one must distinguish between two types of approach. In the first place, there had simply been so-called 'clearance', consisting of a superficial cleaning-up of the remains, the strengthening of walls, with the description and planning of the site. This was a common method in Protestant countries, where hundreds of these buildings were abandoned after the sixteenth century, with the purpose of making these buildings presentable for public display. This has been replaced by 'proper' archaeological research, on different levels. The commonest level was just the study of the main buildings, especially the church, with less often the whole monastery being taken into consideration. Rarer has been the study of not only the main buildings but also the surrounding areas, including workshops, economic infrastructure (mills, cellars, etc), relic-landscapes and villages or towns that had developed links with the monastery. Some of the best known examples of such projects are: San Vincenzo in Volturno, Italy (Hodges 1997); Saint Denis, France (Wyss & Meyer 1996); and Bordesley Abbey, England (Rahtz & Hirst 1976; Hirst et al 1983).

Church Organisation

Taking into consideration this long span of four hundred years, three different periods can be established: (1) the pre-Carolingian (700-51); (2) from the Carolingian to Pope Gregory VII's reform (751-1075); and (3) the Church from 1075 to 1200.

The pre-Carolingian period (700-751)

During this first stage the strong influence of the late Roman period must be kept in mind, as well as a close relationship with, and dependency on, the Byzantine Emperor. Continuity and the permanent expansion of Christianity are the most remarkable characteristics of this period, prime examples being the influence of Irish and Anglo-Saxon missionary monks among the Germanic tribes (Frisians, Saxons, Alamans, Thuringians and Bavarians). National churches at that time were controlled by the rulers, who chose bishops and abbots from their own circles, leading to the common practice of simony (the buying and selling of ecclesiastical appointments).

From the Carolingian period to Pope Gregory VII's reform (751-1054)

In 751, after the Pope had broken away from his dependency on the Byzantine Emperor, he came to a military agreement with the first Carolingian king, Pippin the Short, after which the Papal State was formed in central Italy.

The Carolingian period witnessed the birth of the first medieval Christian culture, when Christianity, the Latin language and Classical traditions became widespread throughout southern England, northern France and Germany. Another important aspect was the fact that the European geographical focus began to swing from the Mediterranean to these northern areas. The expansion of Christianity was one of the most important aims of the Frankish emperor. This was the situation in the conquest of Saxony and in the wars against the Avars. The first bishopric founded in central and southern Germany, east of the Elbe, was Hamburg, which was fundamental in this process of expansion at the beginning of the ninth century. The Latin Church, from the ninth century onwards, was simply an administrative structure auxiliary to the Carolingian Empire - bishoprics in towns, monasteries in the country, missions to new frontiers and territories (such as Saxony). Religion was definitively linked to political structure. This situation, characteristic of the eighth and ninth centuries, intensified after 932 with the coronation of the first Ottonian Emperor, Otto I. The Church's basic structure consisted of the bishop being responsible for his town and diocese, with the archbishop controlling the most important town (or metropolis) in the area. In the tenth century, the papacy was not protected by any royal power, so from 850 to 1050 it linked itself to the interests of local aristocratic families or to the German Emperor.

Christianity expanded at this time to the east and north, through the Germanic and Slavic territories. The most decisive period was between 950 and 1050 (see above). The basis of this expansion was the Magdeburg bishopric, created in 968 by Otto I. So, during the first half of the eleventh century, Latin Christianity was introduced into the northern and eastern borders of the German Empire and then into the territories of the Scandinavians and Slavs.

Education and art were also deemed important within bishops' palaces and their development was encouraged (cf. Fig 13.6). We know how significant some bishops became in their dioceses, especially under the German Emperors and afterwards.

The Church from 1075 to 1200

Pope Gregory VII published a decree called *Dictatus Papae* (1075), which contained the new philosophy of the universal (i.e. Catholic) Church and this provides the key to understanding a renewal in the Latin Church. It signified the abolition of simonies and the cohabitation of the clergy with women. It also contained the official declaration concerning the superiority of the Pope over the Emperor. This document generated serious confrontation between both institutions – Papacy and Empire – throughout the rest of the Middle Ages, but in reality pre-eminence varied, depending on the personalities of Emperor and Pope at any given time. Pope Gregory VII imposed the Roman liturgy, giving rise to institutional and cultural uniformity across Latin Europe.

During the eleventh century the papacy emerged as the visible leader of Christendom (Lynch 1992, 159), the most obvious example of this being the First Crusade (1096-99), when thousands of monks, soldiers and common people went to Palestine to conquer the Holy Land which was then in the hands of Seljuk Turks.

The Basilewsky 'situla', or holy-water bucket, was produced c980 for the visit of Otto II to Milan **Fig 13.6** *Cathedral and used for his ceremonial anointing; it is carved from ivory, with twelve scenes from the Passion of Christ, and originally had a metal handle (height: 16cm), as well as a separate metal bucket inside it (© Victoria & Albert Museum).*

Monasticism

Monasticism was a central feature in religious life that contributed to the expansion of Christianity, to the preservation of classical culture and to the colonisation of new or deserted lands.

Ireland was deeply Christianised from the seventh century (with the process of conversion having started in the fifth), but it developed a special form of Christianity due

Fig 13.7 *The west front of the 9th-century monastic church at Corvey, in Saxony (photo: M Valor).*

to the national church being based on different monasteries (Edwards 1990, chapter 6). In the seventh and eighth centuries these monks spread this new religion across the Continent, in northern France and in Germany, and so they founded monasteries such as Fulda, Reichenau or St Gall. Many of these monks died as martyrs and later became saints. At this time, monasticism had many different rules and each foundation was independent with the abbot having supreme authority.

With Charlemagne, the monastic situation changed. From 817 onwards, only the Rule of St Benedict was allowed, and all missionaries were sent by Rome. A very important event took place in 909 with the foundation of the Benedictine monastery at Cluny in Burgundy. This monastery depended directly on the Pope; monks could elect their own abbots, without interference from local potentates, and liturgical prayer was extraordinarily developed. The mother house of Cluny established a network of monasteries not only in France but also in Italy, Germany (Fig 13.7) and England (Mullins 2006). So, Cluniac Benedictine monasticism became a unifying element in Europe; Cluny was, in fact, the first international monastic institution. Education, libraries and the transcription of manuscripts were the most important tasks of these communities, dedicated to prayer and work. Monasteries were cultural centres where Classical culture was partly preserved and where new artistic styles were developed, expressed in all media (painting, sculpture and architecture).

The tenth century was a most decisive period for the Christianisation of Slavic countries such as Poland or Hungary. In these cases, not only through monasticism, but also through the foundation of bishoprics (see above).

A new step was taken in 1098 with the foundation of Cîteaux and the establishment of a new monastic order, situated in isolated areas in the countryside, living in strict poverty and giving more importance to work (Pressouyvre 1994). The Cistercians experienced rapid expansion throughout Latin Europe (beginning in 1113), developing a most effective network among their many hundreds of houses. They colonised all the new territories and frontiers, which meant that they spread not only the religion, but also the culture of medieval Latin Christianity in all its forms.

The monastery, as an architectural structure, implies an efficient organization of space (see Chapter 14). It contains places for prayer, meeting, study, eating, sleeping and storage. The way these areas were organised evolved in such a way that the phenomenon requires close examination. For example, archaeological research in Italy has revealed thats during the eighth century and at the beginning of the ninth, the size and decoration of the buildings began to become more complex, as in the case of San Vincenzo al Volturno (Fig 14.4). Some examples dating from this period are built around a vast quadrangular space (cf. Fig. 14.3) which was a model used in private houses during the late Roman period. Most of these monasteries were built in fertile valleys, near important roads or in urban surroundings.

In France, most of the excavated monasteries are Cistercian. Commonly, research is linked to the church and to the study of cloister and conventual buildings. Little work has been devoted to 'peripheral' areas, such as the water-supply, fish-ponds, or monastic workshops (blacksmiths, glass manufacture, pottery kilns, tile-making, etc). Other virtually unknown aspects are faunal and botanical remains, ceramics and glassware. Monastic burials are also very important to help reconstruct the particular history of each building. Thus we know that abbots, benefactors and other high-status individuals are buried in privileged areas (church, chapter-house and cloister). Ordinary members of the community and others are buried outside these areas. In fact, utilising paleo-anthropological analyses (see Box 15.1), information may be obtained about social and economic aspects as well as demographic statistics. An example of such research has taken place in the abbey of St Victor in Marseille, in Provence (Boe & Verhaege 1977).

Pilgrimage

Medieval Christians believed that relics preserved holy virtue which could be transmitted to those who touch them. For this reason we have witnessed, throughout the centuries, the expansion of strong popular religious beliefs in which Christian faith and superstition were mixed. In fact, pilgrimages were a phenomenon that developed within Christianity from the fourth century, but they became more common during the early Middle Ages (see Box 13.2).

The worship of relics was especially intense with the Carolingians, when a large number were introduced into the Empire from Rome or the Near East. In this way the commerce of relics emerged as a wealth-based activity (see p 299). Saints, missionaries, martyrs and confessors were venerated in cathedrals, parish churches and monasteries

BOX 13.2   PILGRIMS

When pilgrimage started, in the eleventh century, to the shrine of St James the Apostle, at Santiago de Compostela (north-west Spain), pilgrims would not have travelled wearing specific dress or bearing signs. However, from the twelfth century onwards, when pilgrimage had increased in popularity, specific costumes and emblems became customary. Both the dress and badges are well known from documentary and pictorial sources, as well as from archaeological finds.

The commonest attire for pilgrims was a short robe, with a fur coat or cloak, a felt hat or a cap, a leather bag, a canteen or pumpkin and, obviously, comfortable shoes (cf. descriptions and pictures: *Liber Sancti Iacobi*, c1139; *Cantigas de Santa María*, thirteenth century). The travellers used to walk with the aid of a staff (*bordón*), as represented in the Pórtico de la Gloria, Compostela.

Pilgrims began to wear a variety of symbolic badges as evidence of their blessed journey. The earliest and commonest symbol of this particular pilgrimage was the scallop shell (*Pecten maximus*, or *jacobeus*), which was an ancient symbol of the female genitalia and a Roman charm (Fig 1). The *Liber Sancti Iacobi* (Whitehill 1944) describes some miracles that resulted from its curative qualities, with the result that the scallop shell became the symbol *par excellence* of the pilgrimage to Compostela (Hohler 1957) and of the protection thus afforded by St James (*crusillae piscium, id est intersigna beati Iacobi*).

The first statues of pilgrims, and of St James the Apostle dressed as a pilgrim, show scallop shells sewn onto a bag (e.g. in the cloister of Santo Domingo de Silos and on the abbey church of Santa Marta de Tera (Spain), in the twelfth century, and Chartres cathedral, c1212), or onto the hat or cloak (León cathedral, c1250).

Scallop shells have also been found by archaeologists in pilgrims' tombs from Compostela (in the cemetery that precedes the Romanesque cathedral of the 1120s) to Scandinavia, from the twelfth century onwards (Andersson 1989; Köster 1983; 1985). These shells usually have two or three holes pierced through them, for sewing.

Subsequently, artificial shells were manufactured, either moulded in a lead-tin alloy or struck (cf. *La Vie de Saint Thomas le Martyr*, c1174); these became fashionable and widespread, so much so that the archbishop of Compostela tried to control and regulate production and so profit from the sales. This was more readily achieved

Fig 1

Pilgrim's scallop shell (Pecten maximus), with two holes for sewing it in place; from a pre-1120 grave (© Pilgrimage Museum, Compostela)

through manufactured shells than natural ones; however, forgeries and illegal sales soon became common, so that prohibitions had to be constantly repeated. These lead-tin (pewter) badges were decorated in relief on one face to emulate the natural model, but had a pin at the back, similar to contemporary brooches.

The murder of Archbishop Thomas Becket in Canterbury cathedral (England), in 1170, was quickly followed by the development of a cult of considerable European importance. This resulted in the sale of such souvenirs to pilgrims as both lead-tin badges and *ampullae*, small vessels for holding holy water (Mitchiner 1986; Spencer 1998). The production of such badges as pilgrim souvenirs became widespread at all important Christian shrines (cf. Fig 2).

Sources: see also Jacomet 1990; Moralejo & López 1993; Osma y Scull 1916; Vázquez, Lacarra & Uría 1948.

By José Avelino Gutiérrez

Fig 2

Lead pilgrim badge (c1170-1200) showing the Virgin as Queen of Heaven, from the Virgin's shrine at Rocamadour, France (© Trustees of the British Museum): not to scale.

throughout Roman Europe. At the same time, relics of saints served as a focal point of devotion motivating the construction of many religious buildings.

Some important pilgrimage sites for that period were the 'Holy Places' of Palestine, Constantinople and Rome; and such monasteries as those at Cologne (Germany); San Vincenzo in Volturno and Bobbio (Italy); St Martin of Tours, Mont St Michel and St Denis (France); Canterbury and Durham (England); Santiago de Compostela (Spain). This kind of religiosity generated a large investment in architecture and material culture. In the case of architecture not only are buildings preserved (churches and monasteries), but also spontaneous or planned urbanism around these buildings. This is the case with St Martin of Tours, or the appearance of new towns like Saint-Denis in Paris (Wyss & Meyer 1997). Material culture is well represented in cathedral and monastery treasuries (as also, today, in museums), where shrines, relics and textiles, for example, reveal the evolution of these objects.

Christian Artefacts

Churches and monasteries preserve not only their architecture, if sometimes altered or restored, but also contain many different types of object relating to liturgy and cult, and sometimes also exotic secular gifts to the church, e.g. altars, fonts (Fig 13.8), sculpture, wall paintings, chalices, reliquaries, incense burners, candlesticks (Fig 15.10), furniture, liturgical vestments and other textiles, horns, jewellery, etc. These objects are much studied by art-historians; however, the artefacts preserved in churches, as well as those recovered during church excavations, also provide considerable potential for archaeological studies. For example, they help us understand the importance of the religious foundations, their background and development; they provide evidence for the changing liturgy and patterns of devotion (e.g. the placing of fonts), of national and international trade, and of national or trans-national workmanship. In addition, certain types of secular object from this period have rarely survived outside churches, e.g. some types

Fig 13.8 *Granite font in the Romanesque church at Nørre Snede, in central Jutland (Denmark), carved in high relief with the bodies of four lions, in two pairs with conjoined human-like heads (height: 100cm), mid-12th century (photo: Horsens Museum/Dept of Medieval and Renaissance Archaeology, University of Aarhus).*

Silver pendant crucifix in the form of a reliquary, on an elaborate chain, from a hoard found on the Swedish island of Öland (height: 8.5cm); the form of the cross itself is Byzantine, but the details of its ornament are Scandinavian, thus illustrating the artistic influence, through Russia, of Greek Orthodox Christianity in north-eastern Europe (© ATA, National Heritage Board, Stockholm).

Fig 13.9

of furniture (cf. Fig 5.10) and vessels such as *aquamaniles*, whereas wall-paintings and other pictorial evidence provide much information on daily life.

However, many Christian artefacts are also known from secular contexts; in particular, personal devotional objects, such as pendant crosses or the so-called 'Saint Brooches' (p 249 & Fig 8.5), were often very popular during, or shortly after, the period of the conversion of a country or region. They occur in all types of metal and at all levels of craftsmanship, given that they would have been in use by all levels of society. Some of the more elaborate would have contained a relic (e.g. Fig 13.9), and others would have been brought back from pilgrimages to foreign lands (Box 13.2).

Islam in the Western Mediterranean Area

Like Christianity, Islam has been an example of integration among many different ethnic groups, cultures and territories. Muslim expansion became less widespread after the year 622 and the final phase in the Western Mediterranean area was the conquest of the Iberian Peninsula, which was renamed al-Andalus from 716 onwards (see Box 2.3). Religion and culture were interconnected and the civilization founded by the Ummayad dynasty, under the Abbasid dynasty in particular, was imposed on the whole Dar al-Islam territory, from India to al-Andalus.

After the Muslim conquest of the Iberian Peninsula (711-16), most towns drew up agreements with the Muslims. This resulted in the local inhabitants being able to maintain their religion, property, religious authority (bishops) and political representatives (*comes*). The majority of the invaders were Berbers, i.e. the inhabitants of Magrib, who had only recently converted to Islam. These were joined by a minority of Arabs originating from the Arabian Peninsula and from the Near East, constituting the dominant military elite and the rulers of the conquered territory. We still do not know for certain the number of these new settlers, as different historians provide very different estimates: up to 400,000, for example, or 150-200,000 (Guichard 1995). The fact remains that up until the eleventh or twelfth century, immigrant populations were still entering al-Andalus. The local Christian population was known then as Mozarabs. Islamisation, or the conversion to Islam, seems to have been a slow process and the situation did not change fundamentally until the eleventh century, when most of the Andalusian population converted to Islam and became known as Muwallads.

It was after the Ummayads emirate (756) that the Andalusian state experienced both Arabicisation and Islamisation, with the Arab language, religion and culture being imposed by the Arab minority. Arabicisation seems to have developed first. The Arab language was compulsory, but only the elite mastered the written word. However, Arabicisation was much more widespread in towns than in rural areas where most inhabitants continued using their own local language.

The construction of mosques is a primary example of the slow process of Islamisation. The best-known case is that of Cordova. Muslims rented half the town's St Vincent Cathedral to use as a mosque, up until 786. Then the Christian building was bought and demolished, and the first Friday mosque built. This is the first mosque, documented in written sources, to have been built in the territory of al-Andalus. Familiarity with the mosque at Cordova is essential in order to understand the development of Andalusian religious architecture. This building was a veritable paradigm, being repeated throughout Western Islam, not only under the Ummayads but up until the end of the Muslim presence in the Iberian Peninsula in 1492.

Documentary evidence for the foundation of mosques in al-Andalus is rare, and few remain. Most of them are Friday mosques – the equivalent of cathedrals in Christian territories. The most important example is the Friday mosque at Cordova, constructed in 786, although it underwent several transformations and extensions until the year 987/88. Other significant examples are Seville's first Friday mosque, Ibn Adabbas, built in 829-30 (Box 14.1), the Madinat al-Zahra mosque, first used for prayer in 941, the Bab Mardum's mosque in Toledo (999-1000), the Aljaferia palace mosque in Saragossa (1049-83), and some other smaller mosques attached to castles (*husun*) and villages (*al-qarya*). Examples of these are the mosque at Almonaster (province of Huelva), the Cuatrovitas mosque (Fig 13.10), at Bollullos de la Mitación (Seville), and Vascos (Navalmoralejo, Toledo).

The suggestion here is that most of the Muslim places of worship were churches converted into mosques. The transformation was easy, consisting in changing the axis and direction of prayer. Churches were oriented to the East, *qibla* and *mihrab* were oriented to the South – the only known exception being the Madinat al-Zahra mosque which is oriented to the East. The reverse occurred after the Christian conquest, when mosques were converted into churches (cf. Fig 13.10). The earliest known instance, in written records, is

The 12th-century Almohad mosque of Cuatrovitas, Bollullos de la Mitación (Seville); this village mosque was converted into a church, c1249 (photo: M Valor).

Fig 13.10

the cathedral at Toledo, although there are many examples of standing Andalusian buildings which have been reused as churches, such as those mentioned above.

Archaeological research has not been extensive and most of the buildings were excavated using non-stratigraphic methods. Scientific projects have been taking place only quite recently (1990s), as is the case with the Friday mosques at Seville and Cordova. It is true that the Madinat al-Zahra mosque was 'excavated' in the 1960s, but this was much more of a clearance than a stratigraphic excavation.

The Guardamar *ribat* in Alicante is an interesting excavated complex (Azuar 1989). The settlement was founded in the mid-tenth century, the *ribat* being a type of religious-military institution which was quite common in medieval Islam. It was built for a community of warrior-monks, devoted to jihad, who spent the remainder of the year in prayer. The existence of several of these *ribats* is known in al-Andalus. They were always located in dangerous places, close to borders, coasts or difficult roads. The *murabitun* (warrior-monks) were not obliged to spend their entire lives at the *ribat*, but only for as long as they chose.

The Guardamar *ribat* (Guardamar del Segura, Alicante) has been undergoing excavation since 1984. A group of twenty-one small mosques in a line has been discovered together with a larger mosque, with two naves. The large settlement, which has only been partially excavated, is surrounded by a thick wall about 5m wide.

The Jewish Religion

In Latin Europe of the early Middle Ages, Jewish archaeology remains underdeveloped in comparison to pagan, Christian and Muslim archaeologies. This situation probably results from a combination of factors: the presence of relatively few Jews in Europe during the period of the eighth-twelfth centuries; and the deliberate removal of any traces of Jews, after the thirteenth century, following their expulsion from many countries. There were Jews living in many regions before the eighth century, with the notable exception of England, where they were introduced from Rouen, by William I after the Norman Conquest (1066), at first exclusively in London. There were, however, ten provincial communities by 1159 (Hillaby 2003).

Jewish communities were localised in towns and were devoted to specific professions, relating to administration and especially finance; commerce, in its many forms (including money-lending), was the common profession for Jews. As a result, whether for voluntary cultural and religious reasons, or for constraints applied by rulers or authorities, Jews lived in a specific part of the town, usually known as the Jewry, which can often be identified today from documentary sources or place-names; however, these were not ghettoes, with Christians and Jews living side by side.

The relationship between communities of Christians and Jews was changeable, but in principle both believed their own religion to be the true one. Jews lived their lives according to the Torah (the Old Testament of the Christian Bible), with the addition of the commentaries recorded in the Talmud. On the other hand, the Muslim religion was generally more tolerant of the Jewish religion, with the exception of some Muslim groups that adhered to a strict interpretation of the Koran and the Hadits (the traditions of the Prophet Mohammed). In the case of al-Andalus, Jewish communities played a prominent role during the conquest of the Iberian Peninsula (711-16) and helped the new rulers to maintain control of the towns and population. Andalusian Jews created a flourishing cultural environment that developed during the tenth and eleventh centuries (Mann et al 1992). Following the domination of al-Andalus by North African dynasties (after 1090), this situation broke down and it seems that all their communities were expelled. The majority installed themselves in the northern Christian kingdoms, thus introducing their particular culture into this part of the Iberian Peninsula.

The archaeological evidence for Jewish people that can be detected is generally related to religion because most manifestations of their daily life are similar to those of Christians. The division of tenements, arrangement of structures within tenements, domestic architecture and material culture in the urban Jewry are largely indistinguishable from those of the host community. The physical remains that can be identified are synagogues, *mikva'ot* (ritual baths), cemeteries with inscribed tombstones, and other religious artefacts.

A synagogue was not an essential building for Jews because a room in an ordinary house, or attached to a house, could be used for worship. The Jewish temple is a place for prayer, not being considered as a house of God, as is the case with Catholic churches. This is a significant difference between the two religions, and one that has important consequences for the buildings needing to be constructed.

Indeed, few European synagogues have been recognised that date earlier than the thirteenth century. One of the most important is at Rouen (France) which was discovered during an excavation in the courtyard of the Palace of Justice, in 1976-77; this consists of a Romanesque building (14.14x5.02m), dating to the first half of the twelfth century (Blumenkranz 1980). The remains of the synagogue at Speyer (Germany) are illustrated in Chapter 1 (Fig 1.4; Heberer 2004), and the medieval synagogues of England have been discussed by Hillaby (1993).

An essential building is, however, the *mikveh* (ritual bath), which must be used by both men and women for purification, according to Mosaic law. The *mikveh* is generally sited in close proximity to the synagogue; two types are known: monumental and cellar. The monumental type has one or two shafts, providing access to the bath by means of staircases, as well as providing a source of air and light. Medieval examples have been identified archaeologically, at (e.g.) Cologne, Speyer and Worms (Germany); Besalú and Tarragona (Spain); Montpellier and Carpentras, near Avignon (France) (Hillaby & Sermon 2004). On the other hand, the simpler cellar-type *mikveh* consists of just a subterranean vaulted chamber with a pool. Examples of this group have been found at Gresham Street and Milk Street, in London (Blair et al 2001; 2002), and at Nuremberg, Rothenburg and Sondershausen (Germany). In some cases they are so small that they are to be identified as baths in private houses.

A further type of Jewish ritual bath is the *bet tohorah*, relating specifically to the washing of the dead, a purification process that should not be undertaken in a *mikveh*. A medieval example (if not precisely dated), now known as Jacob's Well, has recently been investigated in Bristol (England); this appears to be a unique discovery in Europe, at least for the time being (Hillaby & Sermon 2004).

The second priority for a medieval Jewish community, after the construction of a *mikveh*, was the establishment of a cemetery, so that the dead could be buried according to their own traditions (although such was not allowed to the provincial Jewries in England until after an edict of Henry II, in 1177). Medieval Jewish cemeteries were located outside the town walls, although sited as close to the Jewry as possible; they were well-enclosed in order to prevent the entry of animals, and the possible desecration of the graves. Tombstones inscribed in Hebrew with Hebrew characters are, of course, clearly identifiable.

The Sephardic tombstones of the Iberian peninsula and southern France lay flat on the ground, conforming to the edict of the Khalif al-Mutawakil (847-61), who wished to prevent confusion between tombs of the faithful and infidel. The medieval gravestones of the Ashkenazi communities of Germany and northern France, on the other hand, were upright. The largest collection, and earliest known examples, lie in the Worms cemetery (Hillaby & Sermon 2004).

A notable example of a medieval Jewish cemetery to have been partially excavated (in England) is that known as the Jewbury, where almost 500 undisturbed bodies were recovered; this was established (outside the walls) for the wealthy community at York, presumably soon after 1177 and had to be extended c1230 (Lilley et al 1994).

There is no specific artistic style by which Jewish communities can be recognised; on the contrary, they assimilated local traditions wherever they were settled. A good example is the Romanesque synagogue at Rouen, mentioned above, or the *mudejar* synagogue of Santa María la Blanca in Toledo (Burgos 1984), built at the beginning of the thirteenth century. On the other hand, inscribed artefacts (such as tombstones) are easily recognisable from their use of Hebrew.

Acknowledgement

The Editors are most grateful to Dr Joe Hillaby (Bristol University) for assistance with the archaeology of Jewish religion.

BIBLIOGRAPHY

Aðalsteinsson, JH (1978) *Under the Cloak. The Acceptance of Christianity with Particular Reference to the Religious Attitudes prevailing at that Time*, Stockholm

Aðalsteinsson, JH (1998) *A Piece of Horse Liver. Myth, Ritual and Folklore in Old Icelandic Sources*, Reykjavík

Andersson, L (1989) *Pilgrimsmärken och vallfart*, Kumla

Andrén, A (1989) 'Dörrar till förgangna myter – en tolkning av de gotländska bildstenarna', in Andrén, A (ed), *Medeltidens födelse*, Vol 1, 287-319

Andrén, A, Jennbert, K and Raudvere, C (eds) (2006) *Old Norse Religion in Long-Term Perspectives: Origins, Changes and Interactions*, Lund

Åqvist, C (1996) 'Hall och harg – det rituella rumet', in Engdahl, K and Kaliff, A (eds), *Religion från stenalder till medeltid*, Linköping, 105-20

Azuar, R et al (1989) *La rábita califal de las Dunas de Guardamar (Alicante)*, Alicante

Bäckman, L and Hultkranz, Å (eds) (1985) *Saami Pre-Christian Religion. Studies on the oldest Traces of Religion among the Saamis*, Stockholm

Bauschatz, P (1982) *The Well and the Tree. World and Time in Early Germanic Culture*, Massachusetts

Bearma, PJ (ed) (1996) *Encyclopaedia of Islam*, Leiden

Bersu, G and Wilson, DM (1966) *Three Viking Graves in the Isle of Man*, Society for Medieval Archaeology, Monograph Series 1, London

Biddle M (1975) 'Excavations at Winchester 1971: tenth and final report', *Antiquaries Journal* 55, 295-337

Biezais, H (1975) 'Baltische Religion', in Biezais, H and Ström, ÅV, *Germanische und Baltische Religion*, Die Religionen der Menschheit 19, 311-74

Blair, I, Hillaby, J, Howell, I, Sermon, R and Watson, B (2001) 'Two medieval Jewish ritual baths, *mikva'ot*, found at Gresham and Milk Street in London', *London & Middlesex Archaeological Society Transactions* 52, 127-37

Blumenkranz, B (ed) (1980) *Art et archéologie des Juifs en France médiévale*, Toulouse

Boe, G de and Verhaege, F (eds) (1997) *Religion and Belief, Papers of the Medieval Europe Conference 1997*, Vol 4, Brugge

Burgos, FC (1984) *Sinagogas Españolas*, Madrid

Carver, M (ed) (2003) *The Cross goes North: Processes of Conversion in Northern Europe, AD300-1300*, York/Woodbridge

Christensen, T (1991) 'Lejre beyond legend – the archaeological evidence', *Journal of Danish Archaeology* 10, 163-85

Chudziak, W (2003) *Mons Sancti Laurentii*, Vol 1, Toruń

Daugudis, V (1995) 'Die Eisenzeitlichen Kultstätten in Litauen', in Kazakevičius, V and Sidrys, R (eds), *Archaeologia Baltica*, Vilnius/Kaunas, 121-46

Diaz-Andreu, M and Keay, S (eds) (1996) *The Archaeology of Iberia: The Dynamics of Change*, London

Düwel, K (1970) 'Germanische Opfer und Opferriten im Spiegel altgermanischer Kultworte', in Jankuhn, H (ed), *Vorgeschichtliche Heiligtümer und Opferplätze in Mittel- und Nordeuropa*, Göttingen, 219-39

Edwards, N (1990) *The Archaeology of Early Medieval Ireland*, London

Faulkes, A (1978) 'Descent from gods', *Medieval Scandinavia* 11, 92-125

Franco Sánchez, F (1997) *Rábitas islámicas. Bibliografía actualizada*, Alicante

Gabriel, I (1988) Zur Innenbebauung von Stargard/Oldenburg, in Müller-Wille, M (ed), *Oldenburg –Wolin –Staraja Ladoga – Novgorod – Kiev. Handel und Handelsverbindungen im südlichen und östlichen Ostseeraum während des frühen Mittelalters*, Bericht Röm-Germ Komm 69, Mainz, 55-86

Gabriel, I (1992) [review of] 'Ewald Schuldt: *Gross Raden. Ein slawischer Tempelort des 9./10. Jahrhunderts in Mecklenburg*, Berlin 1985', *Zeitschrift für Ostforschung* 41:3, 423-5.

Galinié, H (1978) 'Archéologie et Topographie Historique de Tours. IV au IX ième siècles', *Zeitschrift für Archäologie des Mittelalters* 6, 33-53

Gieysztor, A (2006, 2nd ed) *Mitologia Słowian*, Warsaw

Gieysztor, A (1984) 'Opfer und Kult in der slawischen Überlieferung', *Frühmittelalterliche Studien* 18, 249-65

Gilchrist, R and Mytum, H (eds) (1993) *Advances in Monastic Archaeology*, British Archaeological Reports 227, Oxford

Graham-Campbell, J (1980) *Viking Artefacts: a Select Catalogue*, London

Gringmuth-Dallmer, E and Hollnagel, A (1971) 'Jungslawische Siedlung mit Kultfiguren auf der Fischerinsel bei Neubrandenburg', *Zeitschrift für Archäologie* 5, 102-33

Grønlie, S (2006) *Íslendingabók – Kristini Saga: The Book of the Icelanders – The Story of the Conversion*, Viking Society for Northern Research Text Series, London

Guichard, P (1995) *La España musulmana. Al-Andalus Omeya (siglos VIII a XI)*, Madrid

Haavio, M (1967) *Suomalainen mytologia*, Helsinki

Heberer, P (2004) 'Die mittelalterliche Synagoge in Speyer. Bauforschung und Rekonstruktion', in Haverkamp, A (ed), *Historisches Museum der Pfalz Speyer, Europas Juden im Mittelalder*, Ostfildern

Hedlund, G (1993) 'Utgravningen 1992', in Duczko, W (ed), *Arkeologi och miljøgeologi i Gamla Uppsala*, Vol I, Occasional Papers in Archaeology 7, Uppsala, 64-9

Herrmann, J (1993) 'Ein Versuch zu Arkona. Tempel und Tempelrekonstruktionen nach schriftlicher Überlieferung und nach Ausgrabungsbefunden im nordwestslawischen Gebiet', *Ausgrabungen und Funde* 38:3, 136-44

Herrmann, J (1998) *Ralswiek auf Rügen. Die slawisch-wikingischen Siedlungen und deren Hinterland. Teil II – Kultplatz, Boot 4, Hof, Propstei, Mühlenberg, Schlossberg und Rugard*, Beiträge zur Ur- und Frühgeschichte Mecklenburg-Vorpommern 33, Lübstorf

Herrmann, J and Heussner, K-U (1991) 'Dendro-chronologie, Archäologie und Frühgeschichte von 6. bis 12. Jh. in den Gebieten zwischen Saale, Elbe und Oder', *Ausgrabungen und Funde* 36:6, 271

Herschend, F (1999) 'Halle', *Reallexicon der Germanischen Altertumskunde* 13, 415-25

Hillaby, J (1993) '*Beth Miqdash Me'at*: the synagogues of medieval England', *Journal of Ecclesiastical History* 44:2, 182-98

Hillaby, J (2003) 'The Jewish colonisation of 12th-century England', in Skinner, PE (ed), *The Jews in Medieval Britain*, Woodbridge, 15-40

Hillaby, J and Sermon, R (2004) 'Jacob's Well, Bristol: *mikveh* or *bet tohorah*?', *Transactions of the Bristol and Gloucester Archaeological Society* 122, 127-52

Hirst, SM, Walsh, D and Wright, SM (1983) *Bordesley Abbey II. Second Report on Excavations at Bordesley Abbey, Redditch, Hereford-Worcestershire*, British Archaeological Reports III, Oxford

Hodges, R (1997) *Light in the Dark Ages: the Rise and Fall of San Vincenzo al Volturno*, Ithaca.

Hohler, C (1957) 'The badge of St James', in Cox, I (ed), *The Scallop: Studies of a Shell and its Influences on Humankind*, London, 49-70

Huldgård, A (1993) 'Altskandinavische Opferrituale und das Problem der Quellen', in Ahlbäck T (ed), *The Problem of Ritual*, Stockholm, 221-59

Huldgård, A (ed) (1997) *Uppsalakulten och Adam av Bremen*, Lund.

Huldgård, A (2001) 'Menschenopfer', *Reallexicon der Germanischen Altertumskunde* 19, 533-46

Huldgård, A (2003) 'Ár – gutes Jahr und Ernteglück – ein Motivkomplex in der altnordischen Literatur und sein religionsgeschichtlicher Hintergrund', in Heizmann, W and van Nahl, A (eds), *Runica – Germanica –Medievalia, Reallexicon der Germanischen Altertumskunde* Ergänzungsband 37, Berlin/New York, 282-308

Hurst, JG (1976) 'Wharram Percy: St Martin's Church', in Addyman, PV and Morris, RK (eds), *The Archaeological Study of Churches*, Council for British Archaeology Research Report 13, 36-9

Insoll, T (1999) *The Archaeology of Islam*, London.

Jacomet, H (1990) 'Le Bourdon, la besace et la coquille', *Archéologia* 258, 42-51

Jankuhn, H (1967) *Archäologische Beobachtungen zu Tier- und Menschenopfern bei den Germanen in der Römischen Keiserzeit,* Göttingen

Jayyusie, SK (ed) (1992) *The Legacy of Muslim Spain*, Leiden

Jiménez Martín, A (ed) (2002) *Magna Hispalensis (I). Recuperación de la aljama almohade*, Granada

Jørgensen, L (2002) 'Kongsgård – kultsted – marked. Overvejelser omkring Tissøkomplekset struktur og funktion', in Jennbert, K, Andrén, A and Ruadvere, C (eds), *Plats och praxis. Studier av nordisk förkristen ritual*, Falun, 215-48

Kahl, H-D (2004) 'Das erloschene Slawentum des Obermeingebietes und sein vorchristlicher Opferbrauch (trebo) im eines mutmaßlich würzburgschen Synodalbeschlusses aus dem 10. Jahrhundert', *Studia Mythologica Slavica* 7, 11-42

Köster, K (1983) *Pilgerzeichen und Pilgermuscheln von mitteralterlichen Santiagostrassen*, Neumünster

Köster, K (1985) 'Les coquilles et enseignes de pèlerinage de Saint-Jacques de Compostelle et les routes de Saint-Jacques en Occident', in *Santiago de Compostela. 1000 ans de pèlerinage européen*, Gand, 85-95

Lamm, JP (1987) 'On the cult of multiple-headed gods in England and in the Baltic area', *Przegląd Archeologiczny* 34, 219-31

Lilley, JM et al (eds) (1994) *The Jewish Burial Ground at Jewbury*, York

Lynch, JH (1992) *The Medieval Church: a Brief History*, London/New York

Mann, VB, Glick, TF and Dodds, JD (eds) (1992) Convivencia: *Jews, Muslims and Christians in Medieval Spain*, New York

Meulengracht-Sørensen, P (1988) 'Loki's senna in Aegir's Hall', in Weber, GW (ed), *Idee, Gestalt, Geschichte. Festschrift Klaus von See*, Odense, 239-59

Meulengracht-Sørensen, P (1991) 'Håkon den gode og guderne. Nogle bemaerkninger om religion og centralmagt i det tiende århundrede – og om religionshistori og kildekritik', in Mortenssen, P and Rasmussen, M (eds), *Fra Stamme til Stat*, Vol 2, Aarhus, 235-43

Mitchiner, M (1986) *Medieval Pilgrim and Secular Badges*, Sanderstead

Modzelewski, K (2004) *Barbarzyńska Europa*, Warsaw

Moralejo, S and López Alsina, F (eds) (1993) *Santiago, Camino de Europa. Culto y Cultura en la Peregrinación a Compostela*, Exhibition Catalogue, Santiago

Moszczyński, A and Szymański, W (1987) 'Ryt Perunowy (?) z Wyszogrodu', *Zotchłani wieków* 53, 140-5

Moździoch, S (2000) 'Archeologiczne ślady kultu pogańskiego na Śląsku wczesnośredniowiecz-nym', in Moździoch, S (ed), *Człowiek, Sacrum, Środowisko. Miejsca kultu we wczesnym średniowie-czu*, Spotkania Bytomskie 4, 155-93

Müller-Wille, M (1984) 'Opferplätze der Wikinger-zeit', *Frühmittelalterliche Studien* 18, 187-221

Müller-Wille, M (1999) *Opferkulte der Germanen und Slawen*, Stuttgart

Mullins, E. (2006) *In Search of Cluny: God's Lost Empire*, Bluebridge

Munch, GS, Johansen, OS and Roesdahl, E (eds) (2003), *Borg in Lofoten. A Chieftain's Farm in North Norway*, Trondheim

Näsström, B-M (2001) *Blot. Tro och offer i det förkristna Norden*, Stockholm

Niles, JD (2007) *Beowulf and Lejre*, Arizona Center for Medieval and Renaissance Studies

Nordahl, E (1996) *... templum, quod Ubsola dicitur... i arkeologisk belysning*, Aun 22, Uppsala

Nylén, E and Lamm, JP (1991) *Bildsteine auf Gotland*, Neumünster: (1988) *Stones, Ships and Symbols*, Stockholm

Olsen, O (1966) *Hørg, Hov og Kirke*, Copenhagen (with English Summary)

Osma y Scull, GJ de (1916) *Catálogo de azabaches com-postelanos, precedido de apuntes sobre los amuletos contra el aojo, las imágenes del apóstol-romero, y la cofradía de los azabacheros de Santiago*, Madrid

Paddenberg, D (2006) 'Parchim – Löddigsee – late Slavonic temple and trading site', in Andrén et al (eds), 229-33

Poisson, J-M (ed) (1992) *Castrum 4. Frontiére et peuplement dans le monde Méditerranée au Moyen Age, Actes de Colloque Trapani (Italia, 1988)*, Madrid/Rome

Pressouyre, L (ed) (1994) *L'Espace cistercienne*, Paris

Price, NS (2002) *The Viking Way. Religion and War in Late Iron Age Scandinavia*, Aun 31, Uppsala

Rahtz, PA and Hirst, SM (1976) *Bordesley Abbey, Redditch, Hereford-Worcestershire. First Report on Excavations 1969-73*, British Archaeological Reports 23, Oxford

Rodwell, W (1989) *Church Archaeology*, London

Rydving, H (1995) *The End of Drum-Time. Religious Change among the Lule Saami, 1670s-1740s*, Uppsala

Schuldt, E (1985) *Gross Raden. Ein slawischer Tempelort des 9./10. Jahrhunderts in Mecklenburg*, Berlin.

Simek, R (1995) *Lexikon der germanischen Mythologie*, Stuttgart

Simek, R (2002) 'Goddesses, mothers, Disir: iconog-raphy and interpretation of the female deity in Scandinavia in the first millennium', in Simek, R, *Mythological Women*, Vienna, 93-124

Simek, R (2003) *Religion und Mythologie der Germanen*, Darmstadt

Słupecki, LP (1994) *Slavonic Pagan Sanctuaries*, Warsaw

Słupecki, LP (1997) 'Au déclin des dieux slaves', in Rouche, M (ed), *Clovis. Histoire et mémoire. La baptême de Clovi, son echo à travers l'histoire*, Vol 2, Paris, 289-314

Słupecki, LP (1998) *Wyrocznie i wróżby pogańskich Skandynawów*, Warsaw

Słupecki, LP (2002) 'Pagan religion and cultural land-scape of Northwestern Slavs in the early Middle-Ages', *Siedlungsforschung. Archäologie – Geschichte – Geographie* 20, 25-40

Słupecki, LP (2003) *Mitologia skandynawska w epoce Wikingów*, Kraków

Słupecki, LP (2006) 'The temple in Rhetra-Riedegost. West Slavic pagan ritual as described at the begin-ning of eleventh century', in Andrén et al (eds), 224-8

Spencer, B (1998) *Pilgrim Souvenirs and Secular Badges from London*, Medieval Finds from Excavations in London 7, London

Staecker, J (1999) *'Rex regum et dominus dominorum'. Die wikingerzeitlichen Kruez- und Krucifixanhänger als Ausdruck der Mission in Altdänemark und Schweden*, Lund Studies in Medieval Archaeology 23, Lund

Steinsland, G (1991) *Det hellige bryllup og norrøn kongeideologi*, Oslo

Strömbäck, D (1935) *Sejd. Tekststudier i nordisk religionshistoria*, Lund

Sundqvist, O (1996) 'Härskaren i kulten under yngre jarnalder', in Engdahl, K and Kaliff, A (eds), *Religion från stenalder till medeltid*, Linköping, 68-88

Sundqvist, O (1998) 'Kultledare och kultfunktionarer e det forntida Skandinavien', in Westerlund, D (ed), *Religioner i Norr. Svensk religionshistorisk årsskrift* 7, 76-104

Sundqvist, O (2002) *Freyr's Offsprings. Rulers and Religion in Ancient Svea Society*, Historia Religionum 21, Uppsala

Sundqvist, O (2003) 'Priester und Priesterinnen', *Reallexicon der Germanischen Altertumskunde* 23, 424-35

Thorn, J (1987) *A Study in Settlement of the Yorkshire Wolds, III. Wharram Percy, the Church of Saint Martin*, London

Turville-Petre, EOG (1964) *Myths and Religion of the North. The Religion of Ancient Scandinavia*, London

Udolph, J and Inslay, J (2001) 'Kultische Namen', *Reallexicon der Germanischen Altertumskunde* 17, 415-35

Vaitkevicius, V (2004) *Studies into the Balts' Sacred Places*, British Archaeological Reports, International Series 1228, Oxford

Valor, M and Tahiri, A (eds) (1999) *Sevilla Almohade*, Madrid

Váňa, Z (1983) 'Gods, demons and shrines', in Váňa, Z, *The World of the Ancient Slavs*, London, 83-103

Various authors (1992) *Religion and Belief.* Pre-printed papers from the conference 'Medieval Archaeology in Europe, 21-24 September 1992', vol 7, York

Vázquez de Parga L, Lacarra, JM and Uría J (1948) *Las peregrinaciones a Santiago de Compostela*, Vol 1, Madrid

Viguera Molins, J (ed) (2001) *El esplendor de los Omeyas cordobeses: la civilización musulmana de Europa Occidental*, Granada

Viguera, J and Castillo, C (eds) (1995) *Al-Andalus y el Mediterráneo*, Barcelona

de Vries, J (1956-57) *Altgermanische Religionsgeschichte*, 2 vols, Berlin

Wamers, E (1997) 'Hammer und Kreuz. Typologische Aspekte einer nordeuropäischen Amulettsitte aus der Zeit der Glaubenwechsels', in Müller-Wille, M (ed), *Rom und Bysanz im Norden. Mission und Glaubenwechsel im Ostseeraum während des 8.-14. Jahrhunderts*, Vol 1, Mainz/Stuttgart, 83-108

Whitehill, WM (ed) (1944) *Liber Sancti Jacobi. Codex Calixtinus*, Santiago de Compostela

Wilson, D (1992) *Anglo-Saxon Paganism*, London/New York

Wyss, N and Meyer-Rodrigues, N (1996) *Atlas Historique de Saint Denis: des Origines au XVIII siècle*, Paris

Zachrisson, I (1984) *De samiska metalldepåerna år 1000-1350 i ljuset av fyndet från Mörtträsket, Lappland*, Archaeology and Environment 3, Umeå (English summary)

Zachrisson, I (1992) 'The Saami in Scandinavia', in Roesdahl, E and Wilson, DM (eds), *From Viking to Crusader: Scandinavia and Europe, 800-1200*, Copenhagen, 72-3

Zoll-Adamikowa, H (1989) [review of] 'E. Schuldt, *Gross Raden*, Berlin 1985', *Germania* 67:1, 259-66

CHAPTER 14

RELIGIOUS BUILDINGS

Tadhg O'Keeffe, with Matthias Untermann

Introduction

Christianity was the dominant religion of the later Roman Empire. Its shift from a minority cult in Asia Minor to the status of 'official' religion in much of Western and Southern Europe was secured under the Emperor Constantine at the start of the fourth century. Although its practice was widely discontinued in the fifth century, when non-Christian Germanic peoples – the so-called 'barbarians' – settled within the empire, it was again the predominant belief system by the end of the seventh century, having recolonised Europe from regions such as Ireland (as described in Chapter 13). From at least the start of the eighth century, then, the overwhelming majority of religious buildings erected in Europe were Christian churches.

The world of medieval Christendom has bequeathed to us an extraordinary heritage. Literally tens of thousands of churches across the Continent have fabric dating from the period between the end of Antiquity and, say, the start of the sixteenth century, by which stage the medieval period is generally regarded as having come to an end. Much of what was built has been lost, thanks in large measure to post-medieval secularisation, but what remains is still staggering in scale and richness. These standing buildings constitute a readily accessible resource for the medieval archaeologist, and in this chapter we shall outline their architectural and topographical development, as well as demonstrate the contribution that archaeological excavation has made to their interpretation.

Although this survey is confined to Christian buildings, it must not be forgotten that Judaism and Islam were very significant belief systems in medieval Europe, even if Jews and Muslims were heavily outnumbered by Christians. Their architectural heritages also merit careful attention, as demonstrated in Chapter 13 (see also Box 14.1).

From Roman to Romanesque

The study of European ecclesiastical architecture from the end of Antiquity to the twelfth century reveals how important Roman culture remained long after the fall of the city of Rome (see Box 4.2). Roman architecture provided the basic design templates for medieval Christian architecture, and this debt is especially apparent in the three cen-

The ninth-century church of San Miguel   **Fig 14.1**
de Lillo (Asturias, Spain) in Visigothic style
(photo: M Valor).

turies prior to the mid-1100s, when the so-called Gothic style began to spread across Europe. Indeed, the international architectural-stylistic fashion which immediately preceded Gothic, during the period 1000-1150, was so obviously based on Roman models that early nineteenth-century scholars described it as 'Romanesque', the term that is still in use today.

There were two basic church plan-types in medieval culture, both with deep roots in Roman architectural history, but with immediate origins in the church architecture of the Constantinian period (306-37). The more common plan-type was oblong, east-west oriented, and aisled, with an apsidal (or multi-apsidal) sanctuary at one end. Most of the great cathedral and monastic churches of the High Middle Ages – basically, the period of Romanesque and Gothic architecture – are of this type, as indeed are the thousands of smaller churches built to provide pastoral care to local communities across Europe. Somewhat less common was the other type, which was centrally planned, being circular or octagonal in form. Ironically, perhaps, the most celebrated building in Christendom, the Holy Sepulchre in Jerusalem (c330), was dominated by a rotunda (Corbo 1981); it was the symbolic and stylistic inspiration for most of Europe's circular and indeed octagonal churches (Bresc-Bautier 1974), the most famous of which is the Emperor Charlemagne's palace church at Aachen (Untermann 1989; see also p 343, and Figs 12.1 & 12.2).

The medieval architectural debt to the Roman world was not confined to plan-types. Round arches, free-standing columns and 'engaged' (or half-cylindrical) piers, and Corinthianesque capitals were among the many features of medieval church architecture that originated in Roman design. The importance of Antique architecture in the medieval mind is also apparent from the Roman *spolia* (recycled fragments of various sizes from older buildings) that one often finds in medieval religious buildings; Aachen

BOX 14.1 THE ALMOHAD FRIDAY MOSQUE OF SEVILLE

Abu Yaqub Yusuf (1163-84), the second Almohad caliph in al-Andalus, expressed his intentions of converting Seville into a great capital city. This project began in 1171 and included plans for a new Friday mosque, the construction of which commenced in the spring of 1172. Almost four years later the building was complete, although in 1184 the caliph ordered the construction of a minaret. He died that same year and his son and successor, Abu Yusuf Yaqub (1184-99), continued work on the tower from 1188 onwards, while at the same time repairing the outer aisles of the prayer-hall (*haram*). Some years later, 1195-96, we know that the courtyard (*sahn*) was extended. Eventually the mosque was finished in 1198, when the minaret was completed with the installation of a *yamur* – four golden balls crowning the tower.

This monument has been well documented in written sources, but little remains of the original building. Specifically, two courtyard aisles and most of the minaret, with the addition of a Renaissance belfry, are still visible. The prayer-hall was demolished after 1405 in order to construct the existing Gothic cathedral. The Islamic decoration and structure of the minaret and courtyard have been restored. It must be pointed out, however, that when the minaret was 'cleaned' in the nineteenth century the whole facing of the tower was removed, including some of the original stucco; it was once again restored in the 1980s.

The fate of the courtyard has been more fortunate. It was restored by the architect Félix Hernández Jimenez, an expert in the architecture of al-Andalus, with twelve different works being

Fig 1

Section of the Friday mosque at Seville (Spain), after excavation (drawing: MA Tabales).

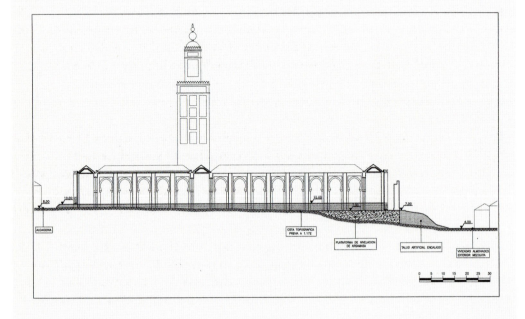

undertaken (1941-73). Due to this restoration, it is now possible to see the many traces that still remain of the former Islamic building.

From the 1980s onwards, systematic restoration works together with archaeological excavation have been taking place. The areas involved are the Almohad prayer-hall (today the Gothic cathedral), the courtyard, the base of the minaret and the area surrounding the mint. This means that we are now in position to reconstruct the original building (Figs 1 & 2). Its surface area can be determined; as can the process of levelling an area of the city where houses and city walls had to be demolished; the number of aisles; how the *qibla* was built; the nature of the foundations; how rainwater was collected and diverted from the roofs to the cistern in the centre of the *sahn*; the system of walls protecting the mosque and *alcazar* from the city; and the latest find, the *mida* or building for ablutions and latrines, located close to the mosque (Fig 3).

As a result of the documentary sources, which provide precise information concerning the building process, and of the restoration works and excavations, a 3-dimensional model has now be reconstructed, showing how the Almohad mosque actually looked (Fig 2). Art-history also plays an important role in the interpretation of these remains; in Morocco, there are some surviving examples from this period, the best known being Koutoubia, in Marrakesh, and the Hasan mosque in Rabat (see pp 390-1).

By Magdalena Valor

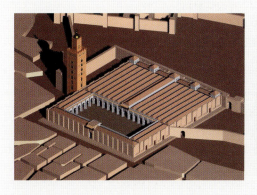

Fig 2

Axonometric and hypothetical reconstruction of the mosque (by A Jiménez, A Almagro & A Fernández, 1999).

Fig 3

*The ablutions building (*mida*) to the east of the mosque, discovered in 1994 under Virgen de los Reyes square (photo: M Valor).*

has the most famous surviving examples of Roman *spolia* (Fig 12.2, and see Box 15.3), but just as celebrated in the Middle Ages were the marble columns which were brought from the Mediterranean to the great mid-tenth-century church at Magdeburg (Kinney 2001; Meckseper 2001).

One critical, if sometimes overlooked, inheritance from the Roman past was the concept of placing a church above a saint's burial-place. At the tomb of St Bonifatius in Fulda, for example, a monumental three-naved basilica, with columns and a majestic transept, was constructed between 802-22 (Jacobsen 1995; Kruse 2002), while in the cemetery grounds a round church dedicated to St Michael was an imitation of the Holy Sepulchre in Jerusalem, itself erected over Christ's tomb. The tombs themselves were normally on display in vaulted crypts, usually sited immediately beneath the main altars of the churches in question and accessible by descending stairs; eighth- and ninth-century crypts were sometimes slightly outside the lines of the churches above them and were 'ring-form', allowing pilgrims and penitents easy movement past the venerable relics (for the variety of crypt-types, see McClendon 2005).

Rome reborn? Churches of the Carolingian renaissance

There were many regional church-building traditions in pre-1000 Europe, such as the Visigothic and Asturian in Iberia (Dodds 1990; Priego 1995; Fig 14.1), and the Anglo-Saxon in England (Fernie 1984), and all of them combine local or indigenous stylistic and technological techniques with traits ultimately derived from Roman work (Untermann 2006). The churches of the Carolingian 'renaissance' do, however, stand out as the most obviously 'Roman' in character of all. The plan of Fulda (founded 774), for example, was clearly inspired by Old St Peter's in Rome (Krautheimer 1942). Yet, to describe Carolingian churches as simply new versions of Roman types would be incorrect. The individual parts of Carolingian churches certainly had Roman pedigrees, but, as whole buildings, the churches were not at all Roman in character. On the contrary, they were generally innovative buildings, pointing assuredly to the future rather than always looking backwards.

One important invention of the Carolingian church builders was the so-called 'Westwork' (a term that is nineteenth-century rather than medieval in date; as 'fictional' it has been heavily criticized by Schönfeld-de Reyes (1999) and has been rejected in Germany and France as a 'Carolingian building type': Untermann 2006; Lobbedey 2002; Sapin 2002). A Westwork is a large, multi-storeyed, building at the west end of a church (McClendon 2005, 184-94). Its function was mainly liturgical, e.g. the Westwork of the now-lost Carolingian abbey church of St Riquier had an upper chapel dedicated to the Saviour, with relics kept within. Unfortunately, the important Westworks of Lorsch (undated), St Denis (dedicated 775) and St Riquier (799) no longer stand, although we do have excavated fragments of each of them and, in the case of St Riquier, informative post-medieval illustrations. Corvey has the only extant Carolingian Westwork (Fig 13.7), but it is quite late in date, from c880 (Lobbedey 2002; Poeschke 2002). Westworks continued to be built through the tenth and eleventh centuries, e.g. a Westwork was erected at Winchester in 974, though it seems to have been replaced within a few years by a two-towered façade, while Tournus in Burgundy still retains its magnificent early eleventh-century Westwork. The influence of Carolingian period and later Westworks can still arguably be detected in massive, Gothic-style, church façades several centuries later (Sapin 2002).

The classic medieval church tower was a related innovation of the Carolingian period, even though towers of some description were used in pre-Carolingian times, e.g. at Nantes, between 535-62. Sometimes towers were attached to Westworks in the Carolingian world, as well as to other parts of churches, while in other instances the Westworks were effectively towers themselves. Whereas classic Carolingian-style Westworks were no longer fashionable in most of Europe by the start of the twelfth century, church towers never went out of fashion. As structures that ascended literally towards Heaven, they had obvious symbolic and liturgical value, a fact reflected in their occasional dedication (as with the Westworks) to the Saviour. They were also necessary for bells; the *casabula* described in 799 as a feature of the original St Denis, for example, was a (timber-built?) bell-tower about 20m high, half of which cleared the roof of the church.

A transitional era? The later tenth century

Most of the surviving church architecture in Europe dates from the period after c1000, a fact which may support the claim, made at the start of the eleventh century by the French cleric Rodolphus Glaber, that the beginning of the second millennium AD was marked by a massive increase in the number of new or substantially reconstructed churches (Landes 2003).

Despite the symbolic importance of the year 1000, it was actually during the preceding half century that truly monumental churches begin to proliferate in Continental Europe, especially in those areas of present-day France and Germany that constituted Lotharingia. The classic plan-type of that period, if one can be isolated, has a double transept, another invention of the Carolingian period. The type is characterised by having transepts (often with apses and crypts) at both the eastern and western ends of the nave. Memleben, founded in 972, is an early example of its classic form (Untermann 2001a), whereas St Michael's at Hildesheim, dating from the period 1010-33 (Cramer, Jacobsen & von Winterfeld 1993), is certainly the best known example.

Romanesque

The so-called Romanesque style of architecture is regarded by many scholars as having emerged in the second quarter of the eleventh century, after the period in which Memleben, Hildesheim and others like them were built. Part of the rationale of scholars for identifying Romanesque as a mid-eleventh-century phenomenon is that it lines up chronologically with the start of the so-called 'twelfth-century renaissance', a renewal of ancient Latin culture that was even more widespread geographically than the Carolingian renaissance of several centuries earlier. In reality, though, the great elev-

Fig 14.2 *The west end of the choir at Durham Cathedral, England (drawing: T O'Keeffe).*

enth-century churches that we describe as Romanesque were part of a continuum of architectural design stretching back into the tenth century and earlier. Indeed, three of the recurring, indeed diagnostic, features of Romanesque architectural design – longitudinal galleries, alternating piers and columns, and wall articulation (Fig 14.2) – appeared first in the tenth century. There is no reason, then, why Hildesheim, one of early medieval Europe's finest buildings, should not be described as Romanesque (cf. Untermann 2006, 197-8). Indeed, a few scholars (most notably the American architectural historian, Kenneth Conant) have argued that Carolingian architecture should be described as Romanesque (Conant 1979).

This debate about the definition of Romanesque and the date of its first appearance has involved many scholars over many years, but we shall make no further contribution to it here. After all, the debate fails to take into account the fact that the term 'Romanesque' is not medieval at all, but was coined in the early 1800s. It is, in other words, a modern invention (Bizzarro 1992). Ecclesiastics and their master-masons a thousand years ago had no such terminology, and there is little evidence that they understood the concept of 'style' in the rather limited, formalist, way that we understand it today. So, while we continue to use the word Romanesque in this chapter, we also warn against too dogmatic an attitude to its definition.

Whatever the problems of terminology, there is no doubt that the great new churches of the eleventh and early twelfth centuries were as indebted to Roman architectural precedent as the word 'Romanesque' implies, and that debt is most obvious in those parts of Europe that had actual Roman buildings still standing in the Middle Ages. The late eleventh- and twelfth-century churches of northern Italy and south-east France (Provence), for example, could easily be misidentified as Roman buildings by untrained eyes. Indeed, Italy and adjacent parts of southern France and north-eastern

Spain formed one of the most dynamic regions of architectural production in Europe in the eleventh century, and it has been argued that many aspects of contemporary architecture elsewhere in Europe – groin vaults and ashlar masonry particularly – actually originated in eleventh-century Italian brick technology (Armi 2003).

Regional variation is critical to understanding the church architecture of the post-1050 era. Every region had its own tradition (cf. Box 14.2), and scholars of medieval church architecture can normally guess accurately a church's location in Europe from a photograph. France alone has, it is argued, several dozen local traditions, and a few very striking regional traditions, one of which – the Norman – spilled over into England in the second half of the eleventh century and from there into Ireland in the early twelfth century.

France and England are two of the five modern countries that were, c1100, essentially the core of Romanesque Europe (Kubach 1975; Stalley 1998). The others were Germany, Italy and Spain. Italian Romanesque churches are, as already noted, very obviously descended from ancient Roman buildings. The Romanesque churches of southern Germany have features that undoubtedly originated across the Alps in northern Italy. The Romanesque churches of the north German lands are obvious descendents of tenth-century (pre-Romanesque) Lotharingian churches. The Romanesque churches of northern Spain, remembering that southern Spain was under Muslim control during this period, have familial links with those of southern and, especially, southwestern, France, and that particular relationship is explained in part by the movement of pilgrims through France to the shrine of St James at Compostela (see Box 13.2).

The end of Romanesque

The Gothic architectural style, which dominated Europe until the sixteenth century, falls outside the scope of this chapter, except to say that it emerged (or was 'invented', as many scholars remark) in the Ile-de-France during the second quarter of the twelfth century, spreading outwards from there during the second half of that century (see below, Fig 14.6). Although its overall affect is quite different, most of its aesthetic and technological features have obvious origins in Romanesque architecture. It is somewhat ironic, however, that the Paris Basin was the birthplace of Gothic, given that it was the one region of France that seems not to have had a strong Romanesque architectural tradition.

As Gothic spread, Romanesque slipped out of fashion, disappearing everywhere by 1200, except on the geographical fringes. Western Ireland had one of the last Romanesque traditions in Europe, but it was discontinued in the second quarter of the thirteenth century, as Gothic ideas diffused from eastern Ireland, a region under English rule (O'Keeffe 2003).

Categories of Christian Architecture

So far church architecture has been discussed without differentiating between different organisational categories. The two principal categories throughout this period were episcopal (cathedrals) and monastic (mainly abbeys and priories, but also nunneries, fri-

BOX 14.2 DANISH ROMANESQUE CHURCHES:

As a result of many archaeological excavations from the 1960s onwards, we now have a fairly good picture of the interior arrangement of the Romanesque village churches of Denmark. The normal parish church from the twelfth century consisted of a nave and chancel, but it was sometimes also provided with an apse and/or a tower (Fig 1). The church was normally furnished with three altars, built in stone, the main (or 'high') altar being at the eastern end of the chancel, with two side-altars flanking the chancel arch (Fig 2).

The high-altar was in many cases provided with a so-called 'golden altar'. In fact, these are made from sheets of thin copper, chased into relief, and then gilded. The known examples are divided into frontals, covering the front of the altar, and retables (often crowned with an arch) placed at the back above the top of the altar. Nine such frontals (from 1135 to c1250) are still preserved from what was the territory of Denmark during the Middle Ages (Fig 3). More important, however, is the fact that fragments of such 'golden altars' are often found during archaeological investigations.

In the nave (and in a few cases in the chancel), there were stone benches along the north and south walls. If the church lacked a tower, there would also be a bench along the western wall, which might be placed on a platform raised one step higher than the floor of the nave. These wall-benches, typically being c40cm both high and wide, are doubtless contemporary with the church, although constructed after the walls had been erected. In one instance, it has been demonstrated that, during a rebuilding in the late twelfth century, free-standing benches had been built parallel with the wall-benches. They seem to disappear from use shortly after 1300.

In eastern Denmark, Scania (now in Sweden) and Zealand, towers were often erected at the western end. There are probably various reasons for this phenomenon, but at least in some instances they had a gallery in the second storey, opening towards the nave, where one could imagine the local lord seated during services.

The floor was in many cases a layer of mortar, often with many repairs, but clay floors are also known. Floors paved with tiles are known from some churches on Zealand and seem to have appeared first at the beginning of the thirteenth century. The font was placed in the middle of the nave on a platform raised one or two steps above floor-level. Romanesque fonts are well preserved in Denmark (e.g. Fig 13.8), although replaced in use today.

Romanesque wall-paintings have been found in so many Danish churches that it must be recognised that such were the norm. These murals

Fig 1

In central Jutland there are numerous 12th-century churches which are of the most simple Romanesque form: nave and choir; none is left untouched, but many have few alterations, as here at Dollerup, near Viborg (photo: HK Kristensen).

were painted in the 'al fresco' technique. They were usually later whitewashed over, but during the last 150 years many have been uncovered and restored. It is the opposite case with stained-glass windows, of which only a couple are preserved; on the other hand, excavations of church-floors have demonstrated that there was originally a lot of painted glass in these Romanesque churches.

In contrast to their modern appearance, the churches would have been dark, but with sparkling colours in the small windows, paintings on all the walls and the sculpture on the font accentuated with colours; the 'golden altar' (with a corresponding cross in the chancel arch) would have reflected the candlelight and the coloured lights from the windows.

Sources: Introduction, *Danmarks Kirker, Vejle Amt* (2004f), 16-21, figs 6-8; Hansen & Morten 1979; Kristensen 1999.

By Hans Krongaard Kristensen

Fig 2

Reconstruction of Butterup, Zealand, showing the original arrangement of the interior looking east (drawing: MA Sørensen).

Fig 3

The frontal from a 'golden altar' in Stadil, Jutland, reused in a Renaissance altar-piece (photo: HK Kristensen).

aries, preceptories, hospitals, etc); however, there were also collegiate churches (ministered by groups of non-monastic priests), local or parish churches, and various types of 'private' church (churches of chantry, estate churches, mortuary chapels, etc). The distinctions between these types or categories were not always very sharp. Cathedrals and monasteries, for example, seem today to be radically different, the former being seats of bishops and the latter places of communal religious observance. Yet, medieval bishops were sometimes members of monastic communities, and it was certainly very common for cathedrals to be staffed by monastic communities, even in sees where there was no tradition of monastic bishops.

Medieval cathedral churches tend to be large buildings. Size usually reflects the size and prosperity of the associated diocesan area, but also the benevolence of the local secular authority. As a general rule, the larger the city – cathedrals are almost all urban establishments – the larger the cathedral church. There is, however, really nothing in cathedral church architecture, other than perhaps a stone-built bishop's chair, that is distinctively or uniquely episcopal. Equally, the architecture of a monastic church is not especially distinctive either. The modern visitor to a great medieval city might not be able to distinguish between its cathedral church and one of its great abbey churches without the aid of modern signage. The fact that medieval cathedrals often had monastic chapters, as already noted, means that looking outside the church for signs is sometimes of no help, given that medieval cathedrals invariably had cloisters, chapter-houses, refectories and various other structures that are associated with monasticism.

Monasteries and monastic planning

Monasticism is nearly as old as Christianity and originated in the same eastern Roman provinces. The monastic ideal, which was to live in community according to a rule, was critical to Christianity's spread across Europe in the first instance, as well as to its recolonisation of 'Dark Age' Europe in the third quarter of the first millennium AD. In the sixth and seventh centuries, for example, the ecclesiastical landscapes of Italy and France were heavily dotted with monasteries. However, the distinctions between hermitages, isolated ascetic monasteries, communities of clerics tending the tombs of saints, and nunneries and convents of women are rather unclear in many parts of Europe before the 800s, if not later, and they may have been equally unclear to contemporaries.

There were some attempts in the seventh and eighth centuries in different parts of Europe to regularise or reform monastic observance (Untermann 2006). It could be argued that these reform movements did not generate particular architectural styles. Equally, it has been argued (Sanderson 2003) that the well-known reform movement of c935, associated with Gorze (near Metz) and impacting directly on Lotharingia and the eastern Franconian realm, had no standardised architectural stylistic manifestation. However, the classic monastic plan of the Middle Ages – the claustral plan – did emerge (at some unknown location) in the eighth century, an era of energetic reforming activity.

The claustral plan was based on a simple principle. A monastery was effectively a machine, and all its parts – its church, its dining-room, its sleeping-space and its meeting-

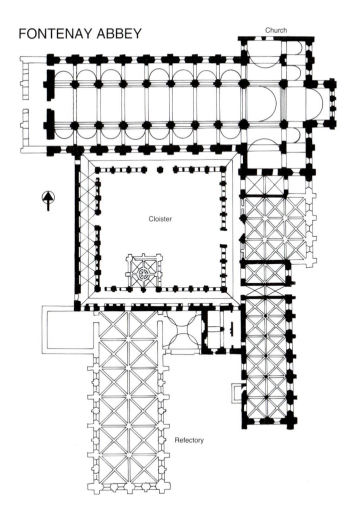

FONTENAY ABBEY

Church

Cloister

Refectory

Plan of the Cistercian monastery at Fontenay (Burgundy). The Cistercian Order originated in Burgundy in the late 11th century and spread rapidly across Europe during the 12th, to outnumber the monasteries of other orders in many parts of the Continent. The order's monasteries were characterised by their austerity, at least in the early years, with claustral planning often being seen in its 'purest' form (drawing: T O'Keeffe).

Fig 14.3

place – were positioned relative to each other around a courtyard (the cloister), according to their importance in the life of the community. The church was normally opposite the refectory on the north side of the cloister, whereas the east side of the cloister usually had the 'chapter-house' (so named because a chapter of the monastic rule was read there daily) and, above it, the dormitory, positioned there so that the community had only a short distance to travel from bed to church in the early hours of the morning (Fig 14.3). This plan-type was adopted by all medieval monastic communities from the early ninth century onwards (although some communities were simply too small to have claustral

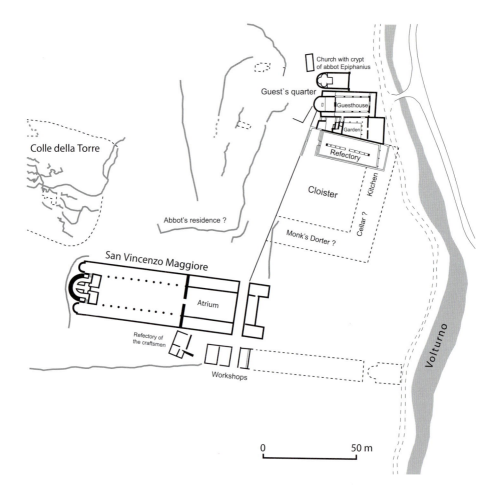

Fig 14.4　*Plan of San Vincenzo al Volturno (Molise), c820. The first Lombardic churches and monastic living-rooms in the north-eastern area were used as guest-quarters after c800; the apses of the new abbey church were orientated towards the West, emulating Old St Peter's in Rome. Enamels, glass objects, jewellery and ivory carvings were produced in the excavated monastic workshops (drawing: M Untermann, after R Hodges & J Mitchell).*

complexes) and arguably reached its apogee in the monasteries of the Cistercian monks during the twelfth century (van der Meer 1965; Fergusson 1984; Heald 2000).

Early manifestations of the claustral plan are a little irregular. For example, the important north Italian abbey of Novalesa (founded in 726) had several buildings arranged in its courtyard, whereas the near contemporary San Vincenzo al Volturno (founded 729) had a detached church, an assembly-room and a large refectory (Fig 14.4), although it is not clear that it had a formal cloister of the type so well known from later contexts (Sennhauser 1996, 17-26, 127-55; Hodges 1997; McClendon 2005, 161). The so-called 'Plan of St Gall', made c825 in the scriptorium of the monastery at Reichenau (Lake Constance), is the drawing of an ideal architectural scheme for a Benedictine mon-

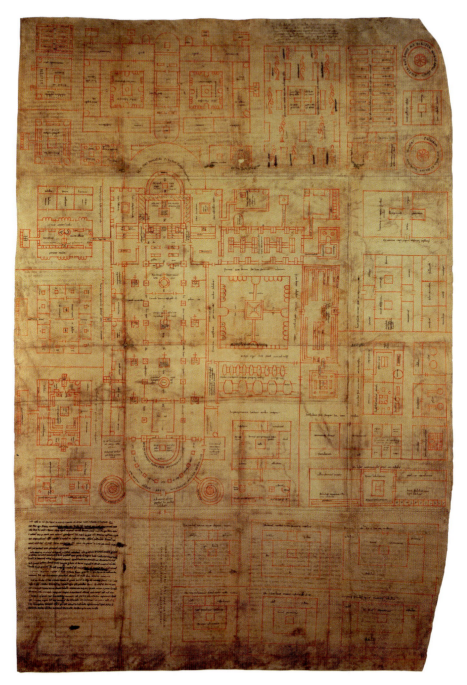

The complete 'Plan of St Gall' (Sankt Galler Stiftsbibliothek).

Fig 14.5

astery, with a precocious claustral plan (Horn & Born 1979; Price 1982; Zettler 1990; Untermann 1996; Ochsenbein & Schmucki 2002). It demonstrates that the classic form had been conceptualised by the early ninth century (Fig 14.5).

Fig 14.6 *St Denis: the east end of this royal abbey church, dating from the 1140s, is one of the most important early Gothic structures in Europe (drawing: T O'Keeffe).*

Rebuildings

Cathedral churches were, of all Christian buildings, the most susceptible to change when new architectural styles were developed during the Middle Ages. Medieval bishops, no doubt encouraged by local secular elites, apparently felt compelled to upgrade and enlarge their cathedrals whenever stylistic fashions changed. Larger ground-plans and superstructures were often necessitated by the numbers coming to worship because, with very few exceptions, the cathedrals of pre-1000 Europe were simply too small to handle the congregations of the eleventh and twelfth centuries. Although not a cathedral church, St Denis, located on the outskirts of Paris, is probably the most famous example of a major church being enlarged to accommodate throngs of visitors (Fig 14.6). It is famous mainly because, in their efforts to enlarge its area for pilgrim traffic, its mason, or rather its abbot, Suger, has been credited as having 'invented' Gothic (for the contemporary perspective, see Panofsky 1979, reasonably contradicted by Markschies 1995).

It is not surprising, then, that earlier medieval (in other words, pre-Romanesque) cathedrals simply do not survive in their original form, and that their original plans – and indeed the plans of their precincts (e.g. Sapin & Berry 1999) – can only be retrieved

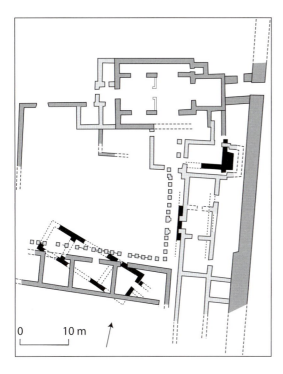

Plan of the monastery at
Landévennec (Brittany). The first
Celtic monastery, from the 7th/8th
century, consisted of isolated
buildings (black); following the
Benedictine reform of 818, the
abbey church, the main building to
the south and the large enclosure
wall to the east were constructed
(dark grey), with the cloister and
the other wings of the monastic core
(grey) being added c850 (drawing:
M Untermann, after P Guigon).

Fig 14.7

0   10 m

by archaeological excavation. The more often a cathedral was modified during the Middle Ages, or the more monumental a cathedral's modification, the more fragmentary the earliest remains are likely to be below ground. Analysis of excavation results is, consequently, often quite difficult. The 'Alte Dom' in Cologne, for example, is now known from long-running excavations to have been a large, three-aisled, church, with apsidal chapels and crypts, but the date of its erection, sometime between 830 and 930, has still not been resolved (Wolff 1996; Untermann 2001a).

Most medieval cathedrals occupy exactly the same sites as their predecessors, even if they have a much larger floor-area; however, the actual location of the original high altar, from the foundation period, tended to be maintained through all phases or periods of reconstruction. There is, then, a rich continuity of use at most episcopal sites. Sometimes, though, discontinuity is evidenced, e.g. the large, Franconian, episcopal churches of the sixth and seventh centuries seem to have survived through the ninth to twelfth centuries, but were then replaced by new constructions which had entirely different alignments (Testini et al 1989; Sapin 1995; Ristow 2001).

The tendency towards complete rebuilding of episcopal churches diminished in the eleventh century. The new Romanesque cathedrals of the eleventh and twelfth centuries generally survived the Middle Ages as Romanesque buildings, although many did have their eastern ends (their main liturgical ends) altered after the Gothic style emerged in the later twelfth century. Durham Cathedral is a good example of this, with its Gothic choir being built in the thirteenth century to replace the original Romanesque one, while the Romanesque nave was left untouched (Fernie 2004).

The same patterns of rebuilding through the Middle Ages are also evident among monastic churches, but less frequently so. Nowhere is the phenomenon of rebuilding more dramatically in evidence than at Cluny, in Burgundy. The monastic community there was founded in 910, following the Rule of St Benedict, but it adapted that Rule to its own needs in the tenth century and, in the process, established a new and extra-ordinarily powerful monastic movement: the Cluniac. Kenneth Conant's excavations at the site of Cluny itself revealed that the original early tenth-century church, known as Cluny I, was too small for the growing community and so was replaced by a new church, Cluny II, built over a period of a quarter of a century, starting in 955. Its replacement, Cluny III, was built over a period of more than four decades (1088-1130) to accommo-date a community of many hundreds. It was located to the north of Cluny II, presum-ably so as to have allowed the latter to remain in use until the larger new building was completed. Cluny II was eventually swallowed up in the claustral courts of Cluny III (Conant 1968; cf. Stratford 1998, 107-32).

Enlargement of Cluny was necessitated by the numbers of people who were join-ing the order. There is a different explanation for the enlargement of the Breton mon-astery of Landévennec, founded in the late eighth century (Guigon 1998, II, 92); there, the original complex, founded by monks from the Celtic West, was remodelled and enlarged when the Rule of St Benedict was introduced under Emperor Louis the Pious in the ninth century (Fig 14.7). Among the most remarkable remodellings of monas-teries from this same period is that of San Vincenzo al Volturno, mentioned above (Fig 14.4). Between 793 and 817, Abbot Joshua erected a large basilica with columns, a funer-ary-atrium and an annular crypt, with the older monastery at the site being renovated and transformed into space for distinguished guests, while its church was converted into a palace with a large hall (Hodges 1997).

By contrast, the first monastery at Petersinsel, in the Bieler Lake (Switzerland), con-sisted of a wooden complex with a single-naved church and a three-winged cloister (of likely tenth-century date). After the island's bequest to Cluny in 1107, this monas-tic complex operated as a provisional lodging for the workmen who, c1030, began the construction of a large church with three apses and transept. After supposed stability problems, the church was torn down and replaced by a smaller structure of similar type (Gutscher et al 1997).

Many monastic communities did not have the resources to reconstruct radically their original buildings, e.g. in eighth-century Franconia and Italy, the older abbey churches were seldom rebuilt at a cost in excess of their original construction costs. In other cases, monastic communities seem to have been happy to retain original Late Antique or early medieval structures, either because they were sufficient for their needs or because they venerated these older structures.

As with cathedrals, the early phases of important monasteries are often known to us from excavation alone, but the excavated evidence is sometimes problematic. The dates of excavated remains can be uncertain, as at San Salvatore in Brescia, where the large church with a one-aisled nave and a transept-arm might possibly be the church of the royal Lombardic convent consecrated in 763 (Bertelli & Brogiolo 2000, 496-530).

Reconstructions based on excavated evidence can also be problematic, e.g. the mid-eighth-century abbey churches of Fulda (Kruse 2002) and Lorsch (Behn 1934; Ericsson & Sanke 2004) have been reconstructed as three-aisled on insufficient evidence.

The Evidence of Excavation

There are two principal ways in which archaeologists study medieval architecture in general: structural examination (of extant walls) and excavation. The first of these involves observation, followed by recording (photographic and measured). Increasingly sophisticated recording technologies have allowed archaeologists to 'see' buildings in great detail. Modern drawings are often executed stone-by-stone and have the accuracy associated with modern engineering projects (cf. Fig 1.4). Such drawings help the archaeologist to determine phases of construction, repair and replacement in complex buildings, while computer technology is available to determine, from these high-accuracy measurements, the original medieval units of measure and proportional systems (Wiemer 1990). An exciting development in recent years has been the radiocarbon dating of mortar, although the technique remains in need of refinement. It has been used on selected buildings in different parts of Europe, such as the episcopal basilica at Stobi, in Macedonia, but the most comprehensive use of it has been at Saint-Benigne, Dijon, where it verified the archaeologists' interpretations of the building and its predecessors (Malone et al 1980). Problems have, however, been encountered with its use in Finland (Hiekkanen 1998). Bricks can potentially be dated by thermoluminescence (Holst 2002).

Excavation is the technique most associated with archaeology, and its deployment at many church sites has yielded much exciting data. One the one hand, it produces finds such as the fragments of large bells from the convent church at Vreden (Drescher 1999) and window glass has been found at San Vincenzo and elsewhere. At St Johannsen, in Switzerland, excavation revealed the postholes of the twelfth-century scaffolding for the mechanism that hammered in the posts of its pile foundation (Mojon 1986). Secondly, excavation produces evidence for constructional phases. For example, excavation was critical to the interpretation of the structural history of a church at Esslingen, near Stuttgart. This began in the seventh/eighth century as a small private church, within which were the burials of the local elite and the tomb of a saint, and then gained collegiate status with the establishment of a monastery by Abbot Fulrad of St Denis, shortly before 766. Subsequently, in the ninth century, this collegiate church was rebuilt as a large single-naved structure, with a long corridor-crypt. In the tenth century, the place of the choir stalls was elevated to the level of the high altar and the crypt expanded; however, by the eleventh/twelfth century, the convent no longer existed, and the church was converted into a parish church by the addition of aisles and a tower (Fehring et al 1995).

The survival rate of Christian architectural fabric from the first millennium AD varies significantly across Europe, but is generally much poorer than for later centuries, thus increasing the importance of evidence from excavation. One major consequence of excavation has been the realisation that timber churches were actually very common across much of the earlier medieval Continent (Ahrens 2001), given that tim-

Fig 14.9 *The interior construction of the 12th-century Norwegian stave-church at Borgund in Sogn (drawing: G Bull; after Bugge 1953).*

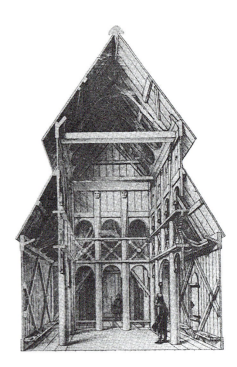

ber-built churches are exceptionally rare survivals in Europe. One such building is that at Greensted, Essex, which was originally dated by dendrochronology to the ninth century (Christie et al 1979); however, a subsequent dating (1995) has suggested that it is from the late eleventh century. The standing stave-built churches of the twelfth century and later in Norway (Fig 14.8) are now unique (Hauglid 1973), although examples of this type are known to have existed in France (Untermann 2001b). The abbey church, cloister and monastic buildings at Reichenau are a good example of what excavation can reveal; these were first constructed in wood and have been dated by dendrochronology to 722 ±10 (Reisser 1960; Zettler 1988). The postholes of an earlier timber church have often been excavated beneath a Romanesque stone building, e.g. the first church built at Jelling, in Denmark, following King Harald's conversion, c965 (Krogh 1982).

There is little sense, however, as one reviews the pan-European evidence, of shared research questions among excavators of churches. Indeed, there is even little pattern to the excavations within particular regions. Thus, for example, although the atria of churches have been partly excavated at Fulda, Kornelimünster and Corvey (Lobbedey 2001), there is astonishingly little archaeological evidence pertaining to contemporary monastic living-quarters at these and other sites in ninth-century Franconia.

Issues for the Future

It is clear that we possess a great deal of knowledge about the architecture of twelfth-century and earlier Christianity, as well as an enlarging knowledge-base about the architectures of the other belief-systems. There are, of course, many important buildings and sites of buildings that still demand our attention, even though they have long been subjects of investigation. Some of these (e.g. St Philibert in Tournus, or St Benigne in Dijon) are likely to remain subjects of research in the long term, simply on account of their obvious architectural importance, while others (e.g. the church of Tewkesbury Abbey in England) present particular problems on account of later destruction of certain parts of them. It is difficult to predict if the number of research-driven excavations within and around extant churches will rise or fall in the next few decades; it should, ideally, rise, as we refine our research questions, but at least it is certain that hitherto unknown churches will continue to be discovered by chance in development-led archaeological excavations across Europe.

What are the key research issues for future students of earlier medieval (pre-Gothic) church architecture? A quick browse through the enormous body of literature that now exists will reveal that many 'traditional' matters – origins, chronology, style-transmissions, conjectural reconstructions – continue to require the attention of archaeologists, with monographs based on in-depth studies of individual buildings continuing to be the corner-posts of research. The pursuit of these issues remains critical to our subject.

However, although basic trends in religious architectural history are now well-mapped, our understanding of those trends needs to be refined, especially at local levels. Much of the archaeological or art-historical literature about medieval religious architecture is concerned with 'great' buildings – those buildings of great structural or aesthetic merit that were of regional, national, or even international, importance in the Middle Ages – but we need to know more about the lesser buildings and about the more localised contexts in which they existed. Moreover, while scholarship has always concentrated on finding and explaining similarities between buildings, it needs to pay equal attention to differences or dissimilarities (e.g. why exactly, does one early ninth-century Carolingian church differ from another, even within the same geographical area?).

Reflecting on the meanings of 'similarity' and 'difference' draws us close to the world of theory. Students of medieval religious architecture have been very resistant to the theoretical turns in archaeology over the past 40 years, even though both the scientism and anthropology that underpinned the so-called 'New Archaeology' of the late 1960s and early 1970s could certainly have been incorporated beneficially into their research. There is an argument today that the theoretical perspectives that have developed in archaeology since the 1980s – phenomenological and gender perspectives, for example – can add much more to the study of religious architecture (Addiss 1987; Gilchrist 1995; O'Keeffe 2007), but it remains to be seen if these ways of thinking will penetrate this traditionally empirical field of research.

BIBLIOGRAPHY

Addiss, JM (1987) *Spatial Organisation in Romanesque Architecture*, Ann Arbor

Ahrens, C (2001) *Die frühen Holzkirchen Europas*, Stuttgart

Armi, CE (2004) *Design and Construction in Romanesque Architecture. First Romanesque Architecture and the Pointed Arch in Burgundy and Northern Italy*, Cambridge

Behn, F (1934) *Die karolingische Klosterkirche von Lorsch an der Bergstraße*, Berlin/Leipzig

Bertelli, C and Brogiolo, GP (eds) (2000) *Il futoro die Longobardi*, Milan

Bizzarro, TW (1992) *Romanesque Architectural Criticism. A Prehistory*, Cambridge

Bresc-Bautier, G (1974) 'Les imitations du St-Sépulchre de Jerusalem (IXe-XVe siècles). Archéologie d'une dévotion', *Revue d'Histoire de la Spiritualité* 50, 319-42

Bugge, A (1953) *Norwegian Stave Churches*, Oslo

Christie, H, Olsen, O and Taylor, HM (1979) 'The wooden church of St. Andrew at Greensted, Essex', *Antiquaries Journal* 59, 92-112

Conant, KJ (1968) *Cluny: les Églises et la Maison du Chef d'Ordre*, Mâcon

Conant, KJ (1979, 2nd ed) *Carolingian and Romanesque Architecture*, Harmondsworth

Corbo, VC (1981) *Il Santo Sepulcro di Gerusaleme*, 3 vols, Jerusalem

Cramer, J, Jacobsen, W and Von Winterfeld, D (1993) 'Die Michaeliskirche', in Brandt, M and Eggebrecht, A (eds), *Bernward von Hildesheim und das Zeitalter der Ottonen* I, Hildesheim, 369-82

Dodds, JD (1990) *Architecture and Ideology in Early Medieval Spain*, Pennsylvania

Ericsson, I and Sanke, M (eds) (2004) *Aktuelle Forschungen zum ehemaligen Reichs- und Königskloster Lorsch*, Darmstadt

Fergusson, P (1984) *Architecture of Solitude: Cistercian Abbeys in Twelfth-Century England*, Princeton

Fehring, GP, Scholkmann, B and Anstett, PR (1995) *Die Stadtkirche St. Dionysius in Esslingen a.N.*, Forschungen und Berichte der Archäologie des Mittelalters in Baden-Württemberg 13, Stuttgart

Fernie, E (1984) *The Architecture of the Anglo-Saxons*, London

Fernie, E (2004) *The Architecture of Norman England*, Oxford

Gilchrist, R (1995) *Contemplation and Action: the Other Monasticism*, London

Guigon, P (1998) *Les Églises du Haut Moyen Âge en Bretagne*, II, Saint-Malo

Gutscher, D, Ueltschi, A and Ulrich-Bochsler, S (1997) *Die St. Petersinsel im Bielersee, ehemaliges Cluniazenser-Priorat*, Bern

Hansen, BA and Morten, AS (1979) 'Den usynlige Kirke', in Egevang, R (ed), *Strejflys over Danmarks bygningskultur*, Copenhagen, 65-82

Hauglid, R (1973) *Norske stavkirker*, Oslo

Heald, D (2000) *Architecture of Silence: Cistercian Abbeys of France*, New York

Hiekkanen, M (1998) 'Problemen med 14C-datering av kalkbruk', *Fornvännen* 1998:2, 142-5

Hodges, R (1997) *Light in the Dark Ages. The Rise and Fall of San Vincenzo al Volturno*, London

Holst, JC (2002) 'Erfahrungen mit der bauhistorischen Anwendung der Thermolumineszenzdatierung', *Jahrbuch für Hausforschung* 49, 241-59

Horn, W and Born, E (1979) *The Plan of St Gall. A Study of the Architecture and Economy of, and Life in, a Paradigmatic Carolingian Monastery*, 3 vols, Los Angeles/London

Kristensen, HK (1999) 'Kirker og klostre', in Ingesman, P, Kjær, U, Madsen, PK and Vellev, J (eds), *Middelalderens Danmark*, Copenhagen, 254-73

Jacobsen, W (1995) 'Zur Frühgeschichte der Quedlinburger Stiftskirche', in Reupert, U, Trajkovits, Th and Weiner, W (eds), *Denkmalkunde und Denkmalpflege. Wissen und Wirken*, Dresden, 63-72

Kinney, D (2001) 'Roman architectural *spolia*', *Proceedings of the American Philosophical Society* 145, 138-50

Krautheimer, R (1942) 'The Carolingian revival of early Christian architecture', *The Art Bulletin* 24, 1-38 [reprinted, with postscript, in idem (1969), *Studies in Early Christian, Medieval and Renaissance Art*, New York, 203-56]

Krogh, KJ (1982) 'The royal Viking-age monuments at Jelling in the light of recent archaeological excavations', *Acta Archaeologica* 53, 183-216

Kruse, KB (2000) *Der Hildesheimer Dom. Grabungen und Bauuntersuchungen auf dem Domhügel 1988 bis 1999*, Hanover

Kubach, HE (1975) *Romanesque Architecture*, New York

Landes, R (2003) 'The white mantle of churches: millennial dynamics, and the written and architectural record', in Hiscock, N (ed), *The White Mantle of Churches. Architecture, Liturgy, and Art around the Millennium*, Turnhout, 249-64

Lobbedey, U (2001) 'Das Atrium der Klosterkirche zu Corvey. Vorbericht zu einer Grabung', in Schmitt, R (ed), *Es thun iher viel fragen. Kunstgeschichte in Mitteldeutschland*, Petersberg, 9-14

Lobbedey, U (2002) 'Westchöre und Westwerke im Kirchenbau der Karolingerzeit', in Godman, P, Jarnut, J and Johanek, P (eds), *Am Vorabend der Kaiserkrönung*, Berlin, 163-91

Malone, C, Valestro, S and Varela, AG (1980) 'Carbon-14 chronology of mortar from excavations in the medieval church of Saint-Benigne, Dijon, France', *Journal of Field Archaeology* 7:3, 329-43

Markschies, Ch (1995) *Gibt es eine "Theologie der gotischen Kathedrale"?*, Abhandlungen der Heidelberger Akademie der Wissenschaften, phil-hist Kl 1995, 1, Heidelberg

McClendon, CB (2005) *The Origins of Medieval Architecture*, New Haven/London

Meckseper, C (2001) 'Magdeburg und die Antike: zur Spolienverwendung im Magdeburger Dom', in Puhle, M (ed), *Otto der Grosse: Magdeburg und Europe*, I, Mainz, 367-80

Möbius, F (1985) *Buticum in Centula*, Abhandlungen der Sächsischen Akademie der Wissenschaften zu Leipzig, phil-hist Kl 71:1, Berlin

Mojon, L (1986) *St. Johannsen/St.-Jean de Cerlier*, Bern

Morris, R (1989; 1998) *Churches in the Landscape*, London

Ochsenbein, P and Schmucki, K (eds) (2002) *Studien zum St. Galler Klosterplan*, St Gallen

O'Keeffe, T (2003) *Romanesque Ireland. Architecture and Ideology in the Twelfth Century*, Dublin

O'Keeffe, T (2007) *Archaeology and the Pan-European Romanesque*, London

Panofsky, E (1979, 2nd ed) *Abbot Suger on the Abbey Church of St Denis and its Art Treasures*, Princeton

Parsons, D (1977) 'The pre-romanesque church of St-Riquier. The documentary evidence', *Journal of the British Archaeological Association* 130, 21-51

Poeschke, J (ed) (2002) *Sinopien und Stuck im Westwerk der karolingischen Klosterkirche von Corvey*, Münster

Price, L (1982) *The Plan of St Gall in Brief*, Los Angeles/London

Priego, CC (1995) *Arte Prerománico de la Monarquía Asturiana*, Oviedo

Reisser, E (1960) *Die frühe Baugeschichte des Münsters zu Reichenau*, Berlin

Ristow, S (2001) *Die frühen Kirchen unter dem Kölner Dom. Befunde und Funde vom 4. Jahrhunderts bis zur Bauzeit des Alten Domes*, Cologne

Sanderson, W (2003) 'Monastic architecture and the Gorze reform reconsidered', in Hiscock, N (ed), *The White Mantle of Churches. Architecture, Liturgy, and Art around the Millennium*, Turnhout, 81-90

Sapin, C (ed) (1995) *La cathédrale de Nevers. Du Baptistère Paléochrétien au Chevet Roman (VIe–XIe siècles)*, Paris

Sapin, C (ed) (2002) *Avant-nefs et espaces d'accueil dans l'église entre le IVe et le XIIe siècle*, Mémoires de la section d'archéologie et d'histoire de l'art 13, Paris

Sapin, C and Berry, W (1999) *Naissance d'un Îlot Urbain. Les Abords de la Cathédrale Saint-Lazare d'Autun du IXe au XVIIIe siècle*, Auxerre

Schefers, H (2004) 'Einige Fragen zur Lorscher Baugeschichte und Archäologie', in Ericsson, I & Sanke (eds), 7-16

Schönfeld-de Reyes, D (1999) *Westwerkprobleme*, Weimar

Sennhauser, HR (ed) (1996) *Wohn- und Wirtschaftsbauten frühmittelalterlicher Klöster*, Zürich

Stalley, R (1998) *Early Medieval Architecture*, Oxford

Stratford, N (1998) *Studies in Burgundian Romanesque Architecture*, London

Testini, P, Cantino Wataghin, G and Pani Ermini, L (1989) 'La cattedrale in Italia', in Duval, N (ed), *Actes du XIe Congrès international d'archéologie chrétienne, Lyon u. a. 1986*, I, Rome, 5-231

Untermann, M (1989) *Der Zentralbau im Mittelalter*, Darmstadt

Untermann, M (1996) 'Das "Mönchshaus" in der früh- und hochmittelalterlichen Klosteranlage', in Sennhauser, HR (ed), *Wohn- und Wirtschaftsbauten frühmittelalterlicher Klöster*, Zurich, 233-57

Untermann, M (2001a) 'Köln und Memleben', in Lieb, S (ed), *Form und Stil. Festschrift für Güther Binding zum 65. Geburtstag*, Darmstadt, 45-55

Untermann, M (2001b) *Forma Ordinis. Die mittelalterliche Baukunst der Zisterzienser*, Munich/Berlin

Untermann, M (2006) *Architektur im frühen Mittelalter*, Darmstadt

Van der Meer, F (1965) *Atlas de l'Ordre Cistercien*, Paris

Weimer, W. (1990) 'Proportion analysis of medieval churches by computer – final success after 50 years of failure?', *Computers and the History of Art* 8:2, 89-108

Wolff, A (ed) (1996) *Die Domgrabung Köln*, Cologne

Zettler, A (1988) *Die frühen Klosterbauten der Reichenau*, Sigmaringen

Zettler, A (1990) 'Der St. Galler Klosterplan. Überlegungen zu seiner Herkunft und Entstehung', in Godman, P and Collins, R (eds), *Charlemagne's Heir. New Perspectives on the Reign of Louis the Pious*, Oxford, 655-87

CHAPTER 15

LIFE, DEATH AND MEMORY

Thomas Meier, with James Graham-Campbell

Life and Disease

With regard to the physical anthropology of the early and High Middle Ages, small-scale research in both time and space is the overwhelmingly important factor because hardly any comparative studies have been undertaken. This is not least because of the differing quality of the available sources, but also because of the varying state of research in different parts of Europe. The study of skeletons provides our main source of knowledge, but this source is limited, on the one hand, by the amount of archaeological investigation and documentation that has taken place of representative and well-preserved burial sites and, on the other, by the somewhat high costs of carrying out intensive anthropological analysis. At present, therefore, anthropological studies deal mainly with individual sites and/or methodology. For the most part, it remains an open question as to whether, or to what extent, these case-studies are representative of a particular region and/or period. Indeed, comparative analyses of medieval populations in England (e.g. York, Wharram Percy, Lincoln, Raunds Furnell and London) have demonstrated that populations in neighbouring areas have experienced very different living conditions. These differences provide important historical information in themselves, but at the same time they demonstrate the local nature of the data and thus the problem that exists in trying to draw a European outline.

Life expectancy and paleo-demography

'Your father is an old man (*senex*), unable to govern the realm', said the young conspirators who were inciting Henry against his father, Emperor Henry IV, who was then 54 years old (*Vita Heinrici IV imperatoris*, ch 9). This is one of the rare medieval remarks concerning what was considered 'normal' life-expectancy. However, as this source was endeavouring to discredit the young rebels, it is hardly useful in anthropological terms. A detailed examination of the Fulda death-rolls has, however, convincingly shown that the monks of this Carolingian monastery died at an average age of c50 years (Schmid 1978). Nevertheless, in most cases written sources, for numerous reasons, do not provide much evidence for the calculation of life-expectancy and thus paleo-demography dur-

Pilsting, near Landau/Isar (Germany): infants' burials in 'post-holes' dispersed throughout the settle- **Fig 15.1**
ment area (8th-10th centuries) (after Kreiner 1989).

ing the early and High Middle Ages. The primary source with which to address these problems is anthropological material.

Paleo-demographic research starts with an estimation of sex and age-at-death of individual skeletons. Whereas the reliable identification of sex is generally possible, through a combination of skeletal morphological indicators (when sufficiently preserved), the determination of age-at-death is more problematic. Apart from individual variability, an individual's stress-load decisively influences the ageing process of the skeleton. Therefore, the biological age, expressed in the morphology of the skeleton, may differ considerably from the chronological age (in absolute years of life). During the period of growth (childhood and youth), a combination of morphological indicators can provide reasonably precise and reliable data, not least in combination with the status of teeth, as a further means of juvenile age-calculation (Scheuer & Black 2000). For adults, however, morphological indicators like tooth-wear, or the closing of bone sutures, presently allow for only a rough estimate of age-at-death (cf. the example of Tirup, Denmark; Boldsen 2005a). A new research agenda (the 'Rostock Manifesto') is in progress in the hope of developing 'more reliable and more vigorously validated age indicators or categories' (Hoppa & Vaupel 2002, 2).

One of these indicators may well be tooth-cementum annulation. This is based on the supposition that every year a further ring of tooth cement is developed at the root of the tooth, fixing it to the jawbone. By counting these 'year'-rings and adding the average

age of eruption of the tooth, the result should give the age-at-death in years (Wittwer-Backofen et al 2004). However, the biological cause of such an annual periodicity of tooth cementum is not yet understood (Renz & Radlanski 2006), and this method still needs standardisation and validation on a historical population under different living conditions from those of today.

A further bias to paleo-demography, directly relating to archaeology, is estimation of infant mortality (Saunders & Barrans 1999). The comparison of medieval demographic data to known pre-industrial populations has resulted in the assumption that there was a very high mortality rate during the first year of life, as well as the next couple of years during the period of weaning, when small children are extremely vulnerable to diarrhoea and infections. However, comparatively few infants are found during excavations of cemeteries and graveyards. There are several possible reasons for this, e.g. dead infants may have been buried away from the rest of the population. Indeed, in some settlements of the late first millennium, infants were buried in 'post-holes', loosely scattered over the settlement area, e.g. at Pilsting, near Landau/Isar, Germany (Fig 15.1), while in the Münsterhof graveyard, Zurich, a remote infants' corner was in use from the mid-tenth century to the first quarter of the eleventh (Schneider et al 1982). This separation of dead infants may result in an archaeological problem in their recognition; remote areas of cemeteries are rarely excavated, and the tiny bones of infants may not be recognized when found in a settlement context. On the other hand, excavations have revealed clusters of infants immediately adjacent to contemporary churches even in the same region, e.g. Igling, Landsberg/Lech, Germany (Fig 15.2); and, in Zurich, prior to the installation of the infants' corner, babies were buried regularly among the adults. In both these cases, the graves of infants have the same or even better chance of being found by excavation as those of adults, implying a statistical over-representation of infants. Another explanation that has been suggested is that infants' graves tended to be very shallow (e.g. Kérpuszta, Hungary) and have therefore been more readily destroyed by the plough or mechanical digger. Finally, even natural decomposition processes can be blamed for poor preservation of immature bones, as has been observed in the Old Slavic (ninth-century) cemetery of Mikulčice (Czech Republic). However, apart from these attempts to explain a discrepancy between our statistical expectations and the excavated data, it might be worth considering whether these 'unfound' infants ever existed, merely owing their 'lives' to our scientific constructs (Stloukal 1989). In this respect, different techniques of deliberately avoiding offspring may be underestimated by demography (Biller 2000). On the other hand, in Iceland, immediately following the official Conversion (c1000), the then current practice of exposing unwanted infants was still permitted for a short period.

In the second step, the data concerning individuals are integrated to form a demographic profile, allowing the calculation of population figures, life-expectancy and other demographic patterns. With regard to the problems of determining age-at-death, however, the researcher tries to estimate a demographic profile 'directly from the distribution of age indicator data themselves' (Hoppa & Vaupel 2002, 17), i.e. morphological and histological age-indicators are not combined to age individuals at death and then

The village cemetery (8th-9th centuries) at Igling, near Landsberg/Lech (Germany), with a cluster of infants immediately surrounding a contemporary wooden church (north to the top): black = children <60cm (© T Meier, Bayerisches Landesamt für Denkmalpflege).

Fig 15.2

used as the basis for a demographic profile, instead this profile is calculated directly from the various indicators, ignoring individuals and their ages (Konigsberg & Frankenberg 2002).

As a third step, it should be possible to infer from these patterns the cultural and eco-logical conditions that this population had been exposed to. As will be obvious, what with the problems of making individual age-at-death calculations, together with the (supposed) deficit of infants, the data-bases for population models are rather weak and so too must be the inferences drawn from them. The results are further obscured by the possible selection of individuals not to be buried in the community's cemetery, by dif-ferent processes of natural decomposition, and by partial or inadequate excavation – not to mention the fact that the small numbers of individuals are not statistically representa-tive in terms of modern demography. To circumvent at least some of these problems, the age-distribution of a concrete population-model was tested against a set of demographic profiles empirically derived from known pre-industrial populations (Weiss 1973; Coale et al 1983). If an age-group was misrepresented, the figure was corrected on the basis of a set of UN-model patterns of mortality, from which a specific pattern was selected by closeness-of-fit to the mortality profile compiled, as well as to the supposed life-condi-tions of the population under study. However, this procedure has forced historic pop-ulations into our expectations of demographic profiles, giving them no chance to show fundamentally different demographic patterns (Meindl & Russel 1998, 389-91).

Unsurprisingly, the calculation of life-expectancy varies considerably between researchers, partly at least because of the methodological problems described above. Overall, many studies suggest that, on average, people mostly died in their early 30s, with women slightly younger than men. However, this figure is not particularly meaningful because life-expectancy increased dramatically if one survived the first few years. Calculating the number of old people – who were essential for providing continuity of cultural knowledge – is, however, faced with the severest of the practical problems and so the results vary widely according to the methods applied by the researcher. Nevertheless, these variations probably do partly reflect reasonable historical differences in time and space, as seemingly there was a tendency for life-expectancy at birth to be in decline from the sixth to the thirteenth centuries, as also from West to East (Langenscheidt 1985, 158-63), with differences being evident on rural, monastic and urban sites. Further research, based on high resolution in both time and space, and utilising standardised techniques of estimating age-at-death, is urgently required.

Population figures are the result of complex demographic processes. It is hardly possible to calculate them from the anthropological analysis of cemeteries as these reflect single settlements, or even only parts of them. Nevertheless, demographic laws generally seem applicable to medieval population development, thus paleo-demographic

Population Estimates (in millions) at Specific Times, 0-1500 A.D.						
Area	0	500	650	1000	1340	1500
Greece and Balkans	5	5	3	5	6	4.5
Italy	7.4	4	2.5	7	10	9
Iberia	6	4	3.5	7	9	8.3
Mediterranean	18.4	13	9	17	25	21.8
France—Low Countries	6	5	3.5	6	19	16
British Isles	0.4	0.5	0.5	2	5	3
Germany-Scandinavia	3.5	3.5	2	4	11.5	7.5
West and Central Europe	9.9	9	5.5	12	35.5	26.5
Slavic	4	5	3			2
Russia				6	8	6
Poland				2	3	2
Hungary	0.5	0.5	0.5	1.5	2	1.5
East Europe	4.5	5.5	3.5	9.5	13	11.5
Total	32.8	27.5	18.0	38.5	73.5	59.8

Sources: Russell, *Late Ancient and Medieval Population*, 148; somewhat revised by articles later: for Balkans in *Journal of Economic and Social History of the Orient* 2 (1960): 269-270; for Italy, J. Beloch, *Bevölkerungsgeschichte Italiens* III (1961): 344-352.

Fig 15.3   *Calculated population figures for the European Middle Ages (after Russell 1985).*

estimates for Europe during the eighth to twelfth centuries assume an exponential growth, which is regarded as typical for pre-industrial populations. The speed of this growth, however, varied enormously between the regions of Europe. For Italy, comparative demographic analysis suggests a more-or-less stable population, growing quite slowly from 4-5 millions, in the sixth century, to 9-10 millions in the fourteenth, prior to the Black Death, with most of the population increase taking place after the renaissance in urban culture during the thirteenth century (Giovannini 2001). In other regions, the population seems to have grown much more quickly, as is indicated by the development of sparsely populated marginal regions (*Landesausbau*). Throughout central Eastern Europe vast areas were affected by the beginning of German settlement; the re-conquest of the Iberian Peninsula opened-up extensive territories for settlement. From the twelfth century onwards, the foundation and growth of medieval towns absorbed masses of people. Simultaneously, famines and price-rises might indicate that population figures had approached the ecological and/or economic limits (Abel 1967, 110f; Russell 1985; Livi-Bacci 1998; for the contemporary perception, cf. Biller 2000).

Putting figures to this general outline is extremely difficult, but attempts may at least give an idea of the order (Fig 15.3). For northern France, central England and parts of Italy, an estimate of c40 persons/km² may be reasonable for the High Middle Ages, whereas in central Eastern Europe figures climbed from c5 to c10 persons/km² during the period from 1000 to the eve of the Black Death.

More precise figures may be calculated when some kind of population record exists. For example, the *Polyptychon Irminonis*, written shortly before 829, for the management of the possessions of the abbey of St-Germain-des-Prés, near Paris, registered complete families, including their children, thus allowing us to calculate precise demographic figures. Another possibility is to calculate the number of farmsteads, based on a thorough archaeological survey of an area. The number of farmsteads can be multiplied by the estimated average number of inhabitants, and the results counter-checked against figures from associated cemeteries and the nutritional potential of the area (crops, livestock, wood, etc) (cf. Bintliff & Sbonias 1999).

Disease

Documentary sources from before the end of the Middle Ages rarely point to any specific diseases. If they do, they hardly describe the sufferings in sufficient detail to make it possible to identify them with the aetiology of modern medicine. Moreover, disease was often regarded as moral punishment, thus being reported in the discourse of religion rather than of medicine.

Again, major information is obtained from skeletal material. Much information on the life of an individual can be revealed by means of a thorough macroscopic analysis. A person may have suffered injurious events, resulting in wounds and fractures. Cuts on the skull and other bones allow the weapon to be identified and the direction of blow reconstructed, with the position and type of fracture indicating the circumstances of the event. For example, a clean fracture in the middle part of the forearm is characteristic of an offensive blow from the front which the person tried to parry, whereas in the case of a chip fracture at the distal end of the forearm the person most probably suffered an unlucky fall. By comparative analysis of different skeletal populations, statistically significant variations in patterns of bone fracture may be revealed, indicating different conditions of life, such as gender, occupation or rural versus urban sites. For example, at the Anglo-Saxon cemetery of Raunds Furnells, in Northamptonshire (England), almost 20% of the population had suffered fractures during their life-times, with clear differences between genders: among males, mainly the collar-bone (*clavicula*) was affected, whereas with females it was the forearm (*ulna/radius*), pointing to different occupations, with different risks of injury. At the contemporary urban site of St Nicholas Shambles, London, only c5% of the individuals had suffered such fractures, showing that farming posed a significantly greater hazard than craft-oriented urban life (Judd & Roberts 1999; for a southern French study, see Mafart 1996).

In addition, many chronic diseases and afflictions leave evidence on the bones, e.g. revealing widespread maladies like periostitis or leprosy, at least when in their advanced state (Aufderheide & Rodríguez-Martín 1998; Boldsen 2005b). Not only diseases, but also those general conditions of life unfavourable to the 'normal' development of the skeleton leave paleo-pathological traces (Larsen 1997; Polet 2003). Repeated hunger or vitamin-deficiency during growth may result in deformations or dissolution of bones (e.g. rickets). A long-term physical overload will ultimately cause visible damage to the stressed bones either by partial or total fracture, by inflammation (arthritis), by new formation of bone material (spondylosis) or by degeneration of the bone with age (arthrosis). At a tenth-century princely burial-site of the Slavonic settlement of Starigard/Oldenburg, Holstein, Germany, degenerative joint disease showed remarkable differences between the genders, indicating that males were occupied with riding (and perhaps fighting), whereas women's work, like weaving, leather- or bone-working, particularly stressed their right hands (Teegen & Schultz 2003).

Not every physical action, however frequently repeated over a long period of time, will necessarily result in a pathological feature. So further information may be obtained from adaptations of bones to such recurring patterns of activity by which the body has responded to this specific strain. Often, these are additional facets of the joints. When they are observed at the knee and metatarsus, they are indicative of work carried out in a squatting position, whereas additional facets at the metacarpus may, for example, indicate weaving. An additional facet at the pelvis is evidence for frequent and prolonged riding and may, therefore, be an anthropological hint as to the high social-status of an individual.

Additional anthropological indicators can be obtained by scientific methods: X-raying may reveal completely healed, but otherwise invisible fractures, allowing a more accurate calculation of such injuries. Again, the general conditions of life are reflected by the bones because, for example, periodical malnutrition during childhood and youth disrupts the growth of bone at the epiphyses, resulting in dark lines of dense bone fabric. X-raying reveals these so called 'Harris lines', possibly elucidating the general circumstances of a premature death, as malnutrition not only restricts growth, but also weakens the immune system.

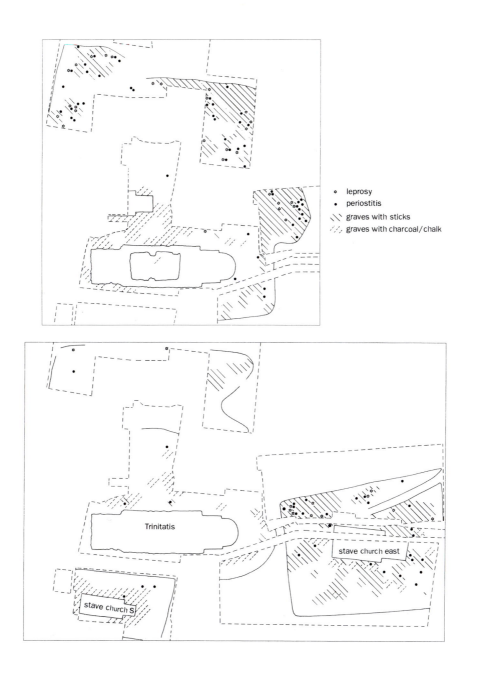

leprosy
periostitis
graves with sticks
graves with charcoal/chalk

Trinitatis

stave church east

stave church S

The cemetery around the Church of the Holy Trinity (Trinitatis), in Lund (Sweden), with the graves marked of those suffering from leprosy or periostitis: (a) for the period c1050-1100 (top); and (b) after 1100 (after Cinthio 2002).

Fig 15.4

BOX 15.1   PUTTING THE PEOPLE IN THE PICTURE:

Human societies are shaped by the environmental and physical constraints of the landscape and biosphere. Human populations are also shaped by intrinsic demographic factors such as size, fertility and mortality rates. Human remains may provide clues to these issues, and thereby add to the analyses of past populations. Methodological advances in biological anthropology, including stable isotope analyses, mathematical modelling of demographic parameters and ancient DNA, may be especially useful in such analyses, as will be illustrated below.

The Greenland Norse

Erik the Red founded the Norse settlements in Greenland in 986. However, contact with Iceland and Norway gradually faded and the settlements lay waste by the fifteenth century. Based on churchyard excavations, it has been calculated that the Norse Greenlanders, on average throughout the settlement period, numbered some 1,500-2,000 people (Lynnerup 1998). This means that the population was small and vulnerable to demographic shifts, even just random events, e.g. the number of child births per year in such a small population would be low, so that random events (such as spates of childhood disease) could have killed some infants, meaning that the overall number of surviving children would be extremely low (or nil). Non-random shifts would be events like emigration and immigration. Indeed, by mathematical modelling, both the initial population increase at the start of the settlement period, as well as a later decrease and ultimate extinction, could be accounted for by 'reasonable' demographic rates (Fig 1). While not disproving that the demise of the Norse settlements was due to some catastrophic event, it does illustrate that changes in a small population, even disappearance, may be brought about by quite unremarkable demographic events.

But why would the Norse leave Greenland? By analysing oxygen isotope values in Norse human dental enamel, we could support the hypothesis of the 'Little Ice Age' (Fricke et al 1995). A colder climate would have had a direct effect on the Norse, probably altering the basis for farming and livestock use. This seems to be reflected by stable isotopes of carbon and nitrogen analyses, which indicate a dietary shift (Arneborg et al 1999).

Early Christian burials in Denmark

An early Christian burial-ground was recently excavated near Roskilde, in Denmark. There was segregation by sex in the churchyard: males were buried to the south and females to the north, as found in other early Christian churchyards. However, the segregation was not absolute: on the north side, several male skeletons could be identified. It has been assumed that these 'misplaced' males may be males with direct familial kinship to nearby females, or of lower standing, or 'newcomers' to an otherwise tightly-knit society.

Ancient DNA analyses were carried out on two 'misplaced' males and the females surrounding them, showing that there was no direct maternal kinship between these males and the juxtaposed females (Fig 2). However, one of the males had a so-called mitochondrial-DNA type (termed a haplogroup) that is extremely rare in Europe. Indeed, the haplogroup is only found east of the Urals and to the south around the Black Sea. Since mitochondrial-DNA is only inherited maternally, this means that this individual came from these areas, or that his mother (or grandmother) did. The other individuals had rather diverse (but not that rare) haplogroups, indicating that the people buried in the churchyard were genetically quite diverse.

Given that the anthropological analyses of the human remains and the subsequent demographic calculations, estimated the size of the once living population to be c200-600 individuals, this means that even small populations at that time could be quite heterogeneous.

Based on the above results, it has been hypothesised that the Kongemarken churchyard was a 'temporary' churchyard, only in use for one or two generations, established by the first Christian inhabitants in the area, and also serving as a churchyard for extraneous Christian people, perhaps called upon as labourers and craftsmen who built the first stone churches in Roskilde, at that time (Christensen & Lynnerup 2004).

By Niels Lynnerup

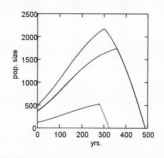

Fig 1

Mathematically modelled population-profile of the Norse settlements in Greenland. The lower curve is the profile for the smaller 'West settlement', which went into extinction first. The middle curve is the larger 'East settlement', also the site of the bishop's seat, which was the last area to be inhabited by the Norse. The upper curve is a summation curve for both settlements.

Fig 2

Plan of the Kongemarken cemetery: DNA analyses were carried out on the individuals shown in the two areas (the A396 burial in Area 1 is the male with a rare haplogroup)

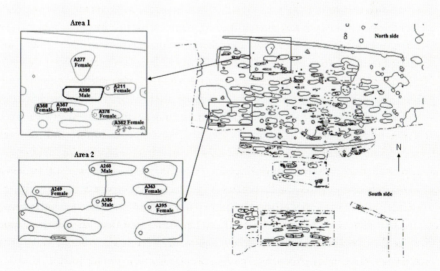

Until recently, diseases with a short course were not detectable by anthropological means because they left no traces on the skeleton, but new techniques of analyzing ancient DNA are making it possible to detect them – at least where good conditions exist for its preservation. Recent attempts have proved (e.g.) diarrhoea, plague and tuberculosis for the late Middle Ages (see Vol 2). It may be presumed that ancient DNA-analyses have the capacity to provide much new information in the future. At present, however, this technique is in its infancy, facing significant technical problems with regards to extraction and contamination, as well as extremely high costs (Herrmann & Hummel 2003).

As physical anthropology contributes so much to our knowledge concerning the health status of medieval populations, this information needs to be compared with the historical and archaeological sources. Archaeologically, an increasing separation of the permanently sick can be perceived throughout the Middle Ages, moving from early medieval integration in the common burial-ground to segregation in late medieval *leprosoria*. This progressive exclusion is illustrated (e.g.) by the huge cemetery around the Church of the Holy Trinity (Trinitatis) in Lund, Sweden. There, during its initial period (c990-1050), citizens who were suffering from leprosy or periostitis were still included in the community, but preferably buried in the marginal areas of the cemetery. During the subsequent period (c1050-1100), their graves were separated from the general graveyard and clustered around a stave-church of unknown name, to the east of the Church of the Holy Trinity (Fig 15.4). Finally, during the period after 1100, such graves are completely absent (Cinthio 2002).

Medical Care

When writing his monastic rule in 529, (St) Benedict laid down in chapter 36 that the care for the sick had to be before and above everything else (*Infirmorum cura ante omnia et super omnia adhibenda est*). This demand, together with the general success of the Benedictine rule, gave rise to centuries of medical practice in monasteries, so that we can speak of a 'period of monastic medicine' up to the twelfth century. The idealised plan of the monastery of St Gall, from c830, allocates much space to the care of the sick; east of the church, there is located a separate infirmary, equipped with its own kitchen, refectory and chapel. Adjacent rooms are designated for bathing and blood-letting, and the doctor's accommodation, together with a pharmacy and an adjacent area for medicinal herbs, were situated in its vicinity (Fig 14.5). These provisions were transformed into reality in the great medieval monasteries. For example, when Cluny (France) was first constructed (c910/27), it was equipped with an infirmary, as were the subsequent phases up to Abbot Petrus Venerabilis (1122-56), who increased the size of the building to create one of largest infirmaries of the Middle Ages, providing room for up to 80 persons.

Herb gardens, difficult (but not impossible) to detect archaeologically, are confirmed by manuscripts among which the writings of the Carolingian abbot, Walafried Strabo (*Hortulus*) and the twelfth-century nun, Hildegard of Bingen (*Physica*; *Causae et curae*), remain well known even today. The wealth of monastic medical texts demonstrates a broad tradition and the careful preservation of mainly Antique medical knowledge (e.g. Pliny, Galen and Celsus). However, this medical knowledge did not go unquestioned. During Late Antiquity, the fathers of the Church discussed intensively whether sickness and medicine were, both alike, part of God's plan of salvation. Was medicine disturbing this plan of salvation? Benedict had to justify engagement with the sick by reference to the Bible (Matthew 25, verses 36 & 40), but during the Carolingian period this remained an obligation; in a Christian world, sickness was mainly explained in religious terms (as punishment for sins or a test), and medicine had to justify its existence by reference to religion. It was not by chance that the plan of St Gall located the infirmary to the east of the church, in a liturgically high-ranking location (Fig 14.5). The spiritual aspect of sickness sometimes even dominated, so that early hospitals provided food, clothes, a bed and 'especially' an opportunity to pray and confess, but (almost) no medical care.

From the eleventh century onwards, there was a growing impact of 'oriental medicine', itself mainly rooted in Antique traditions. On the one hand, this impact resulted from the military contact of the Crusades, confronting Christian warriors with the superior wound-treating skills and techniques of Arab physicians (Mitchell 2004). Additionally, in an atmosphere of growing religious fanaticism, mass-pilgrimage to the Holy Land became a regular phenomenon, giving rise to the establishment of hospital orders, who themselves took a leading part in the Crusades (e.g. the 'Order of the Hospitalers of St John of Jerusalem'). On the other hand, in southern Italy, the 'School of Salerno' had been established, mainly under the direction of monks from Monte Cassino, which was already famous in the tenth century, far beyond Italy, for its computation and practical skills in medicine. On the eve of the First Crusade, Constantinus Africanus, originally a trader in herbs from Carthage and later a monk at Monte Cassino, collected and translated the most important books on oriental medicine, for the School, during the 1070s and 1080s. Some decades later, Gerard of Cremona added translations of the works of Avicenna, finally opening Europe to Antique medical knowledge transformed by oriental science (Schipperges 1964). Salerno was the prototype for the medical faculties that were later established at universities, after the study of medicine and the practice of surgery were forbidden to clerics by several councils during the twelfth and thirteenth centuries (see Vol 2).

Besides these written cultures of medicine, a wealth of medical knowledge also seems to have been stored among ordinary people. As physical anthropology demonstrates, bone fractures, wounds and even complicated amputations were, in many cases, performed and tended adequately. Persons disabled due to accidents, sickness or age were looked after and survived for a long time. However, due to an almost total lack of documentary sources, we know little about these medical practitioners who probably learned their skills through some kind of apprenticeship. At least, like the clerical exponents of medicine, they obviously shared the common conviction of a broad spiritual dimension of disease. At least partly, this was rooted in pre-Christian times, as Old English charms (Deegan & Scragg 1989), e.g. *Lacnunga* and Bald's *Leechbook*, as well as Old German spells, e.g. *Merseburger Zaubersprüche*, and Old Norse *galdrar* invoke the intervention of pagan gods like Wodan/Odin. The theoretical framework of this medical practice is hard to reconstruct, but, besides pagan conceptions, a strong influence of Antique traditions, as well as of oriental knowledge, becomes apparent (Kieckhefer 1990). One of many vivid examples of the intermingling work of traditions are magical finger-rings, many made of precious material and/or attributable to the eleventh/twelfth-century elite, which are inscribed with 'THEBALGUTGUTANI', or a derivative of this term. The same formula is used in a few Old English charms. It may finally go back to Aramaic, expressing some kind of wish, later transformed by popular etymology into a cure against gout (Michelly 1987).

Death and Burial

Rites de passage

As with medicine, we learn most about death rites from sources written by clerics. They paint a scene full of priests and monks, the last minutes dominated by prayer and gospels, the moribund dying as a sinner. A funeral, directed by the Church and focussing on Christian rites of humility and pardon, was what then followed (Rowell 1977; Paxton 1990; Treffort 1996). However, Schmitt (1990) has pointed to the miniatures in the tenth-century *Waremundo Codex* that vividly depict the death and burial of a layman (Fig 15.5). Here, religious persons are limited to a marginal role, while in High (and late) Medieval epics and dirges (*planctus*), the bereavement of the surviving friends is widely lamented, whereas care for the religious welfare of the souls of the dead is reduced to only a few words (Meier 2002). So our conventional idea of religiously dominated rites of death and funeral may mainly be a mirror of clerics' wishes, probably matching reality in monastic practice, but with a limited impact on the great majority of people.

Places of burial

During the early medieval period, the dead were buried outside the settlement (Fig 3.8). With the establishment of the Christian Church, clerics struggled to control the realm of the dead. With a broad variety of transitional phenomena, the cemeteries outside the settlements were finally abandoned. For the future, the dead were to be buried in a graveyard around a church, one often built at the centre of a settlement (Fig 15.2). The obligatory connection between burial and the Church was fixed by ecclesiastical jurisdiction, as well as with the right of burial normally reserved for a parochial church (Treffort 1996). Nevertheless, archaeology normally reveals graves in the vicinity of almost any religious building, be it a parochial or a subsidiary church, or even a chapel.

Despite the Christian ideal of equality and humility, a graveyard can be understood as a career space. Different areas of a graveyard were allocated to different social ranks. For example, especially in Northern Europe, many graveyards were organized according to sex, with females to the north of the church (the lesser direction) and males to the south. This lay-out seems to have expressed a general attitude towards gender in the respective societies (Staecker 2000), whereas the over-proportion of male burials in rural cemeter-

The death and burial of a layman from miniatures in the 10th-century Waremundo Codex (© Ivrea, Capitulary Library MS 86, fol 191-206v, after Schmitt 1990).

Fig 15.5

ies and of females in urban cemeteries does not seem to be intentional, but to reflect gendered spaces of living and working. Monasteries had cemeteries of their own, normally situated to the east of the church, or within the cloister, and restricted to the members of the institution. Indeed, archaeological investigations have revealed monastic cemeteries with mainly, but never exclusively, burials of males (monks) or females (nuns).

At the elite end of society, nobles and high clerics actively avoided the graveyards of common people, taking care to be buried within a church or, at least, at a symbolic site adjacent to it (see Box 15.2). At the other end of the social scale, those of lowest status were emphatically excluded from the communal burial site. This would happen to pagans and foreigners (if baptism was doubtful), to executed criminals, at least in case of a dishonorable mode of death (cf. Box 12.1), or to other dishonorable persons, e.g. at the Sutton Hoo execution-site, in England (Carver 1998, 137f). In many regions of Europe, neonates were also excluded (see above), presumably because they had not been baptized.

Grave-markers and memorials

With the collapse of Antiquity, the tradition of erecting tombstones ceased in most parts of Europe, leaving the majority of graves without a permanent marker for most of the early and High Middle Ages. For the nobility of the Mediterranean, however, the collapse of Antique memorial inscriptions did not last for long. Rome and the papacy proved to be an especially strong link in the return, or even survival, of epitaphs for the highest classes of laity and clergy (see Box 15.3). In many parts of France, it was not long before the nobility joined in this southern European tradition, whereas in the northern and western parts of Britain a tradition of inscribed grave-markers had survived from its origins in the Roman period, spreading also to Ireland (Edwards 1990, 102-4, 161f). However, in most parts of Northern and Eastern Europe, even the graves of the highest classes remained without permanent markers. From documentary sources, we learn that, inside churches, burning lamps, ephemeral structures and carpets laid out on the days of memorial, and at masses, could effectively mark the sites of graves without leaving any archaeological trace (Kroos 1984). If the aspect of burial and memory dominated the perception of a church, the building as a whole could function as a grave-marker, sometimes dominating an area and turning it into a memorial landscape.

From the twelfth century onwards, the interest of kings and bishops in permanent grave-markers increased. Low *tumbae*, no higher than the knee, and early altar-tombs were introduced, probably drawing on the iconography of altars and shrines. Occasionally, these tombs were equipped with engraved effigies, in the form of memorial brasses, or with sculptures, in the form of *gisants*, providing the basis for a highly differentiated interplay between social groups. Whereas in France, where the use of the memorial (or monumental) brass, and of sculpture, was originally restricted to the king, it took some time before the nobility was able to acquire this symbol. In the German Empire, the emperors strictly avoided such sculptural memorials because the first one was used by Rudolf of Swabia (†1080) (Fig 15.6), who was an usurper, with the result that they became a symbol of opposition to royal power (Meier 2002).

Brass memorial of Rudolf of Swabia (†1080), **Fig 15.6**
in the Cathedral of Merseburg, Germany
(© Vereinigte Domstifter zu Merseburg und
Naumburg und des Kollegiatstifts Zeitz,
Bildarchiv Merseburg).

This tendency of nobility to want a permanent grave-marker seems to be in strong contrast to the great majority of burials in graveyards. Archaeologically, almost no durable marking of graves is known, except for some rare cases, e.g. in a Carolingian cemetery at Poigny, France, or in a Slavic cemetery of the eleventh century at Speinshart, Germany, which has small uninscribed steles of stone. On the other hand, secondary burial within the same grave was common (presumably because of biological or social relations with the deceased), leading to the assumption that many graves must have been marked as otherwise it would not have been possible to re-locate them accurately. These markers may have been paving slabs or edgings of stone, as at Poigny, or wooden structures, but, as the ancient ground-surface has normally been completely erased, these presumed markers can rarely be proved.

As described below, King Harald of Denmark, when converted to Christianity, erected a memorial stone to his parents – the first great sculpted stone to stand in his realm (Fig 15.9). This monument spawned imitations by the late tenth-century Danish elite, but the greatest concentration of rune-stones in Scandinavia is to be found in the Swedish province of Uppland, where some 1,300 are known, mostly dating from the eleventh century (Moltke 1985; Jansson 1987). However, these are normally memorial stones, set up in public places, and rarely mark graves.

BOX 15.2   ENACTING RESURRECTION: THE RELIGIOUS

During the Merovingian period, burial within a church was a widespread phenomenon among the upper classes. With the Carolingian renaissance, however, church-burial was restricted to ecclesiastics and laymen of merit (Fig 1). Then, for several centuries, because laying claim to special merit was regarded as sinful pride, the interior of many churches remained (almost) free of graves until the High Middle Ages (Sapin 1996; Scholkmann 2003).

Accordingly, the upper ranks of society construed different concepts of high-quality burial-places, generally marked by their immediate proximity to a church building. The entrance area became one of the most favoured places: e.g. King Pippin (†768) was buried in front of the portal of St Denis; and Charlemagne's grave (†814) was situated in the atrium of his palatine chapel at Aachen. Likewise, many senior Carolingian ecclesiastics chose to be buried near the portals of their churches. On the one hand, this position demonstrated Christian humility, both by staying outside the church and by allowing the corpse to be literally trampled-on

by the church-goers. On the other hand, this site ensured remembrance, as people entering the church would be reminded of the dead over whom they were walking. What is more, the church itself represented 'Celestial Jerusalem', and those lying in front of its portal could be equated with those souls waiting to attain purity (*non valde boni*) in front of the gates of Heavenly City, but waiting in secure knowledge of their future permission to enter (Angenendt 1994). The position in front of a church entrance, sometimes within a narthex or a 'Westwork' (see pp 402-3), was therefore to remain a favourite burial-place throughout the High Middle Ages in the West (Dierkens 2002; e.g. the royal burials at San Isidoro, in León; and the tombs of the dukes of Burgundy, at Cîteaux).

Another option, for getting as close as possible to the interior of a church and its relics, was a grave inside an annexe. This was closely related to burial in front of the entrance because the souls of the faithful were believed to wait, not only in front of the gates of Celestial Jerusalem, but also in her forecourts. As a result, either spe-

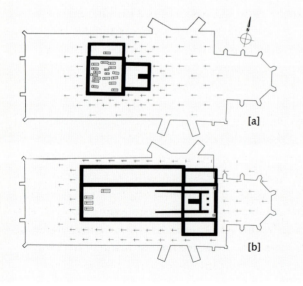

[a]

[b]

Fig 1

Esslingen/Neckar (Germany): an urban parish church, [a] Phase I (pre-777), with 17 burials inside the church and the tomb of Holy Vitalis in the choir; and [b] Phase II (late 9th century, with annexes up to the 12th century), with only four burials at the west end of the nave (© Landesdenkmalamt Baden-Württemberg, Stuttgart).

cial buildings for burial purposes were attached to the church, giving rise to private oratories and mausoleums (sometimes housing several generations of a family), or some parts of the church building were interpreted as representing the forecourts of Celestial Jerusalem and so could therefore be used for burial (e.g. the tombs of the kings of Navarre, at San Juan de la Peña). The narthex, sacristy and even the westernmost end of the nave were chosen for burial in 'the forecourts', extending the idea of a burial 'on the threshold' (*ad limina*) to both sides of the church entrance.

In the Byzantine Orthodox East, burial inside a church had already been banned in the Late Antique period, resulting in the construction of external porticos and proper mausoleums (Grierson 1962), which influenced the customs of (South-) East Europe and the Mediterranean region. There, kings and noblemen were interred, or their sarcophagi lined up, alongside the aisles

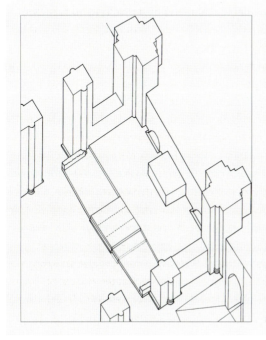

until the late Middle Ages, whereas in Central and Western Europe these were but transitional burial-sites, mainly used in the tenth century, although in some regions re-used subsequently during the Crusades. Apart from representing the forecourts of Celestial Jerusalem, the outer walls of a church were believed to conduct sound especially well, so that a person buried alongside the wall would benefit particularly from the chants and prayers of the clergy.

In Central and Western Europe, the graves of meritorious laymen re-entered the nave from the tenth century onwards. Soon, the place in front of an altar, and especially the one situated at the east end of the nave, became the most favoured burial-site, with the Altar of the Holy Rood being surmounted by a huge cross (Fig 2). This is the location alluded to in *Revelations*, with the 24 seniors sitting at the feet of the Celestial throne (*Apocalypse*, 4.4) and the holy martyrs resting underneath the altar in front of God's throne (ibid, 6.9). At the opening of the Seventh Seal, an angel offers incense at this altar, while all the saints are praying, the incense from the prayers rises to the throne of God (ibid, 8.3f). Those buried in front of the Altar of the Holy Rood could thus be equated with the seniors and holy martyrs in the immediate face of God (Meier 2004).

By Thomas Meier

Fig 2

Speyer (Germany): the Cathedral of St Mary, an isometric reconstruction of the imperial burial-site at the east end of the nave, in front of the Altar of the Holy Rood (c1060–c1090/1100); a chancel-screen, ambo and triumphal cross are mentioned, but are impossible to reconstruct (© Thomas Meier).

Fig 15.7 *Rock-cut graves (c12th century) at the Priory of Carluc, France (photo: T Meier).*

Types of burial

The manner in which a grave was constructed varied widely throughout Europe. It was dependent on the social status of the deceased, with more elaborate and consuming constructions for the upper classes, as well as varying by period and region. In this connection, regional traditions and available materials appear to have been the prime factors. Only against this back-drop can the development through time be fully understood, as well as the different means of expressing status.

A good example is provided by graves cut into rock. This type is mainly confined to southern France (Fig 15.7), parts of the Iberian Peninsula and the Balkans, being regions with widespread outcrops of rock that are quite easy to cut. Nevertheless, the production of one grave was highly work-intensive compared to simply digging a grave in other regions, causing the multiple reuse of each rock-grave. In spite of the high costs of rock-cut graves, this was the regular type of grave in some regions. The prestigious container for an upper-class burial in these regions was the sarcophagus, likewise falling back on the easy availability of stone in combination with a living Antique tradition. In other regions of Europe that had formerly been parts of the Roman Empire, the supply of sarcophagi ran short during the early Middle Ages, but during the Carolingian renaissance, as well as during the late tenth and eleventh centuries, sarcophagi were imported again into Central Europe, or even newly produced in Western Europe, where they are to be contrasted with earthen burials, even if sometimes lined with stones.

Another example is provided by the introduction of bricks (pp 230-2). As many areas, especially in Northern Europe, were poor in building stone, bricks offered the first opportunity to build more solid graves. With their first appearance during the twelfth

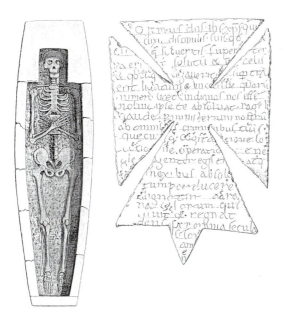

Grave of Reginald at   **Fig 15.8**
Bouteilles, France (c12th
century), containing a skel-
eton with arms crossed on
the breast and a lead tablet
with a formula of absolution
(after Cochet 1856).

century, this material became the prestigious choice for burials of the highest social class in regions short of stone, e.g. the royal graves at Ringsted, in Denmark.

However, not every kind of grave-structure was of social significance, e.g. head-niches within stone sarcophagi (cf. Fig 15.8), as well as in earthen burials, are typical for the Romanesque period, but without social implications. Probably, these niches served to keep the eyes of the deceased looking East, towards the Coming of Christ on the Day of Judgement.

As with the grave-types, the position of the corpse, and especially of the arms, varied greatly on a regional and even on a local level. Given that the laying-out of a corpse was independent of natural resources, a general trend becomes obvious – at least statistically. In general, all burials were directed to the east, meaning that the corpse was laid on its back, with the head to the west so that the eyes were directed to sunrise. The meaning of what constituted 'east' might depend on local circumstances (e.g. adjacent buildings, rocks or riverbanks) and varied between approximately north-east and south-east. Several attempts to determine the season of burial, from variation in the individual 'eastern' direction of graves, are hardly convincing.

Not only the direction of the corpse but also the position of the arms seem to follow a general tendency. At first, during the early Middle Ages, the arms were stretched parallel to the body, then the hands were folded on the pelvis, later on the abdomen; finally, the hands were placed on the shoulders with the arms forming a cross on the chest (Fig 15.8).

While this sequence is similar in many parts of Europe, the dating of each stage is quite different. In France, the transition from Stage 1 (arms parallel to body) to Stage 2 (hands on the pelvis) seems to have started already in the seventh century, to finish with Stage 4 (hands on the shoulders) in the twelfth century (Durand 1988). In Jutland (Denmark), on the other hand, the transition started as late as the 1250s and finished c1500 (Kieffer-Olsen 1993). With respect to this enormous difference in dating, it is most unlikely that the transition of the position of arms can be linked to any general change in religious belief (cf. Kieffer-Olsen 1993, the spreading of the idea of purgatory).

Grave-goods

During Antiquity and the early Middle Ages, it was usual to equip the deceased with grave-goods, most probably as a reflection of his/her social position. This custom ceased approximately with the abandonment of the old cemeteries outside the settlements (see above). The date of this fundamental transition varies widely: in the Mediterranean it took place during the fifth century; it can be dated to the later seventh century in Western Europe; to the tenth and eleventh centuries in the North and in the Western Slavonic regions; while in Finland and the Baltic the transition did not happen before the fourteenth century, or even not until early modern times. This change of burial custom coincides strikingly with the consolidation of Christianity in the respective regions and may thus express a general change in attitude towards death and the dead.

With the High Middle Ages a new approach to furnishing the deceased with grave-goods developed in Western Europe. In contrast to the early Middle Ages, when the dead were furnished with their personal possessions, mainly their clothing, at this time either symbolic objects or objects of status were deposited in the graves.

Such symbolic objects may be jars (northern France, southern Scandinavia, western Slavonic area) or glass vessels (southern France) filled with charcoal for incense, or with holy water, to keep away malevolent ghosts and to symbolise the Christian life and death of the deceased (Madsen 1983). For the same purpose, pilgrims' shells (*Pecten maximus*) (France, southern Scandinavia, southern Germany), and probably staffs (British Isles and Scandinavia), accompanied the corpse, indicating a pilgrim (see Box 13.2). An eloquent inclusion, proving a death according to Christian rites, was the deposition of a lead tablet along with the dead, citing the formula of absolution or the creed, both key-elements of the last rites that had been conferred on the dying (Fig 15.8). This type of inclusion may be interpreted as equipment for the Last Judgement, stating that the soul of the dead was worthy of entering heaven (Meier 1998).

Another type of symbolic grave-good was coins, the only type of grave-furnishing that spread over the whole of Europe, although at very different dates. This custom began in Burgundy around the eighth century, becoming quite common in Western (Central) Europe during the High Middle Ages; however, it took until early modern times before the symbolic deposition of coins was popular in the Baltic. Roughly, the practice expanded in parallel with the abandonment of grave-goods, but with a delay of approximately two to four centuries. As with the dating, the interpretation of this custom varies widely. In the light of Classical texts, these coins are interpreted as a pagan survival, being meant as an entrance fee to the hereafter (Charon's coin). This interpretation is, however, quite probably just an invention of Renaissance scholars, when Classical texts and ideas were being rediscovered. Instead, in many regions, especially in central Eastern Europe during modern times, the deposition of coins in graves was connected to some kind of symbolic resolution of the earthly possessions of the deceased, so that he/she did not have to come back – a kind of symbolic legal transaction.

In the German Empire, from the early eleventh century onwards, there developed a completely different idea of how to equip the dead. There, grave-goods were restricted to the highest ranks of society, who were buried with the insignia of their earthly power, either religious (chalice, paten, mitre, crosier and ring) or secular (crown, sceptre and orb; cf. Box 12.2), while the great majority of society remained without any grave-goods until the later Middle Ages (see Vol 2). In contrast to the symbolic and spiritual grave-goods mentioned above, these types of furnishings were intentionally temporal. This argument is strengthened because these graves are sometimes also furnished with an inscribed lead tablet, but now mainly stating the name, status and merits of the dead rather than anything religious. It is a matter of debate whether these were meant as equipment for the hereafter, for they could have been intended as a display of social status included with respect to any future opening of the grave (Meier 2002).

Memory

'Let us now praise famous men, and our fathers that begat us' (*Ecclesiasticus* 44, 1). This exhortation from the Old Testament serves as a reminder that oral tradition continued to play an important role in the transmission of memories well into the medieval period. Until national histories were actually written down, the recitation of genealogies and the delivery of praise poems was an important aspect of life in the hall.

Part of a verse preserved in the Icelandic text, *Hávamál*, which contains poems thought to have been composed during the Viking period, states that:

> Only your kin
> will proudly carve
> a memorial at the main gate.

While clearly a sound generalisation, this was not necessarily always the case, even in the Viking period. Memorials to the dead have been considered above, but not all memorials were necessarily raised for this purpose, or for this purpose alone. In the eleventh century, a Swedish landowner, in Uppland, constructed a causeway and erected four rune-stones, two at each end, proclaiming that: 'Jarlabanke had these stones put up in memory of himself in his own lifetime. And he made this causeway for his soul's sake. And he owned the whole of Täby by himself. May God help his soul.' (Jansson 1962, 86-7).

One of the most famous carved stones still standing in the North is the great three-sided granite monument at Jelling in Jutland (Fig 15.9). This was raised by King Harald Bluetooth of Denmark, in about 965, ostensibly as memorial to his parents, but in reality to ensure that he was remembered for his own deeds (Roesdahl 2001). The inscrip-

Fig 15.9 *The large runestone at Jelling (Denmark) erected by King Harald, after he had become Christian, in memory of his parents King Gorm and Queen Thyre, who had died as pagans; the smaller runestone, in the foreground, is that erected by Gorm to commemorate his wife (photo: E Roesdahl).*

tion, in Scandinavian runes, may be translated as follows: 'King Harald commanded this monument to be made in memory of Gorm his father and in memory of Thyre his mother – that Harald who won for himself the whole of Denmark, and Norway, and made the Danes Christian.'

Harald was proud to be the first Christian king of Denmark (see also p 379), but Christian rulers and nobility everywhere were keen to do good deeds by endowing monasteries and churches, and presenting them with treasures, in return for which masses and prayers would be said for the benefit of their souls. In 777, Duke Tassilo of Bavaria founded the monastery of Kremsmünster; together with his wife, Liutpirc, daughter of the Lombard king Desiderius, he presented it with a fine chalice which bears their names, presumably before he was deposed by Charlemagne in 788 (Haseloff 1951).

As a further example, one might consider the inscription on an ornate Irish reliquary, the Cross of Cong, made to house a relic of the True Cross (Murray 2006):

This early 12th-century candlestick, **Fig 15.10**
which is the finest surviving piece
of English Romanesque metalwork,
has a Latin inscription around its
stem (Williamson 1986, 108-9),
referring to its presentation by Abbot
Peter (†1113) and his 'flock' to the
Benedictine monastery at Gloucester
(©Victoria & Albert Museum).

+ By this cross is covered the cross on which the creator of the world suffered/
Pray for Muiredach Ua Dubthaig, Senior Ecclesiatic of Ireland/
Pray for Tairdelbach Ua Chonchobair [Turlough O'Connor], King of Ireland
by whom was made this ornament/
Pray for Domnall mac Flannacáin Uí Dubthaig [O'Duffy], from the borders of
Connacht, successor of Commán and Ciarán, by whom was made this ornament/
Pray for Máel Ísu mac Bratáin Uí Echach, who made this ornament/
+ By this cross is covered the cross on which the creator of the world suffered

Turlough O'Connor, King of Connaught, who commissioned this Cross, which was
made at Roscommon c1123 (by the last named individual), was one of the most important political figures in twelfth-century Ireland. Returning to the Continent, it is only
necessary to introduce Joanna Story's 'Box' (15.3), which describes the manner in which
Charlemagne was concerned to be remembered in his relationship with Rome, following
the death of Pope Hadrian I, on the eve of his coronation as Emperor.

BOX 15.3   CHARLEMAGNE AND THE EPITAPH OF POPE HADRIAN I

Hadrian I was the longest-lived pope of the Middle Ages; his pontificate lasted nearly 24 years, from February 772 until Christmas 795. His long rule gave him great influence over the papacy at a crucial phase in its development, when the papacy began to become a major landholder in central Italy, laying the foundations of the Papal States of later centuries. Important too was the alliance that Hadrian cultivated with Charlemagne, King of the Franks (from 768) and Lombards (from 774), and Emperor from 800 until 814. The bond between these two men helped to shift the axis of power in early medieval Europe away from the Byzantine Emperor in Constantinople towards the new imperial power north of the Alps.

When Hadrian died, Charlemagne commissioned a fabulous inscription to grace the Pope's tomb (Fig 1). This was the first time that a foreign power had become involved in the commemoration of a pontiff in Rome, and shows Charlemagne's concern to control publicly the way in which Hadrian (and his links with the Carolingian dynasty) should be remembered by posterity. The epigraphy and poetry of the Epitaph deliberately recalled Classical and Late Antique styles, as if to emphasise the cultural connections between Carolingian Francia and Imperial Rome.

Hadrian's Epitaph survives today in the portico of St Peter's in the Vatican; it is one of very few objects to have been redisplayed from the old fourth-century basilica that was replaced in the sixteenth and seventeenth centuries. One of the most remarkable aspects of the inscription is the large black stone of which it is made. This was an unusual aesthetic choice in the late eighth century that, with the once-golden lettering of the inscription, recalls the purple pages of some deluxe Late Antique and Carolingian manuscripts.

A combination of fossil analysis and geochemical calculations shows that the black limestone

Fig 1

The Epitaph of Pope Hadrian I, now in the portico of St Peter's, Rome (© Istituto suore Benedettine di Priscilla, Rome).

used for the Epitaph came from quarries in the middle Meuse valley in Belgium, from an area in which Charlemagne's family had owned estates for many generations. The choice of a black stone for the papal Epitaph recalled the black columns of the palace chapel that had been built in (nearby) Aachen in the 790s (Fig 12.2); these were, however, imperial *spolia*. Hadrian had given

Charlemagne's architects permission to reuse marbles from Ravenna for his building projects in Francia; that they chose columns made from the rarest, black Egyptian porphyry suggests that they had selected stones only from the most prestigious imperial buildings in the city.

The black stone of the Pope's Epitaph, quarried from Charlemagne's own lands, showed the Roman viewers of the inscription that the Frankish king also had access to scarce, imperial-style resources in his own homeland. Through the careful choice of materials as well as the form of the poetry and lettering (Figs 2 & 3), the Carolingians demonstrated their mastery of imperial aesthetics and the age-old messages of power inherent in the control of scarce resources: an eloquent demonstration of the 'renewal of Empire'.

We do not know for sure when Hadrian's Epitaph arrived in Rome, but it is most likely to have been in place over the tomb in Hadrian's oratory in the south transept by Christmas Day 800, when Charlemagne was crowned in front of the *confessio* of St Peter by Hadrian's successor, Pope Leo III, as the first Emperor in the West since the fifth century.

Sources: Rossi 1888; LeClerq 1924-53; Ramackers 1964; Rubeis 2001; Story et al 2005.

By Joanna Story

Fig 2

Detail of the Epitaph showing Charlemagne's name (photo: J Story).

Fig 3

Coin (pre-772) showing the early form of Charlemagne's monogram, as on the Epitaph (© Fitzwilliam Museum, Cambridge).

To be remembered after one's fleeting life on Earth, whether pagan or Christian, Moslem or Jew, was what medieval men and women might hope for on departure for their after-life. Let us conclude with a complete verse from *Hávamál*:

Cattle die
kinsmen die
all men are mortal.
Words of praise
will never perish
nor a noble name.

Acknowledgement

We are especially thankful to Niels Lynnerup, Laboratory of Biological Anthropology, Copenhagen, not only for contributing Box 15.1, on 'Putting the people in the picture', but even more for his most valuable assistance with the part on anthropological methods.

BIBLIOGRAPHY

Abel, W (1967, 2nd ed) *Geschichte der deutschen Landwirtschaft vom frühen Mittelalter bis zum 19. Jahrhundert*, Deutsche Agrargeschichte 2, Stuttgart

Alexandre-Bidon, D and Treffort C (eds) (1993) *A Réveiller les Morts. La Mort au Quotidien dans l'Occident Médiéval*, Lyon

Angenendt, A (1994) '*In porticu ecclesiae sepultus*. Ein Beispiel von himmlisch-irdischer Spiegelung', in Keller, H and Staubach, N (eds), *Iconologia sacra. Mythos, Bildkunst und Dichtung in der Religions- und Sozialgeschichte Alteuropas = Festschrift für Karl Hauck zum 75. Geburtstag*, Arbeiten zur Frühmittelalterforschung 23, Berlin/New York, 68-80

Arneborg, J, Heinemeier, J, Lynnerup, N, Nielsen, HL, Rud, N and Sveinbjornsdottir, AE (1999) 'Change in diet of the Greenland Vikings determined from stable carbon isotope analysis and C-14 dating of their bones', *Radiocarbon* 41, 157-68

Aufderheide, AC and Rodríguez-Martín, C (1998) *The Cambridge Encyclopedia of Human Paleopathology*, Cambridge/New York

Biller, P (2000) *The Measure of Multitude: Population in Medieval Thought*, Oxford

Binski, P (1996) *Medieval Death: Ritual and Representation*, London

Bintliff, J and Sbonias, K (eds) (1999) *Reconstructing Past Population Trends in Mediterranean Europe (3000 BC-AD 1800)*, The Archaeology of Mediterranean Landscapes 1, Oxford

Boldsen, JL (2005a) 'Analysis of dental attrition and mortality in the medieval village of Tirup, Denmark', *American Journal of Physical Anthropology* 126, 169-76

Boldsen, JL (2005b) 'Leprosy and mortality in the medieval Danish village of Tirup', *American Journal of Physical Anthropology* 126, 159-68

Carver, M (1998) *Sutton Hoo. Burial Ground of Kings?*, London

Christensen, T and Lynnerup N (2004) 'Kirkegården i Kongemarken', in Lund, N (ed), *Kristendommen i Danmark før 1050*, Roskilde, 142-52 (summary in English)

Cinthio, M (2002) *De första stadsborna. Medeltida gravar och människor i Lund*, Stockholm

Coale, AJ, Demeny, P and Vaughan, B (1983) *Regional Model Life Tables and Stable Populations*, New York

Cochet, J-B (1856) 'Sépultures chrétiennes de la période Anglo-Normande, trouvées à Bouteilles, près Dieppe, en 1855', *Archaeologia* 35, 258-66

Colvin, H (1991) *Architecture and the After-Life*, New Haven/London

Cox, M and Mays, S (eds) (2000) *Human Osteology in Archaeology and Forensic Science*, London

Crook, J (2000) *The Architectural Setting of the Cult of Saints in the Early Christian West c.300-c. 1200*, Oxford

Daniell, C (1997) *Death and Burial in Medieval England, 1066-1550*, London/New York

Deegan, M and Scragg, DG (1989) *Medicine in Early Medieval England: Four Papers*, Manchester Centre for Medieval Studies, Manchester

Dierkens, A (2002) 'Avant-corps, Galilées, Massifs occidentaux: quelques remarques méthodologiques en guise de conclusions', in Sapin, C (ed), *Avant-nefs & Espaces d'accueil dans l'église entre IVe et XIIe siècle*, Paris, 495-503

Durand, M (1988) *Archéologie du Cimetière Médiéval au Sud-Est de l'Oise du VIIème au XVIème siècle. Relations avec l'Habitat, Évolution de Rites et des Pratiques Funéraires, Paléodémographie*, Revue Archéologique de Picardie, Numéro Spécial, Chevrières

Edwards, N (1990) *The Archaeology of Early Medieval Ireland*, London

Fricke, HC, O'Neil, JR and Lynnerup, N (1995) 'Oxygen isotope composition of human tooth enamel from medieval Greenland: linking climate and society', *Geology* 23, 869-72

Galinié, H and Zadora-Rio, E (eds) (1996) *Archéologie du Cimetière Chrétien. Actes du 2e Colloque ARCHEA*, Revue Archéologique du Centre de la France, Supplément 11, Tours

Giovannini, F (2001) *Natalità, Mortalità e Demografia dell'Italia Medievale sulla Base dei Dati Archeologici*, British Archaeological Reports, International Series 950, Oxford

Grierson, P (1962) 'The tombs and obits of the Byzantine emperors (337-1042)', *Dumbarton Oaks Papers* 16, 3-60

Grupe, G, Christiansen, K, Schröder, I and Wittwer-Backofen, U (2005) *Anthropologie. Ein einführendes Lehrbuch*, Berlin/Heidelberg

Hadley, DM (2001) *Death in Medieval England: an Archaeology*, Stroud

Haseloff, G (1951) *Der Tassilokelch*, Münchner Beiträge zur Vor- und Frühgeschichte 1, Munich

Herrmann, B and Hummel, S (2003) 'Ancient DNA can identify disease elements', in Greenblatt, CL and Spigelman, M (eds), *Emerging Pathogens. The Archaeology, Ecology, and Evolution of Infectious Disease*, Oxford/New York, 143-9

Hoppa, RD and Vaupel, JW (eds) (2002) *Paleodemography. Age Distributions from Skeletal Samples*, Cambridge Studies in Biological and Evolutionary Anthropology 31, Cambridge

Jankrift, KP (2003) *Krankheit und Heilkunde im Mittelalter*, Darmstadt

Jansson, SBF (1962; 1987, 2nd ed) *Runes in Sweden*, Stockholm

Judd, MA and Roberts, CA (1999) 'Fracture trauma in a medieval British farming village', *American Journal of Physical Anthropology* 109, 229-43

Kieckhefer, R (1990) *Magic in the Middle Ages*, Cambridge

Kieffer-Olsen, J (1993) *Grav og gravskik I det middelalterlige Danmark – 8 kirkegårdsudgravninger*, Højbjerg

Konigsberg, LW and Frankenberg, SR (2002) 'Deconstructing death in paleodemography', *American Journal of Physical Anthropology* 117, 297-309

Kreiner, L (1989), 'Eine früh- bis hochmittelalterliche Ortswüstung bei Pilsting, Lkr. Dingolfing-Landau', in Schmotz, K (ed), *Vorträge des 7. Niederbayerischen Archäologentages*, Deggendorf, 107-17

Kroos, R (1984), 'Grabbräuche – Grabbilder', in Schmid, K and Wollasch, J (eds), *Memoria. Der geschichtliche Zeugniswert des liturgischen Gedenkens im Mittelalter*, Münstersche Mittelalter-Schriften 48, Munich, 285-353

Langenscheidt, F (1985) *Methodenkritische Untersuchungen zur Paläodemographie am Beispiel zweier fränkischer Gräberfelder*, Materialien zur Bevölkerungswissenschaft, Sonderheft 2, Wiesbaden

Larsen, CS (1997) *Bioarchaeology. Interpreting Behavior from the Human Skeleton*, Cambridge Studies in Biological Anthropology 21, Cambridge

LeClerq, H (1924-53) 'Hadrien I (epitaph de)', in *Dictionnaire d'Archéologie Chrétienne et de Liturgie*, Paris, Vol VI:2, cols 1964-7

Livi-Bacci, M (1998) *La Popolazione nella Storia d'Europa*, Rome

Lynnerup, N (1998) *The Greenland Norse = Meddelelser om Grønland*, Man & Society Series, 24

Madsen, PK (1983) 'A French connection: Danish funerary pots – a group of medieval pottery', *Journal of Danish Archaeology* 2, 171-83

Mafart, B-Y (1996) 'Rôle de la pathologie dans l'organisation des nécropoles médiévales', in Galinié, H and Zadora-Rio, E (eds) (1996), *Archéologie du Cimetière Chrétien. Actes du 2e Colloque ARCHEA Orléans 1994*, Revue Archéologique du Centre de la France, Supplément 11, Tours, 95-102

Meier, T (1998) 'Inschrifttafeln aus mittelalterlichen Gräbern. Einige Thesen zu ihrer Aussagekraft', in Boe, G de and Verhaeghe, F (eds), *Papers of the 'Medieval Europe Brugge 1997' Conference 2. Death and Burial in Medieval Europe* (IAP Rapporten 2), Zellik, 43-53

Meier, T (2002) *Die Archäologie des mittelalterlichen Königsgrabes im christlichen Europa*, Mittelalter-Forschungen 8, Stuttgart

Meier, T (2004) 'Ambivalenz im Raum. Zur Disposition mittelalterlicher Herrschergräber' in Staecker, J (ed), *The European Frontier. Clashes and Compromises in the Middle Ages*, Lund Studies in Medieval Archaeology 33 = CCC Papers 7, Lund, 127-44

Meindl, RS and Russel KF (1998) 'Recent advances in method and theory in paleodemography', *Annual Review of Anthropology* 27, 375-99

Michelly, R (1987) 'Der Spandauer Thebal-Ring', in von Müller, A and von Müller-Muči, K (eds), *Ausgrabungen und Funde auf dem Burgwall in Berlin-Spandau*, Berliner Beiträge zur Vor- und Frühgeschichte 5 = Archäologisch-historische Forschungen in Spandau 2, Berlin, 64-81

Mitchell, PD (2004) *Medicine in the Crusades. Warfare, Wounds and the Medieval Surgeon*, Cambridge

Moltke, E (1985) *Runes and their Origin: Denmark and Elsewhere*, Copenhagen

Murray, G (2006) 'The Cross of Cong and some aspects of goldsmithing in pre-Norman Ireland', *Historical Metallurgy* 40:1, 49-67

Paxton, FS (1990) *Christianizing Death. The Creation of a Ritual Process in Early Medieval Europe*, Ithaca/London

Polet, C (2003) 'Les dents et les ossements humains révélateurs des vécus', in Noël, R, Paquay, I and Sosson, J-P (eds), *Au-delà de l'Écrit. Les Hommes et leurs Vécus Matériels au Moyen Âge à la Lumière des Sciences et des Techniques. Nouvelles Perspectives*, Actes du Colloque international de Marche-en-Famenne 2002, Tournhout, 364-403

Ramackers, J (1964) 'Die Werkstattheimat der Grabplatte Papst Hadrians I', *Romische Quartalschrift* 59, 36-78

Renz, H and Radlanski RJ (2006) 'Incremental lines in root cementum of human teeth – A reliable age marker?', *Homo. Journal of Comparative Human Biology* 57, 29-50

Roesdahl, E (2001) 'Jelling', in Crabtree, PJ (ed), *Medieval Archaeology: an Encyclopedia*, New York, 192-4

Rossi, GB de (1888) 'L'inscription du tombeau d'Hadrien I', *Mélanges d'Archéologie et d'Histoire de l'École Française de Rome* 8, 478-501

Rowell, G (1977) *The Liturgy of Christian Burial: an Introductory Survey of the Historical Development of Christian Burial Rites*, Alcuin Club 59, London

Rubeis, F de (2001) 'Epigrafi a Roma dall'età classica all'alto medioevo', in Arena, MS, Delogu, P, Paroli, L, Ricci, M, Saguì, L and Venditelli, L (eds), *Roma dall'Antichità al Medioevo. Archeologia e Storia*, Rome, 104-21 (at pp 112-13, fig 83).

Rudbeck L, Gilbert, MTP, Willerslev, E, Hansen, AJ, Lynnerup, N, Christensen, T and Dissing, J (2005) 'mtDNA analysis of human remains from a 1,000 years old Danish Christian cemetery', *American Journal of Physical Anthropology* 128:2, 424-9

Russell, JC (1985) *The Control of Late Ancient and Medieval Population*, Philadelphia

Sapin, C (1996) 'Dans l'église ou hors l'église, quel choix pour l'inhumé?', in Galinié, H and Zadora-Rio, E (eds), *Archéologie du Cimetière Chrétien. Actes du 2e Colloque ARCHEA Orléans 1994*, Revue Archéologique du Centre de la France, Supplément 11, Tours, 65-78

Saunders, SR and Barrans, L (1999) 'What can be done about the infant category in skeletal samples?', in Hoppa, RD and Fitzgerald, CM (eds), *Human Growth in the Past. Studies from Bones and Teeth*, Cambridge Studies in Biological and Evolutionary Anthropology 25, Cambridge, 183-209

Scheuer, S and Black, S (2000) *Developmental Juvenile Osteology*, San Diego

Schipperges, H (1964) *Die Assimilation der arabischen Medizin durch das lateinische Mittelalter*, Sudhoffs Archiv Beihefte 3, Wiesbaden

Schmid, K (ed) (1978) *Die Klostergemeinschaft von Fulda im früheren Mittelalter*, Münstersche Mittelalter-Schriften 8, Munich

Schmitt, J-C (1990) *La Raison des Gestes dans l'Occident Médiéval*, Paris

Schneider, J, Gutscher, D, Etter, H and Hanser J (1982) *Der Münsterhof in Zürich. Bericht über die vom Städtischen Büro für Archäologie durchgeführten Stadtkernforschungen 1977/78*, Schweizer Beiträge zur Kulturgeschichte und Archäologie des Mittelalters 9/10, Olten/Freiburg

Scholkmann, B (2003) 'Die Kirche als Bestattungsplatz. Zur Interpretation von Bestattungen im Kirchenraum', in Jarnut, J and Wemhoff, M (eds), *Erinnerungskultur im Bestattungsritual. Archäologisch-Historisches Forum*, Mittelalter Studien 3, Munich, 189-218

Staecker, J (2000) 'Die normierte Bestattung – Gotlands Kirchfriedhöfe im Spiegel mittelalterlicher Normen und Gesetze', in Ruhe, D and Spieß, K-H (eds), *Prozesse der Normbildung und Normveränderung im Mittelalterlichen Europa*, Stuttgart, 119-59

Story, J et al (2005) 'Charlemagne's black marble: the origins of the Epitaph of Pope Hadrian I', *Papers of the British School at Rome* 73, 157-90

Stloukal, M (1989) 'Problems of incorrect numbers of cases in palaeodemographic analysis', *Historická demografie* 13, 7-24

Teegen, W-R and Schultz M (2003) *Geschlechtsabhängige Arbeitsverteilung in slawischen Gräberfeldern nach Aussage der Gelenkerkrankungen* (Leipziger online-Beiträge zur Ur- und Frühgeschichtlichen Archäologie 3), Leipzig [http://www.uni-leipzig.de/~ufg/reihe/files/teegen_schultz.pdf (29.3.2005)]

Treffort, C (1996) *L'Église Carolingienne et la Mort. Christianisme, Rites Funéraires et Partiques Commémoratives*, Collection d'Histoire et d'Archéologie Médiévales 3, Lyon

Valdez del Alamo, E with Stamatis Prendergast, C (eds) (2000) *Memory and the Medieval Tomb*, Aldershot

Weiss, KM (1973) 'Demographic models for anthropology', *Memoirs of the Society for American Archaeology* 27 = *American Antiquity* 38.2

Williamson, P (ed) (1986) *The Medieval Treasury: the Art of the Middle Ages in the Victoria & Albert Museum*, London

Wittwer-Backofen, U, Gampe, J and Vaupel, JW (2004) 'Tooth cementum annulation for age estimation: results from a large known-age validation study', *American Journal of Physical Anthropology* 123, 119-29

James Graham-Campbell

It was at the court of Charlemagne that the ancient term of 'Europe' was revived to describe the Carolingian world, as opposed to Byzantium, or the rest of Christendom or the pagan lands. The concept, however, proved to be an ephemeral one, lasting no longer than the Empire of Charlemagne himself. On the other hand, during the nineteenth and twentieth centuries, Charlemagne – Karl der Grosse, Charles the Great – has been periodically regarded as a prototype 'European'; for example, the Council of Europe's prize 'for services to the cause of European unity' is presented in his name. In fact, the idea of 'Europe' is otherwise a relatively modern one, a cultural concept taking hold only after the Middle Ages to replace the earlier one of 'Christendom' (cf. N Davies, *Europe: a History*, Oxford University Press, 1996).

In ancient legend, Europa was seduced by Zeus, the Father of the Gods, while disguised as a white bull. Her homeland was Phoenicia (modern south Lebanon), whence she was borne westwards by Zeus, in the path of the sun, thereby transferring (as one might suppose) the essence of civilisation from the Ancient Near East to the Aegean. There she gave birth to Minos, Lord of Crete, which resulted in her being considered to be the mother of the earliest branch of Mediterranean civilisation. It was thus the Hellenes who first came to use 'Europe' as the name for their new world to the west of Asia Minor.

By definition, an underlying value judgement concerning Christianity runs throughout this book, one that relates more to the eleventh century than to the twenty-first – now a millennium apart. Indeed, even before the eleventh century, our medieval forebears believed that becoming part of 'European civilisation' necessitated conversion to Christianity, a religion that had emerged during the period of the Roman Empire. However one might consider such a viewpoint today, the essential fact is that, during the period under consideration, Christianity was the major force for change – in the process spreading a largely common culture that included literacy.

This archaeological survey commenced with the eighth century, in part at any rate for the reason that much of what was to become Roman Catholic Europe already formed part of 'Western Christendom'. However, as has been described above, the process of Latin Christianisation was still incomplete by the end of the twelfth century (e.g. King Waldemar of the Danes was victorious in the Estonian Crusade only in 1219; the baptism of Lithuania awaited the fourteenth century, and that of the Saami even longer; with the Moslems not being finally evicted from Spain until 1492).

Conversion brought about fundamental changes in beliefs and social conduct and thus also to the rituals of everyday existence, such as baptism and burial, although there is evidence enough for adaptation (as with pagan festivals). As just noted, Conversion was accompanied by literacy, gradually providing some at least with access not only to Latin literature in the form of the Bible and theological works, but also to the whole world of Late Antique scholarship and literature. The 'twelfth-century renaissance' demonstrated that there was value to secular learning and the university became a new phenomenon of the High Middle Ages – that at Bologna was founded in 1088 (although refounded in 1215), followed by five more during the twelfth century (including both Paris and Oxford).

The stories of Charlemagne's journey to Rome in 800 (his fifth to Italy), when he was crowned Holy Roman Emperor, and that telling of his elephant which came from Egypt to Pisa (both recounted above), illuminate important aspects of medieval European communications, Christian origins and Muslim connections, at the turn of a century. The ninth century saw the commencement of the Norse settlement of the North Atlantic islands: Europe was growing in size, even counting Greenland as an extension for some centuries, as also the Holy Places (whilst Crusader kingdoms). By the end of our period, however, other journeys were being made that made Europe seem smaller, such as that undertaken by the Norwegian king, Sigurd 'the Jerusalem-traveller'. His sailing route from the North Sea to the Holy Land took him, by way of Santiago de Compostela, through the Straits of Gibraltar and across the Mediterranean to reach Jerusalem in 1110.

For the German Empire, the twelfth century might be considered to have terminated when Frederick Barbarossa died in 1190. Although Barbarossa had failed by some years to achieve the length of Charlemagne's reign (768-814), he had been on the throne since 1152. On the occasion of Charlemagne's canonisation, it was he who ordered his predecessor's chapel at Aachen to be turned into his shrine. When the new saint's remains were transferred to a golden casket in 1165, Barbarossa presented a vast wheel-shaped chandelier to hang over the imperial throne, as a symbolic 'Crown of Lights'.

Barbarossa was, indeed, a veritable 'European' successor to Charlemagne, although he likewise reigned only over part of Europe. He also was crowned Emperor (even if twice excommunicated by the Pope), wielding extensive power for dynastic reasons, being the son of a Hohenstaufen Duke of Swabia and of a Guelph princess of Bavaria, and marrying the heiress of the Franche-Comté and Arles. He died by drowning in a river in Asia Minor, while taking part in the Third Crusade. But if there is one historical event that might be picked on with which to mark the close of this survey, it is the Fourth Crusade.

The Fourth Crusade was intended to attack Muslim Egypt in 1203, but was diverted by the Doge of Venice, Enrico Dandolo, to storm Christian Constantinople with the intention of restoring Alexius IV to the Byzantine throne, and to share in its wealth. While Dandolo was negotiating with the leaders of the Crusade about the cost for transporting them to the East, he had at the same time sent a diplomatic mission to Cairo to negotiate a trade agreement with the Sultan, promising that Venice would not enable such an expedition to be launched against him. Alexius gained his throne, only to be murdered shortly afterwards in a palace revolution. In 1204, Constantinople was stormed once again; this time it was comprehensively sacked. The two Christian 'Europes' had come into violent collision.

The contents of this book clearly demonstrate that, by the end of the twelfth century, the 'Europeanisation' of Europe was well under way – and was indeed gathering momentum. Developments in urbanism and feudalism considered here, combined with the forces of religion, were the catalysts for economic and cultural change, the pace of which was getting faster thanks to improvements in the mechanisms of communication that made possible the ever more rapid transmission of yet more goods and ideas.

INDEX OF AUTHORS

James Graham-Campbell

A page number in italic refers to an illustration.

Emporia: cf. trading-centres

Europe (definitions)   13-14, 46, *47*, 450-2

Europeanisation   259, 452

Ewers: cf. *aquamanile*

Excavation (& recording)   29-41, *32-6, 38-40*, 76-7, 380-1, 391, 413, 414-17; cf. buildings archaeology; Harris Matrix; urban (& waterfront) archaeology

Execution (cemeteries)   352-3, *353*, 434

Fairs   142, 144, 297-8, 307; cf. markets

Farms (farmsteads)   *33, 59*, 78, 83-4; 89-90, *91*, 92-5, *103-4*, 104-5, 137, 144, 150, *156*, 162-4, *162*, 169-70; defended 139, 335, 338-9; cf. houses (rural); ring-forts; villas (Carolingian)

Feasting   171-2, 177, 354-6, 371-2, 375

Fences   89, 90, *91*, 97, 140, *140-1*, 377; *park pale* 351

Feudalism   316, 324

Fields (field systems)   83, 96-7, 100, 105; cf. crop rotation

Fire-places: cf. hearths

Fish (& shellfish)   50, 73, 185-6, 200, 201-3; hatchery (& ponds) 185, 385

'Fish-event horizon' (trade)   202-3, 312

Flax   193, 208

Floors (floor-layers/levels)   85, 88, 92, 156, 157, 161, 163, 377, 406

Fonts   388, *388*, 406, *407*; cf. baptism

Food (preparation & consumption)   163-4, 172, 174, 177, 186, 264, 310-11; cf. bake-houses; feasting; kitchens; ovens

Food preservation   183, 188-90, 196, 202-3, 232, 312; cf. herbs; honey; salt; storage

Food production   181, 192-3; cf. arable farming; pastoral farming

Food storage: cf. storage

Footwear   271, 312, 386; shoemakers 123, 127, 210

Fords   264, 266, 268, 353

Forest (*silva*): cf. deer-parks, woodland

Fortifications   112, 316-41, 343, 352; cf. bridges; castles; forts (& fortresses); gatehouses; keeps; linear earthworks; *longphorts*; mottes; refuge-sites; ring-forts; Slavic strongholds; urban defences

Forts   171, *171*, 292, 297, 316-19, *317*, 322-3, *333*, 352; fortresses (circular & geometric/Trelleborg type) 74, 139, 318-19, *319*; rectangular 335; temporary 322, 331; cf. refuge-sites; *longphorts*; ring-forts

Forum ware   227, *228*

Fossa Carolina: cf. canals

Fruits (& nuts)   *184*, 187-8, 196; cf. orchards

Fulling   146; cf. cloth production

Funerals: cf. death (& burial rites)

'Funnel-beakers'   239, 242-3, *242*; cf. glass (vessels)

Furs   50, 200, 272, 303, 306, 309, 350

Furnaces (iron)   210, 221, *222*

Furniture (& furnishings)   161, 163-4, *173*, 176-7, 245, 246, *248*, 255, 280; cf. benches; chairs; chests; cupboards; stools

Games, gaming-pieces (pastimes & sports)   163, 178, 257-8, *258*, 259, 353, 356-7, *357*; cf. chess

Gardens (& orchards)   131, 133, 187, 191, 194; monastic, 194, *411*; cf. herb gardens; urban/suburban 157, 187, 194

Garrisons   139, 318-19

Gatehouses (castles)   320, 326, 333, 334, *334, 338*, 347

Gerefa 92

German/Salian Empire, emperors   51, 66, *70, 72*, 134, 142, 150, 230, 249, 258-9, 301, 349, 358-61, 382, *383, 434, 435*, 451

Gifts (& gift-exchange)   217, 241, 273, 294, 298, 302, 309, 354, 356, 359, 388, 442-5, *443-4*

Glass: manufacture   137, 213-14, *213*, 239, 242-3, 296, 297, 309; scrap 273, 293; vessels 140, 177, 192, 239, 242-4, *242-3*, 303, 356, 440; cf. beads; window-glass

Glaze   192, 212, 226-7, 240, 299-300

Goats: cf. animals (as food)

Gold (gilding & goldsmiths)   46, 115, 119, 123, 127, 128, 141, 252, 292, 254, 298, 349, 359, 360, 367-8, 406-7, *407*; cf. precious metals

Gothic architecture   231-2, 405, 412-13, *412*

Grain (trade)   131, 289, 292, 296, 312

Granaries   92, 189, 329, 335; cf. silos; storage

Grapes (& vines)   131, 87-8, 197, 199, 301; cf. wine

Grave-goods   15, 161, 176, 200, 237, 244, 248, 250-1, *250*, 253, 267, *267*, 270, 280, *281-2*, 358, 359-60, *360, 362*, 373, 386, *386, 439*, 440-1; funerary crowns 360, *360*

Grave-markers   393, 434-5; cf. memorials

Graves (& graveyards): cf. burials; churchyards

'Great Schism'   14

Greek Orthodox religion: cf. Orthodox Church

'Green-and-brown decorated' pottery (el-Andalus)   240-1, *240-1*

Groves (sacred): cf. paganism

Grubenhaüser: cf. SFBs

Guilds (craft & merchants)   127, 307

Guldgubbar   367-8

Papacy, papal state, popes (Rome)   14, 15, 66, 131, 342, 381-2, 384, 434, 443-5, 444-5, 451; Basilica of St Peter 131, 444-5

Palaces   *34-5*, 117, 119, 123, *124*, 136, 138-9, *138*, *143*, 144, 145, 147, 150, 175, 224, 335, 342-50, *344-7*, 351, 352, 390, 414; bishop's 131, 345-6, 348-50, 382

Paleo-demography   420-5, 428-9

Paleo-pathology   127, 385, 426; cf. physical anthropology

Parish system   103, 147, 127, 378, 379

Pastimes: cf. games

Pastoral farming (animal husbandry, livestock & stock breeding)   53, 56-7, 60, 62, 64-5, 87, 90, 92-3, 95, 97, 100, 183, 185, 197-8, 200; cf. animals (as food); byres; field systems

Pattern-welding (iron)   222-3, *223*, 255

Pendants   250, *251*, 368, 389, *389*; cf. amulets; horse-pendants

Pfalz (*palatium*): cf. palaces

Physical anthropology   43, 420-30, 431; cf. paleo-pathology

Picks   4 (see *Cover*), 255

'Picture-stones' (Gotlandic)   303, 367, 369, *369*, 372

Pigs, pigsties (pork)   50, 92, 131, 182, 183, 185, 198, 200

Pilgrimage, pilgrims   126-7, 128, 133, 263, 271, 301, 385-8, 405, 412, 440, 451; badges 386-7, *387*; bottles (canteens & flasks) 245, 271, 386; shells 386-7, *386*, 440; staffs (sticks) 271, 386, 440

Pingsdorf ware   144, 226, *227*, 308

Piracy   273, 277, 289; cf. Vikings

Pit-houses: cf. SFBs

Plague: cf. disease

Plan of St Gall   164-6, *165*, 175, 194, 224, 349, 410-11, *411*

Plants   49-50

Plates (platters): cf. tableware

Platforms: cf. benches

Plots: rural 63-4, 84, 89-90, *91*, *94*, *103*, 170; urban (& properties) 111, 117, 125-6, *125*, 132, 134, *135*, 137-8, 140, *140-1*, 144, 145, 147, 150, 166, *167*, 168, 177

Ploughs (tillage)   97-8, *99*, 255; cf. coulter; harrow

Pole-lathe: cf. lathe-turning

Polyptyques   79-80, 101, 425

Pope (Bishop of Rome): cf. papacy

Population estimates   114, 121, 122, 131, 141, 144-5, 289-90, 390, 422-5, 428-9

Portcullises   320, 333, 334

Potsherds   97, 161, 163-4, 177, *188*, 191; cf. ceramics

Pottery kilns   118, 211-12, *211*, 291, 294, 297

'Prague Culture'   63

Precious (noble) metals   177, 244, 293; church treasuries 388; temple treasures 378; treasure-chamber 343; cf. coins; gold; hoards; silver

'Productive sites'   307-8; cf. fairs; markets

Properties (urban): cf. plots

Quarries   120, 300, 444

Quays: cf. harbours

Quernstones (rotary hand-querns)   101, 146, 163, 164, 189, 303, 310; basalt (lava) 48, 119, 140, 146, 293, *298*, 299, *309*, 310, *310*

Radiocarbon dating (C14)   43, *202-3*, 415

Reading: cf. writing

Recording: cf. buildings archaeology; excavation; Harris Matrix

Refectories (monastic)   409-10, *409-11*, 430

Refuge-sites   316-18, *317*, 320, 321, 323, 332

Regalia (royal): crowns   357-8, *357-8*, 360, *360*, *362*, *387*, 441; orbs 358, *358*, 360, *360*, *435*, 441; sceptres 358-60, *360*, *362*, *387*, *435*, 441; cf. coronation; seals; swords; thrones

Reindeer   50, 64, 200

Relics (& reliquaries)   299, 356, 385, 388-9, *389*, 402, 436, 442-3; cf. shrines

Religions   366-97; cf. Christianity; Greek Orthodox Church; Islam; Jewish; paganism; Roman Catholic Church

Ribats   391

Riding gear: cf. horse-harness; saddles; spurs; stirrups

Rigging: cf. ropes; sails

Rings: arm   250, 370, *370*; finger 242, 251, 441; magical 370, *370*, 432

Ring-forts (Ireland)   *56*, 78, 325, 339, 352

Ring-works   325-7, *327*

Rituals (pagan)   366-7, *369*, 371-5, 378

Roads   104-5, 120, 128, *135*, 136, 146, 150, 262, 264, 265-6, *265*, 353; cf. street-systems

Roasting pits (& furnaces)   *96*, 210

Roman Catholic (Latin) Church   13, 63, 66, 71, 381-2, 450; cf. Christianity

Roman Empire (& continuity)   13-15, 19, 51, 54, 56-7, 104-5, 111-12, 116-18, 120-1, 123, *124*, 129-34, *130*, 136, 139, 142, 144, 149, 154-5, 164, 166, 175, 193-4, 196, 199, 214, 221, 224, 228, 230, 237, 239, 261-2, 266, 273, 275, 279, 284, 289-95, 297, 301, 302, 317-18, 320-2, 339, 342-4, 348, 351, 355, 358, 380-1, 385, 398-9, 402, 404, 408, 434, 438, 444

PEOPLE AND PLACES INDEX

Mette Sørensen

In this index, Å has the alphabetical position of A and Æ as AE; Ö and Ø are treated as O.